## THE INSTITUTE FOR POLISH–JEWISH STUDIES

The Institute for Polish–Jewish Studies in Oxford and its sister organization, the American Association for Polish–Jewish Studies, which publish *Polin*, were established after the International Conference on Polish–Jewish Studies held in Oxford in September 1984. The scholars present on that occasion, from Israel, Poland, western Europe, North America, and South Africa, wished to establish a framework for the study of the Polish Jewish past on an interdisciplinary basis and in a manner which transcended exclusive national, religious, and ethnic perspectives. In addition to *Polin*, the Institute and Association have sponsored the publication of over twenty books on Polish Jewish topics, and have helped organize international conferences at the Jagiellonian University in Cracow, the Hebrew University in Jerusalem, the University of Łódź, and the Institute for the Study of Human Sciences in Vienna. They have also encouraged academic exchanges between Israel, Poland, the United States, and western Europe and have sought to aid in the training of a new generation of scholars of Polish Jewry.

The American Association for Polish–Jewish Studies is based in Boston, Massachusetts, and is linked with the Department of Near Eastern and Judaic Studies, Brandeis University, Waltham, Massachusetts.

———

*This publication has been supported by
a donation in memory of*
DR GEORGE WEBBER
*(1899–1982)*
*scholar, Hebraist, jurist*

THE LITTMAN LIBRARY OF
JEWISH CIVILIZATION

MANAGING EDITOR
*Connie Webber*

*Dedicated to the memory of*
LOUIS THOMAS SIDNEY LITTMAN
*who founded the Littman Library*
*for the love of God*
*and in memory of his father*
JOSEPH AARON LITTMAN
יהא זכרם ברוך

'*Get wisdom, get understanding:*
*Forsake her not and she shall preserve thee*'
PROV. 4: 5

# POLIN
## STUDIES IN POLISH JEWRY
### VOLUME TEN

# Jews in Early Modern Poland

Edited by
### GERSHON DAVID HUNDERT

*Published for*
The Institute for Polish–Jewish Studies

London · Portland, Oregon
## The Littman Library of Jewish Civilization
**1997**

*The Littman Library of Jewish Civilization*

*Published in the United Kingdom by*
*Vallentine Mitchell & Co. Ltd.*
*Newbury House, 900 Eastern Avenue,*
*London IG2 7HH*

*Published in the United States and Canada by*
*Vallentine Mitchell & Co. Ltd.*
*c/o ISBS, 5804 N.E. Hassalo Street,*
*Portland, Oregon 97213–3644*

*A catalogue record for this book is available from the British Library*

*Library of Congress Cataloging-in-Publication Data applied for*
*ISSN 0268 1056*
*ISBN 1-874774-31-5*

*Publishing co-ordinator: Janet Moth*
*Copy-editing: Laurien Berkeley*
*Proof-reading: Anna Zaranko*
*Design: Pete Russell, Faringdon, Oxon.*
*Typeset by Footnote Graphics, Warminster, Wilts.*
*Printed in Great Britain on acid-free paper by*
*The Alden Press, Oxford*

Articles appearing in this publication are abstracted and indexed in
*Historical Abstracts* and *America: History and Life*

*This tenth volume of* POLIN *is dedicated to*

IRENE AND RICHARD PIPES

*on the occasion of their*
*fiftieth wedding anniversary*

# Editors and Advisers

# Preface

THIS is the tenth volume of *Polin*, and the first to appear in paperback—a sign of our confidence in the growing interest in the area, particularly among the new generation, and of the changes taking place in Polish–Jewish relations. This is clear too from the lecture given by Krzysztof Śliwiński, Polish Ambassador to the Jewish Diaspora, under the auspices of the Institute for Polish–Jewish Studies, which is reproduced in this volume.

Plans for future volumes of *Polin* are well advanced. This will be the last to be devoted principally to a single theme. The editors have come to the conclusion that to devote such a large proportion of each volume to one theme has meant that very few other articles could be published, and that the length of time between the submission of articles on other topics and their publication had become inordinately long. In addition, the rapid development of scholarship in the field of Polish–Jewish studies has meant that, even if the bulk of an issue was devoted to a single theme, it was impossible to provide a comprehensive overview of the subject. We will still retain clusters of articles on topics we regard as central to our subject, however. Volume 11 will have such a cluster on aspects and experiences of Judaism in Poland; volume 12 will highlight the triangular relationship of Poles, Jews, and Ukrainians in Galicia between 1772 and 1914; and volume 13 will feature a cluster of articles on the Holocaust on the Polish lands. We should welcome articles on these topics, as well as on all other relevant issues. We should also welcome any criticisms or suggestions for improvement. In particular, we should be very grateful for assistance in extending our coverage to the areas of Ukraine, Belarus, and Lithuania, both in the period in which these countries were part of the Polish–Lithuanian Commonwealth and subsequently.

As with previous issues, this present volume could not have appeared without the untiring assistance of many individuals. In particular, we should like to express our gratitude to Dr Jonathan Webber, Treasurer of the Institute for Polish–Jewish Studies, to Professor Jehuda Reinharz, President of Brandeis University, and to Mrs Irene Pipes, President of the American Association for Polish–Jewish Studies. Anna Zaranko and Jolanta Kisler-Goldstein have kept mistakes in the Polish language to a minimum.

Finally we should like to express our sadness at the passing of Professor Lucjan Dobroszycki, a member of our editorial board and one of the great Polish Jewish scholars of our time; of Professor Szyja Bronsztejn, who did so much to create the study of the Jewish past in Lower Silesia; and of Julian Stryjkowski, one of the greatest Jewish writers of the post-war period.

A.P.

# POLIN

Gentle Polin (Poland), ancient land of Torah and learning
From the day Ephraim first departed from Judah

*From a* selihah *by Rabbi Moshe Katz Geral*
*of the exiles of Poland, head of the Beth Din of the*
*Holy Congregation of Metz*

We did not know, but our fathers told us, how the exiles of Israel came to the land of Polin (Poland).

When Israel saw how its sufferings were constantly renewed, oppression increased, persecutions multiplied, and how the evil authorities piled decree on decree and followed expulsion with expulsion, so that there was no way to escape the enemies of Israel, they went out on the road and sought an answer from the paths of the wide world: which is the correct road to traverse to find rest for the soul. Then a piece of paper fell from heaven, and on it the words:

*Go to Polaniya* (Poland).

So they came to the land of Polin and they gave a mountain of gold to the king, and he received them with great honour. And God had mercy on them, so that they found favour with the king and the nobles. And the king gave them permission to reside in all the lands of his kingdom, to trade over its length and breadth, and to serve God according to the precepts of their religion. And the king protected them against every foe and enemy.

And Israel lived in Polin in tranquillity for a long time. They devoted themselves to trade and handicrafts. And God sent a blessing on them so that they were blessed in the land, and their name was exalted among the peoples. And they traded with the surrounding countries and they also struck coins with inscriptions in the holy language and the language of the country. These are the coins which have on them a lion rampant towards the right. And on the coins are the words 'Mieszko, King of Poland' or 'Mieszko, Król of Poland'. The Poles call their king 'Król'.

When they came from the land of the Franks, they found a wood in the land, and on every tree one tractate of the Talmud was incised. This is the forest of

Kawczyń, which is near Lublin. And every man said to his neighbour, 'We have come to the land where our ancestors dwelt before the Torah and revelation were granted.'

And those who seek for names say: 'This is why it is called Polin. For thus spoke Israel when they came to the land, "Here rest for the night [*Po lin*]." And this means that we shall rest here until we are all gathered into the Land of Israel.'

Since this is the tradition, we accept it as such.

S. Y. AGNON, 1916

# Contents

## PART I

## JEWS IN EARLY MODERN POLAND

# Towards a Polish–Jewish Dialogue
## The Way Forward

*Polish Ambassador to the Jewish Diaspora*

*A lecture given at King's College London on 20 November 1996
under the auspices of the Institute for Polish–Jewish Studies and the
Polish Cultural Institute*

Ten years ago, in the first issue of *Polin*, Rafael Scharf wrote:

No-one is under any illusion that the few thousand Jews remaining in Poland, who openly consider themselves to be such and who, as it were, apologize for being alive, are not physically and spiritually a community in terminal decline. They have no schools, no synagogues, no rabbis, no contact with Israel, no leadership, no future. It has to be admitted, albeit regrettably, that world Jewry has ceased to care for them: they have been written off as lost. Therefore, from the Jewish point of view, we are talking not about current affairs but exclusively about history.[1]

The title of Rafael Scharf's paper was 'In Anger and in Sorrow: Towards a Polish–Jewish Dialogue'. Ten years ago the world looked, and was, just as he described it. Poland at that time had a very different political regime, and no one could possibly have foreseen how profoundly and how soon the situation would change.

Today there are about 10,000 people living in Poland who consider themselves (and who are considered to be) Jews. There are nine religious congregations, operating under an umbrella organization called the Union of Jewish Religious Congregations; seven functioning synagogues, and other synagogue buildings being reconstructed; three rabbis; and there is also a new Association of Polish Jews, which means that the Jewish life of the community is no longer limited to religious congregations and the state-sponsored Social and Cultural Association of Polish Jews.

A Jewish primary school has been operating since 1994 with the support of the Lauder Foundation. For the first time since the Second World War there is a Union of Polish Jewish Students. No one could have imagined, even ten years

[1] Polin, vol. 1 (1986), 270.

ago, that such an organization could have about 150 active members. There is even a Maccabi Sports Club. And there is the Association of Holocaust Children with about 700 members.

There are two or three, or even five or six (depending on how you define them) interesting publications. One of them, *Yidele*, is published by the Students Union. A new monthly, *Midrasz*, has emerged, and existing publications also continue to flourish.

The life of institutions runs in parallel with the life of the community. The Lauder Foundation is actively engaged in the field. It is organized by Rabbi Michael Schudrich, who has been in Poland for several years now. Summer and winter camps are held annually, each attended by 400–500 participants who go to learn or relearn the Jewish tradition. The newest idea of the Lauder Foundation is to revitalize one of Warsaw's former 'Jewish streets', in the vicinity of the synagogue, Yiddish theatre, and other Jewish institutions, to provide a Jewish centre with offices, apartments, restaurants, and social and cultural facilities.

In addition to all this, Poland of course has a great many Jewish visitors.

Compared with the richness of Jewish life in Poland in the past, today's community and the scale of its activities is tiny. However, a country with 10,000 Jews, three rabbis, seven synagogues, and active social and cultural associations undoubtedly has a Jewish community of some importance, a community that is certainly very much alive. Poland's Jewish community is also growing, so it is no longer possible to describe it as a community in 'terminal decline'. Quite the opposite.

There are many other aspects of life in Poland that would also have been hard to imagine ten years ago. At that time, there was still a kind of official silence about everything concerning Jews and Jewish life. There were some exceptions, due either to the activity of the Opposition or to some special government initiative— for example, to mark the anniversary of the Warsaw Ghetto Uprising. But for years and years there was official silence—or worse, official lies—about this part of Polish history, this part of *Jewish* history. Things now are very different.

Let me try to give you an idea of the sort of Jewish cultural events that now take place in Poland—only an idea, because there are more events than I can mention in the time at my disposal tonight. There is the Festival of Jewish Culture in Cracow, extending over a week or ten days. This enormously important event, which has been held annually for several years now, attracts many thousands of people to concerts, lectures, plays, and so on. It is probably the most important event of its kind in eastern Europe, and quite a number of foreign visitors, from countries such as Ukraine and Slovakia, come to Poland for this experience of Jewish cultural life.

Cracow's Centre for Jewish Culture, established by the Judaica Foundation in November 1993, has done a tremendous amount, and many of the programmes it organizes are on Jewish themes. In its first three years of operation, it has organized more than 600 events such as lectures, concerts, and seminars. The Centre is also involved in running New York University's summer school in Cracow, a two-week programme that has run for three consecutive years now. It has a serious curriculum, and students receive academic credit for the course.

There are Polish centres for Jewish studies too, at the Jagiellonian University in Cracow and at the University of Warsaw. The Jagiellonian University's School of European Studies has started to run courses on the sociology of the Holocaust and on Jewish culture and identity. At Warsaw University there is a competition for the best theses written on Jewish topics, which is now in its third successive year. A total of forty-six Master's dissertations and ten doctoral theses were presented this year, which is a measure of the number of research projects conducted annually in Poland in this field.

And then there is the Jewish Historical Institute, ZIH, whose very existence has in the past been under threat on a number of occasions, but which is now engaged in a great many important activities. In the coming year it will receive a well-deserved government subvention of about $400,000. In addition to its regular work as a research institute and a museum, it has for four years been running a special programme of courses for Polish teachers of history and literature. Each course lasts two or three weeks and is attended by about twenty teachers. This extremely important and well-organized enterprise is already contributing to changing the ways in which the Jewish past in Poland is presented to Polish schoolchildren and students.

The Jewish Historical Institute has also been involved in launching a huge new project, the Museum of Jewish History in Poland, which will be located in Warsaw. Until his recent death, the honorary president of the museum was Chaim Herzog. There is a distinguished organizing committee, and the City of Warsaw has allocated the museum a prominent site near the famous Ghetto Uprising monument. The Polish Government has pledged $150,000 to this project. Construction has already started, and the first part of the museum is supposed to open in the year 2000. This prediction may be too optimistic, but the project will certainly take years rather than decades to complete.

There are also new initiatives at a constitutional level. For example, the Polish Parliament has introduced a Declaration on the Anniversary of the Warsaw Ghetto Uprising and a Declaration concerning the Holocaust. The level of government concern is also indicated by the prime minister's presence, along with representatives of a great many local and church authorities, at the fiftieth anniversary of the Kielce pogrom.

There have been important non-governmental initiatives too—publications, films, and theatre performances that have brought a knowledge of Jewish topics to a wider audience. Of particular interest was an initiative undertaken by the Shalom Foundation, which issued a public appeal for people to send in photographs of Jewish friends or relatives from before the war. This created the basis for an extremely moving exhibition entitled 'And I Still See their Faces'. It was an enormous success, with the biggest attendance of any exhibition in Warsaw for three years.

In the last two years more than 500 serious titles have been published on Jewish history, literature, and culture. Poland holds the world record for publishing translations from Yiddish: more books have been published in Poland in translation from Yiddish than in the United States or in Israel. The Foundation for Polish Culture, which each year awards prizes to the best books published in Poland, has this year selected four books that were either written by Jewish authors or discuss the problems of Polish Jews. I mention only in passing that one of these books, *A Child in a Landscape*, is of special importance to me because it was written by someone who was a student of mine when I was still teaching biology, Roman Gren. I know him and his family very well. The fact that so many books have been published illustrates the huge interest in Jewish affairs in Poland: there are a great many people who want to read these books and who are willing to buy them.

There are many other initiatives. They include the Foundation for Judaica in Łódź (whose functions include the renovation of the city's Jewish cemetery, one of the largest and most beautiful in Europe), and Jewish cultural festivals in Warsaw, in Torun, and in Gdansk. The three-day festival in Gdansk, called the Festival of the Holy Torah and the Holy Bible, is of particular interest because its various events were held in a church, a synagogue, and a municipal building; moreover, it was in Gdansk that Father Jankowski preached his infamous sermon. The fact that a couple of thousand people participated in the festival, including a rabbi and Jewish and Christian intellectuals, and that the Archbishop was present, shows perhaps that ordinary people in Gdansk are somewhat more tolerant than Father Jankowski. His stance is very regrettable indeed, and, though I understand the significance of the presence of the then president of Poland at this sermon, it was a very unfortunate incident. Things like that do sometimes happen in life; but as the cultural festival and all the other developments I have mentioned show, many more positive things are happening. I am constantly receiving invitations from foundations, councils, and commissions concerned with Jewish topics; for example, I recently received an invitation to a meeting in the main hall of Wrocław University to commemorate the anniversary of Kristallnacht. All this is now part of normal life in Poland. Among other things it demonstrates the current degree of interest in this part of the past by both younger and older generations.

I also receive mail from London. In fact, I was recently sent a publication by the Institute for Jewish Policy Research which reported that in Cracow 'there is growing interest in Jewish music and culture amongst non-Jews, which coexists with endemic Polish antisemitism. There are even crazes for kosher vodka, beer, and mineral water, which are perceived to be more pure than other alternatives on the market.' Perhaps I might be allowed to make a comment about this. The journalist Ruth Gruber, a dear friend of mine of many years' standing, has identified an unhealthy tendency, in both Poland and Germany, towards a perverted philosemitism which idealizes Jews as exotic and abnormal. I would qualify this by saying that, though there are popular crazes for kosher vodka and so on, such things are really marginal. The fact is that we are now witnessing a persistent phenomenon that is extremely important from the cultural, political, moral, spiritual, and religious points of view. There is an openness and a deep interest in this part of *our common past* that is really much greater and more important than a transient craze for kosher vodka: it runs much deeper.

In my opinion, the time is now right to insist that there is a significant degree of philosemitism in Poland, and not only to counterbalance antisemitism. Many of us actually regard it as a basic duty to say that, for many reasons of history, we do feel a special friendship towards Jews and are aware of the many problems that face them, both in Israel and in the Diaspora. It may be late, but we in Poland now need a feeling of deep solidarity with Jews and the Jewish past—with the Holocaust. Because we as a nation and a country witnessed this tragedy, everything that concerns Jews and Polish–Jewish relations occurs somehow against the background of what happened then. But while I call for friendship and solidarity I also see that Jewish suffering is still present in memory: that calls for sympathy and a regard for people's feelings.

Another very clear and obvious fact is that the Jewish past in Poland—extending over 800 years—is an important part of *Polish* history. For mostly political reasons, this was for many years a closed topic and was therefore difficult to explore and to understand. However, the new generation has established a powerful trend towards a revival of interest in this history—the history of our country as it is now.

A decade or so ago I had a collaborator, now in the United States, who became interested in this subject as a young man. A colleague of his—a student of architecture—called him one day with the news that he had discovered a most beautiful oriental cemetery in Warsaw. He thought it was probably a Muslim cemetery, but could offer no explanation as to why something like this should be in Warsaw. In fact, of course, it was a Jewish cemetery. It now seems quite remarkable that only ten years ago a bright 20-year-old student of architecture had never heard that hundreds of thousands of Jews had lived in Warsaw before the war. He had no notion of what had happened because the past was partially closed to him.

For all of us, perhaps, the past has been partially closed, and we now have to think about our moral, spiritual, cultural, and other obligations.

There are indeed many things to think about. Only ten years ago, Rafael Scharf said, as I mentioned at the beginning, that 'we are talking not about current affairs but exclusively about history'. Well, I have been trying to fulfil my mission as Poland's ambassador to the Jewish Diaspora for just over a year now, and God only knows how many problems, conflicts, and crises we have had in that time. In my experience it would be quite wrong to say that we are talking exclusively about history. It is clear that there *are* problems, problems that have to be solved on different levels; but the significant fact is that, ten years ago, it was not possible even to imagine talking about Polish–Jewish relations other than in the context of distant history.

I want here to introduce, though perhaps I shouldn't, a political remark. Being in contact with the leaders of many Jewish organizations, often from the United States, I have come to realize that, by and large, Jews feel that the political left has been more positive towards the problems of the Jewish community than the traditional political right. I understand why the family on the political left may be considered more attractive; in Poland, however, one cannot give the left exclusive credit for all progress—it is not that simple. We must remember that the good work that has been done has only been possible because of the political transformation, initiated by the anti-Communist democratic opposition, that has taken place in Poland during the last couple of years. It is only within the framework of democracy that one has the right to choose one's political family.

The basic fact is that Poland is still developing as a democratic country. But even in Poland there are people—inside the Jewish community too—who tell me that democracy is in some ways worse, because under the former regime there would never have been the skinhead demonstrations that there are now. This is true: in a state in which the police are everywhere there is no freedom of demonstration, so there are no skinhead demonstrations. But such a state also has censors, and some articles are never published. So I prefer democracy with all its shortcomings to the artificial situation of the past, when neither pleasant nor unpleasant demonstrations were possible and intellectual life and dialogue were directed by the office of the censors.

Talking about problems, there is one big problem I have not yet mentioned: the so-called supermarket proposed in Auschwitz. The controversy is important because it has shown how complex and how deeply rooted the 'Auschwitz effect' is. Auschwitz was of course the biggest concentration and extermination camp. It is *the* symbol of the Holocaust. In Polish memory, it is also a symbol of the Nazi occupation of Poland. We are now more or less sure about the relative proportions of the victims: about one million Jews were murdered there, out of a total prisoner population of about 1.4 or 1.5 million. Of those 400,000–500,000 Auschwitz prisoners who were not Jews, about 200,000–300,000 were killed. One-third of them were Polish Christians. There is no doubt that Auschwitz has a special place in the collective Jewish memory, but the Polish memory cannot be neglected either.

Auschwitz presents complex problems. First, there is the question of preserving the site, making it possible to commemorate the victims and to show new generations both the crime and how it was committed; this is a significant educational function that has to be considered. Also, the need to accommodate half a million visitors each year causes problems not only for the museum but for the town of Oświęcim adjoining the camp, and for the surrounding villages too. Finally, there is the sheer physical size of the area—191 hectares.

In the light of all this, and for many other reasons, in September 1996 the government of Poland adopted its Strategic Governmental Programme for Auschwitz, which is meant to ensure that most of these complicated problems will be solved in the course of the next ten years. The cost of the whole project is estimated at about $100 million, but to start with (i.e. in 1997) we will need about $9 million, and the cost of the initial basic works will be about $20 million. The authorities will proceed with money from central government, local government, and from many private organizations, foundations, and so on.

The first task is to tackle the problem of transport facilities—traffic management, roads, and so on. Things cannot continue as they are now. The second task is to undertake thorough research into what is called the *protecting zone*, and then doing what is necessary to maintain it as it should be maintained.

Then there is the problem of making special legislation for Auschwitz in the Polish Parliament because of its special international and national importance. Up to now responsibility for Auschwitz has been divided between different government ministers, such as the minister of culture and the local governor, but very soon we expect to create the post of special government representative for Auschwitz. Tremendous efforts are being made, and it seems that things are going in the right direction. However, I cannot at this point say much about the views of the Jewish community on this plan: not until the imminent meeting at the Holocaust Museum in Washington, where the draft project will be discussed by delegates from the major institutions such as Yad Vashem, the US Holocaust Memorial Museum, and so on.

Another important problem is the restitution of Jewish communal property, by which I mean the property owned by religious communities. Legislation on this issue, as part of wider legislation concerning relations between the state and the Jewish religious communities, is now before Parliament.[2] Government sources estimate that there are just over 1,000 cemeteries and approximately 228 synagogues, about 70 other houses of prayer, and about 150 other relevant buildings. All these properties will have to be examined case by case by a special regulatory commission. Clearly, today's Jewish community, which is small relative to the task of dealing with such considerable communal assets, would have real difficulty in coping with these matters, case by case; the legislation therefore provides for the creation of a foundation that will operate with the participation of people nominated by institutions abroad. The World Jewish Restitution Organization, mentioned by name in the legislation, will be invited to participate; both the Polish government and the Jewish community consider this necessary for prac-

---

[2] The legislation was voted through by Parliament in February 1997 and signed by the President.

tical reasons. The idea is that any income from this property should be used to protect the Jewish heritage in Poland, both cultural and religious, and to promote the functioning of institutions.

I now turn to points of conflict. Mostly in the United States but also elsewhere, the film *Shtetl*—about the little Jewish *shtetl* of Brańsk during the war—led to an explosion of emotion among Poles and Jews. Another event that had enormous impact was the statement made by Eli Wiesel in Kielce during the commemoration held to mark the fiftieth anniversary of the pogrom. Instead of words of reconciliation we heard demands for the immediate removal of crosses and other religious symbols from the Auschwitz site. Its impact was considerable partly because of the timing, partly because of the words he used, and partly because of the difficulty of accommodating his demands. A further point of conflict has emerged over articles published about what happened in the *shtetl* of Ejszyszki after the war: a regrettable incident in which a Jewish woman and her child perished has given rise to the groundless accusation that the Home Army—the most important element in the Polish resistance—and the Government-in-exile—ordered the annihilation of those Polish Jews who had escaped the German Nazi persecutions.

Let me now say something about these matters, as briefly as I can. I have said that there is antisemitism in Poland: of that there is no doubt. There are many opinions about this antisemitism. The Polish Academy of Science recently published a study entitled *Are Poles Antisemites?* This was the first serious sociological research on the subject in Poland for many years, and many distinguished scholars participated in it. They found that no more than 4–7 per cent of the respondents to their survey could be considered deep-rooted Christian 'traditional antisemites'. They also found that this category correlated very closely with people over 60 who were poorly educated and living in closed communities on the margins of society. This suggests that this sort of traditional antisemitism, which we must regret, is no longer a social problem and is dying out. It also shows that the Church as an institution is not teaching what might be considered as the roots of such antisemitic opinions. These findings are very important. A much bigger problem is that about 17 per cent of respondents were identified as being 'modern antisemites'. The identifying statement here was to the effect that they hated or disliked Jews because they considered that they were leading world politics in the wrong direction. (I would note that this antisemitism is in fact not so 'modern', because it is based on arguments of the kind found in the notorious *Protocols of the Elders of Zion*.) I must emphasize that there is nothing particularly Polish in the argument of this 17 per cent. It is the sort of general argument that one finds whenever antisemitism is encountered in the Western world. The problem exists and must be dealt with.

However, there is one phenomenon I want to stress, and that is the spontaneous, or more or less spontaneous, hostility towards Jews that one finds sometimes in the press, very often in declarations by American Poles (the Polish American Congress), and often in the letters I receive.

A serious discussion about the past is possible—even if it is not always a glorious past as far as Poles are concerned. One can discuss Kielce and one can talk a lot and teach a lot about the Holocaust. There are points on which some Poles are very sensitive, and they have some right to be, but we have to fight this because it provokes very negative emotions and makes progress extremely difficult. On the other hand we have the general (I would say visceral) Jewish reaction that identifies Poland as the country of the Holocaust—for example, in the use of the phrase 'the Polish extermination camps'. This approach is seen in *Shtetl*, and elsewhere: the Holocaust is mentioned without a word about the situation of Poland during the war, for example that Poland was under Nazi occupation or that the war was a war for Poland.

I don't want to go further into this question now, except to say that people sometimes dismiss all such sensitivities as an example of a kind of persecution complex. But it is not quite so. There are many Poles who feel that it is particularly unjust when the many Polish victims of Auschwitz are forgotten, or the Warsaw uprising of 1944 in which 200,000 people died is overlooked. This is a very sensitive point.

I should like to conclude, however, by saying that there is a consensus among the major political forces in Poland in their determination to work towards an improvement in the field of Polish–Jewish relations, and also a sincere commitment to making Poland mature in its democracy among the family of democratic countries, which implies securing the rights of minorities, general freedom, religious freedom, and cultural rights.

It is significant that at least those political parties that are represented in our Parliament—that is, the great majority—share a consensus in this field. This means that there is no split between the Opposition and the ruling coalition.

I mention political forces because, when I started in this job, I was frequently told that I was starting something that was so difficult and so frustrating that after a year I would give up or go crazy. Nothing like that has happened. On the contrary, I have found great support—though one has to persevere to see that this support exists. I was told that things would be difficult because my roots were in opposition politics, but I have never yet experienced the slightest moral problem in working as a civil servant for a ruling coalition of another political persuasion.

I know that the direction I am following is the right one. I have enormous support from the Polish press and from the media generally. I would say that 90 per cent of the Polish media are more than fair in the way in which they handle these matters. Of course, the stance of the remaining 10 per cent is regrettable, but they are not opinion-formers and their circulation is very limited. Among them is a Catholic daily in Warsaw that accuses me of being philosemitic. I find this terribly unjust—how can a Christian accuse someone of loving too much?

Indeed, I regret not loving enough. Why is it a sin to love too much? I can find nothing to support that view in the Gospels.

I have had a huge measure of support from the educated people of Poland. I have met with great understanding in the universities, among the readers of the books I have mentioned, and among all those who have attended my lectures. I have been given support from a good part of the Church, including eminent bishops and members of the Polish hierarchy, who from the very beginning have declared their sympathy for my work. I have found that people from all over the world are willing to give me support and help, which is of course very encouraging. And I have found, to my great surprise, that a story about my appointment was published in a Tanzanian paper, and a Japanese journalist has asked to interview me about Polish–Jewish relations!

All this has helped me to realize that among the important reasons for trying to make progress in this Polish–Jewish dialogue—yes, even 'in anger and in sorrow', to quote Rafael Scharf again—is a duty towards the world, the origin of which I can only partly understand.

What happens between the Jews and Poland—with all its attendant problems, quarrels, and opinions—is of interest throughout the world. It seems to be important to humanity as a whole. Perhaps it is the curiosity value of a quarrel that attracts interest; perhaps it is something else. I am not certain.

And so I would say that we Poles have this obligation to do our best not only for ourselves but for something more general—perhaps for humanity as a whole. With the support that we have, we can be sure that a lot can be done without calling for impossible efforts.

# Note on Transliteration, Names, and Place-Names

## Transliteration

An attempt has been made to achieve consistency in the transliteration of Hebrew words. The following are the key distinguishing features of the system that has been adopted:

1. No distinction is made between *aleph* and *ayin*; both are represented by an apostrophe, and only when they appear in an intervocalic position.

2. *Veit* is written *v*; *ḥet* is written *ḥ*; *yod* is written *y* when it functions as a consonant and *i* when it occurs as a vowel; *khaf* is written *kh*; *tsadi* is written *ts*; *kof* is written *k*.

3. The *dagesh ḥazak*, represented in some transliteration systems by doubling the letter, is not represented, except in words that have more or less acquired normative English spellings that include doubling, such as Hallel, kabbalah, Kaddish, Kiddush, rabbi, Sukkot, and Yom Kippur.

4. The *sheva na* is represented by an *e*.

5. Hebrew prefixes, prepositions, and conjunctions are not followed by hyphens when they are transliterated, thus *betoledot ha'am hayehudi*.

6. Capital letters are not used in the transliteration of Hebrew except for the first word in the titles of books and the names of people, places, institutions, and generally as in the conventions of the English language.

7. The names of individuals are transliterated following the above rules unless the individual concerned followed a different usage.

8. For Yiddish, the transcription adopted follows the YIVO system—except for the names of people, where the spellings they themselves used have been retained.

## Place-names

In general, place-names are spelt in the correct Polish way. This enables readers to find the places on maps and to correlate information with Polish sources. The main exceptions are Warsaw and Cracow, both of which have accepted English spellings, and place-names that have become part of the way in which individual Jews have come to be known—in which case the Yiddish form of the place-name has been used, as they themselves would have done.

# Figures

# Abbreviations

| | |
|---|---|
| AGAD | Archiwum Główne Akt Dawnych (Central Archives for Ancient History), Warsaw |
| AP | Archiwum Państwowe |
| *BŻIH* | *Biuletyn Żydowskiego Instytutu Historycznego* |
| *JJGL* | *Jahrbuch für jüdische Geschichte und Literatur* |
| *JJLG* | *Jahrbuch der jüdisch-literarischen Gesellschaft* |
| *MDSC* | *Materiały do dziejów Sejmu Czteroletniego*, vi, A. Eisenbach, J. Michalski, and E. Rostworowski (Wrocław, 1969) |
| *MGWJ* | *Monatsschrift für Geschichte und Wissenschaft des Judentums* |
| NKVD | Narodni Komitet Vnutriennykh Diel (National Committee for Internal Affairs: the Soviet secret police) |
| PAN | Polska Akademia Nauk (Polish Academy of Sciences) |
| *PH* | *Przegląd Historyczny* |
| PPS | Polska Partia Socjalistyczna (Polish Socialist Party) |
| R. | Rabbi |
| *Resp.* | *Responsa* |
| *SHB* | *Shivḥei haBesht: In Praise of the Baal Shem Tov*, trans. and ed. D. Ben-Amos and J. Mintz (Bloomington, Ind., 1971) |
| Tsisho | Tsentrale Yidishe Shul Organizatsye (Central Jewish School Organization; the school system of the Jewish Labour Bund) |

# Introduction

## GERSHON DAVID HUNDERT

When we use the words 'Frenchman', 'Englishman', 'Spaniard', we include all of the inhabitants of France, England, and Spain because each individual is a constituent part of those states. It is not the same in Poland, as I have observed. The three classes that make up the inhabitants do not constitute a nation. The nation is made up exclusively of the nobility, called here the *szlachta*. The second class, that is, the Jews, are foreign to the state and merely serve the material interests of the first class. The third class [the peasants] are simply the property of the first.

HUBERT VAUTRIN

THIS passage from the observations of a French former Jesuit who spent five years in Poland from 1777 reflects the author's perception of the significance of the Jewish presence in Poland as it appeared to an outsider.[1] Some might wonder at the prominence given to Jews, who are usually thought of as a minority population, but who are presented here as comprising one of only three 'classes'. It should be recalled, though, that in the second half of the eighteenth century Jews in Poland–Lithuania numbered about 750,000; even more significantly they made up about half of the urban population of the country. Since Jews were distributed unevenly, increasing in numbers roughly as one moved from west to east, their prominence and visibility were substantial indeed.

The passage depicts Jews as playing a role analogous to a colonized group in the economy of the Polish–Lithuanian Commonwealth. That is, their skills were exploited in the service of the powerful, and the profits drained off for the benefit of the hegemonic group. To be sure, the link between Jews and the more powerful noblemen of Poland–Lithuania was one of the most salient and crucial characteristics of the early modern period. Jews tended to settle in the 'private' towns under the jurisdiction and ownership of the great aristocrats, where they received more extensive privileges and more effective protection than in the 'royal' towns, and where, generally, the economic situation was more promising. This phenomenon was encouraged by the great magnates themselves because, as Vautrin noted, it served their material interests. Moreover, if one reads the sermons and other literary output of Jews, one finds innumerable references to 'our long and bitter exile'.

[1] The work is collected in Maria Cholewo-Flandrin (ed.), *La Pologne du XVIII siècle vue par un précepteur français, Hubert Vautrin* (Paris, 1966), 185. The translation is mine.

If, however, we seek to understand the Jews' own view of themselves, a more complex and rather different picture emerges, for they did not see themselves exclusively as passive victims. The references to the bitterness of exile should be understood as having a dual connotation. They not only lament Jewish suffering; they also provide a certain oblique comfort by encoding the conviction of Jewish cultural and moral superiority over the Gentiles. The following passage from *Sefer tseror haḥayim* by Ḥayim Ḥaike ben Aharon of Zamość, first published in Berlin in 1770, illustrates this point:

'These are the people of the Lord, yet they had to leave His land' [Ezek. 36: 20]. The explanation of this passage is similar to the response of one of the noblemen of Poland to the Jews, who were 'goring' [attacking] each other before him: 'Why are you here? When you were exiled from your land your enemies drove you far away and not to nearby areas. This was because in those days the residents of Poland were immoral in their ways and the noblemen saw that the Jews were restrained. So they brought the Jews to this country to learn from their deeds. And now, since your ways are more immoral than those of the Gentiles here in the pursuit of honours and disputes, why are you here?' Thus is it written [Yoma 86*a*]: 'It was said to them, is this the people of God famous for their godliness?' And so we should read, 'they had to leave the land *to which they were exiled*'. Since now they were worse than them, the Jews did not stay there to teach the Gentiles their ways, and what were they doing there.[2]

What makes even temporary settlement during exile possible is the People of Israel being an example, by its good qualities, to the nation amongst whose people it lives. Now, when Jews are even worse than their neighbours, the Polish nobleman may well ask, 'What are you doing here?' It should be noted, at least parenthetically, that the historical construction in the passage specifically has the nobility bringing Jews to Poland in the first place; Jews were brought to Poland to serve the interests of the *szlachta*. However, this imaginary vignette from a book by an eighteenth-century preacher illustrates the point just made. Implicit in the preacher's message is the unquestionable moral superiority of Jews, but his use of hyperbole to rebuke his people has him putting in the mouth of the *szlachcic* the unimaginable idea that Jews were even less moral than the people of the land.

These passages are cited here to support the perhaps self-evident assertion that an understanding of the Jewish experience in early modern Poland is possible only on the basis of both internal and external sources. The articles in this volume, and particularly those by Thomas Hubka on the wooden synagogues, Jacob Goldberg on marriage practices, and Daniel Stone on knowledge of foreign languages, lead inexorably to the conclusion that to see the Polish Jewish community as wholly insular and divorced from what was going on around them leads to falsification and distortion. Though Hubka makes a daring attempt to tease out the particular elements of contemporary Jewish culture that informed the uniqueness of the

---

[2] (Lublin, 1908), 19. The translation is mine.

remarkable synagogues he describes, they were the product of collaboration between Jewish and Christian architects and artists working within the cultural vocabulary of the period.[3]

Jacob Goldberg's analysis of Jewish marriage in the eighteenth century on the basis of contemporary opinion and the census materials of 1791 is a treasury of new and important material on the subject. We see a certain convergence of opinion between Jewish and Christian Enlightenment representatives on some aspects of marriage in Jewish society, and singularly important new data are presented on the incidence of early marriage in the Jewish population and the vicissitudes in the practice of young couples living in the home of their parents.

On a related subject, but in an entirely different vein, Elimelech Westreich presents an intricate and searching analysis of Polish rabbinical treatments of the medieval Ashkenazi ban on polygamy. He describes the existence of two schools of thought in the late sixteenth century, one adhering strictly to the Ashkenazi tradition, the second more open to the influence of other Jewish cultural spheres. The history of *halakhah* has not been represented before in the pages of *Polin*, and one hopes that this venture will facilitate cross-pollination between, for example, social and economic historians and those who work within the field of Jewish cultural history. Another example of this kind is Israel Ta-Shma's bold hypothesis, based on painstaking research among medieval manuscripts, linking the origins of Polish Jewry with efforts to found new communities by ḥasidei Ashkenaz. His conclusions are likely to foster debates related both to the nature of ḥasidei Ashkenaz and to the beginnings of Jewish settlement in Poland.

In a pathbreaking initial probe of the effect of printing on the Ashkenazi cultural élite, Elchanan Reiner opens an exceedingly important subject. While the impact of the making of books and printing has long been a central issue in the history of European culture in general, it is genuinely surprising that Jewish culture, which is so profoundly literary, has not been examined in this light up to now.

Just as Thomas Hubka's article suggests that the explosion of interest in kabbalah in Jewish society during the late seventeenth and eighteenth centuries may have informed the architecture of the synagogues, so too Chava Weissler finds kabbalistic influence on the Yiddish prayers recited by women during the same period. Between 1660 and 1770 there were sixteen different editions of just one of the works cited by Weissler; *Hemdat yamim*. In this study we learn more about the spiritual world of Jewish women and in particular about the life and work of the most famous author of Yiddish prayers for women, Sarah bas Tovim. Weissler also reminds us once again of the importance of the cemetery and the 'presence' of the dead in the lives of early modern Jews. (Buried in a footnote in

---

[3] There were Jewish artists who worked in non-Jewish contexts. See e.g. Hanna Widacka, 'Działalność Hirsza Leybowicza i innych rytowników na dworze nieświeskim Michała Kazimierza Radziwiłła "Rybeńki" w świetle badań archiwalnych', *Biuletyn historii sztuki*, 39 (1977), 62–72.

that article is the information that Jews used to say Sarah bas Tovim was the ancestor of Julian Tuwim!)

The most dramatic expression of the popularization of kabbalah in eastern Europe was the appearance in the latter half of the eighteenth century of a growing popular movement of religious revival that became known as hasidism. In a hard-headed, consistently objective, and careful article of great importance, Moshe Rosman subjects to rigorous critical analysis perhaps the most studied document related to early hasidism known as *Shivḥei haBesht*: the collection of legends and stories about the putative founder of the movement, Israel Ba'al Shem Tov.

In a letter attributed to him Israel Ba'al Shem Tov referred directly to the sufferings of Jews because of the accusation of ritual murder. In a major contribution to scholarship, Zenon Guldon and Jacek Wijaczka assemble in their article a systematic review of all the available information about this murderous libel in Polish lands between 1500 and 1800. It is the first scholarly review of the subject for many decades and prepares the way for further research and analysis. While the blood libels were manifestations of widespread popular hostility to Jews, the data collected by Daniel Stone in his study of the knowledge of foreign language among eighteenth-century Jews suggests that there were many individual cases of Jews who had learned the language of their neighbours.

The New Views section, in addition to Israel Ta-Shma's article mentioned above, comprises three noteworthy studies: Paul Coates delivers a thorough and thought-provoking review of the depiction of Polish–Jewish relations in recent Polish cinema; on the basis of newly opened archives in the former Soviet Union, Gertrud Pickhan presents a picture of the poignant and disturbing fate of Henryk Erlich and Wiktor Alter at the hands of the NKVD; and Chone Shmeruk's erudite study explains *mayufes*, a custom he terms 'a window on Polish–Jewish relations'.

In the section Review Essays section there is a debate between Tomasz Gąsowski and the late Artur Eisenbach on the latter's book on Jewish emancipation in Poland. Eisenbach's reply represents probably his last publication. Chone Shmeruk reviews two books on I. B. Singer that recently appeared in Poland, and Nechama Tec reviews several books on Auschwitz. The volume concludes with twenty-nine shorter book reviews, followed by the Bibliography of Polish Jewish Studies for 1994.

# PART I

# Jews in Early Modern Poland

# Jewish Marriage in Eighteenth-Century Poland

## JACOB GOLDBERG

### POLISH ATTITUDES TO JEWISH MARRIAGE

IN the eighteenth century marriage was viewed differently from how it is today, and practices often varied among different religious groups. Jews as well as many non-Jews, however, acknowledged that Jewish marriages embodied a good, stable model and praised them as examples to be emulated in an era when immorality and marital breakdown seemed to threaten the institution.

Recent historical research justifies the view that 'the history of households, families and blood relations has a decisive influence on historical–social changes,'[1] and annals surviving from the era of the Polish–Lithuanian Commonwealth clearly show that this generalization is also true of Jewish marriages in that period. In this study of the complex, multifaceted nature of Jewish marriage, the sources and published research available on the subject of Jewish families of the time,[2] as well as for earlier periods, have been examined. I have also reviewed published work on the subject of problems historically encountered by married couples in the Polish–Lithuanian Commonwealth[3] and in west European

---

[1] P. Laslett, 'Familie und Industrialisierung: "Eine stärke Theorie"', in W. Conze (ed.), *Sozialgeschichte der Familie in der Neuzeit Europas* (Stuttgart, 1976), 31.

[2] D. Biale, 'Eros and Enlightenment: Love against Marriage in the East European Jewish Enlightenment', *Polin*, 1 (1986), 49–67; id., *Eros and the Jews: From Biblical Israel to Contemporary America* (New York, 1992); G. Hundert, 'Jewish Children and Childhood in Early Modern East Central Europe', in D. Kraemer (ed.), *The Jewish Family: Metaphor and Memory* (New York, 1989); id., 'Population and Society in Eighteenth-Century Poland', in J. Michalski (ed.), *Lud żydowski w narodzie polskim* (Warsaw, 1994).

[3] W. Abraham, 'Z dziejów prawa małżeńskiego w Polsce: Zezwolenia panującego lub panów na małżeństwa poddanych i świeckie opłaty małżeńskie', in *Księga pamiątkowa ku czci Bolesława Orzechowicza*, i (Lwów, 1916); K. Wierzbicka-Michalska, 'Małżeństwa wśród chłopów w drugiej połowie XVIII wieku', *Kultura i Społeczeństwo*, 1/3 (1959), 125–44; M. Koczerska, *Rodzina szlachecka w Polsce późnego średniowiecza* (Warsaw, 1975); I. Gleysztorowa, *Wstęp do demografii staropolskiej* (Warsaw, 1976), 105–7, 252–60; M. Bogucka, 'Rodzina w polskim mieszcie XVI–XVII wieku: Wprowadzenie w problematykę', *PH* 74 (1983), 495–506; A. Wyczański, *Polska Rzeczą Pospolitą szlachecką* (Warsaw, 1991), 137–40, 255, 373–7; J. Topolski, *Polska w czasach nowożytnych: Od środkowoeuropejskiej potęgi do utraty niepodległości 1501–1795* (Poznań, 1994), 80–2.

countries, as well as early research on the history of marriage now being carried out in Russia.[4]

In the second half of the eighteenth century Polish townspeople as well as the first maskilim were equally convinced of the significance and almost universal role of marriage. In 1561 Mrowiński-Płoczywlos, councillor of Kazimierz, near Cracow, wrote a pamphlet called *The Married Couple*, in which he said: 'The strengths and very existence of towns in the Polish Commonwealth depend on marriages.'[5] He went on to add that 'there is no other kind of love as honest, as sacrosanct, as passionate as that between a husband and wife, and no power on earth can be considered greater than marital love'.[6] Two hundred years later Jakub Kalmanson, a Warsaw maskil, doctor, and translator from Hebrew to Polish, was making a similar statement. Kalmanson viewed contemporary discussions in the Polish–Lithuanian Commonwealth of political reforms and of Jewish marriage as closely related to a number of general contemporary problems. He wrote: 'in a society, marriage is the most important status people attain, a state that has the greatest influence on social customs and sets the future course of their happiness, a fact attested to by age-old proven practice'.[7] This idea, which was expressed by Polish as well as Jewish writers, is supported by the role of marriage in the economic structure of the eighteenth century when workshops and other enterprises often formed an integral part of households.[8]

Expressions of praise for the marital state and for the sixteenth- to eighteenth-century model of marriage have been peripheral to the interests of historians carrying out research into family life, who have concentrated rather on problems connected with the structure and typology of the family. For example, the high value the Socialist thinker August Bebel placed on the Jewish family, and the tributes he paid to it, have been quite forgotten. In *Die Frau und der Sozialismus* (1920) Bebel wrote that 'during the long period of suffering which [Jews] were subjected to throughout the Christian Middle Ages, they developed a kind of close family life which nowadays serves as a model for the whole bourgeois

---

[4] D. L. Ransel (ed.), *The Family in Imperial Russia: New Lines of Historical Research* (Chicago, 1976).

[5] J. Mrowiński-Płoczywlos, *Stadło małżeńskie 1561*, ed. Z. Celichowski (Cracow, 1890), 17.

[6] Ibid. 3.

[7] J. Kalmanson, *Uwagi nad niniejszym stanem Żydów polskich i ich wydoskonaleniem* (Warsaw, 1797), 50–1.

[8] O. Brunner, 'Das "ganze Haus" und die europäische "Oekonomik"', in his *Neue Wege der Sozialgeschichte: Vorträge und Aufsätze* (Göttingen, 1956), 36, 38, 40; R. Hill and H. Becker, *Marriage and the Family* (Boston, 1962), 679; P. Laslett, 'The Family as a Public and Private Institution: A Historical Perspective', *Journal of Marriage and the Family*, 35 (1973), 481–4; id., 'Familie und Industrialisierung', 14; H. Medick, 'Zur strukturellen Funktion von Haushalt und Familie im Übergang von der traditionellen Agrargesellschaft zum industriellen Kapitalismus: Die protoindustrielle Familienwirtschaft', in Conze (ed.), *Sozialgeschichte der Familie*; Bogucka, 'Rodzina', 496–8; A. Wyrobisz, 'Rodzina w mieście doby przedprzemysłowej a życie gospodarcze: Przegląd badań i problemów', *PH* 72 (1986), 309.

world'.[9] Similarly, Werner Sombart's theory, published in two books in the same year as Bebel's, that the archetypal Jewish family and marriage played an important role in the social and economic changes that characterized the emergence of capitalism has also been ignored.[10]

Jacob Katz maintains that traditional Jewish marriage was based on the realistic premiss that, generally speaking, most people are incapable of curbing their sexual drive, and the Jewish practice of marrying at a young age was intended to prevent extramarital sexual relationships. The ideal age for girls to be married was 16, while for boys it was 18.[11] This allowed young people to begin their sexual lives in a married state. In addition, early marriage made it possible for newly married couples to start their married lives while their parents were still alive. This was important because the shorter life expectancy in those days made it otherwise unlikely that parents would live to see their children married, or that they would be able to help the young couple survive financially.[12]

Jewish unions did not take account of romantic sentiments since it was assumed that teenagers did not possess sufficient life experience to be able to choose the right partners for themselves. So such decisions were left to their more experienced parents,[13] who based their choices on accepted contemporary rational economic criteria,[14] much like the arranged marriages prevalent in other European societies.[15]

Yet, even in much earlier times, Jewish marriages, particularly those of Polish Jews, were recognized as embodying all desirable matrimonial attributes.[16] In the course of the eighteenth century Jewish marital practices attracted the attention of all levels of Polish society, as well as of leading maskilim in other countries.[17] At the turn of the seventeenth century, Sebastian Petrycy of Pilzno, a townsman and leading Polish scholar, had a high opinion of Jewish marriage. Although he hated

---

[9] A. Bebel, *Die Frau und der Sozialismus* (Stuttgart, 1920), 56.

[10] W. Sombart, *Die Juden und das Wirtschaftsleben* (Munich, 1920), 274, 278–9, 292–3; W. Sombart, *Der Bourgeois: Zur Geistesgeschichte der modernen Wirtschaftsmenschen* (Leipzig, 1920), 335, 359–60. One of the exceptions is the book by H. Möller, *Die kleinbürgerliche Familie im 18 Jahrhundert: Verhalten und Gruppenkultur* (Berlin, 1969), which approaches these problems from the point of view of ethnography.

[11] J. Katz, *Masoret umashber* (Jerusalem, 1962), 172.

[12] Ibid. 166–7. 'In other religions a disposition of that kind would lead its possessor into either the desert or a monastic cell, into any life of "chastity" in the sense of a total abstinence from sexual intercourse or sexual perversion. But finding himself in this position, a pious Jew jumps straight into the matrimonial bed, the men at the age of 15 and girls at 12' (Sombart, *Die Juden und das Wirtschaftsleben*, 265, 274, 279).

[13] Katz, *Masoret umashber*, 60; for analogous phenomena in Russia, cf. P. Czap, Jr., 'Marriage and the Peasant Joint Family in the Era of Serfdom', in D. Ransel (ed.), *The Family in Imperial Russia*, 121.

[14] Katz, *Masoret umashber*, 166.

[15] Ibid., 167; cf. Sombart, *Die Juden und das Wirtschaftsleben*, 265, 274, 279.

[16] D. Friedländer, *Aktenstücke die Reform der jüdischen Kolonien in der prussischen Staaten betreffend* (Berlin, 1793), 114. [17] Ibid.

Jews and even accused them of ritual murder and other crimes,[18] Petrycy recommended the apparent advantages of their marriages. In his main scholarly work he wrote that 'Solon enjoined that a husband and wife should have marital relations no more than three times a month, which will lead to children coming much faster. Also, a married couple that lives abstemiously tends to be healthier. Jews are so fertile because they do not come together very often.'[19] His research on this subject was based both on reading and on direct observation of the large Jewish families in Kazimierz, where he spent most of his life and where there was the largest concentration of Jews in the Commonwealth at that time.[20] Petrycy believed that the country's demographic potential could be improved if Poles imitated Jewish marital practices. Once the impoverished Polish town dwellers began to imitate the examples of the gentry, however, no other civic representatives praised Jewish marriages in the way Petrycy did. It was only during the period of the Polish Enlightenment that the model of Jewish marriage was promoted on a wider scale because it conformed to popular ideas based on contemporary mercantilist and cameralist principles. The doctrines of the physiocrats, also popular in Poland in the second half of the eighteenth century, also contributed to the favourable regard for Jewish marriage practice. The physiocrats maintained that a rise in population would provide a panacea for the social and economic maladies afflicting the Commonwealth.[21] They believed increased peace and harmony among married couples would favour an increased birth-rate, which would eventually result in a rise in the population.[22] Among those who shared these views was Stanisław Poniatowski, the father and namesake of the last Polish king. In his plan for social and political reforms in the middle of the eighteenth century, he exhorted 'everyone to marry and work for the common good' and not to remain in an unmarried state too long.[23] Instructions issued to administrators in charge of the Roś estates, for example, told them to make certain that any widowed peasant should 'not remain without a wife any longer than six months and [that he] should

[18] K. Bartoszewicz, *Antysemityzm w literaturze polskiej XV–XVII wieku* (Warsaw, 1914), 127; P. Czartoryski, 'Stanowisko Sebastiana Petrycego w naukach ekonomicznych', in *Sebastian Petrycy uczony doby Odrodzenia* (Wrocław, 1957), 105; R. Wołoszyński, 'Poglądy społeczne i polityczne Sebastiana Petrycego', ibid. 255–6.

[19] Sebastian Petrycy, *Polityki arystotelesowej to jest rządu Rzeczypospolitej z dokładem ksiąg ośmioro*, ii (Cracow, 1605), 249.

[20] Czartoryski, *Stanowisko Sebastiana Petrycego*, 105.

[21] E. Lipiński, *Studia nad historią polskiej myśli ekonomicznej* (Warsaw, 1956), 425–6; J. Wybicki, *Listy patriotyczne*, ed. K. Opałek (Wrocław, 1955); J. Lechicka, *Józef Wybicki: Życie i twórczość* (Toruń, 1962), 202–3.

[22] *Monitor*, no. 57 (1768), 463–5; J. F. Nax, 'Wykład początkowych prawideł ekonomiki politycznej z przystosowaniem przepisów gospodarstwa narodowego do onego wydźwignienia i polepszenia stosownie do aktualnego stanu w którym rzeczy zostają', in his *Wybór pism*, ed. E. Sierpiński (Warsaw, 1956), 97–9.

[23] S. Poniatowski, 'List ziemianina do pewnego przyjaciela z inszego województwa', in K. Kantecki, *Stanisław Poniatowski kasztelan krakowski, ojciec Stanisława Augusta*, ii (Poznań, 1880), p. C.

be ordered to marry under the penalty of being evicted from his farm'.[24] Such exhortations did not fall on fertile ground in the agrarian society of the Commonwealth, however. For a peasant household to survive in those days, both spouses had to work the land.

However, there were barriers to marriage, including statutory proscriptions and limitations on the social structure of the Commonwealth. A few marriages did take place between couples one of whom may have come from the gentry and the other from the urban or peasant class,[25] but such marriages were widely disapproved of among the gentry, and Andrzej Zamoyski and Józef Wybicki's plan to abolish the ban on marriage between partners from different social backgrounds was categorically rejected by the Sejm in 1780.[26] The most painful examples of such restrictions applied to children of serfs and inhabitants of small towns owned by the nobility, who were banned from leaving their native place to marry anyone who lived on estates belonging to other noblemen, even if they were of the same social class. The only marriage partners they could choose were serfs who belonged to the same master.[27]

In the different circles of Polish society this situation produced ever more lively discussions on the problems of Jewish marriages in the Commonwealth and the ethics governing cohabitation between husbands and wives. Hugo Kołłątaj, the Lithuanian deputy chancellor and a leading luminary of the Polish Enlightenment, left a broadly conceived, but unfortunately unfinished, scholarly work devoted to these problems.[28] The *Monitor*, a contemporary periodical, published material intended to prove a causal relationship between the observance of moral principles in marriage and a potential growth in the birth-rate. One article published in the *Monitor* in 1768 states that 'public abstemiousness is the most crucial factor in population growth. Experience teaches us that dissolute relation-

[24] 'Instrukcja dla komisarza dóbr Roś, 24. VI. 1804', in B. Baranowski, J. Bartyś, A. Keckowa, and J. Leskiewicz (eds.), *Instrukcje gospodarcze dla dóbr magnackich i szlacheckich z XII–XIX wieku*, i (Wrocław, 1958), 459; cf. W. Kula, 'La Seigneurie et la familie paysanne dans la Pologne du XVIIIe siècle', *Annales, économies, sociétés, civilisations*, 27 (1972), 949–58; and D. Gaunt and G. Lofgren, 'Remarriage in the Nordic Countries: The Cultural and Socio-economic Background', in J. Dupaquier, *Marriage and Remarriage in Populations of the Past* (London, 1981), 51.

[25] W. Dworzaczek, 'Przenikanie szlachty do stanu mieszczańskiego w Wielkopolsce w XVI i XVII wieku', *PH* 47/4 (1956), 693; T. Opas, 'Z problemów awansu społecznego mieszczan w XVII i XVIII wieku', *PH* 65/3 (1974), 465–77.

[26] F. Trojanowski, *Uwagi na niektóre punkta nowoutworzonego prawa i dowody, że mimo j.w.: Zamoyskiego musieli być umieszczone* (n.p., 1780); E. Borkowska-Bagieńska, *Zbiór praw sądowych Andrzeja Zamoyskiego* (Poznań, 1986), 172–3.

[27] Abraham, 'Z dziejów prawa małżeńskiego w Polsce', i, 35, 37; J. Bergerówna, *Księżna pani na Kocku i Siemiatyczach (Działalność gospodarcza i społeczna Anny z Sapiehów Jabłonowskiej)* (Lwów, 1936), 259, 361; J. Rafacz, *Ustrój wsi samorządnej małopolskiej w XVIII wieku* (Lublin, 1922); W. Dworzaczek, *'Dobrowolne' poddaństwo chłopów* (Warsaw, 1952), 92–8; A. Konieczny, 'Ograniczenia swobody w zawieraniu małżeństw wśród chłopów na Górnym Śląsku w połowie XVIII i na początku XIX wieku', *Studia śląskie*, i (1958), 102–8.

[28] H. Kołłątaj, *Porządek fizyczno–moralny*, ed. K. Opałek (Warsaw, 1955), 197.

ships contribute but very little to this growth, or can even result in a fall in the country's birth rate'.[29] Discussions on these questions reached such a pitch that the political subjects previously dominating the Polish theatre of the Enlightenment period were replaced by plays about love and marriage, praising middle-class virtues and the ideal marriage arising out of them.[30]

However, though the *Monitor*, in an earlier article in 1768, proclaimed that 'present day virtues are becoming more appealing and vices less offensive because of the prevailing good taste and refinement of our age',[31] there was evidence that behaviour seen by contemporary public opinion as symptomatic of a progressive decline in moral values was becoming more and more common. This was one of the effects of accelerating population mobility which, despite the limits imposed on the serflike peasants and on some of the residents of towns owned by the gentry, resulted in many people losing their sense of stability, alienating them from traditional, generally accepted moral standards. The decline in moral values led to an increase in premarital sex[32] and adultery, and even in bigamy;[33] and along with these the number of cases of venereal infection also began to rise. The effects were most pronounced in the expanding urban centre of Warsaw and its suburbs,[34] with individual mobility more apparent than in other parts of the country.

In 1789 the Four Year Sejm created a number of Commissions of Civil and Military Order to oversee the cities. They were designed to combat immorality, but these stopped short of implementing the death sentence for adultery required by the Magdeburg law,[35] although the committees were set up to eradicate marital infidelity.

In the same period, Jan Bohomolec, who had led the battle against superstition and belief in devils and witches,[36] was the parish priest of the Praga and Skaryszew church (which are now suburbs of Warsaw). These districts were

---

[29] *Monitor*, 7 (1768), 453–64.

[30] M. Klimowicz, *Początki teatru stanisławowskiego 1765–1773* (Warsaw, 1965), 180, 209–12, 219, 230.                      [31] *Monitor*, 4 (1768), 28.

[32] W. Borejko, *Pamiętnik*, ed. M. Grabowski (Warsaw, 1845), 37–8.

[33] F. Karpiński, *Pamiętniki* (n.p., 1890), 81; *Monitor*, 3 (1768), 17–18; AGAD, Księga miejska Uniejowa, no. 25, fo. 171.

[34] [M. D. Krajewski], *Podolanka wychowana w stanie natury, życie i przypadki swoje opisująca* (Lwów, 1784), 72–3; id., *Dzwon staropolskiej fabryki* ([Warsaw], 1791), 35–7; 'In Warsaw, it is customary to behave in a depraved way and the resulting excesses, as is the case in all capital cities, are more extreme and more widespread than they are in the provinces' (F. L. de la Fontaine, 'Über Freudenmädchen und Lustseuche', in his *Chirurgisch–medicinische Abhandlungen verschiedenen Inhalts Polen betreffend* (Breslau, 1792), 129; J. U. Niemcewicz, *Pamiętniki czasów moich*, ed. J. Dihm, i (Warsaw, 1957), 41; A. Ostrowski, *Żywot Tomasza Ostrowskiego*, i (Paris, 1836), 65; J. Michalski, '"Warszawa" czyli o antystołecznych nastrojach w czasach Stanisława Augusta', *Warszawa XVIII wieku*, i (Warsaw, 1972), 46, 49, 51, 77–8.

[35] Cf. B. Groicki, *Porządek sądów i spraw miejskich prawa majdeburskiego w Koronie Polskiej*, ed. K. Koranyi (Warsaw, 1953), 207–8; J. Riabinin, *Prawo małżeńskie wedle praktyki miejskiej lubelskiej w XVII wieku* (Lwów, 1933), 15–17.

[36] W. Smoleński, *Przewrót umysłowy w Polsce wieku xviii* (Warsaw, 1949), 56–8, 63, 82, 312.

places of the kind where there were significant deviations from traditional standards of behaviour, and Bohomolec urged his parishioners to model their marital life on that of the Jews. In his sermons he emphasized that Jews 'get married solely to procreate their own nation, which they believe is the only one that worships the one true God and makes Him known to other nations'.[37] This statement was based on his observations of the Jewish community concentrated in Praga (Jews were banned from living in Warsaw itself at that time), where Bohomolec was carrying out his pastoral duties. In those days Bohomolec's sermons were rare events, and his admiration for Jewish marriage, proclaimed from the pulpit, the most effective contemporary mass medium,[38] would most certainly have reached virtually every member of the Polish community in the parish.

But the most adulatory statements on Jewish marriage were made by the Revd Stanisław Staszic, a burgher and prominent figure of the Polish Enlightenment, whose interest in the institution was that of a philosopher. He wrote in his main work, *Ród ludzki* (The Human Race):

even now, among these few remaining wandering Jews . . . we find certain relationships closely linked to serenity, family happiness, the real aspirations of marriage and the value of national customs . . . They do not indulge in debauchery, profligacy, widespread adultery and fornication. They stand out among all the European nations among whom they live for their continence. Among them one does not find drunkenness and gluttony, but rather modest behaviour among the young, *fidelity in marriage* and the most intense love both on the part of children for their parents and parents for their children.[39]

Elsewhere he also wrote that the Jews 'stand head and shoulders above any of us in exercising their status as fathers and husbands in marriages'.[40]

The evaluation of Jewish marriage by Sebastian Petrycy and Stanisław Staszic, who wrote nearly two centuries apart, have in common that, while each was a leading Polish scholar who took the anti-Jewish stance characteristic of the Polish urban middle classes,[41] this did not prevent them from expressing genuine admiration for the virtues of Jewish marriage. But there were differences in their orientation.

[37] J. C. Bohomolec, 'Nauka dla włościan o zacności stanu małżeńskiego przez Jana Chryzostoma proboszcza Pragi i Skaryszewa, własnoręcznie w testamencie jego napisana rok 1793', in A. Wejnert (ed.), *Starożytności Warszawy*, iv (Warsaw, 1856), 132; E. Ringelblum, 'A prager galekh vegn yidishn familien-lebn', in his *Kapiteln Geshikhte fun amolikn yidshn lebn in Poyln*, ed. J. Shatzky (Buenos Aires, 1953), 105–7; cf. J. Goldberg, 'Poles and Jews in the Seventeenth and Eighteenth Centuries: Rejection or Acceptance', *Jahrbücher für Geschichte Osteuropas*, 22 (1974), 256.

[38] J. Tazbir, 'Rola żywego słowa w polskiej propagandzie wyznaniowej', *Kwartalnik Historyczny*, 87 (1980), 293, 295, 305–6.

[39] S. Staszic, *Ród ludzki*, ed. Z. Daszkowski and B. Suchodolski, iii (Warsaw, 1959), 288–9; emphasis added.

[40] S. Staszic, 'O przyczynach szkodliwości Żydów i o środkach usposobienia ich, aby się społeczeństwu użytecznemi stali', *Gazeta Wiejska*, 26 (1818), 201–8; 27: 209–16; 28: 217–24; *Pamiętnik Warszawski*, 4 (1816), 408; cf. Goldberg, *Poles and Jews*, 257.

[41] Petrycy, *Polityki arystotelesowej*, 249.

Staszic evaluated all aspects of family relationships between Jews very favourably, while Petrycy was only interested in the details relating to how they lived as husband and wife and the resulting high birth-rate. Staszic's treatment of the subject was influenced by three factors that did not exist in Petrycy's time: (1) the concept of morality and evaluation of the institution of marriage according to the ideology of the Enlightenment most clearly defined by the pseudonymous French *philosophe* M. Morelly in his *Code de la nature*; (2) contemporary Polish judgements on the virtues of Jewish marriage; and (3) the increasing breakdown of marriage among Polish Catholics in the eighteenth century, which prompted Staszic's unfavourable comparison with traditional matrimonial practices among Jews.

These virtues had already been described by the maskil Jakub Kalmanson, who insisted that 'It is still possible to observe happiness among members of this nation, even though they are forced to wander far and wide. Jewish marriage is not dominated by the family arguments, scandalous scenes and licentious debauchery seen among other nations as a result of the shameful practices of our age.'[42] Kalmanson stated: 'The marital state is one of the religious and secular rituals carefully and elegantly observed by the Jewish nation and provides a kind of proof of this nation's true pedigree, and for this it is particularly worthy of even greater reverence and respect than all others.'[43] This statement does not differ substantially from that of Staszic quoted above. Even such a famous representative of the Haskalah in Germany as David Friedländer wrote that Polish Jews are famous for 'the sanctity of their marriages'.[44] But this sanctity was not always unblemished; there were some rare, but well-documented, incidents that deviated from the ideals described above, and both men and women were implicated.[45]

During the sixteenth and seventeenth centuries more permissive practices were encouraged by the Italian Jews arriving in Poland, but the practices did not take root in the Jewish community, despite the lament of the preacher Tsevi Hirsh Koidonover about declining morals among the Jews.[46] In sources from the second half of the eighteenth century there are more frequent references to behaviour that deviated from traditional standards of married life among Polish Jews. Certainly the social and economic changes that exerted such a strong influence on the life of Polish families to some extent also influenced the Jewish community in the Commonwealth. For example, in 1750 in Tarnów a Jewish resident sent an official complaint to Duchess Barbara Sanguszko, the lady of that town, which related the following story: 'While on my way back from the Brody market, rumours reached my ears that in my absence a local *ziemski* [a delegate to the regional Jewish council] had visited my wife in our shop when she was alone all

[42] [Kalmanson], *Uwagi nad niniejszym stanem Żydów polskich*, 51.                [43] Ibid.

[44] Friedländer, *Aktenstücke die Reform der jüdischen Kolonien betreffend*, 114.

[45] M. Bałaban, 'Umysłowość i moralność żydostwa polskiego w XVI wieku', in *Kultura staropolska* (Cracow, 1932), 632.                                                        [46] Ibid.

night; and he was seen to leave her at midnight dressed only in a shirt and a Polish nobleman's robe. With all due respect.'[47] In her turn, the duchess ordered the rabbinical court to carry out a special investigation into the case.[48]

Towards the end of the century Warsaw Jews were directing similar complaints to the president of Warsaw, Ignacy Zakrzewski.[49] There are also recorded cases of Jewish girls losing their virginity before marriage. The rabbinical court records include the names of girls who allegedly fell while climbing trees and lost their virginity in this way. These rabbinical affidavits were intended to rehabilitate the victimized girls,[50] who would otherwise have been particularly likely to encounter difficulties when trying to find a husband.[51]

Jewish community elders and the Wojewoda's courts also attempted to prevent any relaxation of moral codes among the Jews, and they dispensed severe punishments to engaged couples who, in defiance of the existing interdictions, indulged in premarital sexual activity. In the second half of the eighteenth century in Lwów, a provincial court sentenced a Jewish youth to sit in a cage outside the synagogue for a whole week and to pay a fine not just for his own indiscretion, but also on behalf of his fiancée, who was named as his 'co-defendant', even though they had been married in the meantime.[52] The records also reveal sexual liaisons between Jewish girls and Poles, as well as wives who deceived their Jewish husbands with Polish townsmen.[53] Cases in which Jewish men entered into sexual liaisons with Polish girls were treated as scandals and were exposed to public criticism.[54] Sometimes it was the extensive travel for study at foreign educational establishments[55] or frequent journeys on brokerage or trading activities under-

[47] 'Sprawa między Abrahamem a Hasklem Wulfem o życie pokątne z żoną Abrahama', AP Cracow, Archiwum Sanguszków, no. 1725.

[48] The final judgment was issued by the landowner's court in Tarnów, which ruled that 'the plaintiff does not agree to call any witnesses to be sworn on the Torah—Abraham Wielopolski (the plaintiff) was sentenced to pay a double fine of 50 gold zlotys to be paid into the coffers of the Duchess' (ibid.).

[49] A. Zahorski, *Ignacy Wyssogota Zakrzewski prezydent Warszawy* (Warsaw, 1963), 263–4.

[50] A. Tcherikover, 'Shimon Dubnovs Arkhiv', *Historishe Shriftn*, 2 (1937), 571.

[51] In 1791, because of the alleged immoral behaviour of a girl, her engagement was broken in Żarki in Małopolska, as can be seen in the entry of the Civil and Military Commission of the Książ and Lelów districts (AP Cracow, IT 175, 209).

[52] Z. Pazdro, *Organizacja i praktyka żydówskich sądów podwojewodzińskich w okresie 1740–1772 roku* (Lwów, 1903), 155–6.

[53] L. Charewiczowa, *Dzieje miasta Złoczowa* (Złoczów, 1929), 63; M. Bałaban, *Historia Żydów w Krakowie i na Kazimierzu 1304–1868*, ii (Cracow, 1936), 518; J. Bartyś, 'Z przeszłości kulturalnej miasteczek południowo-wschodniej Wielkopolski w XVIII wieku', *Prace i Materiały Etnograficzne*, 13 (1959), 341; Klimowicz, *Początki teatru*, 152.

[54] 'For raping a girl, Jakub, a Jewish proprietor in Bolesławiec, was sentenced to pay the victim 100 zlotys and two cows, 2 zlotys costs, and one week in the stocks. However, the girl also got 50 lashes for *failing to shout* and was banished from the town' (W. Patykiewicz, 'Archidiakonat wielunski', *Wiadomości diecezjalne* (Częstochowa), 1 (1958), 37; emphasis added); 'While a Jew who was suspected of adultery with a Christian had to pay a fine of 50 *grzywny* to the Roman Catholic Church and 20 to the Armenian Church' (Charewiczowa, *Dzieje miasta Złoczowa*, 63).

[55] We find the following entry in the census of the Jewish population in Działoszyn (Wieluń

taken by Jewish men that resulted in the breakdown of their marriages.[56] The 1791 population census records in the town of Chrzanów in the Małopolska region list several Jewish women's names, each followed by a brief and unequivocal entry stating that 'the husband had gone away'.[57] At about the same time, the magistrate in Sieradz issued documents to two Jews (one of them to a man whose son-in-law had vanished without trace, and the other to his travelling companion) requesting that 'these travellers, who are looking for their sons-in-law in various large and small towns and villages, should not be molested by anyone on their way'.[58]

Although such incidents were far from widespread, there were, nevertheless, demands for action by the maskilim, who were striving to counter these tendencies in three ways: (1) by introducing measures to preserve traditional family values, (2) by modernizing ways of arranging marriages, and (3) by addressing the subject of the age of marriage. The very principles that had been traditionally recognized as essential for preserving custom and happy marriage were now pointed to by reformers from the Enlightenment camp in Poland in the eighteenth century as the main reason for the repeated deviation from the generally admired virtues of Jewish marriage in the Commonwealth.

Jakub Kalmanson condemned the methods used by the Jewish community and maintained that only the threat of severe punishment would prevent the complete destruction of traditional marital values. At the same time he warned that

as soon as the restraints the law imposes on them [the Jews] and the fear of excommunication recedes . . . should the horror at the spectre of adultery, rape, and any similar type of seduction disappear, or the punishments for these offences and others of this type cease, we would soon see among the present descendants of the ancient Hebrews the same excesses and crimes that are openly and shamelessly perpetrated by other European nations.[59]

Kalmanson, an advocate of the Jewish Enlightenment movement, also attacked the method of selecting marriage partners. As part of his plans for the social and cultural reform of Polish Jews, he proposed that parents cease the arbitrary practice of selecting marriage partners for their children, because 'it is impossible to create such unions without the knowledge of and against the will of those persons who are to be united. This step requires complete freedom of choice and very serious thought.'[60] For its time, this was a radical idea: to introduce such

region): 'Bluma, a married woman, Wulf Szaykowicz, her husband who is studying in Abszerdam [Amsterdam], *who does not want to return*' (AGAD, Wieluńskie varia, no. 6, fo. 80; emphasis added).

[56] Declaration by a nobleman from the Cracow province in 1792: 'The proprietor of an inn, Mosiek Herszlikowicz, is on his way to the Moscow province; it is not known if he is still alive' (AP Cracow, IT 191a; not paginated).

[57] Ibid.; cf. an analogous case in M. Bałaban, *Die Judenstadt von Lublin* (Berlin, 1919), 78.

[58] AGAD, Księga miejska Sieradza, no. 65 (not paginated).

[59] [Kalmanson], *Uwagi nad niniejszym stanem Żydów polskich*, 51.                      [60] Ibid.

basic changes in family relationships among the Commonwealth Jews also carried a more general message, since arranged marriages continued to be widely practised among other European nations.

The Jewish custom of marrying young also met with strong criticism from the maskilim and from others outside the Jewish community. Abraham Hirszowicz, a maskil and official of the court of King Stanisław Augustus, joined the debate, and in his *Plan for the Reform and Betterment of Customs among the Jewish Residents of the Polish Kingdom*, he wrote that

there is no other country apart from Poland where Jews marry their children so very young, because this is the way that the parents make an arrangement where one side agrees to give a dowry and pay for the wedding and the other side promises to provide the clothes and other presents, and they draw up marriage contracts according to such an agreement, counting on the fact that the children will give all this back to them when they grow up. In the meantime, the parents may become impoverished or go completely bankrupt, and the children have no profession and are not trained or able to carry out any work or trade. When none of the promised clothes, presents, or agreed dowry materializes, and they have no proper education, they begin to quarrel among themselves, which often results in separations and divorces. Frequently, a husband will abandon his wife and set off blindly into the wide world, becoming a vagabond and prevaricator because he has not learned any other way of making a living.[61]

Hirszowicz maintained that the existing circumstances made it impossible for a teenage couple to earn a living, and in many cases the parents were not in any position to help them because they simply did not have the financial means to do so. His arguments, which were directly opposed to traditional beliefs, were intended to show that marriages between juvenile partners not only did not create happiness, but were in fact the main cause for the steady economic decline of a large sector of the Polish Jewish community.

The causal relationship between the absence of occupational training for men and their marital problems, which Hirszowicz emphasized so strongly, coincided almost exactly with remarks on the subject of marriages in Polish society made by Stefan Garczyński, a *wojewoda* of Poznań and representative and early advocate of the Enlightenment in the Commonwealth. In his book *The Anatomy of the Polish Commonwealth*,[62] which went through several editions in the mid-eighteenth century, Garczyński says:

I agree that in Poland most marriages are in an appalling state, but why is this so? It is because our compatriots have a tendency not to persevere at anything, and none knows

---

[61] A. Hirszowicz, 'Projekt do reformy i poprawy obyczajów', in *MDSC* 523.

[62] L. Wegner, 'Stefan Garczyński wojewoda poznański i dzieło jego "Anatomia Rzeczypospolitej Polskiej", 1706–1755', *Roczniki Towarzystwa Przyjaciół Nauk Poznańskiego*, 6 (1871); E. Rostworowski, 'Spór Stefana Garczyńskiego z braćmi Załuskimi o rolę duchowieństwa w "Anatomii Rzeczypospolitej"', in his *O naprawę Rzeczypospolitej XVII–XVIII wieku* (Warsaw, 1965), 214–16.

how to concentrate on or keep to any one trade or profession; as soon as he drops one, he attempts to pick up another without having mastered the first.[63]

Abraham Hirszowicz found analogous problems in the way Jewish families were organized—problems that Garczyński had already observed in Polish families several decades earlier. Garczyński thought Polish irresponsibility was the origin of these problems, but Hirszowicz perceived early marriage as the cause of such shortcomings in the Jewish family.

Jakub Kalmanson also described the 'custom among Jews offered by these sanctified unions: in place of the expected benefits there was nothing but agonizing slavery for the wretched victims who had been forced into a state of bondage against their will'.[64] Perhaps there are echoes of the author's own experiences here, for the early maskilim in Poland were themselves still being married according to traditional custom. Information about this subject can be gleaned from three eighteenth-century memoirs, all written by Jews living in the Commonwealth. Two of the memoirs were written when the authors were young and had divorced their first wives. One of them was Dov Ber from Bolechów, who was married at the age of 12,[65] and the other was Salomon Maimon, who came from the Radziwiłł estates in Belarus and later became an important philosopher and Kant scholar.[66] The author of the third memoir was Moshe Wassercug, a Jew from Wielkopolska, who was married at 18.[67] Based on his own experiences, Maimon wrote down his reflections on the Jewish custom of early marriage.[68]

Apart from Maimon, none of the maskilim who had criticized the custom of early marriage among Jews ever mentioned the biological consequences of such early marriages, despite the fact that they were all keen observers of contemporary society, and two, Salomon Polonus and Jakub Kalmanson, were medical doctors. As early as the seventeenth and eighteenth centuries, some doctors outside the Jewish community wrote about the unfavourable biological and psychological effects of marriages between juvenile partners, based on contemporary interpretations. Sebastian Petrycy, who was both a medical doctor and a philosopher, while praising the high birth-rate among Jews, pointed out that 'in France babies of low birth weight are common because of the custom of marrying early, and this applies equally to the Jews'.[69] At the end of the eighteenth century, F. L. de la Fontaine, a naturalized Polish medical doctor from Alsace, wrote that the custom of marrying early was causing a deterioration in the biological condition of the

---

[63] S. Garczyński, *Anatomia Rzeczypospolitej Polskiej* (Warsaw, 1747), 101–2.

[64] [Kalmanson], *Uwagi nad niniejszym stanem Żydów polskich*, 51.

[65] Dov miBolekhov, *Zikhronot*, ed. M. Wischnitzer (Berlin, 1922), 45.

[66] S. Maimon, *Gesammelte Werke*, ed. M. Verr, i (Hildesheim, 1965), 553–4.

[67] 'Korot Moshe Wassercug', ed. H. Loewe, *Jahrbücher für jüdische Literatur und Geschichte*, 2 (1910), 2.

[68] Maimon, *Gesammelte Werke*, 553–4.

[69] Petrycy, *Polityki arystotelesowej*, 249.

Jewish population in the Commonwealth,[70] though it must be pointed out that de la Fontaine and others writing at the time also suggested other causes[71] for this state, and that it did not differ significantly from the predominantly poor physical condition of the Polish population as a whole in the eighteenth century.[72]

The problem of early marriage became the subject of the social and cultural reform projects directed at the Jewish population in Poland drawn up by both Poles and maskilim during the Four Year Sejm. A directive promulgated in 1790 by the deputation for Jewish reforms appointed by this Sejm recommended that

Rabbis should refuse to marry people who are too young, because they produce children before they can afford to feed them. Those wanting to marry should be required to have at least 2,000 zlotys in ready cash or some steady income from business, a trade, or agriculture. This should result in a reduction in the number of loafers, paupers, and criminal offenders who are usually impoverished, making it possible for people to multiply and populate the country with useful citizens rather than encumber it even further.[73]

A further directive announced by the same deputation in 1791 banned marriage for women under 12 and for men under 18.[74] The maskilim also drew up concrete proposals in their reform plans for setting a minimum age for Jewish marriages. Kalmanson proposed that girls under 14 and boys under 16 should not be allowed to marry.[75] The remaining two maskilim wanted to set the minimum age even higher, with Hirszowicz demanding a minimum age for girls of 15 and 18 for their partners.[76] Like Hirszowicz, Salomon Polonus thought that boys ought to be at least 18 and girls 16 before they were allowed to marry.[77] These proposals were not intended to eliminate the Jewish custom of early marriage entirely, but they were intended to do away with the practice of arranged marriages.

The maskilim attempted to combine the need for changing the age structure of partners entering marriage with the value of productiveness, and they insisted that this change would improve the circumstances of the Jewish community in the Commonwealth. Hirszowicz argued that the measures might make it possible for

---

[70] De la Fontaine, *Chirurgisch–medicinische Abhandlungen*, 151–2.

[71] 'The unemployed Jew, exhausted, in poor health, puts himself, his progeny, his house, and the area where he resides at risk of infection' (ibid.); J. J. Kausch, 'Wizerunek narodu polskiego: Opis podróży ze Śląska do Krakowa w Małopolsce', in W. Zawadzki (ed.), *Polska stanisławowska w oczach cudzoziemców* (Warsaw, 1963), 341; M. Butrymowicz, 'Sposób uformowania Żydów polskich w pożytecznych krajowi obywatelów', in *MDSC* 84.

[72] Z. Kuchowicz, *Z badań nad stanem biologicznym społeczeństwa polskiego od schyłku XV do końca XVIII wieku* (Łódź, 1972), 69–73.

[73] 'Punkta do Prześwietnej Deputacyi reformę Żydów ukladającej roku 1790 podane', in *MDSC* 230.

[74] 'Reforma Żydów: Projekt od Deputacyi do tego wyznaczonej', in *MDSC* 224; J. Michalski, 'Sejmowe projekty reformy położenia ludności żydowskiej w Polsce w latach 1789–1792', in Michalski (ed.), *Lud żydówski w narodzie polskim* (Warsaw, 1994), 27.

[75] [Kalmanson], *Uwagi nad niniejszym stanem Żydów polskich*, 52.

[76] Hirszowicz, *Projekt do reformy i poprawy obyczajów*, 523.

[77] Salomon Polonus, 'Projekt względem reformy Zydów', in *MDSC* 429.

young Jews to complete their primary education and to learn a trade, which would create better material conditions for the young partners: 'at this age [i.e. somewhat older] they will have more sense and will try to earn their bread, and they will have more chance to achieve this'.[78] Kalmanson thought that before being allowed to marry, every man should obtain a school-leaving certificate and a testimonial from a trade guild stating that he had completed his term of apprenticeship; he should also demonstrate a good knowledge of Polish.[79] Salomon Polonus put forward similar proposals, adding that every 'woman intending to marry should be capable of carrying out women's work such as spinning, sewing, mending, etc.'.[80]

The proposed legislation by Polonus and Hirszowicz to control Jewish marriages was paralleled in the maskilim's efforts to increase the level of government interference in the internal life of the Jewish community. Creation of new administrative organs in the Commonwealth in the second half of the eighteenth century generated conditions that made it possible to implement these proposals. Nevertheless, proposals by Jews as well as Poles during the Four Year Sejm to change the structure of Jewish marriage marked a new departure in social and cultural reform plans for Polish Jews in the Commonwealth. The maskilim's aim was not just to remove the marital problems caused by the immaturity of the partners and thereby reduce the number of divorces, but also to change the overall occupational structure: to stabilize and improve the economic situation of the Jewish population and help it draw closer to the mainstream of Polish culture. These proposals show that the problem of Jewish marriage constituted a crucial contemporary issue, not only because it was part of the reform plans but also through its importance compared with other issues facing the Jewish community in the Commonwealth.

Ironically, at the same time there were attempts to introduce various obstacles to the institution of Jewish marriage which were unrelated to the Jewish reform plans. Criticisms of the Jewish practice of marrying early were voiced not only by some minor writers[81] but also by the leading Polish writer and poet of the Enlightenment, Bishop Ignacy Krasicki.[82] Jewish marriages became the main object of anti-Jewish attacks and the principal target of the proposed repressive measures (which were intended as a means to impose additional taxes as well as limit the growth of the Jewish population in the Commonwealth). The revenue and population control potential became apparent during the 1730s and 1740s, when there was a sudden need to raise funds to increase the size of the armed forces. A resolution of the regional council in Halicz in 1736 which banned marriage for under-age Jews was clearly repressive.[83] At the Sejm of 1744, Horain, the

---

[78] Hirszowicz, *Projekt do reformy*, 523.

[79] [Kalmanson], *Uwagi nad niniejszym stanem Żydów polskich*, 52.

[80] Polonus, 'Projekt względem reformy Żydów', 429.

[81] W. Smoleński, *Stan i sprawa Żydów polskich w xviii wieku* (Warsaw, 1876), 14.

[82] I. Krasicki, *Pan podstoli* (Cracow, 1927), 362.

[83] *Akta grodzkie i ziemskie z czasów Rzeczypospolitej Polskiej*, xxv (Lwów, 1935), 146.

delegate from the Wilno region, combined financial considerations with repressive measures against Jews by suggesting that 'in order to reduce the number
of Jews, Jews should not get married until they are at least 30. If they want to get
married before 30, both the bridegroom and bride should pay a fine amounting to
the number of thalers equal to the number of years remaining to their thirtieth
birthdays'.[84]

Neither the resolution of the regional council in Halicz nor delegate Horain's
proposal provoked any further response. A further proposal by the prominent
magnates Andrzej Zamoyski and Józef Wybicki, part of the legal reform plan prohibiting early Jewish marriage to reduce the Jewish population in the country, was
also rejected, but on other grounds.[85] Following a long debate in the 1775 Sejm,
still another proposal to regulate Jewish marriage was considered which would
have prevented Jews unable to pay their taxes from marrying.[86] It, too, was never
implemented.

Following the second partition of Poland attempts were also made to enact
similar repressive legislation in the newly formed province of southern Prussia
(Südpreussen).[87] In Silesia repressive measures were considered[88] to give the
rulers of this dictatorial state the power to interfere in the private lives of the
population.[89] None of these proposals produced any practical results because the
Jews knew how to react effectively to news of any projected reform plans, whether
they were prepared by the maskilim or representatives of the Polish Enlightenment or Prussians: the strategy was to marry off their under-age children quickly
to escape any impending restrictions.[90]

The repressive measures directed against Jewish marriage applied different
criteria to the Jewish community than to other inhabitants. In an era when population theories linked a rise in living standards and economic improvement to
increased demographic potential, the intention of such restrictions was to bring
about a decline in the Jewish population by limiting the freedom of the Jews to

---

[84] 'Dyaryusz sejmu ordynaryjnego, sześcioniedzielnego grodzieńskiego in anno 1744', in M.
Skibiński (ed.), *Europa a Polska w dobie wojny o sukcesyę austryacką w latach 1740–1745*, ii (Cracow,
1912), 316.

[85] A. Zamoyski, *Zbiór praw sądowych*, ed. W. Dutkiewicz (Warsaw, 1874), 262; cf. Borkowska-
Bagienska, *Zbiór praw sądowych Andrzeja Zamoyskiego*, 135–7.

[86] *Volumina Legum*, viii. 95; Uniwersał Komisji Skarbu Koronnego, AGAD, Ostrzeszów
Grodzie Rel. Obl., no. 16, fo. 58.

[87] I. Bartfeld, 'Przyczynki do historii Żydów w Prusach południowych i nowowschodnich
1793–1806', MA thesis, Żydowski Instytut Historyczny, Warsaw 40, 65; J. Wąsicki, *Ziemie polskie
pod zaborem pruskim: Prusy południowe 1793–1806* (Wrocław, 1957), 109, 292–3.

[88] F. A. Zimmermann, *Geschichte der Verfassung der Juden im Herzogthum Schlesien* (Breslau,
1791), 35, 40–1, 48, 59, 75–8; J. Ziekursch, *Die Ergebnisse der friderizianischen Städteverwaltung und
die Städteordnung Steins* (Jena, 1908), 63, 65, 67.

[89] G. Ostreich, 'Strukturprobleme des europäischen Absolutismus', *Vierteljahrschrift für Sozial-
und Wirtschaftsgeschichte*, 55 (1968), 331, 337, 343.

[90] Ibid. 36–58.

marry. Even well-publicized statements by respected leaders about the exemplary character of Jewish marriages could do nothing to prevent the restrictions.

## THE AGE OF MARRIAGE AND THE MARRIAGE MARKET: THE 1791 CENSUS

What knowledge we have about the age at which Jews married in the past is based on sources that contain information about individual Jewish marriages. Such sources alone do not provide realistic estimates about the scale of the phenomenon or about changes in the structure of Jewish marriage in this period. To study these aspects, demographic sources must be examined. There are a number of serious obstacles here, however: sources such as these are not as easily available for the Jewish population as they are for the Christian population (e.g. surviving parish records[91] and lists of members of Roman Catholic parishes). These were required by Church authorities, and contained registers of newly married couples, and sometimes even the age of the couples when they married.[92] But, although reform plans of the Four Year Sejm called for permanent registers of the Jewish population indicating their civil state,[93] it was not until the introduction of the Napoleonic Code in the era of the Grand Duchy of Warsaw that attempts were made to implement this proposal.

The first register of Jewish inhabitants of the Polish Commonwealth dates to 1764–5, and it preceded any widespread use of registers for the general public. With only a few exceptions, however, dates of birth were not included.[94] Information about age was omitted until a general census for the whole population of the Polish Commonwealth was introduced in 1790–2. By then the newly formed administrative organs, as well as the authors of the reforms, finally realized that without comprehensive data on demographic structure it would not be possible to govern the country properly. Thus on 15 December 1789, following a

---

[91] K. Dobrowolski, 'Znaczenie metryk kościelnych dla badań naukowych', *Rocznik Towarzystwa Heraldycznego we Lwowie*, 5 (1921), 93; K. Mika, 'Ruch naturalny i rozwój zaludnienia Krakowa w drugiej połowie XVIII wieku', *Przeszłość Demograficzna Polski*, 2 (1969), 123, 127; E. Brodnicka, 'Ludność parafii Wieleń nad Notecią w drugiej połowie XVIII wieku', *Przeszłość Demograficzna Polski*, 2 (1969), 181, 184; J. Kowalczyk, 'Wartość źródłowa metryk parafii Serniki (pow. Lubartów) z lat 1697–1865', *Przeszłość Demograficzna Polski*, 3 (1970), 63–114; J. Kowalczyk, 'Jeszcze o wartości źródłowej metryk parafii Serniki z lat 1697–1865', *Przeszłość Demograficzna Polski*, 7 (1975), 277–92; Gieysztorowa, *Wstęp*, 116–44; id., 'Rodzina staropolska w świetle badań demograficznych: Zarys problematyki', *Społeczeństwo Staropolskie*, 2 (1979), 159–75.

[92] B. Kumor, 'Metryki parafialne w archiwach diecezjalnych', *Kwartalnik Historii Kultury Materialnej*, 14 (1966), 65–75; B. Kumor, 'Nieznane źródła do statystyki ludności diecezji krakowskiej w XVIII wieku', *Przeszłość Demograficzna Polski*, 4 (1971), 21–57.

[93] 'Urządzenie ludu żydowskiego w całym narodzie polskim', in *MDSC* 497; cf. Michalski, 'Sejmowe projekty reformy', 39.

[94] Raphael Mahler, *Yidn in amolikn Poyln in likht fun tsifern*, i (Warsaw, 1958), 75–6.

resolution by the Four Year Sejm, a law was passed calling for an annual census of the entire Polish Commonwealth. It was to include 'the sex, age, and place of residence of each person'.[95] The recently formed regional and district Commissions of Civil and Military Order were given the task of managing and implementing the law.[96] There was indeed a population census in this period, but it was not wholly accurate, nor was it carried out everywhere.[97] Nearly all of this material was destroyed by fire during the Second World War. Only records from the Cracow province,[98] the Wieluń territory in the western Wielkopolska region, the Ostrzeszów district,[99] and the Radziejów district survived, and for Radziejów the record does not include the Jewish population.[100] The surviving material has not yet been used to investigate the history of the Jewish population in Poland.

The most complete list among the surviving material is a 1791 census containing data for 4,980 Jewish inhabitants of fifteen towns and 212 villages. This sample is representative of the Jewish population on a national scale, as it covers two separate regions with towns and villages of various sizes, and the data provide the basis for a legitimate investigation of the age of marriage of Polish Jews. The two regions comprise: eleven towns in Cracow province, i.e. Będzin, Chrzanów, Częstochowa, Działoszyce, Janów, Kazimierz near Cracow, Książ, Lelów, Modrzejów, Niwska, and Pilica, and 196 villages; four towns in the Wieleń territory and the Ostrzeszów district, i.e. Borek, Kępno, Praszka, and Wieruszów, and fifteen villages in that region.

Among the Jewish population included in the study, there are 1,660 residents of Kazimierz, comprising 33.3 per cent of the total, and 2,108 people, or 55.8 per cent of the Jewish population studied, who lived in fourteen other small towns. Data relating to 1,212 individuals, comprising 24 per cent of the total number, however, refer to Jews living in villages. The village Jews included proprietors of leased public houses, brewers and distillers and their employees, skilled workers, and teachers. The average number of Jewish residents in a village was between five and six, i.e. one family in each village. The numbers for Jewish residents of villages are probably underestimated. They suggest that, with varying degrees of success, various subterfuges were used to avoid being included in the census. Dov

---

[95] *Volumina Legum*, ix (Cracow, 1889), 153; 'Schema do spisywania metryk, chrztów, szlubów i pogrzebów', Ossolineum, no. 275/II, fos. 25ᵛ–26ᵛ.

[96] T. Korzon, 'Komisje Porządkowe Cywilno–Wojskowe wojewódzkie i powiatowe w latach 1790–1792', in his *Odrodzenie w upadku: Wybór pism historycznych*, ed. M. Serejski and A. F. Grabski (Warsaw, 1975); W Szaj, 'Organizacja i działalność administracyjna wielkopolskich Komisji Porządkowych Cywilno–Wojskowych 1789–1792', *Studia i Materiały do Dziejów Wielkopolski i Pomorza*, 23 (1976), 85–102.

[97] S. Krzyżanowski, 'Ludność Krakowa z końcem XVIII wieku', in Józef Czech (ed.), *Kalendarz krakowski na rok 1902* (Cracow, 1902), 51.

[98] AP Cracow, IT 112A, IT 121 A, IT 187, IT 191A.

[99] AGAD, Akta Komisji Cywilno–Wojskowej Ziemi Wieluńskiej i Powiatu Ostrzeszowskiego, nos. 1–5.

[100] AGAD, Akta Komisji Cywilno-Wojskowej Powiatu Radziejowskiego.

from Bolechów confirms this fact in his memoir,[101] as does the anti-Jewish text published in 1792, which says 'every Jew who earns his livelihood from a leased public house, either in a village or in town, keeps a mob of rabble who, during the head count, hide in the cellars, pigsties, mountains, forests and even inside chests (this I have seen with my own eyes)'.[102]

The fear that the census would serve as a basis for increasing taxes and for introducing anti-Jewish restrictions and repressive measures was current among Jews and was not entirely without basis. According to the census programme devised by the Commissions for Civil and Military Order, 'clergymen belonging to the Greek, non-Uniate faith, Evangelical and Augsburg Confession pastors [must keep] christening, marriage, and death registers and Tartar, Karaite, Jewish, or any other clergy are obligated to report births, marriages, and deaths'.[103] In fact, the census in towns belonging to the Crown was mostly carried out by municipal employees; in villages belonging to the Crown, it was conducted by the subprefects, clerks, or leaseholders. In towns and villages owned by the nobility, it was the landowners who were supposed to take the census, but they shifted the responsibility on to administrative staff employed on their estates. In some places the Jews counted their compatriots, contravening the regulations,[104] making it easier to conceal people. Nevertheless, those who took the census of the Jewish population according to the instructions of the Commissions for Civil and Military Order generally carried out their tasks conscientiously. Moreover, they were well informed about prevailing local circumstances. Thus, the information they collected on occupation, living conditions, and family members deserves to be treated with more respect than material collected in the course of earlier censuses of Jewish inhabitants, which did not include any reference to age, and which had been done by external commissioners.

It is important, however, to treat any data pertaining to age with a certain degree of scepticism, because they were based on verbal declarations by the individual concerned, or by an immediate family member, and in those days knowledge of one's age was by no means universal. The records show that in 1761 one resident of Łęczyca declared that 'I am quite old, but I do not remember how old',[105] and at the turn of the eighteenth century Roch Sikorski from Bielsko in the Podlasie province wrote the following entry in his memoir: 'I am thirty-eight or thirty-nine and I am not sure which'.[106] Although such knowledge and the ability to count was more commonly found among Jews than among the Polish inhabitants of small towns or peasants, even Jews had gaps in their memory, and

---

[101] Dov miBolekhov, *Zikhronot*, 89.

[102] *Katechizm o Żydach i neofitach*, in *MDSC* 469.

[103] 1791, Ossolineum, no. 275/II.

[104] AP Cracow, IT 121 A, 495, 536.

[105] Declaration by Stanisław Zwoliński, AGAD, Księga miejska Łęczycy, no. 23.

[106] '*Łyki*' i '*koltuny*': *Pamiętnik mieszczanina podlaskiego 1790–1816*, ed. K. Bartoszewicz (Warsaw, n.d.), 53.

some deliberately falsified their returns. As would be expected, censuses of the Jewish population carried out under such circumstances contained a number of distortions and inaccuracies, but on the whole these were limited to aspects related to external appearance. Polish Jews of that era are supposed to have aged very early, but it was married juveniles who were more likely to say they were older than they actually were. It can be assumed that generally the scale of discrepancies between real and declared ages for Jews would not have exceeded five years. So, the margin of error in calculations based on censuses carried out in such circumstances can be kept to a minimum by dividing the entire population included in the census into five-year age groups.

Tables 1–5 show that in the eighteenth century the proportion of women to men was different from what it is today. The disproportion between the sexes in 1791 among the Christian population in the Wieluń parish varied between 1.6 per cent and 14.6 per cent (Table 11),[107] while among the Jewish population (according to data available for the old Cracow province, Wieluń territory, and the Ostrzeszów district) the difference was between 0.6 per cent and 12.3 per cent (Table 1). In Poland after the Second World War these differences amounted to less than 5 per cent.[108] The disproportion among the sexes is different for each age group: among 15- to 19-year-olds, women represented 54.5 per cent of the population, but among the 30- to 34-year-olds, they represented only 46.8 per cent. In the over-59 age group, however, women represented only 37.7 per cent (Table 1). Thus, women were in the majority in the younger sector of the Jewish population in the Polish Commonwealth in the eighteenth century, while men predominated in the over-30 group.

K. Bartnicka noticed a similar proportion among 2,455 Christians living in the Wieleń parish in 1791, which included residents of the town as well as eleven outlying villages.[109] But among the Christian population in Warsaw, men only begin to form the majority over the age of 35.[110] Researchers also have at their disposal data on the number, ages, and sex of deceased Christians—information that is generally unavailable for the Jewish population. Accordingly, Bartnicka was able to establish that in the 20–25 age group there was a higher mortality rate for men than women, and that in the 25–54 age group women had a higher mortality.[111] Despite the lack of data on the number of deaths for the Jewish population, we can assume that the mortality rate for Jewish women would not be any lower than for Christian women, and was probably higher. This is supported by a number of facts discussed below.

As in the Christian community, the ratio of Jewish women to men decreased

[107] E. Bartnicka, 'Ludność parafii Wieleń', 179–202.
[108] *Małżeństwa w latach 1960–1965* (Warsaw, 1967), 28.
[109] Ibid.
[110] C. Kukło, *Rodzina w osiemnastowiecznej Warszawie* (Białystok, 1991), 71.
[111] Bartnicka, 'Ludność parafii Wieleń', 201.

after the age of 29 (Tables 1–5). Towards the end of the eighteenth century the medical doctor F. L. de la Fontaine attributed this at least in part to the frequency of childbirth among Jewish women,[112] which caused extreme physical exhaustion. There were also many cases of puerperal fever. In his book of medical advice written in Yiddish in the second half of the eighteenth century, the Jewish doctor Moshe Markuze also indicated that 'ignorant midwives kill many babies and their mothers as well, or just one of them. I have seen it many times myself.'[113] At the beginning of the nineteenth century Tadeusz Czacki, the first Polish scholar to investigate Jewish history and culture, wrote that 'not a single trained midwife could be found anywhere in Poland, and because of this many Jewish women died in childbirth'.[114]

To what extent did the high mortality rate for young Jewish women influence the duration of marriages among Polish Jews in the eighteenth century? Among the Christian population of the Wieleń parish, the average marriage lasted eleven to fifteen years,[115] and in the Warsaw parish of the Holy Cross, it lasted on average ten to fifteen years.[116] These are not significant differences and are within the confines of statistical error. It is impossible to estimate the number of years an average Jewish marriage lasted in Poland because there are no reliable sources containing this information. Although most marriages were entered into at a much younger age than was the practice for the Christian population, the greater frequency of births and their dangers probably cancelled out the difference. Under such conditions many Jewish marriages ended while the husband and wife were still young or only middle-aged. Second and even third marriages were quite common among Polish Jews, just as they were among the Christian population in Poland and in other European countries at the time,[117] resulting in an ever-increasing number of orphans, semi-orphans, and stepchildren, which must have influenced relationships within Jewish families, particularly in those where widows and widowers had remarried.[118]

I have not assigned five-year age groups to people under the age of 15 because it was much easier to conceal children from the census officials.[119] Among those

[112] De la Fontaine, *Chirurgisch–medizinische Abhandlungen*, 148.

[113] 'Nokh shteln fun Moshe Markuze "Sefer Refues"', in N. Prylucki (ed.), *Zamlbikher fur yidisher folklor, filologiye un kulturgeshikhte* (Warsaw, 1917), 30–1.

[114] T. Czacki, *Rozprawa o Żydach i karaitach* (Cracow, 1860), 118–19.

[115] Bartnicka, 'Ludność parafii Wieleń', 190.

[116] Kukło, *Rodzina w osiemnastowiecznej Warszawie*, 181.

[117] Bartnicka, 'Ludność parafii Wieleń', 189–90, 214; S. Akerman, 'The Importance of Remarriage in the Seventeenth and Eighteenth Centuries', in Songer and Dupaquier (eds.), *Marriage*, 164; J. Knodel, 'Remarriage and Marital Fertility in Germany during the Eighteenth and Nineteenth Centuries', ibid. 604; H. Palli, 'Illegitimacy and Remarriage in Estonia during the Eighteenth Century', ibid. 475.                                    [118] Ibid. 1–11.

[119] Sometimes whole groups of children were concealed, which is attested to by a laconic but significant note included in the 1765 census of the Jewish population referring to 'Children found on the banks of the river Vistula' (AGAD, Płock Grodzkie Obl., no. 26, fo. 54ᵛ; J. Kleczynski, *Liczba głów*

who were concealed, which included about 50,000 Jews from the Wielkopolska, Małopolska, and Mazowsze regions,[120] the majority were juveniles. It was more difficult to conceal young married couples than young single people, particularly as news of a marriage or wedding would reach not just the local Jews but also the local Polish population. Because of this, the numbers recorded for juvenile Jewish marriages may well have been realistic. In my investigations I was able to find reference only to eight married girls and one married boy among the group under 15. Even if some of these claimed to be older than they really were, they would have been included in the next age group. Thus, the conclusion that as many as 76.3 per cent of men did not marry before they were 20 is justified;[121] 57.9 per cent of girls in the same age group were not married (Table 6). Among the Jewish inhabitants of two of the regions investigated, Kazimierz had the highest percentage of marriages in which the husband or wife was under 20 (73.6 per cent of the women and 28.8 per cent of the men; see Table 8). The fact that Kazimierz had the largest concentration of Jews in eighteenth-century Poland must also be taken into account, since the ratio of married people in the same age groups in smaller towns is different from what it is in the cities: 20 per cent of the men and 11.3 per cent of the women (Table 9).

From this it is evident that the ratios for Polish Jews differed from that for the Christian population; further, it is well known that town dwellers generally married later than peasants.[122] Townsmen believed that a man should only get married after he had learned a trade and achieved financial independence. The traditional Jewish custom, however, involved no such precondition, which led to the criticism mentioned earlier from followers of the Enlightenment among Poles and Jews. Another reason for the prevalence of early marriage among Jews in large urban centres that played a more important role in the Jewish community than among Christians: in the larger Jewish poplation centres it was easier to find

*żydowskich w Krakowie z taryf roku 1765* (Cracow, 1898), 5; *Katechizm o Żydach i neofitach*, in *MDSC* 469; R. Rybarski, *Skarbowość Polski w dobie rozbiorów* (Cracow, 1937), 224–5.

[120] E. Vielrose, 'Ludność Polski od X do XVIII wieku', *Kwartalnik Historii Kultury Materialnej*, 5 (1957), 17; Z. Guldon and N. Krikuń, 'Przyczynek do krytyki spisów ludności żydowskiej z końca XVIII wieku', *Studia Źródłoznawcze*, 13 (1978), 153–8; Z. Guldon, 'Ludność Żydówska w miastach województwa sandomierskiego w II połowie XVII wieku', *BŻIH* 123–4 (1982), 20–1; Z. Guldon and J. Wijaczka, 'Die Zahlenmässige Stärke der Juden in Polen–Litauen im 16.–18. Jahrhundert', *Trumah–Zeitschrift der Hochschule für jüdische Studien*, 4 (1994), 91–101.

[121] The civil state of eight Jews arrested in Warsaw between 1789 and 1793 appeared to be very similar; one of them stated that he was married at the age of 22, two said they were 24, three were 25, and one was 27 (*Z rontem marszałkowskim przez Warszawę: Zeznania oskarżonych z lat 1787–1794*, ed. Z. Turska (Warsaw, 1961), 41, 67, 111, 112, 130, 180, 229).

[122] General remarks about this phenomenon found in many societies were published some years ago by H. Reif in 'Theoretischer Kontext und Ziele: Methoden und Eingrenzung der Untersuchung', in J. Kocka *et al.* (eds.), *Familie und soziale Plazierung. Studien zum Verhältnis von Familie, sozialer Mobilitat und Heiratsverhalten an westfalfischen Beispielen in späten 18 und 19 Jahrhundert* (Bielefeld, 1980), 61.

suitable partners for children than in small towns or in villages. It is also generally recognized that the majority of Jews lived in small towns in which there were simply not enough marriageable candidates of either sex. What used to happen was that marriageable young men visiting a small town would become the objects of rivalry among parents with marriageable daughters.[123] This provided fertile ground for enterprising matchmakers who on market day would attempt to bring together partners, sometimes from far-off places. This made it possible for marriages to be arranged not only among rich families[124] but among the poorer sector as well.

All this was further complicated by interdictions issued by the lords of the manor that affected the towns belonging to them. Taking advantage of their feudal authority, the lords tried to prohibit children of local Jewish inhabitants from marrying people from other estates to prevent their subjects from leaving their place of birth and moving to an area that belonged to a different lord. If the newly married pair decided to remain where they were, it could cause an increase in the population in the towns and villages belonging to that lord. For similar reasons lords of small towns and landed estates banned the children of townsmen and peasants from marrying lieges belonging to other landlords. Such practices were partly influenced by contemporary mercantile ideas opposed to taking dowries out of the country.[125] This was frequently interpreted as an injunction forbidding the transfer of capital and valuables belonging to Jews or town residents to estates belonging to other lords.[126]

Stanisław Poniatowski, father of King Stanisław August, echoed this view in the charter he granted the Jewish community in Jazłowiec in Podolia, his family estate. In it he stipulated that 'in conformity with the law applied in other towns with regard to those who send their children away to other states, *and who give them dowries and thus impoverish the town*, I order to the full extent of this law, all Jews from Jazłowiec to make every effort to settle their children in the immediate vicinity'.[127] And indeed, the landowners of Sokołów Podlaski even demanded one-tenth to one-quarter of the total amount of the dowries of Jewish brides who moved elsewhere.[128] In Opatów similar sums were deducted by the Jewish com-

---

[123] See a description of such an incident in the small town of Żarki in Małopolska in 1791 in AP Cracow, IT 175, 209.

[124] According to Katz, *Masoret umashber*, 127, 141.

[125] Lipiński, *Studia nad historią polskiej myśli ekonomicznej*, 205–490; id., *Merkantylistyczna myśl ekonomiczna w Polsce XVI i XVII wieku*, in his *Wybór pism*, ed. J. Górski and E. Lipiński (Warsaw, 1958); J. Górski, *Poglądy polskiej merkantylistycznej myśli ekonomicznej XVI i XVII wieku* (Wrocław, 1958); E. Stańczak, *Kamera saska za czasów Augusta III* (Warsaw, 1973), 15–30.

[126] Uchwała sejmiku województwa sieradzkiego 9.2.1764, Biblioteka Polskiej Akademii Nauk w Krakowie, Teki Pawińskiego, lauda sieradzkie, no. 4, fo. 432.

[127] J. Goldberg (ed.), *Jewish Privileges in the Polish Commonwealth* (Jerusalem, 1985), 105; emphasis added.

[128] 'Ordynacja dla starozakonnych obywatelów Sokołowa, die 24 Iunii roku 1777', Biblioteka Polskiej Akademii Nauk w Krakowie, MS 1716b, fos. 99ʳ–101ᵛ.

munity.[129] Anyone attempting to evade this levy was liable to severe punishment,[130] since part of the income from this source was passed on to the landowner to whom the town belonged.[131] The lord's clerks were alert to any signs of newly married couples attempting to leave their home town and denounced them to the lord or his confidants.[132]

There is also some other information on interdictions affecting marriages with non-local residents that were issued by the landowners in Lask[133] and Rzeszów.[134] Such limitations placed severe restrictions on the mobility of the Jewish population and made it very difficult for them to marry in accordance with their traditions. So when Jan Gniński decided that he wanted to attract Jewish settlers to Gniń, the new town he had just founded, he issued a charter to the Jewish community's assembly of elders in 1680 in which he included the following statement: 'They will also be allowed to get married wherever they please and to marry off their daughters and send them off anywhere they like.'[135]

All the impediments designed to prevent dowries of Jewish brides going beyond the borders of the lord's estates resulted in much later marriages than for residents of towns, where no such restrictions were present. The impediments also led to a higher ratio of married men than women (Table 7), a most exceptional phenomenon for the Jewish community of those times for several age groups among the Jewish inhabitants of the noble estates. It was particularly true for people between 20 and 24.

The correlation between the size and character of a place, including the number of Jews living there and the differences in the ages of the partners, was also observed. The greatest age differences between husbands and wives occurred in Kazimierz, which had the largest number of Jews of all places discussed here. The proportion of wives older than their husbands could be as large as 15 per cent, with the overall average being 10 per cent, and only 9 per cent in the villages (Table 14). This was because it was much easier to find husbands for Jewish girls in Kazimierz than in the smaller towns and villages.

One research paper about the demographic relationships in the small town of Brzeżany in the eastern region of the Commonwealth and its surrounding villages and an analogous work describing the parish of Wieleń can be used to compare the ages of Jewish and Christian marriages in the eighteenth century. In Brzeżany and

---

[129] G. D. Hundert, *The Jews in a Polish Private Town: The Case of Opatów in the Eighteenth Century* (Baltimore, 1992), 97.

[130] AGAD, Archiwum Gospodarcze Wilanowskie, no. I/74.

[131] Ibid., no. I/109. As a result, dowry tax payments amounted to only 0.4 per cent of the Jewish community's annual income in Opatów: Hundert, *The Jews in a Polish Private Town*, 97.

[132] Letter to the Governor of the Opatów estates, 4 Mar. 1738, AP Cracow, Archiwum Sanguszków, no. 331/7.

[133] AP Cracow, Archiwum Siedliszowieckie Załuskich, no. 209, 1–2.

[134] J. Pęczkowski, *Dzieje miasta Rzeszowa do końca XVIII wieku* (Rzeszów, 1913), 70.

[135] AP Cracow, Varia no. 83, 13.

its surrounding area, between 1784 and 1800, 10 per cent of newly married Christians were between 16 and 20, and 40.7 per cent were between 21 and 25.[136] However, only 3.3 per cent of the married men in the parish of Wieleń in 1791 were under 19, and 21 per cent were between 20 and 24.[137] Comparing these data reveals that in Brzeżany and its surrounding area in the east of the Commonwealth men married younger than in the parish of Wieleń. Jews tended to marry younger than Christian inhabitants of towns or peasants in both locations. The married group aged between 15 and 19 (which, taking account of evasion, probably included a small percentage of people who married younger than 15), comprised 19.2 per cent of men. In the 20–24 age group, 76.3 per cent were already married (Table 6). The differences in the ages of marriage between the nobility and Jews was even greater, because noblemen frequently married late.[138]

There was an even greater difference between the ages at which Christian and Jewish women married. In Brzeżany and the surrounding villages between 1784 and 1800, 4 per cent of Christian town and peasant women married before their fifteenth birthday, and 54.1 per cent married between 16 and 20.[139] In 1791 in the parish of Wieleń, approximately 25 per cent of Christian women of the same social classes married before they were 19, while just under 50 per cent married between 20 and 24.[140] Among Jewish women aged between 15 and 19 (as with the men, this included a small number of married girls younger than 15), 42.1 per cent were already married (Table 6). It is very likely that the differences between the ages of married Jewish women and noblewomen were significantly smaller, as the latter, unlike their male counterparts, tended to be married off earlier.[141]

Although marriages between people where both wife and husband were under 20 were probably not the rule, they were not infrequent in the Polish Commonwealth of the eighteenth century. This was only partly the result of changing customs and the emergence of new ideas in the Jewish community. What was primarily responsible for the change was the difficult economic situation of Polish Jews, which delayed marriage for many young people.[142] Some extreme cases have been reported, such as the one in Poznań in 1717 where a particularly difficult economic situation caused the local elder to urge Jews to postpone all marriages for three years.[143]

[136] B. Puczyński, 'Ludność Brzeżan i okolicy w XVII i XVIII wieku', *Przeszłość Demograficzna Polski*, 5 (1972), 23.

[137] Bartnicka, 'Ludność parafii Wieleń', 183.

[138] J. S. Bystroń, *Dzieje obyczajów w dawnej Polsce: Wiek XVI–XVIII* (Warsaw, 1960), ii. 130; W. Woynowski, *Pamflet obyczajowy w czasach Stanisława Augusta* (Wrocław, 1973), 120–1.

[139] Puczyński, 'Ludność Brzeżan', 23.

[140] Brodnicka, 'Ludność parafii Wieleń', 183.

[141] Bystroń, *Dzieje obyczajów w dawnej Polsce*, ii. 132–4; M. Starzeński, *Na schyłku dni Rzeczypospolitej: Kartki z pamiętnika Michała Starzeńskiego 1775–1795*, ed. H. Mościcki (Warsaw, 1914), 8.

[142] Hundert, 'Jewish Children and Childhood', 9; id., *The Jews in a Polish Private Town*, 76.

[143] J. Perles, 'Geschichte der Juden in Posen', *MGWJ* 14 (1865), 133.

## *KEST*: MARRIED COUPLES LIVING AT HOME

The word *kest* was used for a situation in which the wife's or husband's parents fed and housed a newly married couple and their offspring for a certain period of time. It was intended to ease the young couple's financial worries and to encourage them to have children and create an economic infrastructure for their future. Custom in Germany dictated that the parents of one of the partners guaranteed to feed the married couple during the first year, and to house them for two years following the marriage.[144] Because newly married Jewish couples in Poland tended to be younger than those in Germany, the average *kest* period was somewhat longer. Jacob Katz estimates that in Poland the parents provided full housing and board for their married children for two to eight years.[145] In Salomon Maimon's autobiography we read that the mother of his intended bride had offered the young pair a full six years of *kest*.[146]

Above all *kest* played a very important role for newly married couples still in their teens who could not earn their own living. Mature married couples as well as teenagers took advantage of this institution, for it provided a period in which married couples could learn how to run a commercial enterprise or practise a trade. The institution also enabled men to devote themselves to traditional studies.

The custom was officially recognized by the landowners of the towns as well as by the provincial administrators representing state authorities. The lords of the town of Rzeszów prohibited their Jewish inhabitants from permanently moving to the places where their new spouses came from, but they did allow them to live there for the duration of the *kest*, on condition that it did not exceed two years.[147] It was impossible for the Rzeszów administrative machinery to enforce their return within the prescribed period, however. Moreover, Ruthenian orders from 1726 and 1762 allowed the rabbis in Lwów to keep married couples in their teens together with their spouses; in addition the young couples were exempted from paying taxes or providing services to the Jewish community. The money thus saved, together with the dowry they received, was intended to create capital to enable them to set up a future commercial venture.[148] This means of securing a living for the married couple was severely criticized by Abraham Hirszowicz.[149]

*Kest* also helped integrate the family with the married couple, their juvenile daughter and son-in-law,[150] and when the parents provided room and board, for somewhat older married couples as well. There were some cases in which an entire family was forced to leave its permanent home and to seek temporary

---

[144] Katz, *Masoret umashber*, 167–8.  
[145] Ibid.  
[146] Maimon, *Gesammelte Werke*, i. 92.  
[147] Pęczowski, *Dzieje miasta Rzeszowa*, 70.  
[148] Pazdro, *Organizacja i praktyka*, 81–182.  
[149] Hirszowicz, *Projekt do reformy i poprawy obyczajów*, 523.  
[150] Katz, *Masoret umashber*, 163.

shelter elsewhere. These cases bear witness to the total integration of such families, which included parents, dependent married children, and their offspring. At such times the father made certain that the whole family stayed together, including their children living at home within the framework of *kest*, their children's spouses, and grandchildren. In one case during the plague in Cracow in 1678, the nobleman Stanisław Krzelczycki-Mrożek allowed a group of Cracow Jews, 'those who have sons-in-law or sons *living at home*', to live (for payment of a sum) in his village (Kierlikówka), 'even providing a house of prayer for them'.[151] This was by no means the only example where the word *kest* was replaced by a term that subsequently fell into disuse, 'living at home' ('ojcowski stół'), which confirms that the institution was known in Polish society.

Katz viewed the situation in which parents lived together with their children as a type of small European family.[152] This arrangement can also be seen as a unit categorized as a multiple family household in the typology developed by Peter Laslett.[153] The institution of living at home created a complex tangle of mutual connections between the husband's or wife's parents and the new family unit now living under one roof. These connections formed the basic element of the internal structure of the resulting extended family.[154] In 1765 14.7 to 17.2 per cent of Jewish married couples were living at home,[155] but by 1791, in the towns, only 13.6 per cent were (Table 17). The fact that people married earlier in places where there were more Jews led to a greater percentage of couples being supported by parents at home. This is corroborated by data from the 1765 census of the Jewish population collected by Raphael Mahler, who found the percentage to be higher in towns than in villages.[156] In 1791, in all towns, 13.6 per cent of married couples lived with their parents, but in Kazimierz the proportion was 19.6 per cent (Table 17). Similarly, the declining trend in the numbers of married couples living at home was more marked among rural than urban Jewish families: in 1765, 10.7 to 12 per cent of rural inhabitants were living with their parents,[157] but in 1791 only 5.8 per cent were (Table 17).

The decline in the numbers of married couples living at home in villages was caused by the deteriorating economic situation, especially for proprietors of leased public houses, brewers, and village distillers. The very difficult economic circumstances of this group are described by the author of an anti-Jewish pamphlet published anonymously in 1792 entitled *Katechizm o Żydach i neofitach* (Home Truths about Jews and Neophytes). He points out that 'practically every one of

---

[151] AP Cracow, Castriensia Sandomiriensia, no. 134, fo. 1899; emphasis added.     [152] Ibid.

[153] P. Laslett, 'The Comparative History of Household and Family', *Journal of Social History*, 4 (1970–1), 75–6; P. Laslett, 'La Famille et le ménage: Approches historiques', *Annales économies, sociétés, civilisations*, 27 (1972), 847–72; T. K. Hareven, 'The Family as Process: The Historical Study of Family Cycle', *Journal of Social History*, 7 (1974), 322–3.

[154] Reif, 'Theoretischer Kontext', 48.     [155] Mahler, *Yidn in amolikn Poyln*, 77–8.

[156] Ibid.     [157] Ibid.

these proprietors, whether in a village or in a town, supports his father or mother, wife, children (that is to say a swarm of brats), a teacher, a brewer, etc., and perhaps a mother-in-law or grandmother as well, *not to mention all the children (or brats), for whom he has to provide food and clothing, they having got married at a very young age*.[158] In his economics handbook published in 1786, A. I. Ogiński describes it similarly:

a Jewish proprietor has to live off his income along with his entire family, including a teacher for his children; in addition he has to save money for a dowry for his daughters and his sons, to pay the Chief Rabbi, to contribute a substantial sum to the group of elders he belongs to, including commission expenses and debts incurred by this group, and to help support these elders, as well as to contribute to the group's legal expenses and religious services.[159]

At the turn of the eighteenth century, in *Leib and Siora—A Jewish Romance*, the poet Julian Ursyn Niemcewicz, conforming to literary convention, cites a letter written by a Jew to his daughter's future father-in-law which states: 'I know that your son David is nearly eleven and my daughter Lilja is eight, let us make arrangements for them to marry. I will give Lilja a dowry of two thousand roubles and after the marriage I will keep my daughter at home while your son David can finish his training as a school teacher.'[160]

Harsh economic circumstances made it increasingly difficult for parents to meet the obligations specified in the marriage agreements. While this reduced the number of early marriages and couples living at home, those young people who did live in such circumstances found it more difficult to become financially independent and leave their parental home to set up on their own. As a result the period of living at home was becoming longer, frequently exceeding the time stipulated in the marriage agreements. Using the 1791 census it is possible to identify those married couples still living at home in which most of the husbands were older than 29. It is reasonable to infer that the majority of these couples had been married for some years but continued to live with parents and were supported by them. Seventy-five of the husbands among the 238 couples living at home included in the census were older than 29. This group comprises only 3.8 per cent of the total marriages studied and 35.5 per cent of all those living at home. Clearly, the institution of living at home was ceasing to be a temporary, short-term arrangement for young people; for a large number of couples it was becoming a permanent way of life. Gradually some of the young married couples were taking over the households of their ageing parents and parents-in-law. In families where

---

[158] *MDSC* 469; emphasis added.

[159] [A. I. Ogiński], 'Instruktarz ekonomiczny dla ludzi będących w służbie gospodarskiej, do druku podany w Warszawie w drukarni Nadwornej J. K. Mci i Przes. Kom. Eduk. Narod. roku 1786', in S. Pawlik (ed.), *Polskie instruktarze ekonomiczne z końca XVII i z XVIII wieku* (Cracow, 1915), i. 252.

[160] J. U. Niemcewicz, *Lejbe i Siora—Romans żydowski* (Cracow, 1885), 23.

the young married couples did manage to become self-sufficient and were able to leave the parental home, their places were taken by newly married younger siblings. Considering the large size of Jewish families in Poland in those days, the intervals between the two arrangements tended to be very short.

To Jewish families, living at home led to a structure different from the one prevalent among Polish families living in towns and villages. A Jewish family that included parents and married children and their progeny living at home could be contrasted with the model of a European urban or peasant family, in which, according to Laslett's definition, 'one marriage equals one household'.[161] S. Songer and J. Dupaquier also note that 'they cannot contract a marriage without founding a new household'.[162] Laslett goes on to say that 'marriage was to be contracted only between couples who have reached adulthood and who possess sufficient experience to be able to manage a self-sufficient household'.[163] In Jewish families marriage rarely coincided with the founding of a new household because it was generally accepted that either the wife's or husband's parents would be providing room and board in their home for the young pair.

No such custom existed in Polish families: married children did not expect to live with their parents or parents-in-law; it was the custom neither among townspeople nor in villages. This is shown by a comparison of data from 1789 for 569 families from three small towns (Brzeźnica, Kłobuck, and Pajęczno) on the border of Małopolska and eastern Wielkopolska. In these towns only eight married couples, 1.5 per cent of all resident families,[164] lived with parents. At this stage of research on the social history of the Polish family these numbers appear representative for the whole country. Among Polish peasants it was also rare for parents and married children to live under one roof because, as a rule, landlords were only too happy to settle newly married couples on their farms, and the latter were expected to perform villein service and pay rent and taxes in return.[165] In this way young peasant married couples were able to acquire a certain degree of independence, but they were also more personally dependent on the landowners and were burdened with all the liabilities of peasants working their own smallholdings. Thus, the structure of Polish peasant families was shaped by the interests and wishes of the nobility, who were able to increase the number of their farmworkers.[166]

Jews living in towns and villages that belonged to noblemen were prohibited from marrying their children to people living in other domains. This may have limited their freedom of choice but did not define the structure of their marriages.

[161] Laslett, 'Familie und Industrialisierung', 18, 25.

[162] Songer and Dupaquier, *Marriage*, 3.

[163] Laslett, 'Familie und Industrialisierung', 13.

[164] *Lustracja województwa krakowskiego 1789*, ed. A. Falniowska-Gradowska and I. Rychlikowa (Wrocław, 1963), ii. 529–41, 575–90.

[165] A. Woźniak, 'Rodzina i gospodarstwo chłopskie na mazowieckiej wsi pańszczyźnianej XVIII wieku', *Etnografia Polska*, 18 (1974), 50.                                    [166] Ibid.

Traditional customs and the restrictive economic circumstances of Jews in the eighteenth century played a much greater role, and this led to fewer married couples living with parents. To a certain extent this also led to a lower birth-rate among Jews, as young couples were less likely to have children before they had their own home,[167] which, until they could become self-sufficient, used to be provided for them through *kest*, or living at home.

*Translated by Theresa Prout*

[167] J. Dupaquier, *Pour la démographie historique* (Paris, 1984), 49; Kukło, *Rodzina w osiemnastowiecznej Warszawie*, 76.

## APPENDIX

**Table 1.** Age distribution of Jewish men and women in the two regions, 1791

| Age | Total no. | Men | | Women | | Age distribution (%) | | Sex ratio (no. of men per 100 women) |
|---|---|---|---|---|---|---|---|---|
| | | No. | % | No. | % | Women | Men | |
| 15–19 | 549 | 250 | 45.5 | 299 | 54.5 | 10.4 | 12.7 | 83.6 |
| 20–24 | 815 | 359 | 44.0 | 456 | 56.0 | 14.9 | 19.4 | 78.7 |
| 25–29 | 557 | 231 | 41.5 | 326 | 58.5 | 9.6 | 13.9 | 70.9 |
| 30–34 | 789 | 420 | 53.2 | 369 | 46.8 | 17.4 | 15.7 | 113.8 |
| 35–39 | 506 | 256 | 50.6 | 250 | 49.4 | 10.6 | 10.6 | 102.4 |
| 40–44 | 568 | 314 | 55.3 | 254 | 44.7 | 13.0 | 10.8 | 123.6 |
| 45–49 | 282 | 161 | 57.1 | 121 | 42.9 | 6.7 | 5.1 | 133.1 |
| 50–54 | 309 | 179 | 57.9 | 130 | 42.1 | 7.4 | 5.5 | 137.7 |
| 55–59 | 102 | 63 | 61.8 | 39 | 38.2 | 2.6 | 1.7 | 161.5 |
| 60+ | 284 | 177 | 62.3 | 107 | 37.7 | 7.4 | 4.6 | 165.4 |
| **Total** | **4,761** | **2,410** | **50.6** | **2,351** | **49.4** | **100.0** | **100.0** | — |

*Source*:   1791 census.

**Table 2.** Age distribution of Jewish men and women in fifteen towns (Kazimierz and fourteen small towns), 1791

| Age | Total no. | Men | | Women | | Age distribution (%) | | Sex ratio (no. of men per 100 women) |
|---|---|---|---|---|---|---|---|---|
| | | No. | % | No. | % | Women | Men | |
| 15–19 | 376 | 158 | 42.0 | 218 | 58.0 | 8.7 | 12.0 | 72.5 |
| 20–24 | 613 | 268 | 43.7 | 345 | 56.3 | 14.8 | 19.0 | 77.7 |
| 25–29 | 431 | 175 | 40.6 | 256 | 59.4 | 9.7 | 14.0 | 68.4 |
| 30–34 | 612 | 322 | 52.6 | 290 | 47.4 | 17.9 | 16.0 | 111.0 |
| 35–39 | 404 | 198 | 49.0 | 206 | 51.0 | 11.0 | 11.3 | 96.1 |
| 40–44 | 428 | 230 | 53.7 | 198 | 46.3 | 12.7 | 10.9 | 116.2 |
| 45–49 | 226 | 123 | 54.4 | 103 | 45.6 | 6.8 | 5.7 | 119.4 |
| 50–54 | 236 | 143 | 80.6 | 93 | 39.4 | 7.9 | 5.1 | 153.7 |
| 55–59 | 86 | 53 | 61.6 | 33 | 38.4 | 2.9 | 1.8 | 160.6 |
| 60+ | 212 | 136 | 64.2 | 76 | 45.8 | 7.6 | 4.2 | 178.9 |
| **Total** | **3,624** | **1,806** | **49.8** | **1,818** | **50.2** | **100.0** | **100.0** | — |

*Source*:   1791 census.

**Table 3.** Age distribution of Jewish men and women in Kazimierz, 1791

| Age | Total no. | Men | | Women | | Age distribution (%) | | Sex ratio (no. of men per 100 women) |
|---|---|---|---|---|---|---|---|---|
| | | No. | % | No. | % | Men | Women | |
| 15–19 | 194 | 73 | 37.6 | 121 | 62.4 | 8.9 | 15.4 | 60.3 |
| 20–24 | 244 | 116 | 47.5 | 128 | 52.5 | 14.9 | 16.3 | 90.6 |
| 25–29 | 157 | 66 | 42.0 | 91 | 58.0 | 8.1 | 11.6 | 72.5 |
| 30–34 | 260 | 133 | 51.2 | 127 | 48.8 | 16.2 | 16.2 | 104.7 |
| 35–39 | 190 | 105 | 55.3 | 85 | 44.7 | 12.9 | 10.8 | 123.5 |
| 40–44 | 235 | 125 | 53.2 | 110 | 46.8 | 15.3 | 14.0 | 113.6 |
| 45–49 | 104 | 59 | 56.7 | 45 | 43.4 | 7.2 | 5.7 | 131.1 |
| 50–54 | 107 | 65 | 60.7 | 42 | 59.3 | 8.0 | 5.4 | 154.8 |
| 55–59 | 41 | 27 | (65.8) | 14 | (34.2) | 3.3 | 1.8 | 192.8 |
| 60+ | 70 | 48 | 68.6 | 22 | 31.4 | 5.9 | 2.8 | (218.2) |
| **Total** | **1,602** | **817** | **60.0** | **785** | **40.0** | **100.0** | **100.0** | — |

*Source*: 1791 census.

**Table 4.** Age distribution of Jewish men and women in fourteen small towns, 1791

| Age | Total no. | Men | | Women | | Age distribution (%) | | Sex ratio (no. of men per 100 women) |
|---|---|---|---|---|---|---|---|---|
| | | No. | % | No. | % | Men | Women | |
| 15–19 | 182 | 85 | 46.7 | 97 | 53.3 | 8.6 | 9.4 | 87.6 |
| 20–24 | 369 | 152 | 41.2 | 217 | 58.8 | 15.4 | 21.0 | 70.0 |
| 25–29 | 274 | 109 | 39.8 | 165 | 61.2 | 11.0 | 16.0 | 66.1 |
| 30–34 | 352 | 189 | 53.7 | 163 | 42.3 | 19.1 | 15.8 | 116.0 |
| 35–39 | 214 | 93 | 43.4 | 121 | 56.6 | 9.4 | 11.7 | 76.8 |
| 40–44 | 193 | 105 | 54.4 | 88 | 45.6 | 10.6 | 8.5 | 119.3 |
| 45–49 | 122 | 64 | 52.4 | 58 | 47.6 | 6.5 | 5.6 | 110.3 |
| 50–54 | 129 | 78 | 60.5 | 51 | 39.5 | 7.9 | 4.9 | 152.9 |
| 55–59 | 45 | 26 | 57.8 | 19 | 42.2 | 2.6 | 1.8 | (136.8) |
| 60+ | 142 | 88 | 62.0 | 54 | 38.0 | 8.9 | 5.3 | 163.0 |
| **Total** | **2,022** | **989** | **48.2** | **1,033** | **51.8** | **100.0** | **100.0** | — |

*Source*: 1791 census.

**Table 5.** Age distribution of Jewish men and women in 212 villages, 1791

| Age | Total no. | Men | | Women | | Age distribution (%) | | Sex ratio (no. of men per 100 women) |
|-----|-----------|-----|---|-------|---|-----|-----|-----|
| | | No. | % | No. | % | Men | Women | |
| 15–19 | 173 | 92 | 53.2 | 81 | 46.8 | 15.2 | 15.2 | 113.6 |
| 20–24 | 202 | 91 | 55.0 | 111 | 45.0 | 15.1 | 20.8 | 82.0 |
| 25–29 | 126 | 56 | 44.4 | 70 | 55.6 | 9.3 | 13.1 | 80.0 |
| 30–34 | 177 | 98 | 55.4 | 79 | 44.6 | 16.2 | 14.8 | 124.0 |
| 35–39 | 102 | 58 | 56.9 | 44 | 43.1 | 9.6 | 8.3 | 131.8 |
| 40–44 | 140 | 84 | 60.0 | 56 | 40.0 | 13.9 | 10.9 | 150.0 |
| 45–49 | 56 | 38 | 67.8 | 18 | 32.2 | 6.3 | 3.4 | (211.1) |
| 50–54 | 73 | 36 | 49.3 | 37 | 50.7 | 6.0 | 6.9 | (97.3) |
| 55–59 | 16 | 10 | 62.5 | 6 | 37.5 | 1.7 | 1.1 | (166.7) |
| 60+ | 72 | 41 | 56.9 | 31 | 43.1 | 6.7 | 5.9 | (132.2) |
| **Total** | **1,137** | **605** | **51.8** | **533** | **48.2** | **100.0** | **100.0** | — |

*Source*: 1791 census.

**Table 6.** Total married Jewish population in the two regions, 1791

| Age | Men | | Women | |
|-----|-----|---|-------|---|
| | No. | % | No. | % |
| 15–19 | 48 | 19.2 | 126 | 42.1 |
| 20–24 | 274 | 76.3 | 381 | 83.6 |
| 25–29 | 209 | 90.5 | 307 | 94.9 |
| 30–34 | 394 | 93.8 | 349 | 94.6 |
| 35–39 | 249 | 97.3 | 239 | 95.6 |
| 40–44 | 297 | 94.6 | 235 | 92.5 |
| 45–49 | 158 | 98.1 | 107 | 88.4 |
| 50–54 | 165 | 92.2 | 114 | 87.7 |
| 55–59 | 57 | 90.5 | 27 | 69.2 |
| 60+ | 155 | 37.6 | 65 | 60.7 |

*Source*: 1791 census.

**Table 7.** Married Jewish population in fifteen towns (Kazimierz and fourteen small towns), 1791

| Age | Men | | Women | |
|-----|-----|---|-------|---|
| | No. | % | No. | % |
| 15–19 | 38 | 24.0 | 100 | 45.9 |
| 20–24 | 224 | 83.6 | 286 | 82.9 |
| 25–29 | 160 | 91.4 | 242 | 94.5 |
| 30–34 | 304 | 94.4 | 276 | 95.2 |
| 35–39 | 192 | 97.0 | 197 | 95.6 |
| 40–44 | 220 | 95.6 | 180 | 90.9 |
| 45–49 | 121 | 98.4 | 91 | 88.3 |
| 50–54 | 135 | 94.4 | 83 | 89.2 |
| 55–59 | 49 | 92.4 | 23 | 69.7 |
| 60+ | 115 | 84.6 | 50 | 65.8 |

*Source*: 1791 census.

**Table 8.** Married Jewish population in Kazimierz, 1791

| Age | Men | | Women | |
|-----|-----|-----|-----|-----|
| | No. | % | No. | % |
| 15–19 | 21 | 28.8 | 89 | 73.6 |
| 20–24 | 99 | 85.3 | 122 | 95.3 |
| 25–29 | 61 | 92.4 | 84 | 92.3 |
| 30–34 | 121 | 91.0 | 122 | 96.1 |
| 35–39 | 101 | 96.2 | 79 | 92.9 |
| 40–44 | 115 | 92.0 | 98 | 89.1 |
| 45–49 | 58 | 98.3 | 40 | 88.9 |
| 50–54 | 58 | 89.2 | 39 | 92.8 |
| 55–59 | 26 | 96.5 | 11 | 78.6 |
| 60+ | 33 | 68.8 | 13 | 59.1 |

*Source*: 1791 census.

**Table 9.** Total married Jewish population in fourteen small towns, 1791

| Age | Men | | Women | |
|-----|-----|-----|-----|-----|
| | No. | % | No. | % |
| 15–19 | 17 | 20.0 | 11 | 11.3 |
| 20–24 | 125 | 96.9 | 164 | 75.6 |
| 25–29 | 99 | 90.8 | 158 | 95.8 |
| 30–34 | 183 | 96.8 | 154 | 94.5 |
| 35–39 | 91 | 97.8 | 118 | 97.5 |
| 40–44 | 105 | 100.0 | 82 | 93.2 |
| 45–49 | 63 | 98.4 | 49 | 84.5 |
| 50–54 | 77 | 98.7 | 44 | 86.3 |
| 55–59 | 23 | 88.5 | 12 | 63.2 |
| 60+ | 82 | 93.2 | 37 | 68.5 |

*Source*: 1791 census.

**Table 10.** Married Jewish population in 212 villages, 1791

| Age | Men | | Women | |
|-----|-----|-----|-----|-----|
| | No. | % | No. | % |
| 15–19 | 10 | 10.9 | 26 | 32.1 |
| 20–24 | 50 | 54.9 | 35 | 31.5 |
| 25–29 | 49 | 87.5 | 65 | 92.8 |
| 30–34 | 90 | 91.8 | 73 | 92.4 |
| 35–39 | 57 | 98.3 | 42 | 95.4 |
| 40–44 | 77 | 91.7 | 55 | 98.2 |
| 45–49 | 37 | 97.4 | 16 | 88.9 |
| 50–54 | 30 | 83.3 | 31 | 83.8 |
| 55–59 | n.a. | n.a. | n.a. | n.a. |
| 60+ | 38 | 92.7 | 16 | 51.6 |

*Source*: 1791 census.

**Table 11.** Relative percentage of men in the Christian and in the Jewish populations, 1791

| Age | Men in the Christian population in the Wieleń parish | Men in the Jewish population in Małopolska and the Wieluń district |
|---|---|---|
| 15–19 | 47.1 | 45.5 |
| 20–24 | 46.6 | 44.0 |
| 25–29 | 41.7 | 41.5 |
| 30–34 | 51.6 | 53.2 |
| 35–39 | 50.0 | 50.6 |
| 40–44 | 56.7 | 55.3 |
| 45–49 | 60.0 | 57.1 |
| 50–54 | 58.0 | 57.0 |
| 55–59 | 60.4 | 61.8 |
| 60+ | 64.6 | 62.3 |

*Source*: 1791 census.

**Table 12.** Early marriages among Jews in Małopolska and in the Wieluń district, 1791 (relative percentage in the 15- to 19-year-old group)

| Region | Men | Women |
|---|---|---|
| In the towns | 24.0 | 45.9 |
| In Kazimierz, near Cracow | 28.8 | 73.6 |
| In the villages | 10.9 | 32.1 |
| **Total** | **19.2** | **42.1** |

*Source*: 1791 census.

**Table 13.** Age differences between married Jews in the two regions, 1791 (total: 1,943 couples)

| Age difference in years | Married men | | Married women | |
|---|---|---|---|---|
| | No. | % | No. | % |
| 1–5 | 938 | 58.3 | 134 | 67.5 |
| 6–10 | 436 | 27.1 | 49 | 25.0 |
| 11–15 | 133 | 8.3 | 6 | 3.0 |
| 16–20 | 63 | 3.9 | 8 | 4.0 |
| 21–25 | 19 | 1.2 | 1 | 0.5 |
| 26+ | 19 | 1.2 | — | — |
| **Total** | **1,608** | **83.7** | **198** | **10.3** |

*Source*: 1791 census.

**Table 14.** Age differences between married Jews in Kazimierz and fourteen small towns, 1791 (total: 1,559 couples)

| Age difference in years | Married men | | Married women | |
|---|---|---|---|---|
| | No. | % | No. | % |
| 1–5 | 796 | 62.3 | 116 | 68.6 |
| 6–10 | 317 | 24.8 | 41 | 24.3 |
| 11–15 | 94 | 7.5 | 6 | 3.5 |
| 16–20 | 44 | 3.4 | 5 | 3.0 |
| 21–25 | 13 | 1.0 | 1 | 0.6 |
| 26+ | 13 | 1.0 | — | — |
| Total | 1,277 | 81.9 | 169 | 10.8 |

*Source*: 1791 census.

**Table 15.** Age differences between married Jews in Kazimierz, 1791 (total: 632 couples)

| Age difference in years | Married men | | Married women | |
|---|---|---|---|---|
| | No. | % | No. | % |
| 1–5 | 316 | 59.0 | 62 | 65.0 |
| 6–10 | 154 | 28.5 | 25 | 26.0 |
| 11–15 | 35 | 6.5 | 4 | 4.5 |
| 16–20 | 22 | 4.0 | 4 | 4.5 |
| 21–25 | 6 | 1.5 | — | — |
| 26+ | 4 | 0.5 | — | — |
| Total | 537 | 85.0 | 95 | 15.0 |

*Source*: 1791 census.

**Table 16.** Age differences between married Jews in 196 villages in the Cracow province, 1791 (total: 360 couples)

| Age difference in years | Married men | | Married women | |
|---|---|---|---|---|
| | No. | % | No. | % |
| 1–5 | 142 | 43.0 | 18 | 62.0 |
| 6–10 | 119 | 36.0 | 8 | 27.5 |
| 11–15 | 39 | 12.0 | — | — |
| 16–20 | 19 | 6.0 | 3 | 10.0 |
| 21–25 | 6 | 1.5 | — | — |
| 26+ | 8 | 1.5 | — | — |
| Total | 333 | 92.5 | 291 | 80.83 |

*Source*: 1791 census.

**Table 17.** Jewish couples living in parents' households in the two regions, 1791

| Area | Couples living in parents' households | | Couples in parents' households with husband under 30 | |
|---|---|---|---|---|
| | No. | % | No. | % |
| Kazimierz | 136 | 19.6 | 99 | 54.7 |
| 14 small towns | 76 | 8.8 | 50 | 20.7 |
| Total | 212 | 13.6 | 149 | 35.3 |
| 212 villages | 26 | 5.8 | 14 | 12.8 |
| Total | 238 | 13.3 | 163 | 30.7 |

*Source*: 1791 census.

**Table 18.** Jewish households in the two districts with married children, 1791

| Area | No. of parents' households with families of married children | With a family of: | | | | | |
|---|---|---|---|---|---|---|---|
| | | 1 child | | 2 children | | 3–4 children | |
| | | No. | % | No. | % | No. | % |
| Kazimierz | 108 | 86 | 79.6 | 16 | 14.8 | 6 | 5.6 |
| 14 small cities | 65 | 55 | 84.6 | 9 | 13.8 | 1 | (2.6) |
| Total | 173 | 141 | 81.5 | 25 | 14.4 | 7 | 4.1 |
| 212 villages | 22 | 19 | 86.5 | 2 | (9.0) | 1 | (4.5) |
| Total | 195 | 160 | 81.6 | 27 | 13.8 | 8 | 4.6 |

*Source:* 1791 census.

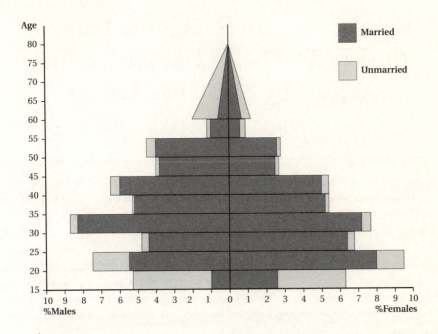

Proportion of the Jewish population in the two regions in 1791 married, by age cohort and gender

# 'For the Human Soul is the Lamp of the Lord': The *Tkhine* for 'Laying Wicks' by Sarah bas Tovim

## CHAVA WEISSLER

WHILE it is difficult to reconstruct the religious lives of Jewish women in any pre-modern era, one important window into the piety of Jewish women in eighteenth-century Poland is through the *tkhines*, the primarily female genre of Yiddish supplicatory prayers.[1] This essay will discuss the work of one author of *tkhines*, the most famous of them all, Sarah bas Tovim. I will begin with a discussion of what can be gleaned about Sarah from her two authentic *tkhine* collections, and then go on to focus on the most beloved portion of one of them, her *tkhine* for making candles of wicks used to measure graves in the cemetery. A comparison of this *tkhine* with other contemporaneous material will elucidate the meaning of the ritual and the *tkhine* that accompanies it.

## THE AUTHOR AND HER WORKS

Sarah, daughter of Mordecai (or sometimes daughter of Isaac or Jacob) of Satanov, great-granddaughter of Mordecai of Brisk (Brześć), known as Sarah bas Tovim,[2] became the emblematic *tkhine* author, and one of her two works,

Prov. 20: 27. Much of the research for this essay was carried out in 1990–1, while I was a Fellow of the Annenberg Research Institute, now the Center for Judaic Studies of the University of Pennsylvania. I want to thank the Center, the library staff, and especially Dr Sol Cohen, for their gracious assistance. My thanks go also to Ross Kraemer and Michael Raposa for their comments on earlier drafts.

[1] The term *tkhine* derives from the Hebrew *tehinah*, supplication. It can designate either an individual supplicatory prayer or a collection of such prayers. For an introduction to the *tkhines*, see my essays 'The Traditional Piety of Ashkenazic Women', in Arthur Green (ed.), *Jewish Spirituality from the Sixteenth Century Revival to the Present*, ii (New York, 1987), 245–75; and 'Prayers in Yiddish and the Religious World of Ashkenazic Women', in Judith Baskin (ed.), *Jewish Women in Historical Perspective* (Detroit, 1991), 159–81. Still valuable is the pioneering study of the *tkhines* by Solomon Freehof, 'Devotional Literature in the Vernacular', *Central Conference of American Rabbis Yearbook*, 33 (1923), 374–424. See also Shmuel Niger, 'Di yidishe literatur un di lezerin', in his *Bleter geshikhte fun der yidisher literatur* (New York, 1959), 35–107.

[2] Sarah's epithet means 'daughter of good or notable people; of good family'. The *tovim* were a type of Jewish communal official, but this seems not to be the direct origin of her epithet. 'Tuwim' is

*Shloyshe sheorim* (The Three Gates), perhaps the most beloved of all *tkhines*. As literary evidence attests, Sarah bas Tovim's *tkhines* eventually became part of the standard knowledge of pious women,[3] and her influence eventually extended much further than her native Podolia. Sarah is an elusive figure: in the course of time, she took on legendary proportions, and some have insisted that she never existed at all.[4] She even became the subject of a short story by Y. L. Peretz, in which she appears as a sort of fairy godmother.[5] The fact that the name of her father (although not her great-grandfather) changes from edition to edition of her work, and the unusual circumstance that no edition mentions a husband,[6] make finding documentation about her quite difficult.[7]

The scepticism about Sarah's existence is rooted in the older scholarly view that no female authors of *tkhines* existed, that all were maskilic fabrications. Yet so

known as a surname among 20th-century Polish Jews; some say that the poet Julian Tuwim (1894–1953) was a descendant of Sarah's (Prof. Dov Noy, personal communication, spring 1985).

[3] In his autobiographical novel *Of Bygone Days*, set in the town of Kapulie (province of Minsk) in the 1840s, the Yiddish writer Shalom Jacob Abramowitsch (Mendele Mokher Seforim, 1835–1917) depicts his mother, a deeply spiritual woman: 'Shloymele's mother Sarah was frail and slight, with small, white hands crisscrossed with tiny purple veins, and the pale face and thin lips of a pious woman. She seemed to be pure spirit, to float rather than walk. She was a learned woman, who knew all kinds of *tkhines*, *tkhines* of the Land of Israel and *tkhines* of Sarah Bas Tovim . . .' (Mendele Mokher Seforim, *Of Bygone Days*, in *A Shtetl and Other Yiddish Novellas*, comp. and ed. Ruth Wisse (New York, 1973), 300). The translation is by Raymond Scheindlin, except that I have substituted the original word 'tkhines' for Scheindlin's translation, 'prayers'.

[4] In the second half of the 19th century, maskilim, who wrote *tkhines* for small sums, used her name on their productions, knowing of her popularity. Because they wrote under her name, some of these maskilim thought Sarah had never existed. The literary historian Israel Zinberg asserts that Sarah bas Tovim was indeed a historical figure; using the statements in her *tkhines* which give the names and places of residence of some of her male ancestors, he hypothesizes that she was probably the great-granddaughter of either Mordecai Zusskind (d. 1684) or Mordecai Gunzberg (d. 1688), both rabbis in Brześć (Zinberg, *History of Jewish Literature*, trans. Bernard Martin (New York: Ktav; Cincinnati: Hebrew Union College Press, 1972–8), vii: *Old Yiddish Literature from its Origins to the Haskalah Period*, 252–4).

[5] 'Der ziveg; oder, Sore bas Tovim', in Y. L. Peretz, *Ale verk*, v: *Folkstimlekhe geshikhtn* (New York, 1947), 372–9. An English translation of this story appears in I. L. Peretz, *The Case against the Wind and Other Stories*, trans. and adapted by Esther Hautzig (New York, 1975), 45–53.

[6] This is extremely unusual. I have only seen one or two other *tkhines* in which no husband was mentioned for the author.

[7] Some, mostly early but undated, editions of *The Three Gates* include the customary formula *shetiḥyeh* ('may she live') after Sarah's name, indicating she was still alive at the time of publication. Of course, editions may be reprinted long after a person's death which continue to contain the formula, but this suggests at least one edition of the work was published during its author's lifetime. Raphael Mahler, in *Der kampf tsvisn haskole un khasides in galitsye* (New York, 1942), 148–50, lists books mentioned by the censor in Lwów, in 1818. The list includes a work entitled *Shloyshe she'orim*, which is probably the *tkhine* by Sarah bas Tovim. (There was another *tkhine* by this title published in the 18th century as an addendum to a work entitled *Naye lange rosh khoydesh bentshn tkhine*, but in the 19th-century editions the title of this addendum seems to change to *Sha'arey dmoes tkhine*.) Other works listed by the censor include *Tsenerene*, *Korbn minkhe*, *Shivḥei haBesht*, *Tkhines uvakoshes*, *Kav hayashar*, *Preger gebete*, *Ma'aneh lashon*, and *Simkhas hanefesh*.

many of them have been historically authenticated that there now seems no real reason to doubt that there was a woman, probably known as Sarah bas Tovim, who composed most or all of the two texts entitled *Tkhine sha'ar hayihed al olomos* (*Tkhine* of the Gate of Unity concerning the Aeons) and *Tkhine shloyshe she'orim* (*Tkhine* of Three Gates). The author repeatedly refers to herself as Sarah within her texts. In *The Three Gates*, she even works her name into an acrostic.[8] All the information we have about her comes from her own texts. Quite unusually, these contain extensive autobiographical sections which enable us to grasp something of her personality and history.

The bibliographical problems associated with Sarah's work are formidable. This is typical of eighteenth- and early nineteenth-century east European *tkhines*, most of which are printed on low-quality paper with poor type and numerous typographical errors, and give no indication of date or place of publication. I have located only two editions of *The Gate of Unity*, neither of which mentions place or date of publication.[9] And as is the case for many *tkhines*, I am unable to identify any edition of the *Tkhine of Three Gates* that I regard as especially good or early, although I can identify some editions as late and bad. Unfortunately, these late, garbled, or rearranged editions include all those with dates of publication. The earliest *dated* edition I have seen was published in Vilna, by Romm, in 1838,[10] but I am convinced, on the basis of typography, that editions were also published in the eighteenth century.

An additional problem is that the publishers of *tkhines* took great liberties with

---

[8] She introduces the first section, or 'gate', of *The Three Gates* with the Hebrew rhyme 'Sha'ar zeh nisyased al sheloshoh mitsvos shenitstavu hanoshim, ushemi Sore beroshei haharuzim' ('This gate is founded on the three women's commandments, and my name, Sarah, is found at the beginning of the verses'). However, most editions print the following section in such a way as to highlight the *sin* and *resh*, the first two letters, skipping the *hé*, the final letter, and highlighting instead a *het* that begins a later paragraph. The *het* is actually in a more logical place for emphasis. It *is* possible that her name was in fact Serah, although that biblical name was very rarely used by east European Jews. Sarah's use of Hebrew here and elsewhere in the text indicates that she had some degree of mastery of the language, although she never wrote extended passages in Hebrew, as did her learned contemporary Leah Horowitz.

[9] On typographical grounds I would place these editions in eastern Europe between 1780 and 1820. The Library of the Jewish Theological Seminary owns a complete copy of one edition; a defective copy of another edition is found in the Library of Agudas Chassidei Chabad. (Two or three pages are missing at the end, including over half of the expanded confession, and all of the *tkhine* for memorial candles. Unfortunately, the extant portions show this to be the better of the two editions.) Interestingly, the author describes herself on the title-page as 'Ikh, ishoh Sarah bas tovim, hameyuheses vehamefursemes' ('I, the renowned woman Sarah bas Tovim, of distinguished ancestry'). *The Three Gates* does not contain quite such bold statements of its author's fame. Of course, such adjectives can always be added by the printer. (Other *tkhines*, by contrast, may state that 'because of her great piety, the modest woman who composed this *tkhine* concealed her name'.)

[10] In the collection of the Jewish National and University Library, Jerusalem, *tkhine* pamphlet collection, R41 A460, vol. i, no. 5. A facsimile of its opening page is printed in the *Encyclopaedia Judaica* (1971), s.v. Bas-Tovim, Sarah. M. Pines, *Histoire de la littérature judeo-allemande* (Paris, 1911), 564, lists an edition published in Sudylków in 1824.

their texts, changing and rearranging them as they saw fit. When no edition can be given clear priority, it is very difficult to establish the correct text,[11] and although all the many extant editions of *The Three Gates* before the mid-nineteenth century contain the same three sections in the same order, this order does not match that described at the beginning of the text itself. Further, some sections of the text are repetitive: two successive paragraphs, for example, may differ somewhat, but contain a large number of nearly identical sentences. The reasons for this are not clear. Sarah could simply be repeating herself, or this could be evidence of a rootedness in oral performance, or it could simply be further evidence of the liberties taken by printers. Finally, the third section of the *tkhine* seems somewhat garbled even in what appear to be early editions. The subject under discussion may change utterly from one sentence to the next.[12] This could be poor editing on Sarah's part, or on the part of the publisher.

The question of authorship has another set of complexities, however. Sarah bas Tovim herself composed only part of her two texts, and compiled other portions from other works. She is quite straightforward about this, and this is more typical of the *tkhine* literature than simple authorship. She says that the *tkhines* contained in *The Gate of Unity* are 'taken out of holy books', thus, in fact, claiming more prestige for them than if they were merely her own invention. Of both of her *tkhines* she says that she 'put them into Yiddish', implying a source in Hebrew.[13] She says of both works that she 'arranged' them. On the other hand, Sarah lays claim to having 'made' the *tkhines*, refers to them as 'both my *tkhines*', and says that they 'came out of' her. Thus, she takes responsibility for these texts, including the portions that she compiled and perhaps reworked, as well as those she actually wrote. An additional complicating factor here is the possible role of the publishers. It may be that some of the passages from other sources have been

[11] The texts used as the basis for my translations and analysis of *The Three Gates* are primarily two undated east European editions, one found in the Jewish National and University Library's *tkhine* pamphlet collection, R41 A460, vol. 8, no. 26, and the other in the Jewish Theological Seminary's uncatalogued *tkhine* collection, bound in a volume with eight other *tkhines*, the first of them entitled *Tkhine koydem tfile*. Both of these editions are problematic, as are all others I have seen. I have also consulted other editions, most of them similarly undated. (The dated editions are all too late to be of much bibliographic value.)

[12] The textual difficulties of even the early editions led me to wonder whether or not the entire work known as the *Tkhine of Three Gates* was in fact the work of one author. I have reached the conclusion that most of it was. Sarah has a number of distinctive stylistic characteristics, most especially, a way of referring to God as 'the dear God, blessed be He and blessed be His Name', the latter phrase appearing as the abbreviation *b'h uv'sh*. One finds this locution throughout the text, except in certain passages which have external sources. (All of these occur in the third section of the text.) Even these are woven together with material in which Sarah's characteristic style appears; this suggests that Sarah herself incorporated them into her text. The only portions about which I am uncertain are two or three paragraphs at the end.

[13] I have not yet identified all of her sources. However, as far as I have been able to determine, all of the material that she incorporates into her texts from Hebrew sources came to her through Yiddish paraphrases. She seems to have been quite well read in Yiddish *musar* literature (ethical writings).

added by a publisher, rather than included by Sarah herself in her original plan. This is made less likely by the fact that all of the early editions of *The Three Gates* contain the same sections in the same order, even though the texts do vary.[14] There are fewer extant editions of *The Gate of Unity*, so it is harder to be certain about the components of the text.

The fact that Sarah uses material from other works allows us to date her *tkhines*. *The Gate of Unity* uses material from Tsevi Hirsch Hotsh's *Naḥalas tsevi* (Inheritance of Tsevi), the Yiddish paraphrase of the Zohar, published in Amsterdam in 1711, and in Żółkiew, closer to home, in 1750. *The Three Gates* paraphrases material from Simon Akiva Ber's *Sefer ma'asei adonai* (Book of the Tales of the Lord), from the 1708 edition. Perhaps most interesting is that Sarah makes use of material from *Ḥemdat yamim* (Days of Delight, first edition Izmir, 1731–2), the anonymous Sabbatean work first published in eastern Europe in Żółkiew in 1740. This guide to the meaning and observance of the Sabbath and festival days was reprinted several times before the recognition of its heretical character caused further publication in Ashkenazi communities to be abandoned, although it did not suppress all interest in the work. I have not yet identified an intermediate source in Yiddish for the material Sarah uses, but there is evidence that there was such a source. None the less, this suggests that *The Three Gates* cannot be any earlier than 1732, unless *Ḥemdat yamim* also drew this passage from an earlier source.[15]

## *The* Tkhine *of the Gate of Unity*

The earlier of Sarah's two works was entitled *Tkhine Sha`ar hayiḥed al olomos* (*Tkhine* of the Gate of Unity concerning the Aeons), a title with mystical overtones, or *Sheker haḥen* (Grace is Deceitful). This *tkhine* seems to have been far less popular than *The Three Gates*, and for good reason: its literary style is more pedestrian and less powerful, and in some ways the contents are less interesting.

[14] Late editions, on the other hand, are often radically altered by the publisher. For example, an edition published in Vilna by Romm in 1859 (included in an anthology entitled *Seder tkhines uvakoshes*, Vilnius, 1860), translated by Norman Tarnor, omits the entire *tkhine* for the making of Yom Kippur candles, and substitutes an altogether different text consisting mainly of paraphrases of selections from the Hebrew liturgy for Yom Kippur. Further, it rearranges the order of the gates, putting the one for Yom Kippur third, thus making it correspond to the order announced on the title-page (Norman Tarnor, 'Three Gates *Tehinno*: A Seventeenth Century Yiddish Prayer', *Judaism*, 40 (1991), 354–67). On the other hand, the edition published in Vilna in 1865 included in *The Merit of our Mothers: A Bilingual Anthology of Jewish Women's Prayers*, compiled and intro. by Tracy Guren Klirs (Cincinnati, 1992), 12–45, contains all of the original text, in the correct order, but with numerous small editorial changes, some of which substantially alter the meaning.

[15] See my essay 'Sabbatian *Tkhines*', in *Voices of the Matriarchs* (Boston, forthcoming). In fact, the passage in question contains an 'internal' date; in the Hebrew original, 1669, and in a *tkhine* that contains a Yiddish paraphrase of the entire passage from *Ḥemdat yamim*, 1735. Sarah probably drew upon the same Yiddish source as this other *tkhine*. However, she only incorporates a portion of the passage, not including the portion with the internal date.

None the less, the introduction and the last *tkhine* in the book, as well as certain other passages, display Sarah's distinctive literary style. This is how the work begins:

O dear women and maids, if you read this *tkhine*, your hearts will rejoice. They are taken out of holy books. By their merit, you will be worthy to enter the Land of Israel. Also I have put down a lovely new *tkhine* that should be said on Mondays and Thursdays and fast days and on the Days of Awe. *Grace is deceitful and beauty is vain.*[16] Beauty is nothing, only righteous deeds are good. *The wisest of women builds her house.*[17] The important thing is that the woman should run the house so that one can study Torah therein, and that she should guide her children *in the straight path* to God's service.

I, poor woman, I have been *scattered and dispersed*,[18] I have had no rest; my heart has moaned within me. I recalled from whence I come and whither I shall go, and where I shall be taken.[19] A great fear came over me, and I begged the living God, blessed be He, *with copious tears*,[20] that the *tkhine* might come out of me.[21]

I, the renowned woman Sarah bas Tovim, of distinguished ancestry, who has no *strange thought*, but has made this *tkhine* only for the sake of the dear God, blessed be He, so that it may be a memorial for me after my death.[22] Whoever reads this *tkhine*, her prayer [*tfile*] will certainly be accepted before God, may His Name be blessed. I, the woman Sarah bas Tovim [daughter of] the rabbinical scholar, learned in Torah, the renowned R. Mordecai, son of the great luminary, R. Isaac, of blessed memory, of the holy community of Satanov, may God protect it.

This introduction sounds several of the themes that reverberate through Sarah's work: a view of women that takes them seriously as religious actors, while honouring their roles as wives and mothers; the significance of her own suffering in her life and in her literary activity; a sense (more clearly expressed here than anywhere else) of her own worth despite the suffering she has endured.

As this introductory material indicates, *The Gate of Unity* contains one long *tkhine* to be recited on Mondays and Thursdays (the days when the Torah is read, sometimes considered minor penitential days) and on fast days. This portion of the text includes, among other things, a Yiddish paraphrase of Ecclesiastes 12: 1–7, and a confession of sins that expands and explicates the standard alphabetic formula. (As far as I have been able to discover, the *tkhine* for Mondays and

[16] Prov. 31: 30. Italic type is used to signify portions of the text that are in Hebrew rather than Yiddish. Often a phrase or sentence will be quoted in Hebrew followed by a paraphrase in Yiddish. All translations of *tkhines* and other works are my own, except for biblical quotations, which usually follow the new Jewish Publication Society translation.

[17] Prov. 14: 1.    [18] Esther 3: 8.    [19] Cf. Avot 3: 1.    [20] Ps. 80: 6.

[21] This passage is in the rhymed prose so typical of Sarah's style: 'Ikh, oreme froy, ikh bin gevezn mefuzar umeforad; hob ikh nit gekont shlumin. Hot mayn harts geton in mir brumen. Hob ikh mikh der mont fun vanen ikh bin gekumen. Un vi ikh vel kumen un vi ikh vel vern genumen. Iz of mir a groyse forkht gekumen. Hob ikh gebetn dem lebndign got borukh hu bidmoes shalish az di tkhine zol fun mir aros kumen.'

[22] This sentence is taken by Zinberg to mean that Sarah was childless, and that she needed to write the *tkhine* because she had no child to say the memorial prayers after her death (*History*, vii. 255 n. 62). I am not sure this inference is justified; many other passages refer to the reciter's husband and children.

Thursdays, although it contains many Hebrew phrases and verses, is not a Yiddish paraphrase of any of the usual penitential prayers and supplications (*seliḥot, taḥanun*) for Mondays and Thursdays.) The work concludes with a *tkhine* to be said before making memorial candles for Yom Kippur, which differs from the prayer for the same occasion found in *The Three Gates*.

## The Tkhine *of Three Gates*

Sarah's second work, *The Three Gates*, is both one of the most popular *tkhines* and also one of the most unusual. By the time she wrote it, Sarah had developed a distinctive and powerful literary voice: she conveys a vivid sense of her personality to the reader. In addition, this one work contains *tkhines* for three of the most popular occasions for which *tkhines* were published in eastern Europe: the three *mitsvot* pertaining primarily to women (the first gate), the penitential season (the second gate), and the new moon (the third gate).[23]

Sarah writes both intimately and intensely. The intimate effect of the *tkhine* is achieved in part by the inclusion of autobiographical material. The author of the *Tkhine of Three Gates* has suffered much in her life, and longs for the redemption that will bring an end not only to her own tribulations, but to the sufferings of all Israel as well. She is an intense and poetic woman, who wants to impart what she has learned, both from books and from life, to other women. The literary power of her work is enhanced by her use of such devices as rhyme, internal rhyme, and assonance.

Sarah opens this *tkhine* with an invocation that expresses her purposes in writing this work, and describes her lot in life. The tribulations at which she hinted in the introduction to *The Gate of Unity* are here spelt out more fully:

I take for my help the living God, blessed be He, who lives for ever and to eternity, and I set out this second beautiful new *tkhine* in Yiddish with great love, with great awe, with trembling and terror, with broken limbs, with great petition, with great . . .[24] May God have mercy upon me and upon all Israel. May I not long be forced to be a wanderer, by the merit of our Mothers Sarah, Rebecca, Rachel, and Leah; and may my own dear mother, Leah, pray to God, blessed be He, for me, that my being a wanderer may be an atonement for me for my sins. May God, blessed be He, forgive me for having talked in synagogue in my youth, during the reading of the dear Torah.

Lord of the whole world, I lay my prayer before You. As I begin to edit my second lovely new *tkhine*, with my entire devotion, and with the entire foundation of my heart,

---

[23] The most popular topic, by far, is that of the penitential season and the Days of Awe. Most other *tkhines* on these themes differ from Sarah's in their overriding concern with confession, penitence, and obtaining God's forgiveness for sin. (As we shall see below, Sarah's *tkhine* for Yom Kippur candles is primarily concerned with obtaining the aid of the dead in bringing about the Messianic redemption.) Other topics that occur frequently, and that Sarah does not address, are the Sabbath (aspects other than kindling Sabbath lights), and prayers for adequate sustenance and livelihood.

[24] A word seems to be missing here in all early editions.

may You protect us from suffering and pain.[25] I pray the dear God, blessed be He, that, just as He heard the prayer of our Fathers and Mothers, He may soon have great mercy on all Israel, and also on the years of my old age, that I not be forced to wander . . . And I beg heaven and earth and all the holy angels to pray for me, that both of my *tkhines* may be accepted; may they become a crown for His holy name upon His head, Amen.[26]

Sarah's intense faith, and difficult life, emerge clearly from this text. She feels that she has been punished for the sins of her youth, especially talking in synagogue, by a life of wandering. The fact of her wandering may be a reflection of the unsettled conditions in eighteenth-century Podolia.[27] Relying on God's mercy, on the merit of the matriarchs, on the intercession of her own deceased mother, Leah, and on the merit of her own act in writing two *tkhines*, Sarah asks God for forgiveness and a peaceful old age. She also asks God to have mercy on the People of Israel, implicitly thus asking for the redemption of the Messianic age.

The sin of talking in synagogue preoccupied Sarah. At the end of the second 'gate', she writes a long excursus on the topic, entitled 'Moral Reproof for the Women'. This portion of the text is particularly rich in autobiographical material, and gives us a sense of her personality, religious concerns, and theology.

I, the woman Sarah, entreat the young women not to chat in the dear synagogue, for it is a great sin. For I remember that the Tanna Rabbi Eliezer ben Rabbi Simeon[28] met the

[25] Much of this *tkhine* is in rhymed prose; this sentence is the first example of rhyme ('mit gantsn grunt fun maynem hartsn, zolstu unz hitn fun payn un shmertsn').

[26] The text refers here to the tradition that the angel Sandalfon fashions a crown for the Holy One out of the prayers of Israel (B. ḥag. 13*b* and *tosafot*, ad.loc.). See Hayyim Liberman, ' "Tkhine imohes" u-"Tkhinas shloyshe sheorim" ', in his *Ohel raḥel* (New York, 1980), 436. Sarah thus claims equality for her *tkhines* with other prayers in Hebrew and Yiddish.

[27] Alternatively, Sarah may have undertaken a life of wandering as a voluntary penance, a common pietistic act at the time. If so, it would be important evidence that women also engaged in this practice. However, Sarah does not use the usual term for such penitential wandering, *golus*, derived from the Hebrew word for 'exile', but instead uses *na venad*, a Hebrew phrase used in Yiddish to express wandering or homelessness. In addition, language she uses elsewhere in the text seems to imply she regarded her homelessness as an involuntary punishment: 'Therefore, I warn you, so that you may not, God forbid, be punished as I was punished, with wandering.' However, to the extent that she was some sort of public religious figure, perhaps a wandering *zogerke* who led women in prayer and rebuked them for their moral shortcomings such as talking in synagogue, she resembles the wandering petty religious intelligentsia described by Joseph Weiss in 'Reshit tsemiḥatah shel haderekh haḥasidit', *Zion*, 16 (1950–1), 46–105.

[28] R. Eleazar (this is the correct form of the name) ben Simeon lived at the end of the second century CE. I have not found any source for the following incident which mentions R. Eleazar. A version of this motif is found in Isaac Ben-Eliakim's *Sefer lev tov* (Prague, 1620), a popular ethical work in Yiddish. (Sarah is quite likely to have read this work.) 'We find in a midrash: R. Yose said, Once I was walking along the way in a field and I saw Elijah the prophet, peace be upon him, and he had four thousand camels with him, all laden. I asked him, With what do you have these camels laden? He spoke thus: I have these camels laden only with destroying angels, who are called wrath and anger. I asked him, For whom have you loaded these camels, or where are you taking them? He spoke thus, I am taking them to hell to repay the people who talk in synagogue *during the prayers*, i.e. from *Barukh she'amar* until after the *Shemoneh esreh*, and after Kaddish that the cantor says after *Raḥum veḥanun*. All of that is termed *during the prayers* [*hilkhot tefilah*].'

officials who led two donkeys carrying punishments. He asked the officials, 'For whose
sake is this?' They said, 'For those people who talk in synagogue between the *Barukh
she'amar* prayer and the end of the *Shemoneh esreh*'.[29] Therefore, I warn you, so that you
may not, God forbid, be punished as I was punished, with wandering. Thus, you should
take proof from me and confess your sins before God, blessed be He.

I also entreat you to have compassion for widows and orphans and proselytes and captives, and for all elderly people, and for all ill people. For just as when you fast, your heart
is bitter, so should you believe that it is bitter for the poor man who has nothing for his wife
and children to eat. Therefore, I entreat you to do this for the sake of the dear God, blessed
be He, that you should see that you have great care. For I, the woman Sarah, hope in God's
blessed Name for great prosperity, and I pray to the dear God, blessed be He, that He may
have great providence for my old age.[30] I have also composed a second lovely *tkhine* so that
I might thereby have atonement for my great sins. Through our recalling of our sins, may
God, blessed be He, send us life.[31]

I remember all the things [I used to do] when I used to come into the dear synagogue, all
dressed up in jewellery. I would do nothing but joke and laugh. Today I remember and
recall that God, blessed be He, does not forgive, as it is written, '*He who is quick to anger,
and extends his wrath*',[32] he waits long and pays quickly. Today, I go wandering, and my
heart moans within me, for I recall that God, blessed be He, will forgive no one. Therefore,
I entreat you to listen to my words and take them to heart. When you enter the dear synagogue, a great terror should overcome you: you should know before Whom you have come
and to Whom you pray, and to Whom you must answer for your life.

I also entreat you to have great compassion for widows and orphans and proselytes and
captives and elderly people, and for ill people. For when you fast, your heart aches; therefore you should believe the poor people—as if he were not in enough distress, it pains him
even more when he sees his wife and children and has nothing with which to refresh them.
Therefore, I, the woman Sarah, entreat that you do this for the sake of the dear God,

---

Another parallel is the following, taken from *Amud ha'avodah* ('The pillar of worship'), which was
appended to an edition of *Sefer hagan* and *Derekh mosheh* (Lwów, 1864). This supplement, extracted
from various ethical works, was compiled by one Abraham ben Judah Leib, in 1802. It is divided into
days; on Day 26 (33*b*) we read: 'In the name of Midrash Shoher Tov: R. Yose ben Kisma said, Once I
was walking on the way, and I met three hundred camels loaded with wrath and anger. And Elijah the
prophet met me and said to me, This is for those who engage in idle chatter in the synagogue.' I have
not yet been able to locate this passage in the midrash named.

[29] *Barukh she'amar* ('Blessed is the one who spoke and the world came into being') begins the core
of the morning service, and this core ends with the *Shemoneh esreh*, the Eighteen Benedictions, which
is recited silently and standing. According to Jewish law, one may not speak during this portion of the
service, but should give one's whole-hearted attention to prayer.

[30] The preceding two sentences were translated from the Jewish National and University Library
edition, not that found at Jewish Theological Seminary, because the text is clearer.

[31] This rhymes in Yiddish: 'Mit dem vos mir tuen oyf unzere zind gedenken, zol Hashem yisbo-
rakh dos lebin shenkin.'

[32] This Hebrew phrase is from the liturgical poem *Vekhol ma'aminim* in the *musaf* service of Rosh
Hashanah (said right after Kedushah; my thanks to Tracy Guren Klirs for this reference). I have
translated it according to the Yiddish interpretation that Sarah gives for it, which corresponds to one
literal sense of the words. However, a more idiomatic translation means almost precisely the opposite:
'He who is wrathful for a short time, and slow to anger'.

blessed be He. May you see that you take great care. For I, like all paupers, hope in God's promise. I also entreat the dear God that He have great care for my old age. May our children not be driven away from us. I have also composed this second lovely new *tkhine* that we may be cured of our sins and of the Angel of Death this year. And because of this merit, may God, blessed be He, send [us] life.

This passage turns the stereotypical critique of women's behaviour in synagogue into an autobiographical account. Unlike many of her contemporaries,[33] Sarah does not simply criticize women's poor behaviour in synagogue; she confesses to it, and testifies to its terrible consequences.

Further, this passage allows us to locate Sarah and her intended audience in a particular socio-economic class. In her youth, Sarah came to synagogue 'all dressed up in jewellery'. This means that, even if she has become impoverished in her old age, she came from a wealthy family. The text addresses other wealthy women: 'For just as when you fast, your heart is bitter, so should you believe that it is bitter for the poor man who has nothing for his wife and children to eat'. The women for whom she writes this have no experience of going hungry. She must make hunger and need concrete for them, by reminding them how they feel on a fast day, when food and drink are forbidden. She reminds them of the obligations of the wealthy: compassion for widows and orphans (who are poor), for proselytes (who may have lost family economic resources as a result of conversion), for captives (who must be ransomed), and for the elderly and the ill (who may also be in need of material assistance).

We also get a glimpse of Sarah's theology from this passage. God is awesome, and punishes sin. One should come before Him in terror and trembling. Yet God is also merciful, if one confesses one's sins, and does good works. Other passages in this text will show us that Sarah also believed that one could establish reciprocal relationships with the dead, so that the matriarchs, patriarchs, and other biblical figures could be made powerful advocates for the living. The closing words of this passage sound a leitmotif which echoes through the second and third gates of the *tkhine*, the hope to be 'cured . . . of the Angel of Death this year'. This is no mere hope for a healthy old age, but for the resurrection of the dead and the eternal life of the Messianic era. This theme and others will reappear in the detailed examination of Sarah's *tkhine* for 'laying the wicks'.

## MEASURING GRAVES AND LAYING WICKS

### *The Texts and the Rituals*

The second gate of *The Three Gates* is rooted in a centuries-old women's ritual. During the High Holiday season (and also in times of illness or trouble) women

---

[33] See e.g. Leah Horowitz's *Tkhine imohes*, which bitterly criticizes the way women spend their time in synagogue comparing their clothing and jewellery.

went to the cemetery, circumambulating and measuring the cemetery or individual graves with candlewicking, reciting *tkhines* while they did so. Between Rosh Hashanah and Yom Kippur, and often on the Eve of Yom Kippur, they made the wicks into candles 'for the living' and 'for the dead', again accompanying the process with *tkhines*. According to some customs, on Yom Kippur the candles were burned at home, while according to others, one or both of them burned in the synagogue. There are hints of this practice in sources going back nearly a thousand years, and it is well attested in literary and ethnographic material over the last three centuries.[34]

While the text in *The Three Gates* is the best-known and most powerful *tkhine* connected with these candles, there are others. Sarah herself composed one of them: the final *tkhine* in *The Gate of Unity* is to be recited before making the candles. A *tkhine* by another author, Simeon Frankfurt, published in his *Sefer haḥayim* (The Book of Life, first edition Amsterdam, 1703) is for the actual measuring of the graves. In addition, several of the later literary and ethnographic sources paraphrase or summarize texts very similar to that found in *The Three Gates* itself. It is quite unusual for any one *tkhine* to be the subject of so many descriptions; this testifies to the tremendous popularity of Sarah's text (and of the practice of making the candles), whether it was attributed to her by later generations or had entered anonymous oral tradition.[35]

In 1906 S. Weissenberg published a description of the ritual of *feldmesn* (measuring the cemetery) complete with photographs.[36] At the behest of any woman who wished to 'order' candles, two, or usually three, women (who specialized in performing the ritual) would measure the cemetery: one, in the middle, would hold two skeins of thread for candlewicks, while the other two would wind up the thread she let fall while walking counter-clockwise around the cemetery. All the while, the woman who had ordered the candles would walk behind them, reciting *tkhines*. (Weissenberg does not give the text.) Alternatively, a poorer

---

[34] The earliest reference that suggests the existence of this custom is a poem by Eleazar of Worms, written in 1197 as an elegy to his wife, Dulcia, murdered by Crusaders. The poem mentions that Dulcia 'makes wicks' and prepares candles for Yom Kippur. See Ivan Marcus, 'Mothers, Martyrs, and Moneymakers: Some Jewish Women in Medieval Europe', *Conservative Judaism*, 38/3 (1986), 34–45. Various other medieval sources, both halakhic and minhagic, refer to aspects of this custom (burning candles for the living and the dead on Yom Kippur, circumambulating the cemetery, and preparing candles from wicks used to measure graves or the cemetery, sometimes for Yom Kippur, and sometimes for someone who is ill). My investigation of this material demonstrated to me how difficult it is to trace women's customs in male sources, a point also noted by Israel Ta-Shma in a chapter on the custom of women covering their eyes while lighting Sabbath candles, 'Kisui ha`einayim be'et hadlakat ner shabat', in his *Minhag ashkenaz hakadmon* (Jerusalem, 1992), 136–41. I hope to publish a separate study of the evidence concerning the historical evolution of the custom of measuring graves with candlewicking to be used for Yom Kippur candles.

[35] There is also the possibility that Sarah transcribed or adapted the text from oral tradition rather than composing it herself. See below.

[36] S. Weissenberg, 'Das Feld- un das Kejwermessen', *Mitteilungen zur jüdischen Volkskunde*, 6 (1906), 39–42. Weissenberg gives the locale for his account as 'southern Russia'.

woman might choose to measure only a single grave (*keyvermesn*), which required the services of only one professional, and smaller amounts of candlewicking and wax.[37]

The measuring finished, the woman would bring the threads home. Later, in the synagogue, on a Monday or a Thursday between Rosh Hashanah and Yom Kippur, they would be made into candles for Yom Kippur; the ritual of making the candles was called *kneytlakh legn* (laying the wicks). A poor woman who knew how to make the candles would receive the wicks. First she would make the candle for the living, or for the healthy. She would take up each wick in turn, while the woman who had asked her to make the candle would say, 'this wick is for my husband, may he live long, this is for my daughter, may she have a good match', and so forth, expressing her wishes for each family member for the coming year.

After laying the wicks for all the relatives and close family friends, they would proceed to the making of the candle for the dead, also called the 'soul candle'. The woman who had asked for the candle to be made would say, over each wick, 'This is for Adam and Eve', 'This is for Abraham and Sarah', and so forth for all of the patriarchs; 'This is for my departed mother, may she have pleasant rest in paradise and be a good advocate for me and my children', 'This is for my [deceased] little son', and so forth. Any wicks left over were made into candles used for Hanukah and a variety of other purposes. The candle for the living was lit at home on the eve of Yom Kippur, to bring good luck for the coming year; other sources say that it was used as an oracle to predict whether the living family members would all live out the year. The candle for the dead was lit in synagogue at the same time.

While Weissenberg's account stems from a time at least a century and a half after Sarah published *The Three Gates*, his summary of the text bears striking similarities to Sarah's own. Other nineteenth- and twentieth-century accounts differ somewhat in the details of the ceremony, but the overall picture of the ritual that emerges is clear.[38] Thus, we may cautiously accept this picture as essentially consistent with the evidence of earlier texts.

[37] Weissenberg does summarize a text for the measuring of a single grave; it is similar to texts collected by Gisela Suliteanu in Romania in the 1960s ('The Traditional System of Melopeic Prose of the Funeral Songs Recited by the Jewish Women of the Socialist Republic of Rumania', in Issachar Ben-Ami (ed.), *Folklore Research Center Studies*, iii (Jerusalem, 1972), 291–349). Suliteanu's texts were simply for the visiting, not the measuring, of parents' graves. The bulk of the article is devoted to the musical notation of the performance of the texts; it is important to remember that *tkhines* were often chanted, rather than simply read.

[38] Additional ethnographic sources: Yehudah Elzet (pseud. of Y. L. Zlotnik), 'Miminhagei Yisrael', in *Reshumot*, 1 (1918), 335–77: 352; H. Chajes, 'Gleybungen un minhogim in farbindung mitn toyt', *Filologishe shriftn*, 2 (1926), cols. 292, 295; Yosef Zelikovitsh, 'Der toyt un zayne bagleyt-momentn in der yidisher etnografye un folklor', *Lodzher visnshaftlekhe shriftn*, 1 (1938), 180–1. Brief mentions are also found in Max Grunwald, 'Aus Hausapotheke und Hexenkuch', *Mitteilungen zur jüdischen Volkskunde*, pt. 1 (1900), 60 n. 201; Dr Lazarus, 'Das Messen', *Mitteilungen zur jüdischen Volkskunde*, pt. 6 (1900), 137; S. An-ski (Shloyme Zanvil Rapaport) *Dos yudishe etnografishe program*

There are two other important pieces of evidence, roughly contemporaneous with Sarah, that confirm this acceptance. The first, slightly earlier than Sarah's text, is the mention of the custom of measuring graves in a legal commentary. Zechariah Mendel ben Arieh Loeb of Cracow (fl. 1671–1707) wrote the commentary *Ba'er heitev* on the Yoreh De'ah section of the *Shulḥan arukh*. In a comment on one of the laws of burial, he first quotes *Sefer ha'agudah*, a legal source written by Alexander Zuslein Hakohen (d. 1349) on the custom of walking the circumference of cemeteries in times of illness, and then says: 'And from this the custom has spread to measure the cemetery's circumference with wicks that are afterwards made into wax candles and given to the synagogue, and this is a good custom.'[39] Zechariah Mendel does not explain the rationale for this custom, nor does he specify whether or not any prayers or supplications were recited during the measuring and candle-making. He does not say whether women or men, or both, performed the ritual. Also, the occasion for the candles is different: this text

(Petrograd, 1915), i: *Der Mentsh, 1641*; and Joshua Trachtenberg, *Jewish Magic and Superstition* (first pub. 1939; Cleveland, Ohio, 1961), 285 n. 6. Literary sources (incl. memoirs): Pauline Wengeroff, *Memoiren einer Grossmutter* (Berlin, 1908–10), i. 103–4; Bella Chagall, *Brenendike likht* (New York, 1945), 77–9. Shmuel Yosef Agnon, *Yamim nora'im* (Jerusalem, 1956), 202–3, paraphrases several sources that deal with this custom, most notably *Mateh efrayim* by Ephraim Zalman Margoliot (to be discussed below). Agnon's paraphrase differs substantially from the original, and includes the detail that the women recall the names of their departed relatives over each wick, especially of those who had been righteous and who could therefore be good advocates for them in heaven. Presumably Agnon added this information from his own observations, or perhaps from other written sources.

Particularly valuable for the sense it gives of the emotional tone of the candle-making ritual is the description found in Abramowitsch, *Of Bygone Days*. While he never attributes the *tkhine* he quotes to any author, Abramowitsch does describe a group of women making the candles, led by Sarah (the character who represents his mother), a learned and pious woman (*Bayamim hahem* (Heb.), 271; *Shloyme Reb Khayyims* (Yiddish), 35–7; *Of Bygone Days* (Eng.), 300–2). Abramowitsch goes on to quote a text that, while apparently based on *The Three Gates*, differs from it in significant details. He also describes how the women weep as they recite the *tkhine*. For a more detailed treatment of Abramowitsch's description of the recitation of the *tkhine*, see my 'The Traditional Piety of Ashkenazic Women', 264–7.

Recent contemporary evidence of the longevity of this *tkhine* is found in *Tkhine imohos* (*Tkhine* of the Matriarchs), published in Brooklyn in 1992, and 'written and adapted' by Jacob Meshullam Grinfeld. This anthology of *tkhines* shows clear traces of the hasidic origin of its editor. For example, it includes a prayer by R. Elimelekh of Lizhensk (Leżajsk). More interestingly for our purposes, it includes a version of Sarah's *tkhine*, as well as a description of the making of candles for Yom Kippur among the women of the Belzer hasidic community in Europe before the Holocaust. Grinfeld's description, found in a footnote on p. 259 of *Tkhine imohes*, reads as follows: 'It was formerly the custom that righteous women would themselves make the candles for Yom Kippur. They made the wicks, dipping them in melted wax several times until the candle was ready. During the making of the candles, they would pray fervently, with great weeping. It was a custom among the *tsadikim* of the Belz dynasty to preach a fiery sermon to the women during the making of the candles. The spiritual arousal among the listeners was so great that their weeping rose to the heart of heaven.' It is interesting that Grinfeld includes this *tkhine*, which runs for three pages, despite that fact that this practice is no longer followed.

[39] Zechariah Mendel ben Arieh Loeb of Cracow, *Ba'er heitev* on *Shulḥan arukh*, Yoreh De'ah 376 (4), s.v. *afar*.

records a custom connected with healing illness, rather than the penitential season.[40] None the less, this suggests that a custom similar to that for which the *tkhine* in *The Three Gates* is the liturgy was in existence by the late seventeenth century. Since we know that other prayers for visiting graves were also in existence by this time (in *Ma'aneh lashon* and *Ma'avar yabok*, for example) it seems reasonable that there might have been prayers to be said for this ritual too.

The second piece of evidence is found in *Mateh efrayim* (first edition Żółkiew, 1835), by Ephraim Zalman Margoliot (1760–1828). Margoliot lived most of his life in Brody, not too far from Satanov, and not much later than Sarah, so his evidence is particularly valuable. He notes that women made candles for use in the synagogue on Yom Kippur on the day before the Eve of Yom Kippur. He specifies that the candles should be attractively made, from good-quality wicks and wax, preferably from white wax, which burns well. He warns that women who sell wicks that they claim have been used to encircle the cemetery often sell inferior merchandise of coarse flax or hemp, which does not burn well.[41] If one wishes to use wicks that have encircled the cemetery, one should arrange in advance for high-quality thread to be used. Margoliot mentions the custom of reciting supplications while making the candles (although he gives no text), and states: 'One should not abolish this custom or mock it, for the custom of Israel is Torah.' Margoliot also specifies that one candle is to be made for each married man and his living family members, called 'the candle of the healthy', and one for departed parents, called 'the soul candle'. Despite the prevalent custom of bringing only the candle of the healthy to synagogue, Margoliot directs that both the candles should burn in the synagogue on Yom Kippur.[42]

Thus, in the text and in the ritual Sarah's text implies, we can recover a level of women's religious creativity that can rarely be approached through the mainly literary genre of *tkhines*: a women's tradition and prayer that represent genuine folk practice. Sarah has composed—or adapted—a liturgy in Yiddish for a religious act of folk origin, apparently created by women. The making of candles for Yom Kippur was by all accounts practised only by women. None the less, Sarah's text repeatedly describes the making of the candles as a *mitsvah*, that is, a divine commandment and obligation, upon women—even though it is not found in any standard halakhic code.[43]

[40] However, Wengeroff, *Memoiren*, i. 104, states that the cemeteries or graves were measured in times of illness, while the actual making of the candles from the wicks used for measuring took place on the Eve of Yom Kippur.

[41] He refers to these women, perhaps with a touch of sarcasm, as *nashim sha'ananot* ('tranquil women', see Isa. 31: 9). This term has a history in midrash and kabbalah.

[42] *Mateh efrayim*, 22a–b.

[43] While the term *mitsvah* can mean a simple good deed as well as a divine commandment, it is clear that Sarah is using it here in the more technical sense of a religious obligation. Evidence for this is found in the close linguistic parallel between her *tkhine* for kindling Sabbath lights (clearly a divine commandment) and the present text. In the first of these, she writes: 'Ribono shel olom, mayn mitsve

In any case, the evidence shows that the candle-making ritual existed for centuries before and after Sarah lived. As with other long-standing rituals, its significance undoubtedly changed and evolved over time. What did it mean in Sarah's texts? Were these meanings contested in her own day?

Since the text from *The Three Gates* is the best-known *tkhine* for this ritual, we shall consider it first. The text begins:

Lord of the world, I pray You, most merciful God, to accept my [observance of] the *mitsvah* of the lights that we will make for the sake of Your holy Name, and for the sake of the holy souls.

*May it be [God's] will* May it be God's will that today, on the Eve of Yom Kippur, we be remembered before you with the *mitsvah* of the lights that we shall make in the synagogue. May we be remembered for good, and may we be worthy to give lights to the Temple, as used to be done. And may the prayers which are said by the light of these candles, be with great devotion and *fear and awe*, that Satan may not hinder our prayer.[44] And may the lights that are made for the sake of the holy souls . . . [words missing?] May they awaken and each inform the next all the way back to the holy patriarchs and matriarchs, who should further inform each other back to Adam and Eve, so that they may rectify the sin by which they brought death to the world. May they arise out of their graves and pray for us that this year may be a good year. For they caused death to enter the world, so it is fitting for them to plead for us that we may be rid of the Angel of Death.

As I lay the next wick for the sake of our Father Noah, it is fitting for him, too, to pray for us, for he was in great trouble. Of him is written: '*For the waters have reached my neck*';[45] the water came up all the way to his neck. May the God who saved him save us from fire and water and from all evil which we fear; may it not, God forbid, come to us.

The *tkhine* then continues with the laying of wicks for Abraham, Sarah, Isaac, Rebecca, Jacob, Rachel (Leah is omitted), Moses, Aaron, David, and Solomon, and for 'all the righteous and pious people who have ever lived', each accompanied by a short paragraph constructed on the model of the one for Noah. In each case, some feature of the person as portrayed in the Bible or later midrashic material is mentioned as making that person an especially appropriate intercessor, and the paragraph concludes with a prayer that is connected in some way with this feature.

fun di lekht on tsindn zol azo on genumen zayn vi di mitsve fun kohen godol ven er hot lekht in libn beys–hamikdosh getsinden . . . ('Lord of the Universe, may my [observance] of the commandment of kindling the lights be accepted like that of the High Priest when he kindled the lights in the dear Temple'). In the latter she writes: 'Ribono shel olom, ikh bet dikh, zeyer der barmiger got, zolst on nemen mayn mitsve fun de lekht vos mir veln makhn fun dayn heylign libn nomen vegn . . .' ('Lord of the world, I pray You, most merciful God, to accept my [observance of] the *mitsvah* of the lights that we will make for the sake of Your holy Name'). In both cases, Sarah is concerned that the performance of the commandment be acceptable to God. Interestingly, Ephraim Zalman Margoliot refers to these candles as 'nerot shel mitsvah' (*Mateh efrayim, 22b*).

[44] There was a belief that Satan would stand in the Heavenly Court on Rosh Hashanah and Yom Kippur to remind God of the sins of the Israelites, thus making God disinclined to accept their prayers.    [45] Ps. 69: 2.

After the laying of all the wicks, the *tkhine* contains some further prayers. It asks for forgiveness of sins, sustenance, and good matches for one's children, but especially for redemption and the resurrection of the dead that accompanies it:

May these lights, which were made for the holy and pure souls, awaken them so that they arise and inform one another back to the holy patriarchs and matriarchs, and further back to Adam and Eve, that they rectify the sin by which they brought death to the whole world. May they arise from their graves and pray for us, that this very year, may it come for good, there may finally be the resurrection of the dead. May [God's] Attribute of Stern Judgement become the Attribute of Mercy; may they be unified.[46] May [the souls] pray for us that the resurrection of the dead will come to pass. And may all the holy and pure angels pray that the dry bones live again,[47] speedily and soon.

This *tkhine* concludes on a similarly eschatological note:

Lord of the world, I pray You, merciful God, accept the lights that we make for the holy pure souls. For each thread that we lay, may You increase life for us. May the holy souls awake out of their graves and pray for us that we may be healthy. It is fitting for us to pray for the dead, for those who died in our own generations, and for those who have died from the time of Adam and Eve on. Today we make candles for the sake of all the souls—for the sake of the souls who lie in the fields and the forests, and for all the martyrs,[48] and for all those who have no children, and for all the little children[49]—so that they may awaken the dry bones; may they come alive speedily and soon! May we be worthy to see the resurrection of the dead this year, Amen, Selah.

The ritual of making the candles for the dead and the living, together with its liturgy, embodies condensed and complex symbolic meanings. The text in *The Three Gates* vibrates with eschatological tension and messianic hopes. It also endows the woman's ritual action in laying the wicks with the power to enlist the aid of the dead in helping her own family and in bringing the redemption. While these themes will be dealt with in passing, I shall focus on the ways this text establishes a relationship of mutual aid and reciprocity between the living and the dead. Such a relationship is also found in Sarah's earlier *tkhine*, *The Gate of Unity*. By contrast, the prayers for the cemetery by the slightly earlier author Simeon Frankfurt portray a more one-sided relationship.

## *The Living and the Dead*

Sarah first lays out the reciprocity between the living and the dead in *The Gate of Unity*:

*May it be Your will* may it be Your will, God, my God, the God of my forebears, Abraham, Isaac, and Jacob, and of Sarah, Rebecca, Rachel, and Leah, the God of righteous men and

---

[46]  This is a standard kabbalistic trope for the final redemption.                [47]  Cf. Ezek. 37: 1–14.

[48]  Many of whom did not receive proper Jewish burial.

[49]  Those without children, which includes those who died as children, presumably have no descendants to make memorial candles for them.

women, of male and female martyrs, [that] for the souls who have already been forgotten, and for the souls who died before their time, in their youth, and for the souls who have no one to make lights for them in the synagogue; may it be Your will, God, my God, that they may have a portion in these lights, so that our lights will not be extinguished; heaven forbid, before the [proper] time. As we have not forgotten the souls who sleep in their graves—we go to entreat them and measure them—thus may we be measured for good in the heavenly court, so that our sentence may be with great mercy, not with anger . . . Therefore we entreat the dear God, blessed be He, that our sentence may be [pronounced] with great mercy, not, heaven forbid, with anger, so that we may not, heaven forbid, leave any little orphans. May these souls inform the souls that sleep in the cave of Machpelah[50] that they should pray for us, that we may have a good year, that we may be worthy to see the red thread turn white,[51] that we may be delivered, and that we may have *a year of mercy for good, Amen.*

The text expresses a touching concern for those Jews who, because they died anonymously and were never given proper burial, or because they were childless, have no one to make candles in their memory. Thus, one element of the reciprocity between living and dead is that the living remember the dead, even those who presumably have been forgotten. They give the dead a portion in the merit of donating candles for the synagogue. (Long-burning candles were especially necessary on Yom Kippur so that people would be able to read the unfamiliar liturgy for the entire holiday, from dusk to darkening dusk.) As a result of this meritorious act, the women making candles hope that their own candles, the oracle for the coming year, will not be extinguished before the holiday is over. Second, the living remember the dead by entreating them and measuring their graves. They thus hope that they will be measured with mercy before the divine court of justice. And finally, by coming to the cemetery, measuring the graves, and entreating the dead, the living hope to rouse the souls of those in that particular cemetery to communicate with other souls, all the way back to the patriarchs and matriarchs, who are buried in the cave of Machpelah in Hebron, to pray for the living. Specifically, the living hope for a good year to come; to see the red thread turn white, both a figure for having their sins forgiven, and a hope to see the restoration of Temple worship in the Messianic era; and finally, to be delivered and redeemed.

What is the origin of this conception of reciprocity between the living and the dead? The Zohar recounts that, when human beings are in trouble, if they weep at the graves of the righteous (later in the passage, it says they should bring a Torah scroll to the cemetery) the dead become concerned, and rouse 'those who sleep in

[50] See Gen. 23, in which Abraham purchases the cave of Machpelah in Hebron as a burial place for his wife, Sarah. According to later Jewish tradition, Adam and Eve, as well as Abraham and Sarah, Isaac and Rebecca, and Jacob and Leah, are buried there.

[51] *Mishnah Yoma* 6: 8, building on Isa. 1: 18. Since this sign that the goat for Azazel had reached the wilderness occurred during the Temple ceremony on Yom Kippur, the wish to be worthy to see it is as much a wish for the restoration of Temple worship in the Messianic era as it is a wish that God may forgive Israel's sins.

Hebron', that is, the patriarchs and matriarchs and Adam and Eve, to plead for mercy for them.[52] Paraphrases of this passage occur in two Yiddish works from which Sarah quotes elsewhere in her works, *Sefer mayse adonai* and *Sefer naḥalas tsevi*, the latter containing more of the relevant material.[53] However, neither of these sources connects this practice to the penitential season; there is some suggestion of association with the new moon. Further, neither of them contains the text of an actual appeal to 'those who sleep in Hebron'. Nor do any of them mention prayers for the Messianic redemption, or the resurrection of the dead; all imply a desire for relief from some temporary difficulty, such as plague or persecution.

However, this passage from the Zohar is also quoted or paraphrased in additional Hebrew sources,[54] among them, *Hemdat yamim*. Particularly interesting is the fact that this work quotes the Zohar passage immediately after the 'Lament for the Exile' that Sarah includes in Yiddish paraphrase in the 'gate' for the new moon. That lament includes powerful pleas to Abraham, Isaac, Jacob, Moses, and the Messiah, to arise and beg God to bring the redemption. Further, the author states that it was his custom to recite the lament, on the eve of the new moon, in the cemetery, and to pray there for redemption. Thus, the actual content of the text of *The Three Gates*, the appeal to the patriarchs and matriarchs, to Adam and Eve, points us back towards the connection with *Hemdat yamim*. This suggests that Sarah could have been given the inspiration for this *tkhine* by a Yiddish work that contained more of *Hemdat yamim* than simply the 'Lament for the Exile'. To the extent that Sarah was influenced by the subterranean Messianic message of *Hemdat yamim*, this might account for the high eschatological tension in her works. Alternatively, she might actually have participated in crypto-Sabbatean circles in Satanov or elsewhere in Podolia, but as yet, there is no way to be certain.

In *The Three Gates*, Sarah takes the general idea of an appeal to those who sleep in Hebron and develops it into a full-fledged plea to various biblical figures (not all of whom are said to be buried in the cave of Machpelah), laying a wick for each

---

[52] Zohar iii. 70*b*–71*a*. Interestingly, the Zohar, as well as later transformations of this passage, uses the phrase *modi'i leho* (inform them) (or its Hebrew equivalent), repeatedly. *The Three Gates* uses *modi'a zayn* ('inform'). This Zohar passage is also one of the sources of the Lurianic pietistic practice of grave prostration. It is not clear to me whether or not *kneytlakh legn* can be considered a women's 'equivalent' of grave prostration. See Lawrence Fine, 'The Contemplative Practice of Yihudim in Lurianic Kabbalah', in Green (ed.), *Jewish Spirituality from the Sixteenth Century Revival to the Present*, 64–98, esp. 79–83.

[53] *Naḥalas tsevi* (Amsterdam, 1711), 'Aḥarei mot'; *Sefer mayse adonai umayse nisim* (Amsterdam, 1723), second excerpt from 'Aḥarei mot'.

[54] Aaron Berechiah of Modena stresses both the satisfaction the dead receive from the visits of their kin, and the fact that they can be awakened to pray for the living, in particular through the ritual of bringing a Torah scroll into the cemetery (*Ma'avar yabok* (n.p., 1732), sect. 3, ch. 24, 40*b*). Explaining and paraphrasing the Zohar (iii. 70*b*–71*a*), he states: 'When people [*benei ha'olam*] are in trouble, and go to the cemetery, the soul [*nefesh*, the lowest of the three parts of the soul, which lingers at the grave site] awakens, and flies [*meshotetet*] and rouses the spirit [*ruaḥ*], and the spirit rouses the aspect of the patriarchs in paradise, and it ascends and rouses the higher soul [*neshamah*], and then the Holy One, blessed be He, has mercy on the world' (sect. 3, ch. 25, 41*a*).

figure. And she further develops the idea of reciprocity between the living and the dead in *The Three Gates*. This text assumes that the dead can aid the living, in some cases simply because God remembers their merit, and in others because of more active intercession:

As I lay the third thread of the wicks for our Father Abraham, whom You saved from the fiery furnace, may You purify us of *sins and trespasses*. May our souls become pure, just as they were given to us, without guilt, *without any fear or terror*, as they came into our bodies.

By the merit of my laying the thread for our Mother Sarah, may God, blessed be He, remember for us the merit of her pain when her dear son Isaac was led away to be bound on the altar. May she[55] be a [good] advocate for us before God, may He be blessed, that this year we not, God forbid, become widows, and that our little children may not, God forbid, be taken away from the world during our lives.

By the merit of our laying a thread for our Father Isaac's sake, may You have compassion for us. You have commanded us to blow the shofar on the New Year: *the horn of a ram, in memory of the binding of Isaac*.[56] May You remember this merit for us, that we may be able to tend to our children's needs, that we may be able to keep them in school, so that they accustom themselves to God's service, to repeat *Amen, may His great Name be blessed for ever and ever*...[57]

By the merit of my laying a thread for our mother Rachel's sake, may You cause to be fulfilled, by her merit, 'Your children shall return to their country',[58] that means, by Rachel's merit, God, blessed be He, will bring us back to our land, Amen. May her merit defend us, that she did not let herself be comforted until the coming of the righteous redeemer, may He come speedily and soon, in our days, Amen...

And by the merit of our laying a thread for our Father Aaron the Priest, and by his merit, may we be worthy to give candles to the Temple. May we live to see how he performs the priestly service. May his merit defend us, and enlighten the eyes of our children and our children's children in the dear Torah, like a light...

The act of laying the wick establishes a connection between the woman and the ancestors of Israel, which allows the woman to claim their aid. As in *The Gate of Unity*, this act creates a reciprocal relationship in which the dead benefit from the meritorious act of providing candles for the synagogue, thereby becoming obligated to help the living.[59] Further, it graphically expresses the connection of the

---

[55] Some editions say 'he', i.e. Isaac.                                    [56] B. RH 16*a*.

[57] This phrase is the congregational response in the Kaddish prayer. The Talmud attaches great importance to this response: 'Whoever answers "May His great Name be blessed" is assured of life in the World to Come' (Ber. 57*a*). The kabbalists discovered mystical significance in the fact that the response contains 'seven words composed of twenty-eight letters. This corresponds to the number of words and letters in the first verse of the Bible... One who responds to the Kaddish with these words becomes, as it were, God's partner in the creation of the world, which is the theme of the first verse in the Scriptures' (Abraham Millgram, *Jewish Worship* (Philadelphia, 1971), 483).        [58] Jer. 31: 17.

[59] Perhaps this parallels the Christian practice of lighting candles for saints. Herman Pollack, however, interprets this ritual differently: 'The act of "measuring the field" would symbolize the "transfer" of ownership of the cemetery grounds to living relatives who thereupon acquired the authority to instruct or direct the dead to aid them' (*Jewish Folkways in Germanic Lands* (Cambridge, Mass., 1971), 48).

woman and the members of her very own family with past generations of Jews, all the way back to the patriarchs and matriarchs, and Adam and Eve. While modern Jewish scholars and theologians have been chary of the idea that the dead can intercede with God for the living, and have tended to collapse this into the concept of *zekhut avot*, ancestral merit, in fact, the concept of the dead as intercessors has had rabbinical proponents from talmudic times.[60] And both views, mixed together, are found in *The Three Gates*: God is asked to remember the merit of Abraham and Isaac (as well as the merit acquired by the woman making the candles), and Sarah is asked to intercede with God.[61]

### East is East and West is West

At a somewhat earlier period, and at the other end of the Ashkenazi world, in Amsterdam, Simeon Frankfurt (a rabbi born in Schwerin, in the Duchy of Mecklenburg, in the first half of the seventeenth century, but active in Amsterdam after 1656) recorded (or, more likely, composed) a different *tkhine* for measuring graves. Frankfurt's text, although superficially similar to Sarah's, in fact portrays a very different relationship between the living and the dead. In 1703 Frankfurt published *Sefer haḥayim* (The Book of Life), which contains prayers for the sick and the dying, for funerals and for visiting the cemetery, and also instructions on how to care for the sick and prepare the dead for burial. The work is intended as a manual for village Jews who do not have easy access to rabbinic authority, and especially for the members of the *ḥevrah kadishah*, the burial society. Frankfurt wrote the work in two sections: the first, in Hebrew, for learned men, and the second, in Yiddish, for women and uneducated men. (The contents of the two sections differ; the Yiddish is not simply a translation of the Hebrew.)

In composing the prayers for visiting graves in *Sefer haḥayim*, Frankfurt drew upon and rewrote earlier material, chiefly *Sefer ma'aneh lashon* (The Right Response, *c*.1615, by Jacob ben Abraham Solomon, a Bohemian rabbi; expanded edition *c*.1658, by Eliezer Liebermann Sofer ben Loeb). His revisions are intended to reconfigure the relationship between the living and the dead as found in these earlier prayers. The text of *Sefer ma'aneh lashon* situates the worshipper

[60] For an example of the discomfort (although also of valuable descriptive material), see Pollack's discussion of the custom of visiting graves (ibid. 47–9), which concludes: 'In the main we shall observe that scholars and rabbis did not always challenge popular views and customs . . . . This is not an accurate statement of the situation; many rabbis actually supported and believed in the efficacy of imploring the dead for aid. Talmudic texts supporting (although not always unequivocally) the intercession of the dead: B. Sot. 34*b*, B. Ta'an. 16*a* and 23*b*. Later sources: *Sefer ḥasidim* (ed. Wistinetzki), 377, no. 1537; *Shulḥan arukh*, Oraḥ ḥayim, 599 (10) with *Ba'er heitev* and *Magen avraham* (primarily opposed to intercession); 579 (3) (*Shulḥan arukh* opposed; *Magen avraham* brings a positive view); 581 (4) with *Ba'er heitev* (opposed); Isaiah Horowitz, *Sha'ar hashamayim* (Amsterdam, 1742), 325*a* (summarizes various customs and positions).

[61] In general, the matriarchs are depicted as somewhat more active in their efforts on behalf of Israel than the patriarchs, but not more than Moses. See Weissler, 'Traditional Piety', 266–7, where I slightly overstated the case.

primarily as a family member who may rightfully appeal to deceased kin for aid. Frankfurt's version of these prayers situates the individual worshipper as a member of the entire people of Israel, and stresses the individual's and the people's direct relationship with God. Further, Frankfurt's prayers downplay the role of the dead as intercessors, and stress instead the benefit the living bring to the dead by their prayers, and, once again, the worshipper's primary relationship with God, not the dead.[62]

There is no prayer for this ritual in *Sefer ma'aneh lashon*,[63] and thus it is not clear what source(s) Frankfurt drew upon. None the less, his version of the prayer for measuring graves can be expected to exhibit the same tendencies as his other prayers for the cemetery:

The women who measure the graves should say this prayer . . .

*I pray You, O Lord my God* I pray you, my dear God, accept my prayer which I pray before You in this holy place [i.e. the cemetery] where lie the pious ones who sleep in the earth. We are come here for the sake of Your glory, and for the sake of the pious souls who are in the light of paradise, and whose bodies rest in the earth, to measure the cemetery and all the graves, so that all may have a part in the candles that we shall bring into the holy synagogue, to honour You with, and that the lamp may bring atonement for the souls, who are called '*the human soul is the lamp of the Lord*' [Prov. 20: 27]. And when we say our prayers in synagogue by [the light of] these [candles], may You accept and receive our plea to forgive all our sins. And may You enlighten us with the light of your presence [Shekhinah]. And may the light be an atonement for the sin of Eve, who extinguished Adam's light, and brought death to the world.[64] O dear God, may You deliver us and enlighten us with the light from Your holy candelabrum in the Temple, and make all the dead live, and do away with death unto eternity, just as You have spoken. Amen, Selah.

And they should begin to measure from the right side, and should measure all the graves with it [the wick], unless [they come to the grave of] someone who did not do right during

---

[62] For further discussion of *Sefer haḥayim* and *Ma'aneh lashon*, see my 'The Living and the Dead: Ashkenazic Family Relations in Light of Hebrew and Yiddish Cemetery Prayers', paper delivered at the annual meeting of the Association for Jewish Studies, Boston, 1986. The relationship between Frankfurt's work and Aaron Berechiah of Modena's *Ma'avar yabok* also requires further examination. I have unfortunately not had an opportunity to examine a doctoral dissertation on Simeon Frankfurt and *Sefer haḥayim* by Shelly Buxbaum (Jewish Theological Seminary, 1991).

The history of the genre of cemetery prayers requires further study. Some of these prayers may be quite old: *Tsiduk hadin* (Venice, 1737) attributes a prayer to be said in the cemetery between Rosh Hashanah and Yom Kippur to R. Israel Isserlein (1390–1460); a prayer to be said at any time of year when visiting the graves of martyrs, and another such prayer for the Ninth of Av, to R. Samuel Archivolti (1515–1611).

[63] At least not in any edition I have examined: All-Yiddish editions (Frankfurt: Johann Kellner, 1724); (Fürth; Itsik ben Leib, 1766); bilingual (Amsterdam: Proops, 1723).

[64] Many rabbinical sources say that the reason women are required to kindle Sabbath lights is to atone for Eve's sin; Eve darkened Adam's light (she made him mortal) by persuading him to eat the forbidden fruit. This view is also found in Yiddish ethical literature, although not in *tkhines* for candle-lighting. See my '*Mizvot* Built into the Body: *Tkhines* for *Niddah*, Pregnancy, and Child-birth', in Howard Eilberg-Schwartz (ed.), *People of the Body* (Albany, NY, 1992), 101–15.

his life. And they should make wax candles from it for the synagogue. And when they have measured, they should say '*May it be Your will, etc.*' and '*You are great, etc.*'[65]

As in later accounts, this text presents a full-blown ritual: the actors are women; there is the text of a prayer; there is a procedure to follow; and the occasion, although unspecified, seems to be the penitential season.[66] And as in *The Three Gates*, the text asks God to receive favourably the prayers recited by the light of the candles, and prays for deliverance from exile and an end to death. Further, this prayer explicitly includes the souls of the dead in the merit of the candles, and mentions Adam and Eve, although not other biblical figures.

The similarities between the two texts suggest that they cannot have arisen entirely independently. However, it is chronologically impossible for Simeon Frankfurt to have used Sarah's text as the basis for his own. *Sefer hahayim* was first published in 1703. The date of publication of *The Three Gates* is unclear, but must be later than 1731–2, the date of publication of *Hemdat yamim*, and is probably later than 1735, the 'internal date' in the Yiddish paraphrase of the 'Lament for the Exile' from *Hemdat yamim* that Sarah quotes. Thus, the thematic similarities between the two texts suggest some common source.

While limitations of space preclude a full discussion here, it is my view that Sarah did not create *de novo* the *tkhine* for *kneytlakh legn*, but reworked a *tkhine* already current in oral tradition, or perhaps in an as yet undiscovered written form—a *tkhine* reworked by Frankfurt, in an altogether different direction, as well.[67] Indeed, the existence of Frankfurt's text is prime evidence for the existence of such a *tkhine*, in oral or written form.

Despite their similarities, Frankfurt's text contrasts sharply with the text of *The Three Gates*. First, this is a text for a different part of the ritual. This prayer is for the act of measuring the graves, while Sarah's prayer is for the making of the

[65] Simeon Frankfurt, *Sefer hahayim* (Amsterdam, 1716), Yiddish sect., 128*b*–129*a*; (Köthen, 1717), Yiddish sect. 55*b*–56*a*.

[66] The *tkhine* immediately preceding this one specifies that 'the women should say this prayer on the Eve of Rosh Hashanah and the Eve of Yom Kippur'.

[67] There are two other possible relationships between these texts. First, perhaps Sarah was familiar with *Sefer hahayim*, and rewrote the *tkhine* she found there. Although this is possible, it seems to me the least likely explanation. It is far more usual for someone to rationalize a text and make it more theologically acceptable by removing certain elements than for someone to take a rationalized text and 'remythologize' it. Further, we know that Frankfurt rewrote other texts. None the less, we cannot utterly dismiss the possibility that Sarah got the idea for her *tkhine* from *Sefer hahayim*.

Second, perhaps *The Three Gates*, or at least this portion of it, is older than 1731. Perhaps the entire third gate, containing the material from *Hemdat yamim*, was added later. But although two key passages of the third gate are taken from other books (and other portions of this gate probably also have similar origins), a careful analysis shows that they were woven together by the same author who composed the rest of the *tkhine*. And even leaving aside the dating of the passage from *Hemdat yamim*, the other passage for which I have identified a source, a description of the women's paradise, is taken from a work published in 1708. This still puts the third gate, and probably the entire work, later than the publication of *Sefer hahayim*.

candles. Second, Sarah's text is much longer, much more dramatic, and has much higher eschatological tension.

Most important is the startling contrast between the valence of key elements in the two texts. Many of the themes found in *The Three Gates* are also found here, but transformed by Frankfurt's reformist programme. For example, Frankfurt stresses atonement as the purpose of bringing the candles into the synagogue; this never appears in Sarah's text. The relationship between the living and the dead portrayed in Frankfurt's text is simple and one-sided: the acts of the living, such as making the candles, can bring benefit to the dead. Frankfurt is very careful here, as in all of the prayers he includes, to make it clear that the living should turn only to God for help, not to the dead. Any benefit for the living is requested directly from God.

*The Three Gates* portrays a more complex and reciprocal relationship between the living and the dead, created by the measuring of the graves and the making of the candles. The ritual empowers women to call upon the dead for aid, and empowers the dead to act: in Sarah's words, the making of the candles has the power to awaken the souls of the dead, and to communicate, even to the patriarchs and matriarchs and Adam and Eve, the plea that they arise from their graves and plead before God for the living. Sarah's text attributes great power to the dead, especially to Adam and Eve to 'rectify the sin by which they brought death to the world'.

For Sarah, then, the sin which brought death to the world belongs to both Adam and Eve, and she attributes to them the power to put it right and bring the Messianic era, the end of death. (To the best of my knowledge, this latter idea is not found in rabbinic sources.) In Frankfurt's text, by contrast, the sin is Eve's alone.[68] Further, the candles are supposed to bring atonement to Eve. Here, she becomes the passive recipient of forgiveness, while in Sarah's text Eve, together with Adam, can be an active bringer of redemption. Thus, in *The Three Gates*, Eve, the matriarchs, and the women reciting the prayers and making the candles all have an active role to play. (So do Adam and the other male figures mentioned.) Perhaps the contrast could be stated as follows: in *Sefer haḥayim*, God is the only real actor; God may choose to respond graciously to the prayers and repentance of the living. In *The Three Gates*, the dead and the living can also act to affect the fate of the individual worshipper, her family, and the People of Israel.[69]

[68] The question of when the sin is described as Eve's and when it is described as Adam's would repay further analysis. In general, it seems to me, when a text is concerned with the nature and fate of humanity, Adam gets 'credit' for the sin, while if the text is concerned with the nature and fate of women in particular, or the relationship between women and men, Eve is blamed for it.

[69] While it is impossible to develop this point fully here, the contrast between Sarah's and Frankfurt's views of the relationship between the living and the dead resembles the contrast between Catholic and Protestant views in early modern France, as described by Natalie Zemon Davis in 'Ghosts, Kin, and Progeny: Some Features of Family Life in Early Modern France', in Alice S. Rossi, Jerome Kagan, and Tamara Hareven (eds.), *The Family* (New York, 1978), 92 ff. Catholics can

## Conclusion

The *tkhines* for measuring graves and making candles for Yom Kippur by Simeon Frankfurt and Sarah bas Tovim give evidence of two sharply differing attitudes about the relations between the living and the dead, and the efficacy of women's ritual performance. In conclusion, let me briefly consider the question of which text is closer to the general range of views on these questions found in eighteenth-century east European *tkhines*. It is safe to say that Frankfurt's west European reformist formulations find little echo in eastern Europe. East European *tkhine* authors generally do believe that the dead can come to the aid of the living; other texts for other occasions display a variety of means of establishing reciprocity with the dead.

One interesting example is the 'Tkhine imohes fun shofar blozn' (*Tkhine* of the Matriarchs for the Blowing of the Shofar) by Serl, daughter of Jacob ben Wolf Kranz (the Dubno Maggid, 1741–1804). Serl makes claims upon the matriarchs because they, like herself and other worshippers who recite her *tkhine*, have had the experiences of hope, loss, and pain entailed in being mothers and daughters:

First we ask our mother Sarah to plead for us in this hour of judgement . . . Have mercy, our mother, on your children. And especially, pray for our little children that they may not be taken away from us. For you know well that it is very bitter when a child is taken away from the mother, as it happened to you. When your son Isaac was taken away from you, it caused you great anguish . . .[70]

Further, other contemporaneous texts stress the efficacy of women's ritual. Sarah Rebecca Rachel Leah (*c.*1710–*c.*1790) daughter of Yokel Horowitz (rabbi of Brody and later of Gros-Glogau) was exceptionally learned, even making use of kabbalistic sources in her discussion of the importance of women's prayer. Like Sarah, Leah Horowitz (as she was usually known) was quite concerned with bringing redemption, and argued that if women pray properly (in synagogue, with weeping) they have the power to hasten the Messianic redemption. Her *Tkhine imohes* (*Tkhine* of the Matriarchs), to be recited on the Sabbath preceding the new moon, contains, in Aramaic and in Yiddish, an appeal to God to remember the merit of each of the matriarchs, and to redeem Israel for their sake.[71]

Interestingly both Serl and Leah used descriptions of graveside appeals to the

appeal to the saints for help, who are expected to aid their deceased kin in purgatory. Further, for Catholics, the dead are simply another 'age group' of the family. Protestants, however, must relate in a more unmediated way to the divine, and tended to develop more individualistic family strategies. Thus Frankfurt's thinking may have been influenced by the Protestant Reformation as well as by political and social changes in western Europe, while Sarah lived in a milieu in which Catholic (and eastern Orthodox) views continued to prevail.

[70] Serl bas Jacob, *Tkhine imohes fun rosh ḥodesh elul* (Lwów, n.d.); the *tkhine* for the shofar is part of this larger text. My translation of excerpts from this text appears in Ellen M. Umansky and Dianne Ashton (eds.), *Four Centuries of Jewish Women's Spirituality* (Boston, 1992), 53–4.

[71] See the chapter on Leah Horowitz in my forthcoming *Voices of the Matriarchs*.

one matriarch who was not buried in the cave of Machpelah, Rachel, as the focal point of their *tkhines*. Serl, whose prayer appealed for the health and welfare of the family, portrayed Joseph at his mother's grave:

And we also ask our mother Rachel to plead for us, that we may be inscribed and sealed for good, and that we may have a year of life, and a year of livelihood. And may we never suffer any sorrow. We know well that you cannot bear to hear of any sorrow. For when your beloved son Joseph was led to Egypt, the Ishmaelites caused him great sorrow, and he fell on your grave and began to weep, 'Mother, mother! have mercy on your child! How can you look on my sorrow, when you had such love for me?' . . . And you could not bear to hear the sorrow of your child, and you answered him, 'My dear child, I hear your cry, and I will always have compassion when I hear your sorrow.' Therefore, have compassion on our sorrow and our anguish, and our trembling before the judgement, and plead for us that we may be inscribed for a good year in which there will be no sorrow, Amen.[72]

Leah, whose *tkhine* prays for the redemption of Israel (understood as the reunification of the Shekhinah and the Holy Blessed One) pictures instead the exiled Israelites at the grave of their matriarch:

O God, just as You answered our forebears, so may You answer us this month . . . by the merit of our faithful mother Rachel, to whom You promised that by her merit, we, the children of Israel, would come out of exile. For when the children of Israel were led into exile, they were led not far from the grave in which our mother Rachel lay. They pleaded with their captors to permit them to go to Rachel's tomb. And when the Israelites came to our mother Rachel, and began to weep and cry, 'Mother, mother, how can you look on while right in front of you we are being led into exile?' Rachel went up before God with a bitter cry, and spoke: 'Lord of the world, Your mercy is certainly greater than the mercy of any human being. Moreover, I had compassion on my sister Leah when my father switched us and gave her to my husband, Jacob, in my place . . . Thus, even more so, it is undoubtedly fitting for You, God, who are compassionate and gracious, to have mercy.' God answered her, 'I acknowledge that you are right, and I will bring your children out of exile.' So may it soon come to pass, for the sake of her merit.[73]

Thus, even without the actual ritual of encircling the graves, and making the candles, the motif of graveside appeals to powerful intercessors clearly lived in the imagination of east European Jewish women.

Despite the similarities between these two texts, there is one area in which they differ sharply, the proper subject for prayer. While Serl's appeal is all for the concrete and the mundane, health and livelihood, Leah sharply condemns this type of prayer as trivial and selfish. For her, influenced by the Jewish mystical tradition, the only true prayer is that for the sake of the Shekhinah. No other prayer can bring the desired redemption.

By contrast, one of the triumphs of Sarah bas Tovim's *tkhine* for making Yom

---

[72] *Tkhine imohes fun rosh ḥodesh elul.* The source of this motif is *Sefer hayashar.*

[73] Sarah Rebecca Rachel Leah Horowitz, *Tkhine imohes* (n.p., n.d.). The source of this motif is Lamentations rabbati, petiḥta 24: 23–5, which builds on Jer. 31: 15–17.

Kippur candles is the remarkable way in which it combines eschatological and domestic concerns. This *tkhine* pleads for purity of soul, deliverance from exile, the resurrection of the dead, and the restoration of Temple worship—in short, for the Messianic redemption. It also asks for sufficient livelihood to keep the children in school and marry them off, just in case the Messiah tarries yet a while longer. Or, in other words, both kinds of concern are legitimized.

And as we have seen, not only does the woman reciting this *tkhine* plead for health, livelihood, and redemption, but her own act helps to bring them about. By laying the wicks and making the candles, she sets up a reciprocal relationship with the dead. She awakens the forebears of Israel and actively enlists their aid. She rouses the matriarchs, patriarchs, and other biblical figures to act as advocates for herself, her family, and all of Israel. She helps to bring the redemption: the advent of the King Messiah, the return of the people of Israel to their land, and the resurrection of the dead. Alongside the clear emotional power of such a prayer, Simeon Frankfurt's rationalized *tkhine* appears dry and sterile.

# The Ban on Polygamy in Polish Rabbinic Thought

## ELIMELECH WESTREICH

### INTRODUCTION

THE Ban of Rabbenu Gershom (R. Gershom ben Judah of Mayence, 960–1028) has been seen by historians as a key determinant of the singularity of Ashkenazi Jewish culture.[1] Hence, analysis of its fate in Poland is a most appropriate means of examining how far Polish rabbis adhered to the Ashkenazi legal tradition.

In sixteenth-century Poland there were two approaches among halakhic scholars: one, represented by R. Solomon Luria (1510–73, known as Maharshal), was closed to other Jewish legal traditions; the second, represented by R. Shalom Shakhna (d. 1558) and his great disciple R. Moses Isserles (c. 1522–72, known as Rema), was, conversely, characterized by openness to other legal traditions. At the turn of the sixteenth century, R. Joel Sirkes (1561–1640) developed a position that harmonized these two approaches.

The Ban of R. Gershom (who was often known also as Me'or Hagolah, 'Light of the Exile') forbade both polygamy and divorcing a woman against her will.[2] Its promulgation brought about a revolutionary change in Ashkenazi Jewish family life and in the body of law that regulated it. R. Asher ben R. Jehiel (known as Rosh), an Ashkenazi rabbi who emigrated to Spain in the early fourteenth century,[3] drew, for the Sefardi Jewish community, a comparison between the Ban and the geonic *takanah* on the rebellious wife, noting that the Ban was of higher status and was considered by Ashkenazi Jews to be on a par with Mosaic Law.[4]

In medieval Ashkenazi tradition, conduct unbefitting a wife, such as rebel-

---

[1] On the Ban of R. Gershom, see H. H. Ben-Sasson (ed.), *History of the Jews in the Middle Ages* (Heb.) (Jerusalem, 1963), 61; M. Elon, *Jewish Law: History, Sources, Principles*, trans. B. Auerbach and M. J. Sykes (Philadelphia, 1994), 783–6; A. Grossman, *Hakhmei Ashkenaz harishonim* (The Early Stages of Ashkenaz), 2nd edn. (Jerusalem, 1989), 127ff.

[2] On the different formulations of the Ban of R. Gershom, see the *Encyclopedia talmudit*, xvii. 757–72; L. Finkelstein, *Jewish Self-Government in the Middle Ages*, 2nd edn. (New York, 1964), 139–47.

[3] A. H. Freimann, *HaRosh: Rabbenu Asher b. Jehiel and his Descendants, their Life and Work* (Heb.) (Jerusalem, 1986), 20–6, 32–41. For a biography of Rosh, cf. Alfred Freimann, 'Ascher ben Yechiel, Sein Leben und Wirken', *JJLG* 12 (1918), 236–317.

[4] *Resp. HaRosh*, 43. 8.

liousness or immodest behaviour, constituted just cause for waiving the Ban. However, in divorce suits based not on the wife's behaviour, but on barrenness, levirate marriage, madness, or the proscription of cohabitation through no fault of the wife ('abandonment of the man'), the Ban was upheld.[5] Even in those cases where cause was found for waiving the Ban, the preference was to waive the enactment forbidding a man to divorce his wife against her will rather than the enactment prohibiting polygamy.[6]

The Ban did not spread to Spain and Provence, except that from the late thirteenth century on, beginning with R. Solomon ben Aderet (known as Rashba), rabbis there acknowledged its authority over Ashkenazi Jews who had moved into the region.[7] However, Rashba considered the Ban an ordinary enactment of the times designed to prevent husbands from arbitrarily hurting their wives.[8] He did not accept its revolutionary impact on the structure of family life, instituting monogamy exclusively and creating halakhic conditions for almost complete equality between spouses. Hence, in all cases in which the husband had halakhic cause, such as levirate marriage, the precept of procreation, or an insane or physically deformed or even insufficiently pious wife, Rashba did not hesitate to maintain that the Ban did not apply.[9] He even declared that the Ban was of limited duration and had expired at the end of the fifth millennium (as reckoned by Jews, i.e. from the creation of the world), that is, in 1240.[10]

Sefardi rulings, especially the time limit set on the Ban, did not penetrate into Ashkenaz in the Middle Ages. Even if the Ashkenazi rabbis knew of such a ruling, they presumably rejected it or ignored it altogether. The first encounter between Ashkenazi rulings and Sefardi legal tradition occurred beyond the borders of Ashkenaz, in fifteenth- and sixteenth-century Italy. The Ashkenazi community formed the majority in the northern part of the country and controlled the yeshivot and the rabbinate throughout the fifteenth century and later. The Sefardi Jews had a marked presence in the south of Italy, and after the expulsion from

[5] With respect to all of these causes, except for levirate marriage, the halakhah was determined in the 12th century and was mentioned in the responsum cited by Maharshal, discussed below in the text to n. 58. On levirate marriage in Ashkenaz, see J. Katz, in his *Halakhah vekabbalah* (Jerusalem, 1984), 136–55. But in the early 14th century Rosh determined unequivocally that in Ashkenaz a married man must be forced to perform *ḥalitsah*, no matter what. E. E. Urbach, 'Responsa of the Rosh in Manuscripts and Printed Editions' (Heb.), *Shenaton hamishpat ha'ivri*, 2 (1975), 17.

[6] *Resp. Maharam* (Prague), 946.

[7] S. Z. Havlin, 'The Takanot of Rabbenu Gershom Me'or Hagolah in Matters of Family Law in Spain and Provence' (Heb.), *Shenaton hamishpat ha'ivri*, 2 (1975), 231ff.; Y. T. Assis, 'The Ban of Rabbenu Gershom and Polygamy in Spain' (Heb.), *Zion*, 46 (1981), 251.

[8] The responsum by Rashba to his disciple R. Jacob Ha'ashkenazi is quoted in full in Havlin, 'The Takanot of Rabbenu Gershom', 230–1.

[9] Ibid. For a comparison of the approaches of the Ashkenazi and Sefardi legal traditions, see my article 'Causes for Waiving the Ban of Rabbenu Gershom in the Late Middle Ages' (Heb.), *Dinei Yisrael*, 16 (1991–2), 91–5.

[10] *Resp. Maharik*, 101. For further discussion, see Havlin, 'The Takanot of Rabbenu Gershom', 230–1 n. 7.

Spain in 1492 began arriving in large numbers. The Italian Jews, who had arrived in the country many generations before and had their own special traditions, formed the majority in the central part of the country; in addition, Italy had smaller Romaniote (Greek-speaking) and Levantine communities.[11] Here for the first time, Ashkenazi tradition had to cope with other traditions, defending its unique legal institutions, especially the Ban, against criticism and challenge. Rashba's view that the Ban was of limited duration was first mentioned in Italy in the work of the French-born R. Joseph Colon (*c.* 1420–80, known as Maharik), who thus brought it to the attention of the halakhic authorities of various countries.[12] Rashba's tradition was enthusiastically adopted by R. Joseph Caro (1488–1575), the greatest halakhic authority in the East, who was active in the Ottoman Empire in the time of Maharshal and R. Shalom Shakhna. R. Caro accepted Rashba's tradition and essentially ruled that the Ban had expired and that Ashkenazi Jews may marry two women, save in Ashkenaz itself, where the restriction still held, but only on the strength of custom and not as a ban or *takanah*.[13]

Polish Jewry viewed itself as part of the Ashkenazi tradition, continuing its spiritual and cultural heritage, and therefore of its legal tradition. At the same time, the Polish Jewish community maintained close ties with two other Jewish centres—Italy and the Ottoman Empire[14]—that did not adhere to the Ashkenazi halakhic tradition. In Italy, as has been mentioned, the Ashkenazi halakhic tradition was quite prominent, but other legal traditions also thrived. In the Ottoman Empire the Sefardi halakhic tradition was gradually taking over, displacing the Romaniote tradition on one side and the Musta'rab (Arabic-speaking) on the other, as well as the Ashkenazi, which had a certain presence there.[15] While disciples of eminent rabbis migrated back and forth between Italy and Poland, the latter also had solid ties with the Ottoman Empire, facilitated by their common border. Thus, the teachings of rabbis from the Ottoman Empire reached Poland either directly or via Italy, where their works were published.[16]

The following analysis examines the response of the early rabbis of Poland to these new traditions, which came into conflict with and contradicted Ashkenazi traditions.

[11] Cf. M. A. Shulvass, *Jewish Life in Italy during the Renaissance* (Heb.) (New York, 1955), 5–13; S. Simonson, *Toledot hayehudim bedukasut Mantoba* (Tel Aviv, 1963), vol. i, pp. v and 3–4. On the existence of various ethnic subgroups, Ashkenazi, Sefardi, and Levantine, in Venice in the 16th century, see D. Karpi, *Betarbut harenaissans uvein homot hageto: Mehkarim betoledot hayehudim be'Italiah bame'ah ha-14–17* (Tel Aviv, 1989), 168, 233.

[12] See n. 10 above.  [13] *Shulhan arukh*, 'Even ha'ezer', 1. 9; *Resp. Beit yosef*, 14.

[14] J. Elbaum, *Petihut vehistagerut: Hayetsirah haruhanit–sifrutit bePolin uve'artsot Ashkenaz beshalhei hame'ah hashesh-esreh* (Jerusalem, 1990), 33–63.

[15] J. Hacker, 'Sephardic Jews in the Ottoman Empire in the Sixteenth Century—Community and Society' (Heb.), in H. Beinart (ed.), *Moreshet Sefarad* (Jerusalem, 1992), 465.

[16] R. Joseph Caro's great works—*Beit yosef* on the *Tur* (1550–9) and the *Shulhan arukh* (1565–6)—were printed in Italy and from there reached Poland.

## THE VALIDITY OF THE BAN IN POLAND

Maharshal addressed Rashba's assertion that the Ban had expired in 1240 in a responsum. The details of the case were as follows: A married Polish Jew left Poland for the city of Palivna, in the Ottoman Empire. There he sought to marry another woman, but the rabbis of the city demanded that he first divorce the wife he had left in Poland. The man sent his wife a writ of divorce, but because of financial claims which she had against her husband, she refused to accept the divorce. In time it became known that the man had married another woman in Palivna. It turned out that he had presented the rabbis of Palivna with written certification from the rabbis of his wife's city, including Maharshal, attesting that he was indeed divorced and therefore nothing precluded him from marrying another woman. The document, however, was discovered to have been forged, although it was not known whether the man had been party to the forgery or had married the second woman in good faith.[17]

The query put to Maharshal was whether the Ban could be invoked to coerce him to divorce his second wife as long as he was still married to his former wife in Poland. The discussion centred on the validity of the Ban and the legal status of the prohibition against marrying two wives. Maharshal rejected the view that the Ban had lapsed, stating, 'With regard to Rashba, writing that he understood the decree of R. Gershom to be valid only until the end of the fifth millennium as cited by Maharik in section [shoresh] 101, these words are unfounded, and are as a fleeting rumour; therefore it [this argument] is rejected.'

Maharshal presented several arguments for rejecting Rashba's view. First, the conditions justifying the Ban in the fifth millennium pertained equally well in the sixth millennium. Second, eminent Ashkenazi rabbis—such as R. Isaac Or Zaru`a, the author of Sefer mordekhai, the author of Sefer mitsvot katan, and others living in the sixth millennium—had upheld the full validity and the legal weight of the Ban. In a more formal argument Maharshal stated that

Most of the takanot of R. Gershom Me'or Hagolah were formulated with no mention of time; moreover, with respect to the takanah on bigamy, he wrote that this can only be permitted with the consent of one hundred sages . . . and even then, they shall not permit it unless they see good reason for doing so . . . How can there be good reason, changing for the better, when, on the contrary, due to our many sins each succeeding generation is more lowly and worsens from day to day?[18]

A great distance separated Maharshal from his contemporary in the East, R. Joseph Caro, who believed that permitting a man to marry two women was fully justified.[19] Maharshal's was a very far-reaching decision, even in comparison to those of rabbis in the Ottoman Empire who held that the validity of the Ban had

---

[17] Resp. Maharshal (Jerusalem, 1969), 14.       [18] Ibid.       [19] See n. 13 above.

not yet expired but, in the case of a man marrying a second woman in good faith, would not force him to divorce.[20]

In Poland R. Shalom Shakhna did not refer to the question of the expiration of the Ban, but his disciple R. Moses Isserles (known as Rema) did address the subject. Rema was a central figure in the world of Polish halakhic scholars in the sixteenth century and his influence shaped the development of the halakhah in Poland for many generations.[21] In complete contrast to Maharshal, Rema accepted the tradition of Rashba, cited by Maharik, regarding the expiration of the Ban. In his work *Darkhei moshe*, Rema wrote: 'In any event, it seems to me that at the present time one does not need the approval of a hundred rabbis to waive [the Ban], since *the period of the edict has already elapsed* and no waiver is necessary at all' (emphasis added).[22] Note that Rema did not claim that the prohibition against polygamy was no longer valid; quite the contrary, it was valid, but the legal basis for it was no longer the Ban of R. Gershom itself, but rather the prevailing custom: 'Therefore, even though in practice the edicts of the Gaon [R. Gershom] are still followed, nevertheless the edict itself has expired and henceforth only has the custom in which the practice is to be strict, and one is not entitled to relax it for them.'[23] Changing the legal basis for prohibiting polygamy resulted in doing away with the need to obtain consent from one hundred rabbis in those cases in which, for any of a number of reasons, a man was granted leave to marry a second wife. Presumably this meant a considerable relief for those men whose reasons were recognized by the courts, saving them from the burden of seeking the signatures of one hundred rabbis—far from an easy task given the conditions of the times. Save for this, it seems that in practice the position of Rema did not differ substantially from that of the medieval Ashkenazi rabbis and Maharshal, who followed in their footsteps.

Basing the proscription of polygamy on custom essentially transferred the proscription from the realm of public law to that of private law,[24] since the theoretical argument justifying the legal force of custom is that it is an implied term, or *umdana demukhah* in the language of halakhic sources—a concept taken from the law of contracts. As R. Yom Tov Al-Ashbili (Ritba), one of the great scholars in fourteenth-century Spain, wrote:

Where the customary practice is only to marry one woman, [a man] is not entitled to marry another woman in addition to his wife, since it is an implied term that she married him with the understanding that he not marry another woman.[25]

[20] *Resp. Mabit*, 2. 15.   [21] A. Ziv, *Rabbi Moses Isserles* (Heb.) (New York, 1972), 21.
[22] *Darkhei moshe, Tur*, 'Even ha'ezer', 1. 10.   [23] Ibid.
[24] In modern legal systems public law includes branches like criminal, constitutional, and administrative law. Private law includes areas such as contracts, torts, family law, and inheritance. In modern western law bigamy comes under criminal law, whereas in Muslim law it comes under private, i.e. contract, law.
[25] Cited in R. Caro, *Beit yosef, Tur*, 'Even ha'ezer', 1. 8.

In response to this Rema wrote:

It seems to me that this refers to a place where the Ban of R. Gershom never spread, but its sources are only the custom. But in a place where the Ban spread, and the Ban is the origin of the proscription by reason of the Ban, even if [a man's] first wife did not object; and never have I encountered polygamy in a place where the Ban was practised even if [a man's] first wife agreed.[26]

According to Ritba, there was no obstacle to a man marrying a second wife after his first had given her consent, since in his view the legal foundation here rested on the law of contracts. Rema, on the other hand, continued to view the prohibition against marrying two women as governed by public law; hence the consent of the first wife permitting her husband to marry a second wife was of no avail.

Ascribing the prohibition against polygamy to the realm of public law has additional implications in the Rema's rulings, namely the sanctions applied to those men who violate the prohibition. In response to R. Caro's assertion in the *Beit yosef* that 'R. Gershom only legislated his decree until the end of the fifth millennium,'[27] Rema wrote, 'This is not done; rather, a man who has married two women is forced to divorce one of them.' He responded in like fashion to R. Caro's statement in the *Shulḥan arukh* that R. Gershom 'only declared the ban until the end of the fifth millennium', writing that

In any case, in these lands the *takanah* and the custom stand and bigamy is not allowed; whoever violates this and marries two women is coerced by bans and ostracism to divorce one of them. Some say that in this era one should not coerce those who violate the Ban of R. Gershom, since the fifth millennium has already passed; but this is not the practice.[28]

R. Mordecai Jaffe (*c.* 1530–1612, known as the Ba'al Halevushim), a disciple of Rema, continued this approach. In *Levush mordekhai* he cited Rema's new interpretation, asserting that since the Ban expired at the end of the fifth millennium, the legal basis for prohibiting polygamy in his day was the force of custom.[29] Like his teacher, Rema, Jaffe held that this change did not have significant implications in terms of actual practice; a bigamist is to be coerced by bans and excommunication to divorce his second wife.[30] The position taken by Rema and R. Mordecai opposes that of the rabbis in the Ottoman Empire during this period, who held that a man who has violated the Ban by marrying a second wife should not be forced to divorce.[31]

---

[26] Ibid. 8.                                    [27] *Darkhei moshe, Tur*, 'Even ha'ezer', 1. 8.

[28] Glosses of Rema, *Shulḥan arukh*, 'Even ha'ezer', 1. 10.

[29] *Levush mordekhai*, 1. 3.                              [30] Ibid. 11.

[31] It surely contradicts the position taken by R. Caro, who permitted Ashkenazi men to marry additional wives without showing any cause (text to n. 13 above), but it also contradicts the position taken by Mabit, who repudiated polygamy without just cause but at the same time was opposed to using coercion against those who violated the Ban (*Resp. Mabit*, 2. 15).

### THE PRECEPT 'TO BE FRUITFUL AND MULTIPLY'

Changing the legal foundation for the prohibition against polygamy was likely to have legal repercussions in those cases in which the man had just cause against his wife, especially in the case of non-feasance of the precept of procreation. As I mentioned in the Introduction, the striking difference between the Ashkenazi and the Sefardi legal tradition in the Middle Ages was manifest in those instances in which the man had a case against his wife. In such instances, the Sefardi tradition readily released the man from the Ban, whereas the Ashkenazi tradition made a waiver of the Ban difficult, granting it only when the cause stemmed directly from the woman's behaviour. In *Darkhei moshe*, Rema presented two approaches to waiving the Ban in cases concerning the commandment of levirate marriage, the precept of procreation, insanity, and women who were only betrothed. In conclusion he wrote:

It seems to me that he who is lenient and bases his judgement on those who waive the Ban has lost nothing; for I have noted above that the decree was not made for fear of a proscription in the Torah itself but is only a plain *takanah*; and if in the case of a scribal *takanah* one can be lenient, then certainly in the case of a plain *takanah* [one can be lenient].[32]

The *takanah*, according to Rashba, was intended simply to 'impose limits on licentious men who abuse their wives'.[33] Since there is no fear of a Torah injunction here, according to the principles of halakhic legislation there is no reason to insist on strictness, and whoever wishes to rule leniently may do so and loses nothing by it. This is a very different approach from that of the Ashkenazi rabbis.

How was this approach reflected in Rema's glosses to the *Shulḥan arukh*, and to what extent did his position reflect a practical trend in halakhic ruling in Poland? The responsa of Polish rabbis discuss the precept of procreation along with insanity as just causes for releasing a man from the Ban; but Rema treated procreation separately and autonomously in his works on legal codification. In *Darkhei moshe*[34] two views are presented on the matter. R. Judah Minz, on the one hand, ruled unequivocally that the Ban is not to be waived by reason of the precept to procreate, while R. Meir of Padua (known as Maharam of Padua) maintained the contrary.[35] Both of these rabbis were Ashkenazim who found their way to northern Italy and headed the Padua yeshiva. The difference, however, was that R. Minz came at a more advanced age and staunchly defended the Ashkenazi tradition against the legal traditions of other Jewish groups, especially the Romaniots.[36] He

---

[32] *Darkhei moshe*, *Tur*, 'Even ha'ezer', 1. 10.      [33] See n. 8 above      [34] *Tur*, 'Even ha'ezer', 1. 10.

[35] *Resp. R. J. Minz*, 10. See also my analysis of the position taken by R. Minz: 'Causes for Waiving the Ban of Rabbenu Gershom in Fifteenth- and Sixteenth-Century Italy' (Heb.), *Meḥkarei mishpat*, 9 (1992), 231–8. *Resp. Maharam of Padua*, 14. 19. The approach of Maharam of Padua is discussed in my article mentioned above in this note, 238–43.

[36] 'Causes for Waiving the Ban of Rabbenu Gershom in Fifteenth- and Sixteenth-Century Italy', 240.

had no qualms about opposing R. Eliyahu Mizrachi,[37] the leading rabbi in the Ottoman Empire, and the latter was eventually forced to accept the stand taken by R. Minz.[38] Maharam of Padua came to Italy as a young man, having studied under R. Jacob Polak (*c.*1460–*c.*1532), the founder of Torah studies in Poland and a scholar known for his independence. Even though he inherited the office held by R. Minz, whose granddaughter he married, he took a completely different approach from that of his predecessor and ruled that the Ban should be waived in order to enable a man to fulfil the precept of procreation. His view was apparently influenced by other legal traditions which he encountered in Italy in the first half of the sixteenth century.

The responsa of these two rabbis, published in 1553 in Venice, came to the attention of Rema. He cited them in *Darkhei moshe* and wrote that 'he who decides leniently has lost nothing'.[39] In his glosses to the *Shulḥan arukh* he presented both approaches again, but refrained from favouring one over the other, nor this time did he note that nothing is lost by a lenient ruling.[40] With respect to the position taken by R. Joseph Caro in the *Shulḥan arukh* that the Ban of R. Gershom did not apply to levirate marriage, Rema added:

The same rule applies in every case where fulfilment of a precept is held in abeyance, as in the case of a man who has lived with his wife for ten years and she has not given birth . . . but there are some who disagree and hold that the Ban of R. Gershom is to be enforced even in the case of a precept and even in the case of levirate marriage.[41]

In his introduction to *Darkhei moshe*, Rema stated that as a matter of principle his discussion, even in those places where he writes 'it seems to me', was not to be taken as a definite ruling, settling a difference of opinion; quite the contrary, his basic principle was: 'one must judge only as one personally sees fit'. Hence when he presented two opinions, his intention was to permit the rabbi adjudicating the specific case to rule according to his own judgement.[42] Perhaps, however, he personally preferred the lenient approach, since he presented it first; and even if he considered the different opinions equally valid, this deviated from the Ashkenazi position of definitely preferring the Ban over fulfilment of the precept to procreate.

To obtain a better understanding of the way Rema arrived at this position, two theoretical arguments used by the Ashkenazi rabbis to substantiate their giving priority to the Ban should be noted. The first argument was that the sin of living outside Israel was the cause of barrenness and made waiving the Ban purposeless. The second was based on an interpretation of a paragraph in the Babylonian Talmud which took it to mean that in their era the precept to procreate should be abrogated.

---

[37] R. Eliyahu Mizrachi's position was published in *Resp. Re'em*, 14.

[38] This is attested by R. Yehiel Kasteliash, in a responsum published by S. Assaf, *Mekorot umeḥkarim betoledot Yisra'el* (Jerusalem, 1946), 209.

[39] *Darkhei moshe*, *Tur*, 'Even ha'ezer', 1. 10. It is clear from the context that he was referring to all the cases mentioned previously, including non-feasance of the precept to procreate, and not only to the case of a betrothed woman, which he discusses before this remark.

[40] 'Even ha'ezer', 1. 10.    [41] Ibid.    [42] Cf. Elon, *Jewish Law*, 1355–6.

Therefore, in opposition to the talmudic ruling,[43] rabbinical courts outside Israel refrained from forcing a man to fulfil the precept to procreate. These arguments also found expression in a responsum of R. Minz[44] with which Rema was quite familiar, but Rema attributed the decisions of rabbinical courts outside Israel to the decline in their strength, which resulted in their not wishing to intervene in family controversies.[45] He did not subscribe to the two justifications given above (and perhaps even opposed them), but the fact that other eminent rabbis adhered to these arguments sufficed to make him feel it necessary to note their position.

## A WIFE'S INSANITY AND ABANDONMENT OF THE HUSBAND

The precept of procreation as cause for waiving the Ban is discussed in Jewish legal sources from Poland only in codexes and theoretical works, but no record exists of any actual case. However, there are responsa from Poland discussing cases where the man used the precept of procreation as an argument, but the true reason for the man's petition was the insanity of his wife or his own abandonment.

A wife's insanity was one of the more common factors in suits for divorce and for permission to marry a second wife. The main argument that a husband proffered in those circumstances was that life with an insane woman was intolerable, or, as the halakhic authorities put it, 'a man and a snake can not live together under the same roof'. Such a condition implied that a wife did not know how to observe properly the laws of menstrual purity and this further justified the husband's petition. If the man had not yet fulfilled the precept of procreation, forced abstinence from cohabiting gave him further legal cause, namely non-feasance of the precept of procreation. The first cause—the intolerable quality of life together—was unique to situations of insanity. The second cause, called 'abandonment of the man', could also exist in the case of gynaecological disorders that prevented the woman from observing the laws of menstrual purity, so that cohabitation would be forbidden by halakhah. The third cause—failure to fulfil the precept of procreation—was more comprehensive and was the commonest, since it pertained whenever there was any deficiency in the fertility of either spouse. Two responsa of early Polish rabbis discuss cases of insanity, and another responsum discusses the man's abandonment due to gynaecological disorders in his wife. Interestingly, however, the only legal argument given in these cases was non-feasance of the precept of procreation, and not the other causes which pertained particularly to these circumstances.

---

[43] See my article 'Polygamy and Forcing the Wife to Accept a Divorce in the Rulings of Eleventh- and Twelfth-Century Ashkenazi Rabbis' (Heb.), *Meḥkarei mishpat*, 6 (1988), 148–50.

[44] See n. 35 above, esp. my article cited there.

[45] Glosses of Rema, *Shulḥan arukh*, 'Even ha'ezer', 1. 3. He based his gloss here on the writings of the Spanish rabbi R. Isaac Sheshet in *Resp. Ribash*, 15.

## The Open Approach

We begin with a discussion of one of the few responsa by R. Shalom Shakhna, whose work was rarely preserved since he refused to commit his rulings to writing.[46] R. Shalom Shakhna was called upon to adjudicate the case of a man who could not cohabit with his wife on account of her insanity and consequently had not yet fulfilled the precept of procreation. Here the only legal argument given in support of the man's petition was non-feasance of the precept to procreate. R. Shalom Shakhna ruled conclusively that the precept of procreation takes precedence over the Ban, and, as attested by R. Joel Sirkes,[47] this position was accepted in actual practice by the rabbis of Frankfurt, Ashkenaz, and Russia.[48] It was a position diametrically opposed to that of the rabbis of medieval Ashkenaz, who refused to accept the argument of non-feasance of the precept to procreate as legal cause for waiving the Ban in cases where the wife was insane.[49] R. Yaakov Molin (known as Maharil), one of the more prominent rabbis of fifteenth-century Ashkenaz, did actually advocate a similar stand in the case of a woman who at times was insane, at times sane, holding that the precept of procreation took precedence over the Ban. But this view remained purely theoretical; in practice he gave precedence to the Ban, since the legal tradition, he said, was opposed to and takes priority over theoretical considerations.[50] R. Shalom Shakhna, in contrast, ruled this way in practice and even went so far as to state that R. Gershom did not enact the Ban in the case of an insane wife, therefore one did not need to obtain consent from one hundred rabbis. It should be noted that R. Shalom Shakhna did not appeal to the other two available arguments—abandonment of the husband and the intolerable situation of living with an insane person. It is quite possible that from his point of view the argument based on procreation was the most convincing since it is based on a Torah precept. The Ashkenazi halakhic tradition was no longer a compelling force in itself, and without theoretical considerations in support of a certain legal outcome, a decision was reached which opposed it. This accords with R. Shalom Shakhna's bias against creating a binding tradition of halakhic rulings. As his son and deputy, R. Israel, attested, R. Shalom Shakhna declined his students' request to commit to writing and publish his rulings and responsa because this would deter other rabbis from deviating from them and make them into binding precepts, inhibiting the judgement of later generations.[51]

R. Shalom Shakhna's approach stands in bold contrast to that of R. Judah

---

[46] See text to n. 51 below.

[47] R. Joel Sirkes, *Bayit ḥadash, Tur*, 'Even ha'ezer', 119, s.v. 'vekatav haRambam'.

[48] Meaning the area of Red Russia, also called Reisin, whose capital was Lwów.

[49] Their responsa are cited by Maharshal and are discussed below, in the text to n. 59.

[50] *Resp. Maharil haḥadashot*, 202; see also my article 'Causes for Waiving the Ban in the Late Middle Ages', 82–3.

[51] *Resp. Rema*, 25; also see the testimony of his disciple R. Hayyim ben R. Betsalel, *Vikuaḥ mayim ḥayim* (Amsterdam, 1912), intro., sect. 2; and A. Zimmer, *R. Ḥayim b. R. Betsalel of Friedburg* (Jerusalem, 1987), 24. For further elaboration, see Elon, *Jewish Law*, 1346–8.

Minz, who was, as mentioned above, a rabbi of Ashkenazi origin active in northern Italy two generations earlier. R. Minz staunchly defended the Ashkenazi tradition against other judicial traditions, even re-interpreting legal sources in order to uphold the Ashkenazi ruling.[52]

Rema accepted the approach of his teacher, R. Shalom Shakhna, deviating from Ashkenazi tradition, and, as noted above, leaving it in the hands of individual judges to decide whether or not to waive the Ban on account of the precept. In the case of an insane wife, Rema's ruling was diametrically opposed to Ashkenazi tradition. Here, he did not advocate giving the judge the option of choosing between the two possibilities; rather, he wrote unequivocally: 'In those cases where the first wife cannot be divorced, such as if she has gone mad or if she may legitimately be divorced but refuses to accept a writ of divorce from her husband, one should rule leniently and permit the husband to marry another woman.'[53] Note that he mentions only insanity as cause for waiving the Ban and does not mention abandonment of the husband or the precept of procreation. That life with an insane wife is intolerable is considered sufficient justification for waiving the Ban and it follows that there is also no need to obtain the consent of one hundred rabbis.

## The Closed Approach

Exactly the opposite stand was taken by Maharshal, who, as some scholars claim,[54] was a great adversary of R. Shalom Shakhna and an older colleague of Rema.[55] A query was directed to Maharshal with regard to waiving the Ban on account of the wife's insanity or abandonment of the husband. His response essentially comprised four rulings pertaining to four separate cases:[56] (1) the direct question addressed to him regarding the man's abandonment; (2) a previous case in which he had been involved concerning a wife's insanity; (3) the response by R. Eliezer ben Joel Halevi of Bonn (known as Ravyah) in a case concerning a wife's insanity; (4) the response of the rabbis of Speyer, Worms, and Mainz (known collectively by the Hebrew acronym 'Shum') in a case concerning a wife's insanity, cited as a precedent by Ravyah.

The explicit question directed to Maharshal concerned a woman who had a discharge of blood as a result of intercourse and could not become ritually clean for her husband, as a result of which her husband was forbidden intercourse with

---

[52] *Resp. R. J. Minz*, 10; for further elaboration, see my article 'Causes for Waiving the Ban of Rabbenu Gershom in Fifteenth- and Sixteenth-Century Italy', 236–8.

[53] Glosses of Rema, 'Even ha'ezer', 1. 10.

[54] H. Graetz, *Geschichte der Juden*, ix (Leipzig, 1866), n. 1 identifies the person alluded to in *Resp. Maharshal*, 16, as R. Shalom Shakhna. See the discussion of E. Reiner, 'The Yeshivas of Poland and Ashkenaz during the Sixteenth and Seventeenth Centuries: Historical Developments' (Heb.), in I. Bartal, E. Mendelsohn, and C. Turniansky (eds.), *Studies in Jewish Culture in Honour of Chone Shmeruk* (Jerusalem, 1993), 54 n. 72.                          [55] Ziv, R. Moses Isserles, 57.

[56] *Resp. Maharshal*, 65.

her for ever. The husband's question was as follows: was it permissible for him to expel her with her *ketubah* against her will, even though R. Gershom decreed that a woman not be divorced against her will; since in this particular instance R. Gershom did not intend his decree to abrogate the precept of procreation? In other words, R. Gershom did indeed decree that a woman may not be divorced against her will, but one can surely not suppose that he would preclude the man from fulfilling the precept of procreation. Note that here, too, as in the case adjudicated by R. Shalom Shakhna, the only argument mentioned is that of failure to procreate. In support of his petition, the husband addressing the query cited a ruling that had been issued near where he lived concerning an insane woman: 'He did not prevent the husband whose wife had become insane from divorcing her by sending a messenger and returning her *ketubah*, with the proviso that if she become sane she receive her writ of divorce, on the grounds of precluding procreation.' Here too, the cause for waiving the Ban is that the precept of procreation could not be kept; other possible causes are not cited.

In his response to the query sent him, Maharshal primarily discussed the precedent on which the husband relied, regarding the insane wife, and only towards the end, in his summation, did he return to the specific issue of the woman who had a discharge of blood and hence was forbidden to her husband. His remarks on the insane woman are very instructive, and therefore are presented here in detail, but first some background on the case itself.

A talmudic scholar who moved to Poland, apparently from Italy, had left his wife, who had become insane, in his country of origin. In Poland a match was proposed for him, but the father and other relatives of the bride-to-be would not consent 'until he bring a waiver from the rabbis permitting him to marry another woman'. The man set to work with verve to obtain the waiver, 'and was heroic as a lion and swift as a gazelle to do their bidding and his own, and prostrated himself before our rabbis that they give him leave to divorce his wife and marry another woman'.

Maharshal, whose opinion was also asked in this case, took the view that he could do nothing: 'I did not feel I could agree with them, nor could I take a stand against them, since I had no way of challenging them halakhically, for their entire view was that R. Gershom Me'or Hagolah did not issue his decree *to supersede the precept of procreation*' (emphasis added).

Those who waived the Ban based their position on the argument that the precept of procreation takes precedence over the Ban and permitted the man to marry another woman. Maharshal did not accept their position, but he could not impose his own view in practice because he lacked concrete justification for his stand. The result was: that the man 'was granted permission to give a writ of divorce, to be entrusted in someone's hands, with the proviso that if she become sane she would receive her writ of divorce and her *ketubah*; and the deed having been done, is done; but I feel pangs of conscience'. This clearly indicates that Maharshal sensed, perhaps intuitively, perhaps because he knew of an inexplicit tradition, that this ruling was a departure from the traditional way followed by the rabbis of Ashkenaz.

Lacking any precedent on which to rely,[57] R. Minz arrived by means of theoretical analysis at a similar outcome to the rabbis of twelfth-century Ashkenaz. Maharshal, however, did not proceed in this way, since the theoretical basis for R. Minz's approach was founded on the two contentions mentioned earlier: the first, that the sin of living outside Israel is what causes barrenness, and therefore divorcing one's first wife or marrying a second wife is of no avail; and the second, based on a paragraph cited in the Talmud,[58] that after the destruction of the Temple one must strive to curtail the prescript of procreation. In his *Yam shel shelomoh*,[59] Maharshal argued explicitly against seeing the sin of living outside Israel as the cause of barrenness. Furthermore, he did not refer to the relevant paragraph from the Talmud in any of his halakhic works and without this basis, he could not develop a body of theory to substantiate his intuition that the Ban should supersede the precept of procreation; hence only an explicit precedent could provide the solid legal foundation needed to back up his judgement. In time he did find a precedent, and in its wake asserted his strongly held view. In his words: 'Several years later, searching in the great book of Ravyah,[60] I found that great rabbis had already ruled against [waiving the Ban] in practice. This is the main point and sums up my response.'[61] Maharshal then cited the responsum of Ravyah, which itself includes the response of the rabbis of Speyer, Worms, and Mainz. Both these responsa discuss similar cases concerning an insane woman whose husband was forbidden to cohabit with her, so that the man had not yet fulfilled the precept of procreation. In both cases it was ruled unequivocally that the Ban was not to be waived in deference to the precept of procreation.[62] The remedy sought in these cases was permission to marry another woman; but Maharshal viewed the Ban's proscription of polygamy and of divorcing a woman against her will as analogous and concluded that just as the rabbis forbade marrying another woman in such circumstances, so too one should forbid divorcing an insane woman against her will. Given these two precedents, there was no longer room for the questioner to suppose that Maharshal might be in favour of waiving the Ban in the case of insanity, although he had not specifically objected to waiving the Ban in the case of the Italian talmudic scholar. Indeed, this is what he wrote: 'It may seem clear to you that leave is given to divorce a woman who has become insane, as you may have concluded from the permission granted to the young talmudic

---

[57] See my article 'Causes for Waiving the Ban of Rabbenu Gershom in Fifteenth- and Sixteenth-Century Italy', 236–8.            [58] Ibid.            [59] *Yev.* ch. 6, sect. 32.

[60] *Sefer Ravyah: Teshuvot* (Bnei-Berak, 1989), 21.            [61] See n. 56, above.

[62] The responsum of the rabbis of Speyer, Worms, and Mainz, which was earlier than that of Ravyah, was unanimous. However, in Ravyah's case, he represented the majority view, but one authority, R. Simḥah of Speyer, held a dissenting view.

scholar, because I remained silent at that time; but henceforth I hold that it is forbidden.'[63]

After establishing his position regarding the insane woman, Maharshal proceeded to address the specific question that had been posed to him: can a woman whose husband is precluded for ever from cohabitating with her be divorced against her will? He responded: 'Also regarding your query, I cannot waive the Ban of R. Gershom and [allow you to] divorce her against her will; for one could say, [it is as if] his field was swept away by a flood.' In other words, Maharshal viewed this case as the decree of fate, and was not prepared to make the wife pay the price by being divorced against her will. He could only propose that: 'The rabbis of that city ought to take the matter in hand and try to find a way of luring her to accept a writ of divorce willingly, using any possible justification or trick.'

It is clear that Maharshal viewed himself as completely bound by the Ashkenazi tradition. Unlike R. Shalom Shakhna, he viewed the rulings of the rabbis of Ashkenaz as binding precedents, and felt that under no circumstances could he rule differently. But what would R. Shalom Shakhna have done had he been aware of these precedents? Presumably this would not have changed his opinion, although it is hard to say definitively. The fact is that rabbis who studied under him followed his approach and were not overly concerned by these two precedents.

This decision fitted Maharshal's high esteem for his Ashkenazi roots and his general tendency to defend the Ashkenazi tradition in other matters, such as the halakhah on phylacteries,[64] flatly refusing to accept the kabbalistic practices that were beginning to penetrate Poland. But this attitude seems, on the surface, to contradict his well-known self-confidence and independence.[65] He himself declared that he would not rely upon any author's interpretation of the Talmud but only upon his own, based upon direct investigation of the text.[66] There is no contradiction here since the spiritual and cultural milieu in which a rabbi is trained comprises his halakhic tradition. It provides the intellectual building-blocks which shape his halakhic world and is, for him, unquestionable. Thus, self-confidence actually motivates the rabbi to be more adamant in defending what has become his own personal asset, an inseparable part of his spiritual–legal world.[67]

[63] See n. 56, above.

[64] See e.g. *Resp. Maharshal*, 98, on his adamant opposition to introducing any change based on kabbalistic consideration in the Ashkenazi practice concerning phylacteries. It is noteworthy that Maharshal was the first to publish a history of the rabbis of Ashkenaz and France in the Middle Ages (*Resp. Maharshal*, 29).

[65] Nothing expresses this more poignantly than his grandiose plan to write a comprehensive composition on the halakhah, *Yam shel shelomoh*. Explicit remarks on this may be found in his introduction to this work. [66] Ibid.

[67] Two other Ashkenazi rabbis who were noted for their great assertiveness and self-confidence— R. Asher ben R. Jehiel (Rosh), and R. Judah Mintz—both strongly defended the Ashkenazi legal tradition. Rosh migrated to Spain in the early 14th century, where he served as chief rabbi of Toledo.

## *The Synthetic Approach*

R. Joel Sirkes, one of the next generation of rabbis, discussed the subject of the Ban in his *Bayit ḥadash*,[68] and essentially presented the stand taken by R. Shalom Shakhna: 'where the precept of procreation is at issue, R. Gershom's decree does not apply at all'. He notes there that 'The rabbis of Frankfurt also wrote a lengthy responsum on this, siding in favour of waiving [the Ban], and all the rabbis of Ashkenaz and Russia agreed with them.'[69] Here R. Sirkes made an original attempt at bridging the opposing views and arriving at a more harmonious approach, lending expression to the independent course pursued by some of his teachers, on the one hand, yet not explicitly contradicting the words of Maharshal, on the other. In principle, he favoured allowing the husband to marry another woman in the spirit of the ruling by R. Shalom Shakhna. Yet whereas R. Shalom Shakhna ruled that the Ban does not apply at all in these circumstances, thus implying that the man is free to marry another woman without any legal severance from his first wife, R. Sirkes demanded that the man file a writ of divorce and deposit the woman's *ketubah*, thus obliging him to obtain permission from one hundred rabbis.[70] He also based the waiver on the precept of procreation, stating that, 'even though R. Gershom Me'or Hagolah banned marrying a second woman in addition to one's wife, he surely did not decree this where the precept is at issue';[71] thus he maintained that the precept of procreation superseded the Ban.[72] R. Sirkes based his remarks on the words of R. Shalom Shakhna, but he was also aware of the rulings and responsa of Maharshal and apparently did not wish to take a stand explicitly contradicting the latter. Hence, he claimed that Maharshal only forbade divorcing an insane woman against her will, but did not forbid marrying another woman. He put it thus: 'As for the leave granted by the Rabbi [Rema] in his glosses to marry an additional wife in the case of an insane woman, Maharshal also acknowledges such leave.'[73]

However, elsewhere in the same work, in a section on divorcing an insane woman, he discusses the position taken by Maharshal, quoting the latter's words

Nevertheless, he defended the Ashkenazi tradition in his rulings on several central issues. At the same time he was extremely independent, not hesitating to challenge the status of the *ge'onim*, to whom even such an astute sage as R. Abraham ben David, the great critic of Maimonides, deferred. The second, R. Mintz, also emigrated from Ashkenaz to a land where he came into contact with different legal traditions. Evidence of his adherence to the Ashkenazi tradition is found directly in the rulings discussed in this article.

[68] A commentary on *Sefer haturim*; discussed in Elon, *Jewish Law*, 1303–4 n. 1.

[69] *Bayit ḥadash*, *Tur*, 'Even ha'ezer', 119, 'Ve'katav ha-rambam'.

[70] *Bayit ḥadash*, *Tur*, 'Even ha'ezer', 1, at the end. R. Sirkes held this to apply also with regard to the commandment of levirate marriage.                                                                 [71] Ibid.

[72] The same holds for the commandment of levirate marriage, namely, that it takes precedence over the Ban; but this was not a question of practical importance in Poland.

[73] *Bayit ḥadash*, *Tur*, 'Even ha'ezer', 1. Similar remarks may be found in his responsa, *Resp. Bayit ḥadash: Hayeshanot*, 78.

as follows: 'Now that we have the ban of R. Gershom prohibiting divorcing a woman against her will and prohibiting polygamy, there is no remedy for him, as Ravyah has ruled in practice and as I have written in my book on *Yevamot*.'[74] While this is a faithful representation of Maharshal's position, it does not accord with R. Sirkes's own interpretation in section 1 of *Bayit ḥadash*.[75] It is unlikely that he simply misunderstood Maharshal, but rather that he was seeking an interpretative approach which could achieve harmony between the various rabbis. The specific question asked of Maharshal was whether abandonment of the husband constituted cause for divorcing against her will a woman who was forbidden to her husband; and to this end the questioner cited the case of an insane woman. R. Sirkes interpreted all of Maharshal's decisions as binding only with respect to cases of divorce from a wife against her will. He did not view Maharshal's remarks pertaining to such cases as binding in other contexts. Hence, he saw no need to draw inferences from the law on divorcing a woman against her will to unrelated judgements about marrying a second wife, even though Maharshal had drawn such inferences himself.

R. Sirkes's approach calls to mind the distinction drawn in Anglo-American law between *ratio decidenti* and *obiter dicta*, between the core of the responsum and asides that are not essential to deciding the case. Since the core of Maharshal's responsum is his discussion of divorcing a woman against her will, all that he says is binding only in that context; whereas his additional opinions voiced on subjects beyond this core are not binding. Just as it is clear to us that Maharshal did not distinguish between divorcing a woman against her will and giving permission to marry a second wife, so too we may assume that R. Sirkes was aware of this. Further on in the same section of the *Bayit ḥadash* in which he had cited Maharshal's words, he again refers to Maharshal's views on a woman who is sometimes mad and sometimes sane, and notes that 'Maharshal took a very strict view regarding this, too . . . and in actual practice one ought to be strict.' Later, however, he adds: 'In any event, one ought to rule strictly specifically regarding divorcing her; however, if he does not divorce her, but rather takes an additional wife, even Maharshal admits that this is not prohibited, as I have written.' R. Sirkes's approach undoubtedly yields a narrow interpretation of the words of

---

[74] *Bayit ḥadash*, *Tur*, 'Even ha'ezer', 119.

[75] This contradiction has been noted by several commentators on the *Shulḥan arukh*. The author of *Ḥelkat meḥokek* (*Shulḥan arukh*, 'Even ha'ezer', 1. 16, and Elon, *Jewish Law*, 1429–30 n. 1), comments on Rema's glosses on the *Shulḥan arukh*, which say that one should rule leniently and permit the man to marry another wife in the case where his wife is insane, noting: 'It has been the practice not to give leave without the [consent] of one hundred rabbis; cf. *Bayit ḥadash*.' Then he adds, 'Also see the responsum of Maharshal, sect. 65, which indicates that, unlike *Bayit ḥadash*, in his opinion one should forbid it.' In other words, the author of *Ḥelkat meḥokek* considers that the *Bayit ḥadash* misunderstood the Maharshal. *Beit shemuel* (*Shulḥan arukh*, 'Even ha'ezer', *Beit shemuel*, 1. 23) makes a similar point in its commentary on sect. 1, and writes with respect to sect. 119 of the *Bayit ḥadash*: 'What he says there, citing Maharshal, contradicts what he writes in this section.'

Maharshal, removing them from their wider context; but this is precisely what he chose to do in order to preserve the continuity of the tradition of Ashkenazi rulings received from Maharshal while at the same time opening the field for the innovative approach which R. Shalom Shakhna adopted and transmitted to his disciples.

R. Sirkes's synthesis is also manifest in curtailing the legal efficacy of the argument of insanity. As mentioned earlier, he required that the husband obtain leave from one hundred rabbis in order to divorce his wife against her will; that he file a writ of divorce in favour of the wife before the Ban could be waived for him; and that he deposit the sum of his wife's *ketubah* in the hands of the court.[76] This approach explicitly opposes that of Rema, who waived the Ban altogether. R. Sirkes largely preserved the spirit of the Ban and rejected bigamy, since filing a writ of divorce and *ketubah* could be viewed as severing the marital relationship from the side of the husband, even if the wife was not yet free to remarry. In such circumstances, one could view the permission to marry another woman as a legal formality designed to overcome the difficulty of the wife not having the legal competence to be divorced. It is true that this did not give the insane woman absolute protection, since her husband essentially had the right to divorce her, but this legal prerogative was extremely limited by the need to obtain the consent of one hundred rabbis. It is worth noting that a hint of this approach can be found in a ruling by R. Simḥah of Speyer, a twelfth-century Ashkenazi, cited in Maharshal's responsum,[77] but his view was rejected by Ravyah and the rabbis of Speyer; Worms, and Mainz, who refused to waive the Ban, even if it were viewed as a pure formality.[78]

The rabbinical community of Poland apparently rejected both the extremely strict approach of Maharshal and the unqualifiedly lenient approach of R. Shalom Shakhna, preferring the intermediate course charted by R. Sirkes, who wrote: 'Thus it was the practice of the rabbis in our times to permit marrying another wife, in addition to the one who had become insane, with the consent of one hundred rabbis; and this has been done several times.'[79]

Note that the legal argument given both by R. Shalom Shakhna and by R. Sirkes for waiving the Ban in the case of insanity was fulfilment of the precept of procreation. According to the ruling given by Rema, each rabbi was free to decide for himself whether or not to accept this as cause for waiving the Ban; but, in all the sources I examined, there was not a single instance in which the Ban was waived solely on this account, where the wife was sane and nothing precluded the couple from cohabiting. Moreover, no petition on these grounds was presented to halakhic scholars, who, nevertheless, did discuss and reject Rema's position. This seems to reflect the existence of a deeply rooted social norm according to which the precept of procreation in itself does not constitute sufficient reason for changing the marital status of a couple. There is positive evidence of this from the

[76] *Tur*, 'Even ha'ezer', 1 and 119.          [77] *Resp. Maharshal*, 65.          [78] Ibid.
[79] *Bayit ḥadash*, *Tur*, 'Even ha'ezer', 1, at the end of the section.

late seventeenth and eighteenth centuries, in addition to the silence of the sources throughout the entire early period in Poland. In fact, the practice was deeply rooted in Ashkenazi society of the Middle Ages,[80] and among the Ashkenazi Jews who migrated to the Ottoman Empire.[81]

## SUMMARY

In this article I examined the Ban of R. Gershom and analysed the attitude of early rabbis in Poland towards the Ashkenazi tradition of halakhic rulings, in light of the fact that the Jews in Poland viewed themselves as belonging to the Ashkenazi community, yet maintained good relations with Jewish centres in Italy and the Ottoman Empire. I investigated whether this fact was reflected in their rulings on a specific issue, either by absorbing influences from other areas or by developing their own independent approach.

Two directions were encountered. Maharshal adhered strictly to the Ashkenazi legal tradition and viewed the Ashkenazi rulings as binding precedents, not to be challenged. This is not surprising, since on various occasions we have seen that Maharshal viewed himself as carrying on the Ashkenazi tradition and defended it strongly against other traditions. The second direction was represented by R. Shalom Shakhna, Rema, and others. There is no doubt that fundamentally they upheld the Ashkenazi tradition, but they were also open to other influences. For example, the Rema and R. Mordecai Jaffe accepted the ruling of Rashba, cited in the responsum of Maharik, that the validity of the Ban had expired, in contrast to Maharshal, who flatly rejected this notion. However, they did not ascribe far-reaching practical implications to this, as R. Joseph Caro, their

---

[80] Ravyah, at the end of his responsum cited by Maharshal (*Resp. Maharshal*, 65), presents a sociological argument in support of his position against waiving the Ban on account of the precept of procreation: 'How many women there are with medical disabilities or barrenness, and how often is there failure to fulfil the precept of procreation; yet we have not heard controversy among them.' On medieval Ashkenaz in general, see my article 'Causes for Waiving the Ban in the Late Middle Ages', 49–52. R. Yehezkel Landau wrote in the second half of the 18th century: 'The fact that for several generations the Ban has not been waived for a man who has spent ten years with his wife, as was done for a man whose wife had become insane, is in my humble opinion due to their concern with the opinion of some of the *posekim* that this law is not applied outside Israel' (*Resp. Noda biyehudah*, Batra edn., sect. 102, p. 55a, s.v. 'omnam ma shelo ira'. Towards the end of the 17th century R. Jonah Landsofer was asked, 'in the case of a man who has spent ten years with his wife and she has not given birth, nor is she capable of bearing, whether it is correct for him to follow *the general practice of the world, that do not try to divorce their wives who have not borne them children*' (*Resp. Me'il tsedakah* (Prague, 1761), n. 33; emphasis added).

[81] At the end of the 16th century the Ashkenazi R. Samuel Yaffe, who was active in Constantinople, adopted the Sefardi position that the Ban should be waived for Ashkenazi Jews on account of the precept of procreation. Nevertheless, he noted that Ashkenazi society was unwilling to accept this ruling, and would not change its practice of not altering marital status in order to fulfil the precept of procreation. This responsum was published by Y. S. Spiegel in *Vayita eshel* (Tel Aviv, 1990).

contemporary in the Land of Israel, did in the *Shulḥan arukh*. They based the prohibition of polygamy on custom, and determined that whoever violates this instruction should be coerced by means of bans and excommunication to divorce his second wife. The impact of non-Ashkenazi sources is more evident in those cases in which the man had legal cause to sue for a waiver of the Ban. In his glosses, the Rema presented two views on the question of whether to waive the Ban on account of the precept of procreation and stated that nothing was lost by deciding leniently. The lenient approach was actually employed in a case where the wife was insane and the husband had not yet fulfilled the precept of procreation. R. Shalom Shakhna had ruled that the Ban is superseded in such a case by the precept of procreation, and according to R. Joel Sirkes, who followed this approach, R. Shalom Shakhna's ruling was supported by rabbis from various localities. This position was diametrically opposed to that of the rabbis of Ashkenaz, as expressed by the ruling of the rabbis of Speyer, Worms, and Mainz in the twelfth century, but accorded with the position taken by Maharik.

Maharshal did indeed take the opposite stand, relying on this ruling, and likewise he opposed permitting a husband who could not cohabit with his wife to divorce her against her will. Nevertheless, a waiver was not given in the case of an intermittently insane wife. R. Sirkes stated in his work on the *Tur*, as well as in his responsum, that in addition to obtaining the consent of one hundred rabbis, a man had to file a writ of divorce and the sum of the *ketubah* as pre-conditions for permission to marry another woman. This approach is a synthesis of the Ashkenazi rabbis' approach, flatly opposing any waiver of the Ban, and the approach first taken by Rashba, viewing the Ban as completely superseded in such a case, especially if the husband had not yet fulfilled the precept of procreation.

It should be noted that no case has come down to us in which the husband petitioned for a waiver of the Ban solely due to his desire to fulfil the precept of procreation. In the cases discussed, the reason for the petition was insanity of the wife or abandonment of the husband, even though the precept of procreation was the only legal cause mentioned. It appears that the changes that emerged in the attitude of the rabbis towards the precept of procreation did not reach the public at large, among whom the deeply-rooted Ashkenazi custom of not filing suit against a woman for being barren persisted.

# The Ashkenazi Élite at the Beginning of the Modern Era: Manuscript versus Printed Book

## ELCHANAN REINER

THE SHIFT from script to print in the sixteenth century heralded a reshaping of Ashkenazi literary models. In this article I shall trace some reactions amongst Ashkenazi intellectuals to this shift, which are indicative of their general attitude to the structural changes in patterns of the transmission of knowledge during the period. My main concern will be with certain developments within intellectual circles, primarily in connection with changes in the way halakhic literature—the core of the Ashkenazi literary canon—was written and transmitted.[1]

### RABBI HAYYIM OF FRIEDBERG AND THE DEBATE ON REMA'S *TORAT ḤATAT*

Hayyim ben Bezalel of Friedberg, brother of Maharal of Prague, was one of the

This essay was first presented as a paper in Feb. 1996 at a research seminar held in the Center for Judaic Studies, University of Pennsylvania, Philadelphia. I am indebted to the directors of the Center—in particular, to Professor David Ruderman and to the members of the Literacy and Learning research group—for the opportunity given me to lecture on the subject; I am also grateful for the fruitful discussion and comments. The paper was part of a research project dealing with how Ashkenazi society coped with the printed book at the beginning of the modern era. The only other material published so far is my article 'Transformations in the Polish and Ashkenazi Yeshivot during the Sixteenth and Seventeenth Centuries and the Dispute over *Pilpul*' (Heb.), in *Keminhag ashkenaz upolin: Sefer yovel leChone Shmeruk* (Jerusalem, 1989), 9–80. Further material has been presented on various occasions and will be published in the future.

[1]  The rabbinic literature in eastern Europe was first described, more or less comprehensively, in the third volume of C. Tchernowitz (Rav Tsa'ir), *Toledot haposekim*, v. iii, *Hashulhan arukh: Hithavvuto vehishtalsheluto 'ad aharonei mefareshav* (New York, 1948). For a brief description of the processes, see M. A. Shulvass, 'The Torah and its Study in Poland and Lithuania' (Heb.), in Y. Heilperin (ed.), *Beit yisrael bepolin*, ii (Jerusalem, 1954), 13–23. For a more comprehensive and ambitious account, see id., *Jewish Culture in Eastern Europe: The Classical Period* (New York, 1975). Jacob Elbaum's book *Petihut vehistagerut* (Jerusalem, 1990), which purports to deal with late 16th-century Jewish literature in Poland and Ashkenaz and has made a tremendous contribution to the study of Jewish literature in Poland in the 16th century, treats halakhic literature only marginally; see ibid. 72–81. S. M. Chones's book *Toledot haposekim* (New York, 1946) is a lexicon arranged by book-titles which contains material of much value for the history of rabbinic literature in the region and at the time under discussion here.

most prominent Ashkenazi scholars of the sixteenth century, and a member of one
of the most distinguished families in Ashkenazi society at the dawn of the modern
era.[2] Reacting to the printing of a halakhic manual—the first of its kind in the
domain of Ashkenazi culture—he wrote:

Just as a person likes only the food that he prepares for himself, in accordance with his own
appetite and taste, not wishing at all to be a guest at another person's table, thus he does
not like another person's rulings unless he agrees with that person. All the more does he
not wish to be dependent upon the books of other authors, whom he does not trust, just as
a person likes only the food that he prepares for himself, in accordance with his own
appetite and taste, and does not aspire to be a guest at their prepared table (*shulḥan arukh*).
And for that reason the ancients refrained from writing any special book to lay down custom and halakhah to the general public. It is therefore quite surprising that the rabbi R.
Moses has written a special book and ignored the things that I have just written about.[3]

This passage is from R. Hayyim's *Vikuaḥ mayim ḥayim*, a sharply polemical
tract against the book *Torat ḥatat* by R. Moses Isserles of Cracow, later known by
the acronym Rema and renowned for the *mapah* (tablecloth) that he spread, so to
speak, over the *Shulḥan arukh*—that ostensibly Sefardi work whose surprising
acceptance in Ashkenazi society was one of the signs of the process I trace here.[4]
The rather clumsy wording of the passage reflects the author's attempt to adhere
as far as possible to the literal meaning of the metaphor *shulḥan arukh*, that is,
'prepared table', and the dishes served up on it. He was, of course, hinting
obliquely at the real, though distant, target of his attack: the book *Shulḥan arukh*,
then coming off the Italian printing-presses.[5]

As for Rema, in the introduction to his *Torat ḥatat* (Cracow, 1559), written
some ten years before the *Mapah* (Cracow, 1578–80), he explained that his intention was to write a book to replace *Sha'arei dura*, a major work of the medieval
Ashkenazi canon, whose study formed part of the basic curriculum in the
medieval Ashkenazi yeshiva.[6] Rema believed that the work was no longer usable

---

[2] For R. Hayyim, see B. L. Sherwin, 'In the Shadows of Greatness: Rabbi Hayyim ben Betsalel of
Friedberg', *Journal of Social Studies*, 37 (1975), 35–60; E. Zimmer, *Rabbi Hayim b.R. Bezalel
miFriedberg aḥi haMaharal miPrag* (Jerusalem, 1987).

[3] Hayyim of Friedberg, *Vikuaḥ mayim ḥayim* (Amsterdam, 1712), intro., p. 1a.

[4] On Rema and his book *Torat ḥatat*, see below the section 'Rema and the Printed Book'.

[5] For the status of *Shulḥan arukh* in Ashkenazi society during the 16th and 17th centuries, see
Tchernowitz, *Hashulḥan arukh: Hithavvuto vehishtalsheluto ad aharonei mefareshav*, which is devoted
in its entirety to the issue. Tchernowitz's account is very comprehensive; under the narrow heading of
'The Dispute over the *Shulḥan arukh*' he subsumes all of the halakhic creativity in the realm of
Ashkenazi culture during the 16th–17th centuries, including topics whose connection with the 'dispute' is indirect and even marginal. He thus misses the opportunity to describe halakhic literature as a
component in the cultural and literary polysystem. The question of the *Shulḥan arukh* is indeed one of
the keys to understanding this polysystem, but by no means the only one. See the section 'Rema and
the *Shulḥan Arukh*' for further discussion of the status of this work in Ashkenazi society.

[6] Concerning *Sha'arei dura*, see I. Ta-Shma, 'Some Characteristics of Rabbinical Literature
in the Fourteenth Century' (Heb.), *Alei sefer*, 4 (1977), 29–31, and see ibid., n. 20 for references
to earlier literature. On this work as a textbook in the Ashkenazi yeshivot and on the standard

and wished to replace it with a new, more systematic text comprehensible to any reader. Rema meant to write a book that, phrased in more modern terms, departed from the customary modes of knowledge transmission of medieval Ashkenazi society and internalized the new communicative values of the printing-press. It was this that aroused the anger of Maharal's brother.

R. Hayyim's bitter reaction was only one manifestation of the far-reaching changes taking place in all areas of intellectual life in Ashkenazi society at the time—a cluster of changes that added up to a crisis.[7] For present purposes I shall concentrate on certain aspects of the stir caused by the advent of print among the three major groups of Ashkenazi intellectuals who dealt primarily with halakhah—the rabbis, heads of yeshivas (*rashei yeshivot*), and Torah scholars (*talmidei ḥakhamim*).

Thus, R. Hayyim viewed books in general as having secondary status, and his caution against writing books was so strong as to sound almost like a prohibition. This position is an expression not so much of Ashkenazi literary tradition as of the apprehension with which some Ashkenazi intellectual circles of the time viewed the transition from scribal to print culture.[8] By 'print culture' I do not mean the instrumental aspects of the phenomenon, but rather the changes that took place in communication media—in particular the availability of printed literary material and its ease of dissemination, so that practically anyone could now obtain any text. Unlike the manuscript, which was inherently exclusive, expensive, and of limited circulation, the accessibility of the printed book made it more difficult to protect, if necessary, the esoteric nature of certain bodies of knowledge. R. Hayyim's objection to writing books, or, at least, his denial of canonical status to the printed book, shows profound awareness of the social implications of the advent of print, and in particular of the possible effect on the stratification of the intellectual élite.

The ideology developed here is intriguing. There is no room, R. Hayyim writes, for the printed manual, as it freezes and rigidifies halakhah, which must remain fluid; further, he seems to be saying that there is no such thing as an authoritative text. Authority is personal, it depends absolutely on the halakhic scholar, the *posek*, who cannot—and may not—rely on precedents. Moreover, authority is

bookshelf of the Ashkenazi yeshiva in general, see my 'Transformations in the Yeshivot', 21 n. 20. And see the section 'Rema and the Printed Book' for a discussion of Rema's attitude to *Sha'arei dura* and passages from his introduction.

[7] Various authors were well aware of the expected—or necessary—changes in patterns of study and knowledge transmission as a result of the advent of print. In this connection see e.g. Maharshal's two introductions to his *Yam shel shelomo*, at the beginning of the volume devoted to tractate Ḥulin (Cracow, 1635). These introductions offer a consideration of the relevant issues different from—and more sophisticated than—that of R. Hayyim.

[8] The prohibition on committing halakhic material to writing was never mentioned among the intellectual élite of Ashkenazi society in the late Middle Ages, except in connection with the teaching of *pilpul* in the yeshivot—and in that case the reason was specifically that such material was not fit to be used for halakhic decisions. See my 'Transformations in the Yeshivot', 18–20 and nn. 17–18.

a unique, one-off affair. The *posek* must thrash out each decision individually, deliberating with the sources and with himself. For a better understanding of R. Hayyim's criticism, let us read what he writes a little further on:

And without doubt he [Rema] was not unaware, moreover, that when we were studying together in the yeshiva of the wondrous Gaon, our teacher R. Shakhna, of blessed memory, and we heard the *She'arim* of Dura from him, we his students entreated him many times that he see fit to compose and collect all the laws of *isur veheter* [laws of forbidden foods and related topics] in the proper order, but he turned down our request, doubtless for the reason I have written.[9]

R. Hayyim, unlike his teacher, had written himself a manual of *isur veheter*:

Some sixteen years ago I, too, undertook to collect all the laws of *isur veheter* from the books of the *posekim*, one here and one there, and I arranged them in the proper order and they became as one in my hand, with the utmost brevity. Now, I had it all put away, sealed up in my storehouses, but the young men who were then in my home stole it from me and copied it secretly. When this became known to me I took that copy away from them in a great fury, because I had composed it for my own needs only, to serve me as an aid and a guard against forgetfulness—not for any other person to rely upon it.[10]

The handwritten or printed book was not an authoritative text, although there was a danger that it might be considered in that light. Meant merely as an aid to its author, without whom the book was meaningless, its authority derived from him and he was also the sole legitimate reader. That was why the mentor of the two disputants, Shalom Shakhna, rejected his disciples' requests to write them a manual; thus the book written by R. Hayyim was meant for him alone and was off limits for his students. Any significance that a text has exists only by virtue of living, direct contact with its writer. Thus the text is a reflection of another, oral text; that oral text is the authoritative one, its source of authority being the fact that it is transmitted from teacher to pupil. Halakhah may be transmitted only through the direct teacher–student dialogue, a context in which the status of the written text is secondary. Once that direct contact has been lost, the text forfeits its authority, even when actually written. Thus the Ashkenazi halakhic tradition is understood—at least, in the mid-sixteenth century—as inherently oral.

  R. Hayyim's critique may be seen as a defence of the élitism of the rabbinical leadership in Ashkenazi society, which viewed the printed book as a threat to the exclusivity of halakhic knowledge. The issuing of a halakhic ruling was defined as a personal, autonomous action of the *posek*, who would never base his decision on authoritative texts other than the Talmud itself. Direct transmission of knowledge from rabbi to disciple ensured that such knowledge would be kept within the domain of the rabbinical élite and its potential successors. The written text was jealously confined to secondary status as one of the *posek*'s personal tools, thus ostensibly guarding against its becoming a threat to the social stratification of the

---

[9] *Vikuaḥ mayim hayim*, 1*b*–2*a*.      [10] Ibid. 4*a*–5*b*.

élite or breaching the closed circle of knowledge, even if it ultimately reached unworthy hands.

The literary corpus to which Hayyim ben Bezalel was referring was supposed to be available only to the circles that created it; for any person outside those circles, it was, quite literally, a closed book.

## RABBI SHALOM SHAKHNA OF LUBLIN AND THE ASHKENAZI TRADITION OF WRITING

Shalom Shakhna, the mentor of the two disputants we have been considering and the greatest head of yeshiva in mid-sixteenth-century Poland, was a disciple of R. Jacob Pollack, the first head of yeshiva known by name in Poland—a semi-mythical figure remembered in the historical memory of Polish Jewry as a 'founder', around whom various foundation legends were woven.[11] The figure of his disciple R. Shalom Shakhna is not far different, and he too figures in many stories.[12] But neither he nor Jacob Pollack were credited with writing any book. Only a few fragments, never collected as a book, were ever ascribed to them.[13] R. Shalom Shakhna's clearly deliberate decision not to write books was explained by his son R. Israel of Lublin, in the following passage:

I was also taught the practical aspects of halakhah by my master and teacher and father, the *ga'on*, rabbi, and luminary of the Diaspora, R. Shalom, known as Shakhno, of blessed memory, may I be an expiation for his decease, who taught many pupils, from one end of the earth to the other; we are sustained from his mouth and drink his waters. And by my very life and soul, many times I requested him, together with many other students, to make a *psak* [=singular of *psakim*, meaning: 'book of halakhic rulings']. And his answer, offered out of much piety and humility—for he was humbler than any man on the face of the earth—was: 'I know that [if I write such a book, future authorities] will rule exclusively as I write, in view of the principle that "The Law is decided according to the last authority," but I do not wish people to rely upon me.' He was referring, for example, to a

[11] For Jacob Pollack and the foundation myths associated with him, see my 'Transformations in the Yeshivot', 47–50, and ibid. n. 17 for earlier literature.

[12] A considerable amount of material about R. Shalom Shakhna was collected by T. Preshel, 'R. Shalom Shakhna of Lublin' (Heb.), *Sinai*, 100 (1987), 682–700.

[13] 16th-century literature preserves various oral traditions attributed to Pollack, transmitted by the next two generations. Some of these traditions originate in his glosses on books studied at the yeshiva: *Sefer mordekhai* and *Sefer mitsvot gadol*, which were still known in the late 1500s in Poland. The only text that has reached us as he wrote it is a writ of excommunication he issued against R. Abraham Mintz; see S. Wiener, *Pesak haherem shel haRav Ya'akov Polak* (1897), in I. T. Eisenstadt, *Da'at kedoshim* (Petersburg, 1897–8). A manuscript containing Shalom Shakhna's glosses on *Seder haget*, a rabbinical handbook on the writing of writs of divorce, is in the possession of the Bodleian Library, Oxford (Opp. 304, Neubauer no. 803). In addition, two of his responsa were printed in Cracow before 1540, not in order to collect his works but for the immediate purpose of imposing judgement on litigants in two concrete cases. The source of the other surviving traditions of Shalom Shakhna's teachings are his glosses to books studied in the yeshivot.

case where there is a controversy among great rabbis, and he would decide between them or sometimes disagree, but the judge can base his decision only on what is before him. Therefore, each person should decide according to that particular time, as he sees fit. For that reason, too, his rabbi, the *ga'on*, our teacher R. Jacob Pollack, also composed no book, neither did those *ge'onim* ever copy in their homes even a responsum that they sent away; moreover, they believed [the writing of a book] would be arrogance on their part.[14]

The son of the mythological head of yeshiva was thus taking the opportunity, about ten years before *Vikuaḥ mayim ḥayim*, to answer a question which, although it had not been explicitly asked, was surely at the back of many people's minds: Why did the two celebrated heads of yeshiva leave no written record of their teachings? How had it happened that, in contrast to all the contemporary authors, the spiritual heritage of Jacob Pollack and Shalom Shakhna was lost for ever? Underlying R. Israel's answer to the unasked question was an argument similar to that of R. Hayyim in his attack on Rema. It was no accident that neither had left any written text; the omission was intentional, for the writing of a book implies deciding the law, and that was what they wished to avoid. The very act of writing freezes the fluidity and relativity of the text, making it something absolute and thus undeservedly authoritative. Halakhic rulings are temporary and should therefore not be committed to writing. In the final analysis, it is a single person who lays down the law, and there is no text that might be consulted in his stead. In justification of this position, the son—and perhaps also the father before him—offered a far-reaching interpretation of the halakhic principle. 'The law is according to the latest scholars': the law is always decided on the basis of the last *posek*. Hence it is not only useless to commit today's conclusion to writing, but even dangerous to this very individualistic, perhaps even anarchistic, principle of religious decisions.[15]

However, R. Israel's clearly enunciated statement, like that of his predecessor R. Hayyim, is only a weak reflection of the medieval Ashkenazi writing tradition. It is primarily a reformulation, reacting to the threatening implications of the printed book for the status of the intellectual élite, on the one hand, and for the status of the traditional Ashkenazi canon, on the other—two things that essentially reduce to one.

## ASHKENAZI LITERATURE IN TRANSITION FROM HANDWRITTEN TO THE PRINTED CULTURE

Because of the advent of the printing-press, the medieval Ashkenazi scholarly tradition, as it had evolved mainly after the Black Death, could not cross over

---

[14] *She'elot uteshuvot haRema* (Cracow, 1640), no. 25, p. 66*b*; ed. A. Siev (Jerusalem, 1971), 156.
[15] On the principle 'The law is according to the later scholars', see M. Elon, *Jewish Law*, iv (Philadelphia, 1994), 1345–8, 1354–6, 1360–6, 1389–94; I. Ta-Shma, 'The Law is according to the Later Scholars: Historical Considerations regarding a Legal Rule' (Heb.), *Shenaton hamishpat haivri* 6–7 (1979–80), 405–23; Y. Yuval, 'Rishonim veaharonim, antiki et moderni', *Zion*, 57 (1992), 369–94.

unchanged to the modern era. The evolution of this tradition since the mid-fourteenth century had been based on a limited canon created, for the most part, within the confines of Ashkenazi culture itself. Among its sources of authority, besides the literary tradition, were local custom, that is, the oral custom of each community, which in fact was largely considered to override the literary tradition. For our purposes the crucial point is that the written text was not necessarily seen as something perfect, authoritative; it generally reflected interpretations and rulings transmitted orally by teachers and heads of yeshivot, or written by the latter for *ad hoc* reference but not as a final, approved source or legal rule. Medieval Ashkenazi culture had definite oral characteristics, and its traditions were therefore fluid and limited in authority, both in time and in scope. Those who passed on these traditions never intended to create a comprehensive, binding legal corpus, as Maimonides' legal code *Mishneh Torah* had been intended to be, and had become in the east and to a considerable extent in the Sefardi world. Before the coming of print, Ashkenazi culture was not based on a fixed text, and certainly had no authoritative canon.[16]

The significance of the crisis caused by the coming of the printing-press can be better appreciated if I elaborate on the notion of text as it existed in medieval Ashkenazi scribal culture. The post-talmudic halakhic text relevant to our purpose, that is, the text that functioned, in the sense that it was studied, read, quoted, cited as precedent or proof-text in legal rulings, was the text as studied in the yeshiva, not as written by its author. It took shape on the basis of a canonical text—generally some halakhic codification from the formative period of Ashkenazi literature in the twelfth and thirteenth centuries, the time of the Tosafists. This is the beginning of the period named for the Rishonim, the 'First or Early authorities', a term which of course signals the primal authority of those authors relative to the Aharonim, the 'Last or Latter authorities'. The basic canonical text being studied at the yeshiva was expanded by the exegesis of the head of yeshiva who taught it. The 'final' text was the canonical text plus the comments, or, as they were usually called *hagahot* (glosses), of the head of yeshiva as recorded by his disciples in the margins (*gilyonot*) of the manuscript page. When the text was copied later, these comments intruded into the body of the main text, where they were absorbed as an integral part.[17]

Thus, for example, one of the main channels of the French Ashkenazi halakhic tradition of the twelfth century was a work compiled towards the end of the

[16] On the ancient Ashkenazi writing tradition, see I. M. Ta-Shma, *Minhag Ashkenaz hakadmon* (Jerusalem, 1992), 13–105; on aspects of Ashkenazi literature after the Black Death, see id., 'Some Characteristics of Rabbinical Literature', 20–41. For a brief discussion of Ashkenazi writing traditions in the 14th century, see my 'Between Ashkenaz and Jerusalem: Ashkenazi Scholars in Erez Israel after the Black Death' (Heb.), *Shalem*, 4 (1984), 28–40.

[17] For references on the phenomenon of *hagahot*, see my 'Transformations in the Yeshivot', n. 10. To the works listed there, add S. Immanuel, 'The Responsa of Maharam of Rotenburg, Prague Edition' (Heb.), *Tarbiz*, 57 (1988), 561 n. 9.

thirteenth century known as *Sefer mordekhai*.[18] From the mid-fourteenth century on, various editions of this book began to appear. They included, in addition to the text proper, sometimes abbreviated and edited, fourteenth-century traditions which, of course, post-dated the completion of the work itself. These works were generally named for the contemporary heads of yeshivas, such as 'The Mordekhai of R. Samuel', 'The Mordekhai of R. Samson', which reflect not only the original source but the mode of its transmission by the fourteenth-century teachers. It was the new, complex text that they produced, which included parts of the original codex together with the teachings of the later authorities, that became authoritative, rather than the original text itself. Despite the marked difference between it and the canonical text, it enjoyed canonical status, albeit limited to a particular locality. It functioned in a well-defined geographical region and was effective only for a limited period. Generally speaking, its lifetime was a single generation, as the text was modified from one generation of heads of yeshivas to the next.[19] In other words, the Ashkenazi text was never finalized but constantly subject to change.[20]

If the life of a halakhic work coincided more or less with the lifetimes of the teacher and his disciples, its geographical sphere of influence was defined by the groups belonging to and in contact with the yeshiva students and former students who had become heads of yeshivas. Just as the texts of the works studied changed vertically, in time, and were named for the various generations of heads of yeshivas, they also varied horizontally. For each geographical area there were characteristic editions of the same work, created and developed in the local yeshivot and representing the regional traditions and custom. Thus, for example, one had the Rhenish Mordekhai, as distinct from the Austrian Mordekhai. Basic to the formation of the medieval Ashkenazi text, therefore, were its oral and regional nature. Such fluid traditions became obsolete with the advent of print, which fixed the text once and for all, in some respects enforcing the formulation of a final binding and authoritative text.

Besides the change in the status of the text due to the advent of print, the traditional Ashkenazi library lost its exclusivity. This library, as we have seen, was based on a limited number of canonical texts. Most of these texts were created where they were actually used and therefore reflected fluid local traditions, which

[18] On this work, see S. Kohn, *Mardochai ben Hillel: Sein Leben und seine Schriften* (Breslau, 1878; first pub. in instalments in *MGWJ* 27–8 (1877–8); also pub. in Heb. trans. in *Sinai*, 9–15 (1943–5) ); E. E. Urbach, *Ba'alei hatosafot*, rev. edn. (Jerusalem, 1980), 556–61; A. Halperin, *Mavo leSefer hamordekhai hashalem* (Jerusalem, 1992).

[19] On the phenomenon of abbreviations in general and the reworked versions of *Sefer hamordekhai* in particular, see Halperin, *Mavo leSefer hamordekhai hashalem*, 125–41, which considers the question in a different light from that considered here; see my 'Between Ashkenaz and Jerusalem'.

[20] For a comparison of the manuscript-copying technique in European universities with the parallel technique in Ashkenazi yeshivot, as described here in brief, see G. Pollard, 'The *Pecia* System in the Medieval Universities', in M. B. Parkes and A. G. Watson (eds.), *Mediaeval Scribes, Manuscripts and Libraries: Essays Presented to N. R. Ker* (London, 1978), 145–61.

came into only partial contact with parallel traditions of halakhic decision and scholarship. It was the local nature of the canon that created its authoritative status and made it into what was known as *minhag hamakom*, literally 'the custom of the place' or 'local custom'.

The authority of the traditional library was severely shaken by its exposure to the foreign literature that began to come off the Italian printing-presses in the late fifteenth century and streamed steadily into the Ashkenazi and Polish yeshivot. Ashkenazi society was now able to read Sefardi biblical and talmudic exegesis, halakhic literature, philosophy, and kabbalah. It was only on account of this process, which peaked in the middle of the sixteenth century, that the *Shulḥan arukh* was accepted by Ashkenazi society a generation later. The patterns of halakhic decision in Ashkenazi society were entirely transformed thereby, and—of particular relevance here—halakhic literature now became available to people who, in the earlier literary situation, could not have achieved the degree of proficiency necessary to make halakhic decisions. All this demonstrates that the advent of printing produced a crisis in Ashkenazi society and a revolution in creative patterns, the structure of the literary canon, and the transmission of traditions that posed an immediate threat to the position of the intellectual élite.

In sum, all the characteristics of the shift from script to print so commonly discussed in literary history—the standardization of texts, exposure of the lower classes to literature, and changes in the structure of the traditional library—may be detected in Ashkenazi society, emphasized by the particular nature of text, book, and canon in that society.[21]

## REMA AND THE PRINTED BOOK

The central figure in the changes that shook Ashkenazi society upon the transition of rabbinical literature from script to print was undoubtedly R. Moses Isserles, Rema, whose book *Torat ḥatat* was the target of the attack by Hayyim ben Bezalel of Friedberg with which I began this article. While other central figures in the rabbinical literature of the time took an antagonistic stand towards print, Rema understood its implications for the future nature of rabbinical literature and proceeded accordingly in his own literary work.[22]

[21] I am referring to the important research done in the past few years in the field of the history of the book, a major landmark in which was the publication of Elizabeth L. Eisenstein, *The Printing Press as an Agent of Change*, i and ii (Cambridge, 1979). Although scholarship in this area has advanced considerably since then, many of the issues and discussions in that book are still influencing modern research in the field.

[22] On Rema and his literary opus, see Chones, *Toledot haposekim*, 174–85; A. Ziev, *Rabbenu Moshe Isserles (Rema)* (New York, 1972). Concerning Solomon Luria (Maharshal), see S. Assaf, 'Something about the Life of Maharshal' (Heb.), in *Louis Ginzberg Jubilee Volume* (New York, 1945), 45–63. It is quite amazing that there is still no satisfactory, comprehensive study of this unique figure or of his unprecedented literary output. Assaf's 'Something about Maharshal' is still a point of departure for any future progress on this intriguing subject.

In his introduction to *Torat ḥatat*, Rema lists his motives for writing the book which was meant to supersede *Sha'arei dura*, a central component of the medieval Ashkenazi canon and a subject of systematic study in Ashkenazi yeshivot:

I bless the Lord who has guided me. My conscience admonishes me at night, to write a book on *isur veheter*, on the laws set forth in *Sha'arei dura*, in so far as that book is widespread and in everyone's hands, presenting a stumbling-block for them. For the *ga'on*, the author of *Sha'arei dura*, composed it for his own generation, great and wise men, and the brevity with which he wrote sufficed for them, and he wrote in his book only those things that he considered innovations or things necessary for that generation . . . But now, owing to the sins of these last generations, his words have become obscure and incomprehensible, as though they had never been. And for that reason the later authorities, of blessed memory, rose up . . . and wrote comments on it in their glosses, so as to instruct the generations how to conduct themselves, even though, in so doing, their writings clashed with one another: one says this and another says that . . . one prohibits and one permits, although they were all given by one shepherd. At any rate, whoever has not the palate to taste their sweet but largely obscure words cannot reach conclusions from these numerous glosses . . . Accordingly, these books have fallen into the hands of many people, small and great, who have interpreted and explained them in different ways. Time comes to an end, but their words are endless, for they have composed for that book commentaries and appendices, and many students have jumped up and attributed nonsensical things to it. Every man did as he pleased in his book—and who shall prevent him? Thereafter these books and words have been printed, and whoever sees them believes they were all uttered at Sinai . . . and the effort of scholars who meant well, to abbreviate and to explain, has caused harm. Therefore have I, Moses . . . seen that it would be good to establish the proper order of all the laws of *isur veheter* that are in *Sha'arei dura* and to commit them to writing in a brief way without lengthy casuistry (*pilpul*) . . . in a manner easily comprehensible to every man, be he small or great.[23]

This bold, almost indiscreet, introduction is a unique text in the history of the Ashkenazi book. Not only does Rema openly discredit one of the works of the medieval Ashkenazi canon, then still serving as the main textbook in the Ashkenazi yeshiva; he openly and deliberately disparages the method of transmission of halakhic tradition that was still in use in the Ashkenazi yeshiva. The poor state of the text in *Sha'arei dura*, as he describes it, was no accident. This was the text as it was supposed to be, in keeping with Ashkenazi scholarly tradition. It was precisely how knowledge in questions of *isur veheter*—the very heart of the legal corpus for which the *posek* was responsible toward his community, as it had accumulated over the many decades of the book's career in the Ashkenazi yeshivot before and during Rema's lifetime—was traditionally preserved and transmitted to the next generation. The glosses to which he refers reflect genuine, legitimate strata of the text as it had evolved; the page was like an archaeological section, cutting across the mound and exposing all its levels. That was how an Ashkenazi text assumed its rightful place in society: one level of commentary superimposed on another,

---

[23] Moses Isserles, *Torat haḥatat* (Cracow, 1569), p. 2*a*–*b*.

without the intervention of any editor's hand that might lighten the increasingly heavy weight bearing down on the original text from one generation to the next. In this way the text became esoteric, accessible to learned scholars only. Such Ashkenazi texts had no didactic pretensions whatever.

Thus the definition of the prospective audience of *Torat ḥatat* as 'every man, be he small or great' seems to undermine the basic principles of the Ashkenazi halakhic text. The same is true of Rema's seemingly innocuous working plan, 'to establish the proper order of all the laws of *isur veheter* that are in *Sha'arei dura* and to commit them to writing in a brief way without lengthy casuistry', but that was also the secret of the work's subsequent popularity. In the very same sentence he declares his intention of writing within the traditional framework, casting the radical potential in traditional moulds: ostensibly, he would merely superimpose one more layer on the canonical book, after the manner of those same predecessors whom he had criticized. Perhaps it was this neutralization of the visibly radical element, the suppression of the sense of novelty in his writing, that enabled Rema to become the single person most responsible for reshaping rabbinical literature in the print era.

In this context it is useful to note as an illustration Rema's philosophical work *Torah ha'olah*, printed in Prague in 1560, only one year after *Torat haḥatat* had been printed in Cracow.[24] Ashkenazi society considered philosophy an extra-canonical discipline, a rather dangerous occupation of undefined status, perhaps bordering on heresy. Rema himself was accused by the greatest scholar of his time, his older relative R. Solomon Luria, the Maharshal, of having taught philosophy at his yeshiva at Cracow.[25] In 1559, only a short time before the publication of *Torat ha'olah*, a fierce controversy broke out in the yeshivot of Prague and Poznań—presumably, indeed, in all the yeshivot of Poland and Ashkenaz—over the study of Maimonides' *Guide of the Perplexed*, and of philosophy in general.[26] The student body split into two groups—those who ardently favoured the study of philosophy, and their opponents, who went so far as to excommunicate the supporters of philosophy. For the anti-philosophy party, the term 'philosophy' denoted not only philosophy proper but the entire corpus of new books then pouring into the Ashkenazi centres of study in Poland and Germany from Italian printing-presses, none of which was listed in the traditional Ashkenazi canon.[27] Anything new was, therefore, philosophy, and philosophy equals, of course, heresy. This dispute over the position of philosophy, like the dispute over halakhic literature with which we

[24] On *Torat ha'olah* and Rema's philosophy, see Y. Ben-Sasson, *Mishnato ha'iyunit shel haRema* (Jerusalem, 1984).

[25] *She'elot uteshuvot haRema*, no. 6, p. 26.

[26] P. Bloch, 'Der Streit um den Moreh des Maimonides in der Gemeinde Posen um die Mitte des 16. Jahrhundert', *MGWJ* 47 (1903), 153–69, 263–79, 346–56.

[27] See my paper 'The Attitude of Ashkenazi Society to the New Science in the Sixteenth Century', submitted to the Conference on Jewish Responses to Early Modern Science, Tel Aviv and Jerusalem, 1995.

are concerned here, also broke out against a background of the upheavals created in the traditional Ashkenazi literary canon by the advent of print and the collapse of the local frameworks of Ashkenazi culture.

Rema's *Torat ha'olah*, written at first sight in the tradition of Jewish Aristotelianism, also reveals its author's affinity with kabbalistic philosophy as it was emerging at that time from the north Italian yeshivot. Nevertheless, though essentially a philosophical work, the book is written in a homiletic rather than philosophical style. Rema chose to clothe his philosophical method in a traditional literary cloak, thereby taking the book out of the disputed area. Such adherence to a traditional genre presumably facilitated the dissemination of the book in the Ashkenazi milieu, which was extremely sensitive to changes. The argument was actually, though unconsciously, over form rather than content. The central bone of contention was the attitude to the old literary canon rather than the question of new halakhic messages or philosophical arguments of one kind or another.

Rema was acutely aware of the frontier between handwritten medieval Ashkenazi literature and the printed Ashkenazi literature at the dawn of the modern era, and was fully cognizant of the inescapable changes that would result from the shift from script to print. He did not, however, create new literary models, but preferred to pour the new content into ostensibly traditional vessels. Thus, for example, his halakhic writing, without exception, remained faithful to canonical texts, as was the norm in past Ashkenazi society. Not one of his works is an independent, self-sufficient text: *Darkhei moshe* is written as glosses on *Arba'ah turim*, the central legal code of the late medieval Ashkenazi world; and the same is true of his glosses on the *Shulḥan arukh*, which is my last subject.

## REMA AND THE *SHULḤAN ARUKH*

The book named *Shulḥan arukh* was written by R. Joseph Caro the Sefardi, in Safed in the years 1555–63, and first printed in Venice in 1565. It was not the author's intention to write a major legal code for *posekim*—the very opposite. Alongside his commentary *Beit yosef* on the *Arba'ah turim*, in which he laid down up-to-date rules of legal decision and filled in gaps remaining since the completion of the *Tur*—the last code completed before his time, in fourteenth-century Spain—he had written the *Shulḥan arukh* as a manual for laymen and students, that is, for the less learned strata of society.[28] That the *Shulḥan arukh*, contrary to

---

[28] 'The great work that I composed on the *Arba'ah turim*, which I have called *Beit yosef*, in which I have included all the laws that may be found in [the works of] all the *posekim*, new and old . . . I have seen fit to collect its teachings in an abbreviated fashion . . . so that the Lord's perfect Torah shall be fluent in the mouths of all men of Israel . . . Moreover, the young students shall study it constantly and memorize its words, so that knowledge acquired in childhood shall be well ordered in their mouths from a young age' (Joseph Caro, *Shulḥan arukh, Orah Hayim*, intro.). On the printing of the work, see R. Margaliyot, 'The First Editions of the *Shulḥan arukh*' (Heb.), in I. Raphael (ed.), *Rabbi Yosef Caro* (Jerusalem, 1969), 89–100.

its author's intentions, became the most authoritative legal code of Jewry is due to Rema. The edition of *Shulḥan arukh* printed in Cracow in 1578–80 included glosses by Rema which—so he explained in the introduction—were intended to introduce Ashkenazi custom into the work of the Sefardi author. The fact that he wove his comments into the main text as glosses indicates—besides upholding the traditional Ashkenazi attitude to a text—that the work itself, meant to serve as a textbook for laymen, had been accepted in Rema's yeshiva at Cracow as a students' reference-book. Instead of the *Arba'ah turim*, the main text for the study of *posekim* in the Ashkenazi yeshiva up to Rema's day, he chose to use the new book, which was free of accumulated layers of glosses and emendations, up to date and lucid, arranged along the same lines as the old *Turim* so that it was easily introduced into the yeshiva curriculum. This was the crucial step in altering the canonical status of the *Shulḥan arukh*. Thus the *Turim* became the second work of the medieval Ashkenazi canon that Rema had replaced with a new book.

Although it is generally accepted that Rema's glosses were intended to supplement the Sefardi text and adjust it to Ashkenazi usage, his work was actually far more complicated. More than just introducing Ashkenazi practice at the appropriate place, he in fact edited and screened it. Quite deliberately, his glosses discarded rather than preserved the bulk of the corpus of Ashkenazi customs left over from the Middle Ages. Because he incorporated only a small part of the Ashkenazi practice into the *Shulḥan arukh*, the material that had not entered the *Shulḥan arukh* gradually disappeared from the consciousness and everyday life of the Ashkenazi community. Rema thus narrowed the local basis of Ashkenazi halakhah and produced a code whose ethnic boundaries were largely blurred. He was therefore largely responsible for the canonization of Ashkenazi practice, having transferred it from the oral realm and placed it on a level with the written halakhah.

The *Shulḥan arukh* proper was in fact never accepted by Ashkenazi society. What was accepted was a new text, the outcome of Rema's efforts. Rema took the foreign text of R. Joseph Caro and met its codificatory threat by treating it in the traditional Ashkenazi manner, by adding layers of accumulated knowledge in such a way that the borders between them and the central text became gradually vaguer. This blurred the primary status of the text, which was transformed from a text meant to be read, hence absolute, to a text meant to be studied, and therefore relative.

A glance at a typical page of the *Shulḥan arukh*, as it took shape among the disciples of Rema and Maharshal or, more precisely, during the seventeenth century, shows that the original text of R. Joseph Caro appears in the middle of the page, surrounded on all sides by commentaries, notes, and glosses, just as if it had been a manuscript of a medieval Ashkenazi halakhic work. Less than 100 years after the printing of Rema's glosses, the original text of the *Shulḥan arukh* was buried under layer upon layer of glosses and comments, which, in keeping with the metaphor of the 'prepared table', came to be known as the *nose'ei kelim*, attendants (literally, vessel- or tool-bearers)—a process initiated by Rema himself. The *nose'ei kelim*, such as *Sefer me'irat enayim*, *Turei zahav* and *Siftei kohen*, became an integral part of the main text, and the authority of the *Shulḥan arukh* extended not only to the text as composed by Joseph Caro, but to the whole collection of texts that had become part of the canon by the very fact of being printed together with that text, first on the page around the text and later at the end of the volume.[29]

I believe that this process was the rule in regard to the acceptance of the printed book among the Ashkenazi intellectual élite: the Ashkenazi halakhic book at the beginning of the modern era retained certain features inherited from the medieval scribal tradition of knowledge transmission. In certain respects it was a kind of printed manuscript, that is, a text which, in the way it took shape, rejected the new communicative values of print culture and created a text with esoteric components, thus protecting its élitist position.

---

[29] On the bibliographical aspects of Rema's *hagahot*, see I. Nissim, 'The *Hagahot* on the *Shulḥan arukh*' (Heb.); Raphael (ed.), *Rabbi Yosef Caro*, 64–88.

# The Accusation of Ritual Murder in Poland, 1500–1800

## ZENON GULDON AND JACEK WIJACZKA

THIS ESSAY is an attempt to describe the occurrences of accusations of ritual murder against Jews between 1500 and 1800 in the territories of Poland. In that period these lands constituted the 'main centre and reserve of world Jewry'.[1]

### THE SIZE OF THE JEWISH POPULATION

It is not easy to determine the exact numbers of the Jewish population in the territories of Poland and the Grand Duchy of Lithuania for the periods covered in this study, but its size can be estimated from extant tax records. Estimates of the Jewish population in the Polish–Lithuanian Commonwealth put it at 500,000 for the mid-seventeenth century, and over one million by the end of the eighteenth century; that is, in the mid-seventeenth century about 30 per cent of world Jewry made its home in Poland–Lithuania, and by the end of the eighteenth century it was home to 44 per cent.[2] Nevertheless, the true size of the population is still open to debate.[3] The amount collected by the per capita tax, a tax first assessed by the Sejm in 1563, is the main basis for determining the size of the Jewish population in the second half of the sixteenth century. The original resolution required payment of 1 zloty from every Jewish person regardless of sex or age, although the indigent were exempted. In Poland in 1569 revenues from the tax were 6,000 zloty, and in 1578 they were 10,000 zloty.[4]

[1] E. M. Rostworowski, 'Żydzi staropolscy: Przywileje i konwertyci (Na marginesie prac Jakuba Goldberga)', *Tygodnik Powszechny*, 2 (1987), 4.

[2] Z. Sułowski, 'Liczebność Żydów na ziemiach polskich', in *Narod-Kościół-kultura: Szkice z historii Polski* (Lublin, 1986), 239.

[3] For more details about these problems, see Z. Guldon, 'Źródła i metody szacunków liczebności ludności żydowskiej w Polsce w XVI–XVIII wieku', *Kwartalnik Historii Kultury Materialnej* (1986), 249–63; Z. Guldon and W. Kowalski, 'Between Tolerance and Abomination: Jews in Sixteenth-Century Poland', in R. B. Waddington and A. H. Williamson (eds.), *The Expulsion of the Jews: 1492 and After* (New York, 1994), 163–6; Z. Guldon and J. Wijaczka, 'Die zahlenmassige Stark der Juden in Polen–Litauen im 16–18 Jahrhundert', *Trumah*, 4 (1994), 91–101.

[4] W. Małcużyński, 'Kilka kartek ze statystyki skarbowej, XVI wieku', *Ekonomista*, 2 (1902), tables 1–4; A. Pawiński, *Skarbowość w Polsce i jej dzieje za Stefana Batorego*, vol. viii of *Źródła dziejowe* (Warsaw, 1881), 176.

Several different demographic estimates were based on the same amount of Jewish taxes.[5] Schiper estimated that there were 75,000 Jews in Poland and 25,000 in the Grand Duchy of Lithuania. S. W. Baron, on the other hand, believed that in the second half of the sixteenth century 150,000 Jews lived in the territories of the Polish–Lithuanian Commonwealth.[6] Even this estimate was further inflated to 300,000 by Z. Sułowski,[7] who later reduced it to 120,000.[8] Comparing data from the tax registers and other sources, M. Horn concluded that because Russian Jews often evaded paying taxes, an estimate based on 3.3 inhabitants for each zloty collected was more accurate.[9] Extrapolating from Horn's findings, H. Samsonowicz recently concluded that there must have been about 20,000 Jews living in Poland in the sixteenth century, based on the collection of over 6,000 zloty in taxes.[10] Along with these estimates, S. A. Bershadski placed the numbers of the Lithuanian Jewry at between 10,000 and 12,000 for that period.[11] Hence, the same source material can yield estimates from 30,000 to 300,000 for the Jewish population in Poland in the second half of the sixteenth century. It is worth noting that of the 1,076 towns in Poland (not including Ukrainian lands), Jewish presence is documented in 294.

Chmielnicki's revolt, as well as the Polish wars with Moscow and Sweden in the mid-seventeenth century, resulted in a significant depletion of the Jewish population.[12] There were statements that between 1648 and 1660 some 100,000 to 180,000 Jews were either killed or emigrated from the Polish–Lithuanian Commonwealth.[13] Perhaps Baron's figure of 350,000 for the number of Jews in the

---

[5] I. Schiper, 'Rozwój ludności żydowskiej na ziemiach Rzeczypospolitej', in Ignacy Schiper, Aryeh Tartakower, and Aleksander Hafftek (eds.), *Żydzi w Polsce odrodzonej*, i (Warsaw, 1932), 29–30. His estimate is accepted by B. D. Weinryb, *The Jews in Poland from 1100 to 1800* (Philadelphia, 1973), 310, and by M. Horn, 'Ludność żydowska w Polsce do końca, XVIII wieku', in Marian Fuks, Zygmunt Hoffman, Maurycy Horn, and Jerzy Tomaszewski (eds.), *Żydzi polscy: Dzieje i kultura* (Warsaw, 1982), 11.

[6] S. W. Baron, *A Social and Religious History of the Jews*, xvi: *Poland–Lithuania, 1500–1650* (New York, 1976), 207; J. I. Israel, *European Jewry in the Age of Mercantilism, 1550–1750* (Oxford, 1985), 27. Israel argues that there were between 100,000 and 150,000 Jews living in the territories of the Polish–Lithuanian Commonwealth.

[7] Sułowski, 'Mechanizmy ekspansji demograficznej Żydów w miastach polskich, XVI–XIX wieku', in *Zeszyty Naukowe Katolickiego Uniwersytetu Lubelskiego*, 3 (1974), table 1.

[8] Sułowski, 'Jewish Population Figures for the Polish Territories during the Last Millennium', in *International Conference on History and Culture of Polish Jews: Abstracts* (Jerusalem, 1988), 110.

[9] Horn, *Żydzi na Rusi Czerwonej w XVI i pierwszej połowie XVII wieku: Działalność gospodarcza na tle rozwoju demograficznego* (Warsaw, 1975), 62.

[10] H. Samsonowicz, 'The Jewish Population in Poland during the Middle Ages', *Dialectics and Humanism*, 1 (1989), 36.

[11] S. A. Bersadski, *Litovskie evrei* (St Petersburg, 1883), 408.

[12] L. Lewin, *Die Judenverfolgungen im zweiten schwedisch–polnischen Kriege, 1655–1659* (Poznań, 1901); J. Schamschon, *Beitrage zur Geschichte der Judenverfolgungen in Polen während der Jahre, 1648–1658* (Berne, 1912); D. Tollet, '1648: Une rupture dans l'histoire juive?' *Tiempo y forma*, series 4 (Historia moderna), vol. vi (Madrid, 1993), 109–27.

[13] Schiper, 'Rozwój ludności żydowskiej', 32.

Commonwealth after the mid-seventeenth century was exaggerated.[14] At least one fact is certain: in the second half of the seventeenth century, a Jewish presence is documented in over 400 Polish towns, and in 1676 the per capita tax was paid by about 20,000 Jews. (By that point, however, children, as well as the elderly and indigent, were exempted from taxes.[15])

In 1765 in the whole of the Polish–Lithuanian Commonwealth, the per capita tax was paid by 587,658 Jews, of which 430,009 lived in Poland. R. Mahler estimated the actual number of Jews in Poland–Lithuania at that time at around 750,000.[16] By the end of the eighteenth century, T. Czacki believed, some 900,000 Jews lived within the territories of Poland (but this is probably an inflated figure).[17]

## BACKGROUND AND SOURCES

In 1235 Jews were accused of having committed ritual murder in the suburbs of Fulda. The accusation that Jews use human blood for their religious rituals was condemned as false in a Golden Bull issued by the emperor in the thirteenth century and in four separate papal edicts by Innocent IV from 1247 to 1253.[18] Moreover, a privilege given to the Jews of Wielkopolska by Bolesław Pobożny in Kalisz in 1264 provided that for falsely accusing a Jew of murdering a Christian child the accuser was to receive the same punishment that would have been applied to the accused Jew had his guilt been proven.[19]

In ritual murder court proceedings from a later period, references were often made to a widely publicized trial in Trent in 1475.[20] In sixteenth-century Poland, procedures for this type of court case were regulated by royal edicts. In 1531, to prevent groundless accusations of host desecration and kidnapping of Christian children levied against Jews, King Zygmunt I ordered that these cases be referred

---

[14] Baron, *A Social and Religious History*, xvi. 207.

[15] Z. Guldon and W. Kowalski, 'Ludność żydowska w miastach polskich w II połowie, XVII wieku', in Jacek Chrobaczyński, Andrzej Jureczko, Michał Śliwa (eds.), *Ojczyzna bliższa i dalsza* (Cracow, 1993), 485–96.

[16] R. Mahler, 'Żydzi w dawnej Polsce w świetle liczb: Struktura demograficzna i społeczno-ekonomiczna Żydów w Koronie w XVIII wieku', *Przeszłość Demograficzna Polski*, 1 (1967), 161.

[17] T. Czacki, *Dzieła*, iii (Poznań, 1845), 254.

[18] For more details, see T. Zaderecki, *Legenda krwi: Analiza krytyczno-historyczna tak zwanego 'mordu rytualnego'* (Warsaw, 1947).

[19] *Kodeks dyplomatyczny Wielkopolski*, i (Poznań, 1877), no. 605: 'Iuxta constitutiones Pape in nomine nostri patris sancti districtius prohibemus, ne de cetero ludei singuli in nostro dominio constituti debeant inculpari, quod humano utantur sanguine, cum iuxta preceptum Legis, ab omni prorsus sanguine se ludei contineant universi. Sed si aliquis ludeus de occasione alicuius pueri Christiani per Christianum fuerit incupatus, tribus Christianis et totidem ludeis convinci debet; et postquam convictus fuerit, tunc ipse ludeus tantummodo pena que sequitur puniatur crimine pro commisso. Si vero ipsum testes supradicti et sua innocencia expurgabit, penam Christianus, quam ludeus pati debuerat, pro calumnia non immerito sustinebit.' For more details, see J. Sieradzki, 'Bolesława Pobożnego statut kaliski z roku 1264 dla Żydów', *Osiemnaście wieków Kalisza* 1 (1960), 133–9.

[20] R. Po-chia Hsia, *Trent 1475: Stories of a Ritual Murder Trial* (New Haven, 1992).

to the highest courts (*ad nos tribunalque nostrum*).[21] After a host desecration trial in Sochaczew (Rawa province) in 1557, King Zygmunt August ordered that all trials of host desecration or ritual murder be heard only by the Sejm court and in the presence of the king.[22] In 1633 King Władysław IV decided that any Jew accused of ritual murder or of host desecration should be imprisoned by the magistrate and turned over to the *starosta* (the territorial administrator appointed by the king). He was to be tried by a special tribunal consisting of a district court and a royal commissioner.[23] The judiciary structure and the rules regulating judicial proceedings were relatively well known. In practice, however, such accusations were brought before the Crown tribunal (established in 1578) and the assessors' court, as well as the district court, the municipal court, and even the manorial court. The judicial problems of these trials are beyond the scope of this study but are well worth investigating.

The marked increase in ritual murder trials in the mid-eighteenth century forced the Jewish Council of Four Lands to send a representative to the Apostolic See in 1758. Both Benedict XI and Clement XIII took the side of the Jews, defending them against the unjust accusations.[24] In 1776 the Sejm prohibited the use of torture: 'It has been proven by frequent experience that in some criminal cases use of confessions obtained through torture constitutes unreliable grounds for convicting the accused, and it is also a cruel way of proving that a person is not guilty.'[25] This resolution was of great significance for future ritual murder trials.

There are relatively few primary sources for ritual murder trials from this period. The sources are, first of all, trial records and court sentences concerning accusations of ritual murder. Much more information about such accusations against Jews and the ritual murder trials can be found in antisemitic literature.[26] Numerous works of this kind contributed to the widespread belief that Jews do, indeed, use Christian blood for ritual purposes. For instance, in 1758 G. Pikulski, a Catholic priest, argued that in Lithuania Jews need 30 gallons of blood and in Poland far more.[27] The works of Father Stefan Żuchowski (1666–1716), a parish priest, archdeacon, and the inquisitor of Sandomierz, stand out in the antisemitic

[21] M. Bersohn (ed.), *Dyplomatariusz dotyczący Żydów w dawnej Polsce na źródłach archiwalnych osnuty, 1388–1782* (Warsaw, 1910), no. 35, p. 484.

[22] S. Kutrzeba, 'Studia do historii sądownictwa w Polsce: Sądownictwo nad Żydami w województwie krakowskim', *Przegląd Prawa i Administracji*, 26 (1901), 940–1.

[23] Ibid. 941.

[24] C. Roth (ed.), *The Ritual Murder Libel and the Jew: The Report by Cardinal Lorenzo Ganganelli (Pope Clement XIV)* (London, n.d.).

[25] *Volumina legum*, viii., 882–3; also M. Klementowski and E. Skrętowicz, 'Z dziejów zniesienia tortur w Polsce', *Studia Kryminologiczne, Kryminalistyczne i Penitancjarne*, 9 (1979).

[26] D. Tollet, 'La Literature antisemite polonaise de 1588 à 1668', *Revue française d'histoire du livre*, 14 (1977), 3–35.

[27] G. Pikulski, *Złość żydowska przeciwko Bogu i bliźniemu, prawdzie i sumnieniu na objaśnienie przeklętych talmudystów na dowód ich zaślepienia i religii dalekiej od Prawa Boskiego przez Mojżesza danego* (Lwów, 1758), 412.

literature. He was appointed commissioner for Jewish affairs at the synod of the Cracow diocese in 1711. As commissioner, he was also in charge of ritual murder cases.[28] Żuchowski's writings became the basis for the works on ritual murder written by Bishop Józef Załuski. He supplemented his writings with information about later trials drawn from contemporary press documents.[29]

The research done to date on this topic has been limited. The recent literature is largely devoted to the history of Jewish settlement, the size of the Jewish population, and its distribution and economic role in particular regions, towns, and latifundia.[30] Also relatively well researched are the activities of the Jewish self-governing body, the *gmina* (*kahal*: (organized) community), of provincial Sejmiki, and of the Council of Four Lands created at the end of the sixteenth century, from which the Council of Lithuanian Jews separated in 1623.[31] Much has also been written about Christian–Jewish relations.[32] There are also a few relevant syntheses of the history of Polish Jewry by S. W. Baron, B. D. Weinryb, and D. Tollet.[33] Amongst works specifically devoted to the ritual murder trials, there are the studies by M. Bałaban,[34] I. Galant,[35] and R. Mahler.[36] In addition, we have discussed some of the problems mentioned above in earlier writings.[37] Nevertheless, there has not yet been any extensive treatment of ritual murder trials in Poland

[28] S. Żuchowski, *Ogłos procesów kryminalnych na Żydach o różne ekscesy, także morderstwo dzieci osobliwie w Sandomierzu w roku 1698 przeświadczone w prześwietnym Trybunale Koronnym przewiedzionych, dla dobra pospolitego wydany* (1700) and *Proces kryminalny o niewinne dziecię Jerzego Krasnowskiego już to trzecie roku 1710 dnia 18 sierpnia w Sendomirzu okrutnie od żydów zamordowane* (*c.* 1720). W. Wójcik, 'Ksiądz Stefan Żuchowski (1666–1716) uczony, pisarz i bibliofil', *Archiwa, biblioteki i muzea kościelne*, 40 (1980), 161–9; W. Muller (ed.), *Relacje o stanie diecezji krakowskiej, 1615–1765* (Lublin, 1978), 111.

[29] J. Załuski, *Morderstwa rytualne w Polsce do połowy, XVIII wieku* (Warsaw, 1914).

[30] M. Aschkewitz, *Zur Geschichte der Juden in Westpreussen* (Marburg, 1987); Z. Guldon and K. Krzystanek, *Ludność żydowska w miastach lewobrzeżnej części województwa sandomierskiego w XVI–viii wieku* (Kielce, 1990); Horn, *Żydzi na Rusi*; G. D. Hundert, *The Jews in a Polish Private Town: The Case of Opatów in the Eighteenth Century* (Baltimore, 1992); A. Leszczyński, *Żydzi ziemi bielskiej od połowy XVII wieku do 1795 roku* (Wrocław, 1980); M. J. Rosman, *The Lords' Jews: Magnate–Jewish Relations in the Polish–Lithuanian Commonwealth during the Eighteenth Century* (Cambridge, Mass., 1991).

[31] J. Goldberg, 'The Jewish Sejm: Origins and Functions', in A. Polonsky, J. Basista, and A. Link-Lenczowski (eds.), *The Jews in Old Poland, 1000–1795* (London, 1993), 147–65; A. Leszczyński, *Sejm Żydów korony, 1623–1764* (Warsaw, 1994).

[32] See J. Goldberg, 'Poles and Jews in the Seventeenth and Eighteenth Centuries: Rejection or Acceptance', *Jahrbücher für Geschichte Osteuropas*, 221 (1974), 248–82; J. Tazbir, 'Żydzi w opinii staropolskiej', in his *Świat panów Pasków* (Łódź, 1986), 213–41.

[33] D. Tollet, *Histoire des juifs en Pologne du XVIe siècle à nos jours* (Paris, 1992).

[34] M. Bałaban, 'Hugo Grotius und die Ritualmordprozesse in Lublin, 1636', in Ismar Elbogen, Josef Meisl, and Mark Wischnitzer (eds.), *Festschrift zu Simon Dubnows siebziegstem Geburstag* (Berlin, 1930), 87–112; M. Bałaban, 'Obvinenija v ritualnych ubijstvach v Polse i Litve', in *Evreiskaia entsiklopedia*, xi. 866–9.

[35] I. Galant, *Dva ritualnych processa po aktam Kievskogo Centralnogo Archiva* (Kiev, 1924).

[36] R. Mahler, 'Z dziejów Żydów w Nowym Sączu w XVII i XVIII wieku', *BŻIH* 56 (1965), 50–8.

[37] Esp. Z. Guldon, and J. Wijaczka, 'Procesy o mordy rytualne na Rusi Czerwonej, Podolu i prawobrzeżnej Ukrainie w XVI–XVIII wieku', *Nasza Przeszłość*, 81 (1994).

comparable to that by R. Po-chia Hsia devoted to such trials in sixteenth-century Germany.[38]

A more precise assessment of the numbers and chronology of ritual murder trials in Poland requires further research. According to Father Żuchowski, there were sixty-eight ritual murders in the period between 1347 and 1710.[39] Yet there is only one encyclopaedia entry, written by W. E. Peuckert, that treats the issue for Europe as a whole—and it is misleading. Peuckert's data, adopted by Po-chia Hsia as approximations, include 101 ritual murder trials in Europe between the twelfth and sixteenth centuries, with as many as fifty-three of these occurring in German-speaking countries and ten in Poland between the twelfth and eighteenth centuries. According to Peuckert, there were only four trials of this kind in Poland from the twelfth to the eighteenth centuries.[40] B. D. Weinryb argued that there were only fifty-nine court cases of ritual murder and host desecration in Poland between the sixteenth and eighteenth centuries,[41] and J. Tazbir presumed that as a result of these trials some 200 to 300 Jews were executed.[42] The entire subject demands a much more detailed treatment based on wider source materials, and we hope this study will serve as a basis for further research.

## THE TRIALS: 1500–1650

The earliest ritual murder trial recorded in the sixteenth century took place in Rawa, a provincial capital. Jewish settlement in the town is first confirmed in 1448.[43] In 1547 two Jews from Rawa, Mojżesz and Abraham, were accused of kidnapping the son of a local tailor and crucifying him. Zygmunt I appointed the commissioners and a judge to be in charge of the investigation and the judicial proceedings.[44] S. Hubicki wrote that both of the accused perished at the stake, and the remaining Jews of Rawa 'were expelled from there for ever and until now none of them can live there'.[45] It was not until 1735 that Jews who 'resettled in the manorial properties' reappeared on the local tax rolls.[46]

---

[38] R. Po-chia Hsia, *The Myth of Ritual Murder: Jews and Magic in Reformation Germany* (New Haven, 1988).

[39] Żuchowski, *Proces*, 146; but see the estimate of eighty-five ritual murders (ibid. 143).

[40] W. E. Peuckert, 'Ritualmord', in *Handwörterbuch des deutsche Aberglaubens*, vii (Berlin, 1935), 727–32.

[41] Weinryb, *The Jews*, 152–3.

[42] J. Tazbir, *Okrucieństwo w nowożytnej Europie* (Warsaw, 1993), 57.

[43] E. Feldman, 'Do statystyki Żydów w dawnej Polsce', *Miesięcznik Żydowski*, 3 (1933), nos. 1–2, p. 133.

[44] Bersohn (ed.), *Dyplomatariusz*, no. 517.

[45] Hubicki, *Żydowskie okrucieństwa nad Najświętszym Sakramentem i dziatkami chrześcijańskimi* (Cracow, 1602), 17; P. Fijałkowski, 'Stosunki żydowsko-chrześcijańskie w województwach łęczyckim i rawskim w XVI–XVII wieku', *BŻIH* 2 (1990), 23.

[46] Biblioteka Czartoryskich w Krakowie, MS 1079, fo. 28. Trzebiński writes that around 1775 a Jewish town was established on *starosta* lands in Zamkowa Wola; W. Trzebiński, *Działalność urbanistyczna magnatów i szlachty w Polsce, xviii wieku* (Warsaw, 1962), 14.

Another early Jewish settlement was established in Kłodawa (Łęczyca province). In 1479 the Jews of Kłodawa were obligated to pay 15 florins in rent charges.[47] During August II's Saxon reign, Jews were accused of committing a ritual murder and, as a consequence, expelled from the town.[48] Father Żuchowski, referring to Syreniusz, states that under King August, Jews murdered a 6-year-old named Dunat and his 7-year-old sister, Dorota.[49] Syreniusz informs us, however, that this incident took place 'under King August in the year of 1547'.[50] There is no mention of any Kłodawa Jews from the mid-sixteenth century until almost the end of the eighteenth century. Only from the census of 1789 is it evident that Jews lived in houses built by the *Starosta*.[51]

The next ritual murder accusation to be found in the literature was made against the Jews of Kcynia (Kalisz province), where a Jewish presence was first documented in 1507.[52] In 1559 the local Jews accused of committing this crime received a letter of protection from the king.[53] No further details of this case are known, but since the 1565 census lists the existence of both a house of study and a synagogue in the town, the events do not seem to have affected the fate of the community.[54]

Other ritual murder trials took place in Podlasie, a province that was created in 1520 and incorporated into Poland in 1569.[55] In 1564 in Bielsko (before the incorporation of Podlasie), Biernat, a Jewish servant of Izaak Brodawka (a leaseholder of the profits from Bielsk and Narwa), was charged with the murder of a young girl from Narwa. Before execution, Biernat declared that the burghers had accused him because they hated the Jews, who were the lease-holders of these towns' profits. The Jews complained about the royal functionaries' actions to Zygmunt August, requesting that he grant them the same rights enjoyed by the Jews of Poland, especially in cases where they were accused of murdering Christian children. Based on the earlier privileges and on the papal statement that Jews do not use Christian blood, the king decided that the ritual murder as well as the sacrilege cases were to be heard exclusively by the king, and only during a general assembly

---

[47] *Matricularum regni Poloniae summaria*, 1 (1905), no. 1.

[48] M. Rawita-Witanowski, *Kłodawa i jej okolice pod względem historyczno-ludoznawczym* (Warsaw, 1904), 93; Fijałkowski, 'Stosunki', 26.

[49] Żuchowski, *Proces*, 92.

[50] S. Syreniusz, *Zielnik herbarzem z języka łacińskiego zowią to jest opisanie własne imion, kształtu, przyrodzenia, skutków i mocy ziół wszelakich* (Cracow, 1613), 1539.

[51] *Lustracja województw wielkopolskich i kujawskich, iii: 1789*, ed. A. Tomczak (with Z. Kędzierska) (Warsaw, 1977), 96.

[52] M. Horn, 'Najstarszy rejestr osiedli żydowskich w Polsce z 1507 roku', *BŻIH* 93 (1974), 13.

[53] A. Heppner and J. Herzberg, *Aus Vergangenheit und Gegenwart der Juden und der jüdischen Gemeinden in den Posener Landen* (Koschmin, 1904), 376.

[54] *Lustracja województw wielkopolskich i kujawskich, ii: 1564–1565*, ed. A. Tomczak (Bydgoszcz, 1963), 273.

[55] It was only in 1616 that Rososz, Kozierady, and Międzyrzec were incorporated into Podlasie. *Źródła dziejowe*, 17, pt. 2 (Warsaw, 1909), 11–12.

in the presence of the royal council. Moreover, accusers were required to support accusations with testimony from at least four Christian and three Jewish witnesses. Anyone failing to present such witnesses would forfeit his own life and possessions.[56]

In 1566 in the Podlasian town of Rososz (Rosochy), Nachim, a Jewish servant of the same leaseholder, Brodawka, was accused of ritual murder. The Jews turned to the Lithuanian deputy chancellor (*podkanclerzy litewski*), Ostaf Wołłowicz, who was also holder of the office of *starostwo* to which Rosochy belonged. Wołłowicz carried out an investigation and presented the king (who was participating in the Sejm in Lublin) with the results. A few Rosochy Jews vouched for Nachim, who was released from prison by the deputy chancellor, who sent his servant to Rosochy to interrogate the witnesses. The burghers of Rosochy testified that Nachim, when returning from Chorodyszcze, took the child on his cart to his house. The witnesses based their testimony on the account told by Lichanka, a 7-year-old Jewish girl, who allegedly declared in the presence of five men and two women that Nachim brought the child home and murdered her with the help of another Jewish man. Lichanka herself, however, said that she knew nothing about the child's murder. After the results of the abduction of the child's body were presented to the Brześć office, the deputy chancellor called all the witnesses and questioned each separately. Their testimonies were contradictory and inconsistent with their earlier statements. On 20 May 1566, during the gathering of the Sejm in Lublin, Zygmunt August declared the charges unfounded and unproved, and he acquitted Nachim and other Jews. The king reminded the assembly that testimony from four Christians and three Jews was required to prove the crime. On 23 May 1566 the king stated once again that the ritual murder accusations made against the Jews in 1564 and 1566 were groundless.[57]

The next ritual murder trial in Podlasie took place in 1577. The Jews of Brześć and Wohyń registered a complaint against Rokotowski, the *wójt* (chief officer of a group of villages) accusing them of violating the privileges given Lithuanian Jews by Zygmunt August and confirmed by Stefan Batory. The *wójt* questioned two Christian women, Maryna and Kachna, who worked as servants in Jewish houses. Maryna stated only that the Wohyń burghers said a Jew, Nachim, had murdered a child. Rokotowski asserted he was not competent to judge the case, and on 14 April 1577, after Nachim had been vouched for, Rokotowski discharged him from jail. Jan Drenicki, Rokotowski's servant, testified that on the day of the funeral he did not see the cross that was reputed to have been carved on the child's body by Nachim. Nevertheless, when the body was exhumed a day after the funeral, a small cross was seen engraved on the child's head.[58]

---

[56] *Regesty i nadpisi: Svod materialov dlja istorii evreev v Rossii*, i, ed. S. A. Bersadskij (St Petersburg, 1899), no. 536; Bałaban, 'Obvinenija', 867.

[57] *Regesty i nadpisi*, nos. 545, 546.　　　　　[58] Ibid., no. 585.

It is possible to reconstruct the ritual murder case in Świniarów, a village in Podlasie that belonged to the nobleman Stefan Pete's wife, Anna Kiszczonka. Both the verdict of the Crown tribunal in Lublin[59] and the description of the execution were preserved.[60]

On 25 March 1598, 'on the Thursday after our Easter', 4-year-old Wojciech, son of the miller Maciej Petrenia, disappeared. Gromek (Aaron) and Izaak (Hajczyk), who had supposedly taken the boy to Woźniki to the inn of Marek Sachowicz (the father of Gromek), were accused of kidnapping the child. A month later the child's body was found in the marshlands by boys looking for ducks' eggs. The leaseholder of the estate, Abraham Skowieski, imprisoned the suspected Jews and lodged a protest with the district court of Mielnik. At that time a Jew named Marek escaped, but 'he was found by 300 men at the same place where the body of the child had previously been found'. On 5 July 1598, following the king's order, the suspected Jews were brought to Lublin. For the first hearings, scheduled for 6 July, 'many Jewish elders came (who knows how quickly) from Cracow, and Lwów, Poznań [bringing] with [them] letters of intercession from the great lords and giving away large gifts'. The accused claimed before the Crown tribunal that Skowieski 'owes 1,000 zloty to Marek and wants to threaten him to get the money back'. One of the accused testified that the miller owed Marek 100 zloty and 'this is why he [together] with the lord goaded each other on against Marek'. Marek himself argued, however, that 'the nobleman did not owe him anything'. The Jews were tortured and 'at first denied [the accusations] but were shaved and pulled harder'. They later gave extensive testimonies, which they confirmed before the tribunal on 10 July.

Joachim, a Jew from Międzyrzecz, was the first one to testify. He said:

There is a Jewish custom that poor Jews are sent to the wealthier ones to receive food. I was sent to Marek in Woźniki, and, having spent much time there, I had permission from Marek to go to the storage and take any food I needed. On Thursday before Easter, when I went to the storage shed to get some bread, I saw there, under the bed on which the Jewish children used to sleep, a new red pot covered by a white cloth. Thinking that it contained honey, I wanted to take some for my bread. But when I tried to put my finger in, I saw that it was not honey but something different, something red. When I left the storage and entered the room, I saw Marek's wife, a Jewess, who was there alone. I asked her what was in the pot under the bed. She told me that it was blood of a Christian child, but not to tell anyone.

[59] The verdict was published by S. Śleszkowski, *Odkrycie zdrad, złośliwych ceremonii, tajemnych rad, praktyk szkodliwych Rzeczypospolitej i strasżliwych zamysłów żydowskich* (Brunsbergae, 1621), 84–7; Żuchowski, *Ogłos*, 175–81; in the German translation, in S. Salmonowicz, 'Niemiecki erudyta barokowy W. E. Tenzel a wyrok Trybunału Koronnego z 1598 roku: Przyczynek do dziejów procesów o tak zwane mordy rytualne w dawnej Polsce', *Odrodzenie i Reformacja w Polsce*, 33 (1988), 268–72.

[60] S. Miczyński, *Zwierciadło korony Polskiej, urazy ciężkie i utrapienie wielkie* (Cracow, 1662), 14–16; Żuchowski, *Ogłos*, 183. K. Bartoszewski, *Antysemityzm w literaturze polskiej, XV–XVII wieku* (Warsaw, 1914), 52–4, takes the description of the trial and the verdict from S. Hubicki.

Continuing his testimony, Joachim also said that Nastaszka,

who has her house near the inn in which Marek lives, said that just before Jewish Easter, while taking beer from the Jewish cellar for the inn, she saw the murdered child under the barrels.

He also testified that he had heard that 'Jews use Christian blood during Easter'.[61]

Gromek testified that Zalman, one of the elders of Międzyrzecz, asked him before the Jewish Easter for 'a Christian child'. Together with Izaak, Gromek kidnapped the boy and brought him to his father's inn in Woźniki. He continued: 'We hid him in the cellar for a few weeks, and then Izaak and Zalman of Międzyrzecz (who by that time had received the information) slaughtered him and then they hired Nastaszka to take away the child['s body]'.[62] Izaak claimed that, having kidnapped and taken the boy to Woźniki, Moszko (a Jew from Międzyrzecz) and Zalman returned from Międzyrzecz. Together they all killed the boy, and took away most of the 'drawn' blood. They left the remains for Izaak, who said that his wife 'put it into unleavened dough'. Supposedly, the Jews also poured blood into wine. Finally, Nastaszka, who had not been tortured, admitted that together with the Jewish woman she 'took the body of the murdered child to the swamps'.[63]

After torture, Gromek expressed a desire to convert, but the tribunal's deputies told him that, even if he was baptized, 'you have to give your throat' (i.e. he would be executed). At that point Gromek said, 'Then I prefer to die as a Jew.'[64] On 11 July the tribunal sentenced the accused to death by quartering, and the execution was carried out the same day in front of the Lublin synagogue.[65] Bernard Maciejowski, bishop of Łuck, ordered that the child's body be buried in Litewniki; later, as bishop of Cracow, he had it moved to a Jesuit church in Lublin. Maciejowski also undertook preparations for the boy's canonization in Rome.[66]

A Jewish presence in Łęczyca was first documented as early as the middle of the fifteenth century. By 1565 Jews owned sixteen private houses, three tenements, and a house of study.[67] P. Mojecki wrote that in 1569, having been tor-

---

[61] Żuchowski, *Ogłos*, 178, 181–2.          [62] Ibid. 179.

[63] Ibid. 179–80.          [64] Bartoszewski, *Antysemityzm*, 55.

[65] Żuchowski, *Ogłos*, 183–4: Tak Marka, włożywszy mu na głowę czerwoną magierkę z piórkiem, na saniach wywieziono za miasto i poćwiertowawszy żywo, ćwierci skoblami dla zdjęcia kat poprzybijał. Syn Marków, lubo się w więzieniu na spodnich obwiesił, z żoną Markową i Hajczykiem zięciem także ćwiertowano. Mojżesz Żydek jako niewinny, ochrzczony wolny został, Mojżesza i Zelmana rabinów dostać nie możono' ('So, Marek was made to wear a red hat with a feather, and was taken outside the city by sleigh and quartered alive. The hangman nailed the pieces with staples for removing the remains. Marek's son hanged himself in prison by his trousers. Marek's wife and Isaak (Hajczyk), his son-in-law, were also quartered. A Jew, Mojżesz, was judged not guilty, baptized, and discharged. The rabbis Mojżesz and Zalman could not be seized').

[66] Miczyński, *Zwierciadło*, 16–17.

[67] *Lustracja województw wielkopolskich i kujawskich*, ii: *1564–1565*, 273.

tured, Wawrzyniec from Bobrowa admitted to selling Jan, the 2-year-old son of Małgorzata Kozanina, who lived in the suburbs of Piotrków (Sieradz province), to a Jew from Łęczyca. Jews were believed to have murdered the boy. The author refers to Piotrków's *wójt* registers, and adds that the king was informed about the incident by Ludwik Decjusz, the governor of Cracow and *wójt* of Piotrków.[68]

On 5 July 1576 Stefan Batory issued an edict to counter the accusation that Jews had murdered a son of the nobleman Studzieński of the Gostynin lands (Rawa province). The king stated that the charges against the Jews accusing them of killing children and of host desecration were groundless, and he warned everyone against making such accusations.[69] P. Fiałkowski argues that this statement relates to the Jews of Gąbin, the only Jewish settlement in this region in the second half of the sixteenth century. It should be pointed out that in 1595 the Jews of Gostynin were also accused of murdering a child. Mojecki writes that two Jews died during torture.[70]

At the end of the sixteenth century, there was a series of ritual murder charges. According to Żuchowski, who refers to Mojecki, S. Hubicki, and Syreniusz, in 1589 the Jews of Tarnów were charged with a ritual murder, but the case was 'hushed up with gold'. The Jews also supposedly stole a child in Zgłobice near the river Dunajec.[71] Syreniusz relates that the incident took place around 1598.[72] A Jewish presence in Tarnów is mentioned for the first time as early as 1445, and in 1577 the Jews paid only 6 zloty per capita in taxes,[73] this low rate of taxation showing that there could not have been a large concentration of Jews there.

Szydłów (in the province of Sandomierz) was another town with a significant population of Jews. The existence of a Jewish cemetery is documented as early as 1470. A census of 1564 lists fourteen Jewish householders (*gospodarze*).[74] According to Żuchowski, in 1590 in Olszowa Wola, the Jews of Szydłów 'also murdered a child. The estate owner was so greedy for money that he only demanded that the Jews give compensation for his subject.'[75] Żuchowski, quoting P. Pruszcz, wrote that the same year in Kurozwęki 'a child killed by the Jews was found buried in the local priests' porch'. From Pruszcz's work, however, it seems that it was the child from Olszowa Wola that was buried in Kurozwęki.[76] In 1597

---

[68] P. Mojecki, *Żydowskie okrucieństwa, mordy i zabobony* (Cracow, 1598), ch. 6.

[69] Bersohn (ed.), *Dyplomatariusz*, no. 146; Fijałkowski, 'Stosunki', 25.

[70] Mojecki, *Żydowskie okrucieństwa*, ch. 6: 'A przedsię w tak oczywistych dowodach i wyznaniu tej bezecnej niewiasty przeklęci Żydowie złotemi perswazyjami inaczej to ludziom wywiedli, że oprócz dwu, co no mękach pozdychali, inni wszyscy bez karania zostawieni.'

[71] Żuchowski, *Proces*, 92; also Mojecki, *Żydowskie okrucieństwa*, ch. 6.

[72] Syreniusz, *Zielnik*, 1539.

[73] Z. Guldon, 'Żydzi wśród chrześcijan w miastach małopolskich w XVI–XVIII wieku', *Nasza Przeszłość*, 78 (1992), 194, 214.

[74] Guldon and Krzystanek, *Ludność żydowska*, 18–19.

[75] Żuchowski, *Proces*, 93; Mojecki, *Żydowskie okrucieństwa*, ch. 6.

[76] Żuchowski, *Proces*, 93; P. H. Pruszcz, *Forteca monarchów i całego Królestwa Polskiego duchowna* (Cracow, 1662), 183.

near Szydłów: 'they [the Jews] stifled the first crime with the Judas sack, and again killed a child, leaving it after untold torment, with pierced eyelids, throat, veins, joints, under the nails, and all other limbs. They [the Jews] sprinkled their synagogue with this new blood and threw away the little body. This account was given by the Jewish elders under torture'.[77]

The earliest ritual murder trial in Ruthenia took place in Sawiń, a small town owned by the bishop of Chełm in 1595. The Cracow community provided financial assistance for this trial, but there is no information about the court proceedings.[78]

In 1569 the town of Piotrków banned Jewish settlement. In 1533 a few of the Piotrków Jews had been executed for murdering a child from the village of Uszczyn. After describing the events of 1590, however, Pruszcz wrote: 'A few years later in Piotrków it [so] happened that the blood of an innocent infant caused a few Jews to be executed and expelled from the homesteads at the foot of the castle. But ignoring the clear edict, the Jews again erect their domiciles there.'[79] By 1626 in Piotrków there was a Jewish street within the city walls.[80]

There were also a number of ritual murder trials at the beginning of the seventeenth century. Syreniusz writes that on 17 May 1601 some Jews captured a 12-year-old girl from the village of Czechry near Warka (Mazovia province), and they 'slaughtered [her and] drew [her] blood'.[81] In 1621 S. Śleszkowski wrote that in Mława (in Płock province) 'eight years ago a Jew killed a Christian infant and was executed because of it'.[82]

In 1606 Jews of Kazimierz Dolny (Lublin province) allegedly bought 2-year-old Wojciech Ozerka from his stepfather in Podgórze (Chełm region). They 'tortured him to death' and then, having 'cut off his little arm and [his] little leg, they dropped him into the waters under the Markuszów castle'.[83] Syreniusz writes that a year later in Zwoleń (Sandomierz province), 'a child of a poor Christian woman was playing with Jewish children. [T]he Jews cut off his flesh in three places and gave him two coins so he would not cry.'[84]

The same source relates that in Staszów in 1610 or 1611 Jews murdered a child, but the local parish priest 'did not have enough power' to punish the guilty.[85] Żuchowski asserted that in 1610 in Staszów,

[77] Żuchowski, *Proces*, 93; Mojecki, *Żydowskie okrucieństwa*, ch. 6.

[78] M. Bałaban, *Historia Żydów w Krakowie i na Kazimierzu, 1304–1868*, 2nd edn., i (Cracow, 1931), 357; M. Bałaban, *Żydowskie miasto w Lublinie* (Lublin, 1991), 48; H. Węgrzynek, 'Ludność żydowska wobec oskarżeń o popełnianie przestępstw o charakterze rytualnym', *Kwartalnik Historyczny*, 101 (1994), 20–1.

[79] Pruszcz, *Forteca*, 183–4, and Żuchowski, *Proces*, 93; also M. Feinkind, *Dzieje Żydów w Piotrkowie Trybunalskim i okolicy od czasów najdawniejszych do chwili obecnej* (Piotrków, 1930), 4; *Piotrkov Trybunalski vehaseviva: Sefer zikaron* (Tel Aviv, 1965), 39.

[80] Feinkind, *Dzieje*, 7.                          [81] Syreniusz, *Zielnik*, 1539.

[82] Śleszkowski, *Odkrycie zdrad*, 96.    [83] Syreniusz, *Zielnik*, 1539; Miczyński, *Zwierciadło*, 17.

[84] Syreniusz, *Zielnik*, 1539.                          [85] Ibid.

A Jew named Szmul kidnapped a male infant playing in the sand and gave him to the Szydłów Jews to be tortured. While they were squeezing out his blood, they were caught in the act by municipal officials. These Jews from Staszów and Szydłów were quartered on the orders of Andrzej Tęczyński, the owner of Staszów. He also ordered that Szmul's daughters be baptized and that the Jews' property be sold to finance the building of a church tower.[86]

The remaining Jews were expelled from the town. The boy's body was buried in St Jacek's chapel in the local church. The inscription says the boy was a son of Jan Kowal and Zuzanna Nierychłowska, and confirms that 'Iudei nominis christiani hostes pellantur Staszovia',[87] that is, that the Jews had been expelled. It was Łukasz Opaliński (d. 1704) who permitted Jews to settle in Staszów once again.[88]

Severe conflicts between Christian and Jewish populations took place in Sochaczew (Rawa province). Between 1426 and 1455 there is mention of a Jewish presence in the region of Sochaczew. In Sochaczew itself, in 1463 a Jewish doctor, Feliks, is mentioned.[89] In 1556 a local Jew, Bieniasz, allegedly convinced Dorota Łazęcka, a maid, to provide him with a host. She was to steal it either from the church in Kozłów or from the Dominicans in Sochaczew. At that time the Archbishop of Gniezno, Mikołaj Dzierzgowski, and the papal nuncio Alojzy Lippomano were in nearby Łowicz. They 'saw to it that such an act would get the punishment it deserves'. By virtue of the verdict of 1557, Dorota and Bieniasz, as well as three other Jews, perished at the stake. Even the Protestants refer to this case in an anonymous document, *O sochaczewskim wymęczonym a wypalonym na Żydzie Bogu i o fałszywych jego cudach* (About Sochaczew's God, tortured and burned by a Jew, and about his false miracles). The document is ascribed to Andrzej Trzecieski or Eustachy Trepka. It was not concerned with defending Jews but with negating the presence of Christ's flesh and blood in the host. In connection with the Sochaczew events in 1557, Zygmunt August ordered that the ritual murder and host desecration cases be heard by the Sejm court.[90]

This was not the first time Jews were charged with desecration of the host. J. Długosz relates that in 1399 a Christian woman stole hosts from the Dominican church in Poznań and sold them to the Jews. After their miraculous retrieval, the bishop of Poznań ordered that a chapel be built in the place where they were found; some time later, Władysław Jagiełło founded a Carmelite cloister and a Corpus Christi church there. The emergence of legends about miraculous hosts and accusations of desecration against the Jews were linked with the development of the cult

[86] Żuchowski, *Proces*, 94–5; Miczyński, *Zwierciadło*, 18.

[87] W. Siek, *Opis historyczny parafii i miasta Staszów* (Staszów, 1990), 23.

[88] Guldon and Krzystanek, *Ludność żydowska*, 48.

[89] Ringelblum, *Żydzi w Warszawie*, i (Warsaw, 1932), 147–8; P. Fijałkowski, 'Żydzi sochaczewscy', *BŻIH* nos. 3–4 (1985), 21.

[90] Fijałkowski, 'Żydzi sochaczewscy', 22–3; J. Tazbir, 'Proces Doroty Łazęckiej', in his *Szlaki kultury polskiej* (Warsaw, 1986), 174–85; H. Węgrzynek, 'Dzieje poznańskiej legendy o profanacji hostii do połowy, XVII wieku', in *Legenda Bożego Ciała: Kronika Miasta Poznania*, 3–4 (1992), 52.

of the Eucharist and establishment of the Corpus Christi holiday in 1264. Jews were accused of host desecration as early as the thirteenth century (in Belitz near Berlin in 1243, as well as in Paris in 1290).[91] There is no indication, however, that it was Jews who perpetrated this act in 1399 in Poznań. Nor is there any confirmation in the town's records or in Boniface IX's papal edicts of 1401 and 1403, Innocent VII's of 1406, or Władysław Jagiełło's charter for the Corpus Christi church in 1406. Only Długosz's chronicle and a sermon given in 1491 by Michał of Janowiec, a monk from Trzemeszno, contain such information about Jews. The alleged host desecration in Poznań in 1399 was made widely known by Tomasz Treter, whose book *Sacratissimi Corporis Christi historia et miracula* (1609) was republished several times in the Latin original as well as in Polish and German translations.[92] In the sixteenth century Jews were also accused of host desecration in Cracow, Kalisz, Kowal, Skierbieszów, Pilica, Oświęcim, Pułtusk, and Bochnia. In 1558 a Protestant pastor from Wschowa was accused of selling a host to the Jews.[93]

On 12 July 1617 the Jews of Sochaczew allegedly bought the son of a woman named Małgorzata for 3½ groszy.[94] They drew the boy's blood and then drowned him in the river Bzura. From the entry in the parish records of the Dominican church, it appears that some of the Jews managed to escape but some were sentenced to death. The boy's mother perished at the stake.[95] In 1877, during restoration of the altar in the church, a small pine coffin was discovered in the mensa of the St Jacek altar. It contained the child's remains along with a note written on parchment that said that these were the remains of Jakub, who was murdered by the Jews.[96] Perhaps these were the events Żuchowski referred to when he wrote that the Jews of Sochaczew 'killed more children than there are houses there. It is a rare year in the past few decades when no children are murdered by them.'[97]

In 1617 Jews were charged with the murder of a child from the village of Siedlcza in the region of Łuków (Lublin province). The Crown tribunal in Lublin sentenced the accused Jew to death. Żuchowski wrote: 'The father of the child suffered more grief [than] justice. If it had not been for the father himself, who noticed that they wanted to substitute a dead Jew for a living one, there would have been a miscarriage of justice. And [thus] he [the Jew] was truly beheaded the second time.'[98]

---

[91] A. Wojtkowski, 'O cudzie trzech hostii i zapomnianym patronie miasta Poznania', *Kronika Miasta Poznania* (1936), 464–89; T. M. Trajdos, 'Legenda Bożego Ciała u poznańskich karmelitów i działalność kultowa klasztoru w I połowie xv wieku', in *Legenda*, 3–4 (1992), 28–9; Węgrzynek, 'Dzieje', 45–7; H. Węgrzynek, 'Oskarżenia przeciw Żydom o morderstwa rytualne i profanowanie hostii w Europie do końca xiv wieku', *BŻIH* (1993), 15–22.

[92] T. Chrzanowski, *Działalność artystyczna Tomasza Tretera* (Warsaw, 1984), 198–200.

[93] Guldon and Kowalski, 'Between Tolerance and Abomination', 175.

[94] 30 groszy = 1 zloty.

[95] L. V. Jaques, 'Sochaczew', in *Ziarno*, 16 (1902), 307; Fijałkowski, 'Żydzi sochaczewscy', 25–6.

[96] Jaques, 'Sochaczew', 307.          [97] S. Żuchowski, *Proces*, 95.

[98] Ibid.; Śleszkowski, *Odkrycie zdrad*, 96.

The first ritual murder case in Podolia took place in 1623. Salomon of Dunajgród lodged a complaint against Elżbieta Kalinowska and her son Marcin, who imprisoned in their Husiatyń castle three Jewish leaseholders: Nisan, Samech, and Marek, and accused them of murdering Christian children. The relatives of the accused Jews requested that the case be heard by the district court of Kamieniec. The Kalinowskis, however, decided to have the case heard in their own court without any judicial proceedings (*absque omni figura iudicii*). The accused Jews were tortured, and although they maintained their innocence, all were sentenced to death and perished at the stake.[99]

In 1626 three Jews of Brzeziny (Łęczyca province) were charged with the murder of Wojciech. The case was heard by the Crown tribunal in Piotrków. Adam Janczewski and Zygmunt Stefan Koniecpolski were sent by the tribunal to hold hearings in Brzeziny. Throughout the interrogation two of the Jews maintained their innocence, and 'during torture they seemed to be in a [kind of] dead sleep'. The third Jew, however, who 'did not leave the inn with them but was preparing fish for them', blamed the boy's murder on the other two. In the course of the interrogation, it was a woman's testimony that was most damning. She testified that she saw Białas of Stryków, the third accused Jew, carrying the body of the murdered boy and then 'throw it through the fence, falling in front of a dog'. The tribunal sentenced the two accused Jews to death at the stake. Białas was to be delivered by Marian Strykowski, the owner of the town of Stryków. The latter 'had to swear that he was not able to deliver him', and that he had been unable to find him.[100]

According to Żuchowski, in 1628 the Jews of Sandomierz were charged with 'kidnapping the child of a pharmacist, drawing his blood and giving his mutilated body to a dog. Afraid that the dog would regurgitate [the body], they gave it poison, which only provoked vomiting, and the signs of the slain child were then evident.'[101] In 1639 in the same town there were anti-Jewish riots, along with looting of the houses in the Jewish quarter.[102]

The ritual murder trials in Cracow, where the Jewish settlement began between 1173 and 1177, require broader treatment. In 1495 Jews were forced to leave Cracow and move to nearby Kazimierz.[103] Długosz relates that in 1407 a priest named Budek accused Jews of murdering a Christian child. The mob attacked the Jewish houses, robbing them of valuables. The king called the councillors to account, and the objects stolen during the riot were taken away from the

---

[99] M. Bałaban, *Żydzi lwowscy na przełomie XVI i XVII wieku* (Lwów, 1906), 506–7; W. Łoziński, *Prawem i lewem*, ii (Lwów, 1904), 63–4.

[100] Biblioteka Kórnicka Polskiej Akademii Nauk, MS 201, fos. 271–2.

[101] Żuchowski, *Proces*, 95.

[102] Z. Guldon and K. Krzystanek, 'Żydzi i Szkoci w Sandomierzu w XVI–XVIII wieku', *Studia Historyczne*, 4 (1988), 531–3.

[103] R. Grodecki, *Polska Piastowska* (Warsaw, 1969), 619–21; S. Kutrzeba, 'Ludność i majątek Kazimierza w końcu XIV stulecia', *Rocznik Krakowski*, 3 (1900), 190.

burghers and gathered in the district treasury. The councillors then took it upon themselves to identify the instigators of the riot, in which most of the artisans had participated. The people asked the municipal council to content itself with the three or four who had already been imprisoned and not to call the whole community to account. The judicial proceedings continued through 1409, and it is not known how the trial ended.[104] This was more a pogrom than a ritual murder trial. In 1508 another Jew perished at the stake for stealing and desecrating a host.[105]

In 1912 M. Bałaban wrote that as the result of an accusation of ritual murder made in Cracow in 1541 or 1542, R. Moses Fiszel perished at the stake.[106] This version has become the accepted one among scholars: J. Tazbir wrote that in 1541 or 1542 R. 'Finkel' (*sic*) perished, and ten years later Izrael Fiszel did so as well.[107] In the second edition of his work (1931), Bałaban wrote that Fiszel was imprisoned in connection with the case against Weiglowa, a woman who perished at the stake in 1539 for converting to Judaism.[108] Bałaban concluded: 'I cannot determine the direct reason for the death of Moses Fiszel. The only thing which is certain is that in 1542 he was no longer alive.'[109] This statement is incorrect, since on 28 May 1543 Fiszel was still litigating a case with Jan Święcicki before the episcopal court.[110]

The first ritual murder trial in Cracow took place in 1631, and resulted in the scholar Anszer Anczel (Anzelm) perishing at the stake.[111] In 1635 Piotr Jurkiewicz, who was accused of stealing silver objects from a church in Cracow, stated that he had sold a host to a Jewish tailor, Jakub Grześlik. *Wojewoda* Jan Tęczyński ordered the Jewish community to deliver the man accused by Jurkiewicz. The *kahal* claimed that the accused had escaped, and after the municipality carried out its own investigation, another Jew who was suspected of committing this criminal act was arrested. Eventually Jurkiewicz was sentenced to death at the stake. Grześlik was sentenced *in absentia* to the same punishment. In his confession Jurkiewicz admitted that he had 'accused him [the Jew], innocently expecting [him] to be discharged'. The authorities, however, still demanded that the suspect Grześlik be handed over. This incident was one of the reasons for the riot in 1637 when seven Jews were killed.[112]

---

[104] Bałaban, *Historia Żydów w Krakowie*, 33–5; J. Ptaśnik, 'Żydzi w Polsce wieków średnich', *Przegląd Warszawski*, 28 (1922), 228–9.

[105] Bałaban, *Historia Żydów w Krakowie*, 100.     [106] Ibid., 1st edn., i (Cracow, 1912), 400, 409.

[107] J. Tazbir, 'Mieszczański pitaval polskiej reformacji', in *Czas, przestrzeń, praca w dawnych miastach* (Warsaw, 1991), 278; also *Polski słownik biograficzny*, vii (Cracow, 1948–58), 20, Weinryb, *The Jews*, 152.

[108] See also J. Tazbir, 'Sprawa Wajglowej w świetle źródeł archiwalnych', in *Historia i współczesność* (Warsaw, 1987), 49–58; W. Urban, *Dwa szkice z dziejów reformacji* (Kielce, 1991), 25–9.

[109] Bałaban, *Historia Żydów w Krakowie*, 2nd edn., i. 128, 130.

[110] *Archiwum Kurii Metropolitalnej w Krakowie*, Acta episcopalia, 20, fo. 172ᵛ.

[111] Bałaban, *Historia Żydów w Krakowie*, 2nd edn., i. 180.

[112] Ibid. 210; compare the recently discovered trial in Ostrowiec, a small town in Sandomierz province. In 1631 two Christians stole twelve hosts and two silver plates from the local church. One thief was caught (the other managed to escape) and he identified a Jew, and a widow in whose house a

In Lublin in 1550 there were 512 Jews living in forty-two houses.[113] Żuchowski states that in 1593 in Lublin, the Jews 'killed Jan of Krasnostawice, a student. A court case began in the district court of Lublin. The Jews appealed *pro conventione generali* (to the Sejm), by which they would give the Lublin boarding school 70 pounds of meat a day.'[114]

Two ritual murder cases were heard by the Crown tribunal in Lublin in 1636. In the first one the Jews were charged with the murder of Maciej, whose mother was a Lublin butcher. The incident supposedly took place before Passover. Bieniasz, son of Pieszak, and Lachman were indicted for the crime. The hearings before the *wójt* court in Lublin lasted from 27 to 30 May 1636. Bieniasz was the first to testify. Even under torture (which included stretching and scorching his body three times), Bieniasz did not confess to killing the child; he stated that Jews do not need Christian blood. The charges against Bieniasz were based mainly on testimony given by Józef Koszut, who was occasionally employed by Bieniasz. Koszut claimed that on that disastrous Sabbath he did not light the candles and that Bieniasz did it himself. Bieniasz, however, defended himself by saying that he lit the candle after the Sabbath. Koszut also testified that on Saturday night Bieniasz talked with other Jews and said to them: 'zu Wasser' (to the water). It is known from another source that the child's body was indeed found in the water. Bieniasz allegedly ordered Józef to leave town, promising to reward him for keeping the secret. Bieniasz did not confirm this. The second accused, Lachman, who leased mills, also maintained his innocence. Bieniasz's wife, Bloma, left town and could not be interrogated, and the testimony of Bieniasz's sister, Fregella, widow of Jakub Cegielnik, did not shed any light on the case. Jan Korpiska, who worked in Jewish butchers' shops, testified that two *nożowniczkowie* (journeymen in a knife-makers' guild) saw Koszut on Sunday morning 'going to the water'.[115] The trial ended successfully for the Jews: 'the tribunal only made them swear [their innocence] and left vindication to God Himself'.[116]

The second trial before the Crown tribunal in Lublin began on 7 August 1636. The accuser lodged a charge against the elders and all of the Lublin *kahal*. The main accused were Marek Markowicz (Mordechaj ben Meir), a barber from Lublin, Jan Smyth, a German Lutheran doctor, and Lewek and Moszko, Marek's servants. They were accused of having used force in performing an operation on Paweł, a lay brother of the Carmelites. The tribunal ordered torture at the *wójt* court. During the interrogation on 11 August 1636, Marek said that on several

monstrance cloth was found, as the people who had commissioned them to do the deed. Both the thief and the widow were burned at the stake; the Jew was acquitted. Archiwum Kurii Metropolitalnej w Krakowie, Acta visitationis capitularis 44, p. 159. (My thanks to W. Kowalski for supplying this information.)

[113] Bałaban, *Historia Żydów w Krakowie*, 2nd edn., 420.     [114] Żuchowski, *Proces*, 93.

[115] AP Lublin, Akta miasta Lublina, 140, fos. 394–413ᵛ. A significant part of these testimonies in German translation was included by Bałaban, 'Hugo Grotius', 92–103.

[116] Żuchowski, *Proces*, 96.

occasions Paweł asked him to operate and remove one of his testicles. The operation was eventually carried out by the German doctor in Marek's house. In the course of the operation, Paweł lost a few drops of blood.[117] Despite this testimony, the tribunal decided that Christian blood was the main purpose of the operation and sentenced Marek to death by quartering. Attempts to seize the other accused were not successful.[118]

This trial had international repercussions. On 19 September 1636 Jerzy Słupecki, a Protestant, wrote a letter to Hugo Grotius. In Grotius' reply, dated 12 December 1636, he stated that accusations that Jews used Christian blood were wrong, and he declared himself against testimony gained through torture.[119]

Thanks to extensive documentation, it is possible to reconstruct the 1639 trial proceedings for the Łęczyca Jews.[120] On 3 May 1639 subjects from the village of Oryszowice (today, Orszewice), which belonged to the Łęczyca chapter, found the body of a boy. The following day they took it to the municipal offices in Łęczyca. It was later identified as the body of the nearly 2-year-old Franciszek, son of Maciej Michałkowicz of Komaszyce, a village owned by Katarzyna Karsznicka. Post-mortem examination of the body by Andrzej Siemsiecki, a barber-surgeon from Łęczyca, revealed several wounds inflicted by *instrumentis tenuibus et subtilibus*. M. Michałkowicz declared that his son had disappeared on the Wednesday before Easter (20 April 1639). Tomasz Kokoszka was accused of kidnapping the boy and selling him to the Jews in Łęczyca. The Jews endeavoured to have the case transferred to the royal court, but the district court did not give its permission. Eventually, the case was heard by the Crown tribunal in Lublin.

The Crown tribunal ordered K. Karsznicka and the *starosta* of Łęczyca to bring Tomasz and the Jews imprisoned in the district prison before the court. The *starosta*, however, did not bring the Jews to the next session of the tribunal on 11 August 1639, and was therefore sentenced to a fine of 100 grzywny,[121] which he had to pay under penalty of banishment. The tribunal decided that the *starosta* should bring them before the court within two weeks.

On 25 August 1639 Lazar Przemyski (Lejzer Rusnak) and a beadle, Meir of Łęczyca, as well as Lazar of Sobota and Tomasz Kokoszka came before the court.

---

[117] For more detailed testimonies given under torture, see AP Lublin, Akta miasta Lublina, 140, fos. 418ᵛ–422; German trans. in Bałaban, 'Hugo Grotius', 103–8: Marek 'pytany wiele krwi wyszło natenczas, gdy doktor tę robotę odprawił, odpowiedział, iż trzy tylko krople wyszły na gacie i samże sobie trzymał gacie i one zawiązał' ('When asked whether much blood had come out when the doctor finished his job, Marek answered that only three drops fell on the trousers and that he [the one who had been operated on] himself had held his trousers and he [also] tied them').
[118] Processus causae inter instigatorem iudicii tribunalis regni et perfidum Marcum Iudaeum in eodem tribunali regni Lublini feria 5 ante festum sancti Laurentii martyris proxima anno currenti 1636 agitatae decretumque in ea contra eundem perfidum Marcum Iudaeum latum (Cracow, 1636).
[119] S. Kot, *Hugo Grotius a Polska: W trzydziestolecie dzieła 'O prawie wojny i pokoju'* (Cracow, 1926), 46; Bałaban, 'Hugo Grotius', 110–12.    [120] Fijałkowski, 'Stosunki', 27–8.
[121] 100 grzywny = 160 zloty.

The tribunal sentenced Kokoszka to torture and sent him to the *wójt* court in Lublin.[122] The Jews were to be gaoled in the municipal gaol and held incommunicado; they were also not allowed to receive any food from the outside.[123] Thanks to a recently discovered official record from the Lublin book of malefactors, we now know in detail the testimony given by Kokoszka before the *wójt* court. On 29 August he confessed before being tortured that he had abducted the child in Komaszyce and taken it to Łęczyca, where he gave him to two Jews, Meir of Łęczyca and Lazar of Sobota. The next day he retrieved the child's body and brought it to the forest near Komaszyce. He also confessed under torture that he had previously kidnapped two other children and sold them to the Jews in Koło and Kutno. The following day, under further torture, he confirmed his earlier testimony.[124] On 1 September Kokoszka confirmed everything before the tribunal and was sentenced to death by quartering. The court decided that both Jews should also be tortured.[125] Kokoszka, who was executed on 2 September, again confirmed his testimony before execution, according to an account given by two assessors from Lublin.[126]

On 2 September the *wójt* court began interrogating Lazar of Sobota, who stated that he lived in Sobota and was not running away from Łęczyca but was returning home. He maintained that he had not participated in murdering the boy and denied that Jews used Christian blood. Lazar also confirmed the testimony previously given by Meir, who had been questioned and tortured. The following day neither Lazar nor Meir pleaded guilty, even though they were tortured continuously.[127] On 6 September Lazar made out his will, in which he stated that the leaseholder of Sobota, Adam Szypowski, had taken several formally signed documents from him that were for varying sums of money as well as other domestic implements. The total amounted to 2,500 zloty. All of these Lazar bequeathed to his wife and children, urging them to recover it from Szypowski.[128] After interrogation and torture, both Jews were sentenced by the tribunal to death by quartering. The third accused, Lazar Przemyski, was sentenced to torture by the tribunal.[129] Despite this, on 7 September Przemyski still maintained his inno-

---

[122] Żuchowski, *Ogłos*, 184–93.　　　　　　　　　　　　[123] Ibid. 193.

[124] AP Lublin, Akta miasta Lublina, 141, fos. 65ᵛ–80ᵛ.

[125] Żuchowski, *Ogłos*, 193–5.　　　　　　　　　　　　[126] Ibid. 196–7.

[127] Meir testified that 'nigdy żydzi nie mordują dzieci chrześcijańskich i nie potrzebują tego i nie widziałem tego dziada (Kokoszki), co powiedział, żeśmy u niego kupili dziecię i nie dałem mu żadnego szeląga za to dziecię' ('Jews never murder Christian children and they do not need to do so. I also did not see this vagabond, Kokoszka, who said that we had bought a child from him. I did not give him any money for the child'). But Lazar, 'pytany jeśli nie wie o dziecięciu i kto je zabił, odpowiedział, że to ten Tomasz płół na mnie i nie wiem ni o czym nic i nie winienem. Pytany kto zamordował to dziecię i na co Żydzi zażywają krwie chrześcijańskiej, odpowiedział że ja nie wiem o tym zabiciu dziecięcia i nie zażywają tej krwie i nie wiem jeżeli kto mordował to dziecię' ('asked whether he knew about the child and who killed it, answered that Tomasz had told lies about him, and that he himself knew nothing and was not guilty') (AP Lublin, 141, fos. 74ᵛ–75, 76ᵛ).

[128] Ibid. fos. 77ᵛ–78.　　　　　　　　　　　　[129] Żuchowski, *Ogłos*, 199.

cence, and the court decided to postpone further torture until 9 September.[130]

On 9 September the Crown tribunal brought in the final verdict. It considered Kokoszka's testimony, which had accused only the two Jews already sentenced to death. In addition, the tribunal took into account the testimony of three other Jews in the court, and decided that both Lazar Przemyski and another defendant, Izaak Samuelowicz, would be judged not guilty of the crime if they swore to their innocence. This was done by each of them separately, in the presence of three Christian and three Jewish witnesses in the Lublin town hall. The other Jews were required to do the same before the authorities of the district office of Łęczyca.[131]

Załuski wrote that the Jews of Łęczyca were charged with ritual murder in 1606, and added that in 1648, Łęczyca Jews murdered a child whom they had previously bought from a beggar. For committing this crime, they perished at the stake.[132] In both cases the remarks most probably referred to the trial of 1639 (discussed above).[133]

The existence of a Jewish community in Przemyśl is attested to as early as the first half of the eleventh century.[134] In 1630 the Jews of Przemyśl were accused of host desecration, and the municipal authorities and the district court carried out an investigation. On 9 May the court crier handed the king's mandate to the *wójt*, ordering the release of the imprisoned Jews. On the same day the king commissioned Jakub Maksymilian Fredro, a prominent nobleman and 'carver esquire' to the royal court, to carry on the investigation. On 18 June 1630 the king ordered the Jewish elders to bring the accused before the *wojewoda* court, adding that in future, cases of this kind should be examined neither by the district nor by the municipal courts.[135]

Several years later, in 1646, a ritual murder trial took place in Przemyśl. On 16 April the Greek Catholic clergy accused Jews of murdering Orcyna, a daughter of Sienko Klimowiat, *wójt* of Bircz Stara. Following the charge by Andrzej Bierecki, the case was heard in the district court of Przemyśl, and subsequently by the Crown tribunal in Lublin. The king's commissioners ordered the case to be transferred to

---

[130] Przemyski: 'Pytany jakim sposobem to dziecię zginęło, które zamordowali Żydzi, fassus, że ja nie wiem, bom nie był przy tym. Pytany na co zażywają Żydzi krwie chrześcijańskiej, fassus, że jak żywo o tym nie wiem, żeby mieli Żydzi zażywać krwie chrześcijańskiej ('Asked how the child that the Jews had murdered died, he said that he did not know because he had not been there. When he was asked the purpose for which Jews use Christian blood, he said that he did not know about Jews using Christian blood') Later on he said, 'Pytany jakim sposobem ten rabin, co tu siedzi, mordował dziecię, czy puszczadłem czy puginalikiem jakim, odpowiedział, że jeśli to ja wiem, Boże karz mnie i żonę moję i wszytko pokolenie moje' ('When he was asked how the rabbi who sits here murdered the child—whether with a scalpel or with a knife—he answered [that] God [should] punish him and his wife, as well as all his children, if he knew') (AP Lublin, 141, fos. 78–80ᵛ).
[131] Żuchowski, *Ogłos*, 199–201.       [132] Załuski, *Morderstwa*, 17, 21.
[133] Fijałkowski, 'Stosunki', 29.
[134] A. Gieysztor, 'The Beginnings of Jewish Settlement in the Polish Lands', in C. Abramsky, M. Jachimczyk, and A. Polonsky (eds.), *The Jews in Poland* (London, 1986), 17–18.
[135] M. Schorr, *Żydzi w Przemyślu do końca XVIII wieku* (Lwów, 1903), nos. 49–63, pp. 117–33.

the royal court, as the king had decided that neither the district court nor the Crown tribunal were competent to examine it. On 23 May 1647 the king *in conventione Regni generali* annulled both the district and the Crown tribunal's decisions and fined Bierecki and Klimowiat 500 grzywny; the accused Jews were acquitted.[136]

Anti-Jewish literature contains references to several murders allegedly committed by Jews in Sandomierz province in 1648 and 1649. These murders were supposed to have occurred in several towns: in Iwaniska,[137] Kije near Pińczów,[138] Niegosławice near Pacanów,[139] Opatów,[140] and Secemin.[141] Żuchowski states that in 1648, in Chwastów (Kijów province), Jews were charged with murdering a child. The case was heard by the tribunal, which acquitted the Jews.[142]

## THE TRIALS: 1650–1750

In the south-eastern territories of Poland, Jews suffered enormously during Chmielnicki's revolt. Some managed to escape to Wołoszczyzna or to reach the other side of the Vistula river, settling in Wielkopolska, Gdańsk, and even beyond the borders of the Polish–Lithuanian Commonwealth. The extent of the losses was best described in a now-forgotten doctoral dissertation by J. Schamschon.[143] Moreover, the Polish–Russian war had devastated the Jewish population not only in the territories of the Grand Duchy of Lithuania,[144] but also in some Polish towns, such as Lublin.[145]

---

[136] Ibid., nos. 75–6, pp. 152–5; AGAD, Metryka Koronna, 201, fos. 187ᵛ–188ᵛ.

[137] Pruszcz, *Forteca*, 184–5: 'Roku 1648 w miasteczku Iwaniskach Żydzi przeklęci dziecię chrześcijańskie uchwyciwszy, wielkie nad nim niemiłosierdzie mieli, bo go srodze szpilkami, igłami i żelazkami ostremi skłuli i krew z niego wytoczyli. Po tymże, aby się dziurki kłute pozatykały, w wosku rozpuszczonym gorącym wymoczywszy, za miasto wyrzucili, które chrześcijanie znalazszy tamże w kościele pochowali. Byli ci przeklętnicy pozwani na trybunał, ale iniustitiati uszli, lecz ich Pan Bóg tego roku sam przez Kozaki justycyjował i krwie się niemowiątek, czego i tam dosyć, pomścił' ('In the year 1648, in the town of Iwaniska, the cursed Jews seized a Christian child and had no mercy on him, because they pierced him hard with pins, needles, and other sharp metal tools, and they drew his blood. Afterwards, they soaked [him] in hot melted wax to seal the holes, and abandoned [him] outside of the town, where the Christians found him and buried him in a church. The cursed ones were called before the tribunal, but they escaped. The same year God in His justice took revenge for the blood of the infants through the Cossacks').

[138] 'Żyd dzieweczkę w drodze siekierą zabił, o co go na trybunale piotrkowskim ćwiertowano' ('A Jew killed a girl with an axe, for which he was quartered by the Piotrków tribunal') (Żuchowski, *Proces*, 96).

[139] 'Dziewka dziecię zarżnąwszy we krwi chustkę umaczała i Żydowi oddała, o co pan Ossowski dzierżawca miasta dał oboje w Piotrkowie justycyjować' ('Having killed the child, the girl soaked a kerchief in blood and gave it to a Jew, for which the leaseholder of the town, Ossowski, sent both of them to the Piotrków court') (ibid. 96). [140] Ibid. 97.

[141] Ibid. [142] Ibid. 96; Pruszcz, *Forteca*, 185.

[143] Schamschon, *Beiträge zur Geschichte der Judenverfolgungen in Polen*, 58–92. [144] Ibid. 92–5.

[145] *Lustracja województwa lubelskiego, 1661*, ed. H. Oprawko and K. Schuster (Warsaw, 1962), 116.

In the ethnic Polish lands, the Jewish population also sustained severe losses during the Polish–Swedish war (1655–60), especially in the pogroms by Czarniecki's armies. The policy of eliminating Lutherans and Jews as traitors to the Commonwealth wherever they were was actively encouraged.[146] At the beginning of the war, many Jews from Wielkopolska, who were afraid of the Swedes, saved their lives by escaping to Silesia. They requested that Emperor Ferdinand III grant them refuge in Silesia. The emperor failed to reply and, once actually in Silesia, Jews repeated their request in a letter dated 19 August 1655 describing their position following the Swedish invasion. Again they asked the emperor to allow them to stay in Silesia, the Czech lands, and Austria. A few days before the new petition was sent, a letter dated 31 July 1655 sent from the Silesian regional office in support of the Jewish request reached the emperor. On 22 August he replied, allowing the Jews of Wielkopolska to stay in Silesia. He demanded, however, that they not be concentrated in one place but should settle in many different towns. The presence of Jews who had fled the Swedes and then the Polish armies is confirmed also in other sources.[147]

Later, in 1656, the Polish armies put entire Jewish communities to the sword, accusing them of collaboration with the Swedes.[148] It is estimated that somewhere between 3,200 and 3,580 Jewish families were murdered in this way.[149] Although this is only an approximation, records from Łęczyca can serve as an example: some sources state that 1,500 to 1,700 Jews were killed there,[150] while another source puts the number closer to 4,000.[151] According to Hebrew sources, over

---

[146] A. Kersten, *Szwedzi pod Jasną Górą, 1655* (Warsaw, 1975), 260.

[147] A. Mosbach (ed.), *Wiadomości do dziejów polskich z Archiwum Prowincji Śląskiej* (Ostrów, 1860), 338; F. Bloch, *Mittlere und neuere Geschichte die Juden in Militsch. Ein Kapitel aus der Geschichte der Niederlassung von Juden in Schlesien* (Breslau, 1926), 4–5, 13–24, 40–1, 47–8; B. Brilling, *Die jüdische Gemeinden Mittelschlesiens* (Stuttgart, 1972), 90, 127.

[148] L. Lewin, 'Die Judenverfolgungen im zweiten schwedisch–polnischen Kriege', *Zeitschrift der historischen Gesellschaft für die Provinz Posen*, 16 (1901), 81–101.

[149] D. Fettke, *Juden und Nichtjuden im 16. und 17. Jahrhundert in Polen* (Frankfurt-on-Main, 1986), 158.

[150] S. Wierzbowski, *Konnotata wypadków w domu i w kraju zaszłych od 1634 do 1689*, ed. J. K. Załuski (Leipzig, 1858), 107; M. Rawita-Witanowski, *Monografia Łęczycy* (Cracow, 1899), 81; Lewin, 'Die Judenverfolgungen'.

[151] E. Raczyński (ed.), *Des noyers Pierre: Portofolio królowej Maryi Ludwiki*, ii (Poznań, 1844), 94, says of the Polish soldiers that 'szczególniej zaś nie przepuszczali żadnemu Żydowi za to, że pomagali wrogom w obronie. W tem zamieszaniu nawet ich żony i dzieci zabijano, a ogień ich jeszcze więcej pochłonął. Zabitych i spalonych leżą na 4 tysiące. Dworzanin królewski nazwiskiem Wulff, podczas tego zamieszania z ludźmi swymi zabierał wszystkie małe dzieci żydowskie, z których wiele już było na pół spalonych i kazał je chrzcić w tej nabożnej myśli, że im to posłuży do zbawienia' ('Above all, they did not spare any Jew for helping the enemy. In the confusion even their wives and children were killed, and more died in the fire. There were about 4,000 killed and burned. In the confusion a royal courtier, Wulff, together with his people, collected all the Jewish children (many of whom were already half-burned) and, intending to assure their salvation, ordered that they be baptized').

fifty Jews were killed in Sandomierz and Dzików in April 1655.[152] Most of the literature assumes that these incidents took place at the end of 1655, and that the slaughter was carried out by Swedes.[153] The issue was resolved by H. Holsten, who wrote that on 2 April 1645, after capturing Sandomierz castle, the Polish armies 'killed over 600 Jews because they were friends (allies) of the Swedes'.[154]

The hostile attitude towards Jews is evidenced in resolutions passed by the Sejmiki. In 1669 the Sejmik of Łęczyca demanded severe punishments for ritual murder and host desecration. When Jews were convicted of these crimes, all their co-religionists were to be expelled from the province and their possessions confiscated.[155] In 1670 the Sejmik of Kujawy demanded that Jews who insulted 'God's Majesty' or committed sacrilege by stealing hosts be expelled.[156] Ironically, the only known case in the Kujawy region where Jews had been accused of host desecration had occurred more than a century before, in 1557.[157]

It should also be noted that there were not many known accusations of ritual murder or host desecration either during the Polish–Swedish war or in the period immediately following. Żuchowski writes that in 1655 the Jews of Klimontów (Sandomierz province) allegedly murdered the son of an innkeeper.[158] In 1666 another ritual murder trial took place in Mościska, and the accused, Abram, was executed.[159] In 1669 there was a trial in Łowicz before the archiepiscopal court. Murzynkowicz, a former monk, confessed that from 1662 to 1669 he would steal hosts and sell them to the Jews in Poznań, Kalisz, Dobra, and Warta. For this Murzynkowicz was burned at the stake.[160]

The literature states that when accusations of ritual murder were made against Jews in Wielkopolska, the Council of Four Lands sent its representative, Jakub, son of Naftali of Gniezno (Kalisz province), to Rome, but very little is known of Jakub's mission. On 26 June 1654 Moses Zacuto wrote a letter introducing Jakub and requested his Italian co-religionists to support the mission. It is also known that Jakub had already been in Venice, where, in 1652, he helped Natan Hannover edit his work. Although Jakub probably did not get to see the Pope, his mission did achieve some results. Most certainly the letter of Giambattista de Martinis, the general of the Dominican order, was a direct result of this mission. This letter,

---

[152] D. Kandel, 'Rzeź Żydów sandomierskich w roku 1655', *Kwartalnik Poświęcony Historii Żydów w Polsce*, I/2 (1912), 111–17.

[153] *Judisches lexicon*, iva (Berlin, 1930), 99; M. Bałaban, *Historia i literatura żydowska ze szczególnym uwzględnieniem historii Żydów w Polsce*, iii (Lwów, 1925), 270; M. Horn, *Powinności wojenne Żydów w Rzeczypospolitej w XVI i XVII wieku* (Warsaw, 1978), 109–10.

[154] H. C. Holsten, *Przygody wojenne, 1655–1666*, ed. T. Wasilewski (Warsaw, 1980), 40.

[155] J. Włodarczyk, *Sejmiki łęczyckie* (Łódź, 1973), 226.

[156] A. Pawiński, *Dzieje ziemi kujawskiej i akta historyczne do nich służące*, ii (Warsaw, 1888), 280.

[157] B. Ulanowski (ed.), *Materiały do ustawodawstwa synodalnego w Polsce w XVI wieku* (Cracow, 1895), 115.                                                          [158] Żuchowski, *Proces*, 97.

[159] Krämer, 'Dzieje Żydów przemyskich na przełomie, XVII–XVIII wieku'; Warsaw, Archiwum Żydowskiego Instytutu Historycznego, Prace magisterskie, sygn. 14, fo. 92.

[160] Żuchowski, *Proces*, 48–50.

dated 9 February 1664, instructed the Polish provincial representative to order the clergy to enlighten the people from their pulpits that the belief that Jews used blood for ritual purposes was false.[161] Nothing in these sources, however, indicates that Jakub's mission was linked to the increase in accusations of ritual murder against the Jews in Wielkopolska.

Information about accusations of ritual murder in the last quarter of the seventeenth century is mainly to be found in the anti-Jewish literature. In 1675 a court in Sandomierz heard the case of a certain Isaac, leaseholder in Brzeźnica, who was apparently accused of attempting to murder a Christian girl, Zofia.[162] Shortly afterwards Jews were charged with ritual murder in Praszka (in the Wieleń region). The accused were sentenced to death by quartering, and the remaining Jews were expelled from town.[163] A ritual murder trial is said to have taken place in Tykocin in the Podlowie region in 1680.[164] In 1689 in the town of Żółkiew, Szczepan Syndlotowicz was allegedly murdered. Ivan, a peasant whom the Jews promised would not be executed and to whom 'nothing would happen even after he is brought to the square [place of execution]', was sentenced to death.[165] In 1694 in Włodzimierz (Volhynia), a Jew accused of killing a child was executed. In the same year in nearby Derewnia, Jews were again accused of murdering a child. The case was examined by the Crown tribunal, and then by the district court in Łuck. Two years later the court in Łuck convicted four Jews and sentenced them to death by quartering. In 1697 in Nowe Miasto (Rawa province), Jews were alleged to have killed an 8-year-old child and escaped from the town.[166]

Father Żuchowski's work makes it possible to reconstruct fairly accurately the ritual murder trial in Sandomierz in 1698. In early April the body of a child was found in the mortuary of the local collegiate church. When the burgrave was informed of the incident, he ordered the body to be 'taken [to his castle] and examined, and it was said to have been a Jewish deed'. The body was then brought to the collegiate church, where it was determined that it was Małgorzata, a daughter of Katarzyna Mroczkowicowa, who had been baptized on 23 June 1695. The municipal investigator called the mother to the town hall, where on 4 April the barber-surgeons of Sandomierz performed an autopsy on the body. Mroczkowicowa declared that the child had died a natural death, but because she had no money to bury her daughter, she secretly placed her body in the mortuary. The court gave credence to her sworn testimony, and her punishment was lenient: Mroczkowicowa was to be confined in a pillory for three days.

---

[161] D. Kaufman, 'Eine Blutbeschuldigung um 1654 in Grosspolen und Jacob b. Naftali aus Gnesen als Sendbote zum Papste nach Rom', *MGWJ* 38 (1894), 89–96; A. Leszczyński, 'Zagraniczne kontakty Sejmu Żydów Korony w XVII i XVIII wieku (do 1764 roku)', *BŻIH* 3–4 (1990), 20.                                                                       [162] Żuchowski, *Proces*, 95.

[163] Ibid. 97.                                                          [164] Bałaban, 'Obvinenia', 868.

[165] Żuchowski, *Proces*, 97. On the Jewish settlement in this town, see the recent work by A. Kazimierczyk, 'The Jews in Żółkiew Domain of Jan III Sobieski', in A. K. Paluch (ed.), *The Jews in Poland*, i (Cracow, 1992), 161–72.                                        [166] Żuchowski, *Proces*, 97–8.

At that point, the bishop of Cracow decided to intervene. He 'ordered the town [municipality] to judge the case differently rather than turn a deaf ear to the calls of the innocent blood'. The proceedings were reconvened, and on 18 April Mroczkowicowa confessed under torture that on the Tuesday before Whitsun (1 April) she had brought her dead child to Aleksander Berek: 'she picked the wounded body up an hour later'. The day after her confession Mroczkowicowa confirmed her statement before the court. But when confronted with Berek, she said, 'this Jew is not guilty of anything, and I myself do not know what I am talking about while in pain'. But on 21 April she again accused Berek.

A dispute began over which court should have jurisdiction in the case: the municipality, district, or perhaps *wojewoda*. Berek appeared at the town hall, where the exhumed body of the child was also brought. Blood began 'pouring' out of the body, confirming the widespread belief that 'long experience attests, as do well-known stories, that blood comes out of a victim's wounds in the presence of the killer'. Berek accused the town's authorities of 'viciously pouring pigeon's blood in the child['s body]' and demanded the right to appeal to the *starosta*. The Sejmik of Sandomierz province also decided on an appeal to the same body.[167]

On 5 May 1698 the judges gathered and ordered that Berek be detained in the cellars of the town hall. The accused Jew presented witnesses, who testified that on 1 April Berek was not even in Sandomierz. On 14 May K. Mroczkowicowa changed her statement, testifying that she had 'confused the time' and that she had brought her daughter's body to Berek on 3 April. At that point Berek sent his son to Lublin to the Crown tribunal, which demanded that the case be sent to them from the district court. The canon, Krzysztof Dembicki, asked the judges 'not to send this case across the river Vistula, [and] added that Jesus also lost his case in the town hall to the Jews once he crossed the river Jordan'. The tribunal summoned the accused Jews to Lublin, however.

On 25 June 1698 the trial began before the tribunal in Lublin, and on 21 July Mroczkowicowa and Berek were put to torture by the court. On 29 July Mroczkowicowa testified that she 'gave the child to the Jew, Berek, and his wife to be murdered because they had been trying to convince her to do it for a long time. And I gave them [the child] alive, and later on I picked it up from them [and it was] dead, [and] without an eye and wounded.' Thus, it was only at that point that Mroczkowicowa accused Berek and his wife of murdering her daughter. Berek did not confess his guilt under torture, denying that Jews use Christian blood for making matzah. The fact that he did not confess was explained as the intervention of Satan: 'Worthy people say that during torture not only the body but also the

---

[167] Biblioteka Polskiej Akademii Nauk w Krakowie, MS 8338, fo. 864: 'Kryminał w mieście Sendomierzu popełniony ratione crudelis necis krwie chrześcijańskiej aby był przez ichmp. oficyalistów grodzkich sendomierskich, których jest zawsze u nas intaminata fides, semoto omni respectu i na żadne względu nie mając protekcyje, według samej był sądzony sprawiedliwości.' The Sejmik vote was on 28 Apr. 1698.

shadow of the tortured man's body should be burned with candles, because it could be that the devil puts the real body in the place of the shadow and something else in the place of the tortured one.' Eventually, both Mroczkowicowa and Berek were sentenced to death. After Berek's decapitation, his head was to be impaled and his body quartered, impaled, and placed by the roadside. In addition, the resolution of the Sandomierz province Sejmik[168] ordered that if Berek's wife was ever caught, she was to be tried by the district court in Nowe Miasto Korczyn.[169]

In the same year Jews were accused of murdering a child in Kodeń (in the Grand Duchy of Lithuania). The child, 3-year-old Maciek Tymoszewicz, son of Tymosz Łukaszewicz and Katarzyna Jachymowa, disappeared on 7 May 1698 after the procession, and his parents accused the Jews. The local *podstarosta*, Andrzej Stefan Rzeszycki, arrested the Jewish elders while some of the Jews escaped town. Szloma Misanowicz, the principal witness for the prosecution, testified that a week after the child had disappeared, and while he was standing sentry near the school (synagogue) and the rabbi's house, Lejb, one of the beadles, brought the child's body and hid it in Froim's house. Misanowicz confessed that together with Boroch they took the child's body 'to the fields', where on 19 May the shepherds found it. The child was buried in St Anna's church in Kodeń. Sapieha, *wojewoda* of Troki and a landowner, was informed of the incident and he 'agreed to order the total destruction of the Jewish synagogue in one hour, so even the foundation would not remain in the ground'. He also ordered the complete destruction of the cemetery. The two Jews, Lejb, the beadle, and the other one, Froim, as the instigators according to the law, were ordered to be tried under the death penalty. The case was heard by the municipal court in Kodeń, which was supplemented with four additional noblemen appointed by the landowner. Misanowicz confirmed his earlier testimony. The accused were subjected to torture on the rack three times and burned by flames. None the less, they did not 'in their stubbornness confess' to murdering the child. The court inflicted the torture again, but even that did not cause the accused to confess. They only cried: 'Even if you were to order us burned to cinders and chop us to pieces we would not say anything, because we know nothing.' Eventually the court sentenced both of them to death by decapitation. The execution took place on 28 May 1698.[170]

In 1699 another ritual murder trial took place in Biała Podlaska (in the Grand Duchy of Lithuania), which was owned by the Radziwiłł family. This time the Jews were charged with killing a 20-year-old man. The owner of the town 'ordered the quartering of the Jewish barbers in front of the synagogue'.[171]

Also in 1699 there was a trial in Piotrków before the Crown tribunal, of Jews of Ciechanów (Mazovia), accused of torturing a child 'to death'.[172]

---

[168] Biblioteka Polskiej Akademii Nauk w Krakowie, MS 8338, fo. 867$^{r-v}$.

[169] Żuchowski, *Ogłos*; J. Gajkowski, 'Procesy o mordy rytualne w Sandomierzu', *Kronika Diecezji Sandomierskiej*, 10 (1917), 81–5.     [170] Żuchowski, *Ogłos*, 163–7.

[171] Ibid. 99.     [172] Żuchowski, *Proces*, 98.

Stefan Żuchowski includes information about accusations of ritual murder at the turn of the eighteenth century. One ritual murder supposedly took place in Kamień near Solec, but there was no trial.[173] In Pińczów a Jew was apparently caught while 'ripping out the veins [from a body] spread on a sheet as if it were a ram [not a human]', but even then there was no trial.[174] A peasant woman from the village of Cergowa sold her child to the Jews of Żmigród (Ruś province).[175] In Krasnocin 'Jews also killed a child, for which forty of them were executed'.[176] In 1703 in Polanica near Bolechów, a Jew allegedly killed a girl.[177] In 1705 the vicar of the town of Grójec (Mazovia) protested to the Czersk district authorities against the Jews of Grójec, accusing them of killing a girl.[178] In 1710 in Mostki (Ruś province) a soldier sold a child to the Jews, but the child was rescued.[179] In the same year Jews were accused of killing a woman from the village of Nisko (Sandomierz province), but there was no trial.[180] Also in 1710 a ritual murder trial took place in Biała Podlaska. At the trial before the municipal court, a vagrant named Paraszke testified that he had sold a girl to the Jews for 12 groszy. Her body was then found behind the house of Zelek Zelmanowic. Zelek was tortured but he did not confess. On 12 April 1710 the court sentenced him to death by quartering. The same punishment was to be applied to his accomplices, who had already run away.[181]

Probably the most famous trial was held in Sandomierz beginning in 1710 and ending in 1713.[182] On 18 August 1710, in the courtyard of the rabbi of Sandomierz, Jakub Herc, the Jews found the body of a child. The elders of the *kahal* advised the rabbi to run away to Raków, and they themselves began to inform people that the burghers had abandoned the body of a child who had died of plague. The burghers, meanwhile, accused the Jews of murdering the boy. The municipal prosecutor, K. Jurkiewicz, sent four magistrates and two priests to search the rabbi's house and carry out an autopsy on the body. Numerous traces of blood were found in the rabbi's house.

Anna Augustynowiczowa, the foster-mother of Jerzy Krasnowski, who was an orphan, testified that he had left the house. Two townswomen informed her that the child's body was behind the rabbi's house, and those who accompanied Augustynowiczowa testified that 'the child did not die of plague, but was killed by the Jews'. Although R. Herc, with his son-in-law Jakub Schario and his son Abraham, had already left Sandomierz, all were captured and brought back to town by people sent to catch them by Father Żuchowski.

On 18 August 1710 Jews allegedly went to Captain Wołkow, who was in command of the Russian dragoons stationed in town, and offered the soldiers 'as much gold as they wanted for hiding the child well'. Since the Russian soldiers refused

---

[173] Ibid. 99.  [174] Ibid.  [175] Ibid.
[176] Ibid.  [177] Ibid. 100.  [178] Ibid. 99.
[179] Ibid. 100.  [180] Ibid. 292.
[181] Ibid. 100, 157–8; Fijałkowski, 'Stosunki', 26, thinks that it is Biała Rawska (Mazovia).
[182] Żuchowski, *Proces*; Gajkowski, *Procesy*, 97–101.

the offer, the Jews accused them of planting the child's body. The Russian soldiers arrested the Jews and wanted to send them to Russia.

On 19 August Żuchowski sent the coffin containing the child's body to Lublin, where on 22 August legal proceedings began before the Crown tribunal. 'When the body was taken from the coffin, fresh blood started pouring out from behind the ear.' The *starosta* of Sandomierz, Aleksander D. Lubomirski, was ordered to bring to Lublin the Jews arrested in Sandomierz. The body of the child was buried in the Lublin collegiate church.

On 24 August the court officials arrived in Sandomierz, and the following day they escorted the arrested Jews to Lublin. On 26 August nine Jews were brought before the tribunal, which ordered them imprisoned in the cellars of the town hall. On 2 September the tribunal decided to put all of them to torture. On 3 September, the executioner began torturing Wolf Jachymowicz, the first accused Jew, but during torture the executioner suddenly died. Żuchowski supposes that he was either poisoned by the Jews or died because of the 'mustiness of the underground prison'. Fearing the plague would break out, the soldiers and the interrogators fled the prison, leaving the arrested Jews behind. Two of them, the rabbi's son-in-law and Szmer, died.

The authorities brought in another executioner from Zamość. Father Żuchowski left Lublin and returned to Sandomierz, where he learned that the Jews had appealed to the Sandomierz *starosta*, claiming that 'they have evidence against a Catholic man who planted the body'. The *wojewoda* of Sandomierz, Stanisław Morsztyn, spoke in defence of the Jews.

On 16 September Żuchowski returned to Lublin, where the torture was to be continued. It lasted until 24 September, but none of the accused pleaded guilty.[183] Only the rabbi's son Abraham, who had been 'flogged while another Jew was stretched [on the rack] came close to admitting guilt, and what he said (that he was afraid of the Jews) gave hope that he would convert'. Two other accused did not survive the torture.

Abraham's fate became the key issue for both sides. Jews accused the crier Tyralski of having 'forced the Jew (Abraham) to testify by inserting pins under his nails'. Abraham himself, however, denied the accusation. On 25 September a hired defender demanded that he be returned to the Jews. Father Żuchowski replied that he could only give him 'to the friars, since the young [boy] had committed himself to becoming a Catholic'. Eventually, the parish priest of the Holy Ghost Church was given charge of Abraham and later baptized him.

On 16 October 1710 plague broke out in Lublin, so the tribunal decided on 22 October to transfer the case to the district of Sandomierz or to Nowe Miasto

---

[183] Sandomierz, Archiwum Kapituły Katedralnej w Sandomierzu, MS 134, fos. 54–62ᵛ. The preserved volume of court proceedings could serve as the basis for a separate monograph on the trial of the Sandomierz Jews.

Korczyn. On 25 October the accused Jews were brought to Sandomierz, where R. Herc had died.

In a letter to the bishop of Cracow, the *wojewoda* of Sandomierz defended the Jews and strongly condemned Father Żuchowski's behaviour, insisting that it was within his (the *wojewoda*'s competence to examine (*prima cognito*) this case. On 23 October, however, the primate promised, at the bishop's request, to exhort the Sejm 'to expel the Jews from Poland as had been done to the Arians previously'.

Although all attempts to resume the trial in the district of Sandomierz were unsuccessful until the end of 1711, it was not a wasted year for Father Żuchowski. The testimony given by Abraham (whose Christian name was now Michał) was essential for later proceedings. In his testimony on 13 February 1711 in the town hall of Sandomierz (subsequently repeated before the district authorities), he gave evidence against the accused Jews. He stated that the Jews of Sandomierz received an order from the Jewish elders of Raków to deliver Christian blood. Later, a neophyte, Serafinowicz, also testified against the Jews.[184]

It was only on 4 January 1712 that the district court finally decided to continue the case against the Sandomierz Jews. On 19 January the Jews asked the court to postpone the hearings, as they were trying to arrange for a defender in Cracow, Przemyśl, and Lwów, and because Kintlewicz, their defender from Lublin, would not be able to reach Sandomierz until 22 January. But the court refused to postpone the trial any further, appointing instead two defenders from Sandomierz. On 20 January the defender from Lublin arrived, and in the afternoon Father Żuchowski was finally able to begin his accusation, which he continued throughout the two following days. In the first part of his speech, Żuchowski tried to prove that 'Jews murder Christian children and they do need their blood.' Then he spoke at length about 'the cruelty and betrayal of the Jews against Christians', mainly giving examples of host desecration and ritual murder. A significant part of his speech was devoted to discussing the reasons why 'the Jews need blood'. He stated that although there were ten reasons why Jews needed blood, it was principally because they hated Christians. After the introductory remarks, Żuchowski moved on to the specific accusations against the Jews of Sandomierz. He said that the Jewish elders of Raków ordered R. Herc to deliver them Christian blood 'under pain of excommunication and removal from [his] rabbinic position'. On 23 January the defender of the Jews rejoined the trial.

The proceedings resumed again on 1 April 1712, when the *wojewoda* of Sandomierz, together with the *starosta* as assessor, ordered the crier to convene the court. Father Żuchowski protested against its composition. The following day *starosta* Lubomirski with *wojewoda* Morsztyn and the castellan of Zawichost, Aleksander Gołuchowski, acting as assessors were in charge of the proceedings. In

---

[184] Cracow, Biblioteka Jagiellońska w Krakowie, MS 101, vol. 1, fo. 175$^{r-v}$.

the afternoon the Jews swore 'that they did not know if the child had been killed by Jews, but they had not killed it'. Father Żuchowski protested, claiming that both the accused Jews and the witnesses took the oath after sunset; moreover, the Jews swore on a [Torah] scroll that was 'not valid, because [it was] worn and soiled [and] they would not read from it in the synagogue'. The Catholic witnesses were supposedly 'drunk from vodka' and bribed by the Jews. Jurkiewicz, who was town prosecutor in 1710, testified in favour of the Jews. The Jews also allegedly bribed the *wojewoda* and *starosta* of Sandomierz.

As a result of the ritual murder accusation made on 28 April 1712, the king ordered the Jews expelled from Sandomierz and the synagogue converted to a Catholic chapel. There is no indication that his order was ever carried out.[185]

Father Żuchowski then began efforts to transfer the trial to the Crown tribunal in Lublin, and on 9 November 1712 the trial was, indeed, resumed. There Father Żuchowski gave an abbreviated version of his previous speech, taking it as a fact that the boy's murder had been committed by Jews, not Catholics, and thus he reasoned that it was justified to put the Jews to torture until they either confessed or pointed to the murderer.[186]

The trial was postponed for some months, and on 10 November 1713 the tribunal sentenced Liczman Majorowicz, Icek Jozwowicz, and David Hirszlowicz to death. After the sentence was announced, it was proposed that the Jews be exempted from capital punishment in exchange for ransom. Even Jews proposed that 'it [would be] better to erect a church and to record that it [was built] because of that crime'. Eventually, however, on 17 November 1713 the execution was carried out.

Żuchowski further wrote that in 1713 Jews had fled from Bydgoszcz after they had killed a child.[187] In Żywiec (Cracow province), Jews were accused of ritual murder as early as 1710, but the owner of Żywiec spoke out in their defence. On 6 February, 1718, 4-year-old Katarzyna, daughter of Wawrzyniec Studentowicz and Franciszka Kotelanka, disappeared. Her body was found on 23 February. During the autopsy, carried out before the municipal authorities, no signs of beating or piercing were seen. The second autopsy, performed in the castle by Jan Korczyński, a barber-surgeon, led to the same conclusion. The body was placed in the church until Franciszek Wielopolski, the estate owner, returned. The

[185] Bersohn (ed.), *Dyplomatariusz*, no. 377; Guldon and Krzystanek, 'Żydzi i Szkoci', 536.

[186] It accorded with the opinion of the bishop of Cracow, who took it as fact that the murder had been committed by Jews. He wrote: 'Ale jeżeli argumentum stringit, to incarcerati Żydzi powinniby byc rei criminis, a jeżeli za wytrzymanemi torturami kładą się liberes, to innych Żydów patratores infanticidii wydać powinni, ponieważ scelus przez Żydów patratum, o czym impossibile aby communitas nie wiedziała, albo ex communitate singulares et consequenter nie mogą być liberi Żydzi a poenis, choćby ci singulares incarcerati wytrzymawszy torturas per evasionem uwolnieni byli, alias póki stawa Żydów w Sendomierzu na tym fundamencie potrzebaby ich brać wszystkich i ad torturas dawać póki non patebit veritas, że Żydzi i którzy zabili' (Żuchowski, *Proces*, 164–5).

[187] Ibid. 100.

inquiry carried out in his presence failed to discover the reason for the child's death, and on 14 March the body was buried under the altar of St Antoni's parish church.[188]

In 1710 Adel of Drohobycz (Ruś), who wanted to save her co-religionists, admitted that she had murdered a child and was executed.[189]

Relatively well known also is the episode in Poznań, in 1736 to 1740. In 1736, 2-year-old Maciej Kazimierz, son of Poznań burgher Wojciech Jabłonowicz, disappeared. His body was found several days later (on 28 April) near the village of Górczyn. Suspicion that the child had been stolen and sold to Jews fell on Helena Sowińska, who was a maid in a Jewish household. She was located on 11 June and arrested together with her 11-year-old daughter. Soon after, a caretaker of the Jewish cemetery, Agnieszka Kubarka, was arrested as well. It was expected that the women, who worked for Jews, would reveal the perpetrators. Neither admitted to kidnapping the boy initially, but the women got into an argument and Sowińska demanded another hearing. On 25 August 1736 she testified that Agnieszka, with Jasiek Parchaty, had been trying to persuade her to kidnap a Christian child and sell it to the Jews. Since she refused, they themselves stole the child. All three of them, including the kidnapped boy, went together to the Jewish quarter, where they handed the child over to the Jews.

On 5 September 1736 municipal guards arrested Arje Lejb Kalahor, a preacher; Jakub, son of Pinkas, a community elder; and two other Jews. The preacher and the elder died during torture, maintaining their innocence. The town authorities arrested five other Jews. Jewish efforts to transfer the case to the royal court were successful. After taking a solemn oath swearing their innocence, that court released the Jews imprisoned in Poznań in the mid-1740s. The final decision in this case was made by August I on 5 August 1740. Only Sowińska, the instigator of the entire affair, was sentenced to two years' imprisonment.[190]

In 1738 in Gniezno (Kalisz province) a Jew named Aleksander was accused of murdering a Christian child. Although no details of this case are known, it was recorded that in 1722 a Jew named Jakub was executed after being charged with insulting the Holy Mother and Jesus Christ.[191]

More information is available about a case heard by the *wójt* court and by the assessor's court of the old town district of Warsaw in 1743. The prosecutor and the mother of the injured boy, 4-year-old Kasper Czubek of Dąbrowa (Gaspari Czubek Dąbroviensis), accused four Jews of stealing the child and taking his

[188] S. Grodziski and I. Dwornicka (eds.), *Chronografia albo dziejopis żywiecki* (Żywiec, 1987), 170, 344–5, 502–3.

[189] J. Caro, *Geschichte der Juden in Lemberg von den aeltesten Zeiten bis nur Theilung Polens in Jahre 1772* (Lwów, 1894), 102.

[190] M. Bałaban, 'Arje Lejb Kalahora (Do procesu poznańskiego w latach, 1736–1740)', in id., *Studia historyczne* (Warsaw, 1927), 141–50; id., *Zur Geschichte der Juden in Polen* (Vienna, 1915), 58–61; J. Perles, 'Geschichte der Juden in Posen', *MGWJ* 14 (1865), 122, 167–70.

[191] A. Warschauer, *Geschichte der Stadt Gnesen* (Poznań, 1918), 193.

blood for ritual purposes. The court ordered that the child be examined by two medical doctors, Henryk Laelhoeffel and Chryzostom Kostrzewski, and by four barber-surgeons, who found five scars.[192]

It is also possible to reconstruct fairly accurately the proceedings of a trial that took place in 1747. Near Zachalich's inn, just outside Michnów (in Volhynia), the body of Antoni, a newcomer, was found. An autopsy performed before the Zasław municipal authorities on 1 April 1747 revealed numerous puncture wounds. As four Jews approached the body, blood began to spurt from it, ostensibly pointing to the perpetrators of the crime. As a consequence, two Jews from Zasław and some leaseholders and innkeepers from nearby towns were accused of the murder. The crime had allegedly been committed in Zachalich's inn, where Antoni had stayed. A special municipal court from Krzemieniec, which included a few burghers from Zasław as well as others, sat in judgement on the Jews in the castle in Zasław. Two of those accused were sentenced to be impaled, one to have his limbs cut off and be impaled, four to be flayed alive and then quartered, and one was sentenced to death by quartering. Two other Jews who had eluded capture were sentenced *in absentia* to flaying alive and quartering. Berek, the innkeeper who pleaded guilty and testified against the others, was to be decapitated by sword. Finally, Zoruch Lejbowicz, a servant at Zachalich's inn who had testified against the others from the very beginning, was said to have been acquitted.[193]

According to I. Galant, Zoruch Lejbowicz was baptized, but he, too, was eventually sentenced to death. The Jews considered Zoruch a Christian, so they did not want to bury him in the Jewish cemetery, and the Christians did not want him in their cemetery either. He was finally buried behind the fence of the Jewish cemetery, and a cross was put on his grave by the Christians. Legend has it that for a long time afterwards Duke Paweł Sanguszko, the owner of the properties, was haunted by the ghosts of the tormented Jews. While driving through Jewish streets he apparently screamed: 'Go away, go away, my victims. Stop being angry.' When representatives of one of the Jewish communities complained that they could not obtain land for a cemetery, he immediately ordered that their request be granted.[194] In any case, it is true that the Jewish community in Zasław became the largest in Volhynia: the 1765 census shows 2,047 Jews in the old city of Zasław, 760 in the new city of Zasław and Józefpole, and 100 in Białogródka.[195]

The next trial that took place in Dunajgród (in Podolia), which was owned by the castellan of Cracow and the grand crown hetman Józef Potocki. Three Jews were accused: Mendel Ejzykowicz, Mendel Zejlikowicz, and Liberman Haskelowicz, as well as a peasant woman, Mandzia, the mother of an 18-month-

[192] F. Giedrojć, *Ekspertyza lekarska w dawnych sądach polskich do końca XVIII stulecia* (Warsaw, 1896), 42–4.

[193] *Dekret w sprawie o zamordowanie okrutne przez Żydów chrześcianina Antoniego pod Zasławiem ferowany w zamku zasławskim dnia 17 kwietnia roku Pańskiego 1747* (n.p., n.d.).

[194] Galant, 'Dva ritualnych procesa', 19.

[195] *Archiv Jugo-Zapadnoj Rossii*, pt. 5, vol. ii (Kiev, 1890), 106.

old boy, Jan. She allegedly came to Dunajgród on 17 April 1748 and offered to sell her son to the Jews.

Two noblemen, appointed by the owner of the town, were to judge the Jews: Aleksander Halecki and Mikołaj Hitnicki, assisted by the municipal court of Kamieniec-Podolski. On Potocki's request Bishop Dembowski appointed his own representative, Tomasz Świrski, a parish priest of Dunajgród. Beside these, eight other noblemen took part in the trial.

The *wójt*, the mayor, and two other burghers participated in the autopsy. Mandzia asked to be acquitted of all charges by the court. The accused Jews argued that they did not need Christian blood for ritual purposes and requested they be released from prison so they could prove their innocence. The prosecutor, basing his argument on Żuchowski's work, as well as on the tribunal's judgement in 1713 in the case of the Sandomierz Jews and the sentence in the 1747 Zasław case, maintained that Jews did use Christian blood and commit ritual murder.

The court decided to interrogate the accused. Mandzia testified that she had come to Dunajgród with her son. Once there she went to Mendel Ejzykowicz, who had offered to take her into service. She told him that she could not accept the offer because of the child. Although at first she claimed she received 3 red zloty,[196] she later denied having said it. The Jew gave her two buckets and sent her to fetch some water in them. When she came back, he gave her vodka and then mixed it with some other beverage. After drinking it, she was not aware of anything that happened and could not tell definitely what she did with the child.

The accused Jews did not admit to killing the child, and confronting them with Mandzia did not prove any more fruitful. Having been tortured, Mandzia claimed that she had left her son in the Jewish house. Even after torture, however, the Jews did not confess their crime. Eventually the Jews were sentenced to one year and six weeks in prison, and Mandzia was sent to receive medical treatment, to be paid for by the municipal authorities and the synagogue.[197] Despite the fact that the court judged the Jews guilty, the punishment they received was exceptionally lenient compared to sentences in other cases of this kind. Finally, in the same year, two other Jews were sentenced to death in the town of Szepietówka (Volhynia).[198]

## THE TRIALS: 1750–1800

The development of Jewish Messianism, which was closely associated with Jakub Frank (1720–91), was very significant for the course of the ritual murder trials in the period 1750–1800. Under the jurisdiction of the bishop of Kamieniec, Mikołaj Dembowski, disputes between Frank and his followers and the rabbis took place first in Kamieniec-Podolski (in 1757) and then in Lwów (in 1759). The

---

[196] 1 red (czerwony) zloty = 1 ducat = 18 zloty.
[197] Galant, 'Dva ritualnych procesa', 21–37.     [198] Mahler, 'Z dziejów', 51.

disputes concentrated on seven points, of which the last is especially relevant here: 'The Talmud teaches us to need Christian blood, and whoever believes in the Talmud should demand it.' Such an interpretation provided a basis for accusing them of committing murders for ritually related reasons.[199]

The first ritual murder trial in the latter half of the eighteenth century took place in Nowy Sącz (Cracow province). Although a Jewish presence was documented as early as the fifteenth century in Nowy Sącz,[200] the town was closed to Jewish settlement in the following century. F. Kiryk and F. Leśniak wrote that in 1600 *starosta* Jerzy Lubomirski confirmed the decision of the municipal authorities to give the square near Szpitalna Street to the Jews for construction of a synagogue. Lubomirski's privilege was issued in 1699.[201] Nevertheless, in 1670 the decree banning Jews from living in the city was confirmed, and it was only in 1673 that Jews were permitted to resettle in the town.

The first ritual murder trial in Nowy Sącz took place in 1751. The main accused, Jakub Habusiewicz, was charged with having committed ritual murders in collusion with Jews from Biecz and Zasław. Habusiewicz was accused of murdering Mateusz Horwin, a student, who had been staying overnight at his inn. Reputedly there were four other Jews from Cracow, Tarnów, and Hungary staying there at that time, as well. In addition, Habusiewicz was also accused of murdering a boy whose body was found by the *wójt* in Żeleźnikowo, as well as of killing Deptowicz. He did not confess to any of the charges: 'Even if you melted me down to gristle, I would not say anything because I know nothing,' he said.[202]

The trial proceedings took place in Żytomierz in 1753, and can be fairly accurately reconstructed. The auxiliary bishop of Kijów and later the bishop of Cracow, Kajetan Sołtyk, played an active role in the trial. In a letter addressed to the archbishop of Lwów, Gerard Wyżycki, Sołtyk informed him that on Good Friday (20 April 1753) the leaseholders from Markowa Wolica, acting on the order of the Jewish elders of Pawołocz, kidnapped 3½-year-old Stefan Studzieński, son of the nobleman Adam and his wife, Ewa (née Wychowska). The boy was allegedly murdered the following day, on the Sabbath, and the Jewish elders ordered the perpetrators to 'take [his body] into the bushes', where it was found on Easter Monday. Bishop Sołtyk imprisoned thirty-one Jewish men and two Jewish women, amongst whom there were 'the richest leaseholders in this land'. The bishop ordered an initial investigation by the Church court into the matter, which would subsequently be sent for trial to the district of Żytomierz.

---

[199] For more details, see A. Czołowski, '*Mord rytualny': Epizod z przeszłości Lwowa* (Lwów, 1899); A. Kraushar, *Frank i frankiści polscy, 1726–1816*, i–ii (Cracow, 1895); J. Doktor, *Jakub Frank i jego nauka na tle kryzysu religijnej tradycji osiemnastowiecznego żydostwa polskiego* (Warsaw, 1991).

[200] I. Schiper, *Studia nad stosunkami gospodarczymi Żydów w Polsce podczas średniowiecza* (Lwów, 1911), 153.

[201] F. Kiryk and F. Leśniak, 'Skupiska żydowskie w miastach małopolskich do końca XVI stulecia', in F. Kiryk (ed.), *Żydzi w Małopolsce* (Przemyśl, 1991), 24–5; J. Goldberg (ed.), *Jewish Privileges in the Polish Commonwealth* (Jerusalem, 1985), no. 35, p. 228.   [202] Mahler, 'Z dziejów', 50–6.

There are a number of other details contained in the sentence issued by the court of Żytomierz on 26 May 1753. The case was examined by Franciszek Ksawery Nitosławski, *podwojewoda* of Kijów, Łukasz Bogdanowicz, the district judge, and Kazimierz Chojecki, the court scribe. The district court examined the accused and afterwards put them to torture. The court found them guilty and decided on a harsh sentence: six of the Jews were to be flayed alive and then quartered, and six others were to be quartered. The Jew from Pawołocz, who had fled, was to be quartered if seized. The court acquitted the remaining Jews.

An account of the executions has survived. After the sentence was read, six of the Jews were led to the gallows. One, who expressed a desire to be baptized with his wife, was given clemency by the court—he was to have been beheaded rather than quartered. Finally, his life was spared at the request of the bishop. The other five Jews were executed. On the following day, six more Jews were brought to the gallows. Three of them were quartered immediately; the other three, who had been baptized shortly before, were beheaded instead. Their bodies were put into coffins and they were given a solemn funeral. A thirteenth accused, the innkeeper Zajwel, who had expressed a desire to be baptized together with his wife and children, was to have been beheaded as well, but his life too was spared as a result of the intervention of the bishop. When the executions were over, the bishop baptized thirteen Jewish men and women and married three Jewish couples.[203] The Jews claimed that the boy they had been accused of murdering had died of an illness and that Bishop Sołtyk had exploited the incident to show his religious zeal as well as for personal reasons. They accused the bishop of having accepted 500 red zloty and sable furs worth 300 ducats in exchange for promising to release the accused.[204]

One of the most well-known ritual murder trials was held in Jampol (Volhynia), when fifteen Jews were charged. The investigation, carried out in 1756 at Kazimierz Radziwiłł's order, revealed that the body found by the river showed no signs of violent death, and that the wounds were inflicted only later on. The court set the Jews free. The bishop of Łuck intervened, however, prompting a new trial in which the accused Jews were put to torture and forced to give false evidence.[205]

One of the accused in that trial, Jakub Selek (Zelek), who had managed to escape from gaol, was sent by the Council of Four Lands to the Apostolic See to implore Pope Benedict XIV to protect the Jews from ritual murder accusations. The document he carried with him detailed unjust charges made against the Jews

---

[203] *Dekret o zamęczenie przez Żydów dziecięcia katolickiego ferowany w grodzie żytomirskim* (n.p., n.d.). Załuski, *Morderstwa*, 27, and N. M. Gelber, 'Die Taufbewegung unter den polnischen Juden im XVIII Jahrhundert', *MGWJ* 32 (1924), 227: both also quote from the trial in Żytomierz in 1745 (although most probably it was the trial of 1753).

[204] K. Rudnicki, *Biskup Kajetan Sołtyk, 1715–1788* (Cracow, 1906), 15–18.

[205] *Encyclopaedia Judaica*, viii (Berlin, 1931), col. 864.

not only at the trial in Jampol, but also in Szepietówka, Zasław, Żytomierz, and in a place near Ostra. The intervention of the Apostolic See was effective, as is evidenced in letters of 9 February 1760 and 21 March 1763 from the papal nuncio Cardinal Corsini de Visconti to Henryk Brühl, the first minister of the court. Both Benedict XIV and the new Pope, Clement XIII, condemned the ritual murder trials. Perhaps one of the most significant statements they made was that there was no evidence that 'Jews need to add human blood to their unleavened bread [called] matzah'.[206]

Before this, however, another trial took place in 1757 in Dzików (in Sandomierz province). There, Jews were accused of kidnapping 15-year-old Bartłomiej Kubacki of Miechocin. Berek, the leaseholder of a brewery in Miechocin, was the main accused. Together with Pinches, another accused, he requested baptism, and they were beheaded rather than having to suffer a slower, more painful execution. Josek, a beadle, and Lejbusz refused to renounce their faith and perished at the stake. One remaining accused died under torture.[207] It should be noted that the 'victim' of the imaginary murder was still alive in 1774.[208]

In 1759 a ritual murder trial took place in Przemyśl. On 27 March, the disappearance was reported of a boy aged 3 years and 10 weeks, Grzegorz, the son of a widow, Ołeńka of Stupnica. On Easter Sunday a local tailor, Jan Karpiński, found the child's body. Seven Jews were accused and charged with the boy's murder at the Pod Garbam Inn in the fields of Stupnica.

Preliminary investigations were held in the Uniate consistory in Przemyśl. From there the case was brought to the court of the municipal council, which on 10 May transferred it to the *landwójt* court for further investigation. None of the

---

[206] *The Ritual Murder Libel*; also Gelber, 'Die Taufbewegung', 228–30; Leszczyński, 'Zagraniczne kontakty', 20; Bersohn (ed.), *Dyplomatariusz*, nos. 307–8, 331–2; M. Horn (ed.), *Regesty dokumentów i ekscerpty z Metryki Koronnej do historii Żydów w Polsce, 1697–1795*, i (Wrocław, 1984), nos. 494, 496.

[207] M. Marczak, 'Obecny powiat tarnobrzeski w świetle metryk parafialnych z XVII i XVIII wieku', offprint from *XI Sprawozdanie Państwowego Gimnazjum im. hetmana Jana Tarnowskiego w Tarnobrzegu* (Tarnobrzeg, 1928), 20: note in the public register of the church in Miechocin: 'Anno 1757 die 19 Aprilis sepultus est Vincentius in ecclesia Dzikoviensi, ante dictus Berek, arendatarius braxatorii Miechocinensis, ante supplicium baptisatus. Item secundus in eadem ecclesia sepultus, pariter baptisatus, dictus Pinches. Supra nominati et infra nominandi crudeliter (ut patuit ex inquisitionibus) necarunt puerum annorum 15, dictum Bartholomaeum Kubacki de Michocin. Szkolnik Josek, Lejbus ad rogum damnati nimio obstinati in sua infidelitate. Tertius Mosiek post corporales confessatas mortuus. Fuerunt et alii plurimi huius nefandi sceleris complices, in quos ex decreto stetit captivatio.'

[208] Biblioteka Czartoryskich, MS IV 803, 'Replika na powództwo ur. instygatora sądowego i jego donosicielów Norków od strony więźniów o dzieciobójstwo obwinionych w sądach Konfederacyi Generalnej Obojga Narodów roku 1774 dana', fos. 29–30: 'Można pozwolić, że Żydzi kiedy dziecię zabili, bo bywają zabójstwa i byli za to sądzeni, ale i tego nie można nie przyznać, że byli za zabójców sądzeni, chociaż cale nie zabijali, jaki jest osobliwszy przykład w sprawie sandomirskiej, gdzie za mniemane zabójstwo chłopca z dóbr hrabiów Tarnowskich z opacznych dowodów osądzono na śmierć i stracono kilku Żydów, a ów człowiek do dziś dnia wielu tutejszym nawet osobom znajomy szczęśliwie żyje i o to do Sądu JO osobno intentowana sprawa.'

accused pleaded guilty. On 14 May 1759 the court found that all of the accused were 'shedders of Christian blood and the murderers of the child in question'. The court sentenced six of them to the block. Only Rechla Beznoska was to remain in the town hall prison in order to obtain information from her about other accomplices.[209]

Another ritual murder trial took place in Krasnystaw in 1761. On 22 April three people went to the district authorities in Krasnystaw. They were Adam Rojecki, representing the owner of Wojsławice, Felicjan Potocki, and two lieges, Marcin and Katarzyna Andrzejuk, from the village of Czarnołozy, the parents of the murdered boy, Mikołaj. They accused the *kahal* of Wojsławice and Lejb Szmujlowicz, an innkeeper at Czarnołozy in the Radziwiłł estate, of murdering the boy.

The trial took place on 9 June 1761 at the district court in Krasnystaw. The accused Jews were tortured before the municipal authorities, with the court assuming that the Jews of Wojsławice and Chełm had decided to obtain Christian blood before the holiday of Pesach. Hence, the court was certain that Mikołaj had been kidnapped. Srul, the innkeeper, was said to have been in charge of abducting the child, taking him to his father-in-law, Lejb Szmujlowicz. The latter took the child to the house of Joś Szmujlowicz, in Wojsławice, where the crime allegedly occurred. Blood from the child's body was to be brought to the community leadership in Brody and Chełm. The body was then hidden by Majer, the butcher, in the 'disgusting dung heap' near Mortek's house; it was later abandoned 'in a swampy place in the bushes' near the child's parents' house.

The Jews not only admitted to committing the act they were accused of, but also to 'other crimes, to killing children, manslaughter, robbing churches, and [what is even more terrifying] to profaning the Holy Sacrament of the Eucharist'. Sender Zyskieluk confessed to having murdered two infants as well as to killing Wawryk, a servant employed by Jews.

The court found Joś Szmujlowicz, Sender Zyskieluk, Lejb Moszkowicz, and Lejb Szmujlowicz, guilty of the crime and 'sentenced them to be quartered alive by the master of public justice (the hangman), and ordered their heads and quarters impaled and placed by the roadside'. R. Herszko Jozefowicz committed suicide by hanging himself in prison before the end of the trial. The court decided that 'his body, which was not deserving of burial, [was to be] tied to a horse's tail by a sworn master of justice, dragged to the square prepared for quartering, burned at the stake, and then his ashes would be thrown in the air and carried by the wind'. The court also ordered that Srul (who managed to escape) be imprisoned, along with other Jews against whom charges were initiated.

Two of the Jews agreed to be baptized. At the request of the Jesuits, the court decided that 'for those who wished to convert, the sentence would be changed from quartering alive to decapitation. For the stubborn ones, however, who

---

[209] Schorr, *Żydzi*, nos. 143–4, pp. 239–43.

deserved no mercy, the severe sentence was confirmed.' At the place of execution, two Jews were immediately baptized and then beheaded, while the two other Jews, having been persuaded by the clergy, were also baptized and beheaded. All four bodies were placed in coffins and transferred to the cemetery chapel. The following day the bishop officiated at a ceremonious funeral. Thus only the rabbi's body was treated according to the original verdict.[210] A Jewish community was founded in Wojsławice in 1780.[211]

In 1761 in Nowy Sącz another ritual murder trial took place. The crime was supposedly committed at the inn in the village of Posadowa. A girl employed at the inn, who was baptized, testified that Josef Bobowski, the innkeeper, murdered a child and quartered the body. As a result of the accusation, Aronowicz, son-in-law of the accused Jew, 'was baptized of his own will' and was sentenced to death by decapitation. Bobowski was sentenced to 'be flayed alive and death by quartering'.[212]

In 1763 several Jews in Kalisz were accused of murdering a girl described as a 'strumpet'.[213] In 1774 Stanisław August gave a letter of protection to Lejb Jankielowicz and two other Jews also accused of murdering a Christian child. They had been tortured before the municipal court in Ostróg (in Volhynia) and then transferred to the district court in Łuck. The king stated that it was not the district court but the royal court that was competent to hear the case, and the royal court was to re-examine it.[214] The final outcome of this case is unknown.

Much better documented is a ritual murder case from the village of Grabie (Mazovia) which took place in 1774. On 30 March in that village (which was owned by the Benedictine abbey in Płock), a 3-year-old girl, Marianna, daughter of Mateusz and Marianna Norek, disappeared. The child's body was found on 5 April between Grabie and the village of Sadków. The girl's uncle, Jędrzej Tryndoch, a cooper, accused local Jews, the innkeeper Jakub Nodkowicz and his wife, of murdering the girl. Tryndoch claimed that it was a ritual murder committed to obtain Christian blood for matzah. Peasants broke into the inn, but they did not find any tools or trace of the crime. The innkeeper and his family were taken to the manor. After being flogged, the innkeeper's children testified that their mother had kidnapped Marianna. Thirteen Jews were imprisoned, including

---

[210] *Złość żydowska w zamęczeniu dzieci katolickich przez list następujący i dekreta grodzkie wydana* (Lublin, 1774).

[211] Goldberg, *Jewish Privileges*, no. 57. As to the later fate of Wojsławice Jews, in 1779 the town became a possession of Humbelina Kurdwanowska, daughter of F. Potocki. Following a fire in 1780, Kurdwanowska gave permission to the Jews there to establish a synagogue, elect a rabbi, and build a school and cemetery. Hence a community was established, and in 1790 there were 182 Jews registered in the town and 244 in the community as a whole. Z. Guldon and L. Stępkowski, 'Spis ludności żydowskiej w 1790 roku', *BŻIH* 3–4 (1986), 128.            [212] Mahler, 'Z dziejów', 56–8.

[213] *Wiadomości Warszawskie*, 7 Sept. 1763, no. 72; Załuski, *Morderstwa*, 29; W. Smoleński, 'Stan i sprawa Żydów polskich w XVIII wieku', in his *Pisma historyczne*, ii (Cracow, 1901), 245.

[214] AGAD, Księgi Kanclerskie, 52, fos. 150–2; Horn, *Regesty*, no. 284.

Jakub Józefowicz, a leaseholder from Sadków who had allegedly brought the kidnapped child to Sadków. On 9 April those under arrest were taken to Warsaw. The court of the general confederation took charge of the case.[215]

Fortunately, the prosecution and defence opinions during the trial have been preserved. The prosecutor claimed that the autopsy showed a number of wounds that pointed to a ritual murder,[216] but it must be noted that the autopsy, carried out on 10 April 1774 by physicians and barber-surgeons at the order of the confederacy court, showed that 'the child had no wound over the entire body that had been inflicted with a pin, either before death or after'. In his long speech, the prosecutor demanded that the accused be put to torture.[217]

The defence pointed out that Passover that year was celebrated between 26 and 28 March, so the child had disappeared after the holiday. He also pointed out that Jews are prohibited from consuming blood in the Bible, the Talmud, and by tradition. He quoted the words of the popes (especially of Clement XIII) and several Polish rulers about ritual murder. Further, the defence said that the prosecutor did not provide any evidence that would point to the guilt of the accused Jews.[218] Finally, referring to Hugo Grotius, he questioned the ability of testimonies gained through torture to discover the truth.[219] On 20 June 1775 the court acquitted all those who had been accused. This trial was of great significance in later discussions about the abolition of torture in judicial proceedings. And indeed a year later the Sejm finally did abolish torture.[220]

---

[215] S. Waltoś, *Owoce zatrutego drzewa: Procesy i wydarzenia, które wstrząsnęły światem* (Cracow, 1978), 95–6.

[216] AGAD, Zbiór Popielów, 'Indukta sprawy o dziecięciobójstwo czyli zamordowanie Marianny z rodziców Norków we wsi Grabiu w województwie mazowieckim, do opactwa płockiego należącej, zrodzonej, przez Żydów inkarceratów dnia 30 miesiąca marca roku 1774 spraktykowane, w sądzie Generalnej Konfederacyi Obojga Narodów w Warszawie publicznie miana', 303, fo. 70: 'dziecię całe skłute, oko lewe z miejsca swego wyjęte, za uszami dziury wydrążone mające, ręce i nogi na krzyż rozpięte, szóstego dnia to jest nazajutrz po świętach żydowskich na rozdrożu znalezione, reprezentowało skutki katuszy swojej, które mordercy żyjącemu zadali, a po wyciśnieniu krwie i duszy jak w nerwach zastygłe zostało, tak martwe wprawdzie, ale żywe morderstwa zostawiło świadki na krzyż ręce i nogi prezentując wyraz chrześcijańskiej ofiary' ('The child [was] pierced all over. [His] left eye was missing, [He] had holes behind [his] ears and [his] arms and legs were stretched into the shape of a cross. [He] was found at the crossroads on the sixth day—one day after the Jewish holy days. [He] showed signs that the torture had been inflicted by the murderers while [he] was still alive. After [his] blood and soul were extracted, even though [he] was already dead, with [his] arms and legs stretched in the form of a cross, [he] remained a testimony to Christian sacrifice').

[217] 'Indukta sprawy', 64–71.                  [218] 'Replika na powództwo', 24–32.

[219] Ibid., 32: 'I sprawiedliwie, bo takowy sposób dochodzenia prawdy przez tortury bardziej ku przytłumieniu niżeli wydaniu prawdy służy. W owych to bowiem ściśniony [w] bólach więzień jest ten, który je wytrzyma albo nie, jeżeli wytrzyma, więc prawdy nie powie, a jeżeli nie będzie mógł wytrzymać, to znowu nieprawdę zezna i choć niewinny z bólu zmyśliwszy występek powie' ('And it is right, because obtaining the truth through torture obscures more than it reveals. The tortured one will either survive the torture or not. If he does survive, he will not tell the truth, but if he cannot endure the torture, he will tell a lie and even if he is innocent he will make things up').

[220] Waltoś, *Owoce*, 97–8.

In 1779 in the village of Goraj (part of the Bogusławice estate of Rafał Wodziński), Małgorzata, wife of Wojciech Grzyb, and Agnieszka Walkówna were accused of selling a 9-year-old girl to Jews from the town of Izbica (Kujawy). The case was heard by the town court, which was brought from the town of Brdów (Kalisz province). Based on testimony 'volunteered' by the accused women and by witnesses, the court established that on 21 September 1778 Małgorzata and Agnieszka went to Izbica. They called at the house of a Jew, Kałdonek (Lachman), who tried to persuade them to sell him a Catholic child. Upon their return to Goraj, Małgorzata persuaded Agnieszka to take Gertruda, daughter of Konstancja, for a walk and bring her to Izbica. On 21 December, after a conversation with Kołdonek and with another Jew, Kopel (Cherszek), Małgorzata agreed to deliver the child in exchange for 15 red zloty. On 29 December Agnieszka gave the girl to the Jews, and her body was later found in the fields. On 23 March 1779 both accused were sentenced by the Brdów court to death by decapitation.[221]

In 1779, in Chrzanów (Cracow province), the body of 4-year-old Katarzyna was found in the courtyard of David Jachimowicz. Her father, Wojciech Wadaś, and a nobleman, Ignacy Szotarski, accused the Jews of 'infanticide because they needed Christian blood'. On 28 January 1780 a protest was lodged in the district office of Cracow by the Jewish elders and congregation of Chrzanów, stating that the accusation was groundless.[222]

Earlier in the case the rabbi of Olkusz, Herszek Zyskielewicz, had sent a memorandum to the permanent council, and from the royal resolution of 21 January 1780, it appears that Zyskielewicz had argued that the child's body was planted by the burghers on one of the Jewish merchants of Chrzanów. The council requested that the owner of the Chrzanów estate, Dobrzyński, acquit the two Jews. He claimed that he was obliged to bring them before the district court in Cracow, whereupon the king ordered the district court to examine the case quickly. How the final stage of the case was resolved is unknown.[223]

The last ritual murder trial took place in Olkusz (Cracow province) in 1787. On Maundy Thursday a Jew met a 10-year-old girl in the marketplace in Olkusz and asked her to deliver a letter to Bolesław. In the forest a young Jew barred her way, 'threw her on the ground, took out a knife, and as he was cutting her throat'

---

[221] J. Wijaczka, 'Proces o sprzedaż dziecka Żydom z Izbicy Kujawskiej z 1779 roku', *Ziemia Kujawska*, 10 (1994), 87–90.

[222] AP Kraków, Castrensia cracoviensia relationes, 211, fos. 110–15; M. Bałaban, 'Żydzi w Olkuszu i gminach parafialnych', in his *Studia historyczne*, 158; J. Pęckowski, *Chrzanów, miasto powiatowe w województwie Krakowskim: Monografia* (Chrzanów, 1934), 150–1.

[223] AP Kraków, Castrensia, 211, fos. 347–9. Zyskielewicz complained that 'iż gdy w mieście Chrzanowie dziecię przypadkiem się zabiło, mieszczanie tamtejsi podrzucili go Żydowi jednemu, kupcowi chrzanowskiemu i to zabójstwo Żydom przypisują. Dzierżawca zaś dóbr pomienionych zaraz dwóch Żydów bez żadnej prawnej konwikcyi do więzienia wtrącić kazał. Doprasza się przeto o nakazanie uwolnienia rzeczonych więźniów o występek nieprzekonanych, którzy pewnie z tego zarzutu się wywiodą w sądzie przyzwoitym.'

was surprised by a coachman. A young Jewish tailor was arrested for attempted murder and was accused of acting on the order of the Jewish elders. While the municipal court sentenced him to death, the elders of the *kahal* were acquitted. The king, who was in Cracow at the time, took an interest in the case. He and several other notables tried to convince S. Wodzicki, who represented the girl's father, that Jews do not use Christian blood. Wodzicki was not convinced, but he bowed to the king's will, and the affair was 'hushed up'.[224]

## REMARKS ON LITHUANIA

Piotr Skarga wrote that in 1574 in the town of Punia, Joachim Smerlowicz, lease-holder of a brewery, murdered 7-year-old Elżbieta, daughter of Urszula from Lublin. The 'affair escaped punishment', however.[225] In 1592 some Jews in Wilno were accused of murdering 5-year-old Szymon Kirkelis.[226] On 24 April 1616 Jews allegedly killed Jan, son of Bartosz, a liege of Krzysztof Oleśnicki, in front of the synagogue. The Jews allegedly gave Oleśnicki eighty times 180 Lithuanian groszy to withdraw his accusation.[227]

In the middle of the seventeenth century, two Jews of Różana were sentenced to death.[228] Four Karaites were charged with the murder of a boy from the town of Szaty in 1679, and the verdict, delivered on 9 January 1680, sentenced them all to death. Later evidence, however, showed that the boy had drowned while swimming.[229] More details are known about the ritual murder trials against Jews of Kodeń (in 1698) and Biała Podlaska (in 1699 and 1710).[230] In 1760 some Jews were accused of murdering a nobleman and the vicar of an Orthodox church named Tuczynowicz. Five of the accused were sentenced to death.[231] In 1766 in the Lida district and in Troki, over 100 Jews were sentenced to death for alleged ritual murders.[232]

## CONCLUSION

This investigation reveals that in Poland between 1547 and 1787 there were eighty-one cases of ritual murder accusation: sixteen in the sixteenth century, thirty-three in the seventeenth century, and thirty-two in the eighteenth century. Not all of the accusations resulted in trials. Much of the information about those accused can only be found in the antisemitic literature of the period. Nevertheless, it should be remembered that most of these accusations took place at

---

[224] S. Wodzicki, *Wspomnienia z przeszłości od roku 1768 do roku 1840* (Cracow, 1873), 198–204; Bałaban, 'Żydzi w Olkuszu', 162–5.

[225] P. Skarga, *Żywoty świętych* (Vilnius, 1579), 289.  [226] Tazbir, 'Okrucieństwo', 56.

[227] S. Śleszkowski, *Odkrycie zdrad*, 95.  [228] Bałaban, 'Obvinenia', 868.

[229] M. Bałaban, 'Karaici w Polsce', in his *Studia historyczne*, 79–81.

[230] See text around nn. 170–1 above for other cases of blood libel in Lithuania.

[231] Załuski, *Morderstwa*, 28–9; Smoleński, *Stan*, 245.  [232] Smoleński, *Stan*, 245.

a time when ritual murder trials in western Europe had been consigned to history.[233]

By the end of the eighteenth century, ritual murder trials had disappeared even from Poland. To a great extent their gradual disappearance was linked with the stand taken by the Apostolic See, as expressed in the papal nuncio's letters of 1760 and 1763, as well as the abolition of torture in court proceedings by the Sejm in 1776.

The ritual murder trials of this period were made possible primarily because of the widespread belief in Jewish infanticide in the Commonwealth. J. Kitowicz's comments are characteristic: 'Freedom without *liberum veto* and Jewish matzo without Christian blood cannot exist'.[234] State policy, as well as the attitude of the king, the Catholic Church, and the *szlachta* (represented in the Sejms and Sejmiki) of the town administration and the landowners towards Jews played an important role in spreading this belief. Added to these was the economic threat posed by the Jewish population. Conflicts between Christians and Jews were much more acute during periods of war and epidemics in the mid-seventeenth and early eighteenth centuries. The superstitious mentality of the period also added to the flames. The more general problem of ritual murder accusations needs to be analysed in the broader context of Christian–Jewish relations, a subject that requires deeper research.

*Translated by Jolanta Kisler-Goldstein*

---

[233] Peuckert, *Ritualmord*, cols. 727–32; see also F. Frank, *Mord rytualny wobec trybunału prawdy i sprawiedliwości* (Warsaw, 1905).

[234] J. Kitowicz, *Opis obyczajów za panowania Augusta III* (Wrocław, 1950), 175.

# Jewish Art and Architecture in the East European Context: The Gwoździec-Chodorów Group of Wooden Synagogues

## THOMAS C. HUBKA

DURING the eighteenth century a unique type of wooden synagogue was built in the medium-sized towns of eastern Europe. Their style was characterized chiefly by a raised wooden ceiling or dome contained within a traditional east European timber roof structure. Although the buildings, along with their communities, were almost completely destroyed by the Nazis, the surviving documentation on the wooden synagogues provides a significant source for interpreting the popular culture of east European Jewry before the advent of modern reform and social movements, and before the rise of hasidism.[1]

The research for this article was funded in part by grants from the National Endowment for the Humanities and the National Endowment for the Arts.

Many people provided helpful suggestions for the article, although the final responsibility is entirely the author's; they include: Michael Steinlauf, Eleonora Bergman, Murray Rosman, Gershon Hundert, Adam Miłobędzki, Elliot Wolfson, Iris Fishof, Maria and Kazimierz Piechotka, Elhanan Reiner, Chone Shmeruck, Carol Krinsky, Shalom Sabar, Zeev Gries, Slawomir Parfianowicz, Iaroslav Isaievych, Stasys Samalavicius, Israel Bartal, Rachel Elior, Joseph Gutmann, Michael Mikos, Marvin Herzog, Marc Epstein, Siergiej Kratzov, Vivian Mann, Edward Van Voolen, David Assaf, Bezalel Narkiss, Mira Friedman, Richard Schoenwald, Jan Jagielski, Elliot Ginsburg, Samuel Heilman, Volodymyr Chornovus, Aliza Cohen-Mushlin, and Jacob Chonigsman.

[1] The origins of the hasidic movement during the middle of the 18th century have received intensive study, and new research has widened the scope of the initial movement beyond the circle of the Ba'al Shem Tov (see e.g. Joseph Weiss, *Studies in Eastern European Jewish Mysticism* (Oxford, 1985), 27–42, Louis Jacobs, *Hasidic Prayer* (London, 1972), 8–9, and Rachel Elior, *The Paradoxical Ascent to God* (Albany, NY, 1993), 8–9). There is little information, however, about the spread of hasidism to the masses of the Jewish people. For example, when and where did a certain percentage of Jewish society adopt hasidic ideas? From the sources available, the acceptance of hasidism by large numbers of Jews occurred some time after initial opposition to it began in *c.*1772 (see Gershom G. Scholem, *Major Trends in Jewish Mysticism* (New York, 1954), 323, 328, 337). Because interior-domed wooden synagogues became popular in east European communities in the first half of the 18th century, before popular acceptance of hasidism, the term 'pre-hasidic' may be applied to them. The issue of the pre-hasidic origins of these synagogues is important because, despite an extensive literature on the history of east European Judaism, far less is known about the masses of the Jewish people before 1800. This

Wooden synagogues have been publicized through scholarly, popular, and photographic sources, and the architecture has been analysed for over a century. In the fifty-year period prior to their destruction in the Second World War, considerable primary documentation was compiled, a significant amount of which survived the war and is now located in east European, Israeli, and newly accessible former Soviet archives.[2] The emergence of the interior-domed synagogue can be dated and subdivided into three historical stages: a gradual, trial-and-error introduction beginning at the end of the seventeenth and in the early eighteenth centuries, a rapid spread throughout the Polish–Lithuanian Commonwealth during the eighteenth century, and a discontinuation of the fully developed form at the beginning of the nineteenth century. Although this article concentrates on the wooden, interior-domed type, it is important to emphasize that there were other forms of the east European synagogue. The complete history of synagogue construction in this region includes many types of wooden and masonry structure, extending over an 800-year period and encompassing millions of Jews in hundreds of cities and towns spread across an enormous area more than double the size of the present Ukraine.[3] The map (Fig. 1) shows the furthest extent of the former Polish–Lithuanian Commonwealth where domed wooden synagogues were constructed.[4] Although integrally related to other types and styles of syna-

population lived primarily in the small towns of the former Polish–Lithuanian Commonwealth and constituted a Jewish popular culture from which these synagogues arose.

[2] See nn. 5 and 7 below.

[3] No complete statistical tabulation of the east European synagogues, including past and present wooden and masonry examples, has been attempted. Surviving masonry synagogues in present Poland have been listed by Eleonora Bergman and Jan Jagielski in 'The Function of Synagogues in the PPR', *Polin*, 5 (1988), 42–3. A complete historical tabulation of wooden synagogues in comparison to other synagogues would require an immense effort, involving case-study research in towns with Jewish populations over approximately fifty people, as listed in Shaul Stampfer, 'The 1764 Census of Polish Jewry', *Bar-Ilan*, 24–5 (1989), 60–147, and expanded by the towns listed in *Słownik geograficzny królestwa polskiego* (Warsaw, 1880). Such a comprehensive inventory has not been completed. Existing surveys of wooden synagogues include Piechotka, *Wooden Synagogues*, 196–210 and [221], Loukomski, *Jewish Art*, 63–5, David Davidovitch, *The Synagogues in Poland and their Destruction* (Jerusalem, 1960), 97, and Yargina, *Wooden Synagogues*, 72–3 (unnumbered). These surveys, however, do not reflect complete historical documentation, but rather a selective editing, based largely on incomplete photographic and architectural survey information. When a complete historical survey is taken of all the synagogues ever built in a medium-sized town (e.g. Eleonora Bergman, 'Góra Kalwaria: The Impact of a Hasidic Cult on the Urban Landscape of a Small Polish Town', *Polin*, 1 (1988), 13–15, 22–3), the greater numbers and complexity of synagogue development through time become evident. Bergman's current research on the synagogues of Warsaw will document an exceedingly complex architectural history where over 300 synagogues and houses of prayer existed in 1900.

[4] Confusion about the region or country of origin is often related to the results of the Polish partitions (1772–95), which divided the Polish–Lithuanian Commonwealth between Russia, Germany, and Austria–Hungary. Most domed wooden synagogues were constructed under the administration and within the culture of the Polish–Lithuanian Commonwealth and even when built after the partitions, the construction techniques and cultural context for these synagogues were largely a continuation of Polish–Lithuanian Commonwealth practices. Other types and styles of wooden synagogue

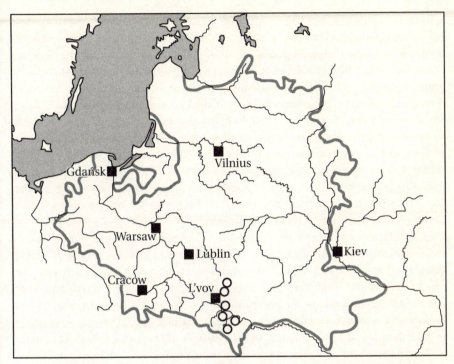

**Fig. 1** Map of eastern Europe showing the furthest extent of the Polish–Lithuanian Commonwealth where wooden synagogues with interior domes were constructed. Markers locate the six case-study towns

gogue, for example the single-vault masonry synagogues from the larger towns, the wooden, interior-domed type achieved a broad unity of similar structures over a wide area during the eighteenth century. Furthermore, while synagogues made out of wood were constructed over a continuous period from the earliest Jewish settlement in at least the thirteenth century until the late 1930s, the emergence of the interior-domed type marks a significant turning-point and refinement in the art of wooden synagogue construction and is related to the rise of a trading-town culture of east European Jewry from the sixteenth to the eighteenth centuries.

This essay concentrates on a specific group of eighteenth-century wooden synagogues—labelled here the Gwoździec–Chodorów group—within their east European context. The goal is to identify the architectural ideas and building

continued to be constructed in eastern Europe, primarily under Russian administration in the Pale of Settlement, e.g. the newly discovered late 19th-century wooden and masonry synagogue (wooden frame, with masonry infill, and stucco exterior) at Velikiye Komyaty, southern Ukraine (Yargina, *Wooden Synagogues*, 65–9). During the 18th century, other types of wooden synagogues were constructed in the countries surrounding the Polish–Lithuanian Commonwealth, including wooden-frame and masonry infill synagogues in Germany (David Davidovitch, *Wandmalereien in alten Synagogen* (Hameln, 1969)), and Switzerland (Carol Krinsky, *Synagogues of Europe* (New York, 1985), 280–2).

traditions which generated these synagogues, and particularly to emphasize the role of ideas from Jewish sources and from the Jewish community in this process. This entails investigating all phases of building development, including sponsorship, inspiration, liturgy, design, construction, and painting, and then differentiating between non-Jewish east European sources and sources from the local and the broader Jewish community. The existing architectural scholarship about wooden synagogues is primarily based upon east European sources and, although Jewish sources are assumed by most scholars, little is actually known about the role of Jews in the design and construction of the wooden synagogues.[5] For example, traditions of the exterior shape and wooden construction of the synagogues have been firmly linked to east European regional architectural traditions, yet, except for the wall paintings, almost nothing is known about the ways Jews may have been involved in the entire building process.

The differentiation between Jewish and non-Jewish sources of design risks a polarized interpretation of the process of architectural design, which is highly integrative and, in the case of the wooden synagogues, combined many types of artistic and cultural tradition.[6] In addition, the emphasis on the Jewish aspects of synagogue design is not meant to minimize the considerable east European contribution which, if weighed in purely architectural terms, must be considered far greater than any Jewish influence. Rather, the role of Jewish ideas requires careful differentiation because their influence on the architecture of the synagogues has been so loosely assumed and insufficiently documented in current scholarship.

## THE GWOŹDZIEC–CHODORÓW GROUP

The Gwoździec–Chodorów group comprises six wooden synagogues built and painted during the late seventeenth century and the first half of the eighteenth in a region surrounding Lwów, Ukraine. The synagogues of Gwoździec and Chodorów have been selected because they are the oldest fully documented

[5] The collective works of Maria and Kazimierz Piechotka contain the most complete record of surviving archival sources and the finest bibliographic guides, especially in *Wooden Synagogues* (Polish edn. 1957; Eng. trans. Warsaw, 1959), 7–8, 48–50, 216–19, and 'Polichromie polskich bóżnic drewnianych', *Polska Sztuka Ludowa*, 43/1–2 (1989), 65–87. I wish to thank Maria and Kazimierz Piechotka for their generous advice and to acknowledge their seminal works on the wooden synagogues. Other extensive bibliographies include David Davidovitch, *Wall-Paintings of Synagogues in Poland* (Heb.) (Jerusalem, 1968), 71–109, George K. Loukomski, *Jewish Art in European Synagogues* (London, 1947), 59–65, and Rachel Wischnitzer, *The Architecture of the European Synagogue* (Philadelphia, 1964), 290–1. New archival information has recently been located in former Soviet collections, e.g. Z. Yargina, *Wooden Synagogues* (Moscow, n.d. [*c.*1993]), 60–4. Various photographic sources exist in public and private collections, e.g. the Tel Aviv Museum of Art, Department of Prints and Drawings, and private collections, e.g. that of Tomasz Wiśniewski, Białystok, Poland.

[6] The necessity of interpreting architectural design as a highly integrative process and the difficulty of isolating individual factors which contribute to that process is emphasized by many architectural theorists, including William Kleinsasser, *Synthesis*, ix (Eugene, Oreg., 1994), 9–24.

interior-domed structures.[7] Most historians have long recognized the basic similarities among the synagogues of this region, including their plans, construction materials and techniques, and exterior and interior style and details. But it is particularly the signed and dated wall paintings that have provided investigators with substantial evidence of their closely associated development. Previous studies have usually classified all east European wooden synagogues within a larger typological building group, including examples from all eras and regions of the former Polish–Lithuanian Commonwealth. Yet considerable regional and temporal variations exist between synagogue types.[8] This research, therefore, concentrates on a smaller, more homogeneous, sample in order to construct a more precise account of their architectural development.

The major characteristics of synagogues from the Gwoździec–Chodorów group are encapsulated in a single example. Kamionka Strumilowa, like most eighteenth-century wooden synagogues, was principally distinguished by an elaborate raised ceiling constructed within a towering timber structure roof (Fig. 2). Built at the beginning of the eighteenth century, the synagogue's interior followed a standard organization featuring a nearly square floor plan (approximately 11 m. × 11.5 m.), defined by hewn log walls and surmounted by a two-tiered, hipped roof supporting a low barrel-vault hung from the centre of the ceiling (Fig. 3).[9]

[7] The six related synagogues are from the towns of Gwoździec, Chodorów, Kamionka Strumilowa, Jabłonów, Jaryczów, and Brzozdowce. Other neighbouring synagogues were closely related but could not be included because of limited documentation. The Jabłonów synagogue was included, despite its lack of a domed ceiling, because in all other respects it is closely related to the other structures. The unity of the Lwów region's synagogues are cited in Piechotka and Piechotka, *Wooden Synagogues*, 18, 34, 196–210, and 'Polichromie', 73–6. Data about the age of the Gwoździec and Chodorów synagogues is analysed by Piechotka, 'Polichromie', 73 nn. 37–8. Newly available archival information in Ukraine reveals similar synagogues in Podolia (east of the Lwów region) which appear to share architectural characteristics with the Gwoździec–Chodorów group, including the towns of Michalpol, Smotrich, Minkovtsy, and Jarochow (D. Shcherbakivsky Collection, Ukrainian Institute for Archaeology, Kiev, and S. Taranushchenko Collection, Central Scientific Library of the Academy of Sciences of Ukraine, Kiev).

[8] All historians of the Polish synagogues have divided the structures into wooden and masonry categories with various subcategories in each group, e.g. Wischnitzer, *The Architecture of the European Synagogue*, 125–47. The Piechotkas made this general distinction but emphasize that there are also many similarities between wooden and masonry types (*Wooden Synagogues*, 35). Adam Miłobędzki ('Architecture in Wood: Technology, Symbolic Content, Art', *Artibus et Historiae*, 19 (1989), 195–8) has proposed a sophisticated analysis of the various types of wooden synagogue, emphasizing that the interior-dome type represented a radical, innovative departure from earlier forms of medieval wood construction. The seemingly obvious grouping of buildings according to construction material is only one of several ways to classify architecture. In many building traditions, a structure is not altered by changes in building materials or usage (see e.g. Thomas C. Hubka, *Big House, Little House, Back House, Barn: The Connected Farm Buildings of New England* (Hanover, NH, 1984), 138–44).

[9] Piechotka and Piechotka, *Wooden Synagogues*, 197–8, and extensive photographs and architectural drawings of the Kamionka Strumilowa synagogue, Tel Aviv Museum of Art, Department of Prints and Drawings.

Fig. 2  Exterior, wooden synagogue, Kamionka Strumilowa, Ukraine.
Tel Aviv Museum of Art

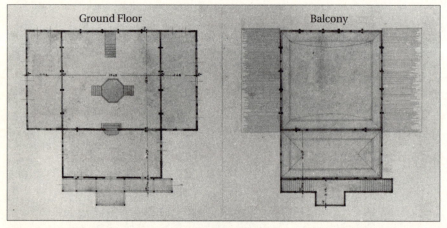

Fig. 3  Plan, wooden synagogue, Kamionka Strumilowa, Ukraine.
Tel Aviv Museum of Art

Similar to most synagogues of the interior-domed type, the major prayer hall at
Kamionka Strumilowa was axially organized between an entrance door in the
middle of the western wall, a centrally located *bimah*, or reader's platform, and an
ark containing the Torah scrolls located in the middle of the eastern wall (Fig. 4).
Various ancillary rooms in low sheds surrounded the main hall, and a women's
gallery with an elaborate exterior balcony was located above the entrance in a
major second-floor room. The broad wooden barrel-vaulted dome, which domi-

**Fig. 4** Section looking east, wooden synagogue, Kamionka Strumilowa, Ukraine.
Tel Aviv Museum of Art

nated the interior space, was a non-structural canopy suspended from the centre of an ingenious structural system modified from the standard east European vernacular timber roof frame. As the roof section drawing reveals (Fig. 5), the outer, structural roof and the inner, applied dome were shaped differently and acted independently of each other following different traditions of building construction and historical development.[10] Through several regional variations, the basic configuration of the interior-domed synagogue, as typified by Kamionka Strumilowa, became a standard formula for the east European wooden synagogue in medium-sized towns of the Polish–Lithuanian Commonwealth throughout the eighteenth century.

[10] The sophistication of the roof truss systems has been widely cited and analysed in detail (see e.g. Piechotka and Piechotka, *Wooden Synagogues*, 38–43). The synagogue-builders demonstrated considerable skill by narrowing the roof trusses of the traditional structural systems in order to accommodate the large domes that extended into the volume of the roof. From a modernist interpretation, several of these synagogues appear to follow a functionalist formula expressing the integration between the internal dome and the supporting roof structure. If many synagogues are compared, however, it is clear that the roof structure and the suspended cupola followed different principles of construction and responded to fundamentally different ideas about the expression of architecture. The fact that the interior dome was attached to, and hung from, the roof truss does not mean that the two systems were highly integrated or followed the same logic of construction.

**Fig. 5** Section looking south, wooden synagogue, Kamionka Strumilowa, Ukraine.
Tel Aviv Museum of Art

## THE DEVELOPMENT OF THE INTERIOR-DOMED
## WOODEN SYNAGOGUES

The development and significance of the interior-domed type of wooden synagogue exemplified by the Gwoździec–Chodorów group and the role of the Jewish
community in this development can be summarized in seven interrelated
hypotheses, each of which will be developed further:

1. Interior-domed wooden synagogues, which were first developed between
*c.*1675 and *c.*1725, represented a major change from previous, pre-1700, synagogues
by incorporating a Baroque-inspired dome into the structural framework of a
traditional vernacular roof structure.

2. While related to various regional structures, such as Polish and Ukrainian
vernacular wooden churches, the interior-domed synagogues were, in their totality, unique structures, unlike any other buildings in their eighteenth-century
small-town environments. The wooden synagogues should, therefore, be interpreted as a unified building type, composed of various regional building vocabularies representing an indigenous creation of their east European Jewish communities.

3. Support and patronage for this new type of synagogue originated in the centres
of Jewish community leadership and rabbinic authority in the medium-sized
towns where they were constructed. They were not produced by isolated, peripheral, or radical elements within the Jewish community.

4. The entire architectural and artistic ensemble of the interior-domed synagogue should be seen as an expression of a mainstream Judaism as popularly practised in the medium-sized towns of the Polish–Lithuanian Commonwealth during the eighteenth century. By the beginning of the nineteenth century, a major portion of this popular culture was transformed by the hasidic movement. The wooden synagogues, therefore, represent a significant material expression of a largely undocumented early eighteenth-century, pre-hasidic, Jewish popular culture.

5. The insertion of an elaborate wooden dome or cupola created a dynamic, vitalized place of worship, the accentuated dome acting to exaggerate the height, lighting effects, and dramatic spatial qualities of the interior. Though related both to late Baroque east European monumental buildings and to Ukrainian folk churches, the synagogues with their wooden domes were unique hybrids unlike any other buildings in their context.

6. While the overall plan and organization followed long-established synagogue precedent, portions of the wooden synagogues' design were also influenced by kabbalistic literature, particularly the Zohar.

7. The organization of the wooden synagogues' elaborate wall paintings was determined by liturgical considerations and included Hebrew inscriptions, primarily daily prayer, set within large text panels. These painted texts were arranged on tapestry-like backgrounds with allegorical animal figures and decorative floral motifs. While stylistic aspects of the paintings are related to east European decorative motifs, the wall paintings primarily express the content and artistic traditions of Jewish sources, and were painted by Jewish artists for the Jewish community.

## EXISTING THEORIES

Maria and Kazimierz Piechotka have produced several of the finest studies of the wooden synagogue, and their scholarship has influenced all subsequent architectural study. Yet scholarly opinion about the synagogues has also been influenced by theories outside the field of architecture, for example, the generally accepted perception of the economic and social decline of east European Jewry following the Chmielnicki massacres of 1648.[11] In the case of the communities that built

---

[11] The well-documented tragedies of the Chmielnicki revolt for the Jewish populations of eastern Poland–Lithuania have unavoidably created the impression that Jewish culture in these regions was irrevocably damaged (as stated in Robert M. Seltzer, *Jewish People, Jewish Thought* (New York, 1980), 480–96). The resurgence of Jewish populations in these same regions within 100 years of the massacres is, however, noted by most demographic historians (e.g. Andrzej Link-Lenczowski, 'The Jewish Population in the Light of the Resolutions of the Dietines in the Sixteenth to the Eighteenth Centuries', in Antony Polonsky, Jakub Basista, and Andrzej Link-Lenczowski (eds.), *The Jews in Old Poland, 1000–1795* (London, 1993), 36–44).

wooden synagogues, a theory of Jewish community decline must be balanced by the record of eighteenth-century economic and social stability in many towns. In the following sections I delineate a group of related theories which have limited the historical analysis of the wooden synagogues before formulating an explanation of the design ideas underlying their development.

## The Perception of the Shtetl

The image of poverty in the small-town, east European Jewish community is widespread, and often uncritically examined. This perception is certainly accurate when applied to the well-documented nineteenth-century economic and social decline of the shtetl community in the Russian 'Pale of Settlement'.[12] However, detailed case-studies of Jewish communities from eastern Europe in the eighteenth century, such as the recent works of Gershon Hundert and Murray Rosman, do not convey a picture of poverty, and certainly do not demonstrate an economic, social, or religious decline.[13] Instead, these studies portray a complex, multicultural, pre-partition environment where Jewish populations increased in private towns under Polish magnate control, and where, in many regions, they developed prosperous economies and a degree of social stability. It was primarily in these medium-sized towns in the eastern regions of the Polish–Lithuanian Commonwealth, beyond the decaying urban centres most often studied by economic and social historians, that Jewish populations soared and their communities built new, indigenous forms of both wooden and masonry synagogues.[14]

The wooden synagogues that were produced in these medium-sized towns

[12] Daniel Beauvois, 'Polish–Jewish Relations in the Territories Annexed by the Russian Empire in the First Half of the Nineteenth Century', in Chimen Abramsky, Maciej Jachimczyk, and Antony Polonsky (eds.), *The Jews in Poland* (Oxford, 1986), 78–90.

[13] Murray Rosman, *The Lords' Jews* (Cambridge, Mass., 1990), 75–105, and Gershon David Hundert, *The Jews in a Polish Private Town* (Baltimore, 1992), 46–68. The social and economic deterioration of east European Jewry after 1648 has been addressed by many historians since S. M. Dubnow, *History of Jews of Russia and Poland* (Philadelphia, 1916), 138–87. Many scholars have based their conclusions about the 18th century on the extremely negative assessments of 19th-century rationalist historians (e.g. Heinrich Graetz, *History of the Jews*, v (Philadelphia, 1956), 51–6, 375–94). While these assessments are correct for the period immediately after the Chmielnicki massacres and for the well-documented declines of the 19th and 20th centuries, economic and demographic research from the 18th century does not support this view (e.g. Rosman, *The Lords' Jews*, 75–105). Because of differences between regions and class cultures, there are varying assessments of the well-being of Polish society in the 18th century. For a negative assessment of the 18th-century era, see Jacek Kochanowicz, 'The Polish Economy and the Evolution of Dependency', in Daniel Chirot (ed.), *The Origins of Backwardness in Eastern Europe* (Berkeley, 1989), 92–130; for a balanced work, see Ignacy Schiper, *Dzieje handlu żydowskiego na ziemiach polskich* (Warsaw, 1937), 1–24; and for a positive assessment, see Jonathan Israel, *European Jewry in the Age of Mercantilism, 1550–1750* (Oxford, 1989), 145–83, esp. 182.

[14] Polish historians have generally not called attention to these regions of magnate prosperity in their otherwise detailed analysis of the 18th century, pre-partition period (e.g. Aleksander Gieysztor, *History of Poland* (Warsaw, 1968), 272–319); an exception is Norman Davies, *Heart of Europe* (Oxford, 1984), 316–54.

were certainly not cheap or inexpensive, as is often assumed. In comparison to buildings of a similar scale in these communities, the wooden synagogues exhibited some of the highest standards of construction, craftsmanship, and technical expertise in their regions.[15] The frequently ornate wood carving of the ark and *bimah* were particularly expensive items in all periods. In the case of the synagogue at Olkienniki, Lithuania, the ark and *bimah*, donated by wealthy community members, displayed craftsmanship of the finest quality in the region comparable to the finest ornamental woodwork produced in Poland during the second half of the eighteenth century.[16]

## The Perception of Wooden Construction

The negative image of wooden construction for synagogues in the trading towns of eastern Europe is commonly shared by generations of immigrants from this region. This perception has been reinforced by contemporary media depictions of the plight of east European Jewry in the nineteenth century, as, for example, in the play and film *Fiddler on the Roof*. In this popularized form, the image of the 'wooden shtetl' and its wooden synagogue has unavoidably become associated with east European backwardness and poverty.

In the eighteenth century, however, the use of wood was certainly not a mark of poverty or backwardness. Although masonry buildings clearly represented the highest standard of building construction, wood was the accepted norm for most structures in all but the largest cities and was even employed in some of the finest palaces, churches, and government buildings of the period.[17] In the medium-sized towns of eastern Europe before 1800, only a few major buildings were built in masonry, and these were usually constructed for the Catholic Church and the Polish nobility or town owners.[18] This general acceptance of wooden structures,

---

[15] The Piechotkas' summary of the complex processes of building and construction techniques is still the finest available (*Wooden Synagogues*, 35–47). Since no documentation of synagogue building accounts has been located, the construction records of similar-scale wooden churches and monumental buildings provide a comparison (see Czesław Krassowski and Adam Miłobędzki, 'Studia nad zabudową miasteczka Ciezkowice', *Kwartalnik Architektury i Urbanistyki*, 2/1 (1957), 33–6; Henryk Samsonowicz, 'Uwagi o budownictwie w Polsce u schylku wieków średnich', *Studia z historii architektury: Sztuki i kultury ofiarowane Adamowi Miłobędzkiemu* (Warsaw, 1989), 117–19; Tadeusz Mankowski, *Fabrica ecclesiae* (Warsaw, 1946), 5–14). Each of these studies details 18th-century construction practices including costs, which were always considerable, and required substantial royal, church, and magnate patronage. No study based on documentation of building construction from 18th-century east European sources has stated or implied that wooden construction on the scale of the wooden synagogues was ever inexpensive.

[16] Shlomo Farber (ed.), *Olkienniki in Flames: A Memorial Book* (Tel Aviv, 1962), 84.

[17] Piechotka and Piechotka, *Wooden Synagogues*, 35.

[18] In Chodorów, which contained a major interior-domed wooden synagogue, detailed property and building maps from 1846 show nine masonry structures out of a total of approximately 350 major buildings in the town centre. Seven of the masonry buildings were owned by either the Catholic Church or the town owner, and two masonry structures may have belonged to Jewish residents (State Archives of the Lwów Region, Lwów, file 186/4/38, fos. 494–510). The author reviewed ten other towns in the Lwów

however, changed in the nineteenth century as masonry structures were increasingly adopted in the medium-sized towns of eastern Europe as a remedy for problems created by fire, overcrowding, and unsanitary conditions. Since this change
in perception coincided with a general worsening of living conditions for the
masses of east European Jewry, particularly in the Russian 'Pale of Settlement',
by the beginning of the twentieth century the wooden shtetl had indeed become a
sign of backwardness and poverty.[19] However, this negative image should not be
applied to the expanding towns that built wooden synagogues in the eighteenth
century, like the synagogues of the Gwoździec–Chodorów group.

## The Relationship between Wooden and Masonry Synagogues

Wooden synagogues have generally been interpreted as derivative of and subordinate to the larger masonry synagogues, but in fact both types date to the
earliest period of Jewish settlement and both have claims to originality and distinctiveness within their long period of intertwined development.[20] While it is
generally true that the inspiration for the shape of the interior wooden dome can
be attributed to historical precedents amongst masonry structures (both synagogues and churches), the increasingly elaborate form of the eighteenth-century
wooden dome combined ideas from many sources to achieve a unique synthesis
not entirely derived from vaulted masonry domes.

Detailed comparisons between wooden and masonry synagogues reveal fundamental differences in shape, lighting characteristics, and overall spatial effect. These
differences are clearly demonstrated in sectional analysis, where the smooth, continuous contours of the typical masonry vault are contrasted with the irregularly stepped,
multi-tiered ceiling, often with deep recesses, of the typical wooden dome (Fig. 6): a
contrast between a structural feature and a non-structural insertion created for spatial
effect. The wooden dome and masonry vault, therefore, produced different types of
spatial experience revealing different conceptions of the space of the synagogue, and
emphasize a basic contrast between the unified structural rationality of the masonry
vault and the vibrant, mysterious complexity of the wooden dome.[21]

region with pre-1939 wooden synagogues; all had similar ratios of wooden buildings to masonry buildings. Even higher percentages of wooden structures existed in the 18th century before these censuses
were taken. Similar conclusions are drawn in Piechotka and Piechotka, *Wooden Synagogues*, 35.

[19] Widely published photographic documentation from the late 19th and 20th centuries depicting
the poverty of east European Jewish communities has unavoidably reinforced the popular and scholarly image of perpetual poverty for these regions (e.g. Lucjan Dobroszycki and Barbara Kirshenblatt-
Gimblett, *Image Before My Eyes* (New York, 1977), 39–101).

[20] The sources and development of the masonry synagogues are analysed by Piechotka and
Piechotka, *Wooden Synagogues*, 23–34, and Wischnitzer, *European Synagogues*, 107–24.

[21] Modernist theory has reinforced the link between structural systems and the idea of simple and
direct expression, yet structural systems have historically expressed many different types of idea. For
example, in the Gothic revival era, structural clarity and its rational expression followed a different,
more elaborate structural logic, as expressed by John Ruskin, *The Seven Lamps of Architecture* (New
York, 1871), 25–56.

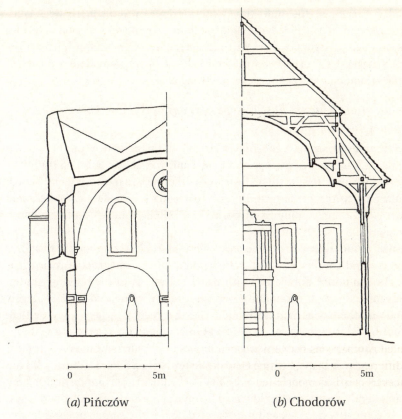

(*a*) Pińczów　　　　　　　　(*b*) Chodorów

**Fig. 6** Roof sections, a comparison of wooden and masonry synagogues.
Based upon drawings from Piechotka and Piechotka, *Wooden Synagogues*

The differences between wooden and masonry vaulting suggest that during the eighteenth century there existed two parallel, frequently intersecting, yet distinct types of east European synagogue: the masonry tradition, which culminated during the seventeenth century in the nine-vault plan type, and the wooden tradition, which culminated during the eighteenth century in the interior-domed type.[22] It remains to be interpreted whether these major architectural differences between wooden and masonry synagogues were reflective of stylistic and aesthetic preferences or were representative of deeper liturgical or cultural differences between the larger towns and cities, where masonry synagogues were primarily built, and the medium-sized towns, where wooden synagogues were primarily built. Whatever the meaning of these differences, the major defining characteristic of

---

[22] The development and significance of the nine-vault plan is analysed in Piechotka and Piechotka, *Wooden Synagogues*, 29–34; Krinsky, *Synagogues of Europe*, 200–25, and Siergiej Kratzov, 'On the Genesis of the Nine-Bay Synagogue', *Jewish Art* (1996).

the wooden synagogue, the multi-tiered interior dome, was distinctly not a component of the typical masonry synagogue (or church) of the same period. The idea that the wooden synagogues were directly derivative of and subordinate to the masonry synagogues must, therefore, be modified to accommodate a theory of parallel development between these major synagogue types.

## The Relationship between East European Wooden Buildings and Wooden Synagogues

Architectural historians have most often attributed the influences on the wooden synagogues to various east European regional and vernacular building traditions from the lands where Jews settled. Two types of source are most frequently cited: vernacular structures of eastern Europe, particularly wooden churches, and monumental Baroque buildings of both the Catholic Church and the Polish aristocracy.[23]

In order to understand the influence of these sources, it is important to appreciate the cultural context in which Jewish communities constructed their synagogues. As a minority population with restricted access to the building trades, buildings for the Jewish community were necessarily influenced by, and largely restricted to, the styles and techniques of the regions where they settled. Therefore Jewish architecture was, and had to be, integrally related to the dominant architectural styles and building techniques of the surrounding region.

But this necessarily derivative nature of the Jewish building vocabulary did not prevent the Jewish communities of the Polish–Lithuanian Commonwealth from producing highly distinctive buildings. The interpretation of this distinctiveness within its context is complex and multifaceted, and is the source of considerable debate and confusion. In order to clarify the issue, a general distinction can be drawn between the influences on the interiors and the exteriors of the wooden synagogues.

### The Exterior

The exteriors of the wooden synagogues, including their structural system, were strongly influenced by the architecture of both vernacular wooden buildings and secular and religious (Christian) structures in the high style.[24] The principal

---

[23] Many investigators who have surveyed only the wooden synagogues have emphasized the relationship to, and derivation from, regional vernacular structures (e.g. Stefan Szyller, *Czy mamy Polską architekturę?* (Warsaw, 1916), 51). The Piechotkas' detailed, comprehensive study (*Wooden Synagogues*, 37–46) presents a much more balanced interpretation, especially emphasizing similarities and differences with regional architecture and the wooden churches.

[24] Piechotka and Piechotka, *Wooden Synagogues*, 35–47; Titus D. Hewryk, *Masterpieces in Wood: Houses of Worship in Ukraine* (New York, 1987), 78–85; summarized in Adam Miłobędzki, *Architektura Polska, XVII wieku* (Warsaw, 1980), 334–8. Several detailed studies by Marian Kornecki demonstrate the similarities and differences between similar-scale 18th-century wooden churches, e.g. 'Małopolskie kościoły drewniane doby baroku, XVIII wieku', *Teka Komisji Urbanistyki i Architektury*, 8 (1979), 117–32.

**Fig. 7** Exterior, wooden church of St George, Drohobych, Ukraine.
Titus D. Hewryk, *Masterpieces in Wood: Houses of Worship in Ukraine*

features borrowed by the builders of wooden synagogues include the shape of the multi-tiered roof, the ornamental decorative woodwork, the twin flanking towers (on some synagogues), the systems of roof-truss framing, and the ubiquitous stacked-log construction systems of the walls. Together, these 'borrowed' characteristics constituted an entire vocabulary of building components, yet even these essential similarities between the wooden synagogues and the surrounding regional architecture did not produce identical buildings. Even when set in the context of their communities and compared with regional buildings, the wooden synagogues were still highly distinctive structures.[25] The plainer, larger, centralized proportions of the typical wooden synagogue contrast with the smaller, usually multi-towered, elongated proportions of a similar-scale regional wooden church (the most frequently compared type of building), exemplified by the Church of St George, Drohobych, Ukraine, in 1659–60 (Figs. 7 and 8). Although the silhouettes and exotic shapes of both churches and synagogues may appear similar to scholars unfamiliar with the vernacular buildings of eastern Europe, closer

[25] Various vernacular building types in eastern Europe share portions of the typical wooden synagogue's construction vocabulary, e.g. the common tavern or inn, as documented in Bohdan Baranowski, *Polska karczma* (Wrocław, 1979), figs. 1–51.

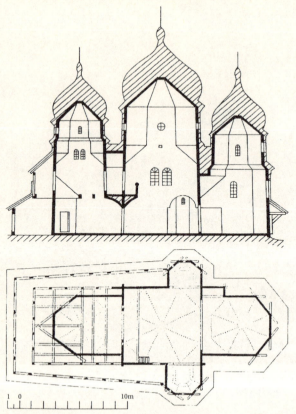

**Fig. 8** Plan and section, wooden church of St George, Drohobych, Ukraine.
Titus D. Hewryk, *Masterpieces in Wood: Houses of Worship in Ukraine*

inspection reveals that, although similar construction vocabularies were employed, their respective builders did not produce similar buildings (compare Figs. 1 and 7).

*The Interior*

The interiors of the wooden synagogues were also strongly influenced by the regional building traditions of eastern Europe, but, despite similarities long noted by architectural investigators, when viewed as a whole, the synagogues' interiors are unique architectural creations and among the most original in the history of synagogue architecture. Detailed analysis reveals that a multitude of east European artistic and architectural sources did indeed provide a basic vocabulary for the builders of the interiors, as is readily apparent, for example, in comparisons of arks and altars, ornamental woodwork, and the decorative motifs of the wall paintings.[26] Nevertheless, these ideas were freely incorporated to produce

---

[26] For example, compare altars in Adam Miłobędzki, *Architektura*, 276–82, and iconostases (altar screens in Orthodox churches) in Hewryk, *Masterpieces*, 30–4, and arks in Piechotka and Piechotka, *Wooden Synagogues*, 52–195 (unnumbered).

hybrid designs, derivative yet original in their totality, and reflective of Jewish artistic and liturgical influences.

A full test of this assertion of the originality of synagogue design would require detailed comparison of many elements of the interior and is beyond the scope of this essay. It is hoped, however, that a brief analysis of the major defining characteristic, the dome, might suffice to demonstrate this thesis. The multi-tiered wooden dome does not at first appear to be related to Jewish sources or influences primarily because precedents were found in most east European religious and secular building traditions. The wooden domes and barrel vaults of vernacular churches, especially the log cupolas of Ukrainian Uniate (Catholic) and Orthodox folk churches, are regional precedents for the synagogues' raised ceilings and have been cited by most scholars.[27] The elaborate Baroque domes of Catholic churches and monumental secular buildings are some of the most consistent components of seventeenth- and eighteenth-century architecture in eastern Europe, and these precedents were particularly influential to the builders of wooden synagogues.[28] Furthermore, as discussed above, the vaulting of the masonry synagogues was one of the most likely sources for the domes of the wooden synagogues. In other words, there was no shortage of raised ceilings and domes from which the eighteenth-century builders could draw their inspiration.

These various models did indeed provide ideas that were skilfully manipulated by synagogue designers. In the most mature period of development, during the late eighteenth century, several east European Baroque spatial devices were adapted in the synagogues to produce a novel, telescoping dome in which blind balconies and deep recesses accentuated the apparent height and depth of the cupola to produce a dramatic sense of spatial mystery (see Figs. 4 and 7).[29] This

[27] Ukrainian wooden churches with log domes were built during the same period and in the same regions as wooden synagogues (see Hewryk, *Masterpieces in Wood*, 22–36; G. N. Logvin, *Monuments of Art in the Soviet Union, Ukraine, and Moldavia* (Russian) (Moscow, 1982), 9–13, and pt. II. *passim*). While providing a clear referential source for the wooden synagogues, these domes are also quite small and dark and are derived from an ancient tradition of log construction. The lighted, soaring volume of the wooden synagogues created an entirely different, more expansive, spatial experience.

[28] Baroque domes in Catholic and Orthodox churches and monumental secular buildings are some of the most consistent features of 17th–19th-century architecture in the Polish–Lithuanian Commonwealth and are analysed in an extensive literature (e.g. Adam Miłobędzki, *Zarys dziejów architektury w Polsce* (Warsaw, 1988), 152–215, and Miłobędzki, *Architektura Polska, passim*.

[29] Accompanying a massive campaign of Jesuit church-building, Italian architects and advanced ideas of the Italian Baroque were imported to the Polish–Lithuanian Commonwealth in the 17th and 18th centuries. This generated a sophisticated Baroque spatial tradition, as, for example, in the work of the architect Tylman van Gameren (Stanisław Mossakowski, *Tylman z Gameren: Architekt polskiego baroku* (Wrocław, 1973), 36–52). Throughout the 18th century, many features of the Italian Baroque were gradually incorporated into the vocabulary of wooden synagogues, reaching a peak of influence in the elaborate, multi-tiered interior domes of the Grodno–Białystok region during the late 1700s (Piechotka and Piechotka, *Wooden Synagogues*, 40–4). In synagogues of this last period of domed construction, neoclassical Baroque details were interwoven with an earlier, more sensuous,

technique differed from standard masonry practices and was without precedent in
the regional wooden architecture of eastern Europe. This exaggeration of the
Baroque technique of spatial foreshortening was perhaps the single most original
architectural feature of the interior-domed wooden synagogue type.

In the earliest examples of domed synagogues in the Gwoździec–Chodorów
group, the deep recesses and dramatic spatial effects of the later synagogues were
only suggested. Yet the spatial character of these earlier domes still differed sub-
stantively from surrounding structures (compare Figs. 4 and 8). Typically the
interior volumes of the synagogues were much wider and their domes much taller
than the domes of the various vernacular churches with which the synagogues are
most closely associated. Furthermore, the majority of Polish and Ukrainian
wooden churches had flat ceilings in all regions and periods. It is important to
note, however, that several other types of east European wooden churches and
secular buildings, such as the Church of the Annunciation, Tomaszów Lubelski,
Poland, 1727,[30] are more closely related to the wooden synagogues, providing
contextual, associative influences. Yet no single tradition can be said to be the
principal source for their architecture.

## THE CONTEXT OF SYNAGOGUE DESIGN

The combination of these theories has tended to limit the perception of wooden
synagogues as significant religious and cultural artefacts of their Jewish communities. This is unfortunate because, as this article demonstrates, they should be considered a product of their communities, and as such, highly reflective of the
dominant mainstream culture of early eighteenth-century Judaism. While individual structures differed slightly in physical appearance and architectural style,
most wooden synagogues of the period were planned and functioned similarly,
reflecting the influence of a common liturgy. A comparison of the towns that built
wooden synagogues at the time also reveals a set of recurring socio-economic
patterns underlying the architectural and cultural unity.[31]

late medieval concept of painted decorated space, as, for example, in the synagogue at Przedbórz,
Poland, 1760.

[30] The Church of the Annunciation united folk and high Baroque traditions in a form similar to
the wooden synagogues but without an interior wooden dome (Miłobędzki, 'Architecture in Wood',
195–7). Another group of structures related to the wooden synagogues was produced in eastern
Ukraine by the Russian Orthodox Church (see Hewryk, *Masterpieces in Wood*, 54–62, and David
Buxton, *The Wooden Churches of Eastern Europe* (Cambridge, 1981), 162–88). These elaborate
churches combined an ancient Ukrainian–Russian log-building tradition with concepts borrowed
from Russian Baroque architecture to produce soaring interior cupolas during the same period as the
domed synagogues (e.g. the Church of the Ascension, Berezin, 1761) (Figs. 10 and 11). Related
Polish churches are analysed in Adolf Szyszko-Bohusz, 'Kościoły w Tomaszowie i Mnichowie',
*Sprawozdania Komisyi do Badania Historii Sztuki w Polsce*, 8/3–4 (1912), 311–26.

[31] Data for three Ukrainian towns, Gwoździec, Jabłonów, and Chodorów, were primarily compiled from documents at the State Archives of the Lwów Region, Lwów; maps and inventory files for

1. During the late seventeenth and eighteenth centuries, large-scale Jewish population increases throughout the Polish–Lithuanian Commonwealth created the need for more and larger synagogues and accelerated the replacement of older, smaller structures in the trading towns of the eastern and southern regions. Population expansion was often accompanied by a change in the status of a town's Jewish community from being one of several minority groups to being the largest minority group.[32] When the interior-domed synagogues were built, their towns often contained Jewish populations that were becoming, or had already become, the numerical majority, with considerable influence, especially in the fields of commerce and trade. From this perspective, the interior-domed wood synagogues may be seen, as I believe their makers intended them to be seen, as the self-confident architectural expressions of expanding, economically vital, predominantly Jewish towns.

2. Synagogue construction was related to population growth, but was most often facilitated by a period of relative economic and social stability. Wooden construction was never inexpensive, and particularly so for the Jewish community, which had restricted access to the building trades.[33] Although it seems to contradict the common perception of post-1648 economic and social decline, the towns which built wooden synagogues experienced a relative social and economic stability, even following the destruction of the Chmielnicki uprisings.[34] This was certainly the case in the towns of the Gwoździec–Chodorów group, as well as for other towns throughout the Polish–Lithuanian Commonwealth where wooden synagogues were built.[35]

each town, and various sources in Ukrainian and Polish research libraries, e.g. a detailed 1712 census for Gwoździec, AGAD, doc. P-23, 242; and the letters of K. Maszkowski, WI-108, Polish Academy of Science Library, Cracow. Data for Olkienniki, Lithuania, were primarily compiled from documents at the Manuscript Division, Library of the Lithuanian Academy of Sciences, including F21–2109, the inventory for Olkienniki, 1749, and UDK-711.424 (474.5), an analysis of the historical development of Olkienniki. Data for Przedbórz were primarily compiled from an unpublished analysis of Przedbórz (in Polish) by Pawel Jaskanis, conducted by the Ministry of Culture, Department of Preservation, Warsaw, and various sources, e.g. C. Goldberg *et al.* (eds.) *Memory Book of the Community of Radomsk and its Region* (Tel Aviv, 1967).

[32] Nearly every work on early modern east European Jewish community demographics confirms this general trend of population growth (e.g. Hundert, *The Jews in a Polish Private Town*, 1–8, and Rosman, *The Lords' Jews*, 39–48). The 1764 census of Polish Jewry has been the basis for many scholarly assessments of the Jewish population trends in eastern Europe (see Stampfer, 'The 1764 Census of Polish Jewry', 41–60). In Chodorów, which contained a well-documented wooden synagogue, the Jewish population in the 1660s was 128; by 1720, a few years after the wooden synagogue had been remodelled and the ceiling painted, the population was 702 (Central Historical State Archives of Lwów, documents 146/85/2368 and 201).

[33] Various restrictions related to building construction and trade are discussed in Gershon David Hundert, 'Jewish Urban Residences in the Polish Commonwealth in the Early Modern Period', *Jewish Journal of Sociology*, 26/1(1984), 27–30.

[34] Hundert, *The Jews in a Polish Private Town*, 36–68; Rosman, *The Lords' Jews*, 37–88.

[35] For example, the 18th-century economic expansion of Przedbórz, where a wooden synagogue was built between 1755 and 1760, is detailed in Jaskanis, MS study of Przedbórz (see n. 31), A1–A63.

**3.** The complexity of the synagogue-building project necessitated unified support from the entire Jewish community of the small towns because construction was frequently initiated within a climate of church and burgher (Christian merchant) competition and hostility. Building restrictions, such as the frequent prohibition limiting Jewish merchants from occupying central commercial districts, often on the town square, also limited construction options[36] and necessitated unified backing from the central communal authorities: the *kahal*, the rabbinate, and a powerful citizenry.[37] Because of the many obstacles, the construction of a wooden synagogue in the early eighteenth century was itself a good indication of the presence of a stable, internally unified, and financially secure Jewish community.

**4.** Approval of the building project, or at least tacit acceptance, by the Polish king, local magnate, church, or other Gentile authorities was also necessary.[38] The evidence suggests that synagogue-building projects in privately owned towns, such as those of the Gwoździec–Chodorów group, often received the active support of the local ruler or magnate, who, despite objections from church and government representatives, frequently benefited from the Jewish community's contribution to the town's economic prosperity.[39] In the royal town of Przedborz, Poland, the Polish monarchy provided financial backing for rebuilding a new wooden synagogue, completed in 1760, after a fire destroyed a previous structure.[40]

An especially telling sign of mainstream institutional support for the building of the wooden synagogues is indirectly evidenced by the existence of well-documented Jewish painters and their painted synagogue interiors. Working in groups or perhaps regional schools, they created sophisticated traditions of synagogue decorative art by incorporating Hebrew texts into profusely decorated wall

Other towns of similar scale are analysed in Hundert, *The Jews in a Polish Private Town*, 46–68, and Rosman, *The Lords' Jews*, 73–105.

[36] Gershon David Hundert, 'The Role of the Jews in Commerce in Early Modern Poland–Lithuania', *Journal of European Economic History*, 162 (1987), 257–64.

[37] In all periods, discord or controversies within the Jewish community could be exploited by Catholic or government authorities, and by merchant competitors, with potentially severe consequences for the entire Jewish community, as detailed in Isaiah Kuperstein, 'Inquiry at Polaniec', *Bar-Ilan*, 24–5 (1989), 25–39.

[38] Rosman, *The Lords' Jews*, 172, 174.

[39] Magnate support for the Jewish populations of their privately owned towns is well documented (Hundert, *The Jews in a Polish Private Town*, 75–85; Rosman *The Lords' Jews*, 136–7, 145–6). Specific documentation on a town owner's support for the construction of a synagogue is cited by Rosman, *The Lords' Jews*, 172. Because of its potentially controversial nature, perhaps such documentation was generally suppressed. A common story told in various legends describes a Polish magnate's support for synagogue construction, e.g. in many of the legends collected by Shlomo An-ski (Shlomo Zainwil Rapoport) and published by Abraham Rechtman, *Jewish Ethnography and Folklore* (Yiddish) (Buenos Aires, 1958), 38–111. It is a story repeated in Jewish community memorial books (e.g. Farber (ed.), *Olkienniki in Flames*, 84).

[40] Piechotka and Piechotka, *Wooden Synagogues*, 206.

paintings.[41] Although specific accounts and references for commissioning these paintings have not been located, the occurrence of an art form incorporating Hebrew inscriptions and prayer, and occupying such a prominent place in the synagogue, could only have occurred with the full co-operation and active sponsorship of the highest authorities in the communities in which they were constructed. In this way the interior-domed synagogues and their elaborate paintings can be interpreted as reflecting the mainstream religious and cultural values of their communities. The painters Joseph son of Yehuda Leib and Israel son of Mordecai from Jarychów, Ukraine, who painted the Gwoździec Synagogue (see below), were probably associated with a school of regional painters active in the Lwów region in the first half of the eighteenth century.[42] Another well-documented painter was Eliezer, the son of Shlomo Katz Sussmann, a cantor from a synagogue in Brody, Ukraine. Between 1732 and 1742 he painted the interiors of several German wooden synagogues, including the Horb Synagogue now preserved at the Israel Museum.[43]

## HISTORICAL DEVELOPMENT

Little is known about the wooden synagogues that preceded the interior-domed type before *c.*1700.[44] While it has generally been correctly assumed that wooden

---

[41] Piechotka and Piechotka, 'Polichromie', 70–6. Well-established schools of Polish and Ukrainian painters existed in Brody during the 17th and 18th centuries (Volodymyr Aleksandrovich, 'Painters' Circles in Brody' (Ukrainian), *Dzvin*, 3/545 (1990), 113–18.

[42] Piechotka and Piechotka, 'Polichromie', 69–70.

[43] Davidovitch, *Wandmalereien in alten Synagogen*, 7–56.

[44] One of the major sources for dating the wooden synagogues was the pre-war documentation of Szymon Zajczyk and his staff (sources partially destroyed) compiled after the Second World War by Maria and Kazimierz Piechotka in *Wooden Synagogues*, 196–210, and supplemented by earlier site investigation sources. Where synagogues can be dated with a degree of accuracy, they were almost all produced within the 18th century. Several other synagogues, for which precise data is lacking, are assumed to have been built during the 17th century. As this research confirms, many wooden synagogues were indeed built before 1700 (see n. 46), but it is doubtful whether any of these structures survived into the late 19th century to be documented by modern historians. Several issues make 17th-century dating problematic for those synagogues that survived into the 20th century: the general lack of written documentation for the 17th century; the practice of remodelling and/or replacing existing synagogues on the same site, especially after destruction by fire; the common tendency of 19th- and early 20th-century antiquarian historians to exaggerate the ancientness of romantic wooden structures; the extreme difficulty of reading the Hebrew method of numerical calculation (the placement of small marks above letters) on the faded painted surfaces of the wooden synagogues; and the strong possibility that early researchers confused the commemorative dates related to the Chmielnicki massacres with construction dates for the synagogues. Whether or not some structures documented in the 20th century were structures that had survived from the 17th century, this research concentrates on the introduction of the wooden dome ceiling into the east European synagogue, and no interior dome can accurately be dated before *c.* 1700, as suggested by Piechotka and Piechotka, *Wooden Synagogues*, 39, and 'Polichromie', 74.

synagogues evolved out of masonry ones, the masonry vault influencing the dome of the wooden synagogues, it should be noted that there were wooden synagogues before several of the earliest known masonry synagogues, so that these wooden precedents may also have influenced later, masonry, synagogues.[45] This pattern of a wooden synagogue preceding a masonry one on the same site occurred in a previously undocumented site in Lwów during the middle of the sixteenth century. A recently discovered drawing cited by Iaroslav Isaievych shows a German diarist's sketch in 1578 of a log synagogue similar to the finer wooden buildings of its period (Fig. 9).[46] This structure was probably the wooden synagogue that burned in 1624 and was replaced in 1632–3 by Lwów's famous Suburban Synagogue, an early example of the nine-vault masonry synagogues.[47] The interior of this early wooden synagogue is unknown, but, based on comparisons with what is known about similar wooden churches and secular buildings of its period, it might have contained a flat ceiling or perhaps a low wooden barrel-vault.[48] Although the drawing of the Lwów structure is a rare representation of a pre-1700 wooden synagogue, it must stand for the many other wooden synagogues known only through documentation.

**Fig. 9** Sixteenth-century drawing, unidentified wooden synagogue, Lwów, Ukraine. Martin Greeneweg's diary, Gdańsk Library

[45] As, for example, in Lwów, 1624–32 (see n. 46), in Gniezno, 1582 (Piechotka and Piechotka, *Wooden Synagogues*, 49), and in Cracow, 1553–7 (Roman Spira, *Rabbis and Jewish Scholars in Poland in the Sixteenth, Seventeenth and Eighteenth Centuries* (Cracow, 1985), 23).

[46] Diary of Martin Greenewegs, Biblioteka Gdańska, Gdańsk, file 406–386/90. The diary is analysed in Iaroslav Isaievych, 'Naidavnishyi istorychnyi opys Lvova', *Zhovten*, 10 (1984), 109–13. I would like to thank Iaroslav Isaievych for bringing this reference to my attention.

[47] Krinsky, *Synagogues of Europe*, 215–16.

[48] Barrel-vaults were continuously employed in Polish church architecture beginning in the 14th and 15th centuries (Hanna Kozaczewska-Golasz, 'Drewniane kolebki w średniowiecznych kościołach Ziemi Chełmińskiej i ich wpływ na architekturę', *Kwartalnik Architektury i Urbanistyki*, 24/2 (1979), 361–70).

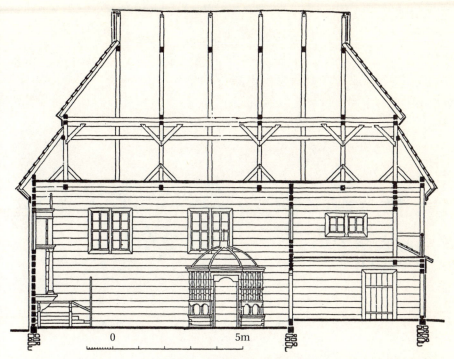

**Fig. 10** Section, wooden synagogue, Jabłonów, Ukraine.
Tel Aviv Museum of Art

The synagogue at Jabłonów, Ukraine, fifty miles south of Lwów, is an example of a wooden synagogue constructed just before the beginning of the eighteenth century. It is similar in appearance to the early Lwów synagogue and is one of the three oldest substantially documented wooden synagogues to have survived into the twentieth century. Built between 1674 and 1700, it is different from most wooden synagogues because it had a flat ceiling suspended from a traditional triangulated structural system that filled the entire roof;[49] significantly, it lacked the raised cupola that was a feature of the later wooden synagogues in its region (Fig. 10). For this reason it is especially important for this study. Because it had a flat ceiling, the interior of the Jabłonów Synagogue closely resembled the traditional churches of the Galician (southern Poland and western Ukrainian) region. It is the unique character of the elaborate wooden dome that is one of the most distinctive characteristics of the wooden synagogues, differentiating them from surrounding buildings.

In striking contrast to the flat ceiling and rectangular shape of the Jabłonów Synagogue are the soaring, tentlike canopy of the Gwoździec Synagogue, and the multi-level vault of the Chodorów Synagogue. Although the three synagogues were built in the same region, decorated by the same school of artists, and probably

**Fig. 11** Exterior, wooden synagogue, Gwoździec, Ukraine.
Tel Aviv Museum of Art

built or remodelled into their final forms within twenty years of each other, the raised canopies of the Gwoździec and Chodorów synagogues represent a dramatic change in the development of the east European synagogue. At Gwoździec, the well-documented construction and painting of the interior dome, between *c.* 1720 and 1729, appears to pinpoint the introduction of an early form of the tent-like cupola into the vocabulary of the common wooden synagogue (Figs. 11 and 12). Several sources confirm the replacement of its original low barrel-vault with a new style of central canopy. Early twentieth-century investigators noted that the original roof structure was not designed to accommodate the new cupola and the roof was seriously weakened when the original beams were cut away for the new cupola.[50] Therefore, at its completion in 1729, the pyramidal ceiling represented an early, experimental model of the domed cupola type of east European synagogue.

The raised ceiling of the Chodorów Synagogue consisted of a steep barrel-vault resting on top of twin projecting coves (Figs. 13 and 14). It is perhaps the most widely recognized wooden synagogue because its elaborate paintings are frequently cited, and a painted model of its ceiling is displayed at the Diaspora Museum, Tel Aviv. Various estimates have been given for the completion of this dome, although dates between 1700 and 1714 are, on the evidence, most likely. It

---

[50] Ibid. 98, based on site investigations of Alois Breier, Max Eisler, and Max Grunwald, *Holzsynagogen in Polen* (Baden-bei-Wien, 1934), 12–14.

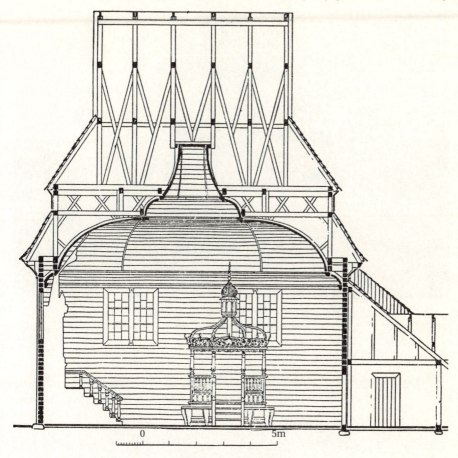

**Fig. 12** Section, wooden synagogue, Gwoździec, Ukraine.
Tel Aviv Museum of Art

is important to emphasize that no painted wooden synagogue cupola can be accurately dated to before 1700, and that most dated cupolas were constructed and painted after 1725,[51] which confirms that the interior domes of the Gwoździec and Chodorów synagogues were early models of a new form of synagogue architecture. Later synagogues followed the general pattern of the Chodorów example, which, in increasingly elaborate configurations, would become the standard model for most eighteenth-century wooden synagogues in the medium-sized towns of the Polish–Lithuanian Commonwealth.

[51] The Piechotkas review the problems of establishing accurate dating before 1700 in 'Polichromie', 72–5. In the case of Chodorów, the existence of a complex triple-tiered dome in a small Ukrainian town far from the major centres of architectural experimentation before 1675 is extremely unlikely (Miłobędzki, *Zarys dziejów architektury w Polsce*, 200–39).

*Thomas C. Hubka*

**Fig. 13** Exterior, wooden synagogue, Chodorów, Ukraine.
Tel Aviv Museum of Art

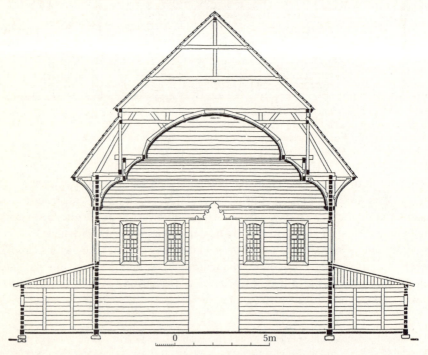

0        5m

**Fig. 14** Section, wooden synagogue, Chodorów, Ukraine.
Tel Aviv Museum of Art

## DESIGN DEVELOPMENT

The absence of any documentation concerning the architects or their designs for the wooden synagogues has puzzled researchers since their initial documentation in the late nineteenth century. While there has been considerable speculation about their identity, especially whether they were Jewish or non-Jewish, there is, at present, no precise information about who these designers were, where they came from, or how the buildings were designed.[52] Fifty years after the destruction of the synagogues, the prospect of identifying individual designers appears extremely remote.

It is still possible, however, to approach the question of design and the role of Jews in the design process by examining the synagogues for the ideas that influenced their making. For example, as emphasized in this article, the exterior form and the construction systems are closely related to east European regional sources, suggesting regional designers or influences, while the interior organization and detailing is closely related to Jewish sources, suggesting Jewish designers or influences.

There can be little question that Jews were highly involved in the design and development of their own synagogues and especially of the interiors; only the method and the degree of participation has resisted explanation. The problem has defied analysis both because of the destruction of the east European communities

---

[52] The identity of the builders and architects, their religion and nationality, and their traditions of construction practices have perplexed all investigators of wooden synagogues. No detailed pre-1800 accounts listing architects or specifying actual synagogue construction have been found. Yet, there are clues from numerous sources related to building construction, e.g. the analysis of carpentry methods and the division of construction labour in structures similar to the wooden synagogues, in Witold Krassowski, 'Ze studiów nad detalami zabytkowych konstrukcji ciesielskich', *Kwartalnik Architektury i Urbanistyki*, 7/1 (1962), 3–20, and the analysis of architect–builder relations in the 17th century in Mankowski, *Fabricaecclesiae*, 36–43. These and other sources document a four-part division of labour typical for late medieval construction: (1) framers (log construction, roof frame, and general carpentry), probably regional associations of Christian woodworkers; (2) finishers (detailed carpentry and decorative woodworking), probably itinerant craftsmen, some possibly of German, and/or Jewish origin; (3) painters (wall paintings), Jewish artists, probably working in regional schools; (4) architects or designers, identity unknown. Many other problems associated with the development of synagogue design could be cited, such as the unknown identity of the originators of the elaborate roof-trussing systems of the larger synagogues. These trusses may have been designed by the architects of local magnates because the advanced structural techniques were not usually employed by the local builders (as implied by Miłobędzki, 'Architecture in Wood', 195–8). The existence of unrecognized Jewish designers for the synagogues should not be excluded, but the seeming lack of recognition by their 18th-century communities is surprising. The absence of construction documentation for the synagogues is also puzzling, but may be attributed to many factors, including, of course, destruction. The scarcity of written documentation in areas outside the major cities could also mean that the synagogues were the product of local builders and local decision-making. Buildings in the small-town centres of the 18th century were also infrequently documented in formal building contracts.

and because of the general lack of design information for pre-1800 synagogues world-wide.[53] All investigators of synagogues would probably agree that traditional Jewish sources guided the layout and organization of the synagogue; this is evident in the general uniformity of synagogues in all eras and regions. Presumably these Jewish design ideas were communicated to professional designers or builders, either through written sources or orally, following unrecorded oral traditions. However, investigation of Jewish literature has not yielded significant evidence of potential design ideas influencing the building of wooden synagogues, or, in large measure, any other type of synagogue.

The scarcity of synagogue building specifications in ancient and medieval literary sources has frequently been referred to, though later sources, such as Joseph Caro's *Shulḥan arukh*, did provide general details about synagogue design.[54] But probably the most influential source of ideas for the design of the east European wooden synagogues, the Zohar, has not been adequately explored. Although frequently studied as an esoteric text, it is, in fact, also a storehouse of pragmatic architectural advice about the synagogue. In my article 'Beit hakeneset beGwoździec—Sha'ar Hashomayim', I present many quotations from the Zohar which appear to have guided (either directly, or indirectly through secondary sources) the architectural organization and detail of the east European synagogue, and especially the wooden synagogues of the Gwoździec–Chodorów group.[55] These guidelines included advice and specifications for many aspects of the synagogue's design, including orientation and siting, specifications for twelve windows in the prayer hall and a special latticed window on the western wall, support for a plan of the four-pillar or clustered-column type of synagogue, general approval of art forms such as wall paintings, encouragement for the adornment of the synagogue, frequent comparisons to the Tabernacle as a model for synagogue design, and the borrowing of stories and images from the Zohar as directives for various architectural details.[56] These specifications were frequently written in a

[53] The scarcity of references to synagogue construction in scriptures has been widely referred to; e.g. 'One of the remarkable aspects of Rabbinical teachings concerning prayer is the paucity of laws dealing with the architecture appropriate to the house of worship' (Joseph M. Baumgarten, 'Art in the Synagogue: Some Talmudic Views', in Harry M. Orlinsky (ed.), *The Synagogue* (New York, 1975), 79); and 'Halakhah governs only very specific components of synagogue design and makes no stipulation for the building's general external appearance' (*Encyclopaedia Judaica*, s.v. 'synagogue').

[54] *Shulḥan arukh*, OH 90. 4, 150. 1–5, and demonstrating the influence of the Zohar.

[55] Thomas C. Hubka, 'The Gate of Heaven: The Influence of the Zohar upon the Art and Architecture of the Gwoździec Synagogue', in Havivah Pedayah (ed.), *Myth in Judaism* (Beersheba, 1996), 263–316.

[56] The following references to synagogue design are taken from what Gershom Scholem has described as the 'main body' of the Zohar in *Kabbalah* (New York, 1974), 220; first printed in three volumes comprising the first Mantua edition and considered to be the primary form for widespread diffusion of the Zohar into eastern Europe, as analysed by Zeev Grieg, 'Sources for the Study of Kabbalah: The Copying and Printing of Kabbalistic Books', *Mahanaim*, NS 6 (1993), 204–11: four

direct didactic fashion so that there is no ambiguity about the intent of the Zohar to influence the organization and construction of the synagogue. In a one-to-one comparison of text and building, the zoharic specifications exactly match many of the building characteristics from the synagogues of the Gwoździec–Chodorów group. For example, each of the six synagogues has the twelve major windows specified by the Zohar. From preliminary study, it appears that the Zohar also influenced other forms of the Polish synagogue, including masonry synagogues, throughout much of the seventeenth and eighteenth centuries.

The close correspondence between the Zohar's guidelines and the actual construction of the synagogues in Poland demonstrates the powerful influence of a work, which, according to Gershom Scholem, achieved canonical status in the Jewish communities of pre-modern eastern Europe.[57] Although some of the Zohar's architectural directives were stated generally and could be applied broadly, for example the strong support for visualization and for beauty in the synagogue, other advice, such as the specifications for twelve major windows in the prayer hall with fifty panes in each window, were directly stated and highly detailed.[58] Unlike scriptural references which were not specifically written about synagogues, but which have been applied to them, for example the frequently cited verse 'Out of the depths I cry to Thee, O Lord' (Ps. 130: 1),[59] the Zohar's architectural instructions were written as if intended to influence synagogue design and construction.[60] The existence of such detailed and significant advice about the construction of the synagogue from such an influential source is a very strong indication of the critical role of Jewish inspiration and Jewish ideas in the design and development of the wooden synagogues. If this hypothesis about the influence of the Zohar is correct, it would connect Jewish sources to the design and development of the wooden synagogue. It also suggests a mechanism for articulating Jewish ideas to regional builders or architects not necessarily familiar with Jewish liturgy or synagogue tradition.

## WALL PAINTINGS

Like all the wooden synagogues of the Gwoździec–Chodorów group, the entire interior surface of the Gwoździec Synagogue was covered with a vibrant tapestry of inscriptional and decorative wall paintings. The paintings of the lower walls, completed in piecemeal fashion between *c*.1675 and 1720, contained a series of elaborately framed panels with Hebrew inscriptions in a serial composition

---

pillars, i. 18*b*; plan, wall paintings, synagogue beautification, ii. 59*b*; the Tabernacle, ii. 231*b*, 232*a*; twelve windows, ii. 251*a*; latticed window, iii. 1144*b*.

[57] Gershom G. Scholem, *Zohar: The Book of Splendor* (New York, 1949), 7.
[58] Zohar, ii. 172*a*.	[59] As cited in *Encyclopaedia Judaica*, s.v. 'synagogues'.
[60] e.g. Zohar ii. 159*b*.

reminiscent of decorated Esther scrolls or title-pages from early printed books (Fig. 15).[61] The paintings of the dome, completed in 1729, display more unified, symmetrical compositions, featuring ethical inscriptions, allegorical animal figures, and floral motifs, culminating in a zodiac at the top of the funnelling, tent-like cupola (Fig. 16).

The painted interiors of synagogues like Gwoździec may appear dense or cluttered to a modern viewer, but in fact they were highly organized in geometric and thematic patterns common to the synagogues of the region and conforming to the accepted aesthetic standards of the period.[62] The central focus of the painters' art was the series of framed text-panels, with ten major panels organized in a standardized arrangement in each synagogue.[63] Most panels contained inscriptions from common prayer with Hebrew letters large enough to be read from any location in the room.[64] Some prayers appear to have been located on particular walls as aids to daily worship. For example, the prayer *Lekhah dodi*, introduced into the common liturgy in the early seventeenth century, was prominently displayed on the western wall of the Chodorów Synagogue (Fig. 17).[65] (At the end of the prayer, the congregation turns toward the western wall.)

The prayer inscriptions were framed in painted architectural surrounds with columns and arches, and bordered with floral patterns. The recurring motif of the inscriptional surround or architectural gate was also one of the most common in sixteenth- to eighteenth-century Jewish decorative art, occurring on gravestones, ritual objects, textiles, *ketubot*, and book art, especially on the title-pages of early Hebrew printed books.[66] Although documentation is lacking, the occurrence of the architectural gate motif surrounding Hebrew texts in the wooden synagogues suggests that the art forms of the Hebrew book exerted a strong influence on the

[61] Traditionally, the text for the Book of Esther is written on a long parchment scroll in sequential columns, often surrounded by decorative frames (see e.g. 18th-century Esther scrolls in Isaiah Shachar, *Jewish Tradition in Art* (Jerusalem, 1971), 153–6).

[62] The practice of covering the entire interior surface of the synagogue with paintings has been associated with pre-modern or pre-industrial cultures and has often been interpreted as *horror vacui* (fear of emptiness). Unfortunately, this widely accepted interpretation has tended to belittle the skilful accomplishments of pre-Renaissance or medieval artists. To describe the artists of the Gwoździec Synagogue as fearful of emptiness would be the equivalent of interpreting modern artists as fearful of complexity and narrative. The compositional style of pre-modern artists, such as those who painted the wooden synagogues, is analysed in E. H. Gombrich, *The Sense of Order* (Ithaca, NY, 1979), 63–94.

[63] My analysis is based on a review of all known interior photographs of the Gwoździec–Chodorów group of synagogues.

[64] At the Gwoździec Synagogue, the letters in the major prayer panels are 3–4 in. high; my estimates based on surviving photographs.

[65] Yehuda Ratshadi, 'The *Lekhah Dodi* of the Kabbalist Rabbi Solomon Alkabez and its Sources', *Mahanaim*, NS 6 (1993), 162–9.

[66] The motif of the architectural gate is analysed by Shalom Sabar, *Mazal tov* (Jerusalem, 1993), 19–25. A comparison of the synagogue paintings to Hebrew manuscript sources was also emphasized by El Lissitzky in 'The Synagogue of Mohilev' (Heb.), *Rimon*, 3 (1923), 12.

**Fig. 15** Painting, western wall, wooden synagogue, Gwoździec, Ukraine.
Tel Aviv Museum of Art

**Fig. 16** Painting, cupola, wooden synagogue, Gwoździec, Ukraine.
Tel Aviv Museum of Art

**Fig. 17**  Paintings, western wall, wooden synagogue, Chodorów, Ukraine.
Tel Aviv Museum of Art

paintings (see Figs. 15 and 17).[67] Their decorative character notwithstanding, the wall paintings of the wooden synagogues were fully integrated into the architectural and liturgical order of the prayer hall. In addition to communicating daily prayer, the paintings of the Gwoździec Synagogue also marked symbolic focal points on the middle of each of the four walls: the Tablets of the Law painted above the ark on the eastern wall, a painted menorah on the southern wall, a

---

[67] Several types of late medieval German manuscripts and early modern east European manuscripts have similar elaborately decorated borders, either as frames for title-pages or as decorative headings throughout the text, as, for example, in the Worms *Maḥzor*, Würzburg, 1272, Jewish National and University Library, MS 781/1, fo. 1*b* (formerly 39*b*); *Erna Michael Haggadah*, German (Middle Rhine), *c.*1400, fo. 40; and examples illustrated in Heinrich Frauberger, *Verzierte hebraische Schrift und jüdischer Buchschmuck*, v and vi (Frankfurt, 1909), 4–45; Bezalel Narkiss, *Hebrew Illuminated Manuscripts* (Jerusalem, 1974), 88–120; and Therese and Mendel Metzger, *Jewish Life in the Middle Ages* (New York, 1982), 20–65.

painted Shew-bread Table on the northern wall, and a latticed, or 'Gate of Heaven', window on the western wall.[68] This arrangement was repeated in all the synagogues of the Gwoździec–Chodorów group and is related to the specifications for the 'holy vessels' of the Tabernacle which was an important model for the architecture and the arrangement of the synagogue during this period.[69]

Despite the presence of considerable stylistic elements from non-Jewish, east European sources (analysed below), the iconography of the paintings primarily depicted Jewish subjects and symbolized Jewish themes for their eighteenth-century communities. In addition to the inscriptions of Hebrew prayer which formed the dominant focus for the painters' art, much of the visual imagery, and especially the animal figures, also had specific meaning for their congregations.[70] Still, the relationship of these images to east European contextual sources remains unclear and subject to considerable speculation. For example, the motif of the deer repeated prominently on the Gwoździec ceiling is one of the most frequently depicted animals in east European folk and national art, but the artists of the Gwoździec Synagogue portrayed a deer turning to look back over its shoulder in a stance long depicted in Jewish sources, such as the Zohar, and possibly referring to the distinctly Jewish story about the abandonment and return of God's mercy to the Israelites (Fig. 18*a*).[71] The image of the deer at Gwoździec, while common to both earlier European and later east European contexts, should be considered an appropriated image, borrowed from regional sources to become transformed by Jewish artists to tell the distinctly Jewish story of God's abandonment of and return to the Israelites.[72]

In another example from the ceiling of Gwoździec, a bird was shown looking directly at three eggs in a nest. Perhaps because the painter was not sure how to depict an ostrich, and he wanted his audience to know what it was, he labelled the bird 'ostrich', in Hebrew (Fig. 18*b*). This painting represents a very close interpretation of a tale about the ostrich's vision which was popularized in several ethical stories such as Tsevi Hirsh Koidonover's widely distributed *Kav hayashar*. The story tells of the ostrich's ability to assist in the birth of its young by the strength of its vision to open its eggs and is used to demonstrate the power of vision for good and evil purposes.[73] While not all images from the painted synagogues can

---

[68] Piechotka and Piechotka, 'Polichromie', 68–70, and Hubka, 'Gate of Heaven'.

[69] Zohar, ii. 231*b*.

[70] Max Grunwald, 'Appendix on Iconography of Paintings in our Synagogues', in Breier *et al.*, *Holzsynagogue in Polen*, 13–21, Davidovitch, *Wall Paintings*, 20–6, and Piechotka and Piechotka, 'Polichromie', 68–9.

[71] A backward-looking deer, for example, is shown in a micrography sketch containing the text of a Masorah from an Ashkenazi bible of 1294; Vatican, Biblioteca Apostolica, Cod. Urbin. ebr. 1, fo. 146ʳ. A similar image is repeatedly described in the Zohar, e.g. ii. 14*a*, and analysed in Hubka, 'Gate of Heaven'.

[72] The usage of appropriated or borrowed images in Jewish art is analysed in several works by Marc Epstein, including '*If lions could carve stones . . .*' *Medieval Jewry and the Allegorization of the Animal Kingdom*, diss., Yale, 1992 (Ann Arbor, Mich., 1993), 33–76, 372–83.

[73] Zwi Hirsch Kaidanover, *Kav hayashar* (Frankfurt am Main, 1705), ch. 2.

(a)                                        (b)

**Fig. 18** Drawings from paintings, deer and ostrich, cupola, wooden synagogue, Gwoździec,
Ukraine. Based on photographs, Tel Aviv Museum of Art

be located so precisely in Jewish literature, I hope to demonstrate in future
research that the majority of the painted animal figures and iconography from the
eighteenth-century Polish synagogues had specific Jewish meaning and symbol-
ism for their audiences.

The qualities of the paintings that constituted their non-Jewish or east
European influences were thus not iconographical but primarily stylistic. Yet,
while these visual motifs were not central to their meaning for Jewish audiences,
they were not artistically insignificant. These characteristics included the overall
compositional organization of the paintings and various decorative and background motifs, including ornamental borders, geometric and floral backgrounds,
and secondary animal figures which can all be related to regional sources and mixtures of the Baroque and Rococo styles of the early eighteenth century. The combined effects of these various stylistic sources was to create a dense, carpet-like
*gestalt* quality throughout the entire interior, which, as noted by most observers,
was similar to the indigenous late medieval folk churches of the region.[74]

When considering both the strong aesthetic impact of these east European
stylistic influences and the scarcity of Jewish stylistic source material from this
period, it is not surprising that the contribution of Jewish artistic sources to the
stylistic character of the paintings would remain undocumented and only suggested. Jewish stylistic sources have, of course, been assumed by many scholars,
but specific references have not been identified, even by those researchers who
actually surveyed the synagogues, analysed the paintings at first hand, and inter-

[74] e.g. Piechotka and Piechotka, 'Polichromie', 65, 73. Parallels can be made to Ukrainian and
Russian folk and Russian Orthodox decorative art traditions, as in G. K. Loukomski, *L'Art decoratif
russe* (Paris, 1928), pll. 7–17, 44–52, 110–33, 172–91. A related tradition of Ukrainian painting of
walls in wooden churches, combining vernacular and high-style influences is preserved at the Church
of St George, Drohobych, mentioned earlier. General parallels may be drawn between the decorative

viewed their communities before their destruction.[75] In my view, the primary reason why potential Jewish sources for the wall paintings have been so difficult to identify is not only the destruction of the synagogues, but that these sources were largely derived from archaic forms of pre-modern Ashkenazi art forms brought into eastern Europe, and about which there is only fragmentary evidence.

In a manner similar to the way in which the Yiddish language was simultaneously preserved and transformed through contact with east European dialects over a long period, the art forms of Ashkenazi Jewry were probably similarly preserved and transformed.[76] For a period of almost 500 years (from approximately 1200 to 1650), waves of German Jews immigrated to eastern Europe, bringing with them their language, religion, and culture, and presumably their art forms. While we know little about the evolution of east European Ashkenazi artistic traditions before 1700, we can observe fully developed Jewish artistic traditions from the eighteenth and nineteenth centuries, for example in gravestone carving, ritual and domestic objects, textiles, and book art.[77] The maturity of these art forms in the eighteenth and nineteenth centuries suggests a long period of artistic development and active institutional support from within the east European Jewish community, probably stretching back for many centuries.[78] The presence of an artistic tradition of long gestation is most powerfully suggested in the paintings of the east European wooden synagogues such as that in Gwoździec (see Figs. 15, 16 and 17). Completely decorated by 1729, it reveals an active, sophisticated, and long-term partnership between Jewish art, architecture, and liturgy.

The synagogues' pre-modern visual vocabulary appears to have been maintained for hundreds of years in eastern Europe by Ashkenazi artists. Although they incorporated elements of current Baroque styles into their compositions, the

painting and woodworking traditions of the Orthodox Church, especially between the construction and painting of the altar and the ark.

[75] e.g. Grunwald, 'Appendix', 1–23.

[76] Alice Faber and Robert D. King, 'Yiddish and the Settlement History of Ashkenazic Jews', in David R. Blumenthal (ed.), *Approaches to Judaism in Medieval Times*, ii (Chico, Calif., 1985), 73–108, and Marvin Herzog, *The Yiddish Language in Northern Poland: Its Geography and History* (Bloomington, Ind., 1965), 235–46.

[77] Catalogues describing the history of Jewish art and the decorative arts often include east European examples (e.g. Shachar, *Jewish Tradition in Art*). Recent access to east European collections has allowed scholars to begin to interpret a vast amount of unrecorded Jewish art (e.g. D. Goberman, *Jewish Tombstones in Ukraine and Moldova* (Moscow, 1993)).

[78] The exact numbers, dates, and motivations for Ashkenazi immigration to eastern Europe have been debated since Dubnow, *History of the Jews*, 13–58. Today it is generally agreed that significant Jewish settlement, mainly from Germanic lands, was well established by the 13th century and was augmented by subsequent waves of settlement (through persecution and invitation) until the middle of the 18th century, as summarized in Bernard D. Weinryb, *The Jews of Poland* (Philadelphia, 1973), 17–32. Considering the strength of this migration, it is not surprising that various forms of Ashkenazi illuminated manuscripts (as well as Sefardi sources in Ashkenazi possession) were imported to Poland through settlement and commerce and that these sources influenced later east European art forms, particularly the synagogue interiors.

Fig. 19 Paintings, northern wall, wooden synagogue, Gwoździec, Ukraine.
Tel Aviv Museum of Art

Gwoździec artists also worked outside the major schools of east European artistic influence. For example, the columns and arches forming the decorative borders for the prayer inscriptions at the Gwoździec Synagogue preserve Romanesque–Byzantine architectural details, such as the chequered and sawtooth patterns of the arches and the basket-weave details of the capitals (Fig. 19).[79] By 1700 these patterns had long since been abandoned by most European artists, but they were preserved by the Gwoździec artists. While various non-Jewish pre-modern sources are of course possible, the dominant presence of these architectural motifs in Hebrew book art suggests a close relationship to Jewish sources. Similar stylistic patterns are evident in the architectural details from the gate motifs of illuminated

[79] For example, similar architectural motifs are found in *Sefer evronot*, Ashkenazi, 1664 (Cincinnati, Hebrew Union College, no. 906), and are continued and developed in elaborate fashion in *Sefer ets Hayim*, Joseph Vital, Podhajce, Ukraine, 1780; Jewish National University Library, Jerusalem, microfilm 38536. The existence of various archaic, late medieval themes is present in many 19th-century east European art works, for example, *Tracing An-sky*, exhibition catalogue, Amsterdam, 1992. The overall composition of the gate motifs from the Gwoździec paintings are also closely related to the typical framed composition of the Sefardi-influenced Italian *ketubah* (marriage contract) (see e.g. Shachar, *Jewish Traditions in Art*, 37–9).

**Fig. 20** Worms *Maḥzor*, Würzburg, 1272. Jewish National and University Library,
Jerusalem, Worms *Maḥzor*, i, fo. 39v.

Jewish manuscripts, such as the famous Ashkenazi Worms *Maḥzor* of 1272 (Fig.
20).[80] Although separated by more than 450 years, the persistence of a medieval
stylistic vocabulary in the wall paintings appears to represent the perseverance of
a Jewish artistic tradition in the east European context. This does not mean, however, that the artists of the Gwoździec Synagogue actually copied from, or even

---

[80] Worms *Maḥzor*, fo. 1*b* (formerly 39*b*). Upon visiting the decorated synagogue at Mohilev,
Belarus, El Lissitzky speculated about the way illustrations of early Hebrew books might have influenced the synagogue paintings: 'Talmudic books and other old printed books with richly decorated
title sheets, illustrations and tailpieces are standing on the bookshelves of old synagogues. In the
olden days, those few pages played the role of today's illustrated magazines, they showed the recognized forms of art' (Lissitzky, 'Synagogues of Mohilev', 12).

knew about, the Worms *Maḥzor*. What it does mean is that they inherited a pre-modern artistic tradition about which little remains except a few aesthetic high points, such as the surviving Hebrew illuminated manuscripts.

One should not, however, expect to find fully preserved examples of late medieval Jewish art painted on the walls of the eighteenth-century synagogues. From the thirteenth century onwards, immigrant Jewish communities from German regions developed an east European Ashkenazi culture in contact with the regional cultures of the Polish–Lithuanian Commonwealth to produce an indigenous Jewish art form whose full flowering is expressed in the rich aesthetic diversity of the wall paintings from the synagogues of the Gwoździec–Chodórow group.[81]

## ABANDONMENT OF THE ART AND ARCHITECTURAL TRADITIONS

While the generative, creative ideas behind the development and spread of the interior-domed wooden synagogues are the primary focus of this study, the abandonment of this tradition provides insights and suggests conclusions about the significance and meaning of these structures for their communities. The high point in the spread of these synagogues occurred in the late eighteenth century in the economically expanding Grodno-Białystok region, between present-day Poland and Belarus. The synagogues of this region have long been recognized as the pinnacle of the interior-domed type, as, for example, the famous synagogue of Wolpa, Belarus (Figs. 21 and 22).[82]

Although large numbers of wooden synagogues continued to be built during the nineteenth century within what was then the Russian Pale of Settlement,[83] many of

[81] The transmission and development of ideas in folk art and culture most often involves the repetition and recombination of traditions through long usage. Change is usually accomplished gradually, and the idea of rapid development is most often inappropriate to the concept and meaning of folk art and culture (Henry Glassie, *The Spirit of Folk Art* (New York, 1989), 198–228; A. J. Gurevich, *Medieval Popular Culture* (Cambridge, 1988), 54–60). The existence of a sophisticated, fully formulated tradition of Jewish folk art on the walls of the Gwoździec Synagogue in 1700 therefore testifies to precursors stretching back in history, probably hundreds of years.

[82] Piechotka and Piechotka, *Wooden Synagogues*, 37–43.

[83] Maria and Kazimierz Piechotka, 'Polish Synagogues in the Nineteenth Century', *Polin*, 2 (1987), 179–98. The amount and types of synagogues built on Russian lands in the 19th century is only beginning to be documented (e.g. in Yargina, *Wooden Synagogues*, figs. 76 and 98 and pp. 65–9). The tradition of wooden dome construction lingered in eastern Europe after 1800, for example, in the masonry synagogues at Kuznica (Białystok region) and Oszmiana, Poland. (Newly investigated Russian sources may add many more structures.) The domed synagogue at Warka, Poland, was built between 1811 and 1817 (Piechotka and Piechotka, *Wooden Synagogues*, 209) and is one of the last fully documented, interior-domed wooden synagogues in the 18th-century tradition. The extensive tradition of the interior-domed synagogue, as a unified art and architectural form, was effectively terminated at the beginning of the 19th century (Piechotka and Piechotka, 'Polish Synagogues in the Nineteenth Century', 183).

**Fig. 21** Exterior, wooden synagogue, Wolpa, Belarus.
State Institute of Art, Warsaw

the elaborate traditions of the interior-domed type of wooden synagogue, such as the detailed painting of the entire surface of the synagogue, were modified and only continued in a diminished form.[84] The interpretation of the complex historical factors that may have contributed to the modification of these artistic traditions

[84] This does not mean that synagogue painting did not continue into the 19th century. In fact, the limited photographic evidence suggests that various motifs and compositional arrangements from the 18th century continued to be employed (see e.g. *Tracing An-sky*, 62–77). However, the fully developed style of iconographic and inscriptional wall paintings, as practised, for example, by the Jarychów school of painters at the beginning of the 18th century, was most probably terminated by 1800. This hypothesis is seemingly contradicted by the continued existence of 18th-century Jewish art forms in other media throughout the 19th century, e.g. in east European tombstones, ritual and domestic objects, and many types of decorated and illustrated literature. It is, perhaps, the special nature of the architectural art, tied so closely to liturgical purposes, that may explain the diminished importance of the synagogue's painted art and the continuation of some of the themes in other forms of artistic expression, such as domestic objects. Further complicating this aesthetic problem is the issue of hasidism and its relationship to the art forms of the 19th-century synagogues. Adequate data are lacking concerning hasidic sponsorship of typical synagogue-building and -remodelling projects, with the exception of a few courts of *tsadikim*, as documented, for example, in Bergman, 'Góra Kalwaria', 14–16 and 20. A related, underexplored issue is the relationship of hasidism to other forms of artistic expression, such as portraiture, as investigated, for example, by Richard Cohen in a lecture, ' "And your eyes shall see your teachers": On the Transformation of the Rabbi into an Icon in the Nineteenth Century', 11th World Congress of Jewish Studies, Jerusalem, 1993.

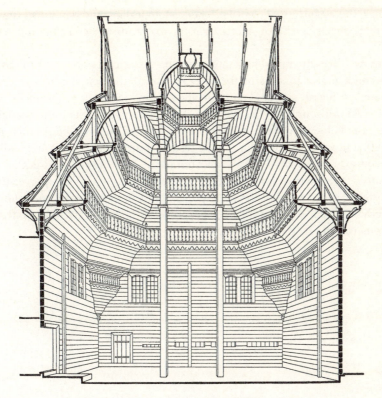

**Fig. 22** Section, wooden synagogue, Wolpa, Belarus.
State Institute of Art, Warsaw

requires extensive research and is beyond the scope of this enquiry. Such factors may have been associated with the spread of hasidism, the advent of the Haskalah movement, or the broad economic and social changes of the modern period.[85] In any case, the extensive art and architectural traditions of the eighteenth-century wooden synagogues were almost totally abandoned by the twentieth century.

The eighteenth-century wooden synagogues that did survive into the late nineteenth and early twentieth centuries were generally not altered by their communities. Indeed, the primary reason why so many eighteenth-century synagogues and their paintings were so well documented in early twentieth-century photographs and measured drawings is that they were left unchanged and were often preserved. The interior-domed wooden synagogues, and particularly their elaborate traditions of decorative art, can thus be seen as the frozen record of a vanished popular Jewish culture from the medium-sized towns of the Polish–Lithuanian Commonwealth. Because of the almost total destruction of many of these com-

---

[85] Aleksander Hertz, *The Jews in Polish Culture* (Evanston, Ill., 1988), 9–25, and Scholem, *Major Trends in Jewish Mysticism*, 325–40.

munities, this architectural record provides an important, and sometimes the only remaining, major source of information for many towns before the nineteenth century.

This essay has attempted to demonstrate that significant portions of the artistic and architectural traditions of the interior-domed wooden synagogues can be attributed to Jewish sources. Without underestimating the critical role of non-Jewish, regional sources to the overall architectural organization, it is possible to identify the influence of Jewish ideas that finally gave these structures their individuality and uniqueness within the larger east European architectural and cultural context. When the critical contribution of these Jewish sources is fully recognized, the interior-domed wooden synagogues can finally be appreciated as the powerful and original expressions of their east European Jewish communities, and perhaps, some of the most original expressions of Jewish art and architecture ever constructed.

# In Praise of the Ba'al Shem Tov:
# A User's Guide to the Editions of
# *Shivḥei haBesht*

## MOSHE ROSMAN

ONE of the most frequently treated subjects in the historiography of Jews in Poland is hasidism.[1] Within this field of research the formative period of the movement, *c.*1740–1815, has until recently received a disproportionate share of scholarly attention. Amongst this scholarship one source has stood out from all the rest, appearing in the majority of studies and itself serving as a frequent object of research. This source is *Shivḥei haBesht* (In Praise of the Ba'al Shem Tov), first published in Kopys in 1814.[2]

A collection of some 250 stories about the putative founder of hasidism, Israel ben Eliezer, the Ba'al Shem Tov, and his associates, *Shivḥei haBesht* has fascinated scholars both because of its vivid depiction of its subjects and because of the complex methodological puzzles it poses.[3] While it is an eminently accessible text, it is also a complex one, particularly when used for historiographical purposes, and over the last 150 years or so scholars have been engaged in a seemingly endless spiral of deconstruction, interpretation, and application of it.[4] The purpose of the

---

[1] The most comprehensive bibliography on hasidism appears in A. Rapoport-Albert (ed.), *Hasidism Reappraised* (London, 1996), 465–91. See also the bibliography at the end of the article 'Hasidism', *Encyclopaedia Judaica*, vii. 1426–7; the bibliographic notes at the end of the ninth volume of the English edition of I. Zinberg, *A History of Jewish Literature*, trans. and ed. B. Martin (Cincinnati, Oh., 1976), 268–76; G. D. Hundert and G. C. Bacon, *The Jews in Poland and Russia* (Bloomington, Ind., 1984), 57–61, 135–7, 158–9; I. Etkes, 'Trends in the Study of the Hasidic Movement' (Heb.), *Jewish Studies*, 31 (1991), 5–19; D. Assaf, 'Polish Hasidism in the Nineteenth Century: State of the Field and Bibliographical Survey' (Heb.), in I. Bartal, R. Elior, and C. Shmeruk (eds.), *Tsadikim ve'anshei ma'aseh* (Jerusalem, 1994), 357–79; Assaf is also editing a collection of basic articles on hasidism which will include some bibliographical updates.

[2] In this article, citations, unless otherwise specified, will come from the English translation *In Praise of the Ba'al Shem Tov (Shivḥei haBesht)*, trans. and ed. D. Ben-Amos and J. Mintz (Bloomington: 1970), based on the Kopys, 1814 text. Henceforth *SHB*.

[3] The stories in the original edition are not enumerated and there are alternative logical ways of dividing the text into discrete 'tales'. Ben-Amos and Mintz counted 251 stories; Rubinstein (*Shivḥei haBesht*, with intro. and annotations (Jerusalem, 1991), based on Kopys, 1814 text) thought the very same material contained only 214 separate units.

[4] For partial bibliographies, see Y. Mondshine, *Shivḥei haBa'al Shem Tov: A Facsimile of a*

discussion which follows is, first, to alert the reader to some important methodological considerations before undertaking historical analysis of *Shivḥei haBesht*; and, secondly, to review the historiographical usefulness of the most significant available editions.

## METHODOLOGICAL ISSUES

The question which has been central to historical studies of *Shivḥei haBesht* has been its reliability as a historical source. Virtually no one accepts the stories at face value. Their obvious mythical content,[5] and the book's very title, proclaim its hagiographic nature, and have induced scepticism among scholars and hasidim alike.

Yehoshua Mondshine, himself a devoted Habad hasid, in summarizing later hasidic responses to *Shivḥei haBesht* (all of which date from the mid-nineteenth century onwards), asserted, 'One can discern the doubts which held sway among the Hasidic community with regard to the degree of reliability . . . of the collection of praises. . . . The various tales should be treated as pleasure-reading material and not as Hasidic literature.'[6]

Academics have been more charitable, with most assigning more than recreational significance to the text, believing that many of the stories are based on events which actually occurred and that they preserve varying degrees of historical information. Where scholars have differed is on how to thresh the historical wheat from the folk-tale chaff. Scholem, Rubinstein, and Etkes seem to judge the stories according to their plausibility.[7] Dubnow has attempted to read the stories as a kind of midrash on reality, reversing exegesis to arrive at the rational reality which underlies the irrational elements. Concerning the story about the Ba'al Shem Tov's miraculous birth, for example, Dubnow assumes that, since the legend says that the Besht's father was taken captive in war and the Besht was born after his safe return, 'a time of turmoil preceded the birth of the founder of hasidism and the child was born after peace returned. In fact the Turkish

*Unique Manuscript, Variant Versions and Appendices* (Jerusalem, 1982), 69–70; M. Rosman, 'The History of a Historical Source: On the Editing of *Shivḥei haBesht*' (Heb.), *Zion*, 58 (1993), 175–6 n. 1 and *passim*.

[5] *SHB*, index of motifs, 290–305; see below, n. 68.

[6] Mondshine, *Facsimile*, 55–6.

[7] Scholem, 'The Historical Image of Israel Ba'al Shem Tov' (Heb.), *Molad*, 18 (1960), 335–56, esp. 346–7; A. Rubinstein, 'A Possibly New Fragment of *Shivḥei haBesht*' (Heb.), *Tarbiz*, 35 (1966), 174–91; 'The Revelation Stories in *Shivḥei haBesht*' (Heb.), *Alei sefer*, 6–7 (1977), 157–86; 'The Mentor of R. Israel Ba'al Shem Tov and the Sources of his Knowledge' (Heb.), *Tarbiz*, 48 (1979), 146–58; 'Notes on *Shivḥei haBesht*' (Heb.), *Sinai*, 86 (1979), 62–71; 'Concerning Three of the Stories in *Shivḥei haBesht*' (Heb.), *Sinai*, 90 (1982), 269–79; I. Etkes, 'Hasidism as a Movement: The First Stage', in B. Safran (ed.), *Hasidism: Continuity or Innovation?* (Cambridge, Mass., 1988), 3–18.

conquest of Podolia ended after the Treaty of Karlowitz in 1699 . . . therefore Israel ben Eliezer was born around this time.'[8]

Dinur sees the stories as symbolic prosopography, embodying the experience of lower-class Jewish society in the life of its hero. As he puts it,

In the stories about the life of the Besht and all of that befell him up until his revelation, hasidic legend incorporated all of the social classes that composed the opposition [to the communal establishment]. . . . His father and mother were refugees and captives, his mother 'out of great poverty' was a midwife . . . the Besht was an orphan who on his life's path went through all of the lower rungs of the social order. . . . [The movement] portrayed its creator and founder in its own image.[9]

Other scholars have painstakingly sought to tease out the historical facts by comparing the stories of *Shivḥei haBesht* with other sources.[10]

Recently, I noted the hagiographic features of *Shivḥei haBesht*.[11] These tend to obscure and subsume any historical material in the service of the author's primary purpose—to exhort readers to adopt a particular mode of behaviour and belief as their own, or to reinforce their traditional beliefs and rituals, rather than to provide a biography of the subject.

This raises the question of authorship. In the case of *Shivḥei haBesht* there were actually two authors, each with his own agenda. The first, the major author, was 'the writer' Dov Ber, the *shoḥet* (ritual slaughterer) of Ilintsy (Linits). He apparently compiled this collection sometime in the 1790s, more than thirty years after the Besht's death.[12] By that time there were many stories in various versions circulating about the famous holy man. Dov Ber, who did not know the Besht personally, decided to compile his collection from what he had heard from people whom he considered to be reliable witnesses.

Reiner has demonstrated, however, that Dov Ber did not write down stories

[8] S. M. Dubnow, *Toledot haḥasidut* (Tel Aviv, 1975), 43; cf. id., 'The Beginnings: The Ba'al Shem Tov (Besht) and the Center in Podolia', in G. D. Hundert (ed.), *Essential Papers on Hasidism* (New York, 1991), 27.

[9] B. Z. Dinur, *Bemifneh hadorot* (Jerusalem, 1972), 140–3. For elucidation of Dinur's view on the nature of this establishment and opposition, see ibid. 92–139; Etkes, 'Hasidism as a Movement', 3–4; and M. J. Rosman, 'An Exploitative Regime and the Opposition to it in Międzyboż c.1730', in S. Almog *et al.* (eds.), *Transition and Change in Modern Jewish History* (Jerusalem, 1987), pp. xi–xxx.

[10] I. Bartal, 'The Aliyah of R. Elazar from Amsterdam to Eretz Yisrael in 1740' (Heb.), in his *Galut ba'arets* (Jerusalem, 1994), 11–34; J. Barnai, 'Some Clarifications on the Land of Israel Stories of *In Praise of the Ba'al Shem Tov*', *Revue des études juives*, 146 (1987), 367–80; M. J. Rosman, 'Międzyboż and Rabbi Israel Ba'al Shem Tov', in Hundert (ed.), *Essential Papers on Hasidism*, 209–25; A. Rubinstein, 'The Letter of the Besht to R. Gershon of Kutow' (Heb.), *Sinai*, 67 (1970), 120–39; C. Shmeruk, 'The Stories about R. Adam Ba'al Shem and their Development in the Versions of *Shivḥei haBesht*' (Heb.), in his *Sifrut Yiddish bepolin* (Jerusalem, 1981), 119–39.

[11] Rosman, 'The History of a Historical Source', 194–7.

[12] Rubinstein, 'Notes on *Shivḥei haBesht*', 63; Rosman, 'The History of a Historical Source', 177–8.

which he heard at random.[13] Rather, he drew upon already formed orally trans-mitted groups of tales, each group being associated with a different teller. The oldest group was apparently initiated soon after the Besht's death and was told by Dov Ber's own father-in-law, Alexander, who for a period of time had been the Besht's scribe, witnessing some of the events he related. A much later group, based on stories told by the hasidim, was compiled by Gedaliah of Ilintsy, probably *c*.1782. These were Dov Ber's two main sources for the stories about the Ba'al Shem Tov himself, and he also added groups concerning some of the Besht's associates, especially Jacob Joseph of Polonnoye (Połonne).

By tracing the identity of the teller of each story group, Reiner has shown that the bulk of the book took shape among the students and associates of Jacob Joseph of Połonne, with Dov Ber's role being that of editor, rather than compiler, select-ing and modifying the pre-existing groups and finally organizing the stories in loose chronological order.

Only one of the constituent groups of stories included in *Shivḥei haBesht* men-tions the most important organizational and doctrinal figure in the second genera-tion of hasidism, Dov Ber, the Maggid of Mezirich (Międzyrzecz) (no connection to Dov Ber of Ilintsy). In the stories of this group appear the last generation of people in *Shivḥei haBesht* (those who were at most only barely contemporary with the Besht, some of whom were still alive when the book was written) and it may have entered the compilation even after Dov Ber of Ilintsy had completed his work. Whether or not this was so, the collection as edited by Dov Ber of Ilintsy primarily reflects the traditions about the Ba'al Shem Tov and others as they were fashioned in the *beit midrash* of Jacob Joseph of Połonne.

Granted that Dov Ber of Ilintsy was not the primary teller, or even compiler, of these hagiographic tales, he was nevertheless their most important transmitter. This is how he stated his objective in doing so:

I myself have noticed as well that in the time between my youth and my old age, every day, miracles have become fewer and marvels have begun to disappear . . . [He then recounts miracles from times past]. . . . Because of all these things, many repented and the faith in the heart of each Jew was strengthened. Now, because of our many sins, the number of pious people is lessened . . . faith has decreased and heresy has been spread in the world. . . . Therefore, I was careful to write down all the awesome things that I heard from truthful people. . . . I wrote it down as a remembrance for my children and their children so that it would be a reminder for them and for all who cling to God . . . to strengthen their faith in God and in His Torah and in the tsadikim.[14]

Dov Ber was alarmed by the crisis which had struck religious belief in his time, and he ascribed it, at least in part, to the lack of miracles. In lieu of actual miracles he hoped that reliable tales about miracles would help to bolster faith. His reason

---

[13] E. Reiner, '*Shivḥei haBesht*: Transmission, Editing and Printing' (Heb.), *Proceedings of the 11th World Congress of Jewish Studies*, division C, vol. ii (Jerusalem, 1994), 145–52.     [14] *SHB* 3–5.

for spreading the stories about the Ba'al Shem Tov was to convince people that miracles once did occur and continue to serve as confirmation of God's existence and continuing involvement with creation. It is therefore understandable why Dov Ber's collection emphasizes miraculous occurrences, which in the nineteenth century were utilized by maskilim to ridicule this book and its hero for their primitive superstitiousness.[15]

The secondary author of *Shivḥei haBesht* was 'the printer' Israel Yoffe of Kopys. By the time of the printing, in late 1814, Dov Ber's basic collection was circulating in different manuscript versions. Israel Yoffe's considerations in deciding to print the book included the following:

After I received these holy striptures about the wonders of God which he revealed through His holy servants—since with the help of God there is no generation without famous tsadikim 'for the Lord will not forsake His people for His great name's sake'— . . . I realized all the benefits which would result from this printing . . . I understood the greatness and the intensity of the desire of those who wished to copy down these holy scriptures. However, I was aware that this manuscript was full of mistakes, and certainly if it had been copied over and over the errors would have increased in number until the meaning of the sentences would have been almost unrecognizable, and so I took great pains to rid it of error.[16]

He would print the book in order to preserve it in an authoritative form and prevent further modification through oral retelling and manuscript copying and rewriting. But Yoffe did not limit himself to putting a manuscript text of the book into printed form. Not having an autograph manuscript and believing that many errors had crept into the existing manuscripts, he decided that it would be proper to emend the text.

Yoffe also created a new opening section of the book, which he placed before Dov Ber's first story.[17] For many years scholars were divided over what precisely he did in producing this new part. Some claimed that he merely reorganized and emended the stories already existing in Dov Ber's collection;[18] others contended that he added a cycle of stories based on Habad traditions.[19] Elsewhere I have attempted to demonstrate that he actually did both.[20] The printer's new opening section was developed in two steps. First, he moved several core stories (regarding the Besht's father, Rabbi Adam, the robbers, and the frog[21]) from the body of the manuscript to the front. Then he wove more stories not in the original manuscript around them. This entire newly minted section he entitled 'The Story of the

---

[15] On the reception of *Shivḥei haBesht*, see Rosman, 'History of a Historical Source', 210–12.

[16] *SHB* 1–2.                                           [17] *SHB* 6–32.

[18] Rubinstein, 'The Revelation Stories', 157–86; id., *Shivḥei haBesht*, 17–19.

[19] Dan, *Hasipur haḥasidi* (Jerusalem, 1975), 64–8; G. Scholem, 'Two Testimonies about Hasidic Groups and the Besht' (Heb.), *Tarbiz*, 20 (1949), 228.

[20] Rosman, 'The History of a Historical Source', 183–94, 202–5.

[21] *SHB*, story numbers: 1a (pp. 9–10), 5, 6, the opening two sentences of 7 (pp. 13–15), and 11 (pp. 23–4).

Besht's [Early] Life and Revelation'.[22] This introduced a feature of conventional biography. In essence Israel Yoffe's added section told the story of how Israel ben Eliezer became the Besht. The tales in the constituent groups of Dov Ber's collection had ignored this early life,[23] for Dov Ber was interested only in the Besht's miracle-making activities. Israel Yoffe, on the other hand, thought it important to recount how the Besht came to acquire his holy status and leadership position because he wanted to show that a leading *tsadik* could be found in every generation.[24] This was probably meant to have implications for Habad—the hasidic group he was associated with—which was embroiled in a major controversy over its leadership and succession at this time.[25]

Another thorny methodological issue which has long been on the scholarly agenda is the relationship between the various editions of the *Shivḥei haBesht* text. Within three years of the publication of the first printing, seven more editions, three in Hebrew (Berdiczów, 1815; Lashchov, 1815; Hrubieszów, 1817) and four in Yiddish (Ostróg, 1815; Korzec, 1816; Nowy Dwór, 1816; Żółkiew, 1816), appeared.[26] The later three Hebrew texts are obviously based on the Kopys text. The Nowy Dwór and Żółkiew Yiddish translations both declare that they are faithful to this text, although upon close inspection it is obvious that there are significant differences.[27]

The Ostróg translation has not been seen by any scholar since Israel Zinberg wrote about it in his *History of Jewish Literature* in the 1930s.[28] The Korzec edition, however, contains a note stating that it is a reprint of the Ostróg translation, so that studies of *Shivḥei haBesht* usually refer to the 'Ostróg–Korzec edition' in Yiddish. For many years it was received wisdom in the scholarly literature that the Ostróg–Korzec edition was so different from the Kopys Hebrew text in terms of the order and selection of the stories, the style and structure of the story-telling, and the meaning of the words that it must be based on a Hebrew text different from the Kopys one. This manuscript text, it was assumed, must have preceded the changes the printer made and thus reflected the 'original' *Shivḥei haBesht* as

[22] Hebrew: 'Seder hahishtalshelut vehitgalut haBesht'; Rubinstein, *Shivḥei haBesht*, 35, 59; cf. trans. in *SHB* 6, 31.

[23] Reiner, 'Transmission, Editing and Printing', 148.

[24] Rosman, 'The History of a Historical Source', 197–202.

[25] See M. Rosman, *Founder of Hasidism: A Quest for the Historical Ba'al Shem Tov* (Berkeley and Los Angeles, 1996), ch. 12, where I argue that this was probably connected to the struggle for succession among the Habad hasidic group following the death of its founding leader, Shneur Zalman of Lyady, in 1813. Israel Yoffe was a close associate of both Shneur Zalman and his son and ultimate successor, Dov Ber of Lubavich. In my opinion, his modification and publication of *Shivḥei haBesht* at the height of the succession controversy was intended to use the example of the Ba'al Shem Tov as a precedent legitimizing the succession of Dov Ber of Lubavich.

[26] For a list of the editions of *Shivḥei haBesht*, see Y. Rafael, '*Shivḥei haBesht*', *Areshet*, 2–3 (1960–1), 358–77, 440–1, (Hebrew).                     [27] Mondshine, *Facsimile*, 22–40.

[28] Yiddish edn. (Vilna, 1936), vol. vii, book 2, pp. 205, 318–21. This material does not appear in the English translation.

written by Dov Ber of Ilintsy. Wherever the Ostróg–Korzec Yiddish differed from the Kopys Hebrew, the Yiddish was to be preferred as reflecting the urtext.[29] Based on this supposition, Rubinstein, in particular, developed the theory that the Yiddish version, presumed to be following the original, showed the Besht as a miracle-worker and charismatic, while the Kopys Hebrew text attempted to portray him as a more scholarly and rational figure because it was composed in the rationalist nineteenth century and was linked through the printer to the more rationally inclined Habad hasidic movement.[30]

Mondshine proved, however, that a comparison with their model of the Nowy Dwór and Żółkiew Yiddish translations, which are declared derivatives of the Kopys Hebrew text, yields differences of the same type as does a comparison between the Ostróg–Korzec and Kopys texts. This is because the kinds of variation from the Hebrew text which Yaari and others detected in the Ostróg–Korzec edition are standard for Yiddish translations of the period.[31] Moreover, some of the apparent differences in the Yiddish text appear to be glosses intended to harmonize the content of the stories of the printer's added opening section with the stories in the body of the writer's collection. For example, in a story placed towards the end of the printer's addition, a representative of the hasidim of Kutów[32] spends the Sabbath with the Besht, during the course of which the Besht reveals himself and commands the guest to go to the hasidim and tell them that

There is a great light living near your community and it will be worthwhile for you to seek him out and bring him to the town. . . . All of them went to his village to invite him to come to town. . . . When they encountered each other they all went to a place in the forest where they made a chair out of the branches of trees. They placed him on the chair and they accepted him as their rabbi.[33]

Yet, in the body of the book, which originated with the writer, Dov Ber of Ilintsy, there is a different version of how the Besht came to be recognized by the hasidim and settle in town. In this story the Besht was brought to town by his brother-in-law, who wished him to be admonished by a woman who was inhabited by a dybbuk (soul of a dead person). When he met the woman, the Besht warned the dybbuk that unless it was silent he would ask permission to use his as yet unrevealed *ba'al shem* powers to exorcise the dybbuk. 'The hasidim who accompanied him said that they would permit him to break his vow and urged him to exorcise the spirit from the woman.' The Besht persuaded the dybbuk to leave the

---

[29] Shmeruk, 'R. Adam Ba'al Shem'; A. Yaari, 'Two Basic Recensions of *Shivḥei haBesht*', *Kiryat sefer*, 39 (1964), 249–72; Rubinstein, 'Revelation Stories'.

[30] Rubinstein, 'Revelation Stories', and in his notes in his edition of *Shivḥei haBesht*.

[31] Mondshine, *Facsimile*, 41–7.

[32] The *SHB* translators, p. 31, following the lead of some earlier scholars, identified the town as Brody. Rubinstein, 'Revelation Stories', 171–3 demonstrated convincingly that it was Kutów; cf. J. Weiss, 'A Circle of Pneumatics in Pre-hasidism', in his *Studies in Eastern European Jewish Mysticism* (Oxford, 1985), 27–42. [33] *SHB* 31.

woman, and 'From that time on they did not let the Besht stay in the village. A certain arrendator [leaseholder] hired him as a *melamed* for his children.'[34]

But was the Besht not already living in the town, having been anointed in the forest ceremony as the rabbi of the hasidim? And as the leader of the hasidim, does it not seem strange that he would take a menial job as a private *melamed*? Did the hasidim not support him? These problems are solved in the Yiddish text, which adds information that makes the two stories consistent: 'And it was after the first feats when he became somewhat famous that they took him out of the village; but despite this he remained poor because he did not wish to accept money for nothing.'[35] Thus the Yiddish text glosses that, owing to his modesty, the Besht could be both rabbi of the hasidim and a lowly *melamed*.

Many of the differences between the Yiddish and the Hebrew editions—failing to identify sources, subtracting stories, and embellishing them with more wonders and miraculous elements—are typical of the recasting of hagiographic stories from a literary language like Hebrew to a vernacular one like Yiddish.[36] In sum, there seems to be no basis for seeing the Ostróg–Korzec text as anything other than a translation based on the Kopys edition. Likewise, Rubinstein's theory of nineteenth-century rationalization of the Ba'al Shem Tov falls away.

There is, however, an independent recension of *Shivḥei haBesht* which does reflect a version of the text which is free of interference by the printer. This is a manuscript which was donated anonymously to the library of the Habad hasidim in Brooklyn in the summer of 1980.[37] This nineteenth-century text contains many significant variations from the printed version, both in the order of the stories and in their content and wording.[38] The differences in order are particularly telling. None of the stories which Israel Yoffe added in the opening section of the printed edition appears in the manuscript and none of those he transplanted to the front of the printed book from later positions shows up at the beginning of the manuscript.

---

[34] *SHB* 35.  [35] Rubinstein, *Shivḥei haBesht*, 65 n. 22.

[36] Mondshine, *Facsimile*, 41–7; Rosman, 'The History of a Historical Source', 181–3.

[37] The genuineness of the manuscript is not established beyond doubt but can be reasonably argued. This version of the stories in the collection contains certain details which are 'statements contrary to interest' for Habad. For example, it indicates that the congregation around the Besht sometimes prayed out loud in ecstasy, where in the printed edition only the Besht himself engages in this practice. The translation (*SHB* 51) is incorrect. Rather than 'He used to utter a great cry and pray louder than anyone else,' it should read, 'He would lead all of them and would pray with a great shout.' The manuscript reads, 'He would lead all of them and they would pray with a great shout' (see Rubinstein, *Shivḥei haBesht*, 86–7). The teachings of the leader of Habad at the time of *Shivḥei haBesht*'s publication—espousing 'normal' prayer—would be better corroborated by the printed version. More interesting is the *pro patria* watermark on the paper, dating it somewhere within the approximate period 1805–14 (see Rosman, 'The History of a Historical Source', 183–5). In order to maximize the apparent authenticity of his text a forger would be expected to use paper which was manufactured in the 18th century, rather than paper that was made close to the date of the appearance of the printed edition, which would make his text appear to be late and thus much less valuable.

[38] See Mondshine, *Facsimile*, 7–18 and *passim*.

It is highly unlikely, however, that this manuscript is a true copy of the version compiled by Dov Ber of Ilintsy. First, it is not complete: many passages found in the original are missing. Secondly, in some places the reading in the printed Kopys text is obviously preferable.[39] Thirdly, based on its probable date, grossly *circa* 1810, it is likely to be one of the manuscripts evidently riddled with mistakes that Israel Yoffe aimed to expose and make obsolete by his act of printing the text. The Habad manuscript is, then, an additional witness to the text that pre-dates the printer's intervention. As such it is helpful in determining where and how the printer left his marks on the text.[40] It is not, however, the urtext, and where it parallels but differs from Kopys, it is not a priori preferable.

Another possible textual witness is the Berdyczów 1815 Hebrew edition. One of the customary endorsements of this book, written by R. Israel Shalom of Lubartów, notes that he brought a manuscript of *Shivḥei haBesht* to the Berdyczów printing-house with the intention of checking the text. In fact the Berdyczów edition contains a superior text of Dov Ber's introduction, as well as an addendum to this introduction, written by Dov Ber's son Yehuda Leib, who was probably the source of the additional manuscript. The Berdyczów text also contains textual variants from the Kopys edition, and some of these are significant. However, there is reason to believe that R. Israel Shalom arrived at the printing-house after the type was already set, so to what extent his manuscript affected the Berdyczów text is not certain.[41]

The result of all of these considerations is that, in setting the text of *Shivḥei haBesht*, one must take into consideration the Habad manuscript and the Berdyczów edition, as well as the Kopys first edition. The Ostróg–Korzec text, like the Nowy Dwór and Żółkiew editions, is not relevant to this process except to see how the early translators understood or interpreted the Hebrew text.

The Yiddish translations are important, however, as preservers of oral traditions about the Besht which may not be reflected in the Hebrew. For example, the Ostróg–Korzec text, which deleted about 40 per cent of the stories which appear in the Kopys edition, contains four stories not in the Hebrew collection. These may very well be tales which circulated as part of the oral corpus concerning the Besht, but Dov Ber, for whatever reason, chose not to include them in his collection. The Yiddish translator freely introduced this material. Similarly, the Berdyczów version deleted one short story for the express reason of modesty; while it added a story which was not in the original collection.[42]

This process of subtraction and addition in subsequent editions illustrates the

[39] Ibid. 7–18.     [40] Rosman, 'The History of a Historical Source', 183–92.

[41] B. Mintz, *Shivḥei haBesht* (Tel Aviv, 1960), 11–12, 17; Rubinstein, *Shivḥei haBesht*, 11–12, and, in the notes, *passim*; Mondshine, *Facsimile*, 47–51.

[42] See Rubinstein, 'Notes on *Shivḥei haBesht*', 68–9, and Mintz, *Shivḥei haBesht*, intro. In *SHB* the deleted passage is on p. 258; the added story appears in the notes on pp. 342–3. The last story in the book is also emended in the Berdyczów text (see Rubinstein, *Shivḥei haBesht*, 315 nn. 15, 17).

common phenomenon of the dynamic relationship between oral tradition and written canon. Only part of an oral tradition is ever included in the written canon, while later editions often incorporate parts that were earlier excluded. Thus what is written down late is not necessarily known late: it may just have been ignored. When it does come to be written down, however, it is shaped by the writer's current concerns.[43]

In the quest to separate the historical wheat from the chaff, therefore, it should be remembered that the later the material is written down, the more it responds to intervening events and accounts and the less accurate it is as a historical record. Thus the extra stories about the Ba'al Shem Tov in the Ostróg–Korzec and Berdyczów texts tell us something about the contents of the Ba'al Shem Tov oral tradition, but probably add little to knowledge about the historical person.[44]

## EDITIONS

From its first appearance *Shivḥei haBesht* proved to be a popular book. The first edition was sold out in much less than one year and a total of eight editions and translations were published within a three-year period. The maskil and enemy of hasidism Josef Perl observed that the book sold as many as 10,000 copies in two years. By the standards of the time, *Shivḥei haBesht* was a best-seller.[45]

Its popularity continued in subsequent generations. In 1960–1, Rafael compiled an (admittedly incomplete) list which numbered forty-nine editions (including translations) and at least five more have appeared in the intervening years.[46] With such a large number of choices the reader, especially the historically minded one, needs to be informed as to what each publication has to offer and what problems it poses. Several of the *Shivḥei haBesht* editions have particular importance or have made a significant impact, and I will direct my attention to these.

*Kopys, 1814.* The first printing of *Shivḥei haBesht* is rare. While Mondshine reproduces much of it photographically, the full original text is available only in a

[43] See Rosman, 'The History of a Historical Source', 181 n. 23, 213 n. 131.

[44] Cf. A. Rapoport-Albert, 'Hagiography with Footnotes', Rapoport-Albert (ed.), in *Essays in Jewish Historiography* (Atlanta, Ga., 1991), 119–59; S. Zfatman, *Bein Ashkenaz leSefarad* (Jerusalem, 1993), 103–4.

[45] J. Perl, *Über das Wesen der Sekte Chassidim*, ed. and trans. A. Rubinstein from German into Hebrew as *Al Mahut Kat hahasidim* (Jerusalem, 1977), 77–8; id., *Ma'asiyot ve'igerot mitsadikim ume'anshei shelomeinu*, ed. C. Shmeruk and S. Verses (Jerusalem, 1970), 29–32. See also the endorsement on the Korzec Yiddish edition, cited by Mondshine, *Facsimile*, 41, implying that both the first Hebrew and the first Yiddish editions of *Shivḥei haBesht* were sold out in less than a year. Likewise, a British missionary journal, *The Jewish Expositor*, 13 (1828), 192, notes that by 1818 three large editions of *Shivḥei haBesht* had sold out. (My thanks to Michael Silber for this reference.)

[46] See Rafael, editions of *Shivḥei haBesht*, n. 26, above. It would be interesting to study the years in which these editions appeared and compare them to the publishing history of hasidic literature in general (see Z. Gries, 'The Jewish Background to Buber's Activity in Shaping the Hasidic Tale' (Heb.), *Jerusalem Studies in Jewish Folklore*, 11–12 (1990), 46–56).

few libraries. The quality of the printing is poor and the pagination is muddled.[47] The text of the 'writer's introduction'[48] is corrupt. Withal, the Kopys edition is still an important source for scholars because no subsequent work has reproduced the entire text with complete accuracy (Rubinstein's edition is close, but not perfect), while many have actually altered or obscured the original text. Anyone seeking to quote, for scholarly purposes, a passage which does not appear in Mondshine's edition had best check Rubinstein's text against this first edition.

*S. A. Horodetzky (Berlin, 1922, Tel Aviv, 1946, 1960).* This is probably the bestselling edition of *Shivḥei haBesht* ever. For many years it occupied pride of place next to the greats of modern Hebrew literature on the bookshelves of Israeli homes. It was the standard text used in school and university courses and most scholarly articles cited it.[49]

Despite its popularity, however, this edition has serious flaws. Horodetzky ends the introduction to his edition by noting, 'The book *Shivḥei haBesht* in the present edition is the very same book; everything is the same as it is in the 1814 Kopys edition. Nothing is missing. What is new in it is *only the order and the form*'[50] (emphasis added). The implications of this self-contradictory statement become plain upon even a first reading of the text. To Horodetzky, *Shivḥei haBesht* was a confused and confusing jumble. 'The various stories are scattered arbitrarily, without any link and connection to a single internal content.'[51] To correct this 'shortcoming', Horodetzky arranges the stories so that 'the book will take on the form of a monograph about the Besht according to popular legends'.[52] He groups the tales according to his own categories (the Besht's early biography and his revelation, his disciples and associates, his activities and wonders, his last days and death, miscellaneous).

By rearranging the stories, Horodetzky takes on the role of editor. In any anthology the order of the elements contributes to the overall effect that the editor wishes to convey. Dov Ber of Ilintsy structured his collection to reinforce the idea of the Besht as miracle-worker. Israel Yoffe changed the order of the stories in order to confront the issue of the Besht's preparation for his role during his early life. Horodetzky, taking a consciously historical approach, attempts to create a quasi-biography about the Besht which will tell his life story from beginning to end. The result is Horodetzky's historical interpretation of *Shivḥei haBesht*, not a faithful rendering of the 1814 edition.[53] In the introduction Horodetzky emphasizes the mythic and spiritual nature of the Besht, and by structuring the text so that

---

[47] See Mondshine, *Facsimile*, 142.     [48] Rubinstein, 'Notes on *Shivḥei haBesht*', 62–71.

[49] e.g. Scholem, 'The Historical Image of Israel Ba'al Shem Tov'. In recognition of this fact, even Mondshine (*Facsimile*), who was severely critical of Horodetzky's work, cross-referenced all passages with their corresponding places in the Horodetzky edition.     [50] p. 28.

[51] Ibid.; he evidently means here an overall organizing principle.     [52] Ibid.

[53] Cf. G. Scholem, 'Two Letters from Eretts Yisrael from 1760 to 1764' (Heb.), *Tarbiz*, 25 (1957), 436 n. 16; Rubinstein, 'A Possibly New Fragment', 188; id., 'Revelation Stories', 181 n. 71.

the stories about the Besht's miraculous activity are concentrated together in the climactic section of the book, Horodetzky reinforces his view of the Besht as primarily a mythic spiritual hero.

Horodetzky's tinkering with the text is not limited to moving the stories around. He also notes that he has changed the 'form'. By this he means that he has corrected 'the most obvious' errors and textual corruptions. While he does not define these, it is evident that he has made extensive changes in the language of the text, apparently with an eye to modernizing it.

First he has corrected grammatical errors and expanded most of the Hebrew acronyms. Such steps may have made the text more accessible to the non-specialist readers Horodetzky had in mind, but they also rob it of much of its original texture and give a false impression of the nature of the Hebrew language in use when the stories were written down. Moreover, these changes render impossible any attempt at deep analysis based on close reading of the text.[54]

Sometimes Horodetzky's efforts at making the text pleasing to modern eyes result in distortion. Thus his expansion of the acronym *bh'k* (p. 140) is *beit hakeneset* (synagogue) when the correct transcription is *beit hakise* (toilet). Certainly not an insignificant slip.[55] Occasionally Horodetzky's emendation of the text slides into interpretation. When faced with a difficult locution he frequently changes it to yield something more easily understood. For example, the puzzling note that 'they sat and they stood' is transcribed by Horodetzky (p. 84) as 'they sat and they studied'.[56] In a few places the line between interpreting and perverting the text is crossed. For example, in the original the printer stated that the beginning stories are 'as *they* heard from his [Shneur Zalman of Lyady's] holy mouth'; Horodetzky prints: '*I* heard from his holy mouth' (p. 39).[57] 'So long as *God* lives' appears in Horodetzky's edition as 'So long as *I* live' (p. 147).[58]

In short, Horodetzky's text is not an accurate reproduction of the original; it is, rather, a reworking. It adds another layer to the text and increases the distance between it and the historical events which may lie behind the stories.

*Binyamin Mintz (Jerusalem, 1960)*. The distinction of this edition is that it is based on the second printing (Berdyczów, 1815) which, as noted above, contains significant variations from the Kopys edition. Mintz follows the order of the Berdyczów text faithfully and allows many acronyms to stand. He has also added

---

[54] e.g. the story about how the Besht revived a dead infant (Horodetzky, 113–14; Kopys, 35*c*; *SHB* 252).

[55] Cf. Kopys edition, 21*a*; *SHB* 164; Mondshine *Facsimile*, 52; Rubinstein, *Shivhei haBesht*, 143. See also Horodetzky, 78, where *m'm* is expanded as if it were *m'k* (*malbushei kalah* = 'bride's clothing') (Kopys, 11*a*; *SHB* 96: 'bridal gown'; Rubinstein, *Shivhei haBesht*, 143); and Horodetzky, 159: *sh'v*, which should be expanded as '*sheti ve'erev*' = 'a Crucifix', is read as *ysh'v* = 'Yeshu' = 'Jesus' (Kopys, 35*b*; *SHB* 251: 'Jesus'; Mondshine, *Facsimile*, 52; Rubinstein, *Shivhei haBesht*, 306 n. 10).

[56] Cf. Kopys, 23*b*; *SHB* 180: 'They sat and they studied'; Rubinstein, *Shivhei haBesht*, 233 n. 20.

[57] Kopys, 1*a*; *SHB* 6: 'As I heard them'; Mondshine, *Facsimile*, 52; Rubinstein, *Shivhei haBesht*, 35 n. 4.          [58] Kopys, 24*d*; *SHB* 191: 'As long as I live'; cf. Mondshine, *Facsimile*, 52.

parenthetical translations or explanations of non-Hebrew or technical terms—certainly an aid for Hebrew readers.

However, in many places Mintz, like Horodetzky, has corrected grammatical errors, modernized the language, and even emended and interpreted the text. This means that a reader interested in comparing the Kopys and Berdyczów texts cannot be sure if a variant reading reflects a difference in the original texts or Mintz's intervention.[59] Moreover, one may wonder whether the subtleties gained or lost by such alternative renderings as 'he will lead him in chains' in place of the original 'he will lower him in chains' (p. 106), or 'bitter crying' instead of 'great crying' (p. 153), justify changing the text.

Sometimes Mintz's attempts at improvement are plainly wrong. For example, following in the path of Horodetzky, he too has misinterpreted acronyms, falling into the 'synagogue'–'toilet' error (p. 116), and expanding *b'g* (*benei gilo*) as if it were *b'b* (*benei beito*)—'members of his household' rather than 'his intimates' (p. 118). Mistakes like changing 'The doctor said, "No"' to 'The doctor said to him' (p. 104),[60] or *Midrash Shemuel* to *Pirkei avot* (p. 70) warn the reader not to take this edition of the text as completely accurate.

Mintz's introduction does provide a short excursus on early editions of *Shivḥei haBesht* (including reproductions of some of the title-pages) and details of the Besht's disciples and associates.[61] In appendices the book also contains other hasidic texts in popular form. These include: 'Igeret hakodesh', the famous letter of the Ba'al Shem Tov to his brother-in-law Gershon of Kutów;[62] selections from *Keter shem tov*, one of the earliest collections of teachings attributed to the Besht;[63] the so-called *Will of the Besht* (*Tsava'at haRivash*, Ostróg, 1793), which is actually a collection of the *Hanhagot* (moral instruction) of the Maggid of Mezerich (Międzyrzecz);[64] *Me'irat einayim*, a collection of statements by hasidic masters about the Besht,[65] here augmented by Mintz; and selections from *Pe'er layesharim*, the book of teachings by the Besht's contemporary Pinhas of Korzec and his disciple Raphael of Bershad.

*Dan Ben-Amos and Jerome Mintz*, In Praise of the Ba'al Shem Tov [Shivḥei haBesht] (*Bloomington, Ind. 1970*). Based on the Kopys first printing, this is the only complete English translation of *Shivḥei haBesht*. In the twenty-five years since its appearance it has been reprinted four times and published in paperback,

---

[59] See the listing of these variants in Mondshine, *Facsimile*, 51, and Rubinstein, *Shivḥei haBesht*, in the notes, *passim*.

[60] In Hebrew 'no' and 'to Him' are homonyms (both pronounced 'lo').

[61] Also not completely accurate; see Rubinstein, *Shivḥei haBesht*, 95.

[62] For translation, analysis, and bibliography, see Rosman, *Founder of Hasidism*, ch. 6.

[63] Compiled by Aaron ben Tsevi Hakohen of Opatów, and first published in Żółkiew, 1794–5; see G. Nigal, 'A Primary Source of Hasidic Story Literature' (Heb.), *Sinai*, 79 (1976), 132–42.

[64] Z. Gries, *Sifrut hahanhagot* (Jerusalem, 1989), 149–230.

[65] First published as the introduction to *Sefer ha Ba'al Shem Tov*, ed. S. M. Wandek (Łódź, 1938; Jerusalem, 1992), the largest anthology of attributed Besht teachings.

and is frequently on college booklists. The translators should be applauded for daring to translate a classic which has always attracted controversy, and thanks to them the audience for *Shivḥei haBesht* has been enlarged manyfold. However, when measured against the yardstick of historiographic utility this now standard translation falls short. I do not quibble with the notion of interpretative rendering—this is part and parcel of any translation. When the Besht says, literally, 'I was separated in bed for fourteen years' (*hayiti parush bamitah y'd shanah*) it could be translated idiomatically as 'I refrained from sleeping with my wife' (p. 258). The translations which damage the credibility of this edition are those that adopt Horodetzky's changes uncritically and, like him, distort the meaning,[66] and Ben-Amos and Mintz display an unwarranted consistency in following Horodetzky's text.

Just as seriously, some translations display a lack of familiarity with pre-modern Hebrew and eighteenth-century history and context. To translate *hakdamot* as 'introductions' (p. 55) rather than the pre-modern 'assertions', or *billet* as 'train ticket' in a story set when a *billet* was a charity voucher and trains had not yet been invented, demonstrates a lack of background knowledge and careful thought.[67]

The indexes of the English translation—a general index including subjects, names, and places, and an index to the teller or source for each tale as cited by the writer and printer—are most useful. They make the book much more accessible to scholars and their utility is not limited to English readers. The folk-motif index can be helpful in distinguishing historical fact from folk-tale.[68] The bibliography was barely adequate in its day and is now outdated. The notes bring basic biblical, rabbinic, and other references and supply historical, geographical, liturgical, theological, and kabbalistic background in modest amounts. They are written for the non-specialist reader and occasionally mislead.[69]

*Yehoshua Mondshine* (*Jerusalem, 1982*). This edition was prompted by the discovery of the manuscript of *Shivḥei haBesht* discussed above. In order to make the manuscript available and to facilitate comparison with the first printing, Mondshine included in his edition both a facsimile of the manuscript and a passage-by-passage comparison of it with the Kopys text. His edition includes photographs of sections of the Kopys text, underlines parallel texts, and places the manuscript's reading alongside. This arrangement virtually guarantees that Mondshine's book will be used only for specialized scholarly purposes. The facsimile is not very inviting to read and the comparative section reproduces only those parts of the printed text which are also in the manuscript.

---

[66] See nn. 55–8 above.

[67] For details of mistranslations, see Rubinstein, according to the index s.v. 'English translation'; and Z. Gries, *Sefer, sofer vesipur be reishit haḥasidut* (Tel Aviv, 1992), 105.

[68] Here a word of caution is in order. As J. Chajes once pointed out to me, some of the story elements which Ben-Amos and Mintz regarded as 'folk literature motifs' actually reflect Jewish traditions and normative Jewish practice. For example, the prohibitions against travelling on the Sabbath or mourning on holidays (*SHB* 291). [69] See n. 67.

While the comparative section efficiently points out the textual variants (and the more important of these are discussed in depth by Mondshine in his introductory material), one possibly significant difference between the printed version and the manuscript is never made obvious. The manuscript differs not only in that it contains a smaller amount of material than the Kopys text and in its variant readings, but also by presenting the material in a somewhat different order. As noted earlier, the order of the stories can affect the overall message of the book. What message did the editor of the manuscript want to convey? Did it differ from that of the writer? Mondshine's edition implies these questions but does not address them.

Mondshine, himself, would probably reject these questions as scholarly overanalysis of the text. His attitude is that scholars have taken *Shivḥei haBesht* altogether too seriously. Thus he makes it clear that the manuscript, while generally superior to the printed text, is not always so. In a brilliant analysis of the Yiddish translations, he demonstrates how they all played fast and loose with the text. Mondshine is even prepared to admit that the printer modified the manuscript he received, although not as radically as most scholars have asserted. The point of all of this is that *Shivḥei haBesht* is not holy writ. It is a collection of edifying and entertaining stories which editors and translators felt free to adapt, resulting in several alternative versions, none of which need be called 'authoritative'.

Moreover, as alluded to above, among hasidim—at least from the mid-nineteenth century onwards—there has been much scepticism with regard to this book. The only people who considered *Shivḥei haBesht* to be 'holy scripture' or the 'canon' of hasidism have been maskilim and modern scholars.[70] In my view the reservations of hasidim with regard to *Shivḥei haBesht* are probably the result of what maskilim like Josef Perl and Judah Leib Mizes did with the text, using it to criticize or even mock hasidism and its founder.[71] The book's initial popularity bespeaks a willingness to credit the stories. The timing of the criticism implies that it was the realization that this book could be used for the purpose of anti-hasidic propaganda that made it suspect in the eyes of believers.[72]

In addition to bringing the *Shivḥei haBesht* manuscript into the public domain, Mondshine's edition renders other valuable services. The analysis clarifies or solves many textual problems, supplying biographical and geographical details which make several problematic stories more readily comprehensible. The bibliography is very useful and Mondshine's appended material about the Besht from other hasidic sources is a worthy supplement to *Shivḥei haBesht*. Finally, he

---

[70]  Mondshine, *Facsimile*, 54–7.

[71]  See J. Perl, *Megaleh temirin* (Vienna, 1819); J. L. Mizes, *Kinat ha'emet* (Vienna, 1928).

[72]  Mondshine (*Facsimile*, 55) reasons that normally holiness grows over time and *a fortiori* later scepticism implies even greater doubts when the book was first published. Such reasoning is not valid here because the intervening ridicule of the maskilim would have interrupted the process of accretion of holiness.

reprints in parallel form the three known versions of the letter from the Besht to his brother-in-law Gershon of Kutów (including one version which Mondshine himself discovered). The whole arrangement greatly facilitates analysis and understanding of this important source.

*Eliyahu C. Carlebach (Jerusalem, 1990)*. Entitled *Sefer shivḥei haBa'al Shem Tov hashalem* (The Complete *Shivḥei haBesht*), this edition was published under the auspices of the Zekher Naftali Institute and is an example of contemporary ultra-Orthodox scholarship. It aims to be a definitive presentation of the text, both correcting all the mistakes of previous editions and adding supplementary material.

With regard to the first objective, the editor never states explicitly which text he has chosen to serve as the basis of this version. Whichever it is, he has corrected it on the basis of 'the Kopys first printing, the Yiddish Ostróg–Korzec printing, both printed in 1814–15, and from other printings and manuscripts, and in some places, after much inquiry and contemplation, I corrected the language myself wherever correction was required' (p. 11). While most of these corrections are indicated by a system of asterisks and appear in a smaller typeface, some are not, and it is difficult to know which correction stems from which source. Moreover, the authority of the anonymous 'printings' and 'manuscripts' (note the plural) is not established, while the use of the Yiddish as a textual witness is, for the reasons explicated earlier, unwarranted. Thus this text is Rabbi Carlebach's undocumented reconstruction of *Shivḥei haBesht* and surpasses Horodetzky's edition as an exercise in interpretation. Any reader who thinks he is reading the original *Shivḥei haBesht* will be much misled.

Carlebach's interpretation is guided by two principles: 'The author did not write the stories as historiography as chroniclers do, but rather to teach by them piety as morality books do. . . . All of his stories are true' (p. 15). For Carlebach, then, this book is both hagiography and history. Unlike the editors of the other editions discussed above, he believes the two can be made completely compatible. His efforts at harmonization are far from convincing.

Probably the most interesting aspect of this edition is the wealth of references it brings from later traditions as part of the effort to reconcile various versions of the stories and to solve textual problems. There are also some useful indexes, maps, and photographs.

*Avraham Rubinstein (Jerusalem, 1991)*. This edition, subtitled 'Annotated and with Commentary', was published posthumously thanks to the near-heroic efforts of the editor's family. Various typographical and other minor errors testify that the manuscript was barely completed before Rubinstein's death. Despite the difficulties these lapses pose, this edition is unquestionably the most usable one there is. The Kopys text is presented in clear type with rubrics provided by Rubinstein which both divide the text into discrete stories and constitute a rough form of interpretation. These features make it easier for the reader to engage with the text.

Accompanying the text on each page are extensive notes. These explain difficult words and concepts; supply realia, background information, and cross-references; outline variant readings; and raise historical, theological, and other issues. Parallel stories from other sources are included in the thirty appendices. There are also facsimiles of book title-pages, some significant archival texts, and other material.

Rubinstein's approach to the text is heavily influenced by his belief, noted above, that the Ostróg–Korzec Yiddish translation is the most reliable version of the text. In his notes he consistently emphasizes the Yiddish readings and the interpretations they imply. However, as already indicated, the Yiddish is not based on any urtext and Rubinstein's theories, assuming that it is, are not tenable.

Rubinstein also had much more confidence in the historicity of the stories than most scholars do, writing that

The information about the Besht's dream inquiries, his celestial journeys, his teacher from the upper spheres, the cancellation of heavenly accusations, his knowledge of the future, his healing of souls, etc.—only the Besht himself could be the original source for them; therefore the close disciples could tell about these mystical events because they learned of them from him himself.

This willingness to accept much of the material in the book as stemming directly from the Besht strikes me as rather credulous, demonstrating an unwarranted enthusiasm for *Shivḥei haBesht* as a historical textbook, rather than a work of hagiography.

Rubinstein was the first to suggest that the Besht filled multiple roles as both a *ba'al shem*-type miracle-worker for the masses and an inspired religious leader who succeeded in gathering an élite group of disciples. This idea has since been developed by Etkes[73] and others. It offers an effective method for conceptualizing the Besht's persona and career.

*Shivḥei haBesht* is a rich and attractive source. As knowledge about hagiography is developed and additional historical sources are discovered, the stories will be subject to novel interpretative efforts and the entire collection will be placed in new perspective. Whatever new interpretations are offered should, however, be based on the text itself.

[73] Emanuel Etkes, 'Mekoman shel hamagiyah uva'alei hashem beḥevrah ha'ashkenazit bemifneh hame'ot ha-17 ha-18', *Zion*, 60 (1995), 69–104.

# Knowledge of Foreign Languages among Eighteenth-Century Polish Jews

## DANIEL STONE

> Jews dress in the Eastern fashion. Their costume is composed of a black dress . . .
> buttoned from neck to waist, and a broad coat which resembles a monastic habit.
> They wear their hair short and their beards long. They wear fur-trimmed caps
> and always walk in slippers, although the climate requires kneeboots. This foreign
> nation, which grows more abundantly here than elsewhere, dresses like this across
> the country.
>
> HUBERT VAUTRIN

THIS comment by Hubert Vautrin, an eighteenth-century French traveller,[1] epitomizes the view of Polish Jews as an isolated community lost in a mixture of religious introspection and commercial development, which interacted minimally with its Polish neighbours, not to speak of more distant peoples such as the Germans or the French. Traditional interpretations of the Enlightenment as providing a sharp break with an ignorant and superstitious past strengthen the image. For Poles, the *Oświecenie* of poets, historians, educators, and political reformers transformed public sentiment, paving the way for the Four Year Diet (1788–92) and the Kościuszko Insurrection (1794). For Jews the Haskalah abandoned a centuries-old preoccupation with religion and allowed them to become Europeans. Moses Mendelssohn's Germany became the centre of the modern Jewish world, while Poland merely provided a reservoir of uninitiated folk who needed to be educated.[2]

This picture requires serious modification. Polish Jews were not isolated in the eighteenth century or in previous centuries. They inhabited an international society of business, medicine, politics, and scholarship. Jews published their works in Hebrew and circulated them across the European continent. Jews also took a major part in international business networks, which carried Jewish merchants to other lands with their Jewish servants and labourers. They travelled to study and

---

[1] Cited in Wacław Zawadzki (ed.), *Polska Stanisławowska w oczach cudzoziemców*, 2 vols. (Warsaw, 1963), i. 812.

[2] Emanuel Ringelblum, *Żydzi w powstaniu kościuszkowskim* (Warsaw [1938]), 18–21, 34.

practise medicine. Within Poland, Jewish occupations demanded extensive contact with the non-Jewish world, as did the political requirements of maintaining a Jewish communal identity. Jews lobbied the Polish kings, parliaments, and provincial dietines to establish, protect, and expand their residential and commercial rights. In the course of the century, Polish Jews developed a significant interest in secular science which foreshadowed the nineteenth-century Jewish stampede out of the ghetto.

While Jewish participation in national and international networks exposed them to the emerging world-view represented by the Enlightenment, Jews were not integrated into any of the state systems of Europe.[3] Polish Jews commonly spoke Yiddish, reserving Hebrew for business, law, and religion. They clung to their separate legal institutions, seeing themselves as a part of the Polish Commonwealth without aspiring to become part of the Polish nation (if we can use that term for the eighteenth century). Jewish schools taught religious subjects exclusively, and much of the Jewish community remained suspicious of anything that did not contribute directly to the traditions, security, and prosperity of the community.

The full question of Jewish tradition and change in eighteenth-century Poland is extraordinarily complex, and the only matter under investigation here is the degree to which Polish Jews knew Polish and European languages such as German, French, and Latin, as well as east European languages such as Russian and Hungarian. The lack of hard evidence precludes a definitive answer to this question. However, the occupational patterns of Polish Jews and their commercial, political, rabbinical, medical, and scientific networks provide indirect indications of probable language knowledge. In addition, Jewish and Gentile memoir literature offers anecdotal evidence of language use.

## BUSINESS CONTACTS

Jews were heavily involved in international trade, and may have handled as much as three-quarters of all exports and imports on their own or on behalf of their royal, noble, and clerical clients. This required regular travel to international trade fairs in neighbouring countries. It also brought foreigners, particularly foreign Jews, to Poland. The linguistic implications are clear, if impossible to quantify.

Hundreds of Polish Jews attended the Leipzig and Frankfurt fairs annually at the end of the eighteenth century. Polish Jews, particularly from western Poland, played a major role in the trade of German-speaking Gdańsk, Szczecin, Elbląg,

---

[3]  See Jacob Katz, *Tradition and Crisis* (New York, 1961), for a general description of 'Jewish society at the end of the Middle Ages'; Bernard D. Weinryb, *The Jews of Poland: A Social and Economic History of the Jewish Community in Poland from 1100–1800* (Philadelphia, 1973); Maurycy Horn, 'Kultura umysłowa Żydów polskich w XV–XVIII wiekach', in *Dzieje Lubelszczyzny*, vi (Warsaw, 1989), 127–66.

and Toruń, while Königsberg and Riga tended to attract Jews from the Grand Duchy of Lithuania. Lithuania also supplied enough merchants to the lucrative Russian trade in furs, tea, and tobacco to require the establishment of a separate Jewish hostel in Moscow in mid-century even while the Ukraine remained the primary focus of Polish Jewish merchants; Russian Jews came to Poland as well. Jews from the Ukraine, Podolia, and Volhynia crossed Poland annually to sell their cattle in Wrocław. Jews were heavily involved in trade with the Austrian Empire, particularly through Brody, which grew extremely rapidly after the first partition to become an important city and the intellectual contact-point between Poland and the Austrian Empire; Jewish merchants and bankers provided protection and patronage for the Jewish Enlightenment. The Hungarian wine trade was substantial.[4]

A typical figure from the end of the eighteenth century was young Józef Perl of Tarnopol, a pioneer of Yiddish literature in the early nineteenth century. Perl's father carried on business activities across the length and breadth of Poland: he imported manufactured goods from Leipzig, sent wood to Gdańsk, and brought wine from Hungary. As a young man, Józef travelled extensively for his father. Jewish emancipation in the West and the debate over Jewish reform in Poland stimulated Perl to study German, French, Latin, mathematics, history, and natural science with Ber Ginzburg of Brody. Perl then established a school which taught Polish, German, and other modern subjects, and he wrote satires against Jewish obscurantism.[5]

International trade brought new Jewish immigrants to Poland from western Europe. Lively contacts with Holland and England rested in the hands of Dutch, German, and English Jews who settled in Warsaw as the capital grew under King Stanisław August Poniatowski. The Dutch Simonis family settled there in 1768 to take up banking and jewellery operations supplying the king, often on credit. Majer Izak Kohen also came from Amsterdam. Szymon Lewi came from Halle, Moses Izak Kies came from Berlin, Szymon Emanuel came from Hamburg, and Lewi (first name unknown) came from Dresden. At least five other German Jews settled in Warsaw in the 1770s and 1780s alone. Several English Jews arrived: Benedict Lewi and two sons of a London rabbi, Joseph and Jacob Pisk. These represented the merchant élite, and it seems likely that they would have been accompanied by family and servants.[6] The creation of Polish synagogues in England and

---

[4] Ignacy Schiper, *Dzieje handlu żydowskiego* (Warsaw, 1937), 232–56, 288–303; Salomon Łastig, *Z dziejów Oświecenia żydowskiego* (Warsaw, 1961), 92–3.

[5] Łastig, *Z dziejów Oświecenia żydowskiego*, 113–26.

[6] Schiper, *Dzieje handlu żydowskiego*, 301–3; Majer Bałaban, *Histoia Żydów w Krakowie i na Kazimierzu, 1304–1868*, 2 vols. (Cracow, 1936), ii. 406–7, 412, 423. Simon Simonis, Moses Levi, and other foreign-born Jews took part in negotiations with King Stanisław August Poniatowski regarding change in the legal status of Jews in 1791–2 (*Materiały do dziejów Sejmu Czteroletniego* [hereafter *MDSC*], 6 vols., vi, ed. A. Eisenbach, J. Michalski, E. Rostworowski, and J. Woliński (Warsaw, 1969), 325, 333).

Holland attests to the number of Polish Jews moving west, among them Juda Litwak, a Dutch mathematician, Izrael Lyons, a professor of oriental languages at Cambridge, and Hyam Hurwicz, a professor at the University of London.[7]

Even far-off America received Polish Jews from the start of the eighteenth century. Haim Salomon, who, according to legend, contributed greatly to the success of the American colonies in the War of Independence, was born in Leszno in 1740. The British arrested Salomon, an army supplier, for spreading sedition among the Hessian mercenaries, but he escaped. He emerged a few years later as the financier who sold American bonds to the French, Dutch, and Spanish governments and handled their securities. Salomon shared his growing fortune with his relatives in Poland, sending them money through a Dutch intermediary. Exchanging letters, Salomon advised his family to study 'the Christian language' to achieve success, while he showed his respect for traditional Hebrew education by offering to support 'any of my brothers' children [who] have a good head to learn Hebrew'. Salomon himself had little formal education, but he learnt Polish, German, French, Italian, and Russian before leaving Europe. Salomon's partner in his early days in New York was Mordecai M. Mordecai from Telsze, Lithuania. Before the Revolution, many Jewish American merchants dealt with Abraham Isaac Abrahams, the son of a Brześć merchant who had settled in London.[8]

Jewish occupational patterns required extensive contact with the local populations of the multinational Polish–Lithuanian Commonwealth. The cream of the business élite in the late eighteenth century were the merchants who supplied the Polish king, state, and great nobles with everything from luxury goods to munitions and, of course, loans. Their activities resembled those of the court Jews (*Hofjuden*) of Germany, who operated on a vast scale and became famous for their luxurious, even princely, way of life which made them forerunners of Jewish emancipation despite their support for traditional Jewish activities. To choose examples which involved Poland, Berend Lehmann financed the election of Augustus II of Saxony to the Polish throne in 1697 and expanded the Leipzig fairs which Polish Jews attended in substantial numbers. Samuel Wertheimer of Vienna was considered the richest Jew in the Austrian Empire. His operations on behalf of the Austrian Crown in Poland included organizing a Polish salt monopoly exporting to the empire. A number of German Jews were encouraged by Frederick II of Prussia to settle in newly conquered Silesia and develop trade with Poland.[9]

[7] I. Lewin, I. Schiper, and A. Tartakower, *Żydzi w Polsce odrodzonej*, 2 vols. (Warsaw, 1933), i. 253; Moses A. Shulvass, *From East to West* (Detroit, 1971), 91–2; Artur Eisenbach, *Z dziejów ludności żydowskiej w Polsce w XVIII i XIX wieku* (Warsaw, 1983), 59–60; Horn, 'Kultura umysłowa Żydów polskich', 164.

[8] Jacob Rader Marcus, *Early American Jewry*, 2 vols. (Philadelphia, 1953), ii. 132–64; id., *The Colonial American Jew, 1492–1776*, 3 vols. (Detroit, 1970), i. 260; ii. 649, 712, 836, 1074, 1086; iii. 1316.

[9] Selma Stern, *The Court Jew* (Philadelphia, 1950), 80, 88–90, 144 ff., 159, 164; F. L. Carsten, 'The Court Jews: A Prelude to Emancipation', *Leo Baeck Institute Year Book*, 3 (1958), 140–58.

The Polish Jewish business agents performed the same functions as the court Jews and sometimes acquired large fortunes, although it is not clear whether they became as secular as their German counterparts. Szmul Zbytkower was the most significant court Jew of Poland; his name appears on the list of eleven Jewish merchants to the court of King Stanisław August Poniatowski, six Jewish suppliers to the Polish army, and six Jewish suppliers to the Russian army stationed in Poland. In addition, four Jews supplied Prussian troops and ten Jews (five of them anonymous) supplied various foreign diplomats in Warsaw.

The personal histories of these Polish court Jews has gone unrecorded for the most part. It is known that Zbytkower had little education, but his third wife, Judith Levy of Frankfurt, knew enough German and French to help her husband deal with the authorities. Berek Joselewicz acted as business agent for Ignacy Massalski, the prince bishop of Wilno, and travelled to France, where he became an enthusiast of revolutionary ideas. Joselewicz organized a Jewish cavalry detachment to fight in the Insurrection of 1794, and later served as an officer in the French army.[10]

Certain Wilno Jews excited the anger of R. Tsevi Hirsh Koidonover (Hersz z Kejdanowa), who published a Hebrew tract in 1705 denouncing 'fathers [who] take greater care that their children learn French and other foreign languages' than religious law. Koidonover made it clear that he was talking about rich Jews with 'florid, fat, and healthy' faces, who can 'indulge in all the pleasures their hearts desire' because they evade their fair share of communal taxes and oppress the poor. In these circles, Jewish women were 'dressing as if they were not Jewish', so that 'it is hard to distinguish between Jewish women and nobles or burghers'. Furthermore, such Jews gave their children non-Jewish names and ignored the laws of *kashrut* when they fraternized with Christians. Both Jewish and Christian clerics objected to mixed social gatherings such as weddings.[11] It is hard to know how many Jews were involved, but the number could only have increased in the course of the eighteenth century in Wilno and many other large settlements.

The vast majority of Polish Jews earned their living by interacting with the Polish population. Between 13 and 15 per cent of Polish Jews worked as estate agents and innkeepers; thousands of them doubled as business agents for Polish nobles. Most of the 35–8 per cent of Jews who worked in trade, 2–3 per cent who worked in transport, 30–2 per cent who worked as artisans, and 16–18 per cent who worked in professions or carried on other activities competed directly with ethnic Poles for customers. Jews managed to make their presence felt even in the few Polish cities which enjoyed the legal right to exclude Jews, especially Warsaw.

---

[10] Schiper, *Dzieje handlu żydowskiego*, 329–30; 'Zbitkower', *Encyclopaedia Judaica*, xvi. 944–5; 'Berek Joselewicz', *Encyclopaedia Judaica*, x. 201–2.

[11] Israel Zinberg, *A History of Jewish Literature*, trans. and ed. Bernard Martin, 12 vols. (Cleveland, Oh., 1972–8), vi. 158–65; Lewin *et al.*, *Żydzi w Polsce Odrodzonej*, i. 249–50.

It seems unlikely that many Jews could have restricted their contacts to the Yiddish-speaking ghetto. Rabbis and other clerical personnel came closest to isolation, although their frequent travels and their positions as community leaders would seem to have required some knowledge of Polish. Almost a third of all Polish Jews lived as isolated individuals and families in villages, particularly in Belarus and Ukraine. Jewish housing in private cities may have been well integrated with Poles.[12]

Jewish contacts with non-Jews may have been particularly close in unincorporated towns and cities, where about three-quarters of all Polish Jews lived. Nobles established these settlements on their properties, often granting them local self-government subject to the ultimate authority of the owner. In order to maximize their revenues, nobles rarely tolerated interference with Jewish interests, even when they personally felt little sympathy for Jews. Such cities rarely produced separate 'Jewish' and 'Polish' neighbourhoods.

## POLITICAL CONTACT

Jews regularly interacted with Poles in politics, presumably in the Polish language. Contact took place on all levels of government. The king and parliament set the privileges governing Jewish communities. Kings (particularly Jan Sobieski and Stanisław August Poniatowski) often intervened to assist Jews in their disputes with local burghers. Royal appointees such as the *wojewoda*, *podwojewoda*, and *starosta* supervised daily activities and heard appeals against verdicts issued by rabbinical courts. Numerous decisions are noted in Maurycy Horn's register of documents from the Metryka Koronna covering the years 1697–1795 under the headings of (1) privileges and limitations concerning Jews or individual Jewish communities; (2) individual privileges; (3) Jewish autonomy; (4) the right to settle or purchase land; (5) economic activities; (6) financial matters; (7) taxes, tariffs, and other financial obligations; (8) criminal and civil matters, and agreements between Jews and Christians; (9) letters of protection; (10) other matters.[13] Some documents report acts by the national government, but others merely register decisions taken by royal cities or courts throughout the country. This clearly does not exhaust the legal interactions of Jews and governments. It does not even raise the matter of interactions occurring in private cities or villages throughout the

---

[12] Eisenbach, *Z dziejów ludności żydowskiej w Polsce w XVII i XIX wieku*, 21; Weinryb, *The Jews of Poland*, 112–18; Emanuel Ringelblum, 'Żydzi w świetle prasy warszawskiej wieku XVIII-go', *Miesięcznik Żydowski*, 1 (1932), 505–6; Murray Jay Rosman, *The Lords' Jews: Magnate–Jewish Relations in the Polish–Lithuanian Commonwealth during the Eighteenth Century* (Cambridge, Mass., 1990), 41–8. For a case-study of a private city, see Gershon David Hundert, *Jews in a Private Polish Town* (Baltimore, 1992).

[13] Maurycy Horn, *Regesty dokumentów i ekscerpty z Metryki Koronnej do Historii Żydów w Polsce*, i: *Czasy Saskie, 1697–1763*; ii: *Rządy Stanisława Augusta, 1764–1795*, pt. 1: *1764–1779* (Wrocław, 1984); iii: *Rządy Stanisława Augusta, 1764–1795*, pt. 2: *1780–1794* (Wrocław, 1988).

country, which must have been very numerous since more than half of all Polish Jews lived under noble jurisdiction.[14]

Jews selected a syndic (*shetadlan*), whose Polish language was considerably better than average, to represent them in meetings with Polish officials. For example, the Jewish community of Słuck boasted in 1761 that

We have found the one whom our souls have been longing for, a wise and reasonable man, from whose mouth flows myrrh, who has the power and authority to stand in the palace of the king and his dignitaries in order to express ideas in a beautiful and eloquent language, whose mouth and heart are equally sincere.[15]

The syndic was well paid and furnished with the means to distribute 'gifts to our lord the king and his nobles'. Numerous seventeenth-century documents show that Jewish representatives regularly attended the parliament and lawcourts to watch over Jewish issues. The practice continued throughout the eighteenth century, as indicated by the somewhat comic example of the Grodno Diet of 1793 which overthrew the constitution of 3 May 1791 and endorsed the Second Partition. Warsaw burghers lobbied hard with Russian and Polish dignitaries to expel the Jews who had settled in Warsaw during the Four Year Diet. As they made the rounds, they invariably stumbled upon a delegation of Jewish representatives engaged in the same activities. Jewish talks with the Russians seem to have been held in French and German.[16] In some cases, Jews in private cities possessed the right to vote for mayors and to participate in city councils.

The debate over the Jewish question during the Four Year Diet revealed a widespread knowledge of Polish and French by Polish Jews: they published quite a few works in both languages, both signed and unsigned.[17] While most of the authors lived in Poland, one of them made his contribution from abroad. Zalkind Hurwicz had moved from Poland to France, where he gained work in the royal library. He won first prize from the Royal Society of Arts and Science of Metz in 1789 (along with works by the *abbé* Henri Grégoire, a political leader in the emancipation of French Jews, and the Protestant lawyer Claude Thierry) for his tract entitled *Apologie des Juifs en réponse à la question: Est-il moyen de rendre les Juifs plus heureux et plus utils en France?* Judging by his embarrassment about having written in 'Sarmatian French', Hurwicz must have written the tract himself. The work was sold in Warsaw immediately and soon appeared in an abridged Polish translation.[18]

[14] Weinryb, *The Jews of Poland*, 120.
[15] Isaac Lewin, 'The Jews' Role in the *Sejm* Elections in Pre-Partition Poland', in *The Jewish Community in Poland* (New York, 1985), 83–6.
[16] Władysław Smoleński, *Mieszczaństwo warszawskie w końcu wieku osiemnastego* (Warsaw, 1976), 204–16.     [17] *MDSC* vi. 188–90, 358–71, 391, 409–21, 526–8.
[18] Ibid. 113; Ringelblum, 'Żydzi w świetle prasy warszawskiej wieku XVIII-go', ii. 73–4; Frances Malino, 'The Right to be Equal: Zalkind Hourwitz and the Revolution of 1789', in Frances Malino and David Sorkin (eds.), *From East and West* (Oxford, 1990), 85–106.

Many leaders of the new Jewish community who participated in the negotiations during the great Diet of 1788–92 for so-called 'Jewish Reform' came from the medical profession. Eliasz Ackord from Wilno studied medicine in Berlin before moving to Warsaw in 1786, and translated into German a well-known but anonymous tract on the Jews. He dedicated his translation to King Stanisław August Poniatowski and added a commentary in which he recommended that Jews attend Polish-language schools. Salomon Polonus, a medical doctor and royal counsellor, published in Wilno in 1792 his own translation of Abbé Grégoire's speech on the emancipation of French Jews plus his own notes and comments, and translations of religious laws. Jakub Kalmanson studied medicine in Germany and France before settling in Warsaw. He acted as the Jewish community's intermediary with the king's representative, Abbé Scipione Piattoli, with whom he negotiated in French. Numerous other meetings were conducted in Polish with Polish dignitaries. Dr Jan Rozenfeld, a royal counsellor, served in the Kościuszko Insurrection and in the Polish legions in Italy.[19]

## RABBINICAL CONTACTS

Polish and other European rabbis travelled extensively throughout Europe as students and as professionals. They not only studied and worked in different places within Poland, but they often went abroad for long periods for study or employment. While settled in one place, they maintained international contacts by corresponding with other rabbis in other parts of Europe. They also corresponded with their families in their place of birth, spreading new ideas and a sense of the breadth of Europe. The correspondence no doubt was carried on in Hebrew with rabbis and in Yiddish with family. Germany provided a special focus for Jewish settlement in mid-century; 500 Polish-born teachers worked in Prussia. Rabbis and other teachers filled a large number of posts in other German states, and local philanthropists often supported promising students from Poland.[20]

For example, Abraham ben Beniamin Zeeb Brzeski came to Poland when the Jews were expelled from Vienna in 1670 and settled in Brześć. From there he carried on an extensive scholarly correspondence with a wide range of Jewish contacts, and published biblical commentaries.[21] Jonathan Eybeschutz travelled in the other direction. He was born in Cracow in 1690 but moved with his family to Moravia when his father assumed a rabbinical post there. A rabbi himself, Eybeschutz worked in Prague, Metz, Altona, Hamburg, and Wandsbeck. His

---

[19] Artur Eisenbach, *Emancypacja Żydów na ziemiach polskich, 1785–1870* (Warsaw, 1988), 43, 73, 99; N. M. Gelber, 'Żydzi a zagadnienie reformy żydów na Sejmie czteroletnim', *Miesięcznik Żydowski*, 2/10 (1931), 327; *MDSC* vi. 310, 421, also 302, 305, 308, 314, 325, 326, 328, 329, 333, 336, 342; Ringelblum, *Żydzi w Powstaniu Kościuszkowskim*, 54.

[20] Shulvass, *From East to West*, 91; Łastig, *Z dziejów Oświecenia żydowskiego*, 92–3.

[21] Mathias Bersohn, *Słownik biograficzny uczonych Żydów Polskich* (Warsaw, 1905, 1983), 17.

scientific interests led him to hold public debates with Christian scholars on astronomy. Other rabbis charged him with kabbalistic heresy, but a synod of Polish rabbis meeting in Lublin (including many of his former students) and the Council of the Four Lands acquitted him. He died in Hamburg in 1764.[22] When Aaron Gordon of Vilna showed scholarly inclinations, his family sent him to Padua to study medicine. He later became August II's doctor. Gordon died early in the eighteenth century.[23]

Moshe bar David, a kabbalist, left Poland in 1741 when he was twenty and 'went to Jerusalem, Cairo, Tiberias, Safed, Aleppo, Ur of the Chaldees, the river Chebar, Mosul, Bagdat, Mt Ararat, Bossora, Ispahan, Cassan, Hamadan, and Surat in India where he lived 2½ years'. He returned to Poland in 1755 for some time before wanderlust struck again. At the age of 50 he turned up in Newport, Rhode Island, carrying a letter of introduction from the Portuguese synagogue in London.[24]

Many Polish rabbis studied in Prague, the centre of Jewish life in the Austrian Empire in the eighteenth century. Ezekiel ben Judah Landau was born in Opatów and worked in Vladimir-Volinsky and Brody before moving to Prague to become the chief rabbi of Bohemia and, in effect, of the Austrian Empire.[25]

## MEDICAL CONTACTS

The traditional Jewish study of medicine linked Polish Jews and Jews in other areas, particularly Italy, where virtually the only university in Europe to accept Jews in numbers from the sixteenth to the eighteenth century was at Padua. The Italian Jewish community was relatively well integrated with Gentile Italian life, and Italian rabbis were particularly known for their knowledge of secular subjects. German universities started admitting Jews in the eighteenth century, particularly the university at Frankfurt-on-Oder, which was near Poland.[26] Students would have learnt Latin for their studies, as well as Italian or German for daily life. Some doctors were also rabbis. In Poland the Jewish élite practised medicine with magnates and other rich Christians as patients. Naturally, they adopted the language, dress, and manners of their patrons.[27]

Dr Mojzes Fortis is an outstanding example of the well-educated doctor. The

[22] Bersohn, *Słownik biograficzny*, 20–1; *Encyclopaedia Judaica*, v. 723, 1075; Hillel Levine, 'Paradise not Surrendered: Jewish Reactions to Copernicus and the Growth of Modern Science', in R. S. Cohen and Marx W. Wartofsky (eds.), *Epistemology and Methodology and the Social Sciences* (Dordrecht, 1984), 214.

[23] Bersohn, *Słownik biograficzny uczonych Żydów Polskich*, 27–8.

[24] Gershon Hundert, 'Characteristics of Jewish Experience in Poland', *Polin*, 1 (1986), 33.

[25] *Encyclopaedia Judaica*, x. 1388–90.

[26] Cecil Roth, *History of the Jews in Italy* (Philadelphia, 1946), 118, 335–6; Eisenbach, *Z dziejów ludności żydowskiej w Polsce w XVIII i XIX wieku*, 57–9; Lewin et al., *Żydzi w Polsce odrodzonej*, i. 289–307.      [27] Lewin et al., *Żydzi w Polsce odrodzonej*, i. 249.

product of a family of Italian and Polish doctors and rabbis, Fortis studied medicine in Latin at Padua, or possibly in Germany. On his return to Poland, he acted as physician to Elżbieta Sieniawska, one of the greatest magnates in eighteenth-century Poland, and also travelled from time to time across the length of Poland to treat other distinguished patients. Fortis supplemented his medical activities with services as Countess Elżbieta Sieniawska's business agent, purchasing luxury goods and even conducting complicated land purchase negotiations on her behalf. He corresponded extensively with Sieniawska in Polish, and even wrote in Polish to her Jewish estate manager. Fortis's Polish correspondence was 'all written in a neat but nonscribal script' and the language was 'perfectly fluent and literate', equal in grammar, usage, and spelling to that of professional scribes.[28]

Tobiasz Kohn was a great traveller. He was born in 1652 in Metz, son of a Polish Jewish doctor and mathematician; his grandfather had been born in Palestine. Tobiasz lost his parents at 8 years of age and returned to the family in Poland, where, growing up, he studied medicine and astronomy. He went to Padua for further study but transferred to Frankfurt-on-Oder to take advantage of financial aid. After completing his courses there, he earned his medical degree from Padua and returned to Poland to practise; he also wrote medical tracts in Hebrew and Latin, which were published in Venice. Because of the Great Northern War (1700–21), Kohn moved to Constantinople and then to Venice. He corresponded with Polish doctors and visited Poland before returning to Constantinople. He died in Jerusalem in 1729.[29]

Mojzesz ben Benjamin Wolf fits a similar, if less exalted, pattern. A doctor from Kalisz, he studied medicine abroad, probably in Germany, and returned to Kalisz, where he eventually died. Wolf wrote medical and pharmacological texts which were published in German in several different cities, as well as in Hebrew. His son followed him as a doctor in Kalisz.[30] Similarly, Yekutiel Gordon of Wilno studied medicine at Padua in the 1730s. While Gordon settled in Amsterdam, his enthusiasm for the kabbalistic doctrines of the Italian rabbi Moses Hayim Luzzatto led him to correspond with several Polish rabbis. Unfortunately, they did not share his enthusiasm and convened a rabbinic court to charge Luzzatto with heresy. Gordon eventually died in Thessaloniki *en route* to Palestine.[31]

Majer Bałaban's study of Cracow Jewry underlines this pattern of foreign travel and knowledge. The Morpurgo family may have been the first family of Jewish doctors to come to Cracow from Italy when they arrived in the mid-seventeenth century. At the same time, Cracow-born doctors started going to Frankfurt to study. In the 1750s and 1760s Dr Aron Kalaher and his brother Mendel Kalaher studied in Frankfurt and returned to treat both Jews and Polish nobles. After Mendel's death, Cracow lacked a Jewish doctor until 1781, when Dr

---

[28] Rosman, *The Lords' Jews*, 147–53, 177–8.
[29] Bersohn, *Słownik biograficzny uczonych Żydów Polskich*, 50–2.  [30] Ibid. 62.
[31] Meyer Waxman, *A History of Jewish Literature*, 6 vols. in 5, iii (1936; repr. New York, 1960), 92.

Szymon Samuelsohn came from Frankfurt. Another Frankfurt graduate, Dr Filip Bondy, settled in Cracow at about the same time. His father, Meszulam Bondy, had been a doctor in Prague and had also practised in Gdańsk. A third medical doctor, Rabbi Marek Szopszowicz, also set up practice. Szopszowicz had received his training from Dr Jędrzej Krapiński, the chief surgeon of Galicia, and was also well versed in botany and chemistry. Competition grew fierce in Cracow as other doctors qualified, forcing some to spread out to lesser towns such as Pińczów, Raków, and Wodzisław, to which they brought their modern medical techniques; they 'also brought western culture to these backward towns'.[32]

Dr Moses Markuze set about bringing western culture to the Jewish masses as well as to Polish Jewish doctors. Born in Königsberg, Markuze settled in Belarus in the Polish–Lithuanian Commonwealth in 1774. He published a medical handbook in 1790 in Yiddish which was up to date as regards medical information and which also sought to impart rationalistic views of nature as well as making a few comments on the place of Jews in Poland. A royal chamberlain, Michał Bobrowski, financed the printing.[33]

## SCIENTIFIC INTERESTS

Jewish interest in medicine provided an entrée into broader scientific areas which often required practitioners to learn Latin and modern west European languages. Throughout most of the eighteenth century scientific thought coexisted quite happily with traditional religious interests in the 'conservative Haskalah', which eventually evolved into 'the wider scope and more revolutionary nature of the ideology of the Berlin Haskalah' led by Moses Mendelssohn but including numerous Polish-born Jews. In this period Jewish scientific work was socially and culturally significant, but it lagged behind the achievements of European science.[34] Mendelssohn was well known to Polish Jews by the 1770s, as indicated by the substantial number of subscribers to his translation of the Torah into German (in Hebrew script). Mendelssohn regularly corresponded with Polish Jews, and wrote to King Stanisław August Poniatowski on behalf of Warsaw's Jews, when Warsaw city authorities prevented Jewish merchants from conducting business in 'New Jerusalem' on the outskirts of Warsaw in 1775; the incident gave its name to Jerusalem Boulevard, or Aleje Jerozolimskie, in modern Warsaw. Polish rabbis

[32] Bałaban, *Historja Żydów w Krakowie i na Kazimierzu, 1304–1868*, 529–38.

[33] Łastig, *Z dziejów Oświecenia żydowskiego*, 106–13.

[34] Isaac Eisenstein-Barzilay, 'The Background of the Berlin Haskalah', in Joseph Leon Blau (ed.), *Essays on Jewish Life and Thought Presented in Honor of Salo Wittmayer Baron* (New York, 1959), 182–97; David E. Fishman, 'A Polish Rabbi Meets the Berlin Haskalah: The Case of R. Barukh Schick', *AJS Review*, 12/1 (Spring 1987), 95–121; Levine, 'Paradise not Surrendered', 203–26. See also David E. Fishman, 'Science Enlightenment and Rabbinic Culture in Belarussian Jewry, 1772–1804', Ph.D. diss., Harvard University, 1985.

generally supported Mendelssohn's scholarly efforts as long as they supplemented Jewish tradition. However, some rabbis concluded in the early 1780s that his programme and that of his supporters threatened to undermine Judaism.[35]

The greatest rabbi of Lithuania, the Wilno Gaon, is reported to have declared also that 'If a man is deficient in the sciences, he will be deficient a hundredfold in the knowledge of Torah, for both Torah and science go together.' He himself learnt no foreign languages and relied on older Hebrew texts (particularly from the Renaissance) for his research in astronomy and mathematics.[36] Rabbi Solomon of Chełm served in the rabbinate of Chełm, Zamość, and Lwów. In his introduction to a biblical commentary published in mid-century, he agreed that traditional Jewish mystics and rabbis were 'devoid of clear and orderly knowledge . . . and contemptuous of common-sense reasoning'. So he studied algebra, geometry, astronomy, logic, and poetry. Like many rabbis, Solomon of Chełm studied medicine, and he ended his career as physician to Count Radziwiłł in Sluck.[37] His pupil Solomon Dubno spent 1767–72 in Amsterdam and Berlin, where Moses Mendelssohn engaged him as tutor to his son Joseph. Dubno encouraged Mendelssohn to complete his Hebrew-script translation of the Torah into German, and provided many of the notes that went into the published text. Dubno moved to Wilno in 1781 but returned to Germany and Amsterdam, where he died in 1813.[38]

Izrael of Zamość was one of the first Polish Jews to move to Berlin to pursue his studies. He was born in 1715 and displayed an unusual aptitude for mathematics and astronomy at an early age. As a mature man, he offended the local community by publishing brochures on the need to enlighten Polish Jews, so he went to Berlin, where he guided the young Moses Mendelssohn in a systematic study of Maimonides and medieval Jewish philosophy. He also became known to the Christian community for his mathematical skills. Izrael moved to Brody late in life and died there in 1772. His cousin, Issacher Falkensohn (Behr), born in Zamość in 1746, became the first Jew to publish poetry in German with his *Gedichte von einem polnischen Juden* (Mietau, 1771). Falkensohn was studying medicine in Königsberg when he came to visit his relative in Berlin, and decided to settle in Germany; he eventually returned to Poland to practise medicine in Mohilew. Jehuda Loeb ben Zew was born in 1764 near Cracow. He studied in Jewish schools but showed such interest in secular studies as to arouse opposition from the community. So ben Zew went to Berlin in 1787 but eventually settled in Wrocław. At the end of the century he wrote grammatical studies and translated

---

[35] Alexander Altmann, *Moses Mendelssohn* (Alabama, 1973), 367, 377, 430–1, 481 ff.; *Encyclopaedia Judaica*, x. 1388–90; William O. McCagg, Jr., *A History of Habsburg Jews, 1670–1918* (Bloomington, Ind., 1989), 22–3.     [36] Waxman, *History of Jewish Literature*, iii. 52.

[37] Eisenstein-Barzilay, 'Background', 184; Altmann, *Moses Mendelssohn*, 354; *Encyclopaedia Judaica*, xiv. 956–7.

[38] *Encyclopaedia Judaica*, vi. 251–2; Altmann, *Moses Mendelssohn*, 354–6, 368 ff.

apocrypha from Chaldean to Hebrew and German. He moved to Vienna late in life to make his living proofreading Hebrew books, but he found time to compile a Hebrew–German, German–Hebrew dictionary. Isaac of Satanów (Isaac Satanower) in Podolia also came to Berlin and wrote a Hebrew–German dictionary and many Hebrew books on religion and philosophy.[39] He never returned to Poland, but he must have been in touch with his family since his younger cousin Mendel Lefin came to Berlin.

Lefin was born in 1749. He came to Berlin in 1780 and met Jewish and Christian philosophers such as Moses Mendelssohn, Solomon Maimon, and Gotthold Lessing. On his return to Poland he lived for a while at Brody before settling in a village on a Czartoryski estate. Prince Adam Kazimierz Czartoryski paid an unaccustomed visit to a crockery shop in the Galician town of Mikołajów and was surprised to see a thick mathematical tome in the German language lying on the counter. The shopkeeper said that it belonged to her husband, Mendel Lefin. Prince Adam soon hired Lefin to tutor his children and helped him publish works such as a Hebrew translation of a Swiss medical tract (with a foreword by Moses Mendelssohn) and a French-language tract on the Jewish question. In the early nineteenth century Lefin wrote a travel book, a book on superstitions, and essays on European and Jewish philosophy.[40]

Lefin spoke little Polish and communicated with Czartoryski in French. His knowledge of French was relatively unusual—the product of Berlin, where Moses Mendelssohn considered French essential and urged his bride to learn the language. Wealthy German Jewish families followed suit, hiring tutors to teach French, geography, arithmetic, bookkeeping, and other secular subjects.[41]

Baruch ben Jakob Szyk (Schick) was born in Szkłów on the Russian border of Belarus and worked as an official of the rabbinical court in Mińsk while studying astronomy and anatomy by himself. He published several Hebrew-language works in Berlin on anatomy, astronomy, and mathematics based on Hebrew and Latin sources. Szyk left Mińsk in 1773 and reappeared in Berlin three years later; there are unsubstantiated stories that he spent the interval studying medicine in London. Unlike most Polish Jewish scholars who went to Berlin to join the Mendelssohn circle, Szyk went to Berlin merely to obtain subsidies for his publications. Naturally, he met Mendelssohn and other leading Jewish and German scholars (indicating that he spoke some German). Berlin money helped him publish a manual of preventative medicine, a Hebrew translation of Euclid, and another translation (this time from English) of a book on algebra, geometry, and

[39] Bersohn, *Słownik biograficzny uczonych Żydów Polskich*, 14, 75–6; Altmann, *Moses Mendelssohn*, 21–3, 336–8, 352–4; Zinberg, *History of Jewish Literature*, viii. 26.

[40] Lastig, *Z dziejów Oswiecenia żydowskiego*, 90–9; *Encyclopaedia Judaica*, xi. 107–8; *MDSC* vi. 409–21.

[41] Solomon Maimon, *An Autobiography*, ed. Moses Hadas (New York, 1947), 79; Zinberg, *History of Jewish Literature*, 9.

trigonometry. Curiously, Szyk became a member of a pseudo-Masonic organization which included aristocrats and Frankists among its members. His interests switched to chemistry late in life.[42]

Back in Poland–Lithuania, Szyk and other Jewish scholars enjoyed financial support from Joshua Zeitlin, a merchant of Szkłów who became a Russian subject after the first partition and gained a large fortune by acting as Prince Grigorii Potemkin's principal business agent in colonizing New Russia and in supplying the Russian army during the Russo-Turkish war of 1788–92. Zeitlin retired to devote himself to scholarship when Potemkin died in 1791. He bought an estate outside Szkłów to house a kind of Hebrew academy of sciences, built up a huge library, and wrote several works himself. Like other Jewish merchants of the region, Zeitlin spoke Russian. Benjamin Zalman Riveles, a disciple of the Gaon of Vilna who abandoned business for study, managed an arboretum on the estate where he grew medicinal plants. Riveles spoke several European languages. Pinhas Elijah Hurwitz from Lwów published a general introduction to modern science in Hebrew in 1797. He knew no foreign languages himself and relied on a friend for translation. After the final partition Naftali Herz Shulman, originally from Wilno, composed a work in Russian on reforming Jewish education. An advocate of using 'pure' German rather than Yiddish, he also knew Latin well.[43]

### THE EVIDENCE OF JEWISH MEMOIRS

The early eighteenth-century wine merchant Ber of Bolechów (in Galicia) learnt Polish in his youth from a Polish noble employed by Ber's father, himself an accomplished linguist who had once acted as translator at a meeting of King Francis II Rakoczy and Hetman Adam Sieniawski. Ber and his father also spoke Hungarian well. Thanks to his fluency in Polish and familiarity with the formal language of official documents, Ber often acted as an intermediary between Jewish communities and Polish nobles or their representatives. He was very proud of his excellent Polish and the secular knowledge which gained him many compliments —and what is more, a favourable response from Polish nobles. As Ber observed,

it is advantageous for every intelligent and educated Jew to have a knowledge of the history of the nations of the world. This will sometimes enable him properly to answer questions directed against the Jewish Law and faith, as has occurred to me several times in my discourses with the nobles and the clergy. In most of the cases I have found the right answer, and it is well known to all that my replies were always convincing.[44]

[42] David E. Fishman, 'A Polish Rabbi Meets the Berlin Haskalah: The Case of R. Barukh Schick', *AJS Review*, 12 (Spring 1987), 95–121; Bersohn, *Słownik biograficzny uczonych Żydów Polskich*, 69–70; Zinberg, *History of Jewish Literature*, viii. 271.

[43] Bersohn, *Słownik biograficzy uczonych Żydów Polskich* 76; Zinberg, *History of Jewish Literature*, viii. 282–3.

[44] *The Memoirs of Ber of Bolechow, 1723–1805*, ed. M. Vishnitzer (London, 1922; repr. New York, 1973), 141–2; see also pp. 65–75, 60, 68, 75, 79–80, 90–1, 165–8.

However, pressure from the Jewish community prevented Ber from pursuing his secular studies further, and he worked in his native province as a wine merchant. He remained interested in languages and history, taking advantage of a fortuitous meeting with a Huguenot clerk in Lwów in about 1750 to exchange German and Hebrew lessons; the two corresponded for years and the clerk later sent Ber a German translation of an English history of ancient Israel which Ber rendered into Hebrew. Ber also knew some Latin.

Thirty years later, the talmudic prodigy Solomon Maimon learnt even more and suffered greatly for it, probably because of his difficult personality. He was born in Nieśwież Belarus in 1754 into a typical bailiff family; his grandfather and father both managed estates, supervised peasants, and carried on trade as business agents for Count Radziwiłł. They interacted on a daily basis with the Belarusian peasants and townspeople, as well as the Polish nobles, learning to speak both languages. (Poorly educated Jews in the countryside spoke 'Russian' rather than Yiddish.) Maimon pursued traditional talmudic studies and succeeded so well that he gained recognition as a rabbi when he was only 11 as well as learning a smattering of history, astronomy, and mathematics.

This narrow intellectual world did not satisfy the young man, but the prejudices of both Poles and Jews prevented him from studying secular subjects openly. This intellectual prodigy proceeded to teach himself German by deciphering the Gothic alphabet. Then Maimon reasoned out the meaning of the words on the basis of their similarity to Yiddish and went on to master complicated philosophical tracts, but when he travelled to Königsberg at the age of 25, he found that supercilious Jewish students laughed at his spoken German. Maimon persisted and, after many tribulations, gained some recognition from Moses Mendelssohn and Immanuel Kant, although personal difficulties made him leave Berlin. He died at the court of a Polish noble in Silesia in 1800. Maimon eventually wrote his memoirs in German, although he had also learnt French. He had taught himself Latin in his youth with the help of medical texts which the chief rabbi of Iwanez (Iwaniec) gave him.[45]

## TRAVELLERS' MEMOIRS

Jews acted as intermediaries between foreign travellers and Poles owing to their knowledge of languages. The following accounts from travellers' reports are likely to be indicative of a widespread situation. In 1767, Erich Ahasverus Lehndorf commented that 'if you need any kind of information, you have to turn to the Jews, who, here and elsewhere, form the most intelligent part of the population. The locals are much more stupid.'[46] Johann Bernouilli reported the same year that his party stopped at a Jewish inn in Lithuania because the innkeeper spoke

[45] Maimon, *Autobiography*, 3–7, 12–13, 19, 34–6, 42, 48, 56–8, 88, 96, 116; Altmann, *Moses Mendelssohn*, 360–4. [46] *Polska Stanisławowska*, ii. 22–4.

German.[47] William Coxe similarly reported in 1778 while travelling in Lithuania, 'If you ask for a translator, they bring a Jew', and noted that the innkeepers and coachmen were Jewish.[48]

The Swedish ambassador to Poland in 1791, Lars Engeström, noted that the first traditionally dressed Jew whom he met in Poland offered his help in touring Cracow. The Jew took Engeström to the cathedral but waited outside when the Swede entered. Engeström thought it a pity because he 'needed a translator badly' inside.[49]

The German traveller Friedrich Schultz had trouble at the Russian border near Kowno. Schultz knew little Russian, while the Jewish population of the border town knew only a little German. A Jewish translator finally appeared who spoke both languages sufficiently well to assist him.[50]

Another German traveller, Johann Erich Biester, came to nearby Wielkopolska in 1791. He noted what seemed to him an extraordinary number of Jews working in a large variety of occupations. In the small towns particularly, Jews were 'the only merchants, pedlars, artisans, translators, and God knows what else!'[51] Similarly, the French traveller Hubert Vautrin commented on a Jewish affinity for foreigners in connection with the fur-trade fair in Sandomierz.[52] Johann Joseph Kausch observed that 'in Polish cities, for each foreigner the Jew fills the role of a hired servant, agent, even guide, and this under the official name of *faktor*'.[53]

Jews also acted as *faktors* for Poles, a situation which led them into relationships that seem odd at first glance. Kausch saw Jewish *faktors* 'keeping watch over each step of every significant Pole' along with the noble's chaplain.[54] Georg Forster also remarked on a Jew who was the inseparable drinking companion of the parish priest.[55]

## POLISH MEMOIRS AND NEWSPAPERS

The voluminous memoirs of Marcin Matuszewicz contain many references to Jews involved in everyday activities without any mention of language. It seems reasonable to assume that he encountered no language barrier. Matuszewicz often employed Jewish coachmen to take him from village to village, and he stopped at Jewish inns. As a local official, he took part in court cases involving Jewish plaintiffs and defendants—again without mentioning language.

The only time Matuszewicz discusses language relates to a singular episode of a noblewoman who liked to read and whose 'woman's reason' failed to interpret the Bible properly, causing her to practise Judaism. After a while, she ran away to Amsterdam with a Jewish estate manager. Her husband followed and also converted to Judaism, perhaps in order to keep in touch with his children.

---

[47] *Polska Stanisławowska*, i. 332.     [48] Ibid. 694.     [49] Ibid. ii. 108.
[50] Ibid. 390–1.     [51] Ibid. 188–9.     [52] Ibid. 730.
[53] Ibid. 368.     [54] Ibid. 321.     [55] Ibid. 95.

Matuszewicz's father visited Amsterdam in 1692, accidentally met the (former) husband on the street, and began a theological debate in Latin. A young Jew 'dressed in the French style' joined in the discussion and then switched to Polish in response to a rude aside by Matuszewicz's companion, Count Jan Radziwiłł. It turned out that the young man came from Cracow and had studied philosophy and theology at the Jagiellonian University, pretending to be a Christian.[56]

In his memoirs Kajetan Koźmian mentions a Polish tutor who fancied himself learned enough in philosophy and theology to proselytize among the Jews. One rabbi slapped his face for his trouble while another Jew told the missionary that he was an ignoramus, apparently in elegant Polish. Otherwise, Koźmian's Jews were coachmen and hangers-on with whom he seems to have encountered no language barriers.[57]

Julian Ursyn Niemcewicz's father also tried to convert Jews when he brought tailors to his estate to make clothes for his family and servants. On one occasion the tailors' complaints that the Polish Bible mistranslated the original so infuriated the elder Niemcewicz that he grabbed their Hebrew text and threw it into the fire. When his anger cooled, he paid its owner twice the value and calmer discussions went on for the rest of the week.[58]

Polish newspapers paid relatively little attention to Jews, and probably few Jews read them. However, a number of advertisements from the 1760s to the 1790s touched on Jews and Jewish matters. Polish newspapers often announced Jewish bankruptcies and property sales. While these may have been aimed at Polish readers, announcements of regional fairs occasionally took the trouble to specify that all customers were invited, although sometimes with limitations. Individual Jewish merchants, most of them foreign, occasionally placed advertisements of items for sale. Book dealers advertised reading material aimed at Jewish readers. One such item was the report of the 1763 appeal by Polish Jews to Pope Clement XIV to outlaw ritual murder trials. Another such item was the campaign to grant civil rights to French Jews during the Revolution; advertisements appeared in Polish papers for Zalkind Hurwicz's French-language brochure advocating Jewish emancipation.

Polish newspapers also reported criminal matters. Froim from Berdyczów advertised for help in locating the Polish bandits who robbed him, but most notices identified Jewish criminals such as the confidence man who spoke good Polish, German, and Yiddish and the Jewish bandit who dressed in Cossack clothes to attack isolated Polish manor-houses. Jewish converts to Christianity from the Frankist movement seemed to produce a disproportionate number of criminals owing to their poverty-stricken background. Quite a few Frankists married Christians, but these marriages often failed.[59]

[56] Marcin Matuszewicz, *Diariusz życia mego*, 2 vols. (Warsaw, 1986), i. 385–6.
[57] Kajetan Koźmian, *Pamiętniki*, 3 vols. (Wrocław, 1972), i. 55, 155, 228.
[58] Julian Ursyn Niemcewicz, *Pamiętniki czasów moich*, 2 vols. (Warsaw, 1958), i. 76–7.
[59] Ringelblum, 'Żydzi w świetle prasy warszawskiej wieku XVIII-go', ii. 68–83.

## HOW WELL DID THE JEWS KNOW NON-JEWISH LANGUAGES?

While it is difficult to say for certain, it seems likely that a large majority spoke Polish fluently but ungrammatically, so that a customer would make the slight effort needed to understand while an unsympathetic listener might draw back.[60] The exception proves the rule. Ber of Bolechów reports an incident in which a rabbi needed help in preparing his side of a lawsuit where an appeal against his legal judgments had been lodged with the king's representative (*podwojewoda*). Since the rabbi knew 'the Polish language a little, but not perfectly', Ber put his position 'in scholarly Polish, such as is used in legal affairs'. He 'also had to write out afresh the verdicts given by the rabbi, as they were full of errors and written in a style foreign to the Polish language'. Ber won the case. On another occasion Ber spoke for a neighbouring Jewish community in a tax dispute because 'nobody understood Polish or could speak it fluently and correctly like a man of intelligence; and only such a man could gain a hearing'. Even the Cracow *syndic* Szymon Szmulowicz wrote Polish in 'a peculiar style'.[61] Some of Countess Sieniawska's Jewish agents wrote Polish with 'sloppy penmanship, poor spelling, grammatical errors, and incorrect usage', defects shared by her non-Jewish employees. They received Polish-language documents and summarized them in Yiddish or Hebrew.[62]

It seems likely that most Polish Jews learnt Polish in a rough-and-ready manner on the spot. The monastic orders which ran most Polish schools until the First Partition did not admit Jews, nor did the Szkoła Rycerska (Royal Cadet School). The schools of the Komisja Edukacji Narodowej (National Education Commission), which took over the formerly Jesuit schools in 1774, had the mandate to educate Polish nobles, although they also admitted some burghers. In 1789 the Commission refused an application to admit Jewish students to schools in Sandomierz because, among other grounds, students might mistreat the Jews. Jewish students could not study Polish in Jewish educational facilities because they did not teach secular subjects such as foreign languages. Of all the lands of the Polish–Lithuanian Commonwealth, only state schools in Galicia admitted Jews to a modernized education, in special German-language schools which sprang up after Joseph II issued his Edict of Toleration in 1789. Some proposals to admit Jews to Polish schools or to encourage Jewish schools to teach Polish were advanced during the debate over the Jewish question during the Four Year Diet.[63]

---

[60] See Maria Brzezina, *Polszczyzna Żydów* (Warsaw, 1986), for a linguistic account of how Jews spoke Polish in the 20th century.

[61] *Ber of Bolechow Memoirs*, 65–6, 133; Ringelblum, *Żydzi w powstaniu kościuszkowskim*, 104.

[62] Rosman, *The Lords' Jews*, 176.

[63] Ambroise Jobert, *La Commission d'éducation nationale en Pologne* (Paris, 1941), 168, 238; Tadeusz Mizia (ed.), *Protokoły posiedzeń Komisji edukacji narodowej 1786–1794* (Wrocław, 1969), 185. *MDSC* vi. 228, 424, 526–8; Majer Bałaban, *Dzieje Żydów w Galicyi* (Lwów, 1914), 56–81.

Although the majority of Jews would not have attended Catholic schools under any circumstances, the number of Jews studying in western Europe, particularly Germany, shows that quite a few would have attended secular Polish schools had they been admitted, even if conservative elements in the Jewish community would have complained. Eighteenth-century Polish Jews were enthusiastically cutting the shackles of the theological way of life and preparing the ground for the remarkable process of emancipation which eventually brought them to prominence as participants in the majority culture. The partitions made it difficult for the Polish state to correct its earlier mistake in excluding Jews, who continued to attend German (or Russian) schools as they became emancipated, although a considerable amount of integration with the Poles occurred as well. As a result, Polish became the first or coequal language for large numbers of Polish Jews only between the two world wars.

Eighteenth-century Polish Jews also learnt German, Russian, Latin, French, and other languages for business purposes and, to a lesser extent, out of intellectual curiosity, while foreign-language knowledge among Catholic Poles was restricted to the élite. This knowledge put Jews from all walks of life in a good position to take advantage of the opportunities presented by the rapid business expansion that took place during the nineteenth century, and does much to explain the continuing prominence of Jews in business. Unfortunately, their independent learning-pattern tended to estrange them from their Polish counterparts and contributed to the separation of the two communities.

# PART II

# New Views

# Walls and Frontiers: Polish Cinema's Portrayal of Polish–Jewish Relations

### PAUL COATES

## INTRODUCTION

THERE are several obvious points at which one might begin to consider the treatment of Polish–Jewish relations in the films of People's Poland and in the Polish Republic, still in its infancy. One might 'begin at the beginning' with *The Last Stop* (1948), Wanda Jakubowska's sobering portrait of concentration camp life; with the first film to touch on the subject by Poland's leading post-war director, Andrzej Wajda, *Samson* (1961); or with Wojciech Has's neglected *The Hour-Glass Sanatorium* (1972), a reverie on the work of Bruno Schulz. Another potential starting-point might be Wajda's *The Wedding* (1972), his film of Stanisław Wyspiański's play in which spirits are summoned by a Jewish woman to invade a *fin-de-siècle* Galician feast. If I start from a different beginning, it is for various reasons.

Jakubowska's film is concerned less with Polish–Jewish relations than with the solidarity forged between women of various nations through their encounter with the camps' brutality; its subject is not what has become known as the Shoah itself. In Wajda's *Samson*, the Jew who wanders beyond the walls of the Warsaw ghetto, finally coming under the wing of a People's Army unit, is less distinctively a Jew than a cipher of alienation: Jewish homelessness dissolves into existential isolation. Jakub Gold's step outside the ghetto is an abstraction from the specificity of Jewishness that transforms him into the archetypal victim—and the abstraction is surely symptomatic of the element of unreality in a work that permits tendentious aggrandizement of the role of the People's Army in the Resistance and ignores the Home Army. (Although accused of falsifying history in other respects, it is only here that Wajda truly distorts it.[1]) The film's prime concern is to exploit the Polish antisemitism of the 1930s to validate the Communist cause. Jakub Gold is no ghetto fighter, but battles, when he does so, only under Communist auspices; and even that effort is a desperate existential plunge into suicidally redemptive action.

---

[1] For a rebuttal of the other accusations, see Michał Mirski's 'Bronię prawdy "Samsona"', *Polityka*, 2 Dec. 1961. Given Mirski's political allegiance, he may not be able to perceive the true weakness of the film. Even if it were visible to him, it is surely not something he would want to stress.

Has's *Hour-Glass Sanatorium*, for its part, does not so much focus on Polish–Jewish relations as unfold an extended hallucination of the life of turn-of-the-century village Jewry; and although the scene in which the timid protagonist—Jan Nowicki's mediumistic personification of the camera eye—crawls out of a cellar into a pogrom's aftermath was almost cut by the censor, the film having been made so shortly after the government-sponsored antisemitic campaign of 1968, its surrealistic self-enclosure makes correlation with reality problematic. In *The Wedding* Rachel's actions, arising out of marginalization as they do, may indeed bespeak a witchlike power of revenge, but Polish–Jewish relations are themselves marginal to the work's hectic panorama of *fin-de-siècle* Galicia.[2] The central concern is with Polish Hamletism.[3]

Why then do I begin, as I do, with a film Wajda made shortly thereafter, *The Promised Land* (1974)? Not simply because the disjunctiveness of Polish–Jewish relations lies at the heart of the Reymont novel on which it is based, but also because—for all its fusion of the febrile and the academic—the interest in these relations displayed by the film marks the first stirring of a theme to be amplified in subsequent years by the Flying University and then Solidarity: the need to claw back from the state the image of a more inclusive pre-war society. Among the things included in that society, of course, had been a large and enormously significant Jewish community. Although certain intellectuals realized that tearing down the state's mendacious version of the past also implied a critique of the tradition of Polish antisemitism, in far too many cases idealization of the inter-war period in the popular consciousness did nothing to prevent the recycling of some of that era's stereotypes, including the resuscitation of the ugly bugbear of *Żydokomuna*—the identification of Jews with Communism. It is possible, I will argue, to read Wajda's *The Promised Land* as a seismograph of this contradiction: consciously espousing the liberal intellectual commitment to do justice to the Jews, but unconsciously loath to relinquish the stereotypes guaranteeing the popular appeal Wajda also craves.

Wajda's film, and the foreign reactions it sparked, illustrate an unfortunate feature of Polish and Jewish discussion of the two peoples' relations: so fraught have those relations often been that the unreasoning passions intellectuals would wish to relegate to the popular consciousness threaten to swamp their own

---

[2] For more on *The Wedding*, see P. Coates, 'Revolutionary Spirits: The Wedding of Wajda and Wyspiański', *Literature/Film Quarterly*, 20/2 (1992), 133–7.

[3] Several other possible starting-points, as well as a panoramic overview of Polish films on this topic, are provided by Lesław Czapliński, 'Tematyka żydowska w powojennym filmie polskim', in *Powiększenie*, 1–4, year 10 (1990), 171–6. Czapliński's aim, which was to produce a survey, along with the brevity of his article, precludes close analysis of the works and their internal tensions. Lack of focus on these tensions, however, can prompt a somewhat dismissive approach, as seen from Czapliński's first sentence: 'The image of the Jewish community in post-war Polish cinema was shaped in a way that was closely dependent upon the general evolution and immediate needs of the official ideological and propaganda line.'

discourse as well. This is exemplified by the tone of a debate between Richard Lukas and David Engel in the *Slavic Review* over the treatment by Poles of Jews during the Second World War,[4] or the reception of Claude Lanzmann's *Shoah* in terms that saw viewers with reservations dubbed antisemites.[5] 'It all begins with a wall', Lech Wałęsa remarked during ceremonies commemorating the fiftieth anniversary of the Warsaw ghetto uprising. He was speaking primarily, of course, of the wall the Nazis erected around the ghetto, but that wall's physical collapse does not preclude the mental persistence of its after-image. Is the mind of a culture a photographic plate, forever scarred by that to which it was once exposed, or can new impressions be made? Just how arduous the assault on the mental wall can be is apparent in the narratives of the films I will be considering and in the reception accorded those of Wajda in particular. The problem scores *The Promised Land* so deeply that it may serve as a master-text of the portion of the Polish and Jewish story told by some of Poland's best films. I will pass from this film to consider two works by his close collaborator Agnieszka Holland—*Angry Harvest* (1984) and *Europa, Europa* (1991)—and then take up the eighth part of Krzysztof Kieślowski's *Decalogue* (1989), and finally Wajda's *Korczak* (1990). That the most powerful and rewarding treatments of the theme by Polish directors emerge during the twilight of People's Poland—and may even, as in the case of Holland's films, be produced beyond its borders—indicates the selectiveness of official versions of the events of 1939–45.[6] My own selectiveness has, I hope, been justified above. Its further justification lies in the complexity and richness of the works; only analysis in some detail can begin to do *them* justice.

## *THE PROMISED LAND*: ANDRZEJ WAJDA'S FAUSTIAN BARGAIN?

Andrzej Wajda's *The Promised Land* is based on Władysław Reymont's novel of the same title about the polyp-like growth of late nineteenth-century Łódź—a metropolitan Moloch, sucking life from the ground and peasants from the soil, its construction's omnipresent scaffolding continually elbowing passers-by into the equally omnipresent mud of the streets. The Fata Morgana of rapid wealth seduces Karol Borowiecki, a gifted textile colourist, Don Juan, and elegant member of the Polish gentry, to cast tradition aside, surpassing in ruthlessness the

[4] For a balanced assessment of the merits of the arguments of the two sides, see Neal Pease, 'New Books on Poles and Jews during the Second World War', *Polish Review*, 33/3 (1988), 347–51.
[5] Thus, for instance, Pauline Kael, whose *New Yorker* review began by stating 'Probably everyone will agree that the subject of a movie should not place it beyond criticism', was rewarded for her careful dissection of the film with an accusation of antisemitism from one of the regular reviewers of the *Village Voice*.
[6] See Tadeusz Szafar's strictures about the omissions in Jerzy Topolski (ed.), *History of Poland* (1976) in 'Anti-Semitism, a Trusty Weapon', Adam Brumberg (ed.), *Poland: Genesis of a Revolution* (New York, 1983), 109–22.

robber barons he tries to imitate. By betraying his *szlachta* background, he becomes, as his Jewish friend Moryc Welt remarks, the biggest *Lodzermensch* of them all. Together with Moryc, and the German Max Baum, he founds a factory that later burns down mysteriously. Unable to stomach the drudgery of rebuilding, he marries the plain, naïve daughter of a German textile millionaire, breaking his engagement to his Polish fiancée. The positivist programme of national reconstruction through *praca u podstaw*—work at the foundations—succeeds materially, but at the cost of moral failure, and offers no solace to Polish national pride, being parasitic on prior German achievement. Reymont's version of positivism would conclude bleakly were it not for the final sentimental volte-face in which Karol, recognizing the emptiness of his life, decides to imitate his ex-fiancée's philanthropy.

Julian Krzyżanowski, the great Polish literary historian, once described Reymont's methods as cinematic. He may have been prompted to do so by the play of looks in the Łódź theatre scene, for instance, which does indeed anticipate the alternation between the shot and reverse shot of classical film grammar. Wajda's use of Reymont's text in the confident early years of Gierek's industrial effort to enrich Poland quickly is doubly piquant. (Perhaps unsurprisingly, given the power over Polish criticism wielded by the censor, the period's Polish reviewers did not make the allegorical connection but seem rather to have been caught up in the film's own expansive fervour.) Although Wajda's version diverges from Reymont's in a myriad ways—some of which I will list—the two major ones concern the plot's reshaping to exonerate Moryc (in Reymont he colludes in the Jewish industrialists' conspiracy against Karol) and the elimination of sources of hope and the possibility of capitalism's self-reform. Indeed, the film takes an almost vulgar Marxist delight in the apocalyptic spectacle of the industrial Sublime, its pulsing score beating out the doom of a capitalist world brimful with contradictions.

For one Polish critic, Janusz Zatorski, *The Promised Land* represents an about-turn in Wajda's career. After a series of films criticizing the Polish gentry, in this work Wajda delineates the suicidal effects of the total negation of tradition.[7] The shifting of the idyllic opening of volume 2 to the film's beginning makes the subsequent passage to Łódź seem like an expulsion from Eden and corroborates Zatorski's reading. Nevertheless, his salutary interpretation overlooks the contradictoriness of a film that upholds tradition on some levels and subverts it on others. Tradition is undermined, for instance, when the Catholic priest, complacently sprinkling Karol's factory with holy water, confronts its scantily clothed female workers and appears pompously shocked; when Karol's father fulminates against his son's violation of 400 years of tradition, becoming the impotent *senex* of melodramatic farce; or whenever images of female nudity obtrude from the work's overripe surface. The drum-rolling Marxism of the menacing close, where Karol

[7] Janusz Zatorski, 'Mazowieckie Klondike', *Kierunki*, 9 Mar. 1975.

orders troops to gun down striking workers, implies the bankruptcy of a ruling class that may have destroyed tradition, but itself has no future: what future there is lies with the shot worker clutching a patch of red flag in the street. Wajda's position is clearly anticlerical in an anti-traditional Marxist tradition. A devastatingly succinct early montage juxtaposes the louring smoke-stacks and industrialists' prayers in Polish, German, and Hebrew (the order suggests that responsibility for Łódź's perversion of humanity lies with the Poles—which is surprising in the context of the narrative, in which Stach Wilczek, the Polish protagonist, is only a millionaire in the making): religion and industrialism join hands in exploitation. Nor is Wajda's variety of adaptation exactly reverent, playing so fast and loose with the logic (assuming it may be dignified as such) of Reymont's plot and characterization as virtually to constitute less an adaptation than a set of variations on his themes. Throughout the film the currents that maintain tradition criss-cross turbulently with the ones that subvert it.

It is surely an index of the film's contradictions that it has been accused both of antisemitism and of seeking to purge Reymont's novel of antisemitism. There is justification for both reactions. In their standard survey of modern Polish cinema, Bolesław Michałek and Frank Turaj comment on these accusations as follows:

But something happened that no one expected, least of all Wajda. After showings in Scandinavia and the United States in 1976, *Land of Promise* was charged with containing antisemitism because of its negative portrayal of the Jews in Lodz [*sic*].[8]

In rebuttal, they argue that

The real conflict in the film has nothing to do with nationalities; it has to do with capital and labour. All this was obscured by the allegations. Wajda, whose record of integrity in matters of human rights and any kind of discrimination, whose conduct during and after the political crisis of 1968 with its distinct elements of antisemitism, should have made him the least likely to be the subject of such charges, was not given credibility. To this day, against any sensible interpretation of the reality of the thing, the film is thought to be antisemitic in Scandinavia and the United States. Interestingly, this is not at all the case in France or Italy, where perhaps Zolaesque realism, with all its candor and completeness, is better understood.[9]

A defence of Wajda's film on the grounds of Zolaesque realism is nevertheless far from compelling. Even if one rejects the argument that Zola's strategies cannot be employed for the production of first-rate art seventy-two years after the novelist's death—after all, whether or not the film is first-rate may well be a separate issue from whether or not it displays prejudice—it is undeniable that an artist

[8] Bolesław Michałek and Frank Turaj, *The Modern Cinema of Poland* (Bloomington, Ind., 1988), 154.

[9] Ibid. In Reymont's work the conflict is primarily one of national groups. 'Polishness' connotes a high culture that is incomprehensible to money-grubbing Jews to the extent that when a rich Jewish girl in love with a selfless Polish doctor realizes the incompatibility of the two cultures, she breaks off the relationship. She knows she would never belong in a Polish salon.

working in the aftermath of the Holocaust ought to consider the effects of stereotypes and racial caricatures used by the fascist regimes of the 1930s, and be circumspect when approaching a work that employs them. At the same time, in so far as stereotyping is a form of generalization, it is not necessarily pernicious. If, as De Tocqueville argues in *Democracy in America*, generalization flourishes in cultures addicted to speed, whose members economically pack a maximum of instances into the portmanteau of a single notion, then it is very much a part of modernity. The condemnation of generalization may itself be a malign generalization about generalization. For generalizations conscious of their status as the opposites of particularities they make no claim to absorb are simply economical modes of thought. The same may apply to the stereotype: its insulation from the concrete renders its users' apparent subscription to antisemitic beliefs quite compatible with humane treatment of all their Jewish acquaintances (perhaps evidence less of hypocrisy than of the logical separation of the abstract and the concrete, the class and the member). The scapegoat is always already nonexistent, and the persistence of antisemitism in countries now without Jews may be less paradoxical than it seems (and may not simply indicate the tendency of ideology to lag behind actuality). The scapegoat is abstract: no single Jew, or even crowd of Jews, is The Jew—who thus becomes Eternal and tantalizingly beyond reach.

Wajda did indeed reflect on the issue of stereotyping. In an interview given during the shooting of the film, he stated, 'It can't be the case that if someone is a Jew he cheats, if a German—he's dull but hard-working. . . . I do not intend to present the differences in their characters in this way.'[10] And so Moryc Welt is no longer the traitor unable to comprehend Karol's willingness to share a financial windfall but, in the words of one critic, 'a fine, loyal, and helpful boy'.[11] Zygmunt Kałużyński, musing on why Wajda's 'dogged darkening of moral perspective' lightens here, concludes that often in his films 'the accent of purity' assumes the form of male friendship.[12] Although Kałużyński lauds the film's recovery of 'a Jewish culture we had long forgotten', it does not occur to him that the change in Moryc's characterization might have been motivated by a desire to avoid antisemitic stereotyping. Could this be because the portrayal of all the film's other Jews partakes of the stereotypical? Wajda transforms the novel's pre-eminent Jew, Moryc, but leaves his milieu untouched, perhaps because antisemitism is so thoroughly woven into Reymont's novel that its complete removal would have caused the tapestry to unravel. The effect is one of aesthetic inconsistency; as in a photomontage, a figure from one space is superimposed on to an incompatible one; a realistic figure is pasted on to the background of satire.

[10] Maria Malatyńska, 'Wejście do "ziemi obiecanej": Rozmowa z Andrzejem Wajdą,' *Życie Literackie*, 5 May 1974.

[11] Wiesław Poczmański, 'Komu obiecano tę ziemię', *Barwy* (Apr. 1975).

[12] Zygmunt Kałużyński, 'Czarna Łódź kolorowa', *Polityka*, 22 Feb. 1975.

The problem arises most clearly in the near-total and verbatim incorporation of two of Reymont's scenes involving Jewish industrialists: Stein's announcement of the death of Victor Hugo, of whom his master has never heard; and the duel of wits between Moryc and Grosglik. In each the industrialist is buffoonish and grasping, and the roles are played in the style of high theatrical farce. Given the film's thoroughgoing rearrangement of Reymont's chronology, its additions to the story, and its shifting and fusion of characters (Grosglik's reasons for preferring Catholicism to Protestantism, for example, are distributed between Moryc and Karol; Kessler incorporates elements of Grosglik, even speaking one of Moryc's lines; Max's declaration that he can read Moryc's infamous intentions from his face is placed in the mouth of Moryc himself), it is all the more surprising that Wajda should have done no more than lightly edit the originals of these scenes. Wajda's transformation of Moryc may indeed have undermined one of the mainstays of Reymont's antisemitic argument, but the theatrical showman in him cannot resist these scenes of pointed farce. Their comedy, however, cannot be entirely innocent now—just as one can no longer laugh at the discomfiture of the Merchant of Venice. Paradoxically, viewers ignorant of the novel may find the narrative at points too elliptical to be fully comprehensible (when Karol's fiancée, Anka, refers to a person with broken ribs, the film's omission of the man's earlier accident at work prevents one from knowing what she means), while those with an awareness of it may find themselves questioning the many arbitrary changes, one of the most glaring being the suicide of Trawiński, who in the novel instead receives a loan from Baum. Their rationale seems to lie in a will to magnify contrast, both within and between images. At the same time, the retention of an absurdly large number of the original characters reduces their parts to rapid walk-ons and augments the speed and indirection of a mode of narration that seeks to overpower and bewilder, mimicking the boom-or-bust atmosphere of Łódź itself. It is a narrative style that fuses the wide-angles of Welles with Eisenstein's politics, farce, and shock-cuts.

Wajda's perspective throughout is relentlessly external. His teeth-baring Borowiecki is free of the inner struggles of Reymont's character, and has no hope of the somewhat sentimental redemption the novelist finally proposed. For Maria Janion, Wajda's ending, in which Karol orders troops to fire on striking workers, is an Ensor-like tableau of grotesque marionettes.[13] The nightmarish quality is heightened by a percussive score and the absence of natural sound; Borowiecki is revealed as a waxwork recruit to the capitalist club of the undead. Whereas Janion speaks of Borowiecki as 'the enigma of internal emptiness', for Poczmański, the encapsulation within him of all the worst features of capitalism amounts to the character's remystification.[14] Wajda's external perspective may even be seen as alarmingly similar to that of Karol, who drains life from everything he touches—Reymont's human

---

[13] Maria Janion, 'Wajda i wartości', *Film*, 2 Mar. 1975.  [14] Poczmański, 'Komu obiecano'.

machine. Here Wajda's approach is surprisingly close to that of the novel itself, which—for all its idealization of the self-sacrificing Polish women whose hands workers kiss unendingly—oscillates between condemnation of Karol and an incorporation into the narrative voice of the contempt so often ascribed to Karol: Wajda's naturalism, like Reymont's, is in part crypto-expressionist. Tadeusz Robak noted the film's allegiance to two styles, 'one true to reality and one inclined to the pamphlet'.[15] The inclination towards reality so often deemed the defining quality of film—by André Bazin or Siegfried Kracauer, for instance—did indeed form part of Wajda's motivation for making *The Promised Land*. Speaking of his wish to record nineteenth-century buildings while that was still possible, he emphasized the pleasure of shooting a historical film with the freedom of movement in real locales more characteristic of a contemporary one,[16] be it in the outlandishly appointed mansions of Piotrkowska Street or in textile factories notoriously still using ancient machines. Many reviewers, meanwhile, would stress the educational value of the necromantic re-creation of Łódź. Yet Wajda's Łódź is clearly also a dreamlike capitalist city of Dreadful Night, where infernal fires shoot from the soil to consume factories, and humanity is mere flesh—orgiastically grasped if female, fed to machines that then spew it forth if male. The insistent wide-angles both provide the space Wajda said was needed by the film's fast-walking, fast-talking protagonists and introduce a sense of vertigo that is reminiscent of the somewhat meretricious hallucinations of Ken Russell, whose name often featured in reviews. The distorting lenses' heightening of speed is accentuated by the fast cuts between contrasting scenes, the movement from one to the next, the twanging of the elastic space those lenses generate. So precipitously does Mada Müller chase Karol through the family palace that she slides in disarray along its floor.

Although Wajda's reworking of Reymont's novel could have sparked as much controversy as had his version of Wyspiański's *The Wedding*, widespread public ignorance of a work far less central to the Polish literary canon confined controversy to the film's explicit eroticism.[17] Teenagers lured by the prospect of a Polish *Last Tango* may have voiced their disappointment, but responses by spectators at Warsaw's Luna and Palladium cinemas and Lublin's Kosmos showed that 'the question of the eroticism in the film arouses most controversy'.[18] Magdalena Enke, a pensioner raised in Łódź, praised the work's verisimilitude in other respects but found these scenes irritating. Their presence may be read in part as Wajda's defiant assertion of his membership of the international film community, which had recently broadened its norms for the representation of sexuality; but

---

[15] Tadeusz Robak, 'Co odkryli Reymont i Wajda', *Życie Literackie*, 9 Mar. 1975.

[16] Malatyńska, 'Wejście do "ziemi obiecanej"'.

[17] One poll showed that 80% of the spectators had not read it.

[18] 'Dlaczego ogladamy "Ziemię obiecaną"', *Sztandar Ludu*, 16 Apr. 1975. These scenes were also criticized by Gierek at a Politbiuro meeting, where he deemed them 'pornographic' (Józef Tejchma, *Kulisy dymisji* (Cracow, 1991), 52).

his inability to foresee the international repercussions of his attempt to rework Reymont's story is indeed ironic. Perhaps in truth the story could not be redeemed, and Borowiecki's Faustian bargain in a sense mirrored Wajda's own. His international success and Oscar nomination brought him more than he had bargained for.

### TRAPS OF IDENTITY: AGNIESZKA HOLLAND

Beginning with her first successful television film, *Niedzielne dzieci* (*Sunday's Children*, 1976), in which a couple seek to circumvent the system by buying a baby destined for abortion, Agnieszka Holland's central theme is entrapment. Here, as later, the fundamental trap, the one that always betrays, is the body itself. It may do so through its femininity (*Sunday's Children*, *A Woman Alone*, *Angry Harvest*), a crippling disability (*A Woman Alone*), Jewishness (circumcision in *Europa, Europa*), or youth (the many children in Holland's films suffer from what Sartre terms the 'existentially false' position of the child). The theme of biological constraint yields a style of naturalistic grittiness. The scenarios are richest when the different traps interlock, as in *Angry Harvest*, where one of the protagonists is Jewish and female, or in *Europa, Europa* which is about a Jew who is also a child.[19]

For Holland, Jewishness—and the Polish–Jewish nexus—is of interest as one factor among many that threaten freedom by placing one in the disempowered position of outsider. The yearning for freedom animating her work is what enables her to function within the mainstream of Polish art of the last two centuries, even as the focus on non-Polish marginal identities and their oppression moves her away from it. In her best films, a powerful and complex dialectic results. It is hardly surprising that the protagonist of *Provincial Actors* identifies so deeply with the hero of Wyspiański's *Liberation* that he contests a director's mindless experimentalism, thereby sabotaging his own attempt to escape the provinces—the setting of so much of Holland's work and another site of entrapment. (The polemic against experimentalism, meanwhile, reflects Holland's recognition of the degree to which in the late 1970s, Polish theatrical experiment had become state-sanctioned freedom promoted at the expense of bluntly comprehensible critiques of the regime.) Nor is it surprising that Holland should have filmed a version of the murder of the pro-Solidarity cleric Father Jerzy Popiełuszko. The priest, too, is trapped in the role—of non-combative male—that virtually predestines him to victimization. Constrained masculinity becomes a problem again in *Europa, Europa*.

*Angry Harvest*, the first of Holland's films to excavate Polish–Jewish relations, offers a biting analysis of a multiform quest for release. 'I really wanted to make a

---

[19] Annette Insdorf analysed the Jew's assimilation with the child in certain films of the 1970s in *Indelible Shadows: Film and the Holocaust* (New York, 1989), 81–97. The Jew's assimilation with the female is analysed in Judith Doneson's 'The Jew as a Female Figure in Holocaust Film', *Shoah*, I/1.

film that related to the Holocaust', Holland remarked—one that would be 'a new
kind of statement about it'.[20] Noting elsewhere how her will to make a film about
the Warsaw ghetto had been frustrated earlier by fear and a sense of the difficulty
of 'reconstructing with false blood and plastic corpses', she attributed her acceptance of the script of *Angry Harvest* to its lack of the 'clichés of SS men with rifles,
deportation and concentration camps'.[21] In it, release is sought as much by the
peasant and would-be priest as by the upper-class Jewish woman he both hides
and torments, and whose presence torments him. War has elevated Leon Wolny
(the surname 'free' is ironic): the father of rich Eugenia once had no time for him
but now he is her protector, and Rubin, a wealthy Jew, kneels before him to beg
money for emigration. Kneeling is very important throughout the film: Wolny
also kneels before Rosa, the Jewish woman who becomes both his Madonna and
his sex object. She is the accessible double of, and sacrificial substitute for, the
declassed Eugenia, since, for all Leon's satisfaction in his rise in status with
respect to Eugenia, he cannot so shake off all vestiges of past respect as to seek *her*
physical possession. After assaulting Rosa, he comments, 'I wouldn't dare do this
to Miss Eugenia.'[22] Leon's attraction to Rosa is the sign of his degradation, however; of the sexual desire that prevents his entry to the priesthood. If the local
priest's sister holds no appeal for him, for all her interest in him, it is not simply
because she is less attractive than Rosa, but also because for Leon religion and sexuality are incompatible. Since sexuality exists beyond the pale, its ideal object is
'la belle Juive': as Sartre remarks, at one level of the imagination of a Leon 'There
is in the words "a beautiful Jewess" a special sexual signification': 'This phrase
carries an aura of rape and massacre.'[23] Sexuality's proscription condemns it to
find expression only during alcoholic frenzy, the Dostoevskian masochism that
causes a protagonist to fling himself into actions he knows he will regret, apparent
power always the prelude to masochistic grovelling, to pleasure in the kneeling
mentioned above. Leon is living in a double bind: 'Please, I'll do anything you
want,' he tells Rosa as he tries to make love. Sex object one moment, she is 'Frau
Rosa' the next. After Rosa's death (she commits suicide rather than suffer transfer
from Leon's now threatened cellar to another hiding-place), unable to deny his
desire, he sets the seal upon its degradation by taking up with the servant girl.

  Leon's relationship with Rosa is so complex and tormented that it is almost
an allegorical enactment of Polish–Jewish relations. When he launches the im-
memorial antisemitic reproach 'The Jews crucified Our Lord', its illogicality—
characteristic of the anti–intellectualism that nurtures anti-Jewish sentiment—is
underscored by her reply that 'Christ was a Jew.' After Leon's nose is bloodied in

---

[20] 'Dialogue on Film', *American Film* (Sept. 1986), 15.    [21] Insdorf, *Indelible Shadows*, 108.
[22] This is an example of the over-explicitness that mars the scenarios of both this film and Holland's
non-Polish work in general. It may be that working outside the Polish context led her to believe that her
presuppositions needed to be made explicit.
[23] Jean-Paul Sartre, *Anti-Semite and Jew* (New York, 1962), 48.

the subsequent fight, she dabs it tenderly and commiserates, 'My poor man, what have they done to you?' If the work is allegorical, its theme is the uneven distribution of sexual, racial, and class power. Rosa terms Leon 'a good man', and the appellation is more than simply ironic. After all—as many Poles might answer Jewish reproaches—in concealing her, he endangers his own life. Cybulkowski's galloping glee at the prospect of obtaining Rubin's orchard clearly appals him. Leon may be read as a composite Protestant and Catholic figure, and hence as Holland's metonym for a Christianity as capable of hypocrisy as of self-sacrifice: her use of German (and a German-speaking border setting) not only distances and makes representable issues arguably too sensitive to air in an exclusively Polish production, but also splices the self-lacerating sense of sin and unknowable interiority native to so much Protestantism into the mentality of the Polish Catholic peasant. Leon's duality corresponds to the constant partiality of all his actions: neither priest nor layman, rich nor poor, good nor evil, he is always riven, locked in a position in between. His sins, those of omission, evoke festering self-discontent rather than the self-evident guilt that cries out for expiation. Consequently, a cloud of self-hatred clings to him. Half-truths rather than lies are his stock-in-trade. He may admit that the racket above Rosa's head during the night was not the German search she imagined, but his failure to name his drunken rage as the true cause leaves Rosa doubting her sanity. When Rubin's daughter later writes from America to thank Leon for the money that ensured her escape (while salving his guilt about Rosa and her father), and adds that she has married Rosa's husband, the irony is excruciating. As Leon buries Rosa in the cellar, his echo of the death-cry of the Jew he venerates as Saviour, 'My God, why have you abandoned me?', emphasizes that because his need was for physical as well as spiritual release, his deity had to be female. The sun as Rosa saw it—eerily intense because so seldom viewed—shines again in the last shot, to highlight the devastating, unbearable fact of her loss.

### IDENTITY SUBMERGED: *EUROPA, EUROPA*

In a key moment in *Europa, Europa*, as Sally (Solomon) Perel and his brother Isaak cross a river while fleeing the Nazi invaders of Poland, a boat from the opposite banks drifts by, laden with Poles in flight from the Red Army. As the boats capsize, Poles swimming for the German and Jews for the Soviet side, Sally's declaration of his own choice of direction is cut short as he sinks beneath the water. He may end up on the Soviet side, but his identity is always in question: he is a Jew born on the same day as the Führer; he is a Komsomol member one day and a Wehrmacht mascot the next; he is sent to an élite academy by the Nazis, who see him as Aryan (after the war, in a scene the film omits, he would attend their reunion dinner!), and mistaken for a war hero by the German platoon behind him as he tries to return to the Soviet side, yet he is saved from execution by the

Soviets because Isaak, who has survived a concentration camp, happens to be nearby and vouches for him. Sally is even more a chameleon than Woody Allen's Zelig. Is he 'really' Komsomol, German, or Jew? Or, as Holland's dry tone would suggest, is he perhaps the first post-modern Holocaust hero, a man without qualities? At points he does indeed consciously play with identities: his practice in a mirror of the Nazi salute speeds up into a soft-shoe shuffle. Identities become personae able to coexist because each rests on a different ground: the German one is linguistic, the Soviet one is ideological, and the Jewish one, biological. Lukács may have seen cinema as standing for humanity's gain of a body at the cost of its soul, but in Sally's case (as Holland remarked to an interviewer), 'his penis saved his soul'.[24] The circumcised body, the sole constant and compass in Sally's life, dictates his final, post-war move to Israel. It becomes his identity's bedrock. And yet that bedrock is precisely what mainstream cinema cannot show. Sally's voice-over then becomes the desperately needed thread through a labyrinth of deceptive appearance. When he sinks under water, that thread slips through our hands.

The gurgling as Sally sinks circumcises his lips. It also censors his words at the behest of what Fredric Jameson would term the political unconscious. To imply that Sally chose a direction would be to contradict the broader emphasis on his lack of options. The film's dreamlike opening, with Sally under water, could almost have been inserted at this point, even though in the opening scene he was swimming dressed in the uniform of the Hitler Youth. Does the repetition of the watery image in these two scenes, which is reiterated later in the film, imply that despite Sally's conscious identification with the Soviets, allegiances are not so clear-cut in the unconscious, where opposites often meet and merge? (In a later dream sequence, Hitler and Stalin dance together.) The link between water and brotherhood frames the film: paralleling the opening scene, in which Isaak joins the swimming Sally, the closing scene shows Isaak and Sally passing water in the rain, followed by an image of the real Solomon Perel beside a river, singing in Hebrew 'How sweet it is to sit surrounded by your brothers.' The suggestion of uterine depths in the first underwater sequence is reinforced by Sally's circumcision in the next one. A child pulls a curtain aside to show the circumcision as theatre, viewed through the glass that is another of the film's leitmotifs.

In his voice-over accompanying these images Sally claims to recall that circumcision, though nobody believes him. The theme of his story's unbelievability recurs at the close, where Isaak counsels against telling it: people will only scoff. Indeed, not until producer Artur Brauner brought him together with Holland did Sally tell his story. Holland herself, meanwhile, may preface the film with the caption 'What follows is a true story' and close with the authenticating image of Sally himself, but the irony and laconicism of her editing style stress its improbability. Her self-confessed emendations of several incidents heighten the tallness of

---

[24]  Amy Taubin, 'Woman of Irony', *Village Voice*, 2 July 1992.

the tale, for instance compressing into one event the arrest and interrogation of Stalin's son, and bringing Sally together with Isaak after the war, rather than with one of his cousins.[25]

The most patent improbability occurs near the end. When Sally's lack of *Volksdeutsche* papers is questioned, he thinks, 'Only a miracle can save me now'—and a bomb obligingly flattens the administrative building he has just left, making confetti of its records. While Holland shows us the bloodied head of his *Hitlerjugend* comrade Gerd crushed by fallen bricks, the wink at the audience caused by the promptitude of this miracle precludes sorrow. Something similar occurs when Robert, the German ex-actor who discovers Sally's identity but lovingly shields him, dies at his side. Sally's voice-over tells us he is devastated, but the camera rises to an impassive overhead shot. The picaresque epic tone stuns emotion, justifying some critics' description of the film as a comic-book.[26] Holland's dryness renders Sally a trickster-survivor, a fairy-tale's charmed youngest son, but even as her use of the anti-psychological conventions of pre-novelistic modes of narration smooths over behavioural improbabilities (it is hard to credit Sally's musing imitation of the hands on a Jewish headstone only a moment after the devastating loss of Leni), at the same time it limns the voice-over's agonizing with an air of the unbelievable.

As Sally's concluding voice-over tells us that on emigrating to Israel he momentarily hesitated before circumcising his sons, we are satisfied more by the witty reprise of the film's opening than by a Zionist sense of home-coming. The sight of the real Sally at a river's side cannot but recall Claude Lanzmann's *Shoah*, which begins with another improbable war survivor, Szymon Srebnik, singing on a river bank. The echo is ambiguous: it can suggest a polemic with Lanzmann as much as a homage to him (after all, Lanzmann's opinion of *Korczak*, as scripted by Holland, had been acerbic), and it may even be unconscious. The real Sally stands like a question mark after the story. Is he also there to show that fictional means can serve a Holocaust story just as well as Lanzmann's painstaking and long-winded devotion to documented 'real time'—with Holland inviting us to rejoice in her own work's difference? There is an inscrutable irony in the fact that the real Sally looks far more stereotypically 'Jewish' than the Marco Hofschneider who has just played him.

In North America critical reaction to *Europa, Europa* cast a largely feminist light on a work in which, for a change, a woman director shows a male naked and charts with black humour the problems of betrayal by one's penis. (Naked males appear in Holland's Polish work also: in *Fever* a leading revolutionary flees unclothed from recognition at the public baths.) Jim Hoberman even interpreted Holland's direction of the combat scenes as an appropriation of male privilege.[27]

[25] *Entretien avec Agnieszka Holland*, press release (Paris, 1990).

[26] Mirosław Przylipak, '*Europa, Europa* trochę jak komiks', *Gazeta Gdańska*, 20 Sept. 1991.

[27] Jim Hoberman, 'Doing the Nazi', *Village Voice*, 2 July 1991.

(I hope it will not be deemed sexist if I say I do not consider these Holland's strongest scenes.) Although feminist theorist Kaja Silverman linked the male voice-over to male privilege and potency,[28] Holland uses it to emphasize the fact of Sally's survival: hearing an opening voice-over conventionally assures us that its speaker has outlived the events that follow.

The attractive Sally may be favoured by the best-looking girl at the Hitler Youth school, but any assertion of potency would betray him. As often, Holland's protagonist is the insider who is really an outsider. Early on Sally perches naked on the rim of the family bath-tub to watch Hitler youths marching down his home street. When one of them sticks out his tongue, Sally does the same (the psycho-analytic implications of this are reminiscent of the girl with extended tongue of Buñuel's *Chien Andalou*). When the window shatters he flees and hides outside in a barrel until his neighbour Kathy brings him a Nazi leather jacket to cover his nakedness—a moment of reality that is more open to dream interpretation than are the two actual dreams Holland includes. Later he will run naked from the German actor Robert. Nakedness means vulnerability, the danger of being oneself (Robert tells Sally it's harder to play oneself than other people). Sally's vicissitudes suggest that the fluidity and experimental quality of adolescent identity may become an asset during wartime, when the opposing parties penalize different identities. Were not the story a real one, one might be tempted to read the film's oneiric quality as marking the wartime incursions as allegorical externalizations of adolescent tensions. If Sally is innocent despite his transgression of his father's injunction to remember who he is, it is partly because adolescence insulates him from full responsibility. When the Russians capture him in Wehrmacht uniform, they deride his claim to being a Jew. They show him photographs of concentration camp victims' skulls: if he were really a Jew, they say, he would look like them. Solomon Perel never saw himself as a hero; his story denies him both potency and heroism. We may learn early on in the film of his sister's wish to be a boy, but Holland is, as it were, that sister's sister, underlining the perils of manhood. Among other things, she offers a richly ironic response to a Jew's postulate of penis envy on the edge of an era when the status of the Jewish male would hardly be enviable.

And what of Polish–Jewish relations? Less important than in *Angry Harvest*, they appear in an acid sketch midway through the film. In the Komsomol orphanage Sally is the insider, the Poles the outsiders. A female instructor mocks their Catholicism, taunting them to demonstrate God's existence by praying for sweets to fall from the ceiling. The fruitless prayer is followed by her own to Stalin, which yields instant results. But the providence that seems to watch over Sally and stage miracles for him (miracles whose deadpan presentation is justified by the

---

[28] Kaja Silverman, 'Dis-embodying the Female Voice', in Mary Ann Doane, Patricia Mellencamp, and Linda Williams (eds.), *Re-vision: Essays in Feminist Film Criticism* (Frederick, Md., 1984), 134.

initial voice-over assuring us of Sally's survival) has the last laugh here too, even though this wonder is not on Sally's behalf: a moment later a bomb shatters the roof. Like George Bernard Shaw, Holland is aware that oppression does not ennoble the oppressed. Zenek, the fair-haired Polish defender of the faith, can also denounce Sally to the Nazis as a Jew. Perhaps there is not one providence but two, with Sally's the stronger: a truck conveniently flattens Zenek before he can reveal too much. Since the Polish–Jewish theme is subordinate to the evocation of the deformities of the century's totalitarianisms, there was little discussion of it on the film's reception. While there were occasional references to it by reviewers outside Poland, there were none by Polish reviewers—a fact that is not especially significant, since a reviewer who overlooks it can hardly be accused of repressing the central theme.

The dryness of *Europa, Europa*, which Holland asserts is modelled on Voltaire's *Candide*, may serve to mediate Sally's story, but it may also dissipate some of the more searching questions the tale raises. For Tadeusz Lubelski, for instance, the film replaces the question of the psychological price exacted by Sally's conformity with the one 'Will he survive?' Since we know he will, 'one watches the film with rather moderate suspense'.[29] Lubelski noted the film's unevenness, lamenting the absence of the incisive analysis of ambiguous motives found in Holland's earlier work.[30] On meeting the real Sally, Holland may have been touched by his memories of his varied unsentimental education,[31] but no such reflection is present in the film. Her distance from the material is almost startling, for the uncertainties of Sally's identity recall those of her own, poised between Polish mother and Jewish father.[32] (Could the distance be a way of denying that resemblance? Could Holland herself be repeating her father's unwillingness to speak of his Jewishness?[33]) The title *Europa, Europa* mirrors that doubleness, but also disavows it by stressing Holland's other duality as a director from 'the other Europe' who works in the west. It is ironically appropriate that the German film industry should have been reluctant to term this a German film. German criticism of its melodramatic qualities is something more complex than a simple use of aesthetic categories to mask rejection of unpleasant material, though in some quarters it was precisely that (the snobbishness about Hollywood that dismisses a 'foreigner's' right to deal with 'German' matters).[34]

[29] Tadeusz Lubelski, 'Cztery wcielenia Salomona Perela', *Kino* (Apr. 1991), 16.       [30] Ibid.

[31] Sally's identities may conflict with one another on occasions, e.g. when he describes religion as 'the opium of the people' while building a Feast of Tabernacles booth with Robert, but there are no hints of misgivings over their shifts and overlaps.       [32] Taubin, 'Woman of Irony'.

[33] Barbara Quart, *Women Directors: The Emergence of a New Cinema* (New York, 1988), 239.

[34] Recently Susan Linville described the German Film Commission's refusal to classify the film as German as motivated by objections to its vertiginous mixing of genres, to the multiple nationalities involved in the production, and to the uncertain identity of Sally Perel himself: 'In effect, lacking pure German blood lines, *Europa, Europa* came to be seen as the product and expression of a kind of cultural miscegenation, as a film body trying to pass as German, and as an impostor not unlike Sally himself' ('*Europa, Europa*: A Test Case for German National Cinema', *Wide Angle*, 16/3 (1995), 40–1). This judgement is an unfortunate simplification of Linville's earlier evocation of an overdetermined

*Europa, Europa* is indeed uneven, as Lubelski and others have noted.[35] It is most suggestive when most compressed, elliptical, and dreamlike. Most oneiric of all are not so much the sequences explicitly coded as dreams as the first ten minutes of the film and the powerful Łódź ghetto sequence, which merits closer consideration. Sally dreams that he should search for his family there, so he takes a tram through the ghetto. In an echo of his earlier etching of a hastily erased Star of David on his school's dormitory window, he scrapes an opening in the tram window-pane's white paint (it is painted over to screen Aryan travellers from defilement by the sight of how the *Unterrasse* lives). The images that flow in and past him are harrowing and hallucinatory, their shadowy edges all the more death-like for their resemblance to the iris of the defunct silent-cinema camera. In the parade of faces, two of the old people Holland has cast are indeed so emaciated that they recall true ghetto inmates. The fleeting representation of the ghetto, whose images slip through the fingers, solves one of the problems that was to vitiate Andrzej Wajda's *Korczak*: the inevitable theatricality of well-fed modern faces presented as inhabitants of a torture chamber.

Sally thinks he sees his mother, but cannot be sure. Later he will learn from Isaak that the family died two weeks after the end of his furlough in Łódź. The faces seen from the tram belong to the dead: the moments shown as present to Sally are uncannily prophetic. To us they seem remote, unattainable, frozen in another time, as if already past, like ghetto photographs viewed in the present yet—achingly—animated, as if their inhabitants might yet live. The moment is one of peering through a narrow aperture that haunts all Holland's films. The boy straining to see through the hole also represents the film-maker and ourselves peering into the past, appalled by our inability to change it and the illusion of presence that feeds the impossible hope that a time-traveller might yet do so. In its fusion of passionate longing and self-awareness, this is the film's most intelligent and most haunting moment.

## THE ODDS AGAINST RECONCILIATION: *DEKALOG 8*

Polish–Jewish relations are engaged more directly in Krzysztof Kieślowski's *Decalogue 8*, which teases out some of the implications of the commandment

German reaction: 'though without doubt the German Film Commission, like the German press before it, rejected and criticized Holland's film partly due to a frustrated desire that Germany not again be identified with its fascist past—and especially not with the depiction of an unidealized Jewish youth— rejection of the film was emphatically overdetermined and also reflected anxieties about the nation's present and future' (ibid. 40). Even here, however, the failure to differentiate the Commission's response from that of such an amalgam entity as 'the German press'—many of whose criticisms were far from simply reactionary—is extremely problematic. In likening these reactions to those of the Freikorps soldiers studied by Klaus Theweleit, Linville simply demonizes them as fascist.

[35] Compare the critic of *Fiches du cinéma*, 1102 (14 Nov. 1990), 7, who writes of 'une mise en scène tantôt bruillone (début du film), tantôt lourde (les rêves)' and of 'longueurs'.

against bearing false witness. The eighth in Kieślowski's sequence of ten one-hour television films begins with the interlocked hands of an adult and child. Darkness is falling, and a musical theme that invites description as Yiddish is playing; we are passing from one courtyard to another. The relationship between the prologue and the rest of the film will long be unclear: a cut into bright sunlight and the morning work-out of Zofia, Warsaw University professor of ethics, reveals nothing. Only much later will the way it haunts the narrative outside which it hovers be understood to represent a wartime trauma's primacy in—and blocking off from—the lives of its protagonists. They are Zofia and Elisabeth, her American Jewish translator. The scene is the only visible trace of Elisabeth's childhood memory of being led to a potential hiding-place only to hear the lady she would know as Zofia say she could not accept her, since to do so would entail lying. Elisabeth cannot comprehend the evolution of the Zofia she knows from the woman of that night, and the disparity torments her.

Elizabeth's earlier attempts to confront Zofia with her deed have been unsuccessful. The way a situation now permits this mirrors Kieślowski's existentialist sense of chance's forming and deforming impact upon choice. (Hence Zofia can say that situations release either good or bad in people.) While auditing Zofia's class, where one student has just recounted the dilemma of the female protagonist of *Decalogue 2*, she hears Zofia conclude discussion of whether the doctor involved should have allowed an abortion by stating: 'the important thing is that the child is alive.' The comment's implications pull her to the front row, tug her experience from her. It emerges tremulously, and is almost cut short by a disruptive student. The interlude with the student is a suspense device, but also more, for it evokes the ease with which the total field of events can frustrate individual intention (a frustration Kieślowski registers at every level of late 1980s Polish life). Zofia will later mention the need to think things through to the end, perhaps because so often they fail to get there of their own accord. Zofia listens agonized, left hand creasing cheek in the posture of Melancholia. The telling so drains Elisabeth herself that when all have left she remains seated, no natural sound on the soundtrack, only the opening Yiddish theme.

Things might end there, with Zofia seemingly compromised irretrievably, but the film thinks them through to the end. Haltingly, against enormous resistance—both in the protagonists and in the situations that continue to threaten to derail their encounter—the dark matter is worked through. Zofia offers Elisabeth a lift to her hotel, but drives her instead to the primal scene of the courtyard. When Elisabeth hides, Zofia's inability to find her becomes consternation, and the way the Yiddish theme evokes *her* anguish suggests (in an undertone that may come to naught, since, after all, films privilege images over their sound-tracks) a sharing of suffering and possible arrival at a place where more of the story can be told, in the teeth of the silence hanging between the two women. Soon after, at Zofia's apartment, an explanation will be offered (not a justification, but a complication of the accuser–accused confrontation): the child's transfer was blocked because of fears that the couple due to shelter her were linked to the Gestapo and might betray the underground organization to which Zofia and her husband belonged. As Oskar Sobański put it:

We are dealing with a double paradox, a paradox within a paradox. By refusing to lie, the film's heroine sentences someone to almost certain death. Yet that refusal to lie . . . is a lie, a false pretext hiding a noble intention that cannot be revealed: to save many human beings at the cost of one life. But that is not the end of it: the danger from which these human beings were meant to be saved was also a result of false witness.[36]

Before giving what she terms a banal explanation, Zofia tells Elisabeth: 'If you crossed the Atlantic expecting a mystery, you'll be disappointed.' While all is indeed resolved on one level, when a mother–daughter relationship crystallizes between Zofia and Elisabeth (the conversation shifts to the second person and Zofia is shot face-on, intimately, from Elisabeth's point of view), it may not be on another level, as the ending shows. This being a Kieślowski film, it is hardly surprising that mystery persists, on another level. On discovering the falsity of the rumour linking the prospective foster couple to the Gestapo, Zofia tries to apologize to the man—'but that is not enough'. Elisabeth's own efforts to address him are stonewalled likewise: a tailor (is it significant for his identification with the Jews that this profession is so often associated with them?), he will not speak of the past, only of making her a dress. Zofia says he has perhaps suffered too much, and Elisabeth terms Poland 'a strange country'. The last image shows him, played by the great Tadeusz Łomnicki, staring through the bars on the window of his run-down shop at the silent spectacle of the two women beside Zofia's car.

Silence prevails in Kieślowski's *Decalogue*: repeatedly events paralyse their protagonists. Yet silence can also reconcile, be sacramental, as when Zofia stands behind Elisabeth, places her hand on her shoulder, and Elisabeth clutches it. In remarking that situations bring out either the good or the bad in people Zofia is not exonerating herself: the bad had to exist for the situation to attract it. She does not think that evening brought out the good in her, and the memory has long tormented her. We do not learn whether her saving of many Jews was a later effort to assuage an anguished conscience. As in all of Kieślowski's work, choices are fearsomely fraught. Perhaps the sole thread through the labyrinth is the importance of children.

Although composed of ten parts and based on the law given at Sinai, Kieślowski's *Decalogue* does not clearly match one film to each commandment. Several episodes dramatize more than one—the most obvious being only a starting-point—or intersect with the expected one only obliquely. Maria Malatyńska discerns 'a certain arbitrariness in the illustration of a particular commandment' and

---

[36] Oskar Sobański, '*Dekalog siedem, Dekalog osiem*', *Film*, 28 Jan. 1990.

sees Kieślowski as aiming less at demonstrating 'the Decalogue's continued presence in each of life's situations' than at using it as 'a pretext for consideration of life under the aspect of its helplessness'.[37] The arbitrariness of the illustration may correspond to the disparity between the protagonists' codes and that of the Commandments, and perhaps even between the Polish *Lebenswelt* and that of the Jews. If single episodes can activate multiple Commandments, this may also echo the Apostle James's assertion that to offend against part of the law was to break it all. Zofia may be in the dock at first, but Catholicism is not. On hearing Elisabeth's story, a student condemns as factitious the reasoning of the couple who refused the child: they could hardly have been Catholic, for the Commandment's intent is to forbid false witness *against one's neighbour*. In the published screenplay—though not in the film—Elisabeth says that after many years she became interested in Catholicism. The screenplay also includes a priest's provision of a false identity card for the Jewish child, ending with Zofia telling a priest—one presumes the same one—that the child is alive. More probably the film's omission of these details is aesthetically rather than ideologically motivated, since Kieślowski is well known for ruthlessly cutting material alien to the conception that emerges in the editing room. The omissions can result in conceptual gaps that augment the air of mystery the director so values.[38]

Jewish and Catholic experiences mingle as well as diverge. I have already mentioned the use of the Yiddish theme when Zofia is distraught at Elisabeth's disappearance. Equally importantly, her unwillingness to use the word 'God' in her work echoes Judaic proscriptions. 'Można nie wątpić nie używając słów', she remarks, almost untranslatably ('One can have no doubts even without using the words'?). The witness figure, whose presence throughout the series suggests a pensive recording angel (the camera slides sideways to find him midway through Elisabeth's story), resembles the invariably winged messengers of Christian iconography less than he does the young men who visit Abraham in the desert. Meanwhile, the gaps in the narrative can recall the enigmatic narrative procedures of the Old Testament, the lack of 'foreground' deemed typical of it by Erich Auerbach. *Decalogue 8* delineates both the possibility of reconciliation and the enormous odds against it. It could so easily not have happened. The final isolation of the tailor, still trapped in his traumas, reminds us of that. A sort of reprise, it shows there are others in need of liberation still.

Perhaps inevitably, the Polish reception of *Decalogue 8* centres less on the Holocaust than on the series as a whole. Those critics who accorded it crucial significance did so primarily on aesthetic grounds, praising the effectiveness of the screenplay (Oskar Sobański) or noting its role as reprise and distillation of the series (Tadeusz Szyma describes its placement as symptomatic of Kieślowski's asymmet-

---

[37] Maria Malatyńska, '*Dekalog*: Kieślowski', *Życie Literackie*, 19 Nov. 1989.
[38] e.g. the interview he gave to *Le Monde* on 16 Sept. 1989, in which he stated that 'en accordant trop d'importance à la raison, nos contemporains ont perdu une dimension de la vie'.

rical composition).[39] The story is more an anecdotal instance of ethical quandaries than the marker of a historical blank spot that calls for *Vergangenheitsbewältigung*. Nevertheless, it is surely significant that the series is distilled in this particular story.

## KORCZAK: THE HEAVEN THAT DOES NOT EXIST

No survey of Polish films concerning Polish–Jewish relations, however partial, can overlook their most recent dramatization by Andrzej Wajda, Poland's most renowned director: *Korczak*. The interplay between Polishness and Jewishness is dramatized even in the names of its subject, Janusz Korczak being also Henryk Goldszmit. When one of his orphanage children terms him 'the greatest living Pole' and another recalls his Jewishness, the first child responds by adding 'and the greatest Jew too'. As in *The Promised Land*, the central role belongs to Wojciech Pszoniak, though his Korczak—stiff with horror at the world's abuse of children, suspicious of the adult world that browbeats them, irascibly primed for their defence—is aeons removed from that sunny, mercurial *macher* Moryc Welt. Since *Korczak* scrupulously avoids any hint of antisemitism, its vilification by sectors of the French press deeply disturbed Wajda, who nobly sought to comprehend it as simply due to divergences in viewpoint: 'otherwise I would have to admit that there is racism both on the one hand and on the other. I would not like to think that and do not do so.'[40]

Danièle Heymann, an initiator of the hostile press reaction, wrote of an 'oneiric ending' that was 'particularly revolting'.[41] In that ending the railway carriage bearing Korczak and his orphans to Treblinka becomes uncoupled from the train, halts in a field, and the children emerge in slow motion, processing under the orphanage's banner. Wajda says that the film ended thus so as not to end it in the gas chambers: his reluctance chimes with the widespread instinct that deems what happened there all but unrepresentable, and is consistent with his realization that even the most exact re-creation of the Warsaw ghetto could never convey the look of its harrowed inhabitants. Alas, the horrifying force of the excerpts from a Goebbels-sponsored documentary Wajda's film incorporates casts it into the shade. If it renders it less like film than theatre, whose actors are always known to be separable from their roles, it also reminds one that only the psychological torment Wajda eschews could have brought ghetto expressions to their faces. Just such torment has of course engendered many of the greatest film performances— one may think of the vicissitudes of Lillian Gish in some of Griffith's works, or Falconetti's in *The Passion of Joan of Arc*—but the nature of Wajda's subject seems rather to have imbued him with tenderness for his actors and a particular sensitivity to the ambiguity of directorial tyranny; admirably restrained, his

---

[39] Tadeusz Szyma, '*Dekalog osiem*', *Tygodnik Powszechny*, 11 Feb. 1990.

[40] 'Z Wajdą o *Korczaku*', *Gazeta Gdańska*, 21–3 Sept. 1991.

[41] Danièle Heymann, 'L'Homme de rêve et l'homme de plomb', *Le Monde*, 13 May 1990.

apologias do not point this out.[42] Positive reviews deemed the ending poetic and in some cases mentioned the legend, circulating in 1943, that the carriage had indeed become uncoupled, permitting Korczak and the children to escape. The existence of that legend invalidates readings of the ending as a self-indulgent, consolatory flourish: rather, it becomes part of the scrupulous re-creation, albeit one that at this point traces the imagination of the past rather than its reality (and unfortunately leaves itself open to misreading by failing clearly to signal the shift to fantasy). In Israel, meanwhile, the image of children bearing a banner with the Star of David could be read as alluding to Israel's persistence, and even to the state's foundation shortly after the Holocaust.

Objections to these closing images nevertheless ignore the statement superimposed upon them, that 'Dr Korczak died with his children in the gas chambers of Treblinka in August 1942.' As often, the film-goer's visual bias can cause an unbalanced response to the mix of media film really comprises. Wajda's detractors failed to grasp the pregnant clash of image and statement in a fusion of dissonant knowledge and all-but-untenable hope of transcendence. Moreover, slow motion's implied 'this is not really happening' (or 'this is happening in a different sense from the way things normally happen') arguably imbues the ending with an aching wish that escape had indeed been possible. It may even be said to imagine escape appropriately, in the form of a child's fantasy. To object to the suggestion of a possible transcendence simultaneously undercut by the title is not necessarily to speak in the name of Korczak himself, who set aside an orphanage room for children to pray as they wished. To deem it escapist is to overlook something noted by Wiktor Woroszylski: that the stylistics of fairy-tale had entered the film even earlier, with the children's march out of the ghetto.[43] Korczak leads a true children's crusade against the ways of this world, and even as the thought of its terminus sobers us, our spirits are strangely exalted by the power of their dream. To reject the ending as an image of 'children going to heaven'—and hence Christian, unacceptable to Jews—is to traduce its ecumenical poetry. What it represents is the hope of transcendence all religions share. Objections to a 'non-Jewish close' are surely further compromised by the half-Jewishness of the script-writer, Agnieszka Holland.

If there *are* grounds for criticism of *Korczak*, they lie less in its close than in its general aesthetic weakness. In eschewing the epic American producers once wished him to make of Korczak's life (a colour production, ghetto scenes reduced to the minimum . . .), and in shackling himself to scrupulous re-creation in monochrome, Wajda denies his own baroque temperament. Perhaps this is only fitting: the brilliance of *The Promised Land* is as humanly dubious as the work of

---

[42] 'Wajda mówi o *Korczaku*', *Gazeta Wyborcza*, 18 Jan. 1991. It is worth noting that Agnieszka Holland's original script places a scene in Majdanek just before the controversial ending. Agnieszka Holland, *Korczak* (Warsaw, 1991), 148–9.

[43] Wiktor Woroszylski, '*Jestem*: Janusza Korczaka i Andrzeja Wajdy', *Kino* (Aug. 1990), 5.

Eisenstein on which it draws. Since Wajda had once proved capable of character studies—think of his fine, taut version of *The Shadow Line*—*Korczak*'s weak characterization and acting surely owe something to the director's age: it has a tired feel, and on release was billed as his last film. More crucial still may be the woodenness of Holland's script, whose dogged placement of the words of Korczak's 'Ghetto Diary' in characters' mouths smacks of declamatory illustrativeness, devoid of actuality's hesitations. Its failure to distinguish between written and spoken modes lends its truth to Korczak's words an air of falsehood. The acting is often stilted also—one glaring instance being the Nazis' roughing-up of Czerniaków. This may be in part the result of Wajda's recorded fear of working with children, never having done so before.[44] (His own formative experiences seem to have been those of wartime adolescence.) The sentimental subplot linking Józef, the orphanage's oldest child, to the blonde Polish Ewa is fatally point-making, in the manner of a movie made for television. Scrupulosity so stifles the film that the imaginative leap into the powerful, poignant ending may have been too surprising for the audience to handle.

Another weakness of Holland's script is a certain inconsequentiality, the result perhaps of close adherence to the episodic structure of the diary. The script is strongest at its close and whenever it breathes the irony so pervasive in Holland's own films. A strong irony links the beginning, where Korczak is shown in his radio role of Old Doctor, stating that 'Whoever pretends to sacrifice himself for a person or thing is a liar,' and the end, where he chooses not to avail himself of an offer of escape. Another is when ex-pupils who have joined the Jewish combat organization reproach him for founding an educational system that leaves them unfit to fight. (Their reservations echo the critique of Father Jerzy Popiełuszko voiced by his chauffeur in Holland's earlier *To Kill a Priest*.) The film's reception was to be marked by irony of a different, more ghastly kind: mechanical reiterations of the charges of antisemitism levelled against *The Promised Land*. If the idealistic doctor–social worker had been a key figure in Reymont's novel, but had not figured in Wajda's brutal apocalypse, *Korczak* makes good the omission by focusing on that character alone, as embodied in Korczak himself. That doctor–social worker had been central to the Żeromski and Prus novels Korczak himself listed among his formative experiences. It is perhaps a shame that Wajda's film tells us nothing of the earlier Korczak, of the process whereby he became so unyielding a defender of children's rights that he allowed them to arraign their teachers in an orphanage's court. Because Henryk Goldszmit remained a Polish writer, resisting the lure of Palestine, the director whom Michałek and Turaj term 'the essential Pole' has every right to tell his story.[45] One should recall Korczak's

---

[44] 'Wajda mówi'. For all Wajda's praise for his child actors, they create a sweet odour of unreality. Contrast the vibrant performance Kieślowski elicits from Wojciech Klata in *Dekalog 1* with the one he gives here as Schlomo.

[45] Michałek and Turaj, *The Modern Cinema of Poland*, 129.

own pride in the fact that a generation of Jewish children had learned to read and write Polish from his *Little Review*. Both Korczak and Wajda seek to reconcile Poles and Jews by demonstrating their compatibility within a single person. It is thus fitting that the wall mentioned during the commemoration of the ghetto uprising should encounter another one, erected by Korczak, with an opposite meaning: 'They've separated us from the rest of the world with a wall,' he comments, 'so we'll separate ourselves from them'—and he walls up the orphanage windows to shield his children from the horror without.

### EPILOGUE: 'FOR TO BEGIN YET AGAIN . . .'

The start of this essay reflected upon the arbitrariness of beginnings. That arbitrariness is apparent in the ways a film my opening survey omitted could have formed an alternative starting-point—or furnished a conclusion—for it compacts within itself elements of all the films considered hitherto. Aleksander Ford's *Ulica Graniczna* (*Border Street*, 1948) should perhaps be placed on one side for more tender, protective reasons: it is a lesser work than the others. Its closing clarion-call can echo the motif of the importance of a child's survival in *Decalogue 8*, while its very improbability is reminiscent of *Europa, Europa*; the complexity of its etching of Polish attitudes to Jews resembles *Angry Harvest*; the images of children in the Warsaw ghetto and the incorporation of newsreel footage anticipate *Korczak*; and the apocalyptic appearance of the Jew in a prayer-shawl—a grandfather prays in Hebrew as burning beams tumble round him—recalls Wajda's *Promised Land*. Moreover, like the 1980s work of Holland and Kieślowski, *Border Street* is not really a product of People's Poland. It stands just before the imposition of the censoring straitjacket Polish cinema would escape only briefly and intermittently until 1989. (Hence Wajda's recent *Ring with a Crowned Eagle* suggests that he now views even *Ashes and Diamonds*, his most renowned work, as a tainted presentation of the aftermath of Soviet 'liberation'.) The onset of orthodoxy occurred during the period of the release of Ford's film and can be seen dawning ominously in Marian Warszałłowicz's description of its ideological shortcomings: 'It is well known that the material aid the Aryan side provided for the ghetto fighters came from the workers' camp, from the organization of the social left—whereas the identity of the people aiding the ghetto is presented as quite anonymous in this film.'[46] Ford's humanism would come to be deemed problematic. A Jew himself, he had broached Jewish themes in the pre-war cinema and would later be driven abroad by the antisemitic campaign of 1968, dying in exile.

*Border Street*: lest the title seem excessively, oppressively symbolic, the narrator begins by stating that the story could have occurred in many streets with other names. Nevertheless, a symbolic dimension is present, one source of the work's

---

[46] Marian Warszałłowicz, '*Ulica Graniczna*: Film arcyludzki', *Film* (1949), no. 12, quoted from Jadwiga Bocheńska *et al.*, *Historia filmu polskiego*, iii (Warsaw, 1974), 158.

operatic heightening. (For all the ubiquitous ruins, this is not a neo-realist film.) The title is re-emphasized at the end, where the narrator's voice returns to echo the Polish children's feeling that Dawidek can never die, for walls cannot separate people, and truth is frontierless. The crossing of ethnic boundaries pervades the film. Good Poles gravitate towards, and are later reclassified as, Jews; malign ones claim German ancestry and toady to the occupation forces. The very first sequence suggests an imminent fusion of high and low, the collapse of the conventional markers separating Poles and Jews: the Polish girl Jadzia may take piano lessons on an upper courtyard floor while Dawidek peers through a ground-level window, but the camera's position before their windows connects them by registering their desire to join in the football game outside. Each does so by eluding a custodial adult, with matching childish disasters as a denouement: the ball's force pushes Dawidek into a water-butt; and when kicked through Jadzia's window it shatters a vase. Although at this point only Dawidek is wet, by the end Jadzia and the other boys will all be wading through the sewers.

Education preoccupies Ford's film, something exemplified in the subplot with the black German shepherd. Fredek, son of the antisemitic Kuśmirak, points out Dawidek to a German soldier and encourages him to let his dog display its talent for worrying Jews. Once the dog has chased Jadzia and Dawidek into the sewers and a stray German bullet has wounded its paw, Jadzia bandages it and tells Dawidek that the dog cannot help biting: it is only doing as it has been taught. Renamed Cyclone, the dog attaches himself to her and comes to her rescue, leading her friends to her and Dawidek in a later sewer scene. Truly effective education, however, begins with the parents. Władek's father, a reserve officer in hiding after the Polish army's defeat, shares the antisemitic prejudices of many pre-war Poles. He refuses to take new clothes as a gift from Dawidek's grandfather. But when German soldiers march in, question the old man about the discarded Polish uniform, and beat him, yet extract nothing from him, the Pole is impressed. The ironic reversal in which the Jew here conceals the Pole typifies the film's sense of the growing interchangeability of Poles and Jews, as both become victims. He later tells Władek that there are Jews like Dawidek's grandfather and Poles like Kuśmirak. Władek's own prejudices, which had turned him against Jadzia when he learned of her part-Jewishness, quickly evaporate.

Although the Germans depicted in *Border Street* have few virtues, they are not the primary object of Ford's criticism; indeed, they are individualized so sketchily as to be simply a many-headed Invader. Ford's deepest scorn is reserved for Poles who renounce national allegiance and curry favour with the Germans. Kuśmirak, for instance, trims his moustache to match Hitler's, slicking his black hair across, in the Führer's style, on learning of the German triumph. In pidgin German his daughter tells a beer-drinking occupier that she too is one of them—and later they marry. With such a father it is no surprise that Fredek steals the photograph of

Jadzia's grandfather from the desk of her doctor father. (The melodrama is a little improbable, it being unclear why Fredek should be perched upon the roof alongside Białek's window. Has his father sent him, or is it a lucky accident? One suspects that it is the melodramatic plot, masquerading as malevolent, cross-eyed Fate, that has sent him.) Reconstituted, its Hebrew dedication translated by an unsuspecting Dawidek, the torn photograph will allow Kuśmirak to blackmail Białek out of his apartment. After dispatching Jadzia to the countryside, Białek, the assimilated Jew, retires to the ghetto (the 'handkerchief' with which he waves her farewell is but one of the film's many symbolic details, unfurling into an armband bearing the Star of David). Later Fredek will join a uniformed gang in pursuit of Jadzia. Waylaid and beaten up by Władek, he loses his Nazi armband, and the Jewish armband lying nearby is taken for his: a German soldier shoots him as a fleeing Jew. Here Ford's melodrama compromises his humanism, for although the latter would accord Fredek the chance to redeem himself, the former sheds few of its tears over a villain's demise. The other children's shock at the sight of the shooting is the shock any death imparts. Could it be that imagination *needs* the Other, the scapegoat, so that the vanishing of the Jewish Other demands a substitute?

Separated at the outset, high and low, Pole and Jew soon become one. The doctor will suffer the fate of the Jews (he now lives *next* to the Libermans, not above them); and Dawidek's uncle Nathan has already fought for the defeated Polish army (near the film's start he is in as much of a hurry at the barber's as Władek's father—who assumes his call-up papers give him priority—because he too is off to the front). Near the end, while fleeing through the sewers, Dawidek, Jadzia, Bronek, and Władek encounter armed partisans (it was surely this scene that prompted Warszałłowicz's objections). Although warned that the ghetto is burning, the partisans wade towards it just the same. When Dawidek decides to follow them, Władek gives him his father's pistol. It is as if the slight 'feminization' of the Jew that had dictated Dawidek's pairing and paralleling with Jadzia has been dispelled by his grasp of the pistol, bringing him into the sphere of heroic action. The children's conviction that he will not die may seem strange, even objectionable: reactions akin to some French journalists' responses to *Korczak* are clearly possible. It may even seem as if what matters for the melodrama is the rescue of Jadzia, the Maiden in Distress. The symbolic heightening that pervades the film, however, surely lends the remark the sense that Dawidek survives as a symbol—whatever really occurs—as an emblem of the Jewish people's heroic persistence. This prevalence of symbol over reality is nevertheless another way of describing the defect many reviewers termed a 'lack of authenticity'.[47] It generates the high opera of the closing scenes. *Border Street* is not a great film: limited

---

[47] Marian Warszałłowicz, '*Ulica Graniczna*: Film arcyludzki', *Film* (1949), no. 12, quoted from Jadwiga Bocheńska *et al.*, *Historia filmu polskiego*, iii (Warsaw, 1974), 158.

formally by theatricality, it is limited conceptually by its depiction of the anti-semite as necessarily pro-Nazi. Kuśmirak's cosiness with the Nazis carries no hint of the existence of a nationalist antisemitism that detests Germans as heartily as it does Jews. For all that, the work has integrity and nobility. One can only echo its final hope that the walls between people must fall, that truth has no borders.

# 'That Incredible History of the Polish Bund Written in a Soviet Prison': The NKVD Files on Henryk Erlich and Wiktor Alter

## GERTRUD PICKHAN

It was only shortly after the German invasion of the Soviet Union in the summer of 1941 that Abram Faynsilber, a member of the General Jewish Worker's Union of Poland, known as the Bund, met Henryk Erlich on a prisoners' transport from Moscow to Saratov. Erlich had been one of the most important representatives of the Polish Bund during the inter-war years and now, like Faynsilber himself, was a prisoner of the NKVD. Erlich was also a member of the Central Committee of the Bund, editor-in-chief of the *Folkstsaytung*, and, with Wiktor Alter, a delegate of the Bund to the Executive Committee of the Socialist International since 1930.

Henryk Erlich, born in 1882 in Lublin and a member of the Bund from 1903, had earned a law degree and worked as a lawyer and publicist in St Petersburg. He became a member of the Executive Committee of the Petrograd Soviet after the February Revolution of 1917. In the summer of 1918 he returned to Poland. Wiktor Alter, who was born in 1890 in Mlawa and joined the Bund in 1904, had finished his engineering studies in Belgium and lived in England during the First World War. From 1919 Erlich and Alter were both on the Central Committee of the Polish Bund and represented their party in various national and international bodies. While Erlich continued his work as a lawyer and wrote at the same time, Alter centred his activities on the Jewish trade union and co-operative movements. With the German Wehrmacht approaching Warsaw, Erlich had left the city on 6–7 September 1939, in accordance with the general advice of the Bund's Central Committee. On 6 October he was arrested in Brześć and charged with anti-Soviet and counter-revolutionary activities.

This article first appeared in a German version: 'Das NKVD-Dossier über Henryk Erlich und Wiktor Alter', in *Berliner Jahrbuch für osteuropäische Geschichte*, 2 (1994), 155–86. In view of the importance of the material, a decision was taken to make an exception to our usual editorial policy and to reprint it in translation in *Polin*.

Ten years after they shared the ordeal of the 1941 prisoners' transport from Moscow, Abram Faynsilber gave an account (in a memorial book for Erlich and Alter, written in Yiddish) of what Erlich had told him about his time in Moscow's NKVD prison:

After two weeks in the Brest-Litovsk prison, Comrade Henryk was brought to Moscow. He was taken to the notorious Lubyanka prison. During the first month he was kept in a one-man cell. Not once was he allowed to enjoy a quiet night's sleep. The interrogations would last from three hours to eighteen hours without a break. Erlich was asked to acknowledge that all his activities were treasonous, hostile to the people, and anti-Soviet.

When they were not successful in this approach, they began to treat him somewhat better for a while. They gave him a cell with another prisoner, then with two others, and later with three. It was at this time that Comrade Erlich wrote from memory the history of the Bund in Poland. (This was after he had actually resolved a number of times not to write it. But after lengthy reflection he decided to do so.) Each day he was led from his cell into a small room which contained a desk, a chair, a pitcher of drinking water, paper, ink, and a pen. The door was shut and no one disturbed him. He was thus able for quite some time to unburden himself of the senseless and painful 'discussion' with the interrogators about socialism and communism, about democracy and revolution. He decided to prove the answer to his tormentors on paper . . .

For several months, Comrade Erlich worked on his twenty-one-year history of the Bund in Poland, *i.e.*, the interval between the First and Second World Wars. Who knows when the GPU archives, drenched in rivers of blood, will become accessible to the Russian people? Who knows when we shall have the good fortune to read that incredible history of the Polish Bund written in a Soviet prison by Comrade Henryk Erlich?[1]

Meanwhile Lucjan Blit, a leading member of the Bund's youth organization during the inter-war years, had also heard about Erlich's Moscow writings. Blit had shared a hotel room in Kuibishev with Erlich and Alter from 29 October to 3 December 1941. They had been evacuated there after their release, together with members of the Polish embassy. On 4 December Erlich and Alter were arrested again. Blit later wrote :

Erlich was convinced that he would never leave the Communist prisons. He decided, therefore, to make use of every item in the indictment to leave behind in written form a document that would, at some point in future—after the GPU archives were opened, just as the tsarist archives had been—convey the truth about the Jewish Labor Bund and its leaders. Erlich wrote a great deal. From what he told me, he had certainly written, in the course of those two years, the equivalent of a large book about the history and ideology of the Bund.[2]

[1] Abram Faynsilber, 'Mitn khaver Erlikh in sovietishe turmes', in Victor Shulman (ed.), *Henrik Erlikh un Viktor Alter: A gedenk-bukh* (New York, 1951), 116–41: 124–5; trans. S. A. Portnoy as 'With Comrade Erlich in Soviet Prison', in *Henryk Erlich and Victor Alter: Two Heroes and Martyrs for Jewish Socialism* (Hoboken, NJ, 1990), 110–35: 119.

[2] Lucjan Blit, 'Henrik Erlikh un Viktor Alter in Soviet-Rusland', in Shulman (ed.), *Henrik Erlikh un Viktor Alter*, 96–115: 103: *Henryk Erlich and Victor Alter*, 96–7. Blit already makes a similar 'statement' in his booklet *The Case of Henryk Erlich and Victor Alter* (London, 1943), 11.

What seemed to be almost beyond imagination became actual. The 'blood-drenched' archives of the GPU, the NKVD, and later the KGB, and now those of the Federal Intelligence Service of the Russian Federation as well, are (partly) open, and what Erlich wrote about the Bund during his imprisonment is available for examination in Moscow.

In the first part of this article I describe the extraordinary experience of working in the KGB archives and survey the Erlich–Alter files; in the second part I document Erlich's history of the Bund, which, because of the circumstances of its creation, is unique.

## THE ERLICH–ALTER FILES IN THE KGB ARCHIVES

In August 1992, after an eight-month struggle with bureaucracy, Viktoria Dubnova, a niece of Henryk Erlich's living in Moscow, was allowed to take notes on the six volumes of the KGB's Erlich–Alter file.[3] She took a particular interest in the last volume, which contained material about the men's second arrest by the NKVD, in Kuibishev, where they had been held from December 1941. From a note written by Maksim Litvinov, Soviet ambassador to the United States, on 23 February 1943, it had generally been assumed that Erlich and Alter had been executed shortly after their second arrest at the end of 1941.[4] This long-held view now had to be revised. In fact, Erlich took his own life in the Kuibishev prison in May of 1942. Wiktor Alter was executed there, but not until 17 February 1943.[5]

In order to find the history of the Bund that Faynsilber and Blit had mentioned, I needed to see the files about Erlich and Alter's first confinement (1939–41). I therefore applied for access to the former KGB's archives, and the German Social Democratic Party (SPD) helped me to arrange a meeting with an official from the Russian embassy in Bonn, which took place in October 1993. (The late Willy Brandt, honorary chairman of the SPD, in his capacity as chairman of the Socialist International, had as recently as April 1992 urged the Russian Federation, as the successor of the USSR, to rehabilitate Erlich and Alter.) By December I obtained permission, through the Russian embassy in Warsaw, to start my research.[6]

---

[3] 'NKVD Documents Shed New Light on Fate of Erlich and Alter', introduction by Lukasz Hirszowicz to *East European Jewish Affairs*, 22 (1992), 65–85; L. Way, 'Exhuming the Buried Past', *Nation*, 1 Mar. 1993, 267–8.

[4] e.g. Nora Levin, *The Jews in the Soviet Union since 1917: Paradox of Survival*, ii (New York, 1990), 364; see also Gertrud Pickhan, 'Auf Befehl Stalins hingerichtet', *Frankfurter Rundschau*, 20 Feb. 1993, 16. For the reactions by the western Allies and the Polish exiles in London to Erlich's and Alter's arrest, see I. Tombs, 'Erlich and Alter: "The Sacco and Vanzetti of the USSR"', *Journal of Contemporary History*, 23 (1988), 531–49.      [5] Hirszowicz, 'NKVD Documents', 75, 82.

[6] I particularly thank H. E. Dingels, head of the International Department at the SPD Executive Committee, for crucial support of my project. I also thank the representatives of the Russian embassies in Bonn and Warsaw for their helpfulness.

When I arrived in Moscow in February 1994, two difficulties remained to be dealt with. First, a responsible official had to be found at Kuznetsky Most 22, where the archives are housed, and also at the Department for Social Relations of the Lubyanka prison itself. Next I learned I could only get access to the files after obtaining personal clearance from Victor Erlich, son of Henryk Erlich, who lives in the United States, a professor emeritus of Slavic studies at Yale University and author of a 1955 study on Russian formalism. With help from the Goethe Institute in Moscow, I was able to contact Victor Erlich, who was kind enough to give his permission promptly.[7]

I worked through five volumes of files marked 'top secret' and 'keep for all time' in a small room that had been set aside for that purpose after the archives were opened to the public (in particular, to the relatives of victims of Stalin's purges). Although this room was open daily from nine to six, it was often over-crowded, and around the middle of February a larger, well-furnished room was made available. The friendly co-operation of the staff was a real surprise, but it is difficult to convey the atmosphere of an archive whose documents contain so much human misery and so much contempt of it. Most of the people reading there came during their lunch breaks or after work looking for final confirmation of the fate of their loved ones, and the interrogation and torture they had endured aimed at forcing absurd confessions so that they might be killed as enemies of the Soviet Union.[8]

Erlich and Alter, however, did not belong to those vast numbers of Stalin's faceless victims. They had been prominent members of the international workers' movement, and after their disappearance many people fought for their release, including the English politician Clement Attlee and the German *émigré* physicist Albert Einstein. It was probably the international reputation of these two prisoners that Stalin had at first wished to exploit which saved them from the 'physical pressure' which until 1953 was still sanctioned in writing in the USSR, and from immediate death. In the summer of 1941 Erlich told Faynsilber that he had not been tortured but that the isolation and constant sleep deprivation had tormented him greatly.[9]

Six accessible volumes in the KGB archives document Erlich and Alter's

---

[7] Jean Alter, son of Wiktor Alter, b. 1925, also lives in the United States. The Russian Intelligence Services (Archival Division) did not seek his permission.

[8] Only recently have NKVD methods begun to come to light, with the publication of some documents from the KGB archives. A. Borshchagovski, for example, describes interrogations and torture of members of the Jewish Anti-Fascist Committee: 'Obvinyaetsia krov: Fragmenty knigi', *Novy Mir*, 10 (1993), 105–51. The 'Polish operation' of the NKVD and the decisions and structures underlying the Great Terror were documented after members of the organization Memorial obtained access to the files; see Ręka Jeżowa, 'Karta', *Niezależne Pismo Historyczne*, 11 (1993), 23–34. The report of the chairman of the Justice Commission of the Russian PEN, A. Waksberg, is available in German translation as *Die Verfolgten Stalins: Aus den Verliesen des KGB* (Hamburg, 1993).

[9] Faynsilber, 'Mitn khaver Erlikh', 125 = 120. Again, the files in the KGB archives yield no evidence of Erlich or Alter having been tortured.

incarceration in the NKVD prisons of Moscow and Kuibishev, their trials in 1941, their deaths in 1942 and 1943, and their rehabilitation by the Soviet authorities in 1990. By a Ministry of State Security decree of 24 January 1952, three volumes of investigation file no. 839 (1941), on Gersh Wolf Moiseyevich Erlich, and two volumes of investigation file no. 460 (1941), on Wiktor Izraelevich Alter, were combined to make up the five volumes of archival investigation file no. 100243.[10] The material in this file gives no hint of who was ultimately responsible for the men's fate, but because of the international concern for these two prisoners, it seems safe to assume that decisions were made at the highest level, in the Politburo, that is, by Stalin himself. According to the official responsible, the KGB archives contain no material about exactly how this came about. Such information probably exists only in the files of the Russian presidential archives, still largely closed.

We now turn to the contents of these five volumes. The first document of the first volume records Henryk Erlich's arrest in Brześć on 4 October 1939.[11] Besides a questionnaire, there is an empty envelope marked 'photographs': these were the official prisoner photographs, frontal and profile, probably taken on 14 October 1939 after Erlich's transfer to Moscow, and found in an envelope containing receipts for everything removed from Erlich on his arrest.[12] In addition, there are twelve interrogation reports for 1 October 1939 to 26 June 1941, each one a typescript followed by its handwritten original.[13]

I think it highly unlikely that these reports cover all of Erlich's interrogations during the first period of custody. It is striking, for example, that the typescript of the interrogation conducted during the night of 21–2 April 1940, which lasted ten hours, should consist of only six pages; either there must have been long breaks or a large part of the proceedings did not find its way into the report. However, the handwritten version, which contains exactly the same text as the typescript, shows Erlich's signature under each of the answers and also at the bottom of every page.[14] Inconsistencies are also found in the interrogation report for 26 June 1941. Not only is there no handwritten version, but the last page of the typescript, which would have stated when the questioning ended and who conducted it, is

[10] This information appears on an additional unnumbered sheet of paper in the first of the five volumes. Each volume has a contents list for the documents and gives its position in the file and its volume number. The documents and pages are numbered in each volume with the exception only of the paginated written notes of Erlich and Alter. The file (839 or 460) is indicated in the citations below, together with the volume, number, and pages cited; all are from archival investigation file 100243. Volume 6, documenting the deaths of Erlich and Alter in 1942, is not considered in this article.

[11] File 839, vol. 1, nos. 1–9, pp. 1–14.

[12] Ibid., nos. 6–9, pp. 8–14. The official photographs of Alter as prisoner, which were missing from a similar envelope, were found 'at a different place' by the responsible official and presented to me.

[13] Ibid., nos. 10–25, pp. 15–260. Sometimes orders from the investigating authorities are found in the middle; see ibid., nos. 11–12, pp. 17–18, and nos. 22–3, pp. 235–8.

[14] Ibid., no. 18, pp. 97–106.

missing.[15] In this context, one more reference to Abram Faynsilber's memoirs is useful. On the men's journey as prisoners of the KGB from Moscow to Saratov at the end of June 1941, Erlich referred to a quite recent interrogation at which Lavrenti Beria had been present in person; and in a last session about two weeks before the transfer to Saratov, Erlich had again been urged to sign a confession but refused to do so.[16] The material in the KGB file, however, neither mentions Beria's presence nor indicates the existence of prefabricated confessions. The question thus arises whether there is a connection between this fact and the missing page, or whether the incompleteness of the documents is just a sign of even the NKVD's disarray after the German invasion of the USSR on 22 June.

The last numbered text document of this volume is the charge against Erlich, written on 24 July 1941.[17] What follows, unnumbered but paginated, are minutes of the preparatory meeting of the military tribunal conducted by the NKVD units of the Volga region in Saratov on 29 July 1941, minutes of the trial on 2 August of the same year, the death sentence, the decree to alter it to a ten-year prison sentence of 22 August, and the order of 29 August and 14 September to release Erlich. The very last batch of papers are Erlich and Alter's rehabilitation documents, issued following a USSR presidential decree of 18 August 1990.[18]

The second volume of documents contains, in its first half, twenty-seven reports of interrogations of several witnesses and prisoners whose testimony was used against Erlich. Particularly interesting is the fact that the first fourteen interrogations, whose reports are only excerpted (containing no indication of where they took place, who did the questioning, etc.), were conducted between 31 December 1937 and 19 August 1938, at a time when Erlich and Alter were still free citizens of the Second Polish Republic.[19] Those individuals questioned were exclusively Jewish prisoners who either had emigrated during the 1920s from Poland to the Soviet Union or were well-known Soviet Jewish activists such as Alexander Chashin, Maks Kiper, and Rubin Pinkus. Most of these witnesses confess to having spied in the USSR for the Polish Secret Service and the Central Committee of the Bund, with Erlich and Alter, of course, at its head. All fourteen documents are signed by NKVD lieutenant Cheremukhin, who also later questioned Erlich seven times in Moscow.[20] The evidence of these interrogations held two years before Erlich and Alter were actually arrested recalls the fact that the

---

[15] File 839, vol. 1, no. 24, pp. 238–48. No. 25 follows directly after pp. 249–60; the missing page of the report from 25 June 1941 must therefore have been removed before the documents were paginated.

[16] Faynsilber, 'Mitn khaver Erlikh', 129–30 = 124–5.

[17] File 839, vol. 1, no. 29, pp. 264–5; p. 267 gives documentary evidence dated 25 July 1941, from which it follows that Erlich had been transferred to the NKVD prison in Saratov.

[18] Ibid. 272–86.  [19] Ibid., vol. 2, nos. 1–14, pp. 1–82.

[20] Ibid., vol. 1, no. 14, p. 67; no. 15, p. 74; no. 16, p. 83; no. 17, p. 92; no. 18, p. 102; no. 19, p. 114; and no. 21, p. 166. On 2 Nov. 1939 Erlich was interrogated by Lt. Krukovski, on 9 July 1940 by Lt. Kozunov, and on 26 June 1941 by Lt. Burlakov; see ibid., no. 13, p. 42; no. 20, p. 128; and no. 25, p. 260.

Bund, already dissolved in the Soviet Union by 1921, had been one of the many objects of Stalin's great purges from 1936 on. According to this evidence, it must have been clear from the beginning that Erlich and Alter had no real chance of survival, although at some point Stalin surely would have liked to exploit their prominence.

Next among the documents are three from 5 October 1939—reports of interrogations obviously conducted immediately after Erlich's arrest in Brześć.[21] The men questioned are Josif Lichtensztejn, Israel-Dawid Kirszbaum, and Israel Zilber, all three from Brześć and, according to their statements, members of the Polish Communist Party (KPP). They seem to have betrayed Erlich to the NKVD. The rest of the interrogation reports, from 1940, with exclusively Jewish witnesses, all but two of whom were prisoners of the NKVD, basically contain statements about alleged anti-Soviet activities on Erlich's part.[22] The notable exception is Chajm Sznicer, who, like Erlich, Alter, and many other Bundists fleeing Germans, had ended up in Soviet jails. Sznicer's second interrogation from 19 May 1940 shows the NKVD's deplorable methods in a particularly harsh light: Sznicer, giving brave answers to his interrogators' questions and clearing Erlich's name, is then confronted with an alleged statement of Erlich's in which he supposedly gives evidence about Sznicer's anti-Soviet activities.[23] Sznicer sadly replies: 'Erlich's statement does not correspond with reality.'[24] (Erlich's alleged statement is nowhere to be found among the reports of his own interrogations or other statements. Erlich does indeed give names of his comrades in Poland when asked to do so, but not once does he link this to any form of denunciation.)

Extracts from Erlich's articles in the *Folkstsaytung*, the central organ of the Bund, conclude the second volume of documents. They were translated from Yiddish into Russian by one Lvovski, member of the NKVD.[25] Erlich told Abram Faynsilber in 1941 that the translations had been tendentiously falsified.[26]

Erlich's handwritten account of aspects of the Polish Bund ('Sobstvennye pokazaniia Erlicha'), some 426 sheets, makes up the third volume of the file. This account, written on and off between November 1939 and May 1941, can be identified as that 'incredible history' of the Bund that Faynsilber mentioned, and is discussed in detail in the final part of this article.

Paralleling volume 1, which deals with Erlich, volume 4 presents materials concerning the arrest and interrogation of Wiktor Alter. First it documents his arrest on 26 September 1939 in Kowel, whence he was transferred to the NKVD prison in Łuck on 22 November and then brought to the 'inner NKVD prison' in Moscow, Butyrki, on 9 December.[27] On the day of his arrival, he filled out an

---

[21] Ibid., vol. 2, nos. 15–17, pp. 83–90.   [22] Ibid., nos. 18–27, pp. 91–173.
[23] Ibid., no. 27, p. 173.   [24] 'Pokazanie Erlicha ne otvetsvuet deistvitelnosti.'
[25] Ibid. 174–211.
[26] Faynsilber, 'Mitn khaver Erlikh', 127 = 121. The file contains only the Russian translation, so comparison with the original is impossible.   [27] File 460, vol. 4, no. 23, pp. 48–9.

NKVD questionnaire and had his fingerprints and photographs taken.[28] The sequence of the following papers is interrupted by some orders of the NKVD's investigating department and consists mainly of handwritten reports of Alter's interrogation in Moscow before his transfer to Kowel and Łuck.[29]

From the interrogation reports, it is striking what different approaches these two leaders of the workers' movement took in dealing with the officials of the NKVD. Henryk Erlich, whom his contemporaries portrayed as a thoughtful and highly educated intellectual, tried to argue, explain, and convince. In Faynsilber's words: 'Comrade Erlich tried to enlighten the Chekist Captain.'[30] The more pragmatically minded Alter does not argue. He does not want to be drawn into pseudo-discussions, and he often refuses to respond at all, especially to questions about other people. The report from 23 November 1939 describes hunger strikes Alter undertook, one from 9 to 11 November and another starting 16 November. As reasons he gives the utter unlawfulness of his incarceration and a decision on his part 'to end this for me quite unbearable situation with my death'.[31] With this, at the very first opportunity he took the most important weapon from his interrogators' hands: the threat of death. Contemporary accounts confirm Alter's assertive nature, which also revealed itself during his time in jail.[32]

Three young witnesses were questioned on 5 June and 1 December 1939 in Łuck. Hanka Turkieltaub, Laja Lajchter, and Mojsej Zilberlicht all claim to be workers, having only seven years of schooling, and members of the KPP. They all accuse Wiktor Alter of being an enemy of the working class, opposing the Soviet Union, and defending Trotskyism.[33]

By a decree of 6 December 1939 Alter was transferred to the 'responsible deputy peoples commissar for state security, Merkulov'. On 20 December NKVD lieutenant Fedotov took him over in Moscow.[34] It was Fedotov who conducted the next fifteen interrogations, between December 1939 and November 1940. In Fedotov's 12 September 1940 order to extend Alter's custody, we read that at this point thirty-three interrogations had taken place.[35] Volume 4 of the file, however, contains only fifteen reports (six sessions in Kowel and Łuck, nine in Moscow), clearly indicating that the material is incomplete. Notes written by

---

[28] File 460, vol. 4, no. 3, pp. 3–4; no. 4, p. 5; no. 5, p. 6. No. 5 is an empty envelope with the inscription 'Paket s fotokartochkami'. Erlich's fingerprints were not included in this file.

[29] Ibid., nos. 7–9, pp. 8–14; nos. 12–14, pp. 17–26.

[30] Faynsilber, 'Mitn khaver Erlikh', 124 = 118.     [31] File 460, vol. 4, no. 12, p. 13.

[32] See J. Gliksman, 'Mitn khaver Viktor Alter in a sovietisher turme', and V. Gabitski, 'Mitn khaver Viktor Alter in a sovietisher turme (zayn tsvah)', in Shulman (ed.), *Henrik Erlikh un Viktor Alter*, 142–61 = 136–55, 167–9 = 161–3.

[33] File 460, vol. 4, nos. 15–20, pp. 46–7. The awkward signatures make one doubt even those seven years of schooling.

[34] Ibid., nos. 21–2, pp. 46–7. Merkulov became People's Commissar for State Security in 1941.

[35] Fedotov's interrogations are ibid., nos. 25–9, pp. 83–123; nos. 31–2, pp. 126–30; no. 38, pp. 141–8; nos. 40–4, pp. 151a–249. The order of 12 Sept. is ibid., no. 39, pp. 150–1.

Alter are inserted into the extended interrogation report for 27 December 1939 in volume 5.[36] Similarly, in Erlich's case the report for 28 August 1940 contains notes he wrote on various days (9, 14, and 16 November 1939).[37]

The last part of this volume is made up of documents of the 1941 trial. Lieutenant Burlakov's statement about the closing of the investigation, dated 31 May 1941, is followed by a wide-ranging written statement by Alter, refuting the charges against him. He rejects the witnesses' account as false, and demands that Wanda Wasilewska be heard and that he be allowed to confront those who testified against him.[38] This confrontation is denied him, with the argument that Alter's anti-Communist and anti-Soviet activities had been sufficiently proven and that the witnesses who had testified against him were already sentenced themselves.[39]

Alter's trial took place in Moscow on 20 July 1941, four weeks after Germany invaded the Soviet Union. He was sentenced to death. The chairman of the secret Military Collegium of the USSR High Court was Military Judge Orlov. In his last words, the defendant, Alter, declared himself not guilty. We also read his declaration that 'I have not yet finished some scientific work in the field of physics that I would wish to leave to the Soviet country for its own uses. To finish the work, I would need another four or five days. I ask the court to grant me this opportunity and repeat that it will be of use to the Soviet Union.'[40] Alter wrote this study while in NKVD custody; it is mentioned in two of his interrogations (14 March 1940 and 24 January 1941).[41] However, the document is nowhere to be found in the KGB archives. Viktoria Dubnova, Erlich's niece, reports that the work (together with an expert opinion written by another physicist under arrest) is in the possession of the Academy of Sciences in Moscow; Alexander Solzhenitsyn gives an account of similar proceedings in his *Gulag Archipelago*.

Following a written objection put before the plenum of the High Court on 22 July 1941 by the well-known deputy chairman of the court, Vasili Ulrich, Alter's death sentence was commuted to ten years' imprisonment.[42] In September 1941 Alter was released with Erlich. One difference between Erlich's and Alter's sentences is striking: Alter's carries the remark that the sentence would be final

---

[36] Ibid., no. 24, pp. 50–82; vol. 5, pp. 194–207.

[37] File 839, vol. 1, no. 21, pp. 136–234; vol. 3, pp. 1–172.

[38] Burlakov's statement is in file 460, vol. 4, no. 50. Alter's is ibid., nos. 51–2, pp. 260–9. Wanda Wasilewska was a prominent member of the Polish Socialist Party and had relatively close links with the Bund. She was co-author of the script of Aleksander Ford's film *Mir kumen on* (1936) about the Medem Hospital in Miedzeszyn, which was run under the auspices of the Bund. In 1943 she was a founding member of the pro-Soviet Association of Polish Patriots. After Erlich and Alter's first arrest, Wasilewska was asked to help. She promised to do so, but warned against too high expectations; see Gliksman, 'Mitn khaver Viktor Alter', 143–4=137–8.

[39] File 460, vol. 4, no. 53, pp. 270–1. These were the same witnesses whose testimony had already served against Erlich. Those reports, or excerpts thereof, are found in file 839, vol. 2, and file 460, vol. 5.

[40] File 460, vol. 4, pp. 285–8: 286.     [41] Ibid., no. 38, pp. 126–7, 141–9.

[42] Ibid. 289–90. For more on V. Ulrich, see Waksberg, *Die Verfolgten Stalins*, 18.

and no appeal allowed,[43] and the alteration was based only on Ulrich's objection. Erlich's sentence, however, contains the line 'An appeal against this sentence can be obtained,' and the sentence was indeed commuted.[44]

Erlich and Alter were tried during the eventful summer of 1941. A brief chronology will allow a clearer picture of those months:

| | |
|---|---|
| 20 July | Alter is tried before the Military Collegium of the USSR High Court in Moscow. |
| 22 July | Alter's death sentence is commuted by the plenum of the High Court; the closing of the investigation against Erlich is reported. |
| 24 July | Erlich is charged. |
| 29 July | The Military Tribunal of the Saratov NKVD unit holds a preparatory meeting. |
| 30 July | Poles and Soviets reach an agreement about diplomatic links and mutual help against Nazi Germany. |
| 2 August | Erlich is tried in Saratov. |
| 14 August | Polish prisoners of war in the Soviet Union are granted amnesty. |
| 22 August | Erlich's death sentence is commuted by the Military Collegium of the High Court in Moscow. |

The handling of the two men's cases does not betray any particular logic. The background will probably only emerge through a study of still inaccessible files in the presidential archives in Moscow. Until that is possible, we can only guess which of these decisions were part of a larger plan and which were made on a day-by-day basis.[45] What, for instance, was the significance of Ulrich's protests? Had a conversion of Erlich's sentence already been decided upon when the death sentence was pronounced? We can only speculate.

The fifth volume of the KGB's Erlich–Alter file begins with five more reports of Alter's interrogations from between 26 and 30 May 1942.[46] Alter is now questioned by Burlakov, who took over the case on 19 May 1941—and who conducted the last known interrogation of Erlich, on 26 June 1941.[47] Whereas at least four different NKVD officials took turns interrogating Erlich, between December 1939 and November 1940 Alter was questioned exclusively by Fedotov, as far as the reports show, and only in May 1941 did Burlakov take over.

Next in the file, used now against Alter, are the same witness statements from 1937, 1938, and 1940 that were already used against Erlich, plus excerpts from the

<hr>

[43] File 460, vol. 4, pp. 288, 291–4.                    [44] File 839, vol. 1, pp. 278–9.

[45] According to Waksberg, *Die Verfolgten Stalins*, 240, 'an incredible number of sentences were pronounced between 5 and 12 July 1940. During these days, all those whose cases had not been closed before were dealt with in a hurry.' At that point, Erlich and Alter were not among them.

[46] File 460, vol. 5, nos. 3–7, pp. 5–58.

[47] Ibid., no. 1, pp. 1–2; file 839, vol. 1, no. 25, pp. 249–60.

*Folkstsaytung.* At the end of volume 5 we find handwritten 'Notes from Wiktor Alter for the NKVD', dated 13 and 21 December 1939 and 10 July 1940.[48] Besides his curriculum vitae, they contain Alter's answers to such questions as 'Why am I a member of the Bund?' and 'Why am I not a Communist?' Alter also writes about the Polish Bund and the 'Jewish question', and about the relationship of the Bund to the KPP, the Polish bourgeoisie, and the USSR. The only type-written document in these notes is an analysis from 10 July 1940 of the 'inner reasons for the breakdown of the Socialist (Second) International and the socialist parties in Europe'.[49] Everything else is written by hand. In comparison with Erlich's handwriting, Alter's is easily decipherable, and in his case, the NKVD has not added any marginal notes or underlined any passages.

## 'SOBSTVENNYE POKAZANIIA ERLICHA'
### NOVEMBER 1939–MAY 1941

Henryk Erlich's history of the Bund, written between 14 November 1939 and 28 May 1941, consists of a total of 426 sheets of paper: 252 of them are handwritten by Erlich; the others are typescripts of the same material. Except for minor typo-graphical errors and details of transcription where Erlich's handwriting was mis-read, the two versions are largely identical. (One recurring 'typographical error', however, deserves note. When writing about pogroms and similar events, Erlich sometimes uses the adjectives 'antisemitic' or 'anti-Jewish'. In the typed version, these words have been changed to 'anti-Soviet'.[50]) Often Erlich's writing in ink is traced over in pen or coloured pencil for better legibility. Sometimes Erlich him-self has crossed out, corrected, or added something. Only the last notes, dated 28 May 1941, are written in pencil, and they are considerably more legible; there exists no typescript for that set.[51]

The NKVD generally used the typed version for their reading. On these pages we find words underlined and comments added in the margins: 'He lies', 'Libel', etc. A close look at the handwriting suggests that at least two people read and commented on Erlich's text, but there are no indications in the file of who they were. My enquiry about this was met by the KGB archives official with the dry remark: 'Not Stalin, but leading officials of the NKVD.'

Except for a few asides, the whole of Erlich's text deals with the Bund during the inter-war years, its work, organizational and personal issues, ideology, and political programme.[52] He wrote the first part between November 1939 and January 1940, with another part between July 1940 and January 1941. Faynsilber states that Erlich had been in solitary confinement for one month after his transfer

---

[48] File 460, vol. 5, nos. 8–23, pp. 59–163; no. 25, pp. 166–92, 194–230, 243–356.
[49] Ibid., no. 25, pp. 231–42.     [50] File 839, vol. 3, pp. 146, 325.     [1] Ibid. 421–6.
[52] The few asides are about people who are not Bund members or about the PPS's relations with various governments; ibid. 175–8, 352–61, 421–6.

to Moscow, and in the winter of 1939–40 had written the history of the Bund. In the spring of 1940 he started—according to Faynsilber—to write the history of the Jewish trade union movement in Poland.[53] For the time between January and early July 1940, however, there are no written notes from Erlich, and in the text itself he only mentions in passing the trade unions. It is impossible to verify whether he did indeed write the history of the unions. The 'incredible history of the Polish Bund', however, is easily identifiable as the text written between late 1939 and early 1940.

Obviously, this party history is different from any similar effort undertaken by party historians or retired party politicians. The NKVD did not let Erlich write as he wished in regard to content and method, but rather made him write in order to provide a document they could use for their own purposes: to justify their persecutions. The text is clearly organized around questions or cues put to the author by the NKVD.[54] Thus the overall structure of his writing is not homogeneous. Passages containing facts and figures about the structure of the Bund alternate with explanations of its political programme. Notes and underlinings added by the NKVD show the latter's special interest in anything concerning the Bund's attitude to the KPP, Comintern, or the Soviet Union.

The first and longest part of Erlich's two-part history consists of seventy-eight sheets and is dated 14 November 1939. Erlich went over it again that day and also on 16 and 23 November, making some additions and corrections.[55] Within this part there are six sections, each one dealing with a different and obviously predetermined topic: the make-up of the Central Committee of the Bund; the Bund's newspapers; the party's actual work; relations between the Bund and other political parties in Poland; the Bund's relationship with the Socialist International; and its relationship with the Polish government.[56]

Erlich begins with the Bund's Central Committee. He lists people elected to the committee at the Bund's last congress in 1935, giving their age, occupation, function, and the position they took during the 1920s on the Bund's joining the Comintern or the Socialist International.[57] Heading his list is Noah Portnoy, the grand old man of the Bund and for many years its chairman. (Here a constantly recurring NKVD question comes up for the first time: 'Where is he now?')

After Portnoy, who during the inter-war years was more of an honorary head, Erlich mentions himself and Alter as the actual leaders of the party. Erlich

[53]  Faynsilber, 'Mitn khaver Erlikh', 125–6 = 119–21.

[54]  According to the responsible official at the KGB archives, none of these questions exists in writing.                                                                    [55]  File 839, vol. 3, pp. 1–172.

[56]  In D. Beyrau's words, neither in Polish nor in any western language does there exist 'a description [of the Bund's inter-war history] worthy of the subject'; see Beyrau, 'Antisemitismus und Judentum in Polen, 1918–1939', *Geschichte und Gesellschaft*, 8 (1982), 212. The fifth and thus far last volume of the Yiddish *Geshikhte fun Bund* (New York, 1981) deals only with events up to the thirty-fifth anniversary of the Bund in 1932. Erlich's notes are even more important, since they deal with the 1930s.

[57]  File 839, vol. 3, pp. 1–3.

describes his own time in Petrograd (1917–18), which had already been discussed in his interrogations. He states that by 1919 he had corrected his original assessment of the October Revolution as 'purely peasant' and arrived at the opinion that 'There has been no larger change in the history of mankind than the October Revolution, and the whole of the international proletariat has to defend it all over the world.'

The NKVD's comment at the mention of Wiktor Alter—'Where is he now? Find out!'—shows that news of his arrest and subsequent detention in Łuck from November 1939 had not yet reached these officials in Moscow. This is surprising, since Alter had been arrested on 26 September. Erlich proceeds to name nine more Central Committee members, as well as numerous former members.

Under the heading 'Organs of the Press', Erlich lists the Yiddish dailies and weeklies of the Bund and its Polish papers from 1918 on.[58] He points out that much sensitive material which would immediately have been censored if it had been in Polish could pass as long as it was in Yiddish. He remarks: 'To talk about the tendency of our papers means to talk about the ideological basis of our party, only we had to be extremely careful with what we wrote.'[59] Here Erlich touches on the Bund's position on the Communists and the Soviet Union (a subject on which he expands further in later texts, of 20 December 1939 and 5 January 1940):

People say the Bund's papers fought against the Communist movement. That is right. But this fight against it had been forced upon us by the Communist movement itself. . . . Today, and after the Communist Party of Poland has been dissolved, we look at the Comintern's motivation for doing so and we can easily see that those terrible KPP methods of fighting were dictated by a third force whose interest it was to ruin the workers' movement.[60]

What may appear confusing today was then a necessary and intricate balancing act: Erlich is attempting simultaneously to criticize the Communists and express solidarity with them. This effort also underlay many of his statements during the inter-war years. It represented the typical conflict of leftist socialists who accepted, in principle, the ideological essentials of the Soviet system but did not want to close their eyes to undemocratic and even inhuman practices.

Continuing, Erlich explains that the Bund's newspapers, in accordance with the party line, had always accepted the achievements of the Soviet Union, particularly its nationalities policy, but they had also voiced their doubts about the odds for success of the planned Jewish autonomous region of Birobidzhan in the Soviet Far East. The Bundists believed the Jewish people of the Soviet Union would not want to move to Birobidzhan, because they did not suffer from unemployment or oppression as a nation.[61] The Bund's press, with Erlich as

---

[58] The name of the Polish magazine *Walka* (which he writes in Cyrillic and Latin letters) changes in the typescript into *Zolka* (ibid. 10).

[59] Ibid.          [60] Ibid. 12–13.          [61] Ibid. 16–17.

editor-in-chief of the *Folkstsaytung* being one of its leading spokesmen, also took a critical view of the splitting of the workers' movement by the Soviet Union. Erlich writes:

The Comintern's fight, backed by the authority of the Soviet Union, against the whole socialist movement, which with a different policy could easily have been turned into a pillar of the Soviet Union, was in our opinion a mistake. . . . This policy was responsible also for the impatience in the Soviet Union itself even towards those socialists who had clearly expressed their wish to contribute to the development of the Soviet Union.[62]

Erlich comments here on an event that occurred less than three months earlier and writes of the critical assessment of the Hitler–Stalin pact that he published in the *Folkstsaytung*. With reference to recent events in western Ukraine and Belarus, he revises his position.[63] These 'recent events' are probably the positive welcome that Ukrainians, Belarusians, and, in some cases, Jews gave the Red Army after their sufferings under the policy of polonization. In this context, he also mentions an interview with Voroshilov, who pointed out that the Polish refusal to let Soviet troops cross its territory had contributed to the German–Soviet non-aggression treaty. 'We thought that these accusations against Poland were justified,' Erlich writes.[64] He adds that he was not able to say so in the *Folkstsaytung* at the time and puts the blame on Polish censorship, declaring that 70 per cent of the newspapers were openly or secretly confiscated. (Comments the NKVD: 'Outrageous lie!')

This part of the text was apparently of particular interest to the NKVD, as indicated by extensive underlining, some question marks, and often quite cynical comments.[65] In a way, this attention sufficiently answers Erlich's question 'Are friendly relations with the Soviet Union really incompatible with some criticism of some particular measures?'[66] We know today that under a tyrant such as Stalin, they were, indeed, incompatible. But Erlich still wanted to discuss specific Soviet measures, and perhaps even to convince his opponents on particular points. Still, he seems not to have held out much hope of that.

For the third topic of his November 1939 writings, Erlich turns to the actual work of the Bund in Poland.[67] One of the most important tasks was to gain new members and new subscribers for its papers. For young recruits, the party organized courses in ideology and politics. With regard to the unions, Erlich states that in Poland and Russia, political parties had come into existence before the trade unions, and the Bund, like all left-wing parties, had been 'forced' to focus its attention on union work (a remark in the margin reads: 'How is that to be understood, "were forced"?'[68]).

In order to support the Jewish national cultural movement, the Bund contributed a great deal to the work of the Central Jewish School Organization (known by the acronym 'Tsisho'). Erlich describes the Central Committee's

---

[62] File 839, vol. 3, 17.     [63] Ibid. 18.          [64] Ibid. 20.          [65] Ibid. 16–20.
[66] Ibid. 18.                  [67] Ibid. 21–9.                              [68] Ibid. 22.

discussions about the nature of Tsisho, an organization in which so many Bundists were active. Should it be generally national, like the parallel Ukrainian movement, or democratic, or restricted to the working class? According to Erlich, the programmatic work of the Bund was mainly concerned with the national question, and in particular with the principle of dictatorship of the proletariat and national cultural autonomy. He does not, however, elaborate here on this point.

With regard to the Bund's dealings with the outside world, Erlich states clearly that its stance towards the Zionist idea was crucial. He points to three periods when the Zionists enjoyed particular support: in 1924–6, during an economic crisis in Poland; in 1929, after attacks on Jewish settlers in Palestine; and, finally, after Hitler came to power in Germany in 1933, throwing the Jews of Poland into despair.[69] The Bund labelled Zionist hopes for a free life in Palestine 'illusions'. Bundists instead believed that antisemitism could be overcome at home, in Poland, but only through a total change in the social conditions, along the lines of the Soviet model.

The party was active in official institutions and also on an extra-parliamentary level. The Bund published and held meetings, both activities quite legal, if sometimes hampered. As another institution in which the Bundists took an active interest until 1926, Erlich mentions the Health Insurance Association.[70] The Bund took part in elections to the Sejm, the city councils, and in *kehilot*, although not regularly. Besides working within the parliamentary system, the Bund used rallies and especially strikes as means of the political struggle, organized together with non-Jewish union bodies wherever possible. Only in 1936, after the Przytyk pogrom, and in 1937, after introduction of the so-called ghetto benches at Polish universities, did the Bund organize strikes and rallies on its own, but some other groups, such as Polish workers, also joined in. Erlich explains that the atmosphere became very tense as a result of Hitler's rise to power and the Spanish Civil War; antisemitism grew, particularly in smaller towns. Campaigns for the regional elections of 1938–9 were already strongly influenced by the threat of war, he writes.[71]

Opening his discussion of the Bund's relations with other political parties, in particular with the Polish Socialist Party (PPS), Erlich reminds his readers of the general need for small parties to seek co-operation with other groups. For the Bund, only other socialist parties could be an option; Erlich rejects any idea of a coalition with bourgeois partners. He records that relations with the PPS were 'dynamic' and, in addition, developed differently at the leadership and local levels. The relationship between the two parties had been 'worse than cold' after 1918. The amalgamation of the Polish and Jewish unions in 1921, later joined by the German and Ukrainian unions in Poland, made some co-operation with the PPS inevitable, although 'not central'. After 1927, when the PPS again ended up on the opposition benches, they, the Bund, and the German and Ukrainian Social Democrats decided to work together in the Sejm election campaign of 1928. But because of

[69] Ibid. 24.                    [70] Ibid. 25.                    [71] Ibid. 25–9.

the rising tide of nationalism in its own ranks, the PPS later abandoned this
policy. Joint tickets for the regional elections of 1938–9 failed again because of the
PPS's refusal to participate. Erlich states that after the beginning of 1938 hardly
any contacts remained between the two parties. The only other potential partners
for the Bund that Erlich mentions were the short-lived Socialist Workers' Party,
led by Bolesław Drobner, and the German Social Democrats in Poland. Only 'formal contacts' existed with Po'alei Tsion Left, a radical Zionist socialist party.[72]

Erlich's notes on the Socialist International were apparently of much more
interest to the NKVD than any of the previous sections. Erlich's statement that
the question of the Bund's international participation had led to much upheaval in
the party is underlined in red.[73] Before the Bund finally joined the Socialist
International in 1930, Erlich had already attended its conferences as a correspond-
ent for the *Folkstsaytung*, in 1923 in Hamburg, 1925 in Marseilles, and 1928 in
Berlin. As a delegate of a member party, he writes that he then participated in
1931 in Hamburg (actually it was in Vienna) and 1933 in Paris and also took part
in meetings of the Executive Committee such as the one in Zurich in 1933. The
Polish government refused the Bund delegates passports to attend the committee's
May 1938 meeting, according to Erlich.[74]

Another point of importance for the NKVD was what Erlich had to say about
his meetings with *émigré* Russian Mensheviks at international conferences. Erlich
writes: 'My first political meeting with the Mensheviks took place in the framework of the Socialist International.' The comment in the margin reads: 'He lies—
that was much earlier.' The significance of this exchange is unclear. For Erlich,
those meetings with old comrades had a certain ambiguity: on the one hand he
met again friends from his time in St Petersburg, but on the other there was a considerable ideological distance between the Mensheviks and the Bund. 'Of course,
I had many talks with certain Mensheviks about many issues. But except for a
certain kind of depression that always comes from meeting people who are cut off
and excluded from real life, not much else stayed with me from these talks. I can
remember only some of them.'[75]

Erlich tries to answer questions about whom the Mensheviks represented and
whether there was still support for them in the Soviet Union, but in his opinion
they were only a party of emigrants, except perhaps for 'some friends living at
several different places in the Soviet Union, to which they have been confined'.
Here again the comment appears: 'He lies.'[76] Erlich is also asked about talks on
peculiarities in the work of socialist parties in Poland, taking into account that
they worked in a country bordering on the Soviet Union, but he cannot recall any
discussions about this.

'There is only one more question left for me to answer,' Erlich continues, referring to the question of relations between the Bund and Polish

---

[72] File 839, vol. 3, pp. 31–7.   [73] Ibid. 38.   [74] Ibid. 40.   [75] Ibid. 40–2.   [76] Ibid. 43.

authorities.[77] He first comments that the Bund, like any other legally operating party, had contact with representatives of the state, for instance when registering public events or official subgroups, publishing, or rejecting repressive measures against the party or protesting against attacks on Jews. Erlich reports a discussion in 1919 with President Moraczewski after severe antisemitic excesses in Poland. A year later, representatives of the Bund intervened again in President Daszyński's office after Bundists had been arrested. By 1926 two more talks had taken place with the Home Secretary about obstructions to the party's work, though with no results.[78] Another three sets of talks occurred at the ministerial level after that: together with Kluszińska, a PPS member of the Sejm, in 1936; after the pogroms in Mińsk Mazowiecki in the same year; and in 1939, when Bundists of the Warsaw city council twice attempted to confer with Education Minister Świętosławski about the introduction of ghetto benches for Jewish university students—'but the Secretary of State found nothing better to say than that we should advise the students to stop refusing to comply with the order', Erlich records.[79] In March 1939 representatives of the Bund appealed to the Employment Minister when 15,000 Polish Jews who had been expelled from Germany were being held under abominable conditions at the Polish border. The Bund asked that at least the children be released, but, as with all previous requests, this, too, was refused.[80]

Several times during the 1930s, Erlich writes, the Bund was summoned to the political department of the Home Office or the Warsaw district council. The topics discussed included the banning of cultural, educational, and sports groups within the Bund, the banning of meetings and events, arrests, and passport refusals. According to Erlich, on two of these occasions the authorities tried to pressure the Bund into adopting a specific policy. In the first case, in 1934, the Bund had been negotiating with the KPP about forming a united front. During one of these meetings a joint statement was prepared at Wiktor Alter's apartment. After the police got hold of this paper, Erlich was interrogated. Warsaw's chief of police, Runge, threatened to repress the Bund if the agreement were signed. Erlich asked Runge why the government, which had never cared much about bloody infighting within the Jewish working class, had now suddenly intervened. Runge replied that the government feared that the Jewish example would revolutionize the Polish workers. He gave the Bund forty-eight hours to consider its options. But by the deadline the problem had solved itself: under pressure from its Politburo, the KPP pulled out of the deal.[81]

The second attempt at blackmailing the Bund came in 1939, when the Bundist Fajner was arrested because of 'tactless' remarks he had made in the city council of Cracow. A member of the government, Sawicki, voiced his opinion that the Bund was in effect sabotaging the Polish government's emigration policy (which was aimed at solving the Jewish question by encouraging Jews to leave the country).

[77] Ibid. 48–62: 48.    [78] Ibid. 49–50.    [79] Ibid. 51.
[80] Ibid. 51–2.                              [81] Ibid. 54–5.

He now wanted to link Fajner's release to a promise by the Bund that it would change its stance on the emigration issue.[82] In this context, Erlich also mentions violent attacks on Bundists, and he suspects official circles of responsibility for them. During the 1937 May Day parade a bomb exploded, and in September of the same year the Bund's headquarters were attacked. Around the same time, the newspaper *Kurier poranny*, which was closely connected with the government, published increasingly ugly written attacks on the Bund.[83]

Again Erlich touches on the Bundists' difficulties in acquiring passports for travelling abroad. After 1938 no more passports were issued for politically motivated trips. He had once planned to go on vacation to Riga with his family to see his father-in-law, the noted historian Simon Dubnow. He obtained the papers only after a formal invitation from Riga, and his travel route was restricted.[84]

So why, then, was the Bund not banned like the Communist Party of Poland? Erlich answers realistically that his party was much less of a threat to the Polish government: 'The Bund is only one of several parties of only one of several national minorities that, taken together, do not represent more than 7 per cent of the whole population of the country.' The Bund only became dangerous where it tried to enter the world of the Polish workers, publishing Polish-language newspapers, and in those cases the official response was immediate and strict repression. He sums up: 'That is the only reason why the Bund could exist legally. But its whole existence during the last twenty years in Poland was a constant struggle against arbitrariness, nearly constant repression, and persecution, a struggle for sheer legal existence.'[85] Members of the Bund were frequently arrested and held in custody, but not Erlich or Alter—according to Erlich, because they were so well known abroad.[86] Again, their reputation was probably an important consideration for Stalin and his henchmen, as well. But the old hatred against the Bund, as a Jewish party of the 'third road' between communism and socialism, must have been even more vital. The roots of this hatred can be traced back to the time of the Russian Social Democratic Workers' Party, which held its first congress in Mińsk in 1898, one year after the Bund came into being. The Bundists played an important role at the Mińsk assembly and their alliance with the Mensheviks against Lenin and his followers was not forgotten.

Some additions and corrections follow Erlich's notes from 14 November 1939. He writes that the Central Committee of the Bund, at its last meeting in Warsaw before the departure on 6–7 September of the more prominent members, had authorized two members who stayed behind, Blum and Klog, to create a new central body of the party and appoint new members.[87] Blum and Klog did indeed later organize the underground work of the Bund in the Warsaw ghetto and during the ghetto uprising. He then names four more members of the Central Committee who were ill and thus had not been very active in its work. Emanuel Sherer, for

[82] File 839, vol. 3, p. 55.      [83] Ibid. 58–9.         [84] Ibid. 59.
[85] Ibid. 61–2.                   [86] Ibid. 162.          [87] Ibid. 142.

instance, had suffered from a mysterious nervous disease for three years that had rendered him incapable of work for the entire previous year: 'His wife, who is totally dedicated to him in a nearly hysterical manner, is pregnant. His arrest would mean a double (triple) catastrophe.'[88]

On 16 November Erlich again discusses the measures the Bund took against the waves of antisemitic propaganda and campaigns that steadily gained strength from the winter of 1935–6 on. He writes about a leaflet in Polish put out by the Central Committee of the Bund and, after some struggle with the censors, distributed all over Poland; unions helped to distribute 450,000 copies. But the Bund, PPS, and unions also distributed leaflets at the regional level in which they all called for a battle against antisemitism. These were often confiscated. The Jewish school organization arranged an exhibition on Jews in Poland, illustrating decades of Jewish presence 'in order to show the place of the Jews in the life of the country'. In this context, the Bund planned a conference about antisemitic attacks, to be held together with Polish workers' organizations. On the eve of the conference and exhibition, however, both were banned as a threat to the state.[89] Erlich also writes more about solidarity actions with the Polish Jews deported from Germany and being held in Zbąszyn. In co-operation with 'radical Polish intellectuals', information sessions were organized. The Bund also helped materially and sent teachers to Zbąszyn.[90]

Adding to his earlier remarks on the relationship between the Bund and the Polish state, Erlich mentions numerous trials against Bundists that he had attended as the defendants' attorney. Particularly notable was the 1937 trial of a former Bund member, Chaskielewicz, in Kałuszyn. Chaskielewicz, who belonged to the Bund's youth organization until joining the army, killed a Polish sergeant while in a state of severe psychological disturbance, Erlich writes. The public prosecutor accused the Bund of educating Jewish youth in a spirit of hatred toward the Polish army and state. A psychiatric diagnosis found the accused to be totally incapable of responsible actions, but it was withdrawn after pressure from the investigating authority and a second expert declared Chaskielewicz partly responsible. An 'atmosphere of great scandal' ensued, but Chaskielewicz was sentenced to death.[91]

Erlich criticizes the PPS's close links with the Polish state. According to him, the PPS felt itself to be a co-founder of the Second Polish Republic and, with others, to be responsible for the fate of the state itself, regardless of the government of the day. Several times members of the PPS had rendered diplomatic assistance to official Poland. For example, in 1926, when the PPS was the opposition party, Herman Diamand helped negotiate a trade agreement with Germany. After the German–Polish mutual non-aggression treaty, the influence of the PPS in Polish foreign policy diminished, as Erlich states, but in 1939 the government nevertheless tried to exploit the PPS's links to the French and British Left for its own

---

[88] Ibid. 143.    [89] Ibid. 147–50.    [90] Ibid. 149–50.    [91] Ibid. 160–2.

purposes. The trip of Mieczysław Niedziałkowski, one of the PPS leaders, who was invited to attend the last Congress of the British Labour Party before the outbreak of the Second World War, received strong support from the same government that refused passports to the Bundists.[92]

The second large block of text, thirty-seven handwritten pages, which Erlich wrote on 3 December 1939 and 5 January 1940, first contains a 'critique of measures of the Comintern and the Soviet government'. The Bund naturally knew about 'the enormous influence exercised by the Soviet government in the Comintern through the Communist Party', but, he writes, he nevertheless prefers to differentiate between the Soviet government and the Comintern. Erlich describes how the establishment of the Comintern was followed with great interest by a large proportion of the workers' movement (the comment in the margin reads: 'like, for instance, by Erlich').[93] But the chance of creating an international organization that would isolate revisionist forces and enhance revolutionary socialism had been lost, he adds. 'On the contrary: the Comintern declared an even more bitter war on the left wing of the socialist movement than it had already done on the right and it destroyed the left wing with the twenty-one points [conditions for joining the Comintern] and forced a large part of it out and into the right camp.' The NKVD comments: 'Libel!' Erlich continues:

In Russia, where the workers' parties until 7 February 1917 existed only as an idea or at most as an apparatus, this policy led, indeed, to the creation of a party (the Bolsheviks) that won the trust of the working class, in an atmosphere of war and revolution. In the west, however, where the Comintern had to deal with old and experienced parties founded long before, in most countries this policy drove the communists into isolation in the ranks of the socialist movement and weakened the left wing.[94]

Erlich sharply criticizes the slogan of social fascism, especially with regard to the German situation (here the NKVD remarks: 'That is the work of enemies inside the Communist Party of Germany'), and he asks, 'Indeed, would the victory of fascism in Germany have been possible, or at least, could Hitler have won so easily, if the German working class had not been so hopelessly divided into two nearly equally strong (and thus weak) parts?' From the very beginning, he points out, the Bund rejected any reformist tendencies, and any coalition with bourgeois partners had been ruled out. However, 'Social democracy was not the left wing of the petit bourgeoisie, let alone the left wing of fascism (social fascism).'[95]

The Bund also criticized the exaggerated role that centralization played in the Comintern's activities. Despite official statements to the contrary, Moscow's orders were often carried out against the will of many national sections, and Erlich thinks this is the reason for the frequent changes at the top of many parties. He also doubts the policy of popular fronts that was adopted in an about-face at the seventh congress of the Comintern in 1935. Erlich saw the Bund's success at the

---

[92] File 839, vol. 3, p. 174.     [93] Ibid. 199.     [94] Ibid. 200.     [95] Ibid. 201–3.

last local government elections in Poland as vindicating its policy of not joining coalitions with bourgeois liberals. The party had achieved brilliant results, taking the absolute majority of the Jewish vote in many cities, 'without the help of qualitatively extremely dubious Jewish democrats (unfortunately there are no better ones in Jewish society)'.[96]

In his criticism of the Soviet government, Erlich first deals with foreign policy and then with domestic policy. He believes that maintaining close diplomatic contacts with representatives of the 'capitalist world' proved totally wrong. He is strongly critical of the warm welcome that Italian architects and engineers received in the Soviet Union after fascism had already won in Italy and the entire Italian labour movement had been wiped out. Again he mentions his criticism of the Hitler–Stalin pact: 'Today I believe that the Soviet Union, unfortunately, could not have acted differently—if we consider not only the policy of Poland and England but also the incredible Polish weakness that soon became evident during the German Blitzkrieg in Poland. And this weakness was probably known before, not only to Germany but also to the Soviet Union.'[97]

The main target of the Bund's criticism, however, was Soviet domestic policy, especially the persecution of socialists and even members of the Communist Party itself. Like Otto Bauer, the Bund believed the Bolsheviks to be the historical party of the Russian working class, but in its eyes the repression of differently minded people was unacceptable. According to Erlich, socialists outside the Soviet Union felt increasingly bitter, and in the Soviet Union itself the intolerance toward socialists 'was bound to lead to restrictions of freedom of political thought in general. It was because of the fight against the socialists that the battle against dissidents in the ranks of the Communist Party itself started and finally led to those well-documented trials against old Bolsheviks.' The devastating comment of the NKVD here: 'Trotskyism'.[98]

Erlich goes on to say that the Moscow trials had deeply disturbed organized workers and democratic intellectuals in Poland. People retreated into passivity, and sympathy with the Soviet Union vanished. For many, this readjustment was a 'personal tragedy'. The Bund did not gloat, but, on the contrary, felt a deep sense of grief and pain. Although avidly read Soviet newspapers reported otherwise, nobody believed that the accused were guilty.

For us trials were an expression of that factional infighting inside the Soviet Communist Party and that intolerance I have discussed before. If that is a crime, we are guilty. But I do not believe this to be a crime. . . . At the end of September I ended up, quite by chance, in the region occupied by Soviet troops. For two weeks I could see for myself what went on. Even those superficial observations confirmed many of the positive things I and my comrades used to treasure about the Soviet Union. But the fact of my arrest and custody (and is it only mine?) must also serve me, unfortunately, as confirmation of those darker sides of Soviet policy that we have always criticized.[99]

[96] Ibid. 206.        [97] Ibid. 210.        [98] Ibid. 213.        [99] Ibid. 216.

Even shortly before his arrest, he had urged his comrades in Pińsk not to renounce their Bund membership but to work loyally with the Soviet occupiers. 'I told them: We hope the Soviet power will tolerate the existence of the Bund, even though this is not very likely. And if they don't, we still will not, under any circumstances, carry out illegal work in a region under Soviet occupation.'[100]

Erlich considers his criticism of Soviet life and the constant battle with the Communist Party of Poland to be the reasons for his arrest. But the Bund, he affirms, had been prepared to co-operate with the Communists, and in some areas this co-operation had in fact materialized. Also, through all of its twenty years of existence in Poland, the Bund always took the view that the Soviet Union was the only country in the world that had actually solved the most urgent problems of the Jewish workers.

'I do not feel any other guilt, neither for myself nor for my party.'[101] With this sentence, Henryk Erlich's writings of the winter of 1939–40 on the history of the inter-war Polish Bund come to an end. But in the summer of 1940 he took up his work once more. On thirty-four handwritten pages dated 5 July, Erlich again characterizes the structure of his party and its position on the Jewish question in Poland.[102]

At its very first congress after the First World War, the Bund agreed on a statute that allowed anybody to join who accepted the political programme and tactical principles of the party. He makes clear the close links with trade unions, which mirrored the fact that, according to him, the main base of Bundist groups in bigger cities were the trade unions. The local party committees were elected once a year at delegate conferences, in smaller towns at general meetings. Like the regional committees, the Central Committee was to be elected once a year, at the party's congress, by simple majority vote. 'The election lists were in fact put together according to the principle of proportional representation, so that the different tendencies present in the party should also be represented in its leading bodies.' One of the last congresses had created the Party Council, an advisory board to exist alongside the Central Committee. This council was also to be elected on the day of the party congress, and its advice was to be sought in particularly difficult matters or conflicts. The Central Committee was not obliged to follow its advice, but according to Erlich it always did. After the first congress it was decided that in the future the party congresses should be held no more often than every other year; in fact, they were held even less frequently.[103]

Next Erlich discusses the position of the Bund on the Jewish question. From the days of the Russian Empire, the Bund had argued 'against a common interest and possible joint actions with so-called world Jewry and against a representation at international Jewish conferences or institutions, not only those on national issues but also those concerned with the workers'. The Bund clearly saw Poland as the centre of its political action, and its co-operation was international in a

---

[100] File 839, vol. 3, p. 217.    [101] Ibid. 218.    [102] Ibid. 267–8.    [103] Ibid. 271–2.

comprehensive and not specifically Jewish way. The Jewish question, in the Bund's view, could only be solved where the Jewish masses lived and worked; any territorial options were rejected. Erlich lists five programmatic demands of his party:

1. total equality as citizens for all Jewish workers and members of the intelligentsia;
2. state funding to enable pauperized Jews to partake in productive work;
3. education in the mother tongue, i.e. Yiddish schools;
4. the right to use Yiddish as a language before courts and administrative authorities;
5. the national cultural autonomy of the Jewish people in Poland.[104]

With this last demand he returns to the project of Birobidzhan, stating that some Bundists believed that the culture of a small minority without its own territory was bound to perish, and these people therefore welcomed the Birobidzhan project. But this position did not find a majority at the Bund's 1935 congress. Most Bundists maintained that migration was a problem caused by poverty, unemployment, and repression. The threat of assimilation was not a sufficient reason for migration.[105]

The Bund's relations with the Jewish community were constantly changing, in Erlich's description. He regards the Jewish *kehilot*, reintroduced in Poland after the First World War, as remnants of the old, Jewish autonomy in the pre-partition period. Polish law prescribed the upholding of religious autonomy as the first duty of the inter-war *kehilot*, but they actually carried out several other functions, such as social work and taxation. The Bund started to run in *kehilot* elections only in the mid-1920s, but with the agreement of the Central Committee it called off its participation in Warsaw, for example, after only a year or eighteen months, as Erlich writes. The Bund ran again in 1936, after a split vote by the Central Committee on the issue (seven to seven), when the Party Council gave the view that participation was advisable.[106]

Erlich describes the dire living conditions of the Jews in drastic terms. General conditions in Poland were marked by unemployment in the cities and landlessness in the country; hygienic and sanitary conditions in the urban working-class quarters and in the country he classifies as catastrophic. In addition to these general conditions, the Jews also suffered from national repression. The establishment of Polish guilds served to force out Jewish artisans as troublesome competitors. In an act of self-defence, the Jews set up committees and societies of their own such as ORT (Obshchestvo Razprostranenia Truda—the Organization for Occupational Retraining) to support apprenticeship training for the youth, and TOZ (Towarzystwo Ochrony Zdrowia—the Society for the Protection of Health) to improve the health of the Jewish people. But these bodies were mainly in the

[104] Ibid. 274–6.   [105] Ibid. 279.   [106] Ibid. 282.

hands of the petty bourgeoisie. Because of growing antisemitism, the Bund had to think over its decision not to co-operate with them. In the end, the Central Committee decided to stand by its principle. One reason was that leftist support might have frightened away American sponsors and could have acted as an invitation to repression by the authorities; another was the Bund's hesitation to support dangerous illusions or channel the activities of the working masses away from the political struggle.[107]

On 1 August 1940 Erlich added some notes on the Bund's newspapers, naming the editorial staff of the *Folkstsaytung* and its foreign and domestic correspondents, and on 15 September he turned to the Bund militia.[108] The Central Committee had approved the setting up of an armed body. Its models were the Austrian Schutzbund and the German (Communist) Rotfront and (Socialist) Reichsbanner. Its task was to provide security at events and public appearances, plus defensive action if fascist organizations should attack. Militias were organized regionally, rather than nation-wide. After attacks by policemen and hooligans on May Day, 1920, the first Bund militia was established in Warsaw to protect party headquarters and other buildings. The Bund militiamen came mainly from trade union groups; Erlich estimates their number for Warsaw alone at four to five hundred. Although possession of arms was prohibited in Poland, a very small proportion of the militia was nevertheless lightly armed. In the 1930s the Bund militiamen could be identified by their grey uniform jackets with a party badge on one arm and a grey cap. The leader of the Warsaw militia was Bernard Goldstein, who left the city together with all the other leading members of the Bund in September 1939 and joined the group around Wiktor Alter. But Goldstein soon returned to occupied Warsaw, where he went through the ghetto uprising and later the Warsaw uprising in 1944.[109]

Erlich's writing dated 26 December 1940 contains some details about the regional distribution of the Bund committees. The Central Committee believed the Bund was insufficiently represented in eastern Poland, except for Wilno, Grodno, and Białystok. But from 1935 on the Bund gained more and more support in all Polish cities. To confirm this, Erlich refers to the election results of 1938–9, when the Bund won 17 out of 20 Jewish seats in Warsaw, 11 out of 15 in Łódź, and 8 out of 9 in Lublin. Results in other cities were similar. Erlich puts the total membership at 15,000, organized in 250 regional groups. (The minimum number of members in a group was ten, 'if I am not mistaken'.) It seems Erlich was also questioned about the Bund's presence in the cities of western Ukraine and Belarus; he names sixteen towns of which the NKVD marked seven with a small tick in the typescript (Vilna, Białystok, Baranowicze, Brześć, Kowel, Przemyśl, and Lwów).[110]

---

[107] File 839, vol. 3, pp. 283–4.      [108] Ibid. 320–2, 324–30.
[109] See Bernard Goldstein, *The Stars Bear Witness* (New York, 1949).
[110] File 839, vol. 3, pp. 385–95.

A whole lesson about party generational conflicts can be learned from Erlich's notes dated 8 January 1940, when he writes about the Yugnt Bund-Tsukunft (Youth Bund Future), which in 1937 had celebrated its twentieth anniversary. Erlich's notes deal mostly with the limits of competence and relations between the youth organization and the party.[111] He writes that the party played 'an enormous role' in the life of the Yugnt Bund. In the party's view, the youth organization was to provide the party youth with a socialist education; in terms of the actual political struggle of the working class, the Yugnt Bund only needed to function as a 'helping organ of the party'. Independent expression was only accepted in questions concerning youth. Some members of the Yugnt Bund were unhappy with these restrictions and requested more freedom of action. In the end, the following formula was agreed on: 'The Yugnt Bund Tsukunft takes its ideological lead from the Bund. Although its members can, of course, discuss all questions of political life wherever they wish, in the centre, the regions, and at their meetings and conferences, they will in all these matters accept the final decision of the party.'[112] Only in cases of clear deviation from the general line of the party would the Bund interfere in areas where the Yugnt Bund was supposed to have full autonomy, for example, in questions of its own internal structure or its relations to other youth organizations. Erlich describes concrete forms of co-operation and concedes, finally, that this also served to revitalize the 'ideological stance' of the party. Delegates of the Bund took part at different levels of executive meetings of the Yugnt Bund in an advisory capacity. Delegates of the Yugnt Bund could also attend the Bund's executive meetings. They participated in meetings of the Party Council and preparatory meetings for party congresses as well.[113]

Next Erlich describes the internal structure of the Yugnt Bund. At the lowest organizational level there were the districts, or *krayzn*. Committees were elected in small towns by the general assembly and in larger cities by delegates from the *krayzn*. At the head of the youth organization stood a central committee elected at national meetings. The structure of the Yugnt Bund was thus parallel to that of the parent party.

Every year a campaign was launched to gain new members. Interested young people were organized into preparation groups, the Greens, before being listed as proper members of the Yugnt Bund. Here older members of the Yugnt Bund or even party members helped with 'supportive socialist teaching'; in big cities educational evening courses in general subjects were also available. Once a year around fifty or sixty young men and women were sent to so-called cadre courses, and summer camps were organized for a healthier life. Teenagers as young as 14 could join the Yugnt Bund. From 18 one could become a member of the Bund itself. To do so, prospective members needed references from two party members; members of the Yugnt Bund needed only a reference from their own

[111] Ibid. 396–403.     [112] Ibid. 398–9.     [113] Ibid. 399–400.

organization. The party retained 'the right to pick this or that activist from the Yungt Bund, if they needed one, and give them tasks to fulfil for the party', but in these matters the Central Committee had to agree beforehand.[114]

According to Erlich, the student groups of the Bund were of considerable importance. There was no central organization, only scattered groups of Bundist students at Polish universities, originally part of the Yugnt Bund. Their importance grew with the increase of militant antisemitism, from the mid-1930s. In view of the 'tragic situation' of the students at their various universities, the Bund then established direct links with them, and their representatives were often invited to discussions with the Central Committee.

With these notes about the Yugnt Bund 'this incredible history of the Polish Bund written down in a Soviet prison by Comrade Henryk Erlich' reaches its end. It is, above all, a moving human testimony. Erlich writes about what had been at the centre of his life for decades—his party, its goals, its ideals—but he had to write under conditions so unbearable that he eventually preferred to put an end to his own life.

There is no doubt that the circumstances of his NKVD custody greatly influenced the papers he left behind. These pages, even though they do not constitute a systematic or structured story of the Bund, form an extraordinarily important historical document in two ways: first, because they document the intellectual argument of the democrat Henryk Erlich with a system that was in many aspects his ideal but whose dictatorial and contemptuous traits, responsible for his arrest in the first place, he also detested deeply; and second, because they contain many details about the Polish Bund, especially during the last years before the Second World War. A proper academic analysis of the Bund's history after 1918 and its critical evaluation is surely something that Erlich himself would have wished.

*Translated by Uta Ruge*

[114] File 839, vol. 3, pp. 401–2.

# *Mayufes*: A Window on Polish–Jewish Relations

## CHONE SHMERUK

FOR centuries *mayufes* was part of the Polish–Jewish experience. In Polish dictionaries and other sources, *mayufes* is usually defined as 'a song sung by Jews at the Sabbath midday meal',[1] or 'a song sung by Jews at certain religious ceremonies';[2] a 'dance';[3] or even a 'ritual Jewish dance'.[4] According to Polish dictionaries *mayufes* derives from the opening words of the well-known Hebrew Sabbath *zemer* (song sung at the Sabbath table) *Mah yofis* ('How fair you are') (in modern Hebrew pronunciation, *Mah yafit*).

None of these definitions takes note of a crucial feature of the concept of *mayufes* in Polish–Jewish culture, however. When a *mayufes* was sung or danced by a Jew (or someone imitating a Jew), it was not at the family Sabbath table. Rather, it was performed before a Polish audience, without any relation to the context or significance of the original Jewish *zemer*.

The Polish historian Janusz Tazbir paints a vivid picture of the *mayufes* show in his discussion of the 'entertaining character who dances the . . . *mayufes*', describing the Jew who is performing as a 'quasi-jester, a crude type who abuses the Polish language in the most amusing away'.[5] The characterization of the

This article first appeared in Polish in a Festschrift in honour of Professor J. A. Gierowski's seventieth birthday entitled *The Jews in Poland*, ed. A. K. Paluch, trans. David Weinfeld (Cracow: Jagiellonian University, Research Center on Jewish History and Culture in Poland, 1992); I presented an expanded version as a lecture on 30 Dec. 1993 in memory of my teacher Professor Ben-Zion Dinur. I would like to thank David Weinfeld for his excellent Hebrew translation, and David Assaf, Israel Bartal, Avraham Greenbaum, and Natan Cohen for their very helpful comments and references, which have been incorporated in the published version. The Hebrew article appeared in *Tarbiz*, 63/1 (1993–4) and was translated into English by Anna Barber. Special thanks to Dr Eugenia Prokóp-Janiec of the Jagiellonian University, without whose help I would have been unable to obtain the many Polish sources used in the article.

[1] J. Karlowicz, A. Kryński, and W. Niedzwiecki (eds.), *Słownik języka polskiego*, ii (Warsaw, 1902), 852. The form *majofis* also appears in parentheses. The dictionary *Nowa księga przysłów i wyrazów przysłowiowych polskich*, iv (Warsaw, 1978), has precisely the same definition on p. 208. A similar explanation can be found in E. Orzeszkowa (ed.), *Z jednego strumienia, nowele* (Warsaw, 1960), 375.

[2] W. Doroszewski and S. Skorupka (eds.), *Słownik języka polskiego*, iv (Warsaw, 1958), 389.

[3] M. Brzezina, *Polszczyzna Żydów* (Warsaw, 1986), 372.

[4] See also the references in J. Tuwim, *Dzieła*, iii: *Jarmark rymów* (Warsaw, 1958), 606.

[5] J. Tazbir, 'Żydzi w opinii staropolskiej', *Świat panów Pasków: Eseje i studia* (Łódź, 1986),

performer as a 'quasi-jester' also includes the persona adopted by the Jew while performing the *mayufes*. Although Tazbir does not cite his sources, the context indicates that he was writing about a phenomenon known as early as the sixteenth or seventeenth century. Although I have not yet discovered any references to *mayufes* before 1763, the later sources show that this dubious form of entertainment—Jews singing or dancing *mayufes* amid heckling by Poles—had been common for some time.[6]

The sources quoted above, as well as Tazbir's comments, do not reveal that *mayufes* represented a traumatic experience for Polish Jewry.[7] As far as Jews were concerned, *mayufes* lost its original meaning as the name of a Sabbath song and was redefined in response to its Polish usage. Within the Jewish world, *mayufes* became a term for toadying or coerced conformity to the expectations of Polish gentry. At times it referred specifically to the degrading abuse of a Jew. The basis for the change was the supposedly entertaining role of the Jew who performed the *mayufes* in response to demands from a non-Jewish public.

This article is an attempt to illuminate the question of *mayufes* from both sides, primarily on the basis of Yiddish and Polish literature. Juxtaposing Jewish sources with Polish texts (which usually do not reveal any awareness of Jewish sensitivities on the subject) may help us to reconstruct, if only in part, a somewhat obscure chapter in the history of Polish–Jewish relations. There is no evidence of *mayufes* beyond the boundaries of the Polish–Jewish encounter.

*Mah yafit* is an ode to the Sabbath composed in twenty-four four-line stanzas. Its verses paraphrase the laws and customs of the day and allude to a number of aggadic motifs relating to Sabbath observance. The song was traditionally sung in Ashkenazi homes at the dinner-table on Friday nights between the fish and meat courses.[8] The first line is an excerpt from the Song of Songs (7: 7): 'How fair and pleasant you are, O loved one, in delights!' The 'loved one', the 'you' that is 'fair and pleasant', is the Sabbath and all its pleasures, such as fish and meat. *Mah yafit*

---

216–17; the article appeared as 'Obraz Żyda w opini polskiej XVI–XVIII wieku', in his *Mity i stereotypy w dziejach Polski* (Warsaw, 1991), 69–70.

[6] A Jewish dance called *majouques* is mentioned by the French engineer Jean-Claude Pingeron in a letter sent from Zamość on 19 Sept. 1763. Pingeron describes a celebration at the house of Prince Czartoryski in which Jews participated. He writes about the end of the festivities, 'Cette cérémonie finie une fois, les meilleurs danseurs d'entre eux dansèrent des danses juives, des polonaises, des cosaques et des majouques' (*Un épisode de la vie des Juifs polonais au dix-huitième siècle: Hommage de Salomon Reinach à M. Joseph Deremberg* (Paris, 1891), 6). This *majouques* is clearly a *mayufes* dance, but the nature of the celebration is less certain. When Gelber republished the French source, he appealed for further information about the event -it described (N. M. Gelber, 'Eine jüdische Huldigung in Polen im 18. Jahrhundert', in *Mitteilungen zur jüdischen Volkskunde*, 21 (1919), 32). I have not found any response to his appeal, however. Gelber's source is also mentioned by J. Stuchevsky, *Hakleizmerim: Toledoteihem, oraḥ-hayeihem viyetsiroteihem* (Jerusalem, 1959), 67.

[7] See J. Tazbir, 'Cruel Laughter', in *The Jews in Poland*, i (Cracow, 1992), 93.

[8] J. D. Eisenstein (ed.), *A Digest of Jewish Laws and Customs* (Heb.) (New York, 1917), 204.

was probably written in the thirteenth century; little is known about its author apart from his name, Mordechai bar Yitshak, which appears in acrostic form in the *zemer*.[9] Of the many sacred Hebrew songs, poems, and hymns written for the Sabbath, only about forty have entered the canon, which consists of the selection of *zemirot* included in the prayer-books of Ashkenazi Jews. To this day, *Mah yafit* often appears in prayer-books and *bentsherls* (collections of songs, blessings, and other liturgical texts for festive meals).

*Mah yafit* was the only Sabbath song to play a formative role in the Polish Jewish experience, but although one of the Polish literary sources unsuccessfully attempts to quote the opening lines,[10] it was not the original text that attracted the interest of the Polish public. The *mayufes* of the eighteenth and nineteenth centuries was a song sung in Polish whose appeal was based on its characteristic instrumental accompaniment and dance. The main attraction, however, was the entertainment provided by a Jew or a performer imitating a Jew.

The pronunciation of *mayufes* preserves the local Yiddish pronunciation of Hebrew at the time, enabling us to identify the geographic boundaries of the phenomenon in Poland. The pronunciation 'mayofes'[11] would point to the Lithuanian–Belarusian dialect (before the division of Poland); the word *mayufes* points to the Yiddish spoken in Mazovia, Wielkopolska, Małopolska, Volhynia, and Podolia.

Jewish sources refer to the *zemer* as 'a special age-old song, very beautiful to listen to'.[12] A number of *zemer* melodies have been preserved, and the musical setting of the original *Mah yafit* probably had a strong rhythm, given the numerous references to dances to the tune of *mayufes*. In the available sources, there is no evidence that dances accompanied the singing of songs at the Sabbath table. Thus, *mayufes*-dancing before a Polish audience probably refers to the coarse, comic movements of the performer, part of an improvised mock-ritual.[13]

[9] *Zemirot shel Shabbat* (Sabbath Songs), ed. and annotated by Naftali ben Menachem (Jerusalem, 1948–9), 26–30, 135–40.

[10] *Nasza ziemia: Przygrywka przez Władysława Chodkiewicza* (St Petersburg, 1859), 206.

[11] See n. 1 above, and A. Z. Idelsohn, *Jewish Music in its Historical Development* (New York, 1944), 384–5; 'Sora kum tancen *majoches*' (Sarah come dance *majoches*), S. Malewicz, 'Betleem na Białej Rusi', *Lud*, 22 (1924), 134. In *Nowa księga*, iii (Warsaw, 1972), however, on p. 989, the proverb goes 'Żeby tobie Żyd *majofis* śpiewał', although a correction notes that this should be *majufes*. Jacob Halevi Lipschitz describes an encounter between Jews and the brother of Tsar Nicholas, Prince Michael Pavlovitch, in Wilkomierz in 1848. Wilkomierz is in the Kovno district, where the Lithuanian–Belarusian dialect of Yiddish was spoken. The prince made fun of the Jews, shouting, 'Zhid! Mah-yafit umah na'amt Shabbat [the first line of the *zemer*], chi tak?' The passage indicates that Prince Michael knew what he was referring to, but the local Jews were simply offended by the cry of 'zhid' and paid no attention to the rest of his words. Lipschitz himself did not respond to this use of *Mah yafit* (*Zikhron Ya'akov: Historiah yehudit beRusiah uvePolin*, 2nd edn. (Bnei Brak, 1967–8), i. 236–8).

[12] Eisenstein (ed.), *Jewish Laws and Customs*, 204.

[13] Some works on the musical dimensions of *mayufes* are Idelsohn, *Jewish Music in its Historical Development*, 384–5, and on the melody, 390. (Idelsohn claims that the tune became popular in the

It seems likely that some *mayufes* performers also sang the original Hebrew version of the song, regaling their audience with an exotic, incomprehensible language. This is suggested by the existence of faulty Hebrew excerpts found in Polish sources. It may be that many Jewish Sabbath songs, not only *Mah yafit*, were called *mayufes*. In at least one case another Sabbath song—*Yom zeh mekhubad* ('This day is honoured') with only minor textual distortions, was presented as *mayufes*, as we see from the following song from Felix Szober's popular 1878 farce *Barnaba Fafuła i Józo Grojseszyk na wystawie paryzkiej* (Barnaba Fafuła and Józo Grojseszyk at the Paris exhibition):

[*Aua appears on stage; the orchestra plays a* mayufes.]

### Mayufes

| | |
|---|---|
| Jam se chybot mikiel jumen, | This day is honoured above all days, |
| Kibaj siubes cyraj lumen, | For on it the Rock of Ages rested. |
| Tajszes jumen tajse malachtichu, | Six days shall you do your labour |
| Jom cha szwitaj taj che echu, | And the seventh day is for your Lord. |
| Szabes taj sanse bojmeluchu, | The Sabbath: do no labour on it |
| Kikotuchu tajses jumen. | For He did all in six days. |
| Jam se chybot mikiel jumen, | This day is honoured above all days, |
| Kibaj siubes cyraj lumen.[14] | For on it the Rock of Ages rested. |

Some remnants of other *mayufes* texts are also preserved, as in Klemens Junosza's story *The Musicians*, in which Sadlowski, a squire, arranges for a Jewish *klezmer* to play at a wedding, offering the following examples:

| | |
|---|---|
| Zagraj—no Żydku— | Play something, Jew-boy |
| Szabas, panie. | Sabbath, sir. |
| Kija na Żyda! | Give him a beating. |
| Zaraz panie.... | Right away, sir!... |
| Lachcium, ciachcium | Lachtzium, tzachtzium, |

Jewish communities of Poland and Germany in the 17th and 18th centuries.) Also M. Nulman, 'Ma Yafith: The Intriguing Fate of the Sabbath Table Hymn', *Journal of Jewish Music and Liturgy*, 1 (1976), 27–38 (musical notation for four different melodies appear on p. 33). Nulman claims it is difficult to know if the melody was accompanied by special choreography or merely by appropriate hand-movements and a few dance-steps. In N. Levin and V. Pasternak (eds.), *Zemirot Anthology* (New York, 1982), the musical notation for a number of different melodies appears on pp. 42–3. Interestingly enough, Chopin mentioned the *mayufes* in a letter written in 1831, where he writes of a Jewish violinist named Herz who regaled his audience with 'Polish music', a rendition of a *mayufes* (F. Niecks, *Frederic Chopin as a Man and Musician* (New York, 1873), i. 183). On pp. 48–9 Niecks includes an anecdote from 1824 that describes Chopin playing a *mayufes* for a group of Jewish merchants in Oborów.

   [14] F. Szober, *Barnaba Fafuła i Józo Grojseszyk na wystawie paryzkiej* (Warsaw, 1878), 119. The character who dances the *mayufes* is supposed to be a Jew in blackface. In an 1889 Polish-language production of Abraham Goldfaden's *Di Kishefmakherin* (The Witch), a *mayufes* was added to the original songs in the play (review by Hanets, *Hatsefirah*, 144 (1889), 591). Yosef Ofer, '"Mayufes", "Mah-yafit" "Veyom zeh mekhubad", *Tarbiz*, 63 (1993–4), 597.

| Bim, bam, bam! | Bim, bam, bam! |
| Gdy pan kaze | When the master orders, |
| To ja gram.[15] | A musician I am. |

The second stanza contains an illusion to the *mayufes*, as we see from the passage 'To the tune of *Mayufes*' that appears in Helena Mniszek's novel *Panicz* (Son of a Lord):

| Niech kto sobie co chce gada | Let everyone prattle as much as he likes |
| Lach tam ti dy ry buru | Lach tam ti dy ry buru |
| Bo co kadryl to parada | For every quadrille is a celebration |
| Lach tam ti dy ry bum.[16] | Lach tam ti dy ry bum. |

This song is sung by a Pole named Richard Denhoff, known in his own circle as a virtuoso performer of *mayufes*. During the rendition, Mniszek writes, 'Denhoff sang it in a comic vein, with great enthusiasm, using comic gestures and making typical faces'.[17]

Do these remnants of lyrics have a Jewish source? It is unlikely they were created by Jews; what is more probable is that they were attributed to Jews by Poles playing the part of Jews. Polish literature may nevertheless contain traces of original Jewish *mayufes* texts in Polish. Our evidence for the existence of such *mayufes* comes from Yiddish literature. In Israel Rabon's story *Mayufes* the following text appears entirely in Polish using the Hebrew alphabet:

| Ma-jufes, *adojni* pan, | How fair you are, my lord squire. |
| Pozdrawiam cie na caly *zman*. | I bless you for all time. |
| Niech ci Bóg posyla *man* | May God send manna from heaven |
| Dla ciebie *un* dla twego ród, | For you and all your countrymen, |
| Kosci dla psy, chleba dla lud, | A bone for your dog, bread for your people |
| Kasztany dla swini, obrok dla koni | Chestnuts for your pigs and fodder for your horses |
| I flaszka *sznapsa* dla Antoni.[18] | And a bottle of schnapps for Anthony. |

The macaronic text, which 'abuses the Polish language in the most amusing way', contains a few Yiddish words: *adoni* (my lord), *zman* (time), *man* (manna), *un* (and), and *sznapsa* (schnapps). It should be noted that in both this song and in the original Hebrew *zemer*, the word 'manna' is repeated a number of times; clearly the use of this word in the Polish text is deliberate.

[15] K. Junosza, *Szkice z natury* (Warsaw, 1908), 24.

[16] H. Mniszek, *Panicz*, ii (Kiev, 1912), 237.

[17] Ibid. 94. Similar success was enjoyed by a man named Siemieradzki (H. Rzewuski, *Denkwürdigkeiten des Pan Soplica* (Leipzig, n.d.), 107). This German translation of the Polish original includes an introduction by Löbenstein, who defines the word *mayufes* as a 'melody frequently played in Poland as a parody, a Polish imitation of a Jewish song'. It is likely that some of these virtuoso *mayufes* performers ended up as actors who specialized in parodying Jewish characters on the Polish stage in the 19th century.

[18] I. Rabon, 'Mayufes', *Haynt*, 126 (1 June 1930). This story, or 'novella', as its author calls it, was reprinted in *Di goldene Keyt*, 121 (1987), 124–32. The song appears on 131–2.

The parodic intent of the poem is obvious from the final three lines, which list schnapps and a variety of foods for both man and beast. Compare these with the traditional Sabbath dishes of fish and meat in the *zemer*.

In Rabon's story, a Jew serving in the Polish army fighting against the Bolsheviks explains where he heard this version of the song:

He went on to recall that his grandfather had come home injured, his face scratched and cut, and that he, Zundl, could not look him in the eye. A sad smile appeared on Grandfather's bloody face, and he said : 'Children, you must learn this song; you must. . . . Every Jew should know it. . . . Things would have gone very badly for me without it. My children, I would not have been left alive! . . . And whenever Grandfather had some spare time, he would sing this *mayufes* to the children'.[19]

There is no reason to doubt the authenticity or accuracy of the *mayufes* of Rabon's story or the grandfather's words about it. Nor is it difficult to imagine a situation in which a passing Jew might be attacked and ordered to perform this Jewish 'blessing' for a Polish landowner and his guests.

At times the performance of this sort of *mayufes* was part of a business deal between a Jew and a Pole. In 'Tu chazy czyli rozmowa o Żydach' (*Ta Hazi*: or, A Conversation about the Jews, 1830) by Stanisław Hoge (before his baptism, Yehezkel Hoge), a Polish lord named Florian haggles with a Jewish pedlar in a Warsaw café over a ring with a blue stone. After some preliminary remarks, the conversation concludes as follows:

JEW.           Okay, for such a learned gentleman, eight.
FLORIAN.       I'm not buying.
JEW.           Seven, my final offer.
FLORIAN.       It isn't even worth six.
JEW.           [*getting up and then returning*]. It cost me more than that, but I have nothing for Shabbes. . . . I have to sell.
FLORIAN.       [*holding out the money*]. Take it, you shyster, for fish—but you have to sing a *mayufes*.
JEW.           [*as he is leaving*]. For such a low price, I should cry.[20]

We never find out if the Jew did sing Florian a *mayufes*, and if he did, what the words were. Nevertheless, Hoge's story provides an example of a less violent demand for this amusement, as the put-upon pedlar protests that he feels more

[19] Rabon, 'Mayufes', 130. The story relates an episode that took place before the First World War in which a Cossack in the town of Staszów forces a Jew to sing and dance a *mayufes* for his commanding officer. Zundl, the grandson, captures the 'very same' Cossack (who is serving in Budyonny's army at that time) and forces him to perform a *mayufes*, teaching his prisoner the words, the melody, and the dance, as they make their way back to Zundl's unit. Is it possible that the *mayufes* was also taken up by Cossacks posted to garrisons in Poland?

[20] *Tu chazy czyli rozmowa o Żydach przez Stanisława Hoge* (Warsaw, 1839), 7–8. The title refers to the Aramaic phrase *ta ḥazi* ('come and see'). On the author of this work, see under 'Hoga, Stanislav', *Encyclopaedia Judaica* (Jerusalem, 1972), vol. viii, col. 814.

like crying. Another type of subtle coercion appears in the lines from Junosza's story (quoted above), in which the Jew must perform on the Sabbath.

*Mayufes* did not disappear after the traditional relationship between Polish landowner and financially dependent Jew came to an end. It was simply adopted by the lower classes, especially in urban settings like the one quoted above from Felix Szober's 1878 farce. Texts containing *mayufes* stories are found even in the period between the two world wars in Poland: I. J. Singer's *The Brothers Ashkenazi*, for example, contains what is perhaps the most poignant *mayufes* story of all. Set in the period immediately following the First World War, Singer's epic novel was a polemical Jewish counterpart to *Ziemia obiecana* (The Promised Land), Władysław St Reymont's openly antisemitic novel about cosmopolitan Łódź, centre of commerce and industry.

The story revolves around the many trials and tribulations of two brothers, Max and Yakub, who, like other Polish nationals, return to Poland from Russia in the wake of the Revolution. At Łapy, just inside the frontier, they are met by armed Polish police under the command of a young lieutenant. When the police begin abusing the brothers, Max and Yakub appeal to the lieutenant for protection, introducing themselves as 'manufacturers and residents of Łódź'. The officer does not believe them, since it is commonly thought that all Jews are Bolsheviks. Ignoring Max's statement that he has just been rescued from the Cheka, the lieutenant orders the brothers to shout 'Death to Leibush Trotsky!' and 'Death to all the Leibushes!' As the gathering crowd enjoys the scene, the officer turns to Max:

'Good', the officer said. 'And now give us a dance, manufacturer and resident of Łódź. A nice little [*mayufes*] for our lads. Step lively now!'

Yakub strained to tear free. 'No, Max!' he cried. Max ignored him. He gazed at his tormentors as one might face a pack of mad dogs and began to whirl awkwardly in a circle.

'Faster! Livelier!' the gentiles cried, clapping their hands in accompaniment. Max spun until his legs gave out and he collapsed.

'Leave him there, and bring the other one,' the lieutenant ordered. The gendarmes led Yakub to the table. He stood there pale but unflinching.

'Now it's your turn. Dance!' the officer ordered. Yakub didn't move. The lieutenant flushed. He was aware of his men watching the contest of wills. After a while he rose from [his] place and seized Yakub by the beard.

'Dance!' he shrieked. 'Dance, you damn Jew!' At that moment Yakub tore loose and slapped the gawky youth so hard that he fell back and struck his head against the wall.[21]

What happened next was inevitable: the enraged, humiliated officer immediately shot and killed Yakub.

*The Brothers Ashkenazi* first appeared as a serial in 1934–5 in the New York

---

[21] I. J. Singer, *Di brider ashkenazi* (New York, 1951), 624–6; the English translation is by Joseph Singer (New York, 1981), 400–2. Also A. Norich, *The Homeless Imagination in the Fiction of Israel Joshua Singer* (Bloomington, Ind., 1991), 44–5.

Yiddish daily *Forverts*. Before being published in book form in Yiddish (Warsaw, 1936; New York, 1937), the novel was translated into Polish and serialized in 1935 in the daily Polish Jewish newspaper, *Nasz przegląd*—without the scene quoted above, which was cut by Polish censors. A blank square appears at the end of the 209th issue of the paper (10 November 1935) in place of the offending portion of the chapter. The passage was also deleted from the third volume of the 1936 Warsaw edition of the novel in Yiddish, and the omission is marked by an ellipsis on page 213.[22]

Whether this passage is based on an actual incident is irrelevant. The Rabon story and I. J. Singer's novel show that violent demands for a *mayufes* were still part of the Polish Jewish experience during the inter-war period. Jewish responses to such demands, however, had changed considerably. The change can be seen not only from Rabon and Singer's fictional characters but also from an item in a Jewish newspaper from 1921 (from the same period referred to by Rabon and Singer). In October 1921 a ballet called *W karczmie* (At the Tavern) was performed in the Teatr Wielki in Warsaw. It included a scene called *Mayufes*, in which the dancers 'turned the performance into a disgusting caricature that should not be allowed in even the cheapest cabaret, let alone a national theatre'. With the Jews in the audience protesting loudly, the rest of the crowd shouted, 'Go on, Jews' and 'On with the performance'. The police came in and arrested ten young Jews. The same incident is described in a Polish daily; there the name of the scene is omitted, and the reporter writes only that, following a Polish folk-dance, 'the Jewish family who owned the tavern began a typical dance. Even though there was nothing offensive about the dance, deafening whistles were heard coming from the upper balconies. This is how the Jews protested this innocent dance.'[23] The Polish newspaper article stated that the Jews came to the performance carrying whistles, anticipating a demonstration; the Polish audience, however, applauded the dancers, and the performance continued. This incident provides a further illustration of, at the very least, the Polish lack of sensitivity to the way *mayufes* was seen by Jews. It is almost certain that the dance deliberately made fun of Jews in an offensive way to provide entertainment for the onlookers.

This incident, like the literary episodes discussed above, represents only partial testimony that the *mayufes* was part of the trauma of Jewish collective memory in Poland. The trauma is further documented through a brief survey of Hebrew and Yiddish dictionaries throughout the twentieth century. The first dictionary of Hebrew terms in Yiddish, published by Spivak and Yehoash in 1911, includes an entry under *Mah yafit* (*mayufes*). After a definition of the term as the name of a

[22] The Polish translation of Singer's novel was recently reprinted in book form from *Nasz przegląd*, and the *mayufes* scene excised by the censor in the 1930s does not appear in this reprint either (I. J. Singer, *Bracia aszkenazy* (Warsaw, 1992), ii. 239).

[23] 'A skandal in groysn teater' (A Scandal in the Great Theatre), *Der Moment*, 234 (13 Oct. 1921); *Kurier Warszawski*, 283 (13 Oct. 1921).

*zemer* sung on Friday nights, the following statement appears in parentheses: 'In bygone days, Polish noblemen seeking entertainment would compel Jews who came to them with requests or on business matters to sing this song.'[24] Similar explanations appear in most present-day Hebrew and Yiddish dictionaries. For example, in his *Digest of Jewish Laws and Customs* (1917), J. D. Eisenstein explains at length:

It is said that Polish lords, the estate owners known as *pritsim*, were fond of hearing this song sung by the 'court Jews' who worked as their leaseholders and commercial agents. When the Polish squire was in high spirits, he would tell his Jew to sing a *mayufes*, and the Polish Jew, who was in the squire's hands, would perform against his will, making himself ridiculous in front of the family and friends of his master. If the Jew refused, he could expect to feel the consequences across his back.[25]

In the *Yiddish–English–Hebrew Dictionary* of 1928, Alexander Harkavy added the following comment to his definition of 'to sing a *mayufes*'—'to cringe, to be servile': 'The origins of *mayufes* have to do with the fact that, at one time, Polish squires (*pritsim*) would force Jews to sing this song as a type of entertainment and the latter, poor souls, would do so most abjectly.'[26]

In his Hebrew dictionary, *Hamilon heḥadash* (1981), Avraham Even-Shoshan includes the phrase 'he sang a *mayufes*' under the Hebrew root *yfh*, defining *mayufes* as a 'popular pejorative term for a person who fawns and grovels before someone more powerful'. Even-Shoshan continues: 'In bygone days, the "court Jews" of Polish landowners (*pritsim*) were forced to sing it [*Mah yafit*] at their masters' feasts in order to entertain those present.'[27] As the writings of Rabon and Singer show, the tendency of the lexicographers to ascribe *mayufes* to the distant past is more a sign of their optimism than of the true situation.

Although Jewish sources, from dictionaries to novels, provide evidence of a humiliating custom, comparable Polish sources do not devote much space to *mayufes* (not even the Polish historian who described the 'quasi-jester' and the antics of the Jew performing a *mayufes* refers to the implications of the custom). Ignoring the element of coercion that was involved, Janusz Tazbir compared the *shabbes goy* to the *mayufes* Jew, writing: 'Here the counterpart of the *shabbes goy* (a Christian who does services for the Jews on Sabbath days for a fee) was the *Majufesjude*. It was in such a contemptuous way that the Jewish community referred to those of their kinsmen who clowned in front of the *goys* [gentiles], often by dancing *mayufes* or telling *schmontzes* [jokes].'[28] These comments by Tazbir are all the more surprising because they appear in an article called 'Cruel

[24] *Yiddish verterbuch, enthalt ale hebreyshe (un chaldeyshe) verter . . . fun Dr. Chaim Spivak un Yehoyosh (S. Blumgarten)* (New York, 1911), 142.

[25] Eisenstein (ed.), *Jewish Laws and Customs*, 204.

[26] A. Harkavy, *Yiddish–English–Hebrew Dictionary* (New York, 1928), 292.

[27] A. Even-Shoshan, *Hamilon heḥadash* (Jerusalem, 1981), iii. 974.

[28] Tazbir, 'Cruel Laughter', 93.

Laughter', which is a catalogue of the types of abuse suffered by Polish Jewry over the centuries.

Is the issue here simply an inability to recognize the factor of coercion in this well-known and widespread phenomenon in Polish Jewish history? The fact that the passage from *The Brothers Ashkenazi* was censored indicates that it was not considered appropriate to write about the custom openly, in Polish or Yiddish. As a result, the *mayufes* episode was removed even from the Yiddish version.

A similar attitude prevailed in Communist Poland. In 1986 the Polish censor deleted a paragraph from the memoirs of Julian Stryjkowski, a Polish writer of Jewish origin, before they were published in the liberal Catholic weekly *Tygodnik powszechny*. These memoirs were explicitly called *My Mayufes in Iowa*: 'Once upon a time in Poland, it was the custom that Jews had to dance before the landowners like performing bears at a fair. The name of the dance was "mayufes", from the Hebrew word "Mah yafit".' Stryjkowski explained in the manuscript of his memoirs that 'Poles would exploit this song to abuse and humiliate the Jew'. The censor also deleted this explanation, thereby obscuring the meaning of the passage and making it difficult for a reader to appreciate the stinging finale of the memoirs and its relationship to the title—'I danced the tragedy of the Jews.'[29]

The new attitude towards the concept of *mayufes* was related to the growth of Jewish national consciousness from the late nineteenth century onwards, a trend reflected in the burgeoning of Jewish national and social movements in eastern Europe. This changed attitude toward *mayufes* made its way into the language of the period; for example, at the beginning of the present century, we find a new entry, *mayufesnik*, in Spivak and Yehoash's Yiddish dictionary of 1911: 'A Jew with no national self-awareness; someone who tries to cover up his Jewish origins or to pass as a non-Jew by denying or disguising his Jewish character traits.'[30]

The word *mayufesnik* and its parallel, *maiufes-yid* (*Majufesjude* in German), are still used today in this sense—not only in Yiddish; writers in the Jewish press still use the term in a polemical sense.[31]

[29] J. Stryjkowski, 'Mój majufes w Iowa', *Tygodnik powszechny*, 51–2 (21–8 Dec. 1986). Stryjkowski supplied the sentence missing from *Tygodnik*. (The published version carried the usual notice by the censor in place of the missing sentence: 'Ustawa z dn. 31. VIII. 81 r., O kontroli publikacji i widowisk, art 2, pkt 3 (Dz. U. nr 20, poz. 99, zm.: 1983 Dz. U. nr 44, poz. 204.)')

[30] Spivak and Yehoash, *Yiddish verterbuch*, 143.

[31] Eisenstein writes (*Jewish Laws and Customs*, 204): 'When Jews wished to describe a Jew so weighed down by the *galut* (Diaspora) that he kowtowed to gentiles, they called him by the insulting term *Mayufes* Jew (*Mayufes-yid*).' Also see I. Elzet, *Der wunder-oytser fun der yiddisher sprakh: Dos Davenen* (Warsaw, 1918), 51. Elzet mentions three parallel terms, *mayufes-zinger*, *mayufes-yid*, and *mayufesnik*, and defines them together as 'today referring to a Jew who has no sense of national honour and sucks up to non-Jews in positions of power (literally, to the *parits*)'. 'Majufesnik' appears as a translation or Polish parallel to 'flatterer' in the play *Tarshish* by Isaac Kacenelson. In the play there is an argument between a young Jew who volunteers to serve in the Russian army during the First World War and his friend who refuses to do so (*Miklat*, 5 (1920–1), 41). The volunteer rejects the accusation that he is a *mayufesnik*, adding, in the Polish translation of the play, 'Nie tańcz, ani nie

As Stryjkowski's piece shows, Polish Jews continue to harbour memories of the *mayufes*. Artur Sandauer's ironic memoirs provide a further example of Polish Jewish sensitivity to *mayufes*. In a chapter called 'Love', he describes a confrontation between a group of antisemitic students and a young Jew during a tryst with his Polish sweetheart. The students have discovered the young man is Jewish and, to prevent any violence, a Polish policeman orders the students to disperse. He then turns to the Jew: 'As for you, what are you doing in the cemetery? You're better off staying at home and singing *mayufesen* [*mejufesy* in the Polish].'[32] Sandauer undoubtedly knew the pejorative term *mayufesnik* and deliberately used the word *mejufesy* to expose the young lover, who fits the definition in Spivak and Yehoash's dictionary. The fact that even under the Communist regime Polish authors of Jewish origin felt compelled to refer to the *mayufes* in their writings bears witness to the profound trauma engendered by the phenomenon. To this very day, the scars are evident among Polish Jews.

*Mayufes* and *mayufesnik* have provoked a wide array of responses over the centuries. Towards the end of his life, the great Yiddish and Hebrew writer Mendele Mokher Sforim (S. J. Abramowitsch) was in the habit of dismissing any type of Jewish lobbying as *mayufes*: 'Trying to intercede with the authorities (*shtadlanut*) doesn't help; in fact, it is harmful—it demeans the Jewish people and smacks of the *mayufes*.'[33]

Unlike his brother, Isaac Bashevis Singer did not see anything humiliating in the custom of *mayufes*, nor did he consider those who performed it despicable toadies. As far as he was concerned, the Jew who sang a *mayufes* in front of the Polish landowner was bullied into doing so, just as a modern Jew might be forced at gunpoint to sing a song. Singer expressed this opinion in 1944, stressing that he had always felt that expressions such as *mayufes-yid* represented an unjustified attack on helpless Jews. If anything, the attack should be aimed against the contemptible squire who enjoyed inflicting humiliation.[34]

śpiewam przed jaśnie panem' ('I don't dance or sing before a lordship') (I. Kacenelson, *Odwrót*, Tłumaczyl z manskryptu, Jan Zandmer (Warsaw, 1923), 41). According to a German definition, 'Daher stammt der Spott- und Schmähname Majufesjuden für solche Juden, die sich vor den polnischen Herren demütigen' (*Jüdisches Lexikon*, iii/1 (Berlin, 1929), 18–34). Also see esp. M. Zobel, *Der Sabbat* (Berlin, 1935), 184, as well as examples from the press: I. J. Singer, 'A frage vos es loynt vegn ir a shmues ton—moderner mayufes', *Literarishe bletter*, 84 (1925), 303–4 (concerning Polish Jewish authors discussed in the Jewish Writers' Association in Warsaw); 'Meir Vilner's mayufes-rede oyf dem komunistishn congress in Moskve', *Forverts* (21 Mar. 1986), 38. An edifying example of the way Jews used the concept of *mayufes* for internal polemical purposes can be seen in Meir Khartiner's anti-assimilationist song 'Ma Jufes' at the end of this article.

[32] A. Sandauer, *Proza* (Warsaw, 1983), 153. Sandauer also published a pamphlet on the difficult, painful position of Polish writers of Jewish origin in the 20th century (Sandauer, *O sytuacji pisarza polskiego pochodzenia żydowskiego w XX wieku: Rzecz którą, nie ja powinienem był napisać* (Warsaw, 1982)).

[33] Mendele Mokher Sforim, *Be'emek habakhah* (Tel Aviv, 1957–8), 249.

[34] I. Varshavski (Isaac Bashevis Singer), 'Mayufes un khutspe', *Forverts* (14 Aug. 1944).

Uri Zvi Greenberg, a modernist poet who wrote in Hebrew and Yiddish, provides one of the most powerful, biting literary expressions of Polish Jewry's collective sensitivity to *mayufes*. His long poem *Kefitsat derekh* can be seen as a last farewell to Christian Europe, following his arrival in Palestine. In the poem Greenberg settles accounts with those responsible for centuries of Jewish suffering in Europe. The Polish Jew is portrayed in the following sarcastic but deeply poignant *mayufes* sketch:

> Here I am again—and again—
> A Jew from Poland,
> So simple, so debased,
> Summoned to feasts in the courtyard of the *parits*.
> A Jew expert in dancing *Mah yafis*.
> . . . The ultimate insult:
> In his courtyard,
> Heavy—
> Legged,
> Dancing
> To the good health
> Of the *parits*.[35]

There was an even more widespread response to the collective trauma of the *mayufes* than those already quoted, however. The evidence suggests that the hasidic movement responded in a concrete, extreme way to this painful memory. As J. D. Eisenstein writes, 'It may be that this is why hasidim no longer include *Mah yafit* among their Sabbath songs.' Some publishers have even excised *Mah yafit* from the prayer-books they printed.[36] A thorough study of this subject in relation to the hasidic movement is still needed, as is a bibliographic search to find the instances where the *Mah yafit* was removed from the prayer-books and *bentsherls*.

Moreover, it is not only the latest incarnations of and responses to *mayufes* that cry out for clarification: the early origins of the phenomenon still remain shrouded in mystery. We do not know exactly when it started or why this song was chosen. Perhaps new sources of Polish Jewish history will be uncovered that will provide

[35] Uri Zvi Greenberg, *Eimah gedolah veyare'aḥ* (Tel Aviv, 1925), 60–1.

[36] Eisenstein (ed.), *Jewish Laws and Customs*, 204. Also, consider the following from A. B. Gottlober's play *Der dektukh* (The Bridal Veil): 'In my day, it was a pleasure to look at a prayer-book, it was so thick! . . . It was full of delicacies! But these newfangled tiny prayer-books are completely useless. My enemies should have to make do with what little there is on their pages. A few measly songs for Friday night and Saturday morning! If a Polish squire wanted to force a Jew to sing *Mah yafit* today, he wouldn't be able to—it's not in the prayer-book' (A. B. Gottlober, *Yiddishe verk* (Vilnius, 1927), 99). Also see Nulman, 'Fate of the Sabbath Table Hymn', 35, as well as Levin and Pasternak, *Zemirot Anthology*, 43, who write: 'As a result of the bitter experiences associated with this tune, the poem itself fell into disuse in many communities and is omitted from many prayer-book editions. The melody is even less frequently found.'

answers. One thing is clear, however: the *mayufes* is only one among the many kinds of interaction between Polish and Jewish culture in Poland. It is unfortunate that this example, which is hardly a source of pride for Poles, continues to be a painful memory for Jews.

*Translated by Anna Barber*

## APPENDIX

*Ma Jufes*
(Kriegsgesang der Assimilanten)

(Dem grossen Dr Buhaj—Lemberg und allen Majufes-Juden in Liebe gewidmet von Mayer Chartiner.)

| | |
|---|---|
| SOLO. Ma jufes! | |
| CHOR. Ma jufes! | |
| SOLO. Schreit-schet, Jüden, mit kawune. | |
| CHOR. Ma jufes! | |
| SOLO. Poilen is in grois sakune; | |
| Ratewets gich die neemune. | |
| CHOR. Ma jufes, ma jufes! | |
| Mj. mj.! | |
| Aufgestannen Zionisten. Mj.! | |
| Tut sich sei gur a Zion glisten, | |
| Reizen of a welt mit Kristen— | |
| Mj. mj.! | |
| Mj. mj.! | |
| Oj, sei stellen sich wie gibboirem—mj.! | |
| Konnen, cholile, noch sein goirem | |
| Mir sollen weren aus faktoirem— | |
| Mj. mj.! | |
| Mj. mj.! | |
| Gewalt, raboissim! Weh geschrigen! Mj. | |
| | |
| Wü wet der Puriz züm vergnigen | |
| Später denn a Moschke kriegen? | |
| Mj. mj.! | |
| Mj. mj.! | |
| Wer wet reinigen fremde stallen? Mj.! | |
| | |
| Wer wet Kuhel schinden, kaalen? | |
| Wer wet machen falsche Wahlen? | |
| Mj. mj.! | |
| Mj. mj.! | |

*Mayufes*
(Battle-cry against the Assimilationists)

(Dedicated to the famous Dr Buhay and all the *mayufes* Jews in Lemberg)

Mayufes!
Mayufes!
Cry out Jews, with fervour.
Mayufes!
Poland is in great danger;
Quickly, save the faith.
Mayufes! Mayufes!
Mayufes. Mayufes!
Zionists have awakened, Mayufes!
Of all things they desire Zion
A world of Christians rises up—
Mayufes! Mayufes!
Mayufes! Mayufes!
Oh, they present themselves as heroes
They can, God forbid, be the cause
Of our ceasing to be brokers—
Mayufes! Mayufes!
Mayufes! Mayufes!
Cry out gentlemen! Cry out in anguish!
Mayufes!
Where will the nobleman for his
Pleasure later find a little Moishe?
Mayufes! Mayufes!
Mayufes! Mayufes!
Who will clean the strangers' stalls?
Mayufes!
Who will skin the community, beat it up?
Who will cast false ballots?
Mayufes! Mayufes!
Mayufes! Mayufes!

| | |
|---|---|
| Lost nischt, Brüder, seit-schet jüngen—Mj! | Do not permit it brothers, be strong men— Mayufes! |
| Zi a chniok, zi a daatsch mit lüngen— | Be an ignorant fanatic, be a force— |
| Moschke müss beim Puriz singen: | Little Moishe must be the one to sing for the nobleman: |
| | |
| Mj. mj.! | Mayufes! Mayufes! |
| Mj. mj.! | Mayufes! Mayufes! |
| Gott beweist üns groisse wünder— | God performs great miracles for us. |
| Mj. mj.! | Mayufes! Mayufes! |
| Hrabia Wojtek mit die kinder | His excellency Wojtek and the children |
| Reichen üns die hand azünder | Stretch out arms to cut us down— |
| Mj. mj.! | Mayufes! Mayufes! |
| Mj. mj.! | Mayufes! Mayufes! |
| Mög der Puriz vün ünz lachen—mj.! | Let the nobleman laugh at us—Mayufes! |
| Kikt nischt of a solche sachen, | Look not upon such things, |
| A du wel mir erscht git machen— | Then you will make me feel better— |
| Mj. mj.! | Mayufes! Mayufes! |
| Mj. mj.! | Mayufes! Mayufes! |
| Sehts, der Puriz hebt dem stecken—mj.! | See, the nobleman picks up his stick— Mayufes! |
| | |
| Oj, dus harz tüt mir sich schreken | Oh, my heart begins to tremble |
| Brüder, gich die t. . .eller lecken— | Brothers, quickly, lick the 'plates'— |
| Mj. mj.! | Mayufes! Mayufes! |
| Mj. mj.! | Mayufes! Mayufes! |
| Mäklerei wet man üns geben—mj.! | They will make us brokers—Mayufes! |
| Schreit-schet, Jüden, se sol asch teeben: | Cry out, Jews, so as to deafen |
| Vivat hrabia Wojtek leben! | Vivat, excellency Wojtek lives! |
| Mj. mj.! | Mayufes! Mayufes! |

*Appendix translated by Esther Frank, McGill University*

# On the History of the Jews in Twelfth- and Thirteenth-Century Poland

ISRAEL M. TA-SHMA

## THE PRESENT STATE OF RESEARCH

JEWISH traders of Ashkenazi origin passed through Poland on their way to Russia on business as early as the first half of the eleventh century. A considerable amount of relevant material on this subject was assembled by Ephraim (Franciszek) Kupfer.[1] These itinerant Jews probably established some permanent settlements in various parts of Poland. Thus, we know of a Jewish presence in Cracow in the first half of the eleventh century. This presence included a regularly functioning religious court (*beit din*), empowered to issue religious rulings, to enforce its decisions, and to impose fines on Jews travelling through the city, in the spirit of—perhaps even inspired by—one of the *takanot* of Rabbenu Gershom Me'or Hagolah. Our information touches upon a financial dispute; the problem, a complicated one, was briefly discussed by R. Judah Hakohen, author of *Sefer hadinin*, a student of R. Gershom who was active in Mainz during the first half of the eleventh century.[2] It is highly significant that most of our historical information about Jews in eleventh-century Poland derives from R. Judah's responsa. This is due to the regular

---

A highly abbreviated presentation of the following account was presented at the First International Congress for the Study of Polish Jewry, held at the Hebrew University, Jerusalem, in Jan. 1988. A Hebrew version of this article was published, in two parts, in *Zion*, 53–4 (1988–9). The present revision includes many additional data and other general updates.

[1] Franciszek Kupfer and Tadeusz Lewicki, *Źródła hebrajskie do dziejów słowian i niektórych innych Ludów środkowej i wschodniej Europy* (Warsaw, 1956). I shall not deal here with sources already considered in the past, except where our understanding of those sources has been modified since the publication of Kupfer and Lewicki's work.

[2] I. Agus, *Urban Civilization in Pre-Crusade Europe* (New York, 1968), 93–7. This information is based on the manuscript version of a responsum of R. Meir ben Barukh of Rothenburg (Prague, 1608), no. 912; see also A. Grossman, *The Early Sages of Ashkenaz* (Heb.) (Jerusalem, 1981), 140 n. 123, 185 n. 45. That the court had authority over visitors to the city is indicated twice in this complex episode: once in the community of Zimri, reported to be in 'Russia', and once again in Cracow or its environs. Cf. the analysis of the story by Agus, *Urban Civilization*.

communications on halakhic matters between him and Polish rabbis, who seem to have considered themselves his disciples. Combined with Polish Jews' observance of the *takanot* of R. Gershom, we thus have evidence of a strong historical and social affinity between these Jews and their co-religionists in Germany—most probably the parent community of the early Jewish settlement in Poland.[3]

The Jewish traders who passed through Poland in the twelfth century included scholars and other individuals versed in religious learning. We have evidence to that effect from R. Eleazar ben Nathan (known as Raban), active in the first half of the twelfth century, and from R. Isaac ben R. Dorbelo, of the second half of the same century, one of the editors of the version of *Maḥzor Vitry* underlying the printed edition. The latter writes: 'Since we are not as well versed . . . as our predecessors, we should be circumspect, lest people accustom themselves to be lazy and rule leniently, as I have seen in the kingdom of Poland among the traders who travel the road.'[4] R. Isaac ben Dorbelo and one of his contemporaries, R. Eleazar ben Isaac of Prague, are mentioned by Bernard D. Weinryb as the first two Jewish scholars to visit Russia 'and possibly Poland' around the end of the twelfth century.[5] R. Eleazar, like his contemporary R. Isaac, was a disciple of Rabbenu Tam.[6]

We possess a letter written by R. Eleazar to R. Judah Heḥasid, vehemently protesting the latter's strictures, in an earlier letter to a Jewish community in eastern Europe, against payment of salaries to cantors. It was then customary 'in most places in Poland, Russia,[7] and Hungary, where, owing to poverty,

[3]  As already pointed out by Agus, *Urban Civilization*.

[4]  Jews' College, London, MS Montefiore 134, *Sefer ba'alei asupot*, Hilkh. Pesah, § 352. Cf. Kupfer and Lewicki, *Źródła hebrajskie*, 152; S. E. Stern, 'Sefer asupot' (Heb.), *Moriah*, 15/5–6 (173–4) (Spring 1987), 5–10. On this important scholar and disciple of Rabbenu Tam, who lived in France and travelled around eastern Europe, see Kupfer and Lewicki, *Źródła hebrajskie*, 148–56; and more recently N. Danzig, 'Excerpts from Geonic Responsa in Works of the Rishonim' (Heb.), *Proceedings of the 9th World Congress of Jewish Studies*, iii (Jerusalem, 1986), 71–8. Another scholar who apparently reached Russia was Raban's colleague R. Ephraim of Regensburg, referred to as the 'teacher' of R. Joel, 'who was there [in the kingdom of Russia] and saw with his own eyes that beer was brought to the priest to mix for idolatrous purposes' (Eleazar ben Joel Halevi of Bonn, *Sefer ravyah*, § 1050; V. Aptowitzer, *Mavo laravyah* (Jerusalem, 1938), 465). R. Joel's other teachers were R. Isaac ben Mordecai (Ribam), R. Moses ben Joel, and R. Samuel ben Natronai. Even though, as Aptowitzer pointed out, we have no direct knowledge of R. Ephraim's presence in Russia, this scholar is nevertheless acquainted with the customs of what he calls 'the land of Yavan' (*Ravyah*, ii. 259). Finally, one of the Machiris was also in Russia; see Zedekiah ben Abraham Harofe, *Shibolei haleket*, ii. 58.

[5]  D. Weinryb, *The Jews of Poland* (Philadelphia, 1972), 24.

[6]  See E. E. Urbach, *Ba'alei hatosafot*, 2nd edn. (Jerusalem, 1980), i. 212–15.

[7]  As defined by R. Benjamin of Tudela, 'the land of Russia' denoted the entire region between Prague and Kiev: 'These are the men of Russia, which is a great empire stretching from the gate of Prague to the gate of Kieff, the large city, which is at the extremity of the empire. It is a land of mountains and forests . . . Thus far reaches the empire of Russia' (M. N. Adler (ed.), *The Itinerary of Benjamin of Tudela* (London, 1907), 80–1). In actual fact, the borders of Kievan Russia extended approximately from the environs of Lwów to the Kiev district. The northern border was not well

there are no Torah scholars, that they hire an intelligent man wherever they can and he serves them as leader in prayer and religious mentor and teacher of their children, and they assure his livelihood in return'. That is to say: 'To levy [payment or food] from those who entertain sons-in-law at their tables, who should give generously, because of the benefit of joy, food and drink . . . And appeals were made for them on Simḥat Torah and Purim.' R. Judah Heḥasid wrote to the Jews in one such place, instructing them to abolish both the hiring of paid cantors and the collection of taxes for that purpose, in the spirit of the old Ashkenazi pietist ideal that considered the function of the cantor as a sacrosanct post. R. Eleazar of Prague took exception to this position, appraising R. Judah of the grave danger that might arise if hired cantors were to relinquish their positions, heaven forfend, leaving their communities 'without Torah, without prayer and without a religious authority'. R. Eleazar ended his letter in a tone of deep concern: 'Even if you retract, I am concerned lest your first views should have been heeded there and misfortune result'.[8] This responsum was written when R. Judah Heḥasid was in the prime of his life, by an older scholar[9] who did not mince words in his criticism of R. Judah: 'May He who forgives iniquity forgive your sin in perpetuity, that you may live and multiply.' We may thus date the responsum to the last years of the twelfth century. Poland is explicitly mentioned, and the letter also provides definite evidence of the existence of Jewish communities at this early date, with some indications of their communal organization and level of religious observance. Later we shall learn some more of R. Judah Heḥasid's contacts with these first Polish communities and how he, rather than a recognized halakhic authority, achieved the profound influence in the region attested by R. Eleazar's letter.[10]

By the last quarter of the twelfth century there was a well-established Jewish community in Cracow, probably a direct descendant of the community whose existence was recorded some 150 years earlier. R. Joel Halevi (d. *c.*1200), father of 'Ravyah', refers in a responsum to a person who was born in Cracow and travelled to his brother in Magdeburg. The man was born around 1175, at

defined, the Hebrew word 'Russia' sometimes extending to Lithuania as well. The southern border was also not precisely drawn; at times it could reach the shores of the Black Sea. The political borders were not clearly delineated, but varied according to the power of the kingdom at any particular time. See below, end of the penultimate section. I am indebted to my friend Dr Elhanan Reiner for this definition, as well as some other excellent advice on the structure of this article.

[8] *Or zaru'a*, i, § 113.　　　　　　　　　　　　[9] Urbach, *Ba'alei hatosafot*, i. 212–15.

[10] The source is cited by Weinryb, *The Jews of Poland*, 24, but his annotation there is defective. The references he cites are concerned with other matters, and the correct—and only—reference for this responsum is omitted. Weinryb's statement that all the sources are preserved 'in a late manuscript only' is quite wrong; as it happens, the MS of *Or zaru'a* is an early one, dating to the 14th century. Moreover, his arguments about the nature of this letter, which he considers contrary to R. Judah Heḥasid's character and figure as it emerges in his writings and as portrayed by Gershom Scholem, are wrong.

the latest, as he travelled to Magdeburg before 1200. Aptowitzer cited this responsum from an unpublished part of Ravyah's responsa.[11]

Our information about the Jewish community in Poland in the eleventh and twelfth centuries is fragmentary and does not provide a basis for a continuous historical account. It is generally believed that there were several 'beginnings', not all of which took root. Continuous Jewish residence in Poland is usually dated from the mid-fifteenth century, though there are increasing indications of a continuous Jewish presence there from the end of the fourteenth century.[12] The sources seem to imply that in 1241, when the Mongolian invasion devastated Poland, the earlier, first Jewish presence, dating to the eleventh and twelfth centuries, disappeared. Later, from the second half of the thirteenth century and during the fourteenth century, there was no organized, rabbinically guided, communal life, and therefore no Polish scholars of this period figure in our literature. Graetz expressed amazement at this situation, as we have copious external evidence for the presence of Jews in thirteenth- and fourteenth-century Poland. Suffice it to mention, for example, the detailed and important privilege granted in 1264 by Duke Bolesław of Kalisz, which was re-validated in these centuries; decisions of the Church in Jewish matters; and coins struck by Jews. However, we lack evidence of 'the pulse of the Jewish heart' there, because of the almost absolute silence of our internal sources, which contribute nothing of substance to our knowledge of Polish Jewish history of the time. As Graetz comments:

Jewish history in the first three centuries of the sixth millennium [of the Jewish calendar, i.e. 1240–1540] . . . in the lands of eastern Europe . . . presents an amazing vision. . . . On the one hand, one learns from the various charters of privilege . . . from government records and decrees, from the writings of chroniclers . . . and from the evidence of travellers [and decisions of the Church] . . . that by the beginning of the sixth millennium, and even earlier, Jewish settlement had made inroads not only in Poland, which was close to western Europe, but also . . . in southern Russia. . . . Besides commerce, they also had a large part in industry, agriculture, trades, and all professions; but the pulse of the Jewish heart, the voice of the Torah, was still unheard in those lands. . . . And that is quite surprising, for the paucity of information and records of historical life persists until the mid-third century [end of the fifteenth century], and there is no trace of Torah study and yeshivot in the Jewish settlement of Lithuania and Poland—the lands which have supplied most Jewish communities, in all other Diaspora lands, with talmudic learning for the past three centuries.[13]

Graetz found the situation puzzling because of the 'direct proportion' that has

[11] Aptowitzer, *Mavo laravyah*, 463. The text has now been published by D. Devlitzki, *Sefer ravyah*, Responsa (Benei Berak, 1989), 68.

[12] E. Kupfer, 'On the Cultural Features of Ashkenazic Jewry and its Scholars in the Fourteenth and Fifteenth Centuries' (Heb.), *Tarbiz*, 42 (1973), 130 n. 110, and the addendum at the end of his article. The first figure in this group was apparently R. David Schweidnitz. See Y. Freiman, *Introduction to Leket yosher* (Berlin, 1903), p. xxv.

[13] Z. Graetz, *Divrei yemei Yisra'el*, trans. S. P. Rabinowitz (Warsaw, 1898), vi. 183–4.

always existed between 'the situation of the nation, wandering and tossed about among the nations in whose midst they lived . . . and the product of its spirit, the heights of its internal ethical and intellectual perfection'.[14] This is clearly not the case in this chapter of Jewish history: the history of the Jews in Poland and Lithuania in the thirteenth and fourteenth centuries is, to all appearances, a success story from the point of view of economic and physical well-being—but lacks any substructure of Torah study and internal, spiritual–cultural creativity. This fact greatly puzzled the historian in Graetz. For him, the silence of the Jewish sources was clear, unequivocal evidence of a life devoid of scholarly creativity—evidence as reliable as any other, material evidence. It did not occur to him to apply, here too, the well-known injunction against drawing conclusions *ex silentio*, as he was convinced that the silence in question was total, unlike other, fortuitous silences of ancient sources. Later historians accepted Graetz's diagnosis. Some went even further, claiming to add this silence to other considerations that indicated, so they believed, that the Jews of Poland in the first stage, i.e. until the Mongolian invasion, had come from Russia or perhaps even beyond, and not from Germany, despite their halakhic connections with that country.

However, despite this seemingly universal agreement, the 'fact' in question is dubious, as the silence on which it relies is far from complete. It is true that printed sources are silent in regard to the first periods of Jewish settlement in Poland; but the situation in manuscripts is quite different, and in fact some of these have recently appeared in print. As we know, the number of Hebrew manuscripts now available is considerable, and research can no longer rely on printed editions alone. True, even the manuscript sources are not too generous in relevant information; but they are certainly not silent. As we deepen our understanding of the nature of the available manuscript sources that have reached us from the Middle Ages, the reason for the relative dearth of 'Polish' material—compared with other countries—becomes clearer. A major cause of this situation is that we lack photographic reproductions of Hebrew manuscripts still buried in various libraries or, in particular, in the possession of the Polish Church. In addition, most of the fragments in bindings of old books and archival envelopes in Poland have yet to see the light of day. Experience has taught us that most of our information about geographically defined areas reaches us through manuscripts originating in those areas. Other reasons will be mentioned below. All the information presented in this article has been garnered over the years, in the course of my browsing—for completely different purposes—through the treasure-house of microfilmed Hebrew manuscripts in the Jewish National and University Library of Jerusalem. I have no doubt that a systematic search would reveal even more. Nevertheless, despite the

[14] Ibid. 183.

small quantity and random nature of the finds, we have sufficient material, I believe, to warrant a preliminary formulation of a quite different thesis about the nature of the Jewish community in thirteenth-century Poland—a thesis that will be much closer to undisputed facts than what we have today.

This apparent silence of the sources, as well as the gaps between the early Jewish presence in Poland during the eleventh and thirteenth centuries, its continuation in the second half of the thirteenth century, and its final consolidation in the fifteenth century, have raised questions about the geographical origins of the first Jews to settle there.[15] It has been suggested that those early Jews were not an offshoot of the Jewish communities in Germany, but a branch of the ancient Jewish centre of Kievan Russia. Eastern Jews—some of them learned in Torah—were living there as early as the twelfth century or before; their roots go back to the ancient Jewish presence in the various parts of Khazaria. The great historical controversy over this issue is well known and need not be discussed here.[16] In this article I shall assemble a variety of

[15] See S. Ettinger, 'Jewish Influence on the Religious Ferment in Eastern Europe at the End of the 15th Century' (Heb.), in S. W. Baron, B. Dinur, I. Halpern, and S. Ettinger (eds.), *Yitzhak F. Baer Jubilee Volume* (Jerusalem, 1960), 228–47: 'The chapter of the Judaizers in Russia enables us to view this [i.e. Polish and Lithuanian] Jewry while it was still driven by its rationalist tendencies.' There were indeed 'rationalist tendencies' as such, an issue that has received considerable support from E. Kupfer, in 'On the Cultural Features of Ashkenazic Jewry', 113 ff.; however, Kupfer's article deals with the Jews of Germany and Bohemia and has nothing to say of the Jews of Kievan Russia or the Byzantine centres.

[16] See S. Ettinger, 'Kievan Russia', in *The World History of the Jewish People*, xi: *The Dark Ages*, ed. C. Roth (Tel Aviv, 1966), 319–24. I would like to rectify a popular error—also marring Ettinger's account—that sees the existence of a R. Moses of Kiev, active around the middle of the 12th century, who quotes Rabbenu Tam and was in contact with R. Samuel ben Ali, head of the academy in Baghdad, as proving that no extensive expulsions of Kievan Jews took place during that period. The truth is that R. Moses was known as 'the Exile' from Kiev; moreover, he does not merely 'quote' Rabbenu Tam, but actually studied under him in France; and his contacts with the Babylonian scholar were maintained from France and not from Kiev. This seemingly surprising fact emerges from the other, less well-known, correspondence of Moses, the Exile of Kiev, and Samuel ben Ali of Baghdad, on the issue of the prohibition on Passover of *ḥamets bemashehu* (mixtures containing minute quantities of leaven); see Aptowitzer, in his notes to *Sefer haravyah*, ii. 77 n. 11, and in 'Addenda and Corrigenda', 18 (repr. in his notes to part II, p. 73). It transpires, therefore, that Moses the Exile was apparently the only Kievan of the time who was learned in Torah—and we have now seen that his rabbinical activity, too, took place in France and not in his native land. However, we have other possible testimony to the existence in the 12th century of a channel of transmission from Babylon through Kiev to Germany, namely, Moses Taku in his *Ketav tamim*. He claims to trace certain ideas of R. Judah Heḥasid to Karaite literature that reached him from the East, and rejects 'the commentators'' idea that [God] creates forms to speak with the prophets. That tradition has survived among the Karaites and the heretics, for thus we find it written in a commentary of theirs to the Pentateuch, which moreover contains calumnious remarks about students of the Mishnah and the Talmud, and we were told that that crooked book came from Babylon to Russia and from Russia it was brought to Regensburg' (MS Paris H711, fo. 28; facs. edn. (Jerusalem, 1984), 55). According to A. Epstein, it was the traveller Petahiah of Regensburg who brought the book with him upon his return from the east (*Mikadmoniyot hayehudim* (Jerusalem, 1957), 240–1). The book thus reached R. Judah Heḥasid, who in fact edited and censored Petahiah's travelogue, as related by Petahiah himself:

Hebrew sources that will tell us more about the existence of an admittedly sparse Jewish presence, including Jews well versed in Torah, in thirteenth-century Poland; about the continuous existence of this presence throughout the twelfth and thirteenth centuries; and, above all, about its Ashkenazi origins and its special, ongoing contacts with the circles of ḥasidei Ashkenaz in Germany. This is not to say that the 'eastern' orientation should be entirely discounted—that is not my intention;[17] but I shall be able to show that the extent of the links between Russia–Poland and Ashkenaz, particularly eastern Ashkenaz, was much greater than believed up to the present. Moreover, I believe that these links were essentially persistent and permanent, rather than a series of random occurrences.

## R. JACOB SVARA OF CRACOW

R. Jacob Svara is the first rabbinical figure known by name from the Polish city of Cracow. He was active there in the first half of the thirteenth century. Although our knowledge of his personality and actions is growing steadily, he is still a largely obscure figure. Attention was first drawn to him by Kupfer.[18] While working at the Institute for Microfilmed Hebrew Manuscripts, he identified an unknown work of a disciple of the tosafist R. Tobias of Vienne in France[19]—an abbreviated version of R. Moses of Coucy's *Sefer mitsvot gadol*,

'In Nineveh there was an astrologer by the name of R. Solomon . . . R. Petaḥiah asked him when the Messiah would come, and he told him: I have already foretold his coming clearly from the stars. But R. Judah Heḥasid did not wish [me] to write [this], lest he be suspected of believing in R. Solomon's predictions.' Incidentally, I have found the entire prophecy, two pages long, in an ancient manuscript, MS Warsaw University 1 (Institute for Microfilmed Hebrew Manuscripts, mic. 32500)—the oldest extant MS of the *Sibuv*. The fragment has now been published by S. Spitzer, in *Alei sefer*, 15 (1988–9), 133–4; and see my comment, ibid. 16 (1989–90), 187. There is yet another reference to Kiev in this early period, in *Sefer haraban*, *Beitzah*, 172*b*: 'It is my view . . . that [such fabrics] are not considered *kilayim* [mixtures], as are made in the land of Greece, and in Kiem I saw some of them without leather underneath . . .'. For 'Kiem' read 'Kiev', as noted by S. Abramson, 'Explanation of Words' (Heb.), *Gevurot haromah: Divrei ḥakhamim leMosheh Ḥayyim Vailer*, ed. Z. Falk (Jerusalem, 1987), 166. The period referred to pre-dates that of Moses the Exile by some fifty years.

[17]  The problem is in fact complicated by the unnoticed fact that Jewish communities in Ashkenaz itself maintained close spiritual–cultural and intellectual contacts with communities in Greece and Byzantium from the mid-10th century and even earlier, not necessarily in connection with Poland, until the middle of the 13th century, as witnessed in the rabbinical literature of those 300 years. The intensity, causes, and significance of those contacts have yet to be determined. I shall treat their history in a forthcoming article. It is not inconceivable that these two sources of influence—Germany and Russia–Kiev–Byzantium—drew from a major common source, at least from the 11th century on.

[18]  E. Kupfer, 'From Far and Near' (Heb.), in I. Klausner, R. Mahler, and D. Sadan (eds.), *Sefer hayovel mugash likhevod Dr. N. M. Gelber* (Tel Aviv, 1963), 218–19.

[19]  For a description of this book, see Urbach, *Ba'alei hatosafot*, i. 488–91, and cf. ibid. concerning R. Jacob Svara.

with halakhic rulings of the author's teacher R. Tobias interpolated.[20] The manuscript reads:

It happened that a woman gave her son to a Jewish wet-nurse, and the wet-nurse was adjured, on behalf of the community, under biblical oath, a grave oath that cannot be annulled, that she would not retract her undertaking to breast-feed the child until it reach the age of 24 months. Upon doing this the mother married a certain *kohen* [person of priestly lineage], named R. Jacob Svara of Cracow, who resided in Poland, a great scholar versed in the entire Talmud, but the great authorities of the time disagreed with him, and were about to excommunicate him. Thereupon he sent responsa to the ends of west and south, and his words reached my teacher R. Tobias. And my teacher instructed, in so far as it is quite obvious that she would not renege, owing to the gravity of the oath, he could not be forced to divorce her, and even if he were not yet married to her, he could a priori marry her.[21]

The episode alluded to here concerns the fate of a woman widowed while still nursing her baby within twenty-four months of its birth. According to Jewish law (Ket. 60*b*), she may not remarry, for fear that she might neglect her baby. Ashkenazi Jewry took this prohibition very seriously throughout the centuries.[22] Such marriages were forbidden even when the couple took all feasible precautions to ensure the infant's rights and welfare, and the rabbis insisted that, if a marriage had nevertheless been performed, it be dissolved by divorce; the couple would be allowed to remarry at the end of the twenty-four-month term. The special feature of the case in question was that R. Jacob of Cracow was a *kohen*, and his 'temporary' divorce would have separated him permanently from his new wife (as a *kohen* may not marry a divorcee). Nevertheless, the halakhic authorities of Ashkenaz insisted that he obey their injunction to divorce his wife and even threatened to excommunicate him should he refuse, despite the fact that he was considered—by them, too—as a 'great scholar versed in the entire Talmud'. In an endeavour to defend his position, R. Jacob sent letters 'to the ends of west and south', and R. Tobias of Vienne supported his stand and completely upheld his actions.

The details of the case are unknown, and there is no surviving trace of the

[20] MS Paris 329. A different version of the book (see Urbach, *Ba'alei hatosafot*) renders a shorter and less specific account of the episode, which is reproduced verbatim, without mentioning the source, in *Piskei rekanati*, § 240. It does not designate the protagonists by name and R. Tobias's ruling is quoted as 'the *geonim* instructed'.                              [21] MS Vat. 176, fo. 51.

[22] The history of this prohibition in rabbinic literature, as well as the reason for the exceptional severity with which it was enforced by Ashkenazi authorities (of all generations), deserve separate discussion. Here, too, as in so many other cases, the root cause was a latent Palestinian tradition; but one must also consider the cruel reality of life in medieval Europe, which meant that a child handed over to a strange wet-nurse was generally doomed to die. See L. DeMausse, 'The Evolution of Childhood', *History of Childhood Quarterly*, 1 (1973), 534–41. And cf. *Mishnah Sotah* 4: 3, which lists certain wives to whom the ordeal of the 'bitter water' is not administered; one of them is a wife still nursing a previous husband's infant—as the marriage itself is not considered properly valid.

correspondence. No doubt the episode was censored by the contemporary Ashkenazi scholars, who completely expunged any expression of the more lenient view from their books. The few surviving responsa, and the few indirect discussions, give only the views of those who favoured the prohibition. Nothing has reached us of R. Jacob's own opinion, as set out in his own language and sent 'to the ends of the earth', which in fact reached the eyes of R. Isaac ben Moses, known as Or Zaru'a, himself ('And I read R. Jacob Cohen's letter and found nothing there that was worthy of response'); the same is true of R. Tobias's responsum permitting the marriage. The responsum of R. Isaac Or Zaru'a, who headed the camp opposing the rabbi of Cracow, was printed in his book;[23] it too censored. The first, informative, part of his letter has been deleted. The text begins *in medias res* and in mid-sentence, clearly indicating that the previous page of the manuscript was torn out. This applies not only to the manuscript on which the printed edition was based, but also to other manuscripts of the work, including MS Cincinnati 154. This manuscript contains the collection of responsa only and is independent of the other manuscripts, as it also includes new responsa found neither in the latter nor in the printed edition. The missing page is present in MS Cincinnati, and it actually enables us to complete the end of the previous responsum, which is missing in the printed edition; but the beginning of our responsum is still missing, here too![24] Next to his own responsum, R. Isaac cited a ruling of R. Moses ben Hisdai of Regensburg, one of the leading scholars of the day, who also wrote in an extreme vein. The case is mentioned in other places, mainly by scholars who copied from the work of R. Tobias's disciple R. Isaac; all these accounts, however, are vague, obscure, and replete with incomprehensible hints, in order to avoid voicing the permissive views.[25]

---

[23] Pt. II, § 740.

[24] Such acts of censorship, and similar ones, were common practice in Ashkenaz even earlier. See my comment in *Kiryat sefer*, 56 (1981), 350–1.

[25] The reader should note that, had R. Tobias's disciple not mentioned his master's name, we would have been unable to attribute this almost unique lenient view to a specific scholar. Cf. R. Yom Tov Ishbili's wording in his novellae to Ket. 60*b*: 'But there are some of the last tosafists, of blessed memory, who wrote that if the nursing mother took an oath on the matter . . . the matter is sufficiently public and it is permitted.' R. Yom Tov wrote his book around 1300–20 and would certainly have been aware of the identity of the tosafist in question. Similarly, R. Nissim, in his comments ad loc., writes 'and the rabbi, of blessed memory, wrote . . .'—deliberately or otherwise omitting the rabbi's name. It is interesting that R. Nissim himself, in his responsum, § 58, firmly prohibited the remarriage of a nursing mother, adding, 'I have been approached on this matter on several occasions, and have prohibited it, particularly after the first case, concerning a prominent member of the Gerona community, and although the matter was extremely grave, I could not agree to grant permission under any circumstances, even though there was a willingness to impose restrictive conditions. Anyone who seeks a pretext to rule leniently in this matter is surely breaching the fence erected by the sages.' So history repeats itself. Both R. Yom Tov and R. Nissim were following in the footsteps of their master R. Solomon ben Adret, who greatly admired the teachings of the French and German scholars (as did *his* master, Naḥmanides); R. Solomon, in his responsum § 723, upheld the prohibition

Urbach dated the episode to around 1245,[26] based on considerations to be clarified presently. However, R. Jacob was already known for his scholarship some ten years previously, as R. Abraham ben Azriel, the author of *Arugat habosem*, who wrote his book in 1234, had heard an explanation of a line in a certain *piyut* 'in the name of R. Jacob of Poland, may he rest in peace', following a quote from a statement by R. Judah Heḥasid. Urbach quite rightly identified the two R. Jacobs, as is indeed beyond any doubt; the reference to him as deceased would then, obviously, be a late interpolation. In Urbach's view, R. Isaac Or Zaru'a wrote his responsum against R. Jacob of Cracow around the year 1245, because in that responsum he does not appeal to any of his great teachers but cites an 'almost unknown' authority: 'In our day the matter depends considerably on our master R. Aaron, for he alone survives in this generation, for in him is Torah, old age, and greatness, and he is worthy of zeal for the honour of the Lord and His Torah, and we shall all concur with him.' This is quite plausible, argues Urbach, if the passage was written towards the end of the author's life, when his great teachers were no longer alive. I shall show later that the phrase 'may he rest in peace' stands on its own merits, the whole episode having occurred before 1234, perhaps as much as ten years earlier. The failure to appeal to his teachers is not conclusive, for the author's most prominent teachers were already dead by the years 1220–5: Ravyah, R. Simḥah of Speyer, R. Judah Heḥasid, and R. Judah Sir Leon; hence there is, of course, no need to go as far back as 1245 to explain the text.

In 1973 Kupfer published a collection of 'Responsa and Rulings' of French and German scholars from MS Bodl. 692,[27] one of them being, 'It happened that a certain woman sinned and had intercourse with her husband while menstrually unclean.' R. Hezekiah ben Jacob of Magdeburg and his court

even for a case in which there were two wet-nurses! Cf. also the responsa of R. Moses Halawa, R. Solomon's disciple, in the last year of his life, and the pupil of his son R. Judah—these responsa were recently published in the collection of R. Moses Halawa's responsa, ed. M. Herschler (Jerusalem, 1987), §§ 137, 142–3. French scholars, on the other hand, were inclined to take a more lenient approach, provided certain reinforcing conditions were observed; but we cannot go into detail here. The questioner in § 137 was R. Shealtiel Hen, and the wording of his question implies that R. Jehiel of Paris, the leading French authority of his time, concurred with R. Tobias of Vienne's permissive view. Another implication from that responsum is that there was also a lenient responsum of R. Solomon Adret, unconnected, of course, with the episode of R. Jacob Hakohen; as yet, however, I have been unable to locate it in the printed editions. The episode is also referred to in the responsa of R. Meir of Rothenburg ( (Lwów, 1860), § 362 = (Prague, 1608), § 864 = *Teshuvot maimoniyot on Sefer nashim*, § 24), but the story has been changed: 'It happened that a *cohen* married a nursing mother . . . and they adjured the nursing mother . . . and this was done on the view of R. Jacob Hakohen of Krakow . . .', as if he himself was not involved in the case; perhaps there were two distinct occasions, one involving himself and another, later one. Also preserved in R. Meir of Rothenburg's responsum are a few rare lines from R. Jacob's own words and the halakhic argument of his opponents.

[26] E. E. Urbach, *Arugat habosem*, iv (Jerusalem, 1963), 120–1.
[27] E. Kupfer, *Teshuvot upesakim* (Jerusalem, 1973), 166.

strictly forbade the woman to maintain conjugal relations with her husband, and revoked her privileges under her *ketubah*, including her property rights. They sent letters to that effect to R. Aaron of Regensburg and R. Jacob ben Solomon of Courson. As transpires from the correspondence, at some time 'the rabbi Jacob Hakohen' intervened in the discussion, suggesting that some compromise be reached between the parties concerning the monetary arrangements, rather than make the woman totally destitute. Finally, however, he 'removed himself from the deliberations', and R. Jacob of Courson therefore held that his view was not binding 'but merely advice'. There is a similar reference in R. Hezekiah's letter, where the scholar in question is called 'the rabbi Jacob son of Shalom'. Kupfer conjectured that the person involved was the same R. Jacob Svara of Cracow, suggesting, moreover, that he was also the scholar mentioned in a responsum (§ 775) of R. Isaac Or Zaru'a addressed to 'the generous R. Aaron' concerning the latter's prospective engagement. At the end of that responsum we read: 'And concerning the fact that he has summoned you to appear before R. [Isaac],[28] think nothing of it, for there resides in your city the rabbi Jacob Hakohen, who is a qualified expert . . .'. Kupfer smoothly assumes that the responsum was sent to Regensburg, as he tacitly identifies 'the generous R. Aaron' with the celebrated sage of that name from Regensburg. That is not possible, however, for it is clear from the salutation at the beginning of the letter that the reference is to a different person, a respected layman ('a youth elevated above the common folk') and nothing more, who would like to cancel a marriage match concluded for his younger son ('that your son, from the day he reached maturity, did not agree to that match'). However, if the identification of R. Jacob Hakohen is correct—and I am inclined to agree—the responsum was most probably addressed to Cracow itself, R. Jacob's place of residence. In that case it is not necessary to assume that he moved from Cracow to Regensburg, or vice versa, in accordance with Kupfer's later correction.

Further progress was made in 1983, again thanks to Kupfer.[29] He was examining fragments of *tosafot* on a thirteenth- or fourteenth-century parchment, found in bindings of old books in Cracow—an interesting coincidence! —whose photographs had reached the Institute for Microfilmed Hebrew Manuscripts. Among these fragments was a marginal gloss to a passage from *tosafot* on tractate *Hulin*, which began, 'And R. Jacob Cohen explained that the wording *le-bet halalo* was used because . . .'. The fragments are identical with a manuscript (Vatican 159) of Ashkenazi *tosafot* on tractate *Hulin*— essentially the same as the presently printed *tosafot*—in which there are several references, both in the body of the text and in marginal glosses, to a

---

[28] Completion based on Hebrew Union College, MS Cincinnati 154 (see above).

[29] E. Kupfer, 'From the Archives of the Institute for Microfilmed Hebrew Manuscripts of the National and Hebrew University Library' (Heb.), *Kirjath sefer*, 59 (1984), 959–60.

scholar identified only by his initials, R.Y.K.[30] It now seems plausible that (at least some occurrences of) these initials should be interpreted as an abbreviation for 'R. Jacob Cohen', rather than 'R. Judah Hakohen' (of Friedburg) as suggested previously. Consequently, it is then very likely that here, too, the scholar involved was that same resident of Cracow, for as yet we know of no other early scholar of the same name. The plausibility is further enhanced by the fact that R. Jacob belonged to the geographical sphere of Saxony–Bohemia—a region whose scholars the editor of MS Vatican 159, R. Eleazar of Tuch,[31] was constantly quoting, as he had studied under them and worked with them.

This identification, if considered sound, opens up another avenue of research and, for the first time, offers us a glimpse of the teachings of this forgotten scholar. The abbreviation R.Y.K. occurs quite frequently in the *Gilyonot tosafot* from the school of R. Eleazar of Tuch (see below), generally in halakhic debate with a scholar whose initials are R.M. Some of these marginal glosses, to several tractates of the Talmud, were recently published from manuscripts by Rabbi M. Blau.[32] The editor has identified R.Y.K. throughout —rightly, I believe—as R. Judah Hakohen of Friedburg. Now MS Vatican 159 also includes these glosses to tractate *Ḥulin*, incorporated in the main text of the *tosafot*, and they, too, feature the name R.Y.K., presumably referring here too to R. Judah Hakohen of Friedburg. However, the fragment that Kupfer discovered explicitly designates R. Jacob Hakohen, perhaps with the express purpose of distinguishing him from the other R.Y.K.s in the book. I am not inclined, therefore, to decipher each occurrence of R.Y.K. in this group of marginal glosses as referring to R. Jacob. Nevertheless, the initials

---

[30] Described and defined by Urbach, *Ba'alei hatosafot*, ii. 666 and n. 28. He believed that the editor was R. Eleazar of Metz.

[31] Contrary to the commonly held view, as expressed by Urbach, *Ba'alei hatosafot*, 581–2, that R. Eleazar was a French scholar (based on interpreting the Hebrew 'Tuch' as Touques), it is quite clear that he was German. His relatives lived in Germany; his associates and close circle were from Magdeburg and the surroundings; and the few known facts and actions that can be connected with him took place there, as may also be seen from Urbach's own account. How did he ever become 'head of the Academy of the land of France'? Rabbi M. Blau argued correctly in this respect. Urbach's counter-argument that 'this place [i.e. Tuchheim] is not mentioned in any source as a place where Jews lived' is no argument, for the same is true of the Normandian village of Touques—'we know nothing whatever of the history of its community' (Urbach, *Ba'alei hatosafot*)—and there is no reason to prefer it over Tuchheim in Germany. Similarly, his statement that 'R. Eliezer's Frenchness is proven by all that is known of him' is inaccurate. On the contrary, it is his 'Germanness' that emerges from all that is known of him, except when he studied under the French tosafists for several years, after which he returned to Germany. The truth of the matter is also evident from his *gilyonot* (marginal glosses) on the *tosafot* to tractate *Baba kama* (Blau made the above statements in his introduction to his edition of those glosses (New York, 1977) ), in which R. Eliezer writes, 'The explanation that was proposed to me in France seems to me extremely far-fetched' (Blau, in his edn., p. 293).

[32] On tractate *Shabbat* (New York, 1978), at the end of an edition of *Sefer habatim*; on tractate *Baba kama*, in *Shitat hakadmonim* (New York, 1977).

may well refer at times to one, at times to the other. The matter deserves further study.

In one of his many publications about medieval Bible exegetes, I. S. Lange referred to MS Paris 260. This manuscript closely resembles the anthology *Moshav zekenim*, published by Rabbi S. Sasson (London, 1959), which includes exegesis of the Torah by the tosafists; the two texts indeed contain many parallel passages.[33] In his study, Lange pointed out several bibliographical and biographical details that are more complete in MS Paris. In appendix v to the article, Lange cited a few examples pertaining to the book of Genesis only; in one of these the name R. Jacob S.B.R., which appears in Genesis 3: 4, replaces the unqualified name R. Jacob at the end of the passage in the printed edition. Lange offers no comment, but this might appear to be a rare reference to R. Jacob Svara[34] of Cracow in connection with the explanation of a biblical verse. This intriguing possibility inspired me to examine the entire manuscript closely, but I found no other such reference. Nevertheless, I discovered that MS Paris (= *Moshav zekenim*) was culled from a variety of sources, among them the Ashkenazi work *Pa'aneah raza* (first pub. Prague, 1607), from whose original version the appellation Jacob S.B.R. is taken. I then proceeded to examine early manuscripts of *Pa'aneah raza*. The printed edition of that work is a highly abbreviated version of the original, as demonstrated mainly by the large, important MS Oxford, Bodl. 3244 in Neubauer's Catalogue. There I found the following sentence: 'The rabbi Jacob of C[racow?] explained in the name of R. Moses of Taku . . .',[35] as well as the reverse, 'R. Moses, who explained in the name of R. Jacob . . .'.[36]

At the end of this manuscript there is a colophon by the author, from which we learn that it was written, or, more precisely, edited, by R. Isaac son of R. Judah Halevi. It is replete with uniquely Ashkenazi—and unfamiliar—material,[37] including much from the school of R. Judah Hehasid and his circle. R. Isaac drew on several collections as his basic sources, which he lists as follows: 'From my teachers, and from the words of R.Y.Z. and his novellae, and from the words of R. Jacob of Orléans and the commentary of our rabbi

[33] I. S. Lange, 'The Book *Moshav zekenim*' (Heb.), *Hama'yan*, Tammuz [5]732 (Summer 1972), 1–39. Cf. ibid., n. 26. Cf. *Moshav zekenim* (London, 1959).

[34] The following passage appears in a manuscript collection of stories in the possession of the National and Hebrew University Library, Jerusalem (8vo 3182): (see below, n. 83): 'There was a certain pious man by the name of S.B.R., and why was he known as S.B.W.R. [!] because he was a learned man (*ba'al sevarah*) . . .'. This is the opening sentence of a fanciful folk-tale whose plot is placed in the time of the (talmudic) sages; nevertheless, one can derive from it (and from the other literary material in this collection) many realia pertaining to Germany of the 13th–14th centuries. And see below, n. 83. And cf. A. Jellinek, *Beit hamidrash*, vi = J. D. Eisenstein, *Otsar midrashim* (New York, 1915), ii. 334 (§ 16): 'A Story of Ben Savar . . .'.

[35] 'Va'era', fo. 52*a*; missing in the printed edn.

[36] 'Beshalah', fo. 58*a*.

[37] I hope to devote a special article to this work and its various manuscripts.

Bekhor Shor and some of what I found in the Garden [a well-known book] . . . and some *peshatim* and *gematriyot* from the words of our rabbi Judah Hehasid and from the words of the rabbi R. Eleazar . . .'. Now material from all the sources that he mentions by name may be located in the text itself dozens of times, if not more, properly designated at the end of each quotation, except for the source that he calls 'R.Y.Z. and his novellae'. To the best of my ability, I have been able to pinpoint only about ten quotations from this source. On the other hand, the dominant figure—on the personal level, rather than the literary—in the book is a scholar referred to as R. Jacob. His name occurs hundreds of times as a source, though presumably not always referring to the same person. It is readily proved that some of the references are to Rabbenu Tam, others to R. Jacob of Orléans and sometimes to other known tosafists. Who is the R.Y.Z. who is cited in the colophon as a basic source but rarely mentioned in the text itself? Upon considering the problem, one immediately recalls a statement by the grandson of R. Samuel Schlettstadt, who, at the end of the fourteenth century, drew up for his own use a long list of abbreviations and acronyms for names of scholars culled from the Hebrew literature at his disposal,[38] based on his own learning experience; and there he wrote, 'The R.Y.Z. in the *gilyonot* is R. Jacob Katz.'[39] The signature R.Y.Z. is common in marginal *tosafot* in *Shitah mekubetset*, in the Ashkenazi glosses (*gilyonot*) to Alfasi's Code, and in glosses on *Sefer mordekhai*, *Sefer mitsvot katan*, and others —a point we shall come back to later. Possibly, then, R. Isaac ben Judah was referring to this very scholar: R.Y.Z. = R. Jacob Katz = R. Jacob Hakohen, so that some of the designations 'R. Jacob' would be referring to the scholar we are discussing here. Alongside R. Jacob's name, and associated with it, one commonly finds in the manuscript *Pa'aneah raza* the names of two other scholars, R. Moses and R. Aaron. Everything suggested here in connection with *Pa'aneah raza* is little more than conjecture, in need of corroboration and proof; I have chosen to include these suggestions in view of their importance, in the hope that time will bring further clarification.

Rabbi Jacob of Cracow belonged to the circle of Judah Hehasid's disciple-companions. This fact emerges from what is apparently the only manuscript of a book of *gematriyot* written by Judah Hehasid's disciples, formerly in the possession of Avraham Epstein and later in the Jewish Community Library, Vienna. Together with most manuscripts in that collection, it was lost during the Holocaust and so far has not resurfaced. Epstein gave a brief description of the manuscript, from which it follows that one of the only three

---

[38] Published by I. Benjacob, 'Shem hagedolim', in *Devarim atikim* (Leipzig, 1844), 7–10.

[39] The enigma of the initials R.Y.Z. is encountered in a variety of contexts in rabbinic literature; the solution is of course not the same everywhere. See M. Kahana, 'Commentaries on the *Sifri* Hidden in Manuscript' (Heb.), in M. Benayahu (ed.), *Studies in Memory of the Rishon Le-Zion R. Yitzhak Nissim* (Jerusalem, 1985), ii. 102 n. 60.

scholars mentioned there by name was 'R. Jacob Hakohen the pious, of blessed memory'.[40]

## R. MOSES POLER

Another forgotten scholar who may be placed in thirteenth-century Poland is R. Moses Poler. He is mentioned in various manuscripts (and here and there in print as well) as Moses Poler, Moses Polak, Moses Polya, Moses Polier, Moses of Pol, and Moses of Polin (i.e. Poland). The sparse data relating to this scholar and his actions were first assembled by A. Marmorstein in a passing note in one of his articles.[41] In light of our increasing knowledge about this scholar, he deserves detailed discussion, which is of necessity preliminary at this stage. He is mentioned several times in an early commentary on the Torah, BL MS 2853, whose author is anonymous but the time of writing is known—the turn of the thirteenth and fourteenth centuries,[42] and it is based on teachings of the tosafists of that time. The same scholar is mentioned in a few other manuscripts,[43] and in a *gilayon* (or set of marginal glosses on the *tosafot*), cited by *Shitah mekubetset* on tractate *Ketubot*.[44] Unfortunately, Bezalel Ashkenazi

---

[40] See A. Z. Schwartz, *Die Hebräischen Handschriften der Nationalbibliothek in Wien* (Leipzig, 1925), no. 234. One of my notebooks contains a comment that R. Jacob Hakohen is mentioned as one of R. Judah Hehasid's teachers(!) in an old manuscript of a Torah commentary known to R. H. Y. D. Azulai, which he copied into one of his books (near the end of the book of Genesis). I was subsequently unable to locate the passage and concluded that my reference involved an error. The reference has now been located in the book *Penei david* (Livorno, 1792), 49a. Cf. S. Emanuel, 'The Lost Halakhic Books of the Tosafists' (Heb.), Ph.D. thesis, Hebrew University, Jerusalem, 1993, 205 n. 10. My colleague Prof. Sid Z. Leiman has called my attention to the following passage in Elijah ben Moses de Vidas, *Reshit hokhmah* (ed. pr. Venice, 1579), 'Sha'ar ha'anavah', ch. 3: 'I heard it told of the Hasid R. Jacob Ashkenazi, of blessed memory, that he was a wonderfully learned scholar, and wished to teach his lore to R. Judah Hehasid. He first tested him in connection with anger, as they had a tradition that one should not transmit the lore save to a person who had been tested for anger and had not displayed anger, and they tested him, six times he suffered and on the seventh he could not resist etc.' The story is also interesting in relation to R. Judah Hehasid's personality. Prof. Moshe Idel has informed me that the hagiographical tales, particularly those about Hasidei Ashkenaz, scattered here and there in *Reshit hokhmah*, were originally part of a lost historical work including an autobiography of R. Isaac of Acre as well as hagiographical tales of famous Jews, mainly from the circles of Hasidei Ashkenaz, collected by R. Isaac during his lifetime. On this book, see A. Goldreich, 'The Book *Me'irat eynayim* by R. Isaac of Akko' (Heb.), Ph.D. thesis, Hebrew University, Jerusalem, 1984, 408–9 nn. 10–11.

[41] A. Marmorstein, 'An Italian Scholar and *Posek*' (Heb.), *Devir*, 2 (1924), 226.

[42] Marmorstein devoted a special article to this manuscript; Urbach, however (*Ba'alei hatosafot*, ii. 486 n. 32), comments: 'All Marmorstein's statements about this manuscript are unacceptable.' Cf. the important work of M. Kahana, 'Prolegomena to a New Edition of *Sifri* Numbers' (Heb.), Ph.D. thesis, Hebrew University, Jerusalem, 1982, 71–6; id., 'Commentaries on the *Sifri*'.

[43] See previous note.

[44] These references in *Shitah mekubetset* were already noted by Zunz, as pointed out by Marmorstein, 'An Italian Scholar', loc. cit. They are of special interest, because this particular *Gilyon tosafot* was edited by R. Eleazar of Tuch himself, i.e. at the end of the 13th century. This is explicitly

cited very sparingly from these marginal notes, both in *Ketubot* and in *Baba kama*. At any rate, one of them reads as follows: 'Our teacher R. Moses Polak posed a difficulty: If the Day of Atonement be postponed to Tuesday, the seventh day of the willow-branch [i.e. Hoshana Rabbah, the seventh day of the Feast of Tabernacles] will fall on the Sabbath day! And our teacher R. Abraham explained: If [the Day of Atonement] fell on Sunday and should be postponed to Monday, it shall not be so postponed.'[45] While in *Shitah mekubetset* on *Baba metzia* we read: 'In a marginal note to the *tosafot* it was written as follows: R. Moses Poler posed a difficulty: Why should he take the oath— after all, the borrower supports him!—or perhaps the text is concerned with a case in which the borrower is related to the owner. And my teacher R. Moses explained that this was a case in which there was some other transaction between them that required an oath.'[46] The same case is mentioned in MS Cambridge 781,[47] a most important manuscript, dealing with forbidden foods etc., by a disciple of R. Eleazar of Worms, yet to be described in the scholarly literature. The text on fo. 186*a* cites this brief exchange in the name of 'the s[aintly] R. Moses Poler . . . and M.H.R.M. explained . . .', the latter being none other than the above-mentioned R. Moses. We have already found 'R. Jacob' deliberating in a similar vein with 'R. Moses', in our discussion of *Pa'aneah raza*. R. Bezalel Ashkenazi mentions him again in *Shitah mekubetset*, and again as *Gilyon tosafot* in his commentary to the same tractate (50*a*). As we have pointed out, R. Bezalel made only scant use of this *gilayon*, and consequently we have very few quotations from the teachings of R. Moses Poler. At any rate, it is interesting that elsewhere R. Bezalel quotes from this *Gilyon tosafot* as follows: 'The difficulty posed in the *tosafot* of R. Samson, as to whether a defiling thought is considered speech [in connection with the sacrificial rite], how does he know . . . ? And R.Y. said in the name of my teacher R. Aaron of Regensburg . . .'. The eastern Ashkenazi provenance of this comment, as might be expected from the nature of the previous *gilayon*, is clear here too. Our data therefore enable us to reconstruct the context with some

stated in *Shitah mekubetset* on Ket. 60*b*. He cites certain *kunteresim* (see below), which systematically criticize the *Gilyon tosafot* here and elsewhere, as follows: 'It is further written in another *Gilyon tosafot* as follows . . . But the *kunteresim* write as follows: That is puzzling: what is the difference between this *gilayon* and the first *gilayon*, as the rabbi R. Eleazar of Tuch wrote them both? . . .' And the statement is also made directly by R. Bezalel Ashkenazi: 'Know that the marginal glosses of the *tosafot* were formulated by R. Eleazar of Tuch, the author of the *tosafot*' (fo. 32). The question of the *gilyonot* and the *kunteresim* is discussed in the new edition of Urbach's *Ba'alei hatosafot*, ii. 628. I disagree with his account on several points, but that is not relevant to the present issue. The *Gilyonot tosafot* of R. Eleazar of Tuch constitute the collected comments and deliberations of the last tosafists, particularly the German contemporaries and compatriots of R. Eleazar of Tuch, as well as his own comments (see n. 31 above), on the main corpus of the *tosafot*, which are mostly French, up to *c*. the mid-13th century. They therefore comprise an independent work of R. Eleazar of Tuch himself, inserted in the margins of his monumental edition of the *tosafot*.

[45] On Ket. 5*a*.                      [46] On Ket. 35*b*.                      [47] Fo. 186*a*.

confidence. R. Eleazar of Tuch died before 1291; he was a nephew of R. Hezekiah of Magdeburg[48] and a disciple of R. Isaac Or Zaru'a. Hence R. Moses was active in the first half of the thirteenth century or a little later, in mid-century.

The same R. Moses is mentioned again in MS Oxford 696—an Ashkenazi collection of rulings on matters of ritual slaughter, written in the region of Regensburg (whose leaders and rabbis the author mentions) around the middle of the thirteenth century. The passage of relevance here, which is headed with the Hebrew letters '*HG*', abbreviating the word *hagahah* (gloss), and ends with the phrase 'thus far the gloss', is part of the main text, like other 'glosses' in this work. It reads as follows: 'Gl[oss] found in a responsum of Rashi: our statement concerning a lobe of the lung . . . But if the meat does not protrude beyond the adhesion, [the meat is] ritually unfit, because it has adhered breadthwise—a tradition transmitted by R. Moses Poler. And if the tubercle is adhering to the ribs, it is ritually unfit—in the name of R. Abraham Ḥladik. Thus far the gloss.' The author reports two halakhic traditions, one in the name of R. Abraham Ḥladik, a leading authority on Jewish law and customs in eastern Ashkenaz in the first half of the thirteenth century, and the other in the name of our R. Moses Poler. Immediately after the gloss, the text states: 'As to what Rashi wrote concerning the little rose-lobe, wherever there is an adhesion the animal is ritually unfit—I received a tradition from my teacher, R. Isaiah di Trani, that this is the case only if it adheres to a lobe . . .'. R. Isaiah di Trani, a colleague of R. Isaac Or Zaru'a, died around 1230–40.[49] Our author is writing, therefore, around the third quarter of the thirteenth century.

A further reference to R. Moses Poler may be found, once more, in MS Oxford 2344 of *Pa'aneaḥ Raza*, which, as we have already stated, is an Ashkenazi commentary on the Torah from the first half of the fourteenth century, including a great variety of eastern Ashkenazi material. Part of the work has been published in print, under the same title, in several editions; but the bulk of it still remains in manuscript—and MS Oxford is one of the most important manuscripts. Indeed, I have already referred to it here for other purposes. At one point in the book we read: 'R. [Moses] Poliera posed a further difficulty, from what we say in [chapter 7 of tractate Ḥul.]: If an unclean fish be found among clean fish, one should throw it away and the remainder is permitted . . . But this raises the difficulty, whether the same reason would not suffice to declare all of the fish unfit. . . . And the difficulty was solved for him by our teacher R. Solomon . . .' (fo. 87*a*). In style, the

[48] Urbach, *Ba'alei hatosafot*, ii. 581–5.

[49] See my article 'Rabbi Isaiah di Trani the Elder and his Contacts with Byzantium and Palestine' (Heb.), *Shalem*, 4 (1984), 411. On R. Abraham Hladik, see S. Spitzer, 'The *Minhagim* of R. Abraham Hladik' (Heb.), *Kovets al yad*, 9 [19] (1980), 151–215.

passage is very similar to that of the discussion cited by R. Bezalel Ashkenazi
in *Shitah mekubetset* (see above), between R. Moses and his colleague R.
Abraham. On fo. 94*a* we read: 'And R. Moses Polier posed the difficulty:
Granted that the phylactery worn on the head is not considered an inter-
position; it should nevertheless be considered as superfluous [priestly] vest-
ments . . . And our teacher R. Solomon explained . . .'. This selfsame passage
is cited in the aforementioned BL MS 2853. Yet another passage in *Pa'aneah
raza* (fo. 89*a*) reads as follows: 'R. Moses Poliera posed a difficulty: Why
should one desecrate the Sabbath by cooking [for an invalid], which is a prohibition punishable by stoning, while one can do the same by telling a non-Jew
. . . And our teacher R. Hayyim explained . . . And our teacher R. Solomon
explained . . .'. And a fourth reference: 'R. Moses Polier posed a difficulty . . .
Why does the Talmud ask in tractate *Bekhorot* . . . One who makes a slit in the
ear of a first-born animal, is his son after him fined or not? . . . And our teacher
R. Solomon explained that this question was asked on behalf of the Rabbis . . .'.
Thus, though we do not know just who this R. Moses Poler was, we are
acquainted with his colleagues: R. Solomon, R. Abraham, R. Hayyim, and
R. Moses—a group of scholars studying and discussing points of law
together, in a yeshiva excelling in Torah and wisdom. However, the yeshiva
need not be in Poland; it is not inconceivable that our R. Moses came from
Poland to study with his colleagues in Germany.

Another reference to R. Moses Poler may be identified in MS Paris,
Alliance 166, which contains a brief, four-page work commenting on
Maimonides' Laws of Ritual Slaughter.[50] The work has an appendix entitled
'Examinations of Our Master Moses Palier, of blessed memory' (fos. 107–9)
very probably the same R. Moses Poler we have been discussing. In my first
search of the card-index at the Institute for Microfilmed Hebrew Manuscripts, this particular work escaped my attention because of the distortion of
the name (spelled here without a *vav*). However, a study of the work confirms
the identification without any doubt. The author refers in his brief commentary to R. Moses Taku ('some authorities [test the adhesion in the lung]
by rubbing it with the hand; R. Moses Tatu (*sic*) did this'); to R. Jacob ben
Nahman of Magdeburg ('This was instituted by R. Jacob ben Nahman of
Magdeburg' [in connection with adhesions in the lung]; 'It happened that a
tubercle was found . . . and the scholar R. Jacob ben R. Nahman permitted it
to be eaten and said . . .'); to 'our teacher R. Ezekiel' ('I heard from our teacher
R. Ezekiel that if the two membranes of the lung have been examined . . .'); to
R. Isaac ('Thus said R. Isaac: I have not heard any prohibition from our rabbis
in this connection . . .'); and to R. Eleazar of Bohemia ('and so I have heard

---

[50] I am indebted to my friend and colleague Dr Simhah Emanuel, who drew my attention to this
passage after he had unearthed this work as part of his Ph.D. thesis, 'The Lost Halakhic Books',
256–7.

that R. Eleazar of Bohemia permits . . .'). All these scholars belong to the group of Polish scholars, as listed below. This person Moses, then, in the brief span of four pages, mentions a fairly large number of local scholars, of the same period and circles discussed here; perhaps he was also personally acquainted with them. Moreover, apart from these particular scholars (and a few earlier tosafists), the author mentions no one else, with one exception: 'And I, the writer, have it on the authority of my teacher R. Shabbetai, of blessed memory . . . that he told me in the name of R. Oshaia of Tran, of blessed memory, who proved from the wording of R. Shabbetai, who said . . .'. Now I have already demonstrated this link of tradition between R. Moses Poler and R. Isaiah di Trani—and on this very same issue—on the basis of another, independent source. It thus transpires that the link was by way of R. Isaiah di Trani's pupil R. Shabbetai, who is also known to us from direct contemporary evidence[51] and may thus be assumed to have studied Torah in his youth, like his illustrious master, in the Torah centres of Germany.[52]

MS Paris, Alliance 166 was written in the year 1627 by 'Benjamin son of . . . Abraham Motal of blessed memory'—none other than the anthologist of the great halakhic collection known as *Tumat yesharim* (Venice, 1622), which contains a rich selection of works by both early and late authorities. The same Benjamin Motal's MS Paris is also a collection of various works on ritual slaughter and related areas, organized as a kind of commentary on Maimonides' Laws of Ritual Slaughter. Moshe Poler's brief work is appended at the end of the collection. Anthologies of this kind on ritual slaughter and the like were very popular among Yemenite scholars of all generations, and they copied this collection, too, together with Moses Poler's brief treatise (distorting the text considerably; one Yemenite manuscript calls our Moses 'Pleiral'). A search of the card-index at the Institute for Microfilmed Hebrew Manuscripts brought up two such Yemenite manuscripts: Bar-Ilan University 235 (Institute Mic. 36593); New York JTS Rab. 589 (Mic. 39280).

---

[51]  See my article 'Rabbi Isaiah di Trani', 414. Incidentally, the source currently before us provides conclusive proof—if such were still needed—for the identification of R. Isaiah ben Immanuel, mentioned in Nathan Kalkish's book *Even sapir*, with the celebrated Isaiah di Trani, author of *Sefer hamakhria*, as I argued in my article. We may thus reject the arguments of S. Hasidah, who, without any basis, challenged the identification in his edition of *Shibolei haleket* by R. Zedekiah ben Abraham the Physician (Jerusalem, 1988), 70 n. 36. Hasidah actually mentions the very passage from Kalkish's work and rejects the identification of the R. Isaiah ben Immanuel referred to there with R. Isaiah di Trani. However, the association of the disciple Shabbetai with both figures clearly corroborates my argument. The sparse material cited in relation to the 'unknown' scholar Isaiah ben Immanuel should also be associated with R. Isaiah di Trani the Elder. For an argument against Hasidah on another count, pointing out the fundamental error responsible for his misconception, see S. Z. Havlin in his 'Survey of New Books and Studies' (Heb.), *Alei sefer*, 15 (1988–9), 157–8.

[52]  The rabbi Shabbetai mentioned by R. Isaiah di Trani is, of course, a different person, apparently known to us from another source. Cf. the Italian work published by S. Assaf, 'From the Teachings of the First Scholars of Italy' (Heb.), *Sinai*, 34 (1964), 15–40.

Two further Yemenite manuscripts of this type are mentioned in the list of Yemenite manuscripts at the Ben-Zvi Institute.[53]

A closer look at the collection of commentaries preceding Moses Poler's work in the Yemenite manuscripts reveals some new data of interest to our topic. Among the many sources from which Motal put his collection together, besides such familiar works as *Arba'ah turim*, *Kolbo*, *Sefer ha'itur*, etc., the anthologist cites quite copiously from a commentary to tractate *Ḥulin* by a R. Dosa, known as *Ner Yisra'el*. Yosef Tobi suggested that this R. Dosa was the son of R. Sa'adya Gaon.[54] However, comparison of the parallel manuscripts indicates that the author in question was R. Dosa the Greek, a Byzantine scholar who lived in the second half of the fourteenth century, studied under Ashkenazi scholars, notably R. Sar-Shalom of Vienna, and wrote, among other things, a commentary on Rashi's commentary to the Torah (still in manuscript).[55] The author's identity is quite clear from the fragments of this commentary to tractate *Ḥulin*—a lost commentary of which nothing was known until now, particularly in connection with the interesting material it contains relating to the Ashkenazi scholars. A description of the personality and activities of this Byzantine scholar would be of considerable interest, but that is not our purpose here. His importance in our present context stems from the fact that, according to the structure of the system of copying and quotation in these Yemenite collections—which cannot be discussed in detail here—it seems almost certain that Moses 'Palier's' 'Laws of Examination' were also copied from R. Dosa's commentaries to tractate *Ḥulin*, not from the original. That is to say: it was R. Dosa the Greek, who studied in Ashkenazi academies under the leading Ashkenazi teachers in the second half of the fourteenth century, who received and transmitted these traditions of Moses Poler from his teachers; the latter presumably knew this material from a more direct source, being removed only by about 100 years from Poler himself. R. Dosa's lost book has thus yielded information about another lost book—that of Moses Poler.[56]

Most recently, a further search produced a quotation from R. Moses Poler's teachings in a book of R. Joseph di Sigora, a disciple of R. Joshua Soncino (brother-in-law of R. Moses Isserles, Rema), in MS Benayahu (Mic. 44725),

[53] Y. Tobi, *Kitvei hayad hateimaniyim bimekhon Ben-Zvi* (Jerusalem, 1982), nos. 121, 379.

[54] Loc. cit.

[55] Bodl. MS Neubauer. A few passages from this manuscript, in which Dosa quotes teachings of his teacher R. Sar-Shalom, were published by S. Spitzer in *Hilkhot uminhagei Maharash* (Jerusalem, 1977), 180–9, based on a previous publication by A. Neubauer in the Dutch journal *Israelitische Letterbode*, 8 (1882–3). See Spitzer's comments in his introduction (p. 17 n. 25). And cf. further id., 'Data on R. Dosa the Greek from his Work on the Torah' (Heb.), in Benayahu (ed.), *Studies in Memory of the Rishon LeZion*, iv. 177–84.

[56] See my article 'On Three Lost Hebrew Books from the Middle Ages' (Heb.), in *Saul Lieberman Memorial Volume* (Jerusalem, 1993), 214–24.

fo. 30*b*. The quotation consists of a question and answer concerning a passage in the first chapter of tractate *Gitin*. Joshua Soncino lived and wrote in Turkey and brought much Ashkenazi material to the attention of Sefardi scholars.

## OTHER TORAH SCHOLARS IN THIRTEENTH-CENTURY POLAND

I will now list other thirteenth-century scholars whose teachings have been cited and who are explicitly associated with Poland. My attention in this article focuses on rabbinical literature only; but it should be noted that contemporary rabbinical sources contain further material, as yet unexploited, bearing on the history of Polish communities in the thirteenth century, both in manuscript and in print. Thus, for example, one finds, in the responsa of R. Hayyim Or Zaru'a (son of R. Isaac Or Zaru'a),[57] a responsum concerning a coercive divorce involving members of the Ludmir community. The responsum, dating back to the last third of the thirteenth century, may be added to an item of information from the year 1171 about 'R. Benjamin the generous of Ludmir', who happened to be in Cologne at the time and fell victim to some kind of accusation.[58] The responsum, in contrast to the case of R. Benjamin, attests to the existence of a regular community with properly appointed leaders and institutions, including official rabbis: R. Isaac and R. Manoah ben Jacob,[59] who were involved in imposing the divorce. Here, too, it is quite clear that the far-off community of Ludmir, in Volhynia province, depended on the halakhic rulings and teachings of German and Bohemian scholars. But concealed in R. Hayyim Or Zaru'a's responsum is yet another revelation: mention is made there of Jews in the nearby town of Chełm, where the recalcitrant husband was staying: 'Finally we sent after the woman and the agent that she should be divorced here in Vladimir [Ludmir], and we urged him that he should divorce [her] himself, but he refused, and to the town of Chełm, too, we decreed that he should be sent for . . .'. I believe this is the earliest testimony in our sources to a Jewish presence in that city.[60]

[57] § 157.        [58] A. Habermann, *Sefer gezerot ashkenaz vetsarfat* (Jerusalem, 1964), 128.

[59] The father's name is lacking in the printed edition but appears in the manuscript of the responsum, at the end of the collection *Simanei or zaru`a*, MS Vat. 148, fo. 155*b*.

[60] Dr David Assaf drew my attention to the rather surprising possibility that R. Joseph *Haḥelmi*, whom Judah ben Shemaryah met in R. Meir of Rothenburg's study-house, was a native of Chełm. See N. Goldfeld, 'A Commentary on the Torah by Judah b. Shemaryah in a Geniza manuscript' (Heb.), *Kovets al yad*, 10 [20] (1982), 144. And cf. S. Eidelberg, 'On the Antiquity of the Communities of Chełm and Ludmir' (Heb.), *Zion*, 31 (1966), 116. At one time I thought to identify a reference to the city of Ostraha in *Or zaru'a*, i. § 112. The responsum in question is concerned with a Jew named Mattathias who inadvertently killed somebody and was banished to another city, where he was received with respect. The printed edition reads, 'Therefore this Mattathias, in so far as he declared that for that event [he was banished], even though the people of Trigom [*benei adam Trigom*]

In this connection, Mr Adi Schremer has called my attention to a passage in *Or zaru'a*, 'Hilkhot terefot', 56*d* (bottom): 'Similarly, R. Gershon . . . and our rabbi Sasson . . . and our rabbi Samuel . . . and R. Isaac ben Judah . . . and in Mainz and Polanit [Poland] it is permitted in accordance with their ruling . . .'. We have yet another relevant source in a responsum of R. Judah Hakohen, author of *Sefer hadinin* (mid-eleventh century), mentioned at the very beginning of this article: 'A certain Jew brought goods from the Land of Polum' included in R. Meir ben Barukh of Rothenburg, *Responsa* (Prague, 1610), § 885)—probably also a reference to Poland.

Let us proceed now with our list of Polish scholars.

*R. Moses ben Ḥisdai.* Also known as R. Moses Taku, R. Moses was one of the central members of ḥasidei Ashkenaz,[61] a man of extraordinary learning who produced a tremendous literary output of high quality in both legal and philosophical genres. He was active in Poland, for Naḥmanides calls him 'the great scholar R. Moses ben R. Ḥisdai of Poland, may he live a long life', stating in his name that 'the wording of this talmudic teaching has been distorted by the students . . .'.[62] As there are good grounds for the assumption that Naḥmanides' novellae to the Talmud had already been written by 1240, it seems likely that R. Moses was still alive at that time. A considerable quantity of information about him was assembled by Urbach,[63] creating a picture of his literary, social, and religious activities. He was active around the cities of Regensburg—where

treated him with respect, it is deemed a true exile.' However, in all the manuscripts that I have examined the text reads, 'even though the people of Ostrigom [benai Ostrigom; the letters would look similar in a badly written text] treated him with respect . . .'. The difficult word was obviously misunderstood by the printers, who mistakenly split it into two. However, my colleagues have pointed out to me that the reference is to the city of Esztergom in western Hungary, home of the oldest Jewish community in that country, known to have existed as early as the 11th century. In fact, R. Isaac Or Zaru'a himself visited Esztergom, as attested in his *Hilkhot nidah*, p. 51*a*.

[61] For a summary of this chapter in his life, see Y. Dan, introduction to facs. edn. of the book *Ketav tamim*, 7–27.          [62] Naḥmanides, *Novellae* to tractate Git. 7*b*.

[63] Urbach, *Ba'alei tosafot*, i. 420–6. The report that R. Moses Taku visited Palestine is extremely dubious, as my friend Dr Elhanan Reiner has shown me. The source is a responsum of R. Bezalel Ashkenazi, § 2, where the respondent quotes from the book *Ketav tamim*: 'Upon our arrival in Palestine . . .', citing several laws concerning agricultural matters which apply only to the Holy Land. However, R. Moses Taku's name is not mentioned at all, and there is no doubt that the scholar concerned is some other person who wrote a similarly named book; indeed, the very same passage is quoted verbatim in two manuscripts as the beginning of a letter by Isaac Hilo, a Spanish scholar of the 13th century, after his journey to Palestine. It is common knowledge that the letter describing a journey to Palestine, purportedly written by Isaac Hilo, is a forgery (see G. Scholem, 'The Book *Shevilei Yerushalayim* Attributed to R. Isaac Hilo is a Forgery' (Heb.), *Me'asef zion*, 6 [1934], 39–53; and see my article 'Matters of Erez-Israel' (Heb.), *Shalem*, 1 [1974], 82–3, and the argument that evolved on the affair in the subsequent two volumes of the journal). However, there was also a genuine letter, but it has not survived—except for its first lines, which match the quotation from *Ketav tamim* word for word. At any rate, further research is needed.

he probably officiated as rabbi; Magdeburg, where he was asked to intervene and resolve a conflict; Tachau (Tachov) in Bohemia (or Dachau in Germany), probably his native town; and Wiener-Neustadt, near Vienna, mentioned (in a later period) as his place of burial. He was also asked to intervene in the above-mentioned episode of R. Jacob Svara of Cracow, concurring in his responsum[64] with the majority view of the scholars who required R. Jacob to divorce his nursing wife, even though, as a *kohen*, he would never be able to remarry her. A description of R. Moses' character, as one of the greatest Torah scholars of his time—and one of the most extreme on the 'right wing' of ḥasidei Ashkenaz—and a full account of the philosophical, literary, and chronological problems that his biography raises require a special study.

*R. Mordecai of Poland and R. Isaac of Poland.* R. Moses Zaltman, son of R. Judah Heḥasid, studied under scholars who had attended his father's discourses on the Torah portions of the week. Known by name among those scholars are R. Mordecai of Poland and R. Isaac of Poland.[65] As implied, these two belong to a broader circle of scholar-companions. The leading figure was undoubtedly 'R. Isaa[c] [ben Ezekiel?] of Russia', who is referred to as such dozens of times. A comparison of parallels indicates that he is identical with R. Isaac of Moriat.[66] Some authorities have identified him with R. Isaac of Chernigov, near Kiev, who was also a disciple of R. Judah Heḥasid; this R. Isaac travelled through Europe, even reaching England, where he told R. Moses ben hanesi'ah that the Hebrew verb *yabem* (to marry one's brother's widow) meant 'sexual intercourse' in Russian. However, there is no support for this identification, and to my mind the identification with R. Isaac of Moriat must stand. Since R. Judah Heḥasid died in 1217, the members of this circle were active in the first half of the thirteenth century.

For the moment we can say nothing further, or more detailed, about these figures. Nevertheless, two further passages might be mentioned. One occurs in MS Gaster 730 (London Or. 9931), fos. 121*a*, 123*b*, where there are a few statements in the name of one 'R. Isaac Poler', whom I am inclined to identify with R. Isaac of Russia (and even if the two are distinct, we may at any rate add a further scholar to our list). The other passages appear in a commentary on the prayers by R. Eleazar of Worms, in manuscript, fo. 21*a*:

Our rabbi Judah Heḥasid asked my teacher R. Rab. (*sic*) Mordecai: Whence do we know that the Holy One commands many angels to guard those who fear Him?—from the verse, 'For

[64] *Or zaru'a*, i, § 740.

[65] I. S. Lange, *Perushei rabbi Yehudah Heḥasid la Torah* (Jerusalem, 1975), Terumah 19: 18; Beshalaḥ 14: 2.

[66] See Lange, *Perushei rabbi Yehudah Heḥasid la Torah*, index, s.v. For his father's name, Ezekiel, see below, text around n. 73. Cf. Kupfer, *Teshuvot upesakim*, 162 n. 14.

He will order His angels to guard you.' And whence do we know that he commands an individual angel?—from the verse 'The angel of the Lord camps around those who fear him.' . . . And he answered him: The verse 'The angel of the Lord camps . . .' refers to the Prince of the Countenance, who stands in the camp and commands the angels under him . . .[67]

In MS Paris 772,[68] however, we read, '. . . asked my teacher R. Y. ben R. Mordecai . . .'. At first sight this would seem to refer to the celebrated R. Isaac ben Mordecai (known as Ribam), one of the greatest tosafists of the generation before R. Judah Heḥasid, a resident of Regensburg, who was surely consulted by R. Judah on occasion. However, R. Eleazar of Worms could not have studied under Ribam; moreover, R. Judah could hardly have consulted him, for chronological reasons: R. Judah himself was still young when the latter was quite an old man. Urbach was therefore fully justified in not listing R. Isaac ben Mordecai as one of R. Eleazar of Worms's teachers, passing over Aptowitzer's statement to that effect in silence.[69] One should therefore prefer the simple reading 'R. Mordecai', as is indeed the case in other manuscripts of the commentary that I have examined. An interesting passage is included in a commentary to *Sefer yetsirah*, attributed to R. Sa'adya (a Franco-German scholar of the twelfth century): 'He made them by weight'—*kaf* and *lamed* occur halfway through the alphabet. . . . 'And He exchanged them all for one'—that is to say, when He made the alphabet, He placed the *alef* at the beginning of the alphabet with all 22 letters . . . and from them derived the alphabet *alef-tav bet-shin* etc . . . And R. Mordecai received [a tradition] that the middle of *alef-lamed bet-mem* was prior to that.'[70] This is not the proper place to discuss the commentary itself, which is a French work from the mid-thirteenth century, as Prof. Moshe Idel has assured me, though the bulk of its material belongs to the beginning of that century. At any rate, it is clear that in the first quarter of the thirteenth century (or slightly before that) there was a scholar named R. Mordecai in the circle of mystics; perhaps this is indeed our R. Mordecai.

R. Mordecai and R. Isaac of Poland are also mentioned in MS Cambridge 53 (Cat. Schiller-Szinessy), fos. 163–4.

*R. Simeon 'Polner' and R. Pinehas of Poland.* Another pair of scholars, active in the third quarter of the thirteenth century, is mentioned in the sermons of

---

[67] Text from MS Moscow 614, fo. 21*a*.       [68] Ed. and pub. M. Herschler (Jerusalem, 1992), 87.

[69] See Urbach, *Ba'alei hatosafot*, i. 389 and 199: 'Ribam was a man of halakhah and we do not know that he was active in any other area, except, perhaps, for a hint that he showed some interest in esoteric lore, as he asked R. Judah Heḥasid a question in angelology', citing the source before us now. This is not quite accurate, for Ribam—if the reference is indeed to him—was asked by Judah Heḥasid and not the opposite. Urbach's comment also contributes a major consideration in favour of our conviction that the person involved was not Ribam. Cf. Aptowitzer, *Ravyah*, introduction, 317 n. 5*a*.

[70] *Sefer yetsirah* (Przemyśl, 1885), end of ch. 2. Cited from BL MS 754, fo. 124*a*. This passage and others are omitted in the printed edition.

R. Hayyim Or Zaru'a: 'I heard from the *h*[*aver*] R. Simeon Polner, may God protect and preserve him, a good mnemonic for Counting the Omer, so as not to forget . . .'; and also: 'I heard from the *h*[*aver*] R. Phineas that in the land of Poland . . .'.[71]

*Rav Aaron and Rav Ezekiel.* The aforementioned responsum of R. Isaac Or Zaru'a concerning R. Jacob Hakohen and his marriage with a nursing woman (ii, § 740) is worded as an open letter and manifesto addressed to all rabbis of the region, but one of the latter is designated in particular by name and specifically urged to act:

Therefore, rabbis of all places, gather together and assemble and force him to divorce her, so that the words of the learned shall not come to nought; in our day the matter depends particularly on our teacher R. Aaron, for he alone remains in this generation, for in him is Torah and great age, and he is worthy of exercising zeal in honour of the Lord and in honour of His Torah, and we shall all sign after him.

As we have pointed out, the first part of the manuscript page was censored at some time in the Middle Ages, and we have no way of identifying the particular addressee. It transpires from the heading, as stated, that it was an open letter, but it is obvious that R. Aaron, and another scholar, named R. Ezekiel (see below), were among those actually named in the salutation. At the end of the letter, after a repeated call to take a stand and act in concert, R. Isaac Or Zaru'a ends his responsum as follows: 'To you, our masters R. Aaron and his yeshiva, and R. Ezekiel, [greetings of] life and peace.' It is quite obvious that these two scholars, like the other anonymous scholars alluded to in the letter, were local residents, for the responsum is worded as follows: 'Therefore, gentlemen, do not shirk your duty and divorce her from him in any way you can, for you surely know that this breach will spread to all places.' It is very doubtful whether the person in question is the celebrated R. Aaron of Regensburg, for the special tone of respect in this responsum is absent in other responsa of R. Isaac Or Zaru'a and his companions sent to the rabbi of Regensburg. I would assume that he and his companion R. Ezekiel were Polish scholars from around Cracow; we may be able to identify them in time. Special attention should be paid to the most unusual honorifics heaped upon R. Aaron, far exceeding the usual verbiage then in vogue. Incidentally, it was presumably to this scholar that R. Avigdor Cohen-Zedek of Vienna was alluding in his responsum, as cited in *Sefer mordekhai* on tractate *Shabbat*, ch. 11 (end):

R. Aaron asked R. Avigdor Kohen-Zedek, instruct us, our rabbi: concerning a cure by a spell, whether it may be pronounced on the Sabbath, if this involves a danger of pounding spices? And thus he replied: Chief of leaders, most honoured among the thirty, prince of fifty, *holy of holies*, builder of ruins and restorer of paths and many more mighty deeds, well versed in the channels of knowledge and wisdom, and nothing he proposes is impossible

---

[71] *Derashot mehar or zaru'a* (Jerusalem, 1974), 73, 84.

for him, *most eminent of the generation*, R. Aaron [. . .], may his memory be for a blessing, for his words are a cure and a remedy. In Sanhedrin, chapter 'ḥelek': It is permitted to rub the stomach with oil and feel it, it is permitted to pronounce spells against snakes and scorpions on the Sabbath, etc. . . . And moreover, our master and rabbi Simḥah [of Speyer] had a disorder of the eyes, and he ordered that spells be pronounced for him even on the Sabbath. Peace be upon you, I, the worm, Avigdor Kohen.[72]

Now, in the printed edition of *Sefer mordekhai*, 'Shabbat', § 385, we read: 'And once our rabbi Simḥah's eyes were unwell, and a certain woman taught the rabbi R. Avigdor Kohen a spell, and he pronounced this spell on the Sabbath twice a day on the eye, once in the morning and once in the evening.' The exceptional laudatory terms used in the salutations indicate quite clearly that we are concerned here with the same person. As to R. Ezekiel—I know nothing. Nevertheless, I have found a reference in a book named *Minhag tov*,[73] written around the year 1275 by an Ashkenazi Jew resident, apparently, in Italy, to a scholar by the name of R. Isaac ben R. Ezekiel of Russia. It is quite intriguing that the name of R. Aaron of Regensburg, too, mentioned above several times, occurs in this book, and the reference is most probably to the same circle or one of its offshoots.

*R. Isaac of Breslau.* This scholar is mentioned in R. Abraham ben Azriel of Bohemia's *Arugat habosem*. Urbach wrote in his introduction to the book: 'The author heard an explanation of a passage in the *Mekhilta* from R. Isaac of Vratislau, that is, Breslau. This scholar was the first Jew in that city to be mentioned in Hebrew literature. In many respects, it was a Polish city.'[74]

*R. Israel of the land of Poland.* This scholar's interpretation of a verse in Exodus (4: 2) is cited in an anonymous collection of exegeses in MS Strasbourg 44.[75] This Ashkenazi collection, written in the fifteenth century, consists for the most part of commentary by R. Judah Heḥasid as reported by his son R. Moses Zaltman. The manuscript was one of Lange's prime sources for his edition of R. Judah's Torah exegesis.[76] Alongside these comments, it includes a selection of further Ashkenazi sources: from commentaries by R. Eleazar of Worms and R. Meir of Rothenburg, as well as from two unknown books: *Maḥaneh Elohim* and *Kupat harokhelim*. Our passage ends with the words: 'Received from Israel, may the Lord protect and preserve him, from the land of Poland, but I added a little to his words.' By all indications, the

---

[72] According to Bodl. MS Neubauer 666, ad loc.

[73] Printed by M. Z. Weiss, 'The Book *Minhag tov* (Based on MS Kaufmann)' (Heb.), *Hatsofeh lehokhmat Yisra'el*, 13 (1929), 217–45; and see my 'Havdalah Made on Bread' (Heb.), in M. Benayahu (ed.), *Rabbi I. Nissim Memorial Volume* (Jerusalem, 1985), i. 145.

[74] Urbach, *Arugat habosem*, iv. 120.

[75] The entire commentary was published by J. Gellis, *Tosafot hashalem* (Jerusalem, 1987), 96.

[76] See above, n. 65.

collection was edited at the turn of the thirteenth and fourteenth centuries, and R. Israel lived in the last quarter of the thirteenth century.

*Eleazar of Lublin.* A scholar named Eleazar of Lu[b?]lin is mentioned at the end of R. Meir of Rothenburg's work *Sefer tashbets* as it appears in the *Rothschild Miscellany*.[77] In fact, many of the numerous works included in that manuscript contain various additions. In the text of *Sefer tashbets*, § 489, we read: 'Rabbi Eleazar of Lulin, may he rest in peace, used to pronounce the blessing whenever he begin to study . . .'. And compare my comments in the description of the *Rothschild Miscellany* introducing the facsimile edition, where I proved that the manuscript from which this passage was copied into the *Miscellany* was written in 1300.[78]

*Asher ben Rabbi Sinai.* An interesting item of information about a Polish scholar, who died young, before being ordained a rabbi, is reported by R. Jacob ben Asher in his celebrated legal code *Arba'ah turim*. A youth named Asher, son of R. Sinai, was studying in R. Asher ben Jehiel's yeshiva at Toledo; on his way home 'to Russia', he died in Sicily. According to R. Asher,

he told them his name, and that he had studied here with us, and showed them *tosafot* [to 'a few tractates that our teacher, the aforementioned rabbi, had composed'; i.e. *tosefot harosh*] that we know he took with him from here. . . . And we attest, and it is known to all members of our group, that since the day he came here no one else has come here to study whose name is Asher, save that same R. Asher son of R. Sinai, and he was from the land of Russia and came here with a certain youth named R. Jonathan.[79]

In another report of this 'student', a companion defines him as 'an important German [Heb.: Ashkenazi] student'.[80] As we have already seen, the term 'Russia'—at least, for Benjamin of Tudela—defines the region between Prague and Kiev, that is, Poland. However, the reference may be to the territories of Silesia in western Poland, rather than the region of Kiev, as possibly indicated by the more complete, detailed account of the event rendered by R. Asher ben Jehiel himself: 'There was also here a certain youth by the name of R. Reuben, and he was from the land of Bohemia, and he was an acquaintance of R. Asher, who had died, who was from the land of Russia.' The event

---

[77] Currently in the Israel Museum, cat. no. 180/51. Possibly the correct reading should be 'of Poland' (mePolin) rather than 'of Lu[b]lin' (meLu[b]lin). R. S. Schneersohn, who is currently editing *Sefer tashbets*, has pointed out to me that in the printed edition § 133 and in many manuscripts this decision is attributed to R. Eliezer of Metz. The Hebrew words *mits* and *lulin* are not so dissimilar from a graphical point of view.

[78] *The Rothschild Miscellany: A Scholarly Commentary* (London, 1989), 53–5.

[79] *Tur*, 'Even ha'ezer', end of ch. 118. The rare name Sinai is rather intriguing. It appears once more—again in connection with Kiev—in an old text published by N. Golb and O. Pritsak, *Khazarian Hebrew Manuscripts of the Tenth Century* (Ithaca, NY, 1982), 14: 'Sinai b. Samuel'.

[80] Ibid.

occurred somewhere between 1306—the year in which R. Asher's yeshiva was founded at Toledo—and *c*.1328, the year of his death.[81]

## POLISH SCHOLARS AND ḤASIDEI ASHKENAZ

A perusal of the list of Polish scholars indicates that in the first half of the thirteenth century the Jews of Poland maintained close contacts with R. Judah Heḥasid, who might be considered their spiritual leader and principal mentor. The situation recalls the intimate link between the Polish Jews and the Torah scholars of Germany in the first half of the eleventh century. Almost every Polish scholar of the thirteenth century who is mentioned (or cited) in our ancient sources is clearly a member of the circle of R. Judah Heḥasid himself or of his successors. This aptly explains R. Judah's rather surprising involvement in the appointment of cantors in the new communities of his disciples or close associates, as described at the beginning of this article. It also clarifies why R. Eleazar ben Isaac of Prague was so concerned that R. Judah's letter to the Polish Jews would cause irreversible harm. The whole surprising picture almost automatically raises the question of Judah Heḥasid's departure from the city of his birth and upbringing, Speyer, to Regensburg. The move apparently took place about thirty years before his death, and we know nothing of its cause or exact date, just as we possess almost no other information about R. Judah Heḥasid's personal biography; we do not even know under what masters of esoteric or exoteric lore he studied. But the move to Regensburg was undoubtedly significant: he would not have departed his birthplace, his family's native town—the celebrated city of Speyer, cradle of Jewish mysticism in all of Germany, the seat of his greatest predecessors in learning and piety—and gone to live in the far-off city of Regensburg without some very cogent reason. True, Regensburg was also renowned for its Torah and learning; prominent scholars had lived there as early as the late eleventh century and certainly in the twelfth century, when it was the home of such famous personalities as R. Isaac ben Abraham, R. Isaac ben Mordecai, and their associates. However, the suggestion that R. Judah Heḥasid uprooted himself from his home town because of economic and physical difficulties in 1196–7 and moved to

---

[81] Asher ben Jeḥiel, *Responsa*, ch. 51, § 2. Our traditional chronology holds that R. Asher died in the year 5081 of the Jewish calendar, i.e. 1320/1. A. Freimann, in his famous essay on R. Asher (*JJLG* 12 [1918], 265–6), argued that he died in 5088 (1327/8), and on that basis Y. Baer (*History of the Jews in Christian Spain* (Heb.) (Jerusalem, 1959), 185) fixed the date as 1327. The source of the traditional date is the book *Tsedah laderekh*, whose author, Menahem ibn Zerah, studied under R. Asher and his sons and should be a reliable authority. None of the proofs cited by Freimann for his later date is wholly valid, while there is clear evidence that 5081 was the last year for which there are reports of R. Asher's activities. See e.g. his *Responsa*, ch. 8, § 11, cited by Freimann, as well as the new fragments published by Urbach in *Shenaton hamishpat ha'ivri*, 2 (1975), 39. And cf. my article, 'Philosophical Considerations in Deciding the Law in Spain' (Heb.), *Sefunot*, 3 [18] (1985), 106–7. Today I would nevertheless be inclined to support the 1327 dating.

Regensburg, where living conditions were more comfortable,[82] clashes with what we know of the man's character from his many letters.

In this connection, we have an interesting observation. A collection of tales from Germany, written in the sixteenth century,[83] contains a few dozen old folk-tales about R. Judah Heḥasid and his miracle-working. It turns out that these miracles all took place in Regensburg; not one of them is reported from the Rhine cities. Moreover, some of the tales feature various prominent personalities of Speyer Jewry, community leaders and rabbis, relatives of R. Judah who came to visit him or happened to come to his Regensburg home, where all these events occurred. Although the tales in the collection are all imaginary, their narrative frames tell us something of life and realia at the time; this is particularly true with regard to names of places and contemporary people. R. Judah, having completed his studies in his home city and established a reputation for himself, moved in middle age to Regensburg, where most of the major events in his life took place. It was there, along the eastern border of Germany, that he exerted his main influence and it was from there that his fame spread. Interestingly enough, all appeals to him for guidance in Jewish law and ethics, as well as all the quotations in these fields, come from the same geographical region,[84] though the material that has survived is far from exhaustive and much of what exists still awaits publication. Thus, for example, one of the main speakers in an early German minhagic book from the thirteenth century, ascribed to the eastern part of the country, is R. Jacob ben Naḥman of Magdeburg.[85] The text reads: 'R. Jacob taught in the name of R. Judah Heḥasid and R. Baruch and R. Abraham'[86] (in connection with how long the baking of matzah on Passover should take). The phrasing is very similar to that of R. Ephraim ben Meir: 'And I decided to send to my masters R. Baruch, and R. Abraham, and the Ḥasid R. Judah, to hear what they might

---

[82] *Germania Judaica*, i (Tübingen, 1963), 293. This account is based on A. Epstein, 'Das talmudische Lexikon *Yiḥusei tanna'im ve'amora'im* aus Speier', *MGWJ* 39 (1895), 449 n. 5. However, Ashkenazi tradition itself considers the move as an 'exile' and punishment for incautious treatment of the mystical literature entrusted to him. I agree whole-heartedly with Ivan Marcus's approach in the introduction to his edition of MS Parma of *Sefer ḥasidim* (Jerusalem, 1985), p. xix n. 45.

[83] N. Brill described the collection at length and copied many passages from it. See N. Brill, 'Beitrage zur jüdische Sagen- und Spruchkunde im Mittelalter', *Jahrbücher für Jüdische Geschichte und Literatur*, 9 (1889), 1–71. He and other scholars learned from this text various details of R. Judah Heḥasid's family connections and some relevant matters of realia. The manuscript is now in the Jewish National and Hebrew University Library, Jerusalem, 8vo 3182.

[84] With the exception of the passage in *Sefer tashbets*, § 219.

[85] Concerning this scholar, see Urbach, *Arugat habosem*, iv. 125–6. R. Jacob was the father of the celebrated halakhic authority R. Hezekiah of Magdeburg, as Urbach wrote there (and accordingly I do not understand why Urbach himself wrote R. Hezekiah's name in his *Tosafists*, ii. 564, as R. Hezekiah b. Jacob b. Meir).

[86] Bodl. MS Neubauer 1150 (Institute for Microfilmed Hebrew Manuscripts, mic. 16610); also MS Vat. 45 (mic. 162), fo. 88.

instruct me on this matter.'[87] All three were members of the Regensburg *beit din*.

The last quarter of the twelfth century was the period of the German *Drang nach Osten*, eastward into Poland. And, as we have seen, all the scholars whose names are identified with Poland in the sources for this period belong to Judah Heḥasid's circle of companions and admirers. It is not inconceivable, therefore, that groups of ḥasidei Ashkenaz moved in an organized—or unorganized—manner to the new, 'Germanized' territories. It is also possible that this organized movement provided one of the main motives for R. Judah's own move to Regensburg: a desire to be as near as possible to his disciples in the new scene of events. The fact that so many of the 'Polish' references have been located in the *gilyonot* literature, whose editor was active around Magdeburg, in Germany, and that some of the chief figures in that literature lived in the same area, supports this conjecture. Moreover, the link with ḥasidei Ashkenaz also helps to explain the background to the literary silence of which we spoke at the beginning of this article. These scholars, who held a unique position in regard to the study and teaching of Torah,[88] confined their pronouncements to brief *ad hoc* sayings, mainly as comments on biblical passages or short, laconic exchanges of views in other areas of halakhah and *aggadah*, as well as *gematriyah* and *notarikon*.

The direct, intimate ties between early Polish Jewry and ḥasidei Ashkenaz in those early generations may provide an apt explanation—as suggested by my friend Prof. Moshe Idel—for a most puzzling phenomenon which is unique to kabbalistic literature in Poland at a later time, when Lurianic kabbalah began to spread in the seventeenth century. Kabbalistic literature in Poland is replete with elements of *notarikon* and *gematriyah*, which generally make their appearance interspersed in kabbalistic texts. They are quite extraneous to kabbalah proper, quite foreign to the original works of Lurianic kabbalah, whether by the mystics of Safed or by their disciples. This phenomenon is so unique to Polish kabbalists that one can immediately attribute the source of any kabbalistic material of this sort to Poland or to Polish writers. Now it is common knowledge that one of the most salient characteristics of the writings of R. Judah Heḥasid, his disciples, and their successors, for many generations, is an almost obsessive preoccupation with *gematriyah*. The close historical link of the early Polish scholars with these circles, as it emerges from our account, may provide a clue to a correct evaluation of the phenomenon in its second, later guise, when scholars of the school actually settled in Poland. Thus, one also perceives a considerable—and surprising—internal continuity of Jewish life in Poland in all periods.

[87] *Sefer ḥasidim*, ed. Wistinetzki, 390.

[88] See my article, 'The Precept of Torah Study as a Religious and Social Problem in *Sefer ḥasidim*' (Heb.), *Shenaton Bar-Ilan*, 14–15 (1977), 98–113.

To summarize: early Jewish settlement in Poland, as we have seen, was intimately bound up with—and most probably an offshoot of—ḥasidut Ashkenaz from its very beginnings. Little wonder, therefore, that those early Polish Jewish scholars modelled their method of study and style of instruction on those of the mainstream German Jewish pietists: brief, mainly oral, ephemeral, *ad hoc* comments, questions, and answers; short-breathed discussions and makeshift arguments between teacher and disciple. These teachings were almost never written down in a systematic literary fashion, but rather transmitted as traditions and occasionally preserved by someone who saw fit to include some of what he had heard, personally or otherwise, in a 'book'. For that reason, the early history of rabbinical literature in Poland, i.e. the early history of the major channel of Jewish cultural expression, is still buried under a heap of as yet unidentified manuscripts, most of them anonymous *collectanea* and miscellanea. Only a scrupulous, methodical comparison of these manuscripts may produce a more coherent description of that 'pulse of the Jewish heart' whose absence so troubled Graetz's historical consciousness.

*Translated by David Louvish*

# PART III

## Reviews

# On Eisenbach on Emancipation

## TOMASZ GĄSOWSKI

THE emancipation of the Jewish population ranks among the most significant of the profound social changes that occurred in Europe during the nineteenth century. Emancipation for the Jews involved gradual acquisition of citizenship, and civil, and finally political, rights. This long process, which evolved over several decades, became the foundation for the formation of the modern Jewish nation, and thus is one of the central issues in contemporary Jewish history.

In each European country, Jewish emancipation proceeded in a different way; its onset, pace, inner dynamics, and final results varied from one state to the next. The lengthy duration of the process was especially characteristic of east central Europe, including the Polish territories. Jewish emancipation within this region generally followed the pattern of changes initiated by the French Revolution, although changes were implemented much more slowly and gradually than within western Europe. Another important difference between east central and western Europe was the frequency and importance of state-sponsored reform imposed from above. Initiatives from the top down were generally inconsistent, often halted or recalled, and largely responsible for the torpid pace of actual reform. In the case of the Polish territories, the non-existence of the previously partitioned Polish state presented an additional problem.

Emancipation means liberation, which, in the case of the Jewish population, was represented by leaving the ghetto. As soon as Jews acquired the ability to settle freely outside the small, isolated, and administratively delimited urban districts, they gained the right to unlimited participation in the economic, social, and political life of the state. This new situation introduced the mass of the Jewish population to European culture, a confrontation that was to have far-reaching consequences.

Two diverse, but parallel, mechanisms brought about emancipation and the consequent clash of cultures. The first was the gradual liquidation, initiated from above, of the legal and fiscal limitations on Jews. The second was the Jews' gradual acquisition, together with fellow subjects, of civil and political rights, a process that often took place under great social pressure and even revolutionary upheaval. The subsequent exercise of these hard-won rights by Jews and others often met with various difficulties and obstacles, and constitutes a separate but important

Dr Gąsowski's review was completed before the death of Professor Eisenbach in Oct. 1992. *Ed.*

chapter in European history. The emancipation of the Jewish population should be understood in the context of the general emancipation and democratization of European communities.

Appreciation of the wider context of Jewish emancipation is one of the basic dimensions of Artur Eisenbach's new work.[1] It is perhaps the crowning achievement of his half-century of research, his first book on the subject having appeared in 1936. Eisenbach's commitment to this subject is matched by his commitment to the Marxist historical method. It is within the Marxist dialectic that Eisenbach found inspiration to construct three cumulative stages of emancipation. These stages are compatible with the Marxist typology of the transition from the feudal to the capitalist system.[2]

Eisenbach's latest study consists of ten chapters corresponding to the chronological and thematic construction that he worked out. The chapters analyse in detail a complex of phenomena, beginning during the European Enlightenment and concluding at the close of the 1860s. Eisenbach mainly emphasizes the legal dimension of emancipation, which he views as playing the key role in the entire process. Adopting periodization from general European history, with minor adjustments for the Polish situation, and referring to the larger European context, he narrates the history of Jewish emancipation simultaneously in the three parts of partitioned Poland. Nor does he neglect the 'fourth partition' of the Polish state, namely, Polish emigration.

Clear presentation of the sequence of events, both local and global (not necessarily contemporaneous), which occurred throughout the broad territories of east central Europe must have been, even for a scholar as well acquainted with the facts and historiography as Eisenbach, a difficult task. The difficulties are compounded by the diversity of social, economic, and political structures in a period of almost nine decades. The struggle with this mass of material is evident in the book. The correlation of a chronological and thematic approach, which is important in historical discourse, is usually controversial, and is so in this case. Eisenbach does not consistently realize his aims. A construction based on three or four clearly defined chronological stages would have more adequately presented all the problems that determined the diversity and characteristic features of the subsequent stages of emancipation. This type of presentation would have facilitated linking the mass of events in the process of emancipation occurring at any given time with the entire process, as well as the principles behind it. Instead, Eisenbach presents a number of chronological and territorial studies that are neither compact nor interconnected.

[1] A. Eisenbach, *Emancypacja Żydów na ziemiach polskich 1785–1870 na tle europejskim* ('The Emancipation of the Jews on Polish Lands against the European Background 1785–1870') (Warsaw: Państwowy Instytut Wydawniczy, 1988), pp. 679, 29 illustrations.

[2] The traditional Marxist typology, which admits only two possibilities of transition from feudalism to capitalism in agriculture, has recently been questioned by J. Jedlicki, in *Jakiej cywilizacji Polacy potrzebują?* (Warsaw, 1988), 129–30.

The broad range of phenomena and events is not presented in a balanced way—partially owing to the state of research in this area. Research findings are presented differently for Russian-partitioned Poland—from the partitioning period through the duchy of Warsaw, the Congress Kingdom, up to the 1860s (including the Wielka Emigracja, the Great Emigration)—than for Austrian and Prussian Poland or the rest of Europe. The first of these chronological and territorial sequences on Russian Poland is based on Eisenbach's long-term, thorough, exhaustive investigations; the last is based on rich new historical literature. Perhaps the difference in treatment of the Jewish problem in Austrian- and Prussian-partitioned Poland may be a result of the dearth of appropriate recent studies and monographs: Eisenbach had to rely on obsolete pre-First World War works. This section of the book is, therefore, somewhat unsatisfactory, especially compared to the erudite comprehensive analysis of Jewish emancipation in the territories under Russian jurisdiction. Eisenbach is hardly responsible for the state of current research, however; my major criticism of the book concerns its construction and organization.

The study has a decidedly analytic character that includes information more appropriate to a textbook. This information swells the number of pages in an already lengthy volume. A specialist will find that some of the statements are trivial; the non-professional reader (the publishing-house and the large number of copies, even for the Polish market, suggest it is targeted at the latter audience) may easily become lost in the excess of detail about the socio-political changes in nineteenth-century Europe. A synthetic approach more suitable for such an edition prevails only in the introductory and concluding chapters and is barely present in the others. The only exception is the short summary in the eighth chapter devoted to the 'Spring of Nations', which functions effectively and points to the possibility of a more synthetic approach to the entire subject. The book is not only overloaded with details and reflections, but even digressions; for example, fragmentary information about Jews and Freemasonry on page 276. Eisenbach's reluctance to set aside the analytic method for a synthetic approach compounds the difficulty of finding a clear construction for the book.

Some of Eisenbach's statements are clearly polemical. The Jewish issue that emerged at the end of the existence of the pre-partition Commonwealth can be viewed in a different way, for example Krystyna Zienkowska's interpretation. She shows that Christian–Jewish conflicts were sharper in the larger towns than in the small, feudal centres, and that the general situation of Jews in Poland compared to the rest of contemporary Europe was not as catastrophic as Eisenbach suggests. On the other hand, Christian citizens' acquisitions after the Four Year Diet did not change the Jewish situation.[3]

Emancipation, taking Jews out of the civilizational ghetto, was accompanied

[3] K. Zienkowska, 'Spór o Nową Jerozolimę', *Kwartalnik Historyczny*, 93 (1986), 351–9.

by cultural changes. There arose a need to redefine Jewish identity to enable existence and development in a thoroughly changed situation. This problem, especially important for the future of the Jewish people, is noted by Eisenbach, but only in a few short and controversial remarks. For example, the interpretation of Jewish national consciousness presented on page 42 is very general and Marxist in tone, which is not appropriate to eighteenth-century Jewry. The group doubtless had a very special consciousness, developed on the basis of the long-lasting Judaic tradition of identity as the Chosen Nation. Unfortunately, Eisenbach does not choose to examine this fascinating problem, even though he retains other, repetitious information.

The presentation of the whole process of emancipation from the point of view of legal and juridical changes results in the book having a somewhat one-sided focus. A larger theory of emancipation, indispensable to understanding Eisenbach's argument, has not been sufficiently developed. Although material on this issue can be found in a few places in the book, the reader must consolidate and confront the various references himself. It seems that in a work of this type, which aims to present the entire problem of emancipation, including the construction of theoretical models, more attention should be devoted to this issue. It is critical, especially since the notion of emancipation itself is very broad, and Eisenbach has not supplied us with a full and clear definition.

There are several obvious mistakes. T. Mencel's work on western Galicia is devoted to territories acquired by Austria after the Third Partition (also known as Nowa Galicia), which were already lost by 1809. The division of Galicia into east and west Galicia, which existed in the nineteenth century, applied only to the territories of the First Partition. Opinions on Jewish participation in the November Uprising, collected on pages 273–4, are contradictory: one source notes Jewish participation as numerous, another as not. The interpretation of changes in the state system in Austria following its defeat in the war against Italy is wrong. It deals primarily with evaluation of the intentions of both the October and the February manifestos. The former, prepared by Agenor Gołuchowski, saw the reconstruction of a federalist state; the latter advocated a return to the centralist conception. During the Four Year Diet, Józef Czalczenski (later removed by Franciszek Wielopolski) was the president of Cracow, while the reference to J. Leskiewicz on page 118 (which is not included in the index) was probably intended to refer to the contemporaneous town councillor J. Laskiewicz, who took the post of city president only after the victory of Targowica.[4] In the comprehensive bibliography, the omission of W. M. Bartel's and J. Bieniarzówna's works on the republic of Cracow is noticeable.

Eisenbach's competence and experience raised expectations that this work would become a milestone in Polish historiography. Instead it is a very depend-

---

[4] *Polski Słownik Biograficzny*, 16 (1971), 522–3.

able, broad, and necessary compendium, but one that is lacking deeper and original reflections and conclusions. This might be because Eisenbach chose to cling to a pattern he established at the beginning of the book, which, rather than providing explanations, tends to over-simplify the complex reality.

*Translated by Joshua Zimmerman, Brandeis University*

# A Reply to Tomasz Gąsowski

## ARTUR EISENBACH

I SHALL adopt the position of *sine ira et studio* regarding the review of my work by Tomasz Gąsowski, whom I do not know personally. I have only read a few of his book reviews that touch on problems of Jewish history and culture. I had the impression both that he was competent to evaluate complex social and cultural processes—particularly those of the nineteenth century—and that he was able to present information about a publication reliably to readers. To err is human. Gąsowski's current review of my book is not accurate in those sections where he discusses the source base and methodological principles that I used to study this complex problem, one that covered a large territory over a long time.

My monograph is the first attempt to present the nearly century-long process of the civic and political emancipation of one group of inhabitants: the Jewish community. I examined this issue not only in the aristocratic Commonwealth and the later three partitions, but in the wider European context as well. To date, no extant work has undertaken an analogous task on the emancipation of other groups, such as peasants and townspeople, and the divisions among them. A reviewer should take this into account and appreciate the magnitude of the task. Mr Gąsowski, however, completely missed this, and instead points out omissions, inaccuracies and errors. Naturally, this makes discussion difficult.

Gąsowski reproaches me for not explaining in my work 'a larger theory of emancipation, indispensable to understanding Eisenbach's argument', although he then admits that 'material on this issue can be found in a few places in the book'. This material was not merely a collection of reflections that the reader must put together himself. In the first chapter, entitled 'Research Principles', I explained extensively not only the scope of the term 'emancipation', but the wider methodological principles of the subject under examination. Moreover, I wrote widely about the views on emancipation among Jewish, French, and German historians. I emphasized that, in contrast to them, I treat the process of Jewish emancipation not separately, but together with two factors: an internal one, that is, the disintegration of the old society as well as the movement to liberate the peasants and townspeople; and an external one, the course of the process of granting equal rights to Jews in different European countries. In addition, I wrote

These words were written shortly before Professor Eisenbach's death in Oct. 1992. *Ed.*

about controversies around theoretical, philosophical, and legal aspects of this problem in chapter 7, while in subsequent chapters I addressed the views and disputes among *émigré* activists as well as those of the Galician liberals and conservatives on the issue of emancipation. The subject of emancipation covers dozens of pages, which is not a small amount. In fact, some readers found it excessive. In this context, I clarified my view about the specificity of Jewish emancipation in the Polish lands.

Following my thinking, Gąsowski writes correctly that '[E]mancipation for the Jews involved gradual acquisition of citizenship, and civil, and finally political, rights.' A few lines after this, however, he restricts the term 'emancipation' and writes: 'emancipation means liberation, which, in the case of the Jewish population, was represented by leaving the ghetto'. And yet, his definition of emancipation greatly narrows the essence of the problem.

Indeed, I devoted a sizeable part of this work to the legal aspect of emancipation because legal acts by the state were decisive factors in the process of attaining civic equality not only for Jews, but for dissidents, peasants, and townspeople in Poland as well, and for different ethnic groups in France and for Catholics in England. I did not limit my work to the legal side of this issue: I presented the emancipation drive in different aspects of mobility (*w różnych pionach ruchliwości*).

As Gąsowski notes, the 'state-sponsored reform imposed from above', which I largely wrote about in my work, played an important role in the emancipation of the Jews, particularly in the states of the Holy Alliance. The reviewer did not notice, however, that I presented the position of government authorities in the context of their policies towards peasants and townspeople because I formulated emancipation as a complex social problem connected with the formation of modern society on Polish lands. I emphasized that the civil equality of Jews was almost always the last link in the process of emancipation taking place in the Polish lands.

Gąsowski's next criticism refers to the content of the material, or the way the work was presented. The correlation of the chronology with a problematic formulation, particularly in a work that addresses many aspects (economic, legal, social, political, and cultural relations) is always difficult and controversial. Even more so is this true of a subject that covers almost the entire hundred-year period of the three Polish partitions, as well as in other countries with different forms of government and political system.

Concerning the difficulties of presenting the material, I explained in the introduction why I divided chapters into certain chronological periods so that each period explains the relations within the three partitions, as well as the situation in other countries at the same time. If I separated individual chapters, it was because they dealt with almost all researched periods, such as the economic and social factors of integration (chapters 4 and 6). Gąsowski believes that 'Eisenbach does not consistently realize' this scheme. In no way did I make an effort to restrict such a rich and complex problem to the rigid framework of a definite construction. The reviewer's opinion, however, that my work is 'a number of chronological and territorial studies that are neither compact nor interconnected' is totally groundless. Gąsowski obviously did not notice that each successive chapter consists of historical periods in chronological order. Within this framework I examined contemporary issues discussed in government circles, the press, and publications both in the partitions and abroad.

Each author has the right to organize material in his own way, especially when that construction helps to facilitate the presentation of the main aspects under examination. Analogous difficulties can be found in the highly sophisticated works of Stefan Kieniewicz. As he confessed in his introduction to *Historia Polski, 1795–1918*, he did not use the model of economic historians who present the three partitions together, because this scheme could not be used for political history. He chose an intermediary way in which sections referring to analogous occurrences in the three partitions were gathered for each chronological period. So each method of presenting material is specific to a particular study. My method makes it possible for readers to understand better the relations and problems specific to each historical period.

Connected with this issue is the typology of ways and methods used to study the transformation of social relations. Mr Gąsowski suggests to readers that the model guiding my work was taken from Marxist methodology. This is not only an undeserved compliment, it is falsification. The reviewer does not explain why my typology, which refers not only to the Jewish population, but to other groups as well, is not useful to understanding and clarifying contemporary social transformations; he does not give a single concrete argument.

In fact, I followed in the footsteps of Polish historians, by no means Marxist, who analysed the different ways in which the feudal structure was transformed to a new form of capitalism in Poland. They took into account only transformations in agrarian relations, however, and differentiated two basic types of development: the Franco-American and the Prussian. It is a broader, multi-layered problem. The transformations extended to all areas of life in Poland and to every part of the population. That is why I expanded the two-part typology to include a separate American type, underlining its particular characteristic; namely, that in the United States no separate legal acts concerning Jews, peasants, and other groups were adopted.

Such a typology is useful because it treats the emancipation of the Jews as an integral element in the liberation movement of all groups of inhabitants and the formation of modern society in Polish lands. Finally, the typology is helpful when comparing the changes in Polish lands with changes occurring in other countries.

I did not build a priori models; I did not deduce them from the theoretical foundations of some ideology; rather, I based the typology on the true course of social transformations taking place in different areas of life. I discussed these in my book. At this point it should be recalled that my typological model was accepted not only by Polish but by non-Polish historians, who acknowledged it as very instructive, making it possible to understand the process of emancipation for different groups of people.[1]

Gąsowski's view is that my work has 'a decidedly analytical character' because it is overloaded with 'details . . . and even digressions'. A few sentences later, he writes that it is possible to find synthesized formulations, but only in some chapters. Well, each reads a book in his own way. None the less, the evaluation of a book, particularly when it is public, should not rely solely on one's own stock of knowledge. Gąsowski would like to have historical works closely unified, synthesized, and uniform. Such a thing exists only as an abstraction.

My book is not an outline history of the Jews in Poland, but a monograph on a particular subject. To understand socio-political changes in Polish lands, as well as in other European countries in a particular period, it is necessary to cite indispensable facts and events without which the reader would have difficulties becoming oriented to these complex problems. Moreover, this book was thought through and worked out with more than just Polish readers in mind. Such issues interest historians and researchers in other humanities disciplines, as well as in other countries. Thus it seemed even more necessary to expand the discussion, because in all works of Polish history information about the Jewish population and its diversity of activities, as well as attitudes towards contemporary political events is meagre.

Gąsowski may have forgotten his earlier objection that my work is overloaded with reflections when he writes that my study lacks 'deeper and original reflections and conclusions'. Such epithets can be attached to any book review that lacks concrete arguments. Regarding objections to digressions and reflections, it is true that I do not avoid them. Every author has the right to such digressions during a presentation. This technique worked well in the explanation of the specifics of the transformation process in Polish lands, especially when comparing the situation in one partition with an analogous situation in other regions or European countries.

I wrote much about the Jewish enlightenment movement that developed in Poland from the end of the eighteenth century. It propagated ideas of assimilation and social integration through improved education, reforms of customs and dress, secularization, and a Jewish cultural revival. In this context, 'a new problem appeared also for groups of maskilim': how to preserve the religious aspects of the Jewish identity along with a reformed and national identity, while adapting to

---

[1] I presented my 'Research Principles' for the first time at the Polish–German Symposium in Warsaw, mid-Mar. 1983. The text was published that same year in *PH* 4 (1983) and was soon after reprinted in historical journals in West Germany, the United States, and Israel. These research principles have so far been published in Polish, German, English, Hebrew, and Yiddish.

civilizing changes and becoming incorporated in the country's general cultural and intellectual currents. It was a dilemma not only for Jews in the Commonwealth and the subsequent three partitions, but also for other religious and ethnic groups living in the Diaspora—even for Polish immigrants in the United States in the twentieth century.

Gąsowski also touched on this issue, stating that the acculturation of Jews brought about 'the need to redefine Jewish identity to enable existence and development in a thoroughly changed situation'. The reviewer admitted that I was aware of the problem of identity, but said that I devoted only 'a few short and controversial remarks' to this question, with which he disagreed. Again, he did not formulate any counter-arguments, but stated that my 'interpretation of Jewish national consciousness . . . is very general and Marxist in tone'.

Above all, my thoughts on the subject of historical consciousness and Jewish national identity and the above-mentioned dilemma refer not only to the eighteenth century, but to the whole period covered in my book; thus, to the nineteenth century as well. I discussed this in the second chapter and in subsequent ones. Moreover, I did not treat the Jews as a 'Chosen Nation'. That biblical characterization is not and cannot be an analytical category in a socio-historical work. A deeper consideration of this theme, as the reviewer postulates, would have increased the denseness of my book.[2]

Gąsowski states, without any justification, that in my work there are 'obvious mistakes'. Let us examine them. He writes that there is no consistency in what I wrote on pages 273–4 about Jewish participation in the November uprising. In fact, I wrote that, according to the sources, many Jews served in different regiments of Kalisz and Mazovia and that forty-three Jews worked in health services during the uprising. In relation to the Jewish population in the kingdom of Poland, however, it was a 'meagre participation', and I explained the reason for this. The attitude of the rebel government towards the issue of civil emancipation did not convince many Jews and peasants to participate in the insurrection.

Gąsowski writes that my interpretation of changes in the political system in Austria after their defeat in the war with Italy is incorrect because it depends on the interpretation of the February and October manifestos. I clearly wrote in my work that Count Agenor Gołuchowski was in charge of preparing the project for state reform by the emperor. He prepared the project, and the emperor signed the manifesto on 20 October 1860 that 'opened the constitutional era in Austria and announced the rebuilding of the country in a federal spirit' (p. 437). I wrote further that this course none the less did not satisfy the opinions of different groups and that, after Gołuchowski was dismissed, Schmerling

---

[2] In another very favourable review of the book in *Nowe Książki*, 11 (1988), however, there was an objection that 'there is relatively little information about the Jewish population' found in my work. The reviewer may have been looking for information about orthodox groups, stating that I wrote very little about them.

prepared a new manifesto of 26 February 1861 that limited the county sejms further.[3]

The reviewer also recalls Krystyna Zienkowska's views on the conflict between two groups of townspeople in Warsaw at the end of the eighteenth century. The different views did not at all centre, as the reviewer suggests, on the sharpness of these conflicts (mainly on the basis of competition) in the small or larger cities. I never wrote about this issue. It is not even an issue for discussion. Gąsowski, none the less, accepts the opinion of Zienkowska that the Jewish situation in Poland at the time of the Four Year Sejm was better than in other European countries. He does not cite one source to support this viewpoint. I will not engage in such a polemic; I only refer to my article in *Kwartalnik historyczny*, no. 2 (1988), in which I argue with Zienkowska.

This problem is much deeper than the conflict between two groups of townspeople in Poland, for it concerns the political consciousness and role of the upper layer of townspeople in Poland as well as in the (mainly royal) cities in the period of major reforms and the formation of a modern middle class. I explained the essence of this problem because it surfaces in the nineteenth century and lasts through the 1870s.

As to the president of Cracow, it was Jan Laskiewicz, although the book printed his name incorrectly (in my earlier work his name is spelled correctly).[4] He was not, however, a councillor, as Gąsowski states, but the president of Cracow. He signed his instruction letter on 16 January 1792 to Józef Jagielski, plenipotentiary of the cities of the province of Cracow, who was then in Warsaw. This letter was published in *Materiały do dziejów Sejmu Czteroletniego* ('Materials on the History of the Four Year Sejm') (Wrocław, 1955–69), vol. v, p. 354, and is sufficient proof to call Laskiewicz the president of Cracow. J. Bieniarzówna wrote[5] that he was president of Cracow during the Targowica period and the Kościuszko uprising, but this does not mean that he had not been president before that time.

As to minor issues, the reviewer's conclusion that the chapters concerning the Austrian and Prussian partitions were incomplete (which allegedly is mainly the result of a lack of monographs on these regions) is puzzling. I did not rely, as the reviewer writes, on studies written before the First World War. I used reliable works by Austrian, German, and Jewish historians, such as J. Toury, W. Hausler, H. Fischer, S. Wenzel, R. Rürup, M. Ashkewicz, and many others published after the Second World War, and I referred to them in my work. The amount of information in studies on certain issues is always relative. Each reader, each researcher, is dependent on the amount of knowledge available about certain

---

[3] An analogous evaluation of this manifesto can be found in S. Kieniewicz, *Historia Polski, 1795–1918* (Warsaw: PWN, 1968).

[4] A. Eisenbach, *Z dziejów ludności żydowskiej w Polsce w XVIII i XIX wieku* (Warsaw, 1983), 85, 312.

[5] See *Polski Słownik Biograficzny*, 16 (1971), 522–3.

Polish regions and will evaluate the facts presented differently. It is the author who must decide if the information given about certain issues is sufficient to explain the problem or situation.

Finally, Gąsowski complains that my bibliography does not include the works of W. M. Bartel and J. Bieniarzówna with regard to Cracow. I used the works of many scholars, not only historians, whom I did not list in my bibliography. The bibliographic literature in six languages included in the appendix is, as I pointed out, a selective bibliography, so I could not include all Polish and non-Polish historical works consulted.

Thus, Gąsowski does not provide accurate information about my book, the many aspects it includes, and its methodological principles. To be sure, he concludes that 'Eisenbach's competence and experience raised expectations that this work would become a milestone in Polish historiography.' I, however, allegedly simplified the subject and adopted a model. The reviewer formulated his views and opinions in a general, arbitrary way, without providing evidence to support his points. In this situation, a desirable and constructive discussion on this important issue becomes almost impossible.

*Translated by Joshua Zimmerman, Brandeis University*

# Two Books on Isaac Bashevis Singer

## CHONE SHMERUK

THE two works considered here, both of which reflect Polish interest in Isaac Bashevis Singer, are of sharply contrasting value. *Singer: Pejzaże pamięci* (A Landscape of Memory) by Agata Tuszyńska reads very well.[1] It is a book that eludes easy categorization because, despite appearances, it is not a standard monograph about a writer.

The most important of the many grounds for criticism of the work is probably that the author does not know the Yiddish language in which Isaac Bashevis Singer composed. It is difficult to conceive of an honest monograph about any writer without knowledge of his language of composition, and since only a part of Singer's *oeuvre* has been translated into English (and from English into other languages), Tuszyńska was thus unable to investigate some of his most significant writings.

As far as I understand Tuszyńska's rather unclear purpose, her goal was to reconstruct the Jewish 'landscape' of Poland that no longer exists, on the basis of the works of Singer. This idea is undoubtedly reasonable, and Singer himself aspired in his works to resurrect the murdered Jews of Poland—witness the following from the introduction to the immensely important cycle of stories entitled *Mentshn oyf mayn veg* (People on my Road):

On the occasion of the murder, Jews had various fantasies like revenging themselves upon the Germans, or saving the Jews. My fantasy was to find a means of resurrecting the murdered. In my fantasy I had an elixir that breathed life into the dead.

Unfortunately, the resurrection of the dead does not lie within the limits of human possibility. But I wanted at least by literary means to resurrect the murdered; to present to Jewish readers pictures of specific men and women with all their features, with the characteristics of individuals. That is, strictly speaking, the aim of everything I write.

I do not know if a serious attempt has been made to evaluate Singer's writings as an attempt to resurrect a murdered world. Tuszyńska's book is certainly not such an attempt.

The cycle *People on my Road* consists of 232 separate stories which were published in the Yiddish newspaper *Forverts* from January 1958 to October 1960. In spite of their conspicuous literary value, the stories of this cycle have not been col-

[1] Agata Tuszyńska, *Singer: Pejaże pamięci* (Gdańsk: Wydawnictwo Marabut, 1994).

lected for publication in the original language, nor have they been translated into English. This is only one case among many of well-known writings by Singer being accessible exclusively to Yiddish readers, and it is doubtful whether Tuszyńska even knew of its existence. The cycle directly touches on her purpose of piecing together lost landscapes, yet there is no reference to it in her book. Familiarity with these stories is absolutely fundamental both for the reconstruction of the landscape and for a monograph on the creations or the life of Singer.

Without access to the full *œuvre* of Singer in his own language, Tuszyńska bases her work on 'memory', as suggested in the title of her book. The statement that memory is deceptive is banal; but it is not banal when this deceptive memory is used in a variety of questionable ways to substitute other, unavailable methods of re-creating the past. The part of the book in question consists of apparent quotations from interviews and statements of people who 'remember': of Poles who remember Jews and of Jews who remember Singer.

There is probably value in warning that Tuszyńska's quotations are distorted and not particularly faithful. She gained herself journalistic renown with the combination of interviews and observations in her book *Kilka portretów z Polską w tle* (A Few Portraits with Poland in the Background) (Gdańsk, 1993). Unfortunately, the citations in that book are also inaccurate and at times quite false. This is confirmed by acquaintances of mine, and is true in my own case as well. To take one example, I could not have told Ms Tuszyńska that on my Warsaw University student identity-card in 1938–9 was the stamp 'Jew' (p. 52), because the stamp in fact read 'seat on the odd side' ('miejsce po stronie nieparzystej'). That may have been equivalent, because Jews were obliged to sit on the odd side, but it is not the same. If Tuszyńska does not grasp this, the precision of her interviews is at the least questionable, and others have no less essential faults to find with the interviews directed by her.

Bearing this in mind, her whole interviewing technique is rendered problematic, not to mention her citations in the book about Singer. In order to connect the pronouncements of Poles about Jews with Singer, Tuszyńska went to places remembered in the biography of the author and of his family. And so to Tomaszów (pp. 143–51, 211–18), because his parents married there, to Radzymin (pp. 69–77), because his family lived there until their departure for Warsaw in 1908. The witnesses she found there testify more to Polish attitudes towards Jews than to the lives of actual Jews. There would not be anything new or special in this if, in fact, the author had succeeded in evoking the atmosphere in which Jews lived in Poland before, during, and after the extermination. This is not achieved because Tuszyńska does not always pay attention to what the quotations say. It is painful to read such gems as the following, which appear entirely without authorial comment:

The Kikes were ugly and loathsome.  (in Radzymin; p. 74)

They drank vodka in silver glasses especially made for this purpose.  (in Tomaszów; p. 146)

. . . [the] guards, those who saved Jewish synagogues, found in them several barrels of Jewish plum brandy. (in Tomaszów; p. 147)

. . . they kept their corpses, not in a lying but in a sitting position . . . (in Tomaszów; pp. 49, 148)

. . . the Germans murdered them in ditches and afterwards carried away suitcases full of dollars and watches. (in Frampol; p. 229)

I fear that there are readers living in Poland who will accept this rubbish at face value.

Among the 'witnesses' and the 'remembering' Poles, there is not one who knew Singer himself or his family. Instead we are provided with the reminiscences of those Jewish writers and journalists who agreed to be interviewed by Tuszyńska—not everyone did. Represented are M. Tsanin, A. Shulman, S. L. Sznajderman, H. Klepfisz, and C. Finkelsztejn. Assuming that the observations presented were genuinely intended to give a picture of Singer, and that they have been transcribed entirely accurately, they turn out to be filled with envy and bitter criticisms of the writer, despite recognition of his greatness. Even aside from misinformation like the reference to Sznajderman meeting Runia in Warsaw after the war (p. 289) when she was not there (p. 278), these assembled comments tell us nothing new about Singer.

These criticisms seem superfluous when one knows that not only was the author himself aware of the criticisms of his works in literary and journalistic circles, but he was able to formulate them better, more succinctly, and more scathingly than any of the critics quoted by Tuszyńska. As early as the 1950s, in one of his lesser books which has only recently been translated into English,[2] he wrote:

There was no end to the complaints against me. I was too pessimistic, too superstitious, too sceptical about the progress of humanity, not devoted enough to socialism, Zionism, Americanism, the battle against antisemitism, activism, the problems of women. Some critics complained that when before my eyes a Jewish state came into being, I buried myself in cobwebs of folklore. They accused me of dragging my readers back to the dark Middle Ages. Well, and why so much interest in sex? Sex has no place in the Yiddish literary tradition.

In the book this ironic speech is placed in the mouth of a writer who is obviously to be identified with Singer himself.

That segment of Krochmalna Street in Warsaw which is known from *My Father's Court*—the street about which Singer wrote so much—no longer exists. This does not prevent Tuszyńska from presenting records of mortgages and title transfers of properties on the street, despite the fact that there is in them absolutely nothing about Singer and his family. The names of the owners of the tenements and the sums for which they changed hands are utterly irrelevant to the

[2] I. B. Singer, *Meshugah* (New York, 1994), 114.

re-creation of the lives of the poor Jews who lived on the original Krochmalna Street. Tuszyńska, though, wants to create the illusion that she has carried out important archival research. Such undertakings make up not a little of the book. Another example of valueless, even misleading, research follows the citation of the record of the wedding of Singer's parents (p. 19). We find a 'wedding picture' that simply could never have existed. It is a pure invention of Ms Tuszyńska. Strictly observant families such as that of Singer's parents, in the latter half of the nineteenth century, would not have had photographs taken.

I have read elsewhere about Tuszyńska's practice of 'borrowing' quotations from Singer.[3] Such borrowings are numerous, and in some cases it is clear that she does not understand what she is citing. Thus, on page 301 we find a quotation from *Mayseh tishevits* (The Last Demon), one of Singer's loveliest stories, without quotation marks or a suggestion of the source. She speaks there of the 'mourning prayer' of the synagogue, which cannot have been in the original Yiddish and does not appear in the English translation. It is Tuszyńska's invention. I shall not now deal with Tuszyńska's source, which is not mentioned in her book. There is a talmudic saying: 'One who says [cites] things in the name of their author brings peace to the world'. Ms Tuszyńska certainly brings no peace to the world, quoting Singer and other authors without acknowledgement.

The creations of Isaac Bashevis Singer have given rise over the years to broad critical interest and literary research. A particular genre of this scholarship is the series of monographs and doctoral dissertations, especially from the United States, and ordinarily based exclusively on English translations of his books. In Poland, research on this prolific writer's works seems to be somewhat neglected, and critics regularly base their remarks on Polish translations from English, despite the fact that the writings of Singer clearly have a special resonance in Poland. Monika Adamczyk-Garbowska very accurately defines that eloquence in her book *Polska Isaaca Bashevisa Singera: Rozstanie i powrót* (The Poland of Isaac Bashevis Singer: Parting and Return),[4] writing that, 'The reception of the works of Bashevis in Poland involves their being read in a more complex way than in other countries because of the close relationship between Singer and our country and because of the tangled history of Polish–Jewish relations' (pp. 143–4). Adamczyk-Garbowska's book is thus greatly to be welcomed. It is not only the first general discussion in Polish of the works of the writer resting on his Yiddish writings as well as their English translations, it also has at its base constant consciousness of the distinctiveness of the reception of Singer in Poland.

The first of the four sections of the book is entitled 'The Polish Period of the Life and Works of Bashevis', and provides the biographical background that is correctly presented as the foundation of his creations. Consideration of his

---

[3] *Twórczość*, 9 (1994), 114–17.
[4] (Lublin: Wydawnictwo Uniwersytetu Marii Curie-Skłsdowskiej, 1994).

knowledge and familiarity with the Polish language and its literature is here presented scrupulously and factually, without the exaggerations and embellishments that are current in criticism of Singer in Poland. Singer's years in Poland up to 1935 remained throughout his life the basis for his work; his departure from Poland took him to a personal Diaspora. To the end, he was immersed thematically in the history, day-to-day experience, and way of life of the Jewish community in Poland.

The two succeeding parts of Adamczyk-Garbowska's book are devoted to her main theme—'the image of Poland and Poles' in Singer's works. With great insight and excellent control of the material, including texts that have never been translated from Yiddish, the author presents the intricate, often illogical and ambivalent image of Poland and Poles in the Singer *œuvre*. Alongside comments on such stories as 'Washerwoman' and 'Pigeons', in which ordinary Polish women are presented with much sympathy and appreciation, she discusses with considerable understanding stories in which Polish characters are portrayed in a decidedly negative fashion. The author rightly sees in this mixture in Singer's historical stories a reflection of contemporary problems about which more than one opinion is expressed in the work of the Jewish writer. One can agree with the author's declaration that 'the matter of the presentation of Poles in Bashevis' compositions is an especially sensitive and important issue for Polish readers' (p. 134). In this context, one has to admire the skill of the author in dealing with difficult and delicate subjects. She disarms the reader when presenting examples of Singer's handling of some Polish Jewish issues that Poles might find insulting with her honest and impartial analysis of the texts she discusses. I should argue that the ability to read the texts in the language in which they were created served the author particularly well in achieving a profound and sensitive reading of Singer's works.

The concluding section, entitled 'The Return of Bashevis', deals with two fundamental problems: the reception of Singer's works in Poland and the quality of the translations into Polish of his work. Both the works of the writer and their criticism have complex significations in Poland. Professor Adamczyk-Garbowska provides an extensive review of Polish criticism of Singer, a subject with which she has intimate familiarity, not omitting sensitive critical views.

As mentioned, Singer's works have usually been translated into Polish from English translations. With appropriate harshness, Adamczyk-Garbowska stresses the unacceptability of this procedure, giving numerous examples of how lack of familiarity with both Yiddish and English and unfamiliarity with the customs and ways of life of Polish Jews have led to distortions and elementary mistakes. Particularly valuable in this chapter are the detailed comparisons of the Polish texts with the original Yiddish. These demonstrate how much closer direct translation from Yiddish to Polish could be in depicting both the Polish background and Jewish customs.

This book is written in a manner that is at once lively, controlled, and factual.

The research is penetrating and sensitive. Like her earlier work on the subject, the book is a major scholarly achievement because the conclusions are based on genuine familiarity with and subtle reading of the texts. The combination of the author's awareness of the problems of translation from translations with her excellent control of Singer's works provides a particularly fruitful basis for her work. In contrast with the fragmentary and usually impressionistic criticism of the works of Singer in Poland, the value of this monograph is obvious.

I am convinced that *Polska Isaac Bashevisa Singera* provides not only an excellent introduction to the works of the writer for the Polish reader, but also that, in an English translation, it would provide the key for western critics to understand the Polish themes in his works. This book will certainly become the corner-stone for criticism and research in Poland on the works of Isaac Bashevis Singer. It should stand as a model for others.

# On Auschwitz

## NECHAMA TEC

'THE dark night is my friend, tears and screams are my songs, the fire of sacrifice is my light, the atmosphere of death is my perfume. Hell is my home.' This is how Zalman Gradowski, a Polish Jew who was a Sonderkommando, one of the prisoners who worked in the crematoria in Auschwitz II–Birkenau, summed up his life in the camp. He perished while taking part in the Sonderkommando revolt of 7 October 1944. Gradowski and some other members of the Sonderkommando buried their diaries near the crematoria in the hope that those who found them would make them known to the world. The authors of these documents had no illusions. They knew that in a short while the Germans would gas them and replace them with a new group of workers. Ready to die, they wanted their diaries to live.

Nathan Cohen's gripping paper 'Diaries of the Sonderkommando' is one of twenty-nine chapters in *Anatomy of the Auschwitz Death Camp*,[1] currently the most comprehensive contribution to the field. Based on impeccable research, this volume is divided into six parts: 'History of the Camp', 'Dimensions of Genocide', 'The Perpetrators', 'The Inmates', 'The Resistance', and 'Auschwitz and the Outside World'.

For each of these sections, Michael Berenbaum provides a concise, informative introduction. The articles are written by twenty-six experts from such diverse fields as architecture, education, history, literature, pharmacy, philosophy, psychology, psychiatry, political science, sociology, theology, and Jewish studies. A meeting-ground for twelve disciplines, these papers cover a wide range of complex issues and show how Auschwitz became the biggest centre of human destruction and degradation. From 1940 to 1945, like a powerful spider, Auschwitz relentlessly wove an ever larger web over German society and German institutions. Research from these papers points to a continually widening German responsibility for the crimes at Auschwitz. On a more abstract level, the book systematically examines the special efforts, meanings, and consequences of extreme domination.

---

[1] Yisrael Gutman and Michael Berenbaum (eds.), *Anatomy of the Auschwitz Death Camp*, comp. and ed. Teresa Swiebocka (Bloomington: Indiana University Press, 1994); *Auschwitz: A History in Photographs*; Eng. edn. prepared by Jonathan Webber and Connie Wilsack (Bloomington: Indiana University Press, and Oświęcim: Auschwitz–Birkenau State 1993); pp. 292; ISBN 0-253-35581-8; $59.95.

In the opening article Yisrael Gutman paints a clear picture of Auschwitz's origins and its historical context and transformations. In 1940 Auschwitz was designed for members of the Polish intelligentsia and the Polish underground. By March 1941, in anticipation of Soviet prisoners of war, Himmler ordered that Auschwitz be extended to Birkenau, three kilometres from the original site. Subsequent expansion came with the projected annihilation of the European Jews, Gypsies, and other groups. Eventually Auschwitz included three main camps: Auschwitz I, Auschwitz II–Birkenau, and Auschwitz III–Monowitz.

As the biggest death factory and a huge labour camp complex, Auschwitz supplied slave labourers to about forty subcamps. Some of these were directly affiliated with Auschwitz; others served as branches of the main complex. Varying in size, with prisoner populations ranging from a dozen to several thousand, these camps were built near industrial enterprises, mines, and foundries.

Gutman's chapter is followed by Shmuel Krakowski's discussion of satellite camps, where extermination through labour became established Nazi policy. Here as elsewhere a disproportionately high number of the victims were Jewish.

Responsibility for the appalling conditions in these camps and the prisoners' high death-rate is shared by German industrial firms and the SS. On page 53 Krakowski identifies some of these firms: 'IG Farbenindustrie and Bismarckhutte, Oberschlesische Hydrierwerke, Siemens-Schuckert, Hermann Göring Werke, Ost Maschinenbau, Grun & Bilfinger, Holzmann, Konigshutter Metallwerke, Emmerich Machold, Borsig Koks-Werke, Rheinmetall Borsig, and Schlesische Feinweberei.'

To the question what made Auschwitz the symbol for the destruction of European Jews, Raul Hilberg offers three partial explanations. First, more Jews died in Auschwitz than in any other single camp (the latest estimate is one million). Secondly, Jewish victims were brought to Auschwitz from different European countries and regions. Thirdly, as a death camp, Auschwitz had the longest history, operating after other killing centres ceased to exist. Hilberg feels that, in itself, this continuity expresses a determination to annihilate the Jews.

Relying on path-breaking research, Robert-Jan van Pelt, in 'A Site in Search of a Mission', shows how much architectural plans can tell about the treatment of prisoners. For example, German architectural blueprints show that more than eight times as much sleeping-space was allotted to a guard than to a prisoner. In addition, Pelt's evidence, combined with information contained in Franciszek Piper's 'Gas Chambers and Crematoria', Jean-Claude Pressac and Robert-Jan van Pelt's 'The Machinery of Mass Murder at Auschwitz', and Andrzej Strzalecki's 'The Plunder of Victims and their Corpses', show how deeply implicated German industries were in the building and perfecting of the death machinery and in the use, not only of the victims' property and labour, but also of parts of their bodies. German industrialists and scientists participated enthusiastically and competitively in the death industry of the Auschwitz complex and all other camps.

Alexander Lasik's 'Historical Sociological Profile of the SS' shows that of the 6,800 SS men and 200 SS women in Auschwitz, two-thirds came from a low-grade occupational background. More important, his research confirms what has been reported for other contexts: namely, that none of the available documents indicate that any punishment was inflicted upon the SS for refusing to harm a prisoner. On the contrary, the evidence shows a consistent willingness on the part of the SS to injure and abuse. This in turn suggests the effectiveness of the camp ideology that aimed at dehumanization and destruction of prisoners. On page 286 Lasik concludes that in Auschwitz 'the first to undergo the dehumanization process, and on a much larger scale, were the SS personnel who served there.'

Gypsies are sometimes referred to as the forgotten victims. Yehuda Bauer's comprehensive account about this group goes a long way to right the record.

It is inevitable that in an extensive collection of papers there will be some overlap. For example, Irena Strzalecka's 'Women', Helena Kubica's 'Children', and Nili Keren's 'The Family Camp' are all concerned with the fate of women and children. Nevertheless, because each researcher brings a different perspective, the result is a more comprehensive treatment of the subject. In addition, whatever repetitions there are in these and other papers help validate the whole.

The papers by Randolph L. Braham on 'Hungarian Jews', Martin Gilbert on 'What was Known and When', and David S. Wyman on 'Why Auschwitz Wasn't Bombed' also deal with similar material, but provide distinct contributions. Collectively they attest to Jewish powerlessness, to German efficiency and duplicity, and to the Allies' unwillingness rather than inability to help. On this last point, particularly relevant is Wyman's conclusion on page 583. It asks: 'How could it be that the governments of the two great Western Democracies knew that a place existed where 2,000 helpless human beings could be killed every 30 minutes, knew that such killings actually did occur over and over again and yet did not feel driven to search for some way to wipe such a scourge from the earth?' Scattered throughout this volume are efforts to answer this very important question.

Of all the death camps, Auschwitz came closest to becoming a system of total domination. Those who experience extreme subjugation are most in need of freedom, but have the least possibility of getting it. Total domination leaves no options for resistance, especially armed resistance that inflicts direct physical damage upon the enemy. In 'Auschwitz Underground' Langbein emphasizes that in Auschwitz the only possible forms of resistance were helping other prisoners, collecting incriminating, illegal evidence, and assisting escape efforts. Despite seemingly insurmountable obstacles, there was an armed rebellion in Auschwitz, a rebellion led by members of the Jewish Sonderkommando. As a result of this uprising, three SS officers died, twelve were wounded, and crematorium IV was destroyed so thoroughly it could never again be used for gassing. Of the Sonderkommando who started and carried out the revolt, none survived. Altogether 451 Sonderkommando lost their lives. Moreover, four young Jewish women who had smuggled in explosives for the rebels were implicated. After being subjected to prolonged torture, all four—Regina Sapirsztein, Ala Gartner, Ester Weissblum, and Rosa Robota—were hanged on 6 January 1945. On 18 January 1945 Soviet troops reached Auschwitz.

A landmark in the Holocaust literature, *Anatomy of the Auschwitz Death Camp* opens the door to other books on the subject. This is attested by the significant contribution of *Auschwitz: A History in Photographs*. As the title suggests, the main portion of the volume is filled with photographs. Some were taken by German photographers, either for official or private use, others by inmates, and still others by Allied pilots. A separate section of the book is devoted to art, mainly paintings and drawings. The artists are former Auschwitz inmates who created the pictures during their incarceration or after the war.

The photograph captions and introductory essays were written by historians who for the most part were associated with the Auschwitz Museum. Of the five essays, three were written by Kazimierz Smolen, a former director of the Auschwitz Museum who had spent four and a half years as a political prisoner in Auschwitz.

The explanations and photographs provide evidence that some Sonder-kommando, far from restricting their illegal activities to fighting and writing, took photographs, which they smuggled out of the camp as further proof of German crimes. From these documents we learn about the intricate co-operative efforts that went into creating, collecting, and hiding the evidence. On page 181 there is a photograph of an aluminium flask and a portion of the text written in Yiddish by Zalman Gradowski, the Jewish Sonderkommando prisoner mentioned above. Next to this photograph is a picture of another flask containing a manuscript by a different Jewish member of the Sonderkommando, Zalman Lewenthal. This second flask was discovered seventeen years after the war, in crematorium III in Auschwitz II–Birkenau.

As a rule, knowledge about people, objects, and events is enhanced by photographs. *Anatomy of the Auschwitz Death Camp* and *Auschwitz: A History in Photographs* sometimes link the written and the visual in a unique way. Thus, for example, Robert J. Lifton and Amy Hacket, in *Anatomy of the Auschwitz Death Camp*, tell about Claus Clauberg, a prominent professor from the University of Kiel, who in 1942 set up a research facility in block 10 of Auschwitz II–Birkenau. There, searching for an effective and inexpensive means of sterilization, Clauberg performed horrible experiments, mostly on young Jewish women. Included in *Auschwitz: A History in Photographs* is a photograph of Clauberg, which imparts a new reality to the written words.

Occasionally a caption illuminates a less well-known aspect of the Auschwitz experience. This is true for the photograph on page 119 that shows a young Hungarian boy with a deep scar. The caption states that the boy's wound was inflicted by an SS man as punishment for attempting to give a slice of bread to a starving woman prisoner.

Art, particularly if illegally created within the camp, attests to the inmates' extraordinary determination to retain a semblance of humanity. Filtered through the artists' eyes, these former inmates of Auschwitz come close to reality, a reality that is often missing from the hastily taken illegal photographs. In these paintings, along with the cruelty of everyday life, is an occasional expression of tenderness and love. This is true of the oil painting on page 242 by Mieczysław Kościelak called *Friendship*, painted in 1948.

This collection also includes a portrait on page 187 of Mala Zimetman, drawn in crayon on cardboard by Zofia Stepien-Bator in 1944. Mala, a young Jewish woman from Belgium, became an Auschwitz legend. In the summer of 1944 she and her Polish lover, Edward Galinski, escaped. After two weeks Mala and Edward were brought back to Auschwitz. Neither broke down under severe torture. During preparations for a public hanging, Mala slapped the face of the attending SS man and cut her wrists. Unlike her lover, who was hanged, Mala died on the way to the gas chamber. The story of Mala and Edward continues to live as a symbol of courage, fearlessness, defiance, and love. Stories about them appear in many Holocaust publications, but none of these tales include pictures. Now, thanks to *Auschwitz: A History in Photographs*, the heroine, Mala, has been given a face.

The two books, *Anatomy of the Auschwitz Death Camp* and *Auschwitz: A History in Photographs*, are important in different ways. In part complementary, in part interdependent, each adds to our understanding of Auschwitz. Both deserve a space on the shelves of all college and public libraries. Both deserve wide readership. The editors and contributors of both books have enhanced our understanding of issues that are important and elusive.

# BOOK REVIEWS

ISRAEL BARTAL, RACHEL ELIOR, AND CHONE
SHMERUK (EDS.)
*Tsadikim ve'anshei ma'aseh: Mehkarim
behasidut Polin*

(Jerusalem: Mosad Bialik, 1994)
pp. 397. ISBN 965-342-618-4

Following the death of R. Dov Ber, the Maggid of Międzyrzecz, in 1772, the late
eighteenth century witnessed the differentiation of the growing hasidic community into a variety of geographically based schools and branches in which its
teachings were adapted to new social settings. During this period, central Poland
was transformed into a major centre of hasidic life and creativity. In their introduction, the editors of *Tsadikim ve'anshei ma'aseh: Mehkarim behasidut Polin*
(Hasidism in Poland) note that from its onset Polish hasidism developed its own
distinctive characteristics. Brought to Poland by the students of the Maggid,
within a generation hasidism was transformed from an extended circle of élite
contemplatives into a broadly based spiritual and social movement, gathering
within its purview adherents from all strata of society and educational backgrounds. This expansion necessitated the creation of new modalities of religious
leadership and forms of interaction between the master and his followers. Where
Shneur Zalman of Lyady formulated an ethico-contemplative discipline accessible to the majority of his adherents, the Galician–Polish model developed by
Elimelekh of Leżajsk and Jacob Halevi Horowitz, the Seer of Lublin, propounded
the centrality of the *tsadik*, or charismatic spiritual master. The *tsadik* was conceived as the terrestrial locus of divine–human interaction, a living conduit of
celestial energy binding the hasid to God through his very being. As the group of
*tsadikim* coalesced into a powerful socio-political institution, its members culti-
vated intricate relationships with the indigenous noble families who retained
considerable influence in post-partition Poland and developed the intricate intercessionary skills requisite to dealing with its varied governments. Furthermore,
the continuing urbanization of Polish society and its Jewish community in the
nineteenth century brought *tsadikim* as a group into increasing confrontation
with such forces of Jewish modernization as the Haskalah and then Zionism
(pp. 9–10).

While rigorous scholarly analysis has been devoted to the issue of hasidism's origins and the mystical theology of its creators, the history and unique spiritual milieu of Polish hasidism has been largely neglected. In *Hasidism in Poland* Israel Bartal, Rachel Elior, and Chone Shmeruk have begun to fill this gap, providing the reader with an extensive anthology of fifteen essays tracing selected aspects of the history, religious thought, and literary dimensions of Polish hasidism from its beginnings until the period between the two world wars.

The first part, focusing on the history of Polish hasidism, commences with translated selections from Ignacy Schiper's history of the Jews in central Poland, produced in the Warsaw ghetto. The other historical essays provide background concerning significant localities (Gershon Hundert on Opatów and Elianora Bergman on Jewish settlement in Góra Kalwarija) and the biographies and political activities of hasidic masters (Yosef Salmon on R. Naftali Tsevi Horowitz of Ropczyce and David Assaf and Israel Bartal on the intercessionary activities of Polish *tsadikim*). The second part, comprising the greater part of the book, examines the literary creativity and inner life of Polish hasidism (Zeev Gries writing on Israel of Kozienice's commentary on *Avot* and Yoram Yakovson on the Sabbath and cosmic unity in Yehudah Aryeh Leib of Góra Kalwarija's *Sefat emet*) and the ideology of the *tsadik* (Rachel Elior and Beracha Zak on the Seer of Lublin and Mendel Piekarz on the anti-Zionist polemics of Natan David of Parczew (d. 1930)). The final part focuses upon the presentation of hasidism in contemporary literature (Chone Shmeruk on the image of the *tsadik* in I. L. Peretz's *Di goldene keyt* (The Golden Chain) and textual history and narrative technique in Martin Buber's *Gog umagog* (For the Sake of Heaven). The volume concludes with a valuable bibliographical survey focusing upon the nineteenth century compiled by David Assaf.

In his discussion of Natan David of Parczew, Mendel Piekarz contends: 'Remove the dimension of the *tsadik* from hasidism and you have removed its soul' (p. 292). Uniting this profoundly variegated work is a series of essays exploring the institution and person of the *tsadik* from socio-historical, theological, and literary perspectives. The research of Elior, Zak, and Salmon reveals that the institution of the *tsadik* rested upon a carefully constructed ideology which motivated its extraordinary range of involvement in both the internal governance of the Jewish community and its interactions with the state. The *tsadik* constituted the translation of a rigorous contemplative practice and mystical experience into a life of charismatic communal leadership and service. It retained the élitism of Międzyrzecz mystical praxis: its call to void the individual ego so that human consciousness might merge with its source in divine wisdom and view the divine light and vitality animating all things. In this state, the Maggid taught that the devotee became a conduit for the manifestation of divine blessing in the world. Elimelekh of Leżajsk and the Seer of Lublin integrated this contemplative practice within an active life of communal leadership. Community was established around the *tsadik*'s person and his ability to publicly manifest salvific power. The *tsadik*'s authority was derived from a charisma put to open test. The Seer taught that the *tsadik* must serve as a near-prophetic medium for the Shekhinah by transmitting 'heavenly Torah'—lucid but automatic discourse creating a bond of shared ecstasy between the illuminate and his auditors (Elior, pp. 188–9). The *tsadik*'s ability to sustain his community with 'progeny, life, and provisions' was equally a matter of public record.

Classical kabbalistic spirituality was very much one of cosmic blessing, in which the contemplative praxis and the performance of the commandments by the religious élite were believed to draw energies of benediction into the world. However, Elimelekh and the Seer took classical ideology and, engaging in an exegetical reconstruction of reality, created full-blown communities around their very persons. Their sense of mystical mission engendered a community based upon reciprocal fealty and trust and a powerful social institution in which the varied charitable services of the *kahal* were subsumed under the rebbe's mantle. The urgent sense of mission motivating this charismatic turn to community finds expression in a letter of Rabbi Naftali Horowitz of Ropczyce praising a student for assuming a rabbinical post and 'dealing with the needs of the community, guiding them, instilling peace between an individual and his neighbour, husband, and wife and through this worshipping God' (Salmon, p. 108).

Both the inroads of rationalism and the declining economic condition of Polish Jewry severely strained this vision of the power of the charismatic holy man in the early twentieth century. In his study of Natan David of Parczew, Mendel Piekarz notes that the Parczewer rebbe attributed this diminution of manifest miracle to the loss of the faith of the masses in their leadership and Zionism's abnegation of Jewry's mystical obligation to remain in exile and raise the holy sparks embedded therein to their primal sources. Both rationalist doubt and the continued hold of hasidic spirituality over the modernizing east European Jewish imagination finds expression in a 'hasidic' play produced by Y. L. Peretz during the first decade of this century which deals with the inner life of a *tsadik*'s family. Chone Shmeruk notes that the multiple drafts of this play share a climactic scene in which the *tsadik* undergoes a crisis of faith in which he doubts his miraculous abilities and calls God to a public test for which he receives no answer. However, the play's final variant, entitled *Di goldene keyt*, commences with a scene in which the *tsadik*'s predecessor, Shlomo, engages in a utopian refusal to make *havdalah* and dances ecstatically with his great-grandchildren, symbolizing hasidism's spiritual grandeur and its unwillingness to compromise with the sullied realities of the world. It is one of the dancing children, now grown, who assumes the role of *tsadik* at the play's end. Shmeruk finds in this final draft indication that Peretz had not wholly abandoned hope in hasidism's future spiritual revival.

In *Hasidism in Poland* the editors have provided a valuable introduction to the history and ideology of a significant and inadequately explored element of the hasidic community and are to be particularly commended for the light which they have shed upon the *tsadik* as a religious, political, and literary figure.

SETH BRODY
*Haverford College*

S. BRONSZTEJN

# Z dziejów ludności żydowskiej na Dolnym Śląsku po II wojnie światowej

(*History of the Jewish Population in Lower Silesia after the Second World War*)

(Wrocław: Wydawnictwo Uniwerwsytetu Wrocławskiego, 1993)
pp. 105. ISBN 83–229–0962–4

Following the end of the Second World War, two groups vied for the leadership of the remnants of Polish Jewry. The first, dominated by Jewish members of the (PPR, Polish Workers Party) who regarded the Jewish street as the primary focus of their political activity, sought to spearhead the rebuilding of a Jewish community in Poland along socialist lines. The second, headed by members of the Zionist youth movements that had played a leading role in organizing armed resistance during the Nazi occupation, opposed efforts to re-establish any sort of Jewish community in Poland on a long-term basis, preferring instead to see surviving Polish Jews commit themselves to reconstructing their lives in a Jewish state in Palestine. One of the principal means by which each of these contenders endeavoured to win adherents was to attempt to prove more adept than the other at meeting the day-to-day needs of the approximately 250,000 Holocaust survivors and repatriates from the Soviet Union who gathered in Poland during the years 1944–6. The Zionists worked towards this goal by establishing a network of informal social service agencies, centred about institutions known as kibbutzim, that provided all Jewish comers with food, clothing, shelter, and psychological support with a mind to channelling them eventually into the ranks of Berichah, the clandestine organization that would guide them out of Poland on their way, it was hoped, to the Jewish homeland. Their rivals, in contrast, placed their hopes in large measure in the creation of an area within the borders of the new Poland where Jews might enjoy especially favourable conditions for settlement, if not a special status altogether. Beginning in mid-1945 they thought that they had found such an area in the newly acquired province of Lower Silesia, and they poured considerable effort into building a strong Jewish community in that region.

During the immediate post-war years each side viewed the other as a serious competitor. The Jewish PPR activists regularly railed against the Zionist concept of what they termed 'emigrationism', claiming that their rivals were artificially sowing panic among Holocaust survivors in order to make them flee Poland in fear. The Zionists, for their part, were concerned that Jews might be seduced by what they regarded as false promises of a bright future in a territory that offered many of the benefits of a Jewish homeland and possessed the additional advantage of being immediately available, unlike Palestine, for large-scale Jewish settlement. As a Palestinian Jew involved in the work of Berichah later explained:

In Poland the Jews enjoyed an abundance of promises of a glorious future. . . . In Lower Silesia and its capital, Wrocław, from which the *Volksdeutsche* (*sic*) had been expelled after the war and 30,000 (*sic*) Jewish refugees settled there, Jewish life began to develop. . . . Within this sea of "guarantees" of a glorious future, which had already begun to be absorbed in the consciousness of the hesitant refugees, we [Zionists] had to show the refugees the truth about the insecurity of their future.[1]

For a while, especially during the first half of 1946, it appeared that the Zionists were losing their battle. In that interval, which coincided with the great repatriation of Polish citizens from the Soviet Union, the Jewish population of Lower Silesia reached upwards of 75,000, an increase from 16,000 at the beginning of the year. By the middle of 1946 Jews were living in forty-three different locations in the area, and they comprised 12–13 per cent of the total population. Their concentration was especially noteworthy in Wrocław and Dzierzoniów, where they represented over a quarter of each town's inhabitants. The intensification of anti-Jewish violence around the time of the referendum on the structure of government in post-war Poland, capped by the Kielce pogrom of 4 July 1946, threw the balance to the Zionist side, as 60,000 Jews, including a number who had previously settled in Lower Silesia, fled the country under Berichah auspices during the ensuing three months. Nevertheless, even in March 1948 there remained over 50,000 Jews in the area (a number that by then represented the majority of Polish Jewry), and for a decade thereafter the region managed to sustain a serious Jewish cultural and organizational life.

Szyja Bronsztejn has been studying the post-war Lower Silesian Jewish community for over thirty years. In the short volume under review he has summarized many of his findings. His book endeavours, first, to explain why the Lower Silesian settlement project was unable to serve as a more effective barrier to emigrationist sentiments among post-war Polish Jewry, and, secondly, to describe how the Jews who remained in the area after the great emigration made a new life for themselves.

The former problem is discussed primarily in the book's first substantive chapter, in the context of an analysis of the changes in the Jewish population of Lower Silesia over time. As it turns out, the author has little new to say on this subject: he enumerates the factors that have been cited since the time of the mass exodus itself—anti-Jewish violence; Zionist convictions on the part of a number of Holocaust survivors and Zionist agitation among the rest; and the desire of

[1]  Efraim Dekel, *Benetivei haberiḥah* (Tel Aviv, 1959) i. 30–3.

survivors to rebuild their lives in the company of relatives abroad—on the basis of a small sampling of secondary and testimonial literature and without much critical reflection. The latter, descriptive task, in contrast, is undertaken with considerably more energy and attention to detail, in separate chapters devoted to demographic trends, education and health care, economic activity, cultural life, and sport. The treatment of these matters is mainly statistical: the ninety-two pages of text include twenty-five tables containing figures on everything from the age and sex distributions of the Lower Silesian Jewish population to the number of programmes on subjects of Jewish interest presented at the Lewartowski People's Club in Wrocław, broken down by type of programme (in absolute numbers and percentages). In fact, most of the book's text consists of commentary on the statistical tables; there is little in the way of sustained narrative. Nor does the presentation appear to reflect any assessment of the relative significance of the data presented; as much space is devoted, for example, to a recitation of the names of Jews who played table tennis and association football (with dates and scores of matches, team rosters, and league rankings) as to a discussion of Jewish employment patterns.

This statistical, purely informational treatment is valuable to the extent that it summarizes verified data that can be employed by future scholars of a more analytical inclination. However, there appears to be reason to question the work of verification, at least for the immediate post-war years. The Provincial Jewish Committee of Lower Silesia gathered voluminous statistical material on the Jews of the region from 1946 to 1949. This material is available in the archives of the Jewish Historical Institute in Warsaw, yet the author has made only scattered reference to small parts of it, relying instead primarily on statistics culled from government sources, which do not always support the Jewish figures. It is highly unlikely that the author was unaware of the existence of this material, since it is mentioned in a number of the secondary works listed in the book's bibliography. One wonders, then, why it has been virtually ignored. Does the author regard the material gathered under Jewish auspices as fundamentally unreliable, as some scholars have suggested? If so, an analysis of its deficiencies in the face of more reliable government-gathered material, including a discussion of the procedures by which both types of material were collected, is essential; in its absence one cannot take the author's findings for the critical 1946–9 period as definitive. Such an analysis by a trained demographer like Bronsztejn would have constituted an especially valuable contribution, as it might have resolved definitively a problem that has continued to trouble researchers in the field.

This shortcoming is serious and unfortunate. Nevertheless, Bronsztejn's book is an essential starting-point for any future research on the Jews of Lower Silesia, and we are indebted to him for its publication.

DAVID ENGEL
*New York University*

ABRAHAM DAVID (ED.)
# A Hebrew Chronicle from Prague, c.1615
Translated by Leon J. Weinberger and Dina Ordan
(Tuscaloosa: University of Alabama Press, Judaic Studies series, 1993)
pp. xiv + 106. ISBN 0–8173–0596–3

In about 1615 an anonymous Jew from Prague composed a short Hebrew chronicle
to recount 'the expulsions, miracles, and . . . other occurrences befalling [the
Jews] in Prague and the other lands of our long exile' (p. 21). Abraham David discovered the manuscript in the Jewish Theological Seminary Library in New York
and published it in 1984. David added glosses, historical notes, and an introduction. By means of extensive references to Jewish and non-Jewish historical
literature, David showed that the chronicle was accurate. The English translation
of this edition is well designed and produced, and the translation itself is very
readable and generally true to the original. (There are some errors: for example,
on page 79, 'between Red and Red' should be 'between Edom and Edom'. The
translation also deletes a number of phrases from the original, as in the entry on
the Peasant's War on page 27.)

The chronicle, like the world-chronicle *Tsemaḥ david* (Prague, 1592) by David
Gans, briefly lists events year by year. Also like *Tsemaḥ david*, it lists events from
both the Jewish and Gentile worlds, and even some meteorological and astro-
nomical events. Unlike *Tsemaḥ david*, however, the 1615 chronicle focuses primarily on *gezerot*, the 'evil decrees' that have befallen the Jews. (David also
included two other documents in this volume, both of them lists of *gezerot*. One
contains *gezerot* occurring from 1096 to 1520, the other from 1488 to 1525.) The
notion of *gezerah* encompasses human as well as divine decrees. The expulsion of
the Jews of 'Rus' (Ukraine) in 1494–9 and the martyrdom of the Jews of Trebitsch
in 1498 (p. 23), for example, are both *gezerot*, as are a flood in the Prague Jewish
Quarter in 1501 (p. 24) and a fire in 1516 (p. 26).

Like David Gans and other Jewish historians of the sixteenth century, the
author of the 1615 chronicle was interested in non-Jewish history. In fact, in the
chronicle's account of the years 1522 to 1537 (pp. 26–44), Jewish misfortunes
recede entirely to the background. (This section of the chronicle was probably copied
from a separate, unknown early sixteenth-century Jewish source; see pp. 34 and
36.) For these years the focus shifts to the politics of the Holy Roman Empire: the
Turkish war, the Italian wars, the Peasants' War, and the Protestant Reformation.
The author speaks his mind, expressing sympathy, for example, with the
Anabaptists: 'They did righteous acts, may God forgive me [for saying so] . . . providing each other's basic needs [and] they desired to learn the laws of Moses' (p. 33).

The chronicle, with its brief annual entries, is not a continuous narrative, but
does give a feeling of immediacy, like a newspaper. To read that in 1577 grain was

very cheap in Bohemia (p. 51), and that on the eve of Sukkot 1609 an emissary from the Ottoman sultan arrived in Prague accompanied by 120 men (p. 61), allows us to see the work for a moment from the perspective of a seventeenth-century Jew.

Of special importance for the history of the Jews of Prague is the account of the 1615 chronicle of a *gezerah* in 1602 (pp. 54–8), which may serve to balance an excessively positive presentation of Jewish life in Prague in its golden age during the reign of Rudolph II. The heads of the Jewish community of Prague were accused of attempting to poison a non-Jew named Nicholas Preiss. The chief rabbi, Judah Loew (known as Maharal), and others were imprisoned, the community was threatened with expulsion, and one Jew died under judicial torture.

The chronicle's final entry (pp. 62–9) on events in 1611, David suggests (p. 7), may actually be based on the author's eyewitness observations. In that year, the Prague Jews were threatened by both sides in a civil war in Prague, but the intervention of the Habsburg monarchs and, the chronicler believes, miraculous divine intervention kept the Prague Jews from harm. (A couple of decades later, Leib Kirchheim of Worms would tell a similar story of the 1614 riots in that city.)

This final entry is in keeping with the goals that the author announces at the head of the chronicle. There he declares that he wishes to recount not only 'expulsions' and misfortunes, but also 'miracles'. The narrative of the civil war of 1611 emphasizes not the sufferings of the Jews, but rather their miraculous deliverance. It is in the line of other seventeenth-century Jewish 'deliverance narratives', a number of them written by Prague Jews, such as the memoir of *Meir hakadosh*, R. Yom Tov Lipman Heller's *Megilat eivah*, and Judah Leib ben Joshua Heschel's Hebrew chronicle of the 1648 siege of Prague called *Milḥamah beshalom*.

Indeed, it is a significant aspect of the historical experience of the Jews of Prague in the seventeenth century that the long series of sixteenth-century *gezerot* was succeeded by a series of public 'deliverances' in 1611, 1620, 1629, and 1648. This experience contrasts with that of Polish Jewry in this period. For them the job of listing *gezerot* was just beginning.

JOSEPH M. DAVIS
*University of Maryland at College Park*

NORMAN DAVIES AND ANTONY POLONSKY (EDS.)
## *Jews in Eastern Poland and the USSR, 1939–1946*

(London: Macmillan, in association with the School of Slavonic and East European Studies, University of London, 1991)
pp. xiv + 426. ISBN 0–333–49128–9

The Jews who lived in the region called eastern Poland in the inter-war period numbered about 1.3 million, and constituted one of the largest Jewish communities in

Europe. Like the other Jews of Poland, they suffered almost total annihilation at the hands of the Nazis. But the circumstances in which this tragedy occurred were unique. Not only did the Jews of eastern Poland have to contend with the Germans, they had to deal with the Poles and Soviets as well. And the triangular relationship of Jews, Poles, and Soviets in the context of the Second World War is the focus of the papers in this volume.

Half of the fourteen papers are based on presentations delivered at the Conference on the History and Culture of Polish Jews, held in Jerusalem in 1988. The other papers were included to provide a fuller treatment of the topic. An extensive but balanced and informative introduction by the editors synthesizes the major points in each paper and highlights the most important and controversial issues. These issues include the role of the Jews in the Soviet administration of eastern Poland, the relationship between Poles and Jews under Soviet occupation (especially the creation of the Anders Army, repatriation from the USSR, and the role of Jewish Communists in the formation of the Soviet-sponsored Polish army), and in Soviet preparations for the occupation of Poland in 1944. Papers by Jan Gross and Aharon Weiss treat, respectively, the political and socio-economic plight of Jews under Soviet occupation. A series of briefer papers deals with population statistics, Jewish issues in Polish literature of the period, the response of Jews in Soviet-occupied lands to Nazi exterminations, Jewish resistance, and the efforts to organize aid for Jewish Polish refugees in the USSR.

The final five papers concentrate on the activities of Jewish and Polish refugees and deportees in the USSR. On the whole, the articles are objective and often based on sources that are not easily accessible. The final section of the book, consisting of about 150 pages, contains very informative documents. Although some of these have already been published in Hebrew, they appear here in English translation for the first time. It is worth noting that the recent appearance of several publications of Soviet documents, most notably Ivan Bilas's *Represyvno-karaina systema v Ukraini, 1917–1953* (The Repressive System of Punishment in Ukraine), 2 vols. (Kiev, 1994) are highly relevant to the issues discussed in this publication, especially concerning the numbers of Jews, Poles, and Ukrainians who were deported to the USSR.

One major conclusion that arises from reading these materials is that the dilemma of the Jews in eastern Poland was far more complex and confusing than anywhere else in Europe. Besides their tragically clear-cut relationship with the Nazis, they had to maintain a difficult relationship, characterized by mutual suspicion, with the Soviets and the Poles. Moreover—an aspect not treated in the book—their relations with the Ukrainian and Belarusian majorities in the region were, to put it mildly, also very complicated. These complexities and tensions exacerbated an already tragic dilemma. As Ben-Zion Pinchuk points out, the Jews of eastern Poland were the only ones who had somewhere to flee: to the USSR. That so few chose this option, even though failure to do so meant almost certain death, was due in part to their unfortunate experiences during the Soviet occupation of 1939–41 and to the disorganization and confusion that the occupation imposed on the Jewish communities.

As the editors note, the events treated in this volume belong to a world that is dead and gone. It is still astonishing to realize that in the area once called eastern Poland there are now practically no Jews, Poles, or Soviets. None the less, the relationship that existed among these three groups during the Second World War reflected (and continues to reflect) issues of great historical significance. The editors and authors of this collection deserve commendation for elucidating thoroughly and fairly a topic that has been neglected too often and too long.

OREST SUBTELNY
*York University*

ARTUR EISENBACH
## *The Emancipation of the Jews in Poland, 1780–1870*
Edited by Antony Polonsky; translated by Janina Dorosz
(Oxford: Basil Blackwell in association with
the Institute for Polish–Jewish Studies, 1991)
pp. l + 623. ISBN 0631178023

The study of Jewish emancipation has long dominated modern Jewish historiography. In *The Emancipation of the Jews in Poland, 1780–1870* Polish historian Artur Eisenbach provides a masterful account of this process in the lands of partitioned Poland. The book is a work of grand synthesis, which securely places the situation of the Jews in Poland in the context of pan-European developments in the late eighteenth and nineteenth centuries.

Eisenbach employs a classic Marxist approach to explain the course of Jewish emancipation in Poland. He argues that emancipation, or the removal of traditional restrictions, and granting the Jews equal civil and political rights, can only take place within the context of the transformation of society from feudal to 'modern'. Thus, emancipation can only occur when the serfs are free, the nobility loses its privilege, and the bourgeoisie becomes strong enough to forge a liberal ideology and demand hegemony in society. Unfortunately, social, economic, and political realities in Poland precluded emancipation until the 1860s. Eisenbach laments the fact that anti-Jewish restrictions prevented the integration of the Jewish and Christian bourgeoisie in Poland. Since Jews were such a numerically significant part of the urban economy, the absence of such integration meant that the Polish bourgeoisie remained small, traditional, and ineffective. Only with the end of feudal privilege and the beginning of a modern, capitalist society in the late 1860s could the Jews in Poland be emancipated.

In some ways it is utterly refreshing and not at all surprising to see such commitment to the Marxist paradigm. After all, the Marxist approach does have much to recommend it. Jewish emancipation did result in large measure from the transformations of society in the late eighteenth and nineteenth centuries. But the Marxist approach in the pure form in which it is presented here is overly simplistic and too deterministic, and ignores other factors that contributed to the emancipation of the Jews in Europe.

Eisenbach presents emancipation as resulting only from the dismantling of a society based on privileged estates. He regards the opposition of the Polish nobility to Jewish emancipation as inevitable, given the desire of the nobles to maintain hegemony. In other countries, however, the nobility accepted Jewish emancipation while still retaining its privileges. In Hungary, for example, the serfs may have been free after 1848, but the manorial economy persisted and the nobles retained political power. The nobles nevertheless approved of Jewish emancipation and they warmly encouraged the Magyarization of the Jews.

Eisenbach's Marxism also makes him underestimate the role of the state acting for its own reasons, not necessarily influenced by bourgeois liberalism. Joseph II's reforms in Austria, for example, which removed many traditional restrictions on the Jews and urged them to Germanize, did not derive from the power of the middle classes to change state policy but rather from the monarch's own desire to centralize and Germanize his state. The state also had an interest in secularizing the Jews long before it freed the serfs. In Bohemia and Moravia in the late eighteenth and early nineteenth centuries, the Austrian government, working with local Jewish leaders, created a network of German Jewish schools that created a large cohort of Germanized, modern Jews by the middle of the nineteenth century.

One of the most perplexing results of Eisenbach's deterministic thesis is his assertion that the Jews in Poland were emancipated by the 1860s, even if only partially in the Congress Kingdom. True, the Jews in Galicia were equal before the law in 1867–8, and the Jews in Prussian Poland also received equality in 1866. But surely the Jews in Congress Poland were not emancipated, not in any real sense, even if the serfs were free and many civic restrictions, including the right to municipal citizenship, were lifted in the early 1860s. Eisenbach's attitude toward the gentile Polish bourgeoisie is similarly problematic. He seems genuinely upset that the urban middle classes did not understand that it was in their economic and political self-interest to tear down anti-Jewish restrictions and so strengthen the power of the middle classes in general. But bourgeois groups in other European countries also retained traditional anti-Jewish prejudices and did not always articulate a liberal ideology with respect to the Jews.

Despite the problems of Eisenbach's idealistic Marxism, his book makes a significant contribution to our understanding not only of the vicissitudes of emancipation in the Polish territories but also of the dynamics of emancipation generally.

Particularly striking is the similarity in the struggle for emancipation in all European countries. For example, Polish advocates of Jewish emancipation demanded that the Jews Polonize and renounce Jewish national identity. Even those who opposed emancipation argued that if the Jews could prove their worthiness, if they could become Poles and cease belonging to the Jewish nation, then perhaps they could gain equality. Advocates and proponents of Jewish emancipation in the German states made exactly the same demands; they expected that Jews would assimilate, Germanize, and renounce their membership in a Jewish nation either as a result of emancipation or as a condition for it. Eisenbach criticizes the Poles, a group themselves subjected to denationalization, for demanding the end of Jewish national identity, and he even labels such demands 'anachronistic' in the 1830s and 1840s. Perhaps such demands were morally anachronistic in those decades, but liberals all over Europe felt no compunction in making them.

Although Eisenbach from time to time exaggerates the Polish loyalties of Polish Jews, his book is admirably free of apologetics. A master of archival materials and secondary literature in many languages, he skilfully keeps track of the different courses of emancipation in the Austrian, Prussian, and Russian parts of Poland. The reader does wish, though, that he had defined 'Poland'. It is obvious that Eisenbach deals only with ethnic Poland (the Congress Kingdom, Poznań, and Galicia), but that means that he ignores those parts of the eighteenth-century Polish–Lithuanian Commonwealth annexed by Russia. While such exclusion might be justified, Eisenbach should have summarized developments in the Pale.

Despite some problems, the scholarly public should warmly welcome this first-rate translation of Eisenbach's excellent survey of Polish Jewish rights in the nineteenth century.

MARSHA ROZENBLIT
*University of Maryland at College Park*

BARBARA ENGELKING
## *Na łące popiołów: Ocaleni z Holocaustu*

(*On a Meadow of Ashes: Survivors of the Holocaust*)

(Warsaw: Cykłady, 1993)
pp. 223. ISBN 8390059223

Many Holocaust survivors have written memoirs, but only some have been published. Many more survivors have been interviewed by scholars, and although thousands of such interviews are in the Yad Vashem archives, very few of these have been published. It is a pity. Interviews are an important source of knowledge, and they are invaluable for gaining an understanding of the horrors of the

Holocaust. The recent book by Barbara Engelking is evidence of the value of this type of historical record.

Engelking interviewed ten Holocaust survivors who now live in Poland, asking about their background, Holocaust experiences, and how they felt about it now. Those interviewed had very different backgrounds and experiences; the only thing they had in common was that they were all among the pitifully few Jewish Holocaust survivors who chose to remain in Poland. Six women and four men were interviewed. Two had come from very poor families, while three had been wealthy; four had been part of the intelligentsia, with one of them having been completely assimilated to Polish society; before the war four had engaged in communist activities: together, a sample of pre-war Jewish society in Poland.

The Holocaust experiences the ten had were also very different. Five had been in the Warsaw ghetto. Three had escaped at the beginning of the war to Lwów and experienced the bloody pogroms organized by the Germans and Ukrainians there. Left with no other choice, they had smuggled themselves back in the Warsaw ghetto. Three of those interviewed had been inmates of the Łódź ghetto, and one of the ghetto in Cracow. Five had been prisoners in a concentration camp, while six had lived for an extended period in 'Aryan' Poland. Six of the Jews who chose to stay in post-war Poland had been part of the underground, with two having belonged to a partisan unit.

Engelking knows the right questions to ask to elicit the facts and horrors about those sad years: the tormenting hunger in the ghettos, the terrifying deportations, the loss of all who were dear, the endless suffering in the concentration camps, the constant fear on the Aryan side. Moreover, while many were very generous with help, others showed brutal enmity.

Perhaps the most instructive parts of the interviews are the descriptions of those who succeeded in escaping from the Warsaw ghetto to the Aryan side. Polish Warsaw was not at all an easy place during the Nazi occupation, and the suffering of the Polish population is well known. Nevertheless, those who escaped from the ghetto considered that place a paradise compared to the ghetto, even before the deportations to the death camps began. As Helena Merenholc put it in answer to Engeling's question: '"What was my impression—the sharp difference between the ghetto and the Aryan side?" "I walked through the streets, and here it was normal. This was my first impression—normality. I was shocked"' (p. 205). Helena Merenholc (who provides perhaps the best interview) gives important insights for some well-known figures in the Warsaw ghetto, such as Janusz Korczak, Adam and Felicja Czerniaków, Stefa Wilczynska, Abraham Gepner, and others.

The statement by Józef Seweryn on page 81 presents a marked contrast to Merenholc. He says: 'I was lucky that as a Jew I didn't come to Birkenau, which was an extermination camp. There, only those who worked by burning and killing their brothers could survive.' If Seweryn meant those who were in the

Sonderkommando, he is mistaken, for those poor souls may have been the most miserable the world has ever seen. They were forced by the Nazis to burn the corpses of the murdered victims. It is nonsense to accuse them of participation in murder, and, in any case, only a few of them survived. They were the only ones who organized an uprising in Auschwitz, and they wrote and hid the famous diaries. These diaries, found after the war, constitute some of the most important evidence of Nazi crimes.

On page 83 there is another highly questionable statement by Seweryn. When asked by Engelking, 'Why, in your opinion, did Hitler want to murder all Jews?' he gave this astonishing answer: 'He himself was seemingly of Jewish extraction. People who wish to hide something show others that this is precisely what they hate. Not only Hitler; certainly, others as well.' Perhaps the book might have been improved if the Seweryn comments had been omitted, even though some sections of the interview were important.

Both Mostowicz and Sznajderman were asked: 'In general, how was the Holocaust possible?' Sznajderman's reply was 'Please, I am neither a historian, nor a sociologist, psychologist, philosopher, or economist. However, should I even be to some extent all of them, still I don't know if I would be able to answer your question. The Holocaust is beyond the categories of usual human minds. Even now, I can neither understand it, nor provide an answer' (p. 187). Mostowicz replied: 'I think, that at each period in my life, my answer would be different. Now, not thinking too much, I would say that the Holocaust was an inherent feature of the human race from its inception. The murder of the South American Indians was also a Holocaust; so was the murder of all the inhabitants of Australia and Tasmania. So was the murder of the Armenians by the Turks . . .' (p. 27).

Is it possible that a man like Mostowicz, with his knowledge and personal experience, does not understand the uniqueness of the Holocaust? Other tragic events, horrible as they were, cannot be compared with the total murder campaign organized by Germany against all Jews, without exception. The hunt for the last hidden infant, the death sentence for all who dared to help, are without precedent in human history. But perhaps Mostowicz answered spontaneously, as he put it, 'not thinking too much'. If he had thought a bit before responding, his answer might have been different.

A statement by Barbara Engelking in the Introduction is also a simplification. There she writes: 'The Nazis questioned many of the archetypes of European culture, as for example the deep inherited belief that it was glorious to die for the Fatherland. This was one of the basic norms obligatory in wartime. Now this principle was shaken—the Jews were deprived of the privilege of a glorious death. In contrast to the Poles, they did not die for the Fatherland' (p. 7).

This is far from the realities of what happened to Jews and Poles during the Second World War. It does not reflect the Jewish or Polish plights under the Nazi occupation, nor Jewish helplessness against the German policy of total extermination or Polish helplessness against the brutal terror. Nevertheless, these remarks do not diminish the value of Engelking's book. She deserves to be praised for her contribution to the understanding of the Holocaust.

SHMUEL KRAKOWSKI
*Yad Vashem, Jerusalem*

BARBARA ENGELKING

# *Zagłada i pamięć*

## (*Shoah and Memory*)

(Warsaw: Wydawnictwo IFiS PAN, 1994)
pp. 315. ISBN 83–85194–98–3

The subtitle of *Zagłada i pamięć*, 'The Holocaust Experience and its Consequences on the Basis of Autobiographical Accounts', is a full and accurate reflection of the contents of this volume. At the end of the book, the summary in English provides a synopsis of each of the five chapters. Chapter 1 shows the differences between the wartime experiences of Poles and Jews: what life was like in the ghetto, on the Aryan side, and in the concentration camps. The author portrays the situation of the Poles as a two-sided conflict against the Germans, while the Jewish situation is presented as a three-sided conflict among Jews, Germans, and Poles. 'The Poles who were at war with the Germans had no need of Jews, but the Jews, if they wanted to escape death from the Germans, could not manage without the Poles.'

The second chapter deals with daily life in the ghetto. The third chapter concentrates on why it happened, a question that cannot be comprehended rationally, especially for the handful who were lucky enough to survive. Chapter 4 deals with psychological scars resulting from the war trauma. Chapter 5 is dedicated to the 'Holocaust and how to preserve its memory'.

Many Holocaust books have been published over the years, but *Zagłada i pamięć* is a uniquely valuable contribution to Holocaust literature. The reader is struck by the rigorous precision of this doctoral thesis. What is even more impressive is the fascinating narrative, along with the analysis. Engelking, an objective and informative scholar, has the right amount of empathy for her subjects. As part of the post-war generation of Polish intellectuals, she writes from a humanist perspective, yet shows remarkable psychological insight into the underlying aspects of humiliation and suffering as experienced by all the Holocaust victims.

Because Polish–Jewish relations evoke a great deal of emotion, along with heated, sometimes even hysterical debates, Engelking's calm, rational voice is very important. That the interviews were conducted in Polish means that nothing was lost in translation. At the same time, the author shows an ability to conceptualize and generalize on the basis of the over forty interviews. Besides the interviews, Engelking uses diaries by such authors as Emanuel Ringelblum, Adam Czerniaków, and Katarzyna Żywulska, along with the many sources listed in the bibliography.

The list of reasons why the *szmalcowniks* (blackmailers) behaved as they did is presented logically and without emotion so that the integrity of the text is preserved. In a similar vein, Engelking enumerates the reasons for altruistic behaviour by those who sheltered and protected Jews at the risk of their own lives. Along with victims and perpetrators, we are introduced to the bystanders, who were essentially indifferent. Engelking gives a meticulous account of what it was really like to live in a ghetto, dealing with the impact of hunger, illness, and death.

What this reviewer found especially enlightening was the description of the cultural life of the ghetto. The half-clandestine activities that promoted learning took place as if death did not exist. There were even some forms of entertainment, such as concerts and plays, as well as an active social life. The special meaning of gossip and rumour is also described, and how they influenced the degree of panic felt by the ghetto's inmates. The portrayal of the tense, yet vibrant, atmosphere is reflected in the alternations between fear and hope.

Most original is the author's approach to the dimension of time and its significance in people's lives: 'The Ghetto was an island within time that ruled itself by its own laws. There was no past. The only past referred to was yesterday, and only a restless and insecure present, as time was one of the forms of totalitarian oppression.' People experienced a kind of distortion of time. Every day intimate contact with death excluded the possibility of the future, and the future was transformed into eternity. As to ghetto morality, the struggle for survival sometimes included survival at the expense of others. It was a diabolical Nazi scheme to use victim against victim, and some Jewish collaborators and policemen degraded themselves by choosing that option. A disturbing memoir by Calel Perechodnik describes the agonizing feelings and choices Jewish policemen had to make.

The conclusion of the book deals with the decision of some Jews to remain in Poland after the war, a position widely criticized by North American Jewry. Some of the Jews who stayed in Poland did so because it was a cemetery of the Jewish nation; some hoped to find a loved one who had survived; some felt a commitment to the new Communist system, which they thought would bring justice to all. In the end those who stayed were treated with contempt by both Poles and Jews. Engelking gives several reasons for the survivors' reluctance to share their experiences with others, including their own children: for the most part they were afraid of being misunderstood or judged by others. After reading *Shoah and Memory*, however, it would be very difficult to judge. An English version of this outstanding Polish document on the Shoah is eagerly anticipated.

TECIA WERBOWSKI
*Montreal*

PETER FAESSLER, THOMAS HELD, AND
DIRK SAWITZKI (EDS.)
*Lemberg–Lwow–Lviv: Eine Stadt im Schnittpunkt*
*europäischer Kulturen*
(Cologne, Böhlau Verlag, 1993)
pp. 207. ISBN 3-412-04292-7

L'viv, the Ukrainian form of the city's name in the official language of the country it is located in today, is a typical city in east central Europe. Like all urban areas in that part of the European continent, L'viv was traditionally inhabited by peoples of different nationalities and religions, who may or may not have been of the same nationality as the administrative authorities of the many states that ruled the area.

L'viv's history begins in 1250, when the Rus' prince and soon-to-be king Danylo of Galicia–Volhynia built what was to become his new capital closer to the river routes that linked the realm northward via the rivers Bug and Vistula to the Baltic Sea, as well as eastward and southward via the rivers Dniester and Prut to the Black Sea. A century later, Galicia was annexed by Poland, where it remained until 1772. From then until 1918, Galicia was an Austrian province in the Habsburg Empire, with L'viv as its administrative centre. Austrian rule was interrupted at the outset of the First World War, when during the fall and winter of 1914–15 the city, together with most of Galicia, was occupied by tsarist Russia. At the close of the war, in November 1918, L'viv was for three weeks the seat of government of the short-lived West Ukrainian People's Republic; then from 1919 to 1939, it was again part of Poland. When Poland fell to Nazi Germany in September 1939, L'viv was annexed by Hitler's temporary ally the Soviet Union. Soviet rule lasted less than two years. From June 1941 to the summer of 1944, the city was part of Nazi Germany's Third Reich, until it was 'reunited' with the Soviet Union, specifically Ukraine, from 1944 to 1991. Since that time it has been part of an independent Ukraine.

Aside from Rus'–Ukrainians, Poles, Austro-Germans, and a few thousand Russians, all of whom represented the states that have ruled L'viv, the city has been home to Germans (from states other than Austria), Armenians, Austrian officials and bureaucrats of varying nationalities (in particular Czechs), and most importantly Jews, who by the outset of the twentieth century comprised 27.7 per cent of the inhabitants. Not surprisingly, and again like most cities in east central Europe, L'viv has had, or in the minds of people of various nationalities still has, many names: L'viv (Ukrainian), Lwów (Polish), Lemberg (German), Lvuv or Lemberik (Yiddish), Lvov (Russian), or, for the reader of documents and architectural inscriptions, Leopolis (Latin).

During most of the twentieth century, many states in east central Europe have tried to eradicate the historical past of the territories that they acquired, frequently by force. Thus, in 1919, when L'viv became part of a restored Poland, the authorities tried to eliminate the former traces of Austrian Habsburg rule as well as Ukrainian organizational life. When the Soviets took over in 1939, Polish institutions were abolished, and both Poles and Ukrainians were deported to Siberia or forced to flee westward. The few years of the German presence (1941–4) witnessed the annihilation of virtually the entire Jewish population and its rich centuries-old institutional and cultural presence. The Soviets after 1945 dismantled all traces of the Polish and Ukrainian 'bourgeois-nationalist' past, while most recently, after 1991, aspects of life that recall the Soviet presence are being replaced by Ukrainian national forms.

Nevertheless, whether through their buildings, cobbled streets, or the memories of residents driven away or killed, cities have a remarkable way of preserving the heritage that their present rulers may try to eliminate. The volume under review, by its very title, *Lemberg–Lwow–Lviv*, is a testament to how the historical past of L'viv remains alive no matter who controls the city. The book actually derives from a series of lectures held in 1990–1 at the Albert-Ludwigs University at Freiburg im Breisgau. Freiburg had recently become a sister-city to L'viv, and the lectures (revised for the book under review) were intended to remind Freiburgers and other Germans of the multinational and multicultural heritage of its urban partner to the east.

With this goal in mind, five of the six essays are descriptive surveys based on a wide body of secondary literature that covers a specific period of the city's history. These include: the long period of Polish rule to 1772 (by Isabel Roeskau-Ryde), the Austrian era and post-First World War era when L'viv became a centre of both the Polish and Ukrainian national revivals (by Rudolf Mark), Jewish life in the nineteenth and twentieth centuries (by Jerzy Holzer), the inter-war period (by Anna-Halja Horbatsch), and the wartime and post-Second World War Soviet period until Ukrainian independence (by Dmytro Zlepko).

The one exception to the survey approach, and the only essay not based on a lecture given in the University of Freiburg series, is Thomas Held's 'From Pogrom to Mass Murder: The Destruction of the Jewish Population of L'viv during World War II'. Although dealing with only three years of German rule from the summer of 1941 to the summer of 1944, Held's essay (pp. 113–66) takes up over a quarter of the volume. It does not present any new evidence, but it is perhaps the most detailed available survey based on virtually all the existing memoir and secondary literature. Its particular virtue is to describe in an impartial manner the role of all participants, whether German, Polish, or Ukrainian, in the killing (and in a few instances saving) of L'viv's Jewry.

Despite the chronological imbalance in the coverage of L'viv's history, the editors of this volume have succeeded in reminding us—and we all need to be reminded over and over again—that cultural and national diversity were the norms in east central Europe. Only nationalist fanatics in the twentieth century tried to change this. And while they may in the process have caused the destruction of hundreds of thousands of lives, in the end they did not succeed in their ultimate goal: the ethnic cleansing of the past. The publication of *Lemberg–Lwow–Lviv*, not to mention the interest of L'viv's present-day Ukrainian majority in all aspects of the city's history, are most welcome developments because they confirm what the perceptive commentator Timothy Garton Ash has recently written: 'In many ways, to propose multiculturalism in Central Europe really is to suggest going forward to the past.'

PAUL ROBERT MAGOCSI
*University of Toronto*

DARRELL J. FASCHING
## The Ethical Challenge of Auschwitz and Hiroshima: Apocalypse or Utopia?
(Albany: State University of New York Press, 1993)
pp. xvi + 357. ISBN 0-7914-1376-4

In the last ten years a growing number of scholars have wrestled with the theological and ethical challenges of Auschwitz and Hiroshima—historical events that have come to symbolize the modern danger of valuing efficiency and accomplishment over human dignity and rights. Elucidating for readers ways in which a wide variety of theologians, ethicists, political theorists, and social critiques have responded to these challenges, Darrell Fasching focuses his work on the problem and the solution, as he understands them. To do so, he draws upon the biblical story of Babel and the contemporary lessons that it offers.

Once, the story tells us, everyone on earth spoke the same language (Gen. 11: 1 ff.). Living close to one another, talking and working with each other, human beings came to recognize the ability and power they possessed. Consequently, 'to make a name for [themselves]', they began to build a city, and within it a tower which, when completed, would reach up to the heavens. Yet, unhappy with these efforts, God confused their tongues. Lacking a common language, they could not now complete the tower and were scattered by the Almighty throughout the world. Fasching convincingly suggests that this tale is, in fact, a meaningful parable for our times. Imagining the inhabitants of Babel as modern men and women, attempting to create a perfect city through their technological prowess and expertise, he insists that God did not see their efforts as sinful but as misguided. The point of the story, Fasching tells us, 'is that utopian transcendence is to be found not in a "finished world" of technological and ideological conformity but in an "unfinished world" of diversity' (p. 2).

The picture of the future that Fasching presents is frightening, yet clear. Cultural visions that emphasize technology's promises but not its dangers have led us, he warns, on a path from Auschwitz to Hiroshima to the brink of 'MAD-ness' (i.e. mutually assured destruction). We have created a secularized myth of human progress without a counter-myth of human responsibility. Thus, Auschwitz 'embodies the demonic use of technology against targeted populations to commit genocide' while 'Hiroshima and Nagasaki represent the last such use of technology, for . . . [if a nuclear] bomb is ever used again, genocide will be transformed into collective suicide or *omnicide*—the destruction of all life' (pp. 28–9). As Fasching sees it, we have erroneously understood the challenge of Auschwitz and Hiroshima to be an absolute Either/Or: an apocalypse of universal annihilation or a utopia of technological achievement. Unwilling to face the first possibility, we have embraced the second, repressing the 'prophetic warnings' that Auschwitz and Hiroshima offer. Yes, Fasching suggests, utopia is possible; but those who believe that technology alone can take us there are deluded, for 'a normless world inevitably ends in apocalyptic self-destruction' (p. 29).

If anything, he continues, citing Jewish theologian Irving Greenberg, Auschwitz and Hiroshima should teach us to distrust any absolutes, *any* final solutions. The real challenge that lies before us is to create a world in which ideological conformity gives way to diversity, and societies are subject to constant critiques that transcend specific cultures. In all probability it will not be perfect, but again, as the story of Babel reveals, the human realm is not meant to be one of absolute perfection; rather, it is one in which human dignity and diversity are preserved through the valuing and sharing of one another's stories. While we may speak different languages, it is crucial, he argues, that we find a way to understand one another. Placing his detailed critique of technological civilization within the framework of ethical and theological discourse, Fasching successfully underscores the extent to which the challenges that lie before us are not merely political, economic, and social. Nor are they limited to any one culture or nation. Here, the urgency of his message is powerfully conveyed and its content quite convincing.

Less convincing, however, is the book's second major theme: a call for the creation of that which Protestant theologian Paul Tillich first described in 1920 as the theology of culture. In light of Fasching's self-described alienation from Christianity, it is understandable that he finds a theology rooted in a particular cultural context, yet not necessarily grounded in any one religious tradition, to be so appealing. As Fasching maintains, theology of culture as 'decentred' or 'alienated', begins by imaginatively standing outside one's own religious tradition in order to see and criticize it from the perspective of the narrative traditions of the 'other', i.e. those whom one's religious tradition considers to be strangers. Yet the more Fasching elaborates upon the need for and content of such a theology, the more he seems to be describing that which may be of particular value to Christians, since, according to him, Christianity has not adequately welcomed 'others in the world whose way of being might, by contrast, cause self-doubt and self-questioning' (p. 7). Left unexplored is what he thinks such a theology might mean for those within a religious tradition such as Judaism (his prime example) that not only values the stranger but also recognizes religious anger as a legitimate expression of faith.

Like Fasching, I believe that Jews and Christians can, and should, learn from one another. I also share his conviction that story-telling is a particularly effective means of sharing both experiences and ideals. Yet just as each 'holy community' has its own language through which stories are told, so each has its own theological language through which problems and challenges are articulated. Fasching, for example, writes: 'After Auschwitz and Hiroshima, speaking from a biblical perspective, we live in a time of a new covenant with the whole of humanity, a covenant whose saving remnant is composed of holy communities such as those found within the narrative traditions of Judaism, Christianity, and Buddhism' (p. 208). While I appreciate his more inclusive use of the terms 'new covenant' and 'saving remnant', the biblical and contemporary perspectives from which I, as a Jew, view these concepts are quite different from his. So, of course, are the perspectives of Buddhists, for whom the whole idea of a 'biblical perspective' lacks either cultural or theological resonance.

Rather than undermining the considerable merits of Fasching's work, this critique in fact underscores its importance, for, as Fasching himself insists, all attempts to create a universal language are doomed to failure. According to Fasching, our best hope, if not our only hope, lies in celebrating that which makes each of our communities unique, while respecting and learning from one another. *The Ethical Challenge of Auschwitz and Hiroshima* does not make easy reading. Yet for those who recognize the great importance of the many social, political, theological, and ethical issues with which Fasching wrestles, this carefully written, thought-provoking work is certainly worth while.

ELLEN M. UMANSKY
*Fairfield University*

P. FIJAŁKOWSKI (ED.)
*Dzieje Żydów w Polsce: Wybór tekstów źródłowych,*
*XI–XVIII wieku*

(Warsaw: Żydowski Instytut Historyczny w Polsce, n.d.)
pp. 132. ISBN 8385888004

This collection of sources on the history of the Jews of the Polish–Lithuanian Commonwealth in the eleventh to eighteenth centuries is one in a series of books concerned with the history of Polish Jewry published by the Żydowski Instytut Historyczny (Jewish Historical Institute) in Poland. Seven books are planned for this series; four have already been published. Fijałkowski's book is the only one that deals with the history of Polish Jewry before the partitions.

This source book, like the series as a whole, is designed as a reference-book for schools and has been included by the Polish Minister of Education on the list of history books for secondary schools. This new trend in the Polish Education Ministry, which includes the history of the Jews of Poland in the curriculum as an integral part of Polish history, is the result of both internal Polish processes and Israeli–Polish co-operation. These new curricula demand new textbooks that reflect up-to-date historical ideas. First and foremost, there is a need to gather existing source material, which until now has been scattered in many books and old publications, or even not published at all.

The majority of the seventy-three documents in this book are drawn from other reference-books and collections. Only three are printed here for the first time, two of which are taken from the archives of the Jewish Historical Institute in Poland. Of the latter, the first document (pp. 27–8) is the privilege to build a synagogue in Lublin granted by King Władysław IV on 16 July 1636 to his court Jew Zwi Hirsh Doktorowicz.[1] The second document (p. 95), dated 1664, is from the crown hetman, Stanisław Potocki, on the subject of pogroms against the Jews in Lwów, in which he defends the Jews. The third document (pp. 39–40), taken from the Central Archives of Old Records in Warsaw (AGAD), is an agreement between the Jews and the townspeople of Myszczynów in 1778. These documents are presented in a concise fashion that suits the needs of the readers.

The collection is divided into four sections: (1) privileges, obligations, and prohibitions; (2) the internal life of the community; (3) means of existence; (4) the nature of coexistence. The criteria determining the division of chapters is not consistent: the first chapter is determined by the nature of the documents, the remaining three by subject. The editor does not explain how or why these divisions were made, leading to a lack of the clarity and systematic framework that is necessary in a reference-book. For example, we find privileges also in chapters 2 and 3. However, important official documents of other types, such as contracts with the *szlachta*, decisions of the *beit din* (rabbinical court), the Magdeburg Law, and wills, are not represented. In the chapter on the means of existence there is no mention of Jewish tenancy on *szlachta* lands at all, although this is mentioned in the chapter on coexistence.

The chapters are organized chronologically. However, in all other respects it is clear that the collection is haphazard. There is no regional representation, and no

---

[1] In fact this document is well known and has been published based on a copy dated 16 July 1638. See B. Mandelsberg-Shildkraut, *Studies in the History of Lublin Jewry* (Tel Aviv, 1965), 92–3; *Pinkas va'ad arba aratstot*, ed. I. Halperin, 2nd edn., rev. Y. Bartal (Jerusalem, 1990), 30; J. Goldberg, *Jewish Privileges in the Polish Commonwealth* (Jerusalem, 1985), 155–6.

representation of other estates—private, ecclesiastical, or royal—with which Jews were involved. In the first chapter, for example, there are privileges from the Polish kings to both the Jewish collectivity and individuals, decisions of various synods, several decisions of the Sejm, and a number of agreements between Jews and townspeople. In contrast to this, however, there is no mention in this chapter of privileges, obligations, or prohibitions which affected Jews in private holdings. This lack is conspicuous because during its peak period Polish–Lithuanian Jewry was concentrated on private estates. The majority of documents in other chapters also relate to the domain of the king.

The second chapter, devoted to the lives of the communities, is made up of a collection of sources which are even more haphazardly arranged. The documents were collected according to availability alone. They include neither Hebrew nor Yiddish material, except for quotes from a few individual sources that have already been translated. There is no mention of any other sources on the history of Jewry in the Polish–Lithuanian Commonwealth, such as the records of communities, councils, and synagogues, etc., responsa, regulations of artisan guilds, and historical relics. The life of the Jewish community and all that is connected to the internal life of the Jews remain unclear. The reader will learn nothing about rabbis, *parnasim*, businessmen, etc. There is no differentiation made among various Jews; instead, a monolithic image is presented of the Jew as an urban trader and money-lender who suffers periodically from religious persecution.

In the third chapter, which deals with the livelihoods of Jews during this period, there is no representation either of the different types of business in which they were involved or of the changes that occurred in Jewish economic life and business during this period. The majority of documents deal with credit and loans, trade, and the leasing of monopolies from the king, a stereotypical and inexact picture. As is known but not mentioned here, from the end of the sixteenth century Jews were increasingly becoming borrowers with interest as opposed to lenders with interest. Similarly, the various products, tradesmen, and trades are also incompletely represented, and there is no representation of the Jewish crafts that developed simultaneously with trade from the sixteenth century onwards. With regard to the leasing of monopolies from the king it is known that the nobility pushed Jews out, in the majority of cases, from the royal monopolies (for example, the selling of salt and currency). However, the leasing of monopolies and lands (mainly as subtenants) on *szlachta* estates developed and became the main factor in the lives of Jews of the Polish–Lithuanian Commonwealth in the sixteenth to eighteenth centuries. This is not mentioned at all. Neither is the role of the Jews as agents, nor their function in the river trade.

The fourth chapter, which is concerned with coexistence, focuses on religious issues. Only a few documents deal with the relationship of Jews to Polish society. Of these, half are devoted to suggestions for the reform of Jewish life from the period of the Four Year Sejm. Primarily, we find mentioned all those things that

disrupted peaceful coexistence: blood libel; conversion to Judaism (which in reality was rare); accusations of desecration of the host; the reaction of the king to the
pogrom against the Jews of Przemyśl in 1561; the priest Piotr Skarga writing on
Jews and Protestants; and Yitshak of Turkey on the religious persecution in
Poland, converts, and the Chmielnicki pogroms. In other words, coexistence is
described as a series of conflicts and religious pogroms, a distorted and lachry-
mose view of the history of the Jews in the Polish Diaspora no longer accepted
even in Jewish historiography.

In addition to the source material, there is a brief summary of the history of the
Jews in Poland during this period, a short glossary, and a suggested reading-list.
The same things are lacking in the historical sketch that are missing in the main
text: a picture of the internal life of the Jewish community and the connections
developing between the Jews and the *szlachta*, and especially the magnates. The
reading-list omits major works in the field of Polish Jewish history, such as:
M. Bałaban, *Żydzi lwowscy na przełomie, XVI-go i XVII-go wieku* (Lwów, 1906);
M. Bałaban, *Historia Żydów w Krakowie i na Kazimierzu, 1304–1868* (Cracow,
1931–6); and M. Schorr, *Żydzi w Przemyślu do końca XVIII wieku* (Lwów, 1903).
However, there are some general works in Polish history in which the Jews appear
that are noted in this short list.

For all this, all beginnings are difficult, and the most important thing is that
here, for the first time, is a collection that addresses a pressing need and which is a
first step in the right direction.

JUDITH KALIK
*Hebrew University, Jerusalem*

DAVID E. FISHMAN
## *Russia's First Modern Jews: The Jews of Shklov*

(New York: New York University Press, 1995)
pp. 195. ISBN 0814726143

One of the tasks facing historians of east European Jewry is to crack the code of its
extraordinary cultural creativity and elasticity. This is no easy assignment, given
the fact that it requires knowledge of two Jewish languages (Hebrew and Yiddish)
and at least Russian or Polish, as well as an intellectual mastery of traditional
and post-traditional genres and idioms. Today's cultural historian is obliged, in
addition, to explore the newly accessible archival documentation in Russia and
elsewhere in eastern Europe. On all these counts, David Fishman's delightful
study of a pivotal experience in east European Jewish cultural development takes
its place as a worthy contribution to the historiographical record.

Fishman guides the reader easily and comfortably through Jewish Shklov at the end of the eighteenth century, using literary material, archival sources, and an interpretative imagination that convincingly bridges the gaps in the written record. In so doing, he makes a good case for viewing Shklov in the 1780s to 1790s as a microcosmic 'anticipation' of the modernizing forces that would affect Russian Jewry as a whole over the next hundred years.

Shklov, in the Mogilev province of White Russia (today Belarus), was an exceptional community, and Fishman is careful to point out just what made it so atypical. Its brush with destiny was determined by its early annexation by Russia in 1772, by its subsequent commercial boom, by the deliberate cultivation there of an advanced cultural outpost of the Russian aristocratic élite, and by the presence of distinguished Jewish scholars, writers, and worldly patrons of Torah and intellectual endeavour of all kinds. Shklov was also fated to play a key role in the battle waged by rabbinical scholars and communal leaders against the nascent hasidic movement in White Russia, which traditionalists viewed as a sectarian threat. Similarly, Shklov leaders played a vital role in the earliest negotiations with the regime over the Jews' civil status. The community thus became a key link in the political and religious affairs of Russian Jewry, a position that was reflected in its brief reign as a centre for Hebrew publishing (prior to the emergence of Vilna as the region's most important focus of scholarly and literary output).

Probably the most fascinating aspect of this book is its description of the interrelationship between traditional Jewish high culture and the new intellectual currents associated with the Hebrew enlightenment (Haskalah). Fishman joins other recent scholars in puncturing the myth of a hermetically divided Jewish world, clearly demarcated between German Jewish modernism and east European traditionalism. His portrait is a nuanced revision that points to the areas of contact between these two socio-geographic milieux.

While the influence of Shklov's moderate modernizing élite was limited to one generation, the account of their activity enriches our understanding of the processes of cultural change as it deepens our appreciation for the diversity of the east European Jewish experience. Along with such studies as Steven Zipperstein's *The Jews of Odessa* (Stanford, Calif., 1986), it also enhances our ability to appreciate the importance of local, regional, and economic factors in Russian Jewish cultural history.

ELI LEDERHENDLER
*Hebrew University, Jerusalem*

JOSEPH HELD (ED.)

# The Columbia History of Eastern Europe in the Twentieth Century

(New York: Columbia University Press, 1992).
pp. lxix + 435. ISBN 0231076967

This book begins with a lengthy chronology of events in eastern Europe from 1918 to 1990. For the purposes of this volume and in the eyes of many historians, the twentieth century started after the end of the First World War and ended in 1990. This short century has made up for the missing decades in redoubled, over-wrought intensity.

The volume brings to print the proceedings of a conference held in 1990 at Rutgers University on this timely topic. It is also a Festschrift of sorts, which is evident from the dedication to Stephen Fischer-Galati, long-time editor *extra-ordinaire* in the field of east European studies in America. For the last few decades, the East European Monographs series and the journal *East European Quarterly*, which Fischer-Galati edited, did more for more scholars in east European studies than possibly all other North American presses and journals put together. While many authors who published in the series (not to mention reviewers) grumbled about its mixed quality and loose copy-editing, both the *Quarterly* and the monographs brought historical and social science research about eastern Europe to the public, when it might otherwise have remained in the proverbial drawer. Until 1989 less specialized presses often turned away east European material, invoking (even from the perspective of the small academic market) its marginality. Through the series and the journal, Fischer-Galati, along with a couple of other editors, kept the field from being completely crushed in the rough waters of the Cold War, when eastern Europe was to the mainstream little more than an after-thought to the Soviet colossus.

Fischer-Galati is logically the author of the volume's introductory essay en-titled 'Eastern Europe in the Twentieth Century: "Old Wine in New Bottles"'. As elsewhere in his prolific work, he is a master of grand generalization. His most important theme here is that democracy in eastern Europe is not now and has never in this century been within easy reach, and that this difficulty with demo-cratic practice has been primarily a function of internal, and not, as others have argued, external, factors. This argument is persuasive and sets the tone for the chapters that follow: Nicholas Pano on Albania, Marin Pundeff on Bulgaria, Sharon Wolchik on Czechoslovakia, Peter Hanak and Joseph Held on Hungary, Andrzej Korbonski on Poland, Trond Gilberg on Romania, Dimitrije Djordjevic on Yugoslavia, and Melvin Croan on Germany (mostly East). Ivan Volgyes concludes the volume with an essay entitled 'Controlled and Uncontrolled Change in Eastern Europe', focusing on the revolutionary changes of 1989.

As always in such volumes, the essays represent many different styles and methodologies. Some chapters cover the historical course more fully than others. Gilberg's survey of Romania's twentieth century is interesting but not at all comprehensive. His focus on the Ceauşescu regime and its antecedents gives short shrift not only to pre-Communist history, but also to most post-war developments. On the other hand, Wolchik, Djordjevic, and Croan treat their respective subjects with admirable balance. Without mentioning each essay individually, suffice it to say that any faculty intending to use the book in courses should be prepared to compensate for the unevenness of collective authorship.

All in all, a volume covering the history of eastern Europe in the turbulent twentieth century is a welcome contribution to the literature. While Joseph Rothschild's *East Central Europe between the Two World Wars* (Seattle, 1974) is still *the* comprehensive survey for the inter-war period, supplemented by his *Return to Diversity* (New York, 1989; 2nd edn. 1993) for the post-war decades, a book that attempts to bring these periods together between two covers deserves commendation.

IRINA LIVEZEANU
*University of Pittsburgh*

EDWARD H. JUDGE
*Easter in Kishinev: Anatomy of a Pogrom*
(New York: New York University Press, 1992)
pp. x + 186. ISBN 0–8147–4193–2

Two tragic days in Kishinev, Sunday 6 and Monday 7 April 1903, influenced not only the fate of the Jews living in this remote Moldavian town, but the political situation in the entire Russian Empire. The death of fifty-one city-dwellers (almost all Jews), the wounding of about 500 others, and the destruction or damaging of a significant number of buildings, depriving thousands of Jewish shopkeepers and artisans of property, were sufficiently tragic. Even more important were the psychological consequences, which affected not only the residents of Kishinev. At the time, the Russian authorities presented themselves as at the very least incapable of assuring the safety of the population. Popular opinion was much more severe. The people believed that the authorities (and maybe even the government) were directly involved and responsible for the tragic anti-Jewish riot. The local tragedy therefore appeared as a major political event.

The author of this book tried to gather all possible evidence concerning the pogrom of 1903. The bibliography includes numerous newspapers, contemporary reports, memoirs, and other prints. There are relatively few archival sources (unfortunately they are not distinguished in the list from other types of source). Maybe future historians will be able to add some more materials from the Russian archives. There is, however, little likelihood that these will change the basic picture that Judge presents in this book.

The structure of the book is simple and logical. The seven chapters are: (1) The Jewish Question in Russia, (2) Kishinev, (3) Agitation and Provocation, (4) Pogrom, (5) Repercussion and Reverberations, (6) The Question of Guilt, and (7) The Causes and Legacy of the Easter Riots. The author analyses the general conditions and atmosphere of Jewish life in Russia, the specific situation of Kishinev with its relatively numerous and growing Jewish population, the events before the pogrom, the story of the two eventful days, and the consequences.

The logical analysis of events and the critical appreciation of the many (often contradictory) sources reflect the conflicts between social classes and religious groups. The local politicians were nonentities (sometimes with good intentions), ambitious men who were trying to exploit events for private aims, or fanatic anti-semites using even transparent lies in their propaganda. The authorities did nothing to prevent the tragedy, in spite of warnings. Later on they were not able to co-ordinate the anti-riot actions of the military and civil power. The central government was afraid of consequences, but antisemitic superstitions made it dif-ficult to act effectively. The presentation of events, critical analysis of sources, and the construction of the book make it a model case-study of a pogrom, deserving imitation by future historians.

The critical analysis of sources allowed Judge to conclude that 'government leaders did not consciously seek to instigate the pogrom' (p. 134). He does not place direct responsibility on the Russian government and local authorities for the riot, but credits them with indirect influence and the sins of creating an atmosphere that made the pogrom possible and of promoting anti-Jewish attitudes.

The arguments presented in the book are convincing. There are, however, several points that require more detailed investigation and comparison with pogroms elsewhere. The author is apt to suggest 'that the outburst was not entirely sponta-neous' (p. 51). The indirect arguments in favour of this thesis are not very con-vincing. There are, however, significant facts (or rather evidence given by the witnesses) that resemble details from other pogroms.

There was a rumour that the emperor allowed the plundering of Jewish houses during the three days (pp. 45–6). Similar rumours were common in other places, even in Poland. For example, in the Rzeszów region (formerly an Austrian province), the peasants, in May 1919, repeated a rumour that the government had allowed two or three days of plundering Jewish houses. There were repeated com-ments about instigators coming from other places (p. 46). Similar rumours about unknown people agitating against Jews were heard after the anti-Jewish riot in

Rzeszów province and in other places. The unpreparedness of police and the inability of local authorities to act were other points repeated in other pogroms. Did the behaviour of a weak, incapable administration create a similar situation here? Did similar events give rise to the same types of rumour before or after a pogrom? Such suppositions are more probable than hypotheses about some kind of conspiracy. The idea (not mentioned by Judge) that a secret centre instigated pogroms in different east European countries is considerably more improbable.

There are some unfortunate sentences in the book, though these have no bearing on the main topic. The presentation of the Jewish privileges in Poland before the partitions (pp. 11–12) is not exact. In fact these 'privileges' (a formal legal term at that time) were a codification of the legal situation of the Jews. The other groups ('estates') of society and individual towns had their own rights (comprised of privileges). This word had a somewhat different meaning in the eighteenth century than it does in the twentieth. Phrases such as 'the "son" of the Jewish God' and 'some Christian "saints"' (p. 5) are examples of unnecessary quotation marks. I understand that the author wanted to draw attention to his critical attitude in regard to Christianity, but doing it in this way seems somewhat out of place, even if one shares his view as an unbelieving *apikoyres*.

JERZY TOMASZEWSKI
*Institute of History, Warsaw University*

## EDWARD KOSSOY AND ABRAHAM OHRY
### *The Feldshers: Medical, Sociological, and Historical Aspects of Practitioners of Medicine with below University Level Education*

(Jerusalem: Magnes Press, 1992)
pp. 250. ISBN 965–223–789–2

In view of the acknowledged though often stereotypical association of Jews with the medical profession, it is surprising that so little serious scholarly attention has been devoted to the study of Jews as physicians or members of allied medical fields. Until the late 1970s almost no general critical assessment of the history of lower-ranking medical personnel existed. Edward Kossoy and Abraham Ohry have made a significant contribution in gathering the diverse materials that they present on the history of feldshers in general and Jewish feldshers in particular.

Though it is unclear until the latter part of the book, the authors have an agenda that no doubt inspired this project. They are, as they state, concerned with the 'implications of the past and present for the future'. Their book is a response to the goal set by the World Health Organization in 1978 to establish global health care by the year 2000. Through their historical evaluation of the role of the feldsher, they set the stage for a debate on the important function that feldshers might fulfil in the future. In addition to the historical material they present, the authors discuss the role of feldshers and feldsher equivalents in contemporary Israeli and Soviet health care systems. They view the feldsher as a model for the kind of medium-level medical worker who might best be able to reach the maximum number of people with basic medical service.

Kossoy and Ohry argue that the nature of this type of health care provider underwent significant transformation over the course of centuries. They trace the feldsher's development from barber-surgeon to mercenary 'Feldscherer' serving as low-ranking military personnel, though neither well trained nor highly skilled, to more highly skilled and educated surgeon. The authors consider various factors, such as the role of political rulers, involved in reshaping and redefining the feldsher. Particular attention is devoted to the development of feldsher education, as well as to the feldshers' 'armory', the repertoire of techniques and treatments they employed.

The authors ambitiously attempt to create an image of the feldsher and his circumstances that is sweeping in its historical and geographical scope from the Middle Ages to the post-Second World War era, in the east and the west, Jewish and non-Jewish. To set their discussion of feldsher practice in context, the authors provide background on a variety of topics including the development of medical professions, talmudic terminology relating to healers and the talmudic pharmacopoeia, and military medical services in Europe. There was a close relationship between the position of feldsher and the military. While this is an important and well-developed point, the analysis as a whole suffers from being stretched in so many directions. The authors present useful information and engaging anecdotes throughout, but the final product is sketchy and unevenly presented.

The scope of the source material is impressive and wide-ranging, though at times it relies too heavily on encyclopaedias. The authors responsibly acknowledge the limitations of their research, particularly for the Soviet Union, which had not yet opened up for such research at the time they were engaged with the project. The medieval woodcuts and other illustrations that the authors chose to accompany their text, while insufficiently documented, add an interesting and entertaining dimension to the book.

The most original research in the book draws on *yizkor bikher*, memorial books the authors scoured for anecdotal materials on Jewish feldshers. The particular material they use had previously been untapped, for the one other short study of Jewish feldshers is a chapter of Emanuel Ringelblum's *Kapitln fun geshikhte* (Buenos Aires, 1953). Kossoy and Ohry present the Jewish feldsher with fond nostalgia: 'There is in the folklore aspect of the character of the Jewish feldsher a relic of the not so distant but already legendary and rapidly fading past. It is our desire to revive this memory.' At this point, the first half of the book appears as a prologue to the section on Jewish feldshers, the topic that is clearly closest to the authors' hearts.

This contribution to our limited vision of Jewish feldshers is welcome, as current scholarship on feldshers, primarily the insightful work of Samuel Ramer, discusses Jews only marginally. The Jewish feldsher was indeed an important figure in the landscape of eastern Europe. At the same time, the authors' emphasis on Jewish feldshers is disproportionate in what purports to be a general study of feldshers. The nature of the relationship between Jewish feldshers and their non-Jewish counterparts merits much further consideration.

*The Feldshers* is especially noteworthy for making accessible to an English-reading public materials about health care in Russia. Delving into Russian archives under current, more conducive political circumstances will no doubt yield information that will expand our understanding of the feldsher's role. This book underscores the value of *yizkor bikher* as a resource for material that illuminates a number of the varied aspects of Jewish society in eastern Europe. The book suggests many areas for further research and is valuable for the diverse sources it has drawn together, a necessary beginning to the study of the feldsher.

LISA EPSTEIN
*Vassar College, Poughkeepsie, New York*

MARK LEVENE
*War, Jews, and the New Europe: The Diplomacy of Lucien Wolf, 1914–1919*
(Oxford: published for the Littman Library by Oxford University Press, 1992)
pp. xvii + 346. ISBN 0-10-710072-4

Lucien Wolf (1857–1930) was undoubtedly an interesting personality, influencing different fields of Jewish life. The book reviewed here analyses his activity during the First World War and the Paris Peace Conference, when the Minorities Treaties were prepared. Mark Levene opens his book with a comment on an apparent paradox: diplomacy 'would normally be considered the prerogative and function of sovereign states' (p. 1). The Jews had no sovereign state and no territory of their own, nor even an internationally acknowledged authority such as the Holy See. It was, however, possible to speak of Jewish diplomacy, and Lucien Wolf was one of the most significant personalities in this field. It should be remarked that the story of the efforts undertaken by Wolf was by no means a unique case of diplomacy without a state. Similar to some extent was nineteenth-century Polish diplomacy when the country was divided among three big powers. The First World War also inspired Czech and Slovak diplomatic efforts; in the crucial year, 1919, there were Belarusian and Ukrainian diplomacies as well, all undertaken without the backing of sovereign states. Probably the existence of a national diplomacy without a state was a characteristic feature of east central European nations, and the Jews belonged to this category as well.

The presentation of the diplomatic efforts of Lucien Wolf required a thorough analysis of the situation of Jews in Great Britain as well as the international activity of the Jewish representatives from several countries. Levene mainly discusses the problems faced by the British Jews and their efforts to help their co-religionists in other countries. The first part of the book deals with these problems before and at the beginning of the war. The next part confronts Britain's traditional Jewish policy with the growing influence of Zionism. The problems connected with the recognition of Jews as a national minority in east central Europe are discussed in the third part of the book. The fourth and last part deals with diplomatic activity aimed at including adequate clauses in the Peace Treaty and the Minorities Treaties in 1919.

The Jews in Great Britain, at least the Jews who were His Majesty's subjects, were integrated into English society, enjoyed full civil rights, and considered themselves Englishmen of the Mosaic faith. Their interest in the fate of Jews in Russia was based on religious solidarity and a conviction that the best way of solving the 'Jewish question' should be based on the British experience. This conviction was shared by the leading British statesmen. At the same time, British Jews were sincerely loyal to their country.

In the opinion of British Jews, the Jews in Russia were an oppressed people, whereas in Germany they enjoyed full civil rights. This created a complicated situation for the Jewish community in Great Britain. Enmity towards imperial Russia led to a kind of sympathy for Germany. This was, however, contrary to British foreign policy, and it was not an easy task to accept the British–Russian alliance. Lucien Wolf, an influential journalist who specialized in foreign relations, met with numerous difficulties and suffered a lack of confidence when he tried to influence the Foreign Office in favour of the Jews in Russia and Romania. The merit of the book is to reveal his complicated efforts and delicate diplomacy, which, however, was by no means successful.

Lucien Wolf, like the majority of British Jews, was critical of Zionist ideology. To accept the idea that the Jews were a nation similar to other nations endangered their integration in English society. Wolf was probably one of the few Jewish politicians in Great Britain ready to find some kind of compromise, maybe even to accept to some extent the notion of the special situation of Jews in east central Europe. The Balfour Declaration represented a defeat of his policy, but he accepted the idea of a Jewish homeland in Palestine as important for British foreign policy at that time.

His victory, as Mark Levene underlines, came with the Minorities Treaties. From the British point of view, it was necessary to eliminate anything that would spark nationalist conflicts in the new states in east central Europe. For Wolf, the Jewish diplomat, this was a chance to help the Jews in these new states. It was possible to join British loyalty with Jewish desires. Levene observes rightly that the Minorities Treaty was the most important convergence of British and Jewish interests, but this common interest was not the case in every instance.

Another problem addressed by Levene's work is the extent of Jewish influence. Levene presents a complex picture of conflicts dividing Jewish societies in every country, involving contradictory ideologies and controversies based in part on personal motives. This lack of unity even on fundamental issues substantially handicapped Jewish politics. The chances of Jewish politicians influencing the Foreign Office were limited: several members of the government were deeply convinced that Jews would not be loyal to Great Britain. Wolf and his associates were often denied the opportunity to meet with influential statesmen. One of the reasons for the mistrust was that many English (as well as French, German, and other European) politicians and intellectuals were deeply convinced of the existence of Jewish international solidarity, financial strength, and hidden power, which enabled them to manipulate world history. At the same time, however, this popular suspicion helped Wolf's diplomacy. Since the international power of Jews was taken for granted, Jewish politicians tried to secure the help of this apparent power for themselves. Wolf did not actually possess any real bargaining power, yet his partners thought otherwise; this was an important source of his influence.

Levene frequently discusses problems connected with Polish history, but this is not his area of expertise, and his sources of information are works written by other historians. One consequence of this is that he misunderstands Polish policy in some cases; these are, nevertheless, of minor importance. Had he gone directly to the Polish sources and literature, he would have been able to add new arguments to support his views. From the point of view of a Polish historian, this study helps explain several elements in Poland's situation in post-war Europe and the attitudes of the major powers towards the reborn republic.

Levene's book is a significant contribution to the diplomatic history of Europe during the First World War, to contemporary Jewish history, and to some extent to the history of Poland.

JERZY TOMASZEWSKI
*Institute of History, Warsaw University*

### STEVEN M. LOWENSTEIN
# The Berlin Jewish Community: Enlightenment, Family and Crisis, 1770–1830

(New York: Oxford University Press, 1994)
pp. xii + 300. ISBN 0-19-508326-1

The political, economic, and cultural modernization of the Jews has been the major focus of modern Jewish historiography. For much of this century Jewish historians have explored the conditions that contributed to the rapid erosion of traditional Jewish patterns of life, particularly in western Europe and in some urban centres of east central Europe, and, more recently, the factors that promoted resistance to modernization. Nowhere is the puzzle of the rapid breakdown of traditional Jewry more striking than in Berlin at the end of the eighteenth century and the beginning of the nineteenth. Yet Steven Lowenstein's major new book is the first scholarly investigation of the dimensions of that breakdown to address fully the interrelations between political, economic, and ideological changes. Moreover, as a creative social historian he weaves private and public lives together, demonstrating that the family was the primary venue for the manifestation of the abandonment of traditional Jewish values. Indeed, family networks promoted both tradition and conversion.

Mining a mix of sources—tax-lists, censuses, baptismal records, and lists of subscriptions to Enlightenment periodicals—Lowenstein offers his readers a splendid collective biography of the Jews of Berlin in this period. He traces the beginnings of 'peaceful', that is, moderate, modernization of the traditional Jewish community before turning to the period of crisis that began in the 1780s and extended into the early 1820s. In fact, he appropriately raises the question why early efforts at modernization in Berlin were relatively free of conflict in comparison with later efforts at change. Central to his story is the emergence in the wake of the Seven Years War of an economic élite that became community leaders. It was this élite that funded the maskilim, the men of the Jewish Enlightenment, and co-operated in the dissemination of their ideas and the building of their institutions. This combination of social élites and intellectual activists hastened the pace of change. Although there remained poor Jews and Orthodox Jews within Berlin, the wealthy set the tone of the community, and wealth tended to correlate with modernizing tendencies.

Lowenstein argues that a number of factors specific to Berlin undermined the process of gradual moderate change. The failure of the modernizing camp to achieve its goal of emancipation led to radicalization. The struggle for emancipation in fact stimulated growing calls by maskilim for Jewish self-improvement and for state intervention. Moreover, the death of Moses Mendelssohn and the economic decline of the old élites removed the forces that had sustained the blend of acculturation and tradition characteristic of the first generation of modernizers. Unable to retain the loyalty of all the members of the community, the rabbis became more adamant in their opposition to acculturation and thereby proved incapable of providing leadership. With no models to follow, no clear alternative to traditional Judaism, the modernizing element among Berlin Jewry lacked a sufficiently broad social context for its new forms of Jewish life.

Most importantly, Lowenstein demonstrates how the situation of the Berlin élite as the first modernizing Jews in Germany led to a dual crisis: a proliferation of illegitimacy and an epidemic of conversions. High illegitimacy rates among Jews reflected the larger society and hence signify increased Jewish acculturation. Tracing intergenerational patterns, he finds a clear connection between support for the Enlightenment and conversion in subsequent generations. He concludes that the absence of a social context and reference group for the modernizers, the sense that there was no middle ground between unacculturated Orthodoxy and total secularization, promoted despair and transgressive behaviour. Although the rate of conversion seems never to have exceeded 7 per cent of the Jewish population, it was perceived as an epidemic because of the high proportion of the wealthy élite among those who chose to leave the Jewish community for the purpose of integrating into German society.

Lowenstein also addresses the question of gender differentiation in the experience of Berlin Jewry, finding that women and men did indeed walk different paths towards modernization. He attributes the gender distinctions to the absence of an institutional framework for enlightened women, while men had numerous organizational supports. In most respects his analysis confirms the findings of Deborah Hertz, author of *Jewish High Society in Old Regime Berlin* (New Haven, 1988), although he points out that the baptism of women occurred for marriages already planned rather than simply to open for themselves the Christian marriage market in general.

Lowenstein concludes his study of the emergence of Berlin as the vanguard community of Jewish modernity with the transformation of Berlin Jewry in the 1830s and 1840s. The mass migration of Jews from the east, the 1823 governmental ban on religious reform, and the abandonment of the community by most descendants of the earlier élite families created a new situation in which Jewish religious and cultural creativity declined. The questions of the shape of Jewish identities, of the limits of assimilation, would be raised many times throughout the modern Jewish world, but Berlin would no longer serve as the source of radically new answers.

This is an important work, necessary reading for all who are interested in the modernization of European Jewry. One wishes only that an editor could have helped Lowenstein in crafting a more elegant book. Too much of Lowenstein's wealth of information is located in his copious footnotes. Moreover, the text is divided into fifteen chapters and a conclusion, which leads to some repetition and suggests a difficulty in constructing a cohesive narrative. This minor criticism aside, Lowenstein's book demonstrates how the methods and perspectives of social history may provide a context vital for the understanding of the nexus of ideologies, economic forces, families, and social change. The heirs of Bałaban, Mahler, Schiper, and Shatzky have much to offer us by applying this model to the yet-to-be-written social history of the Jews of Poland.

PAULA E. HYMAN
*Yale University*

## PAUL ROBERT MAGOCSI
## *Historical Atlas of East Central Europe*

(*A History of East Central Europe*, i)

Cartographic design by Geoffrey J. Matthews
(Seattle: University of Washington Press; published in Canada by
University of Toronto Press, 1993)
pp. xiv + 218, maps, tables, source list, bibliography, and index.
ISBN 0–295–97248–3

This is the keystone of the yet to be completed series *A History of East Central Europe*, edited by the late Donald W. Treadgold and Peter Sugar. In quarto format, it consists of eighty-nine maps, thirty-five of them full-page, arranged in fifty sections. Each is accompanied by an explanatory text. Together, they describe the region between central Germany and Russia's western border and from the southern Baltic to western Anatolia, from the time of the later Roman Empire to the early 1990s.

The work is based on a catholic array of sources, including Manteuffel, Czaplinski, and Ladogorski on the historical geography of Poland, and Beinart, as well as de Lange and Gilbert, on the region's Jews. Economic, demographic, ecclesiastical, legal, and cultural history and political and military change are covered; and, though specialists might wish for fuller treatment of the eighteenth century, the balance between periods is on the whole well judged. The results of Dr Magocsi's labours are presented on well-designed, brightly coloured plates, often rich with data yet always readable. Furthermore, the work can be used as a much-needed gazetteer of place names since it provides up to a dozen linguistic variants (including Yiddish) for every town. In this respect, too, the *Historical Atlas of East Central Europe* fills a long-felt gap.

Historical atlases of eastern Europe tend to favour political geography and military history, and a similar tendency is detectable in this work. But it is neither narrow in approach nor topically restricted. Magocsi provides good clutches of maps on the commonly neglected medieval and early modern periods for cities; on the spread of German settlement and German law; on the Reformation and Counter-Reformation; on the dissemination of schools and printing-presses; and on ecclesiastical jurisdictions (which, however, fails to draw attention to the singularities of the Catholic Church in Germany). It is also good to see Venice given due attention as a colonial power of some importance in the region.

The thematic maps covering the modern period are rich in interest. They include canal-cutting and railway-building; the growth of population and cities; cultural and educational, as well as economic, development; administrative structures; and, not least, ethno-linguistic distribution, including ethnic cleansing and population movements during and after the Second World War. The final map showing east central Europe in 1992 recognizes the break-up of Yugoslavia, Czechoslovakia, and the Soviet Union.

For all its considerable merits, however, the work has shortcomings. Some of these derive from the very nature of the enterprise. Mapping favours hard edges and coherent shapes. Uncertainties are difficult to represent cartographically: the results tend to look messy, unattractive. Yet our knowledge of east central Europe, especially of the earlier periods, is uneven and in parts defective. Magocsi overcomes the problem in describing the territorial origins of the Slavs by depicting the conclusions of several (though not all) differing authorities; and he is careful to designate some of the early medieval boundaries as 'approximate'. Yet this is not quite enough. During much of the medieval period, frontiers tended to be unstable: territorial claims were disputed; access to trade routes tended to be as important as control of territory; power over people was sometimes preferable to ownership of land; and local lords might wield more power than the monarchs to whom they are ascribed. Political entities were often in flux, and historians cannot always agree where to draw their confines. In such circumstances, the presentation of clear-cut 'international' boundaries can be misleading.

But if the atlas occasionally communicates more than it should, it is sometimes less informative than it might be. Current rainfall, vegetation, and land use are given, but there is no attempt to describe ecological change (despite the fact that sources for this exist). Also disappointing is the failure to address the social dimension more fully. Reference is made to Cossacks, but other similar frontier groups such as hajduks and uskoks are overlooked (though not the Austrian military frontier system); and social structure is largely ignored. There is no reference to the number of clergy or how the size of the noble class fluctuated from place to place and over the years; there is nothing on serfdom, even though its introduction and abolition constitute historical patterns of significance.

There are shortcomings in the text as well. The term 'feudalism' (at least in Marc Bloch's classic formulation) is misapplied; and the level of historical explanation is sometimes superficial, especially in the description of the decline of Byzantium and the alliance of Lithuania with Poland rather than Muscovy. The Chmielnicki revolt is attributed to 'misunderstanding'; the Muscovite siege of Riga in 1654 is overlooked; the first partition of Poland is indulgent to Prussia, and not all military historians will agree that Sobieski was 'instrumental' in relieving Vienna in 1683.

Problems also arise in the treatment of ethnogenesis. Serbs and Croats may have been as early in their ethnic distinctiveness as Magocsi suggests, but they were not always easily distinguishable on the ground; and Map 20*d*, which purports to show linguistic-based ethnicity about 1700, is anachronistic, presenting clear-cut divisions between Czechs and Germans that did not exist even as late as the twentieth century. The fact that nationalities in some areas were intermixed without clear boundaries is acknowledged (p. 87). Yet the problem of how to ascribe multilinguals (outside Austria, where census-takers were careful to distinguish between language used at work and in the home) is not addressed. Furthermore, the table comparing ethnolinguistic–cultural composition in Poland in 1931 and 1991 (p. 131) is of questionable value, not only on account of the depredations of the Holocaust and German occupation, but because of the changed borders and the fact that the figures for 1991 are estimates.

There is some imbalance in thematic coverage at certain points. The treatment of Protestants in the modern period is skimpy, though that of the Greek Catholics is always commendably full. Universities, academies of arts and sciences, and national museums and theatres are all pinpointed, but not that channel for cosmopolitan (and revolutionary) culture, the opera-house. And the section on industrial development in the Soviet period fails to mention the oil-price revolution as a factor in energy policy and the region's changing fortunes.

But errors and imperfections will find their way into any undertaking as broad in scope as this one. They can be corrected in a new edition, for which there will surely be a demand. The region is again unstable; institutions are failing; populations are on the move. Yet work still continues on filling in the blanks in historical maps (in the Polish Academy of Sciences as elsewhere). It is to be hoped that Magocsi will be able to incorporate these developments in the course of updating and revising his invaluable work.

PHILIP LONGWORTH
*McGill University*

JERZY MICHALSKI (ED.)
*Lud żydowski w narodzie polskim: Materiały sesji naukowej w Warszawie, 15–16 Wrzesien 1992*

(Warsaw: Instytut Historii Polskiej, Akademii Nauk, and Center for Research on the History and Culture of Polish Jews, Hebrew University, 1994)
pp. 120. ISBN 8–3900–8468–6

This useful volume, entitled *The Jewish People in the Polish Nation*, includes six papers by noted specialists on eighteenth-century Jewish and Polish history from a conference that took place in Warsaw in 1992. One paper is in English and five are in Polish.

The English-language article by Gershon David Hundert, 'Population and Society in Eighteenth-Century Poland', boldly challenges two generally accepted ideas. First, Hundert argues that rapid Jewish population growth stemmed primarily from the relative prosperity that allowed early marriage and provided the conditions for children to survive. Hundert slides into the related topic of class struggle within the Jewish community, suggesting that instances of apparent class conflict between rich and poor Jews really represented conflicts between patrician factions that mobilized the lower classes to help them.

Jerzy Michalski painstakingly re-examines 'Parliamentary Reform Bills concerning the Position of the Jewish People in Poland in the Years 1789–1792'. He challenges Eisenbach's recent critique of Polish reform, concluding that the Polish parliament would have given Jews civic and political rights if the 1792 Polish–Russian war had not ended the Four Year Diet.

Jakub Goldberg provides an original study entitled 'The First Political Movement among Polish Jews: Jewish Plenipotentiaries during the Four-Year Diet'. Communal representatives from all parts of the Commonwealth gathered in Warsaw to counteract the Christian middle-class lobby, and they developed their own ideas about how to integrate Jews into the Polish constitutional system. Goldberg traces the evolution of Jewish ideas and notes the group's organizational difficulties, arguing that their activities demonstrated the political maturity of eighteenth-century Polish Jews.

Stanisław Grodziski analyses the 'Legal Position of Jews in Galicia' between 1772 and 1790. He finds that Maria Theresa's and Joseph II's reform measures Germanized Galician Jews to a considerable degree and gained their loyalty. However, Grodziski argues, the Habsburgs failed at their primary goal, which was to assimilate the Jews, who took advantage of new possibilities for social and economic advance while steadfastly refusing to abandon their identity.

Krystyna Zienkowska discusses 'The Stereotype of the Jew in Polish Political Writing in the Second Half of the Eighteenth Century'. Zienkowska illustrates unfavourable stereotypes of Jews in late eighteenth-century Polish writings, arguing that such stereotypes were common throughout Europe. Examining English political literary writings for comparison, she finds Polish antisemitic stereotypes 'considerably more civilized and lacking that dose of poisonousness, aggression, and hate, that characterized . . . many other countries'.

Finally, Zdzisław Libera analyses 'Jews in Polish Literature in the Late Enlightenment Period'. He finds that the late eighteenth-century Polish writers accused Jews of pursuing parasitic economic occupations and cheating their customers. Jewish participation in the 1794 insurrection and the Napoleonic wars changed Polish attitudes, inspiring early nineteenth-century authors to introduce patriotic Jewish heroes in their plays and novels. Such literature criticized both

Polish antisemitism and traditional Jewish separatism (especially hasidism), laying the foundation for literary stereotypes in the positivist period.

DANIEL STONE
*University of Winnipeg*

CLARE MOORE (ED.)
## *The Visual Dimension: Aspects of Jewish Art*
(Published in memory of Isaiah Shachar, 1935–1977)
(Boulder, Colo.: Westview Press; published in co-operation with the
Oxford Centre for Postgraduate Hebrew Studies, 1993)
pp. xv + 184, figures and colour plates. ISBN 0-8133-1259-0

It is a credit to the authors of the papers collected in this elegantly produced volume that their work is as relevant today as it was years ago, when it was presented at a conference held on October 23–5 1977 in Oxford under the aegis of the Oxford Centre for Postgraduate Hebrew Studies and the Tarbuth Foundation. Unfortunately, the reason for the perennial freshness of these essays is that the field these papers deal with has not advanced very far beyond what was cutting-edge in 1977.

It is disappointing that the field of Jewish art has not attracted more attention in the wider context of Judaic studies or art history in general. With the significant exception of work such as that found in *Art and its Uses: The Visual Image and Modern Jewish Society*, Studies in Contemporary Jewry, vi, edited by Richard I. Cohen (New York, 1990), developments in the field of Jewish art have by and large been far outstripped by those in general art history. This is due in large part to the fact that the preoccupations of historians of Jewish art, as evidenced in the present volume, have hardly changed since the publication of the previous significant anthologies of essays on Jewish art and iconography in the 1960s. These include enquiries into what had constituted 'Jewish art', the reconstruction of antique Jewish models presumed lost on the basis of evidence in medieval Jewish and Christian art, the cataloguing or motif indexing of iconographic elements based on textual parallels, issues in collecting, fakes, and forgeries.

Joseph Guttman's corner-stone essay 'Is there a Jewish Art?' is a further recapitulation of an issue he has dealt with in print many times before. Yet this time it is something of a summa that seeks to call off the search for some Jungian *Ur-Judentum* in nudes of Modigliani. What he neglects to suggest is that it might be more fruitful to concentrate on issues of greater moment that are current in the various fields of general art history. Thus, Guttman's essay is ultimately valuable more for this overview than for its conclusion, which has remained unchanged since his essays on the topic in the 1960s. Now, as then, his conclusions are nebulously drawn: ultimately for Guttman, Jewish art must be the cumulative reflection of the experience of the Jewish people, whenever, wherever, and among whomever they lived. This might make for good American reform theology if we substitute 'Judaism' for 'Jewish art', but as an art-historical definition it is not very useful.

Vidosava Nedomacki's response to Guttman is generally well reasoned, though in her zeal to insist that 'every work created by Jewish artists belongs to the art of Jewish people', she tends to excess. Distinctions must be made between art created by anyone for use in a Jewish context (Jewish art) and art created by Jews for contexts that are not necessarily recognizable or indigenously Jewish (art by Jewish artists). Nedomacki deems it 'absurd' that Jewish *sacralia* made by non-Jews be considered 'Jewish art'.

Yet non-Jews in fact do produce Jewish *sacralia* when they are commissioned to do so. Of course, we can obviate the entire problem by completely avoiding the temptation to fit various objects in rigid categories of our own creation, and instead ask specific questions about the specific objects: What do such commissions tell us about patron–client relations, religious attitudes, economics? Do wealthy Jewish clients hire non-Jewish artists, and do the less wealthy make do with native or folk artists? Should commissions from non-Jews be read as evidence of a certain class snobbery, or do they indicate a dearth of competent Jewish artists? If there are themes of pagan or Christian motifs in Jewish art, we need to ask an entire category of questions about adoption and adaptation of motifs by minority societies. If they are created for Christian patrons, they are not within the realm of Jewish art, but of art produced by Jews. These questions are not addressed at all.

The body of the volume is composed of essays on specific art-historical problems. Ursula Schubert's 'The Continuation of Ancient Jewish Art in the Middle Ages' is successful in conveying a definite sense that certain iconographic elements in early and medieval Christian art are ultimately Jewish in origin. But there is a lack of concrete evidence for this thesis, save for a very few isolated examples of a now lost Jewish iconography in antiquity and some alleged textual transmissions, which are often impossible to confirm with any degree of precision. In addition, Schubert's essay leaves unanswered those questions that are most intriguing about Jewish art. We have a fairly thorough picture of *what* was transmitted; it still remains to determine precisely *how* it was transmitted or *why* the particular midrashim in question should have been chosen by Christians in the first place. Dr Schubert's work has advanced considerably since this essay was published, and she is actively moving in those directions.

Therese Metzger's survey 'The Iconography of the Hebrew Psalter from the Thirteenth to the Fifteenth Century' is a comprehensive and illuminating description of previously neglected images. Like her list of the Bodleian manuscripts (co-edited by her husband), which appears as an appendix to this volume, it reveals her great strengths in producing an engaging catalogue. Metzger's conclusions point to a dearth of well-established cycles of psalter illumination among Jews, but to myriad interesting, if isolated, examples of iconography that are often quite creative in presenting very literal visual clues about the psalms they illustrate. Yet, here she stops. She speculates little on the reasons for the lack of established psalm cycle illustrations, or upon literal illustration in connection with contemporary trends in exegesis and perhaps polemics. I would hate to think that Metzger has abandoned this vein. It should be mined, albeit with a full understanding of ancient and contemporary psalm commentaries, lest Elliot Horowitz's now classic critique of Metzger's work as being long on art but short on knowledge of medieval Jewish texts still holds true.

Helen Rosenau's work on the 'Architecture of the Synagogue in Neoclassicism and Historicism' is a worthy expansion of the material she examined in her book *The Vision of the Temple* (London, 1979). One wishes Rosenau had lived to work beyond her general speculation on the reasons for changing architectural taste among Jews, to go back and examine, in so far as this is possible, individual cases and communities in more depth and detail to determine the specific indigenous mentalities that influenced their choice of the neoclassical aesthetic.

Alfred Moldovan's 'Foolishness, Fakes, and Forgeries in Jewish Art: An Introduction to the Discussion on Judaica Conservation and Collecting Today' is self-consciously didactic and polemical, more suitable for a column on Judaica-collecting than the serious context in which it appears.

The volume closes with Bernard Blumenkrantz's programme urging establishment of a central archive of Jewish art, a project whose European incarnation has not yet progressed beyond planning. Such a project remains a desideratum, yet it is strange that there is no mention in the book of the efforts of the Center for Jewish Art in Jerusalem, which has been attempting to realize this dream for over a decade. Those who know the Jewish art would recognize the familiar political divisions involved here. Would it not be wise for the Diaspora and the Jewish homeland to collaborate on such projects rather than be torn by factionalism, squabbles over potential donors, and rivalry over 'authentic expertise'?

On the whole, the anthology feels preliminary and too loosely knit. It might have been better to insist on some more thematic consistency for the essays and to have picked a theme with some theoretical depth beyond the customary, tired issues these essays explore. More's the pity, since this volume is dedicated to Isaiah Shachar's memory, and Shachar, as Chimen Abramsky points out in his evocative preface, was truly a prescient innovator in bringing to the field the questions that need to be asked. Perhaps the direction of scholarship represented here is very different than it would have been had Shachar lived and been mentor to more students. He might have been able to produce a work using the relatively rich and undiscovered country of Jewish art as a medium for gaining access to the mentalities of its creators, its patrons, and its intended audience, a work that might have accomplished for Jewish cultural studies what Simon Schama's *An Embarrassment of Riches* (New York, 1987) did for general cultural studies.

It is telling, then, that some of the freshest and most perceptive comments throughout this volume occur when the authors and editors mention Shachar; it is as if his very name breathes the promise of new horizons in examining the visual dimension of Jewish culture. The present volume, however, beautifully produced and expertly prepared as it is, regrettably falls short of these horizons.

MARC MICHAEL EPSTEIN
*Vassar College, Poughkeepsie, New York*

GEDALYAH NIGAL
# *Magic, Mysticism, and Hasidism*
Translated by Edward Levin (Northvale, NJ: Jason Aronson, 1994).
pp. xiii + 281. ISBN 1-56821-033-7

Nigal's thorough and provocative analysis of magical practices in Judaism offers the reader a startling array of data and discourse on the methods of practical mysticism from rabbinical times to the twentieth century.

The book is essentially divided into two parts. The first (chapters 1–4) traces the history of *Ba'alei shem*, or wonder-workers, *kefitsat ha derekh*, *gilgul* (transmigration of souls—metempsychosis), dybbuks (souls of the dead), and exorcism. Nigal writes as a historian of ideas, mapping the changing formulations of similar ideas across historical and ideological boundaries. In the second part Nigal writes as a folklorist, comparing and contrasting stories as they develop from pre-hasidic literature to the hasidic story, and as they move between Christianity and Judaism. In his introduction, Nigal presents his overarching thesis regarding the hasidic story: 'There is nothing new, because everything was already present in previous stories. The innovation in the hasidic story consisted of the recomposition of these elements and their appearance in new situations' (p. xiii). Yet later on he states: 'All that changed in the hasidic story is that the active central figure is no longer the early *baal shem* but the Baal Shem Tov, or a hasidic *tzadik*' (pp. 170–1). This later definition reflects his theory regarding the uniqueness of magical practices in hasidism. 'Beginning with the Baal Shem Tov, the hasidic story contained the idea that the *tzadik* sees from afar, knows from afar everything that happens, and is even capable of acting from a distance, facts that presumably cancel the need for *kefitzat ha-derekh*' (p. 48). This distinction is not only historical in nature, according to Nigal, but emerges as a difference between stories and practices of non-hasidic wonder-workers such as Rabbi Jonathan Eybeschuetz, who was a contemporary of the early hasidic *tsadikim*, and the hasidic masters after the

Ba'al Shem Tov. The hasidic master is not merely a wonder-worker or adept in the recitation of magical formulas, but a man with superhuman powers whose proficiency affects the way the hasidic story develops (see e.g. p. 214). According to Nigal, the unique character of the hasidic story is that its central figure is this unprecedented *tsadik*. For example, commenting on the hasidic version of a story of the lost son common in central Europe, Nigal notes, 'The lost son is a hasidic story *only* because the hasidic personality giving the amulet is a hasidic *tzadik*' (p. 211; emphasis added). Thus the use of amulets, which has a rich history in Jewish mystical circles, takes on a different character when it is administered by the hasidic *tsadik* rather than the traditional Jewish healer.

A second important contribution of this study is Nigal's contention that the sixteenth-century Safed circle of kabbalists, led by R. Isaac Luria and R. Hayim Vital, serve as the bridge between medieval magical practices and their reformulation in hasidic literature. Although the ideological influence of the Safed circle on hasidim is well documented, Nigal illustrates that the hasidic story should also be seen through the prism of the Safed school. The focus on *gilgul* serves as a good test-case. While the Lurianic kabbalists popularized *gilgul* and made it the subtext of many stories in their hagiographic literature, the hasidic rendering offers a unique feature. Whereas the Safed versions have the master revealing the past lives of his pupils and clients, the hasidic *tsadik* also has the knowledge of future migrations and is able to converse with these reincarnated souls, helping them correct their imperfections (pp. 54–5). The ontological distinction between the hasidic *tsadik* and what preceded him thus adds an innovative spirit to practical mysticism in its hasidic garb.

Although the erudition and research of this study is unsurpassed in English literature on this subject, there are a number of methodological issues which I find problematic in Nigal's presentation. First, I think the reader is sometimes inundated with cases and data, much of which lack adequate analysis. This is particularly true in chapter 4 on dybbuks, possession, and exorcism. This chapter reads like a shopping-list of case-studies, sometimes going on for pages before any analysis is rendered. Although Nigal states his thesis clearly in a number of places throughout the book, the reader sometimes finds the distinctions between the hasidic *tsadik* and the pre-hasidic wonder-worker muddled. Moreover, Sefardi and Ashkenazi practices and stories are often listed side by side. Are there any substantive differences between Sefardi magical practices which emerged in Muslim lands and Ashkenazi practices which emerged in Christian lands? Nigal is silent on this important matter. This affects his analysis of hasidism as well. The Safed circle, the bridge between the medieval literature and the hasidic story, is largely Sefardi in nature, flourishing in Palestine in the mid-sixteenth century. Are we to believe that hasidic practices are only or even primarily influenced by the Safed circle and not also by the older traditions of Ḥasidei Ashkenaz (the thirteenth-century German pietists), who had a profound impact on all of

Ashkenazi Jewry? One example of this is that many of the cases he cites come from the southern Moravian city of Nikolsburg, the seat of the Moravian rabbinate and a city which inherited a rich tradition from the pre-Lurianic German pietism. One can hardly read four of five pages of Nigal's study without coming across the city of Nikolsburg, yet he does not seem to view this phenomenon as significant.

A second issue refers to his comparative analysis of Jewish and Christian tales in the later part of the book. Although Nigal does indeed point to basic differences between Christian and Jewish variants (p. 161), his analysis sometimes seems speculative and leaves certain basic questions unanswered. The shared literary device of the story and the interaction between simple Jews and Christians in the market-places of eastern Europe lends itself to a complex set of issues for the folklorist. Although Nigal gives these issues close attention in other scholarly studies, here he leaves many of them unresolved. However, this is a sterling piece of scholarship written in a way that can benefit the scholar and non-scholar alike. Nigal has given us a window into the obscure world of Jewish magic that will shatter conventional notions of the Jewish mind and Jewish spirituality.

SHAUL MAGID
*Jewish Theological Seminary, New York*

## MAGDALENA OPALSKI AND ISRAEL BARTAL
### Poles and Jews: A Failed Brotherhood

(Hanover, NH: Brandeis University Press, 1992)
pp. 191. ISBN 0874516013

The idea was simple enough: proceeding from the assumption that to some degree literature reflects popular values and attitudes, Magdalena Opalski would sift Polish writing for portrayals of Jews, while Israel Bartal would do the same for Polish personages in Yiddish and Hebrew literature. The special impetus for the comparison was the short-lived interval of Polish–Jewish 'brotherhood' that preceded the 1863 Polish insurrection against tsarist Russia. In an effort to secure Jewish support, the Poles had promised the Jews full equality. Many Jews, for their part, took active part in the Polish military effort. The uprising failed, and in the decades that followed Polish–Jewish relations deteriorated. The two communities grew further and further apart, not least during the twenty years of Polish independence between the two world wars.

Professors Opalski and Bartal, both experienced scholars in their fields (she, the author of a study of the Jewish tavern-keeper in nineteenth-century Polish writing, he, of a forthcoming monograph on the portrayal of gentile society in Hebrew and Yiddish fiction) were quite aware of the strikingly asymmetrical nature of the materials they probed. Secular Jewish writing, both Hebrew and Yiddish, is largely a relatively recent phenomenon, dating back only to the latter part of the nineteenth century, at which time it was also supplemented by Russian Jewish prose, drama, and verse. Moreover, all of it reflected one particular ideological stance, that of the Jewish Enlightenment (Haskalah), a movement born in Germany that strove to reconcile religious tradition with secular modernity. Opponents of that tendency, the steadfast Orthodox—whether hasidim or mitnagedim—produced no secular writing at all. In contrast, Polish literature was already flourishing during the Renaissance and the Reformation, and was inspired by a variety of religious values and political creeds. Fortunately, these methodological difficulties failed to dissuade the two scholars from undertaking their exceptionally challenging project, which required a huge amount of research. Their persistence was rewarded. The slim volume Magdalena Opalski and Israel Bartal have produced is a most valuable contribution to Polish, as well as Jewish, history and literary scholarship, and also to general literary sociology.

As Bartal reminds us, Haskalah authors unanimously preferred multinational monarchies to uninational states, viewing Poland 'as the least likely to grant full civil rights to the Jews. Austrian legislation and the reforms of [Tsar] Alexander II are extensively cited in support of the view' (p. 97). Accordingly, Jewish portrayals of the Polish uprising of 1863—whatever the ideological disagreements among individual authors—were uniformly unfriendly:

They all depict the Polish side as corrupt, unstable, weak, and unrealistic. They all view Polish nationalism as intolerant, too demanding and too Christian. In [the novelist] Smolenskin's eyes the latter is also too 'French', by which he means too Catholic and too centralized . . . In all of the Jewish works under study, disillusionment with the Poles leads their positive heroes [who were usually assimilationist Jews] to reassess their attitudes toward and rediscover the bonds tying them to their own people. The overall ideological evaluation of these characters clearly leans toward Jewish nationalism.   (pp. 96–7)

One might add yet another reason for the Jews' apparent preference for Poland's Russian- and German-speaking occupiers in the mid-nineteenth century. When facing a choice between two competing ethnic communities, minorities tend to gravitate towards those they perceive as culturally more developed and offering better prospects for professional and economic advancement. This, it so happens, is attested by sociological processes within twentieth-century Polish Diaspora. In Canada, Poles assimilate into the English community, not the French. In Belgium, they gravitate toward the French, not the Flemish speakers.

Some of the values of Jewish Haskalah writers were close to those espoused by Polish positivism. These included a criticism of ghetto life, the concept of a secular society, and an emphasis on modern education. What set them apart was the positivists' assumption that Jews would welcome the prospect of total assimilation into Polish society, a goal in fact accepted by only a tiny minority of the country's Jews. The vast majority might have been willing to accept varying degrees of acculturation, religious and cultural, but not a total disappearance of the Jews as a distinct community. It is for this reason that the otherwise philosemitic writings of Bolesław Prus, Maria Konopnicka, and, above all, Eliza Orzeszkowa met with guarded reception among Poland's Jews.

The decline of Polish positivism toward the end of the nineteenth century coincided with the end of Haskalah. The young generation of Jewish authors was generally inspired by ideas of social radicalism and, in response to the upsurge of antisemitism in the gentile camp, of a nascent, defiant Jewish nationalism. The radicalism inspired the appearance in Yiddish fiction of sympathetic Polish gentile personages, victims of social injustice. Occasionally such oppressed and exploited Christian peasants and artisans appear side by side with the new type of villain, who were the modern antisemites. Such is the case of two leading Yiddish authors, Y. L. Peretz and Mendele Mokher Seforim (whom Professor Bartal identifies as 'Shalom Yaakov Abramowitz', his real but rarely used name), for whom the menacing shadow of contemporary Jew-hating ideologies resurrected memories of enemies of yore, such as the drunken and cruel Polish landowner. A striking scene in Peretz's play *At Night at the Old Market-place* (1902) depicts a grotesque dance of Polish noblemen and Catholic priests with dead Jewish girls. The message was clear enough: east is east, and west is west, and never the twain shall meet. Incongruously, a sympathetic Yiddish portrait of the Polish uprising of 1863 appeared much later, in the 1920s, in two novels of Joseph Opatoshu, *In Polish Forests* and *1863*. Significantly, both were published in New York.

The sympathetic Jewish protagonists from the prose of Orzeszkowa and Prus are descended from the most celebrated single Jewish character in all of Polish literature, the idealized innkeeper and courageous Polish patriot Jankiel in Adam Mickiewicz's *Pan Tadeusz*. (Regrettably, Professor Opalski side-steps Jadwiga Maurer's claim that Poland's national poet was himself of Frankist, and hence of Jewish, origin, an apposite claim in this context.) Unlike the positivists' 'good Jews', Mickiewicz's Jankiel is traditionally religious (a rabbi's assistant, no less) and displays no assimilationist tendencies.

Conventional wisdom ascribes most blame for popular antisemitism in nineteenth-century Russian-occupied Poland to the Jews' failure to assimilate and to economic friction engendered by the destruction of traditional agrarian society and its replacement by capitalist institutions. Professor Opalski's research demonstrates the need to revise this view. She writes:

contemporary fiction, especially works by Józef Ignacy Kraszewski, popularized the negative perception of *assimilated* Jews in the process of the capitalist restructuring of society. Denunciations of the *shortcomings of assimilation* on the one hand and demands for the *total Polonization of Jews* as a pre-condition for their receiving full civil rights on the other, reflected the ambiguity of the Polish authors' attitudes toward assimilation. (p. 17, emphasis added)

In fact this ambivalence antedates the arrival of capitalism. One year after the publication of *Pan Tadeusz*, Zygmunt Krasiński's *Undivine Comedy* (1835) depicted an evil conspiracy of Jewish converts to Catholicism—that is, of completely assimilated Jews—against the Christian world order. Emergence of capitalism begot numerous literary villainous assimilated Jews: 'the portrayal of the Jewish banker as a villain was firmly established in Polish fiction . . . and betrayed an intense preoccupation with the upward mobility of Jews in general' (p. 25). Krasiński's Jewish conspiracy, this time aimed specifically against Poland—resurfaced in Julian Ursyn Niemcewicz's *The Year 3333: or, The Incredible Dream* (1858), in which Warsaw becomes Moszkopolis (in honour of its Jewish ruler), Poland is renamed Palestine, and the country's language is changed to an ugly mixture of Yiddish and French.

In theory, individual Jews could assimilate, although, as Professor Opalski warns, 'the list of Polish prerequisites for integration grew longer and was constantly modified': 'The ideal young Jew's road to total Polonization typically included moving to Warsaw, acquiring a modern Polish education, falling in love with a Pole, rejecting his Jewish heritage (a special emphasis is placed on its capitalistic and linguistic aspects) except for religion, and participating in a crusade aimed at promoting Polish interests among Jews' (p. 71).

Somewhat surprisingly, nineteenth-century writing, in Polish, as well as Hebrew and Yiddish, features a great many inter-faith love stories. Very significantly, 'In Polish and Jewish works alike, the romances *never end in intermarriage*' (p. 94, emphasis added). Professors Opalski and Bartal found not a single exception.

MAURICE FRIEDBERG
*University of Illinois at Urbana-Champaign*

EUGENIA PROKÓP-JANIEC
## Międzywojenna literatura polsko-żydowska jako zjawisko kulturowe i artystyczne
(*Interwar Polish Jewish Literature as a Cultural and Artistic Phenomenon*)

(Cracow: Universitas, 1992)
pp. 340. ISBN 8370520707

Without the language of the country in which we live we are culturally poorer; without Hebrew we lose our past; without Yiddish we are not a people.

Y. L. PERETZ

The centuries-long Jewish presence in Poland could not pass unnoticed in Polish literature, yet writing about the Jews in Polish was for a long time the exclusive domain of Poles. This is why the image of the Jews created in that literature was far from objective and was founded mainly on stereotypes and clichés established over the ages, functioning completely inside Polish society's firm beliefs about Jewish traditions, life, and customs. Even if an author aimed to re-evaluate prevailing opinion about Jews, he too often had equally erroneous ideas, and would end up strengthening existing stereotypes, whether he intended to or not.

A number of literary critics have noted that Polish literature tended to portray the Jewish intelligentsia, to which it had easy access, while Yiddish literature tended to portray the Jewish masses, to which it had easy access. The world of ordinary Jews, inhabitants of the shtetl or the urban poor, was described by Jewish writers rather than by Poles. Jewish spirituality remained beyond the interest and understanding of Polish writers. Assumptions that are based on only superficial observations, without any solid basis of knowledge or understanding, tend to be mistaken, so it is small wonder that Polish literature never gave a very accurate picture of Jewish life.

The first work of a Polish Jew in Polish was published in 1782, and a relatively large number of Jews became very active in Polish literature and literary criticism from the nineteenth century. Since Polish Jewry was almost entirely Yiddish-speaking, however, it was not until the beginning of the twentieth century that the increase in the number of Jews writing in Polish became marked.

Those Jews who wrote about Polish literature in the mid-nineteenth century did not generally deal with Jewish topics. When they did, as for example in the works of Julian Klaczko, Henryk Merzbach, and Aleksander Kraushar, they abandoned the subject very quickly, perhaps as part of their quest for assimilation. Requests from other individuals to describe Jewish life and tradition and to make them more accessible to non-Jewish (Polish) neighbours met with no response.

A few authors, however, while writing in Polish, remained faithful to their Jewish heritage. *Interwar Polish Jewish Literature as a Cultural and Artistic Phenomenon* is the first monograph on this trend, which flourished particularly between the two world wars. It reveals many important details on the subject that were previously unknown to both Polish and western readers.

To someone who thinks about pre-Holocaust Jewish life in Poland, or in eastern Europe in general, in terms of shtetl culture, this book comes as a complete surprise. There is hardly any trace of 'Yidn fun a gants yor' (everyday Jews) from Sholem Aleichem's mythical town of Kasrilevke, nor of *sheydim* (demons) or *rukhes* (spirits) from Singer's stories.

The first part of the book describes the discussion that took place at the turn of the century among Polish Jewish writers writing in Polish. It was Jewish themes and the national and cultural self-identification of the authors that differentiated Polish Jewish literature from Polish writing. A strong wave of nationalistic feeling during this period was reflected in the newly emerging Jewish press in Polish. Periodicals such as *Rocznik żydowski*, *Moriah*, and *Almanach żydowski*, unlike the earlier *Izraelita* or *Ojczyzna*, which adhered to maskilic views, focused on the renaissance of Jewish culture, and sought ideological support from cultural Zionism (similar to that emphasized by Martin Buber). The authors' affirmation of Jewish culture and the Jewish system of values exposed them to attacks from assimilationists who were very critical of literature in Polish that tended to the Zionist point of view.

During the inter-war period the authors who wrote in Polish while maintaining a Jewish identity developed a new form of Jewish creativity. This led to another distinction: between Polish Jewish writers and Polish writers of Jewish origin who were not at all interested in Jewish topics.

Generally speaking, the ideological framework of the Polish Jewish press in inter-war Poland was very supportive of Zionism, although it was certainly less political than the contemporary Yiddish press in Poland. There were a large number of Polish Jewish newspapers and magazines that supported Polish Jewish writers throughout the period from 1918 to 1928 and even after 1928, when this literature went beyond the columns of the Polish Jewish press.

This press aimed not to compete with the Hebrew and Yiddish media at the time, but rather to supplement them. One of its missions was to 'inform the intelligent spheres among Jewry about current problems', as well as to 'inform the Polish Christian intelligentsia properly about these aspects of our life, about which they usually do not know anything at all'. From today's perspective, it seems to have been destined to fail. Many years later Adolf Rudnicki, the famous Jewish author who wrote in Polish and died in Warsaw in 1990, could still write: 'Incredible. How was it possible to live together for a thousand years and know nothing about one another. Nothing.'

The beginning of the 1930s brought more interest in Polish Jewish cultural life, probably linked to the fact that the new generation of writers entering this literature issued new programmes and aesthetic manifestos, and increased the quality of their literary production. Lwów, Cracow, and Warsaw, the three main centres of the Polish Jewish press, now also became the focal points of pre-war literary and cultural life.

Not surprisingly, Galician literary circles were the first and most vital to be established. The Jewish intelligentsia of Galicia was well-read, educated in Polish schools, yet not cut off from their Jewish roots. The assimilationists, however, did not succeed in dominating the Jewish scene. Neither Cracow nor Warsaw had its own literary group equivalent to the Galician Wzlot, which included all the poets writing in Polish and Yiddish, as well as literary critics, journalists, and artists. Among these was Dov Sztock, later the famous Israeli historian Dov Sadan.

Both of the prestigious newspapers *Chwila* and *Nowy dziennik* opened their columns to young readers and writers. It was Janusz Korczak himself who supported this young literary group and who later became the editor of *Mały przegląd* (part of *Nasz przegląd*, appearing in Warsaw), which exclusively published the texts of its young readers.

By 1933 a heated discussion between two groups of Polish-speaking Jewish intelligentsia had emerged, which led to two diverging visions of Polish Jewish literature. The first was represented by Roman Brandstaetter, who advocated the kind of art that, instead of simply elaborating on Jewish topics, included and propagated the ideas of national revival. He suggested co-operation between Polish Jewish writers (of course he meant only those who had strong Jewish identity: 'Polish Jewish poets are the Jews who "feel at home" in Polish culture, not the Poles of Jewish persuasion') and the Jewish National Fund. Brandstaetter also called for Zionist involvement, using in support of his ideas the names of other active west European writers such as Elsa Lasker-Schuler, Hugo Zuckermann, Edmond Fleg, and André Spire. The goals of this literature, in other words, were similar to those of Hebrew literature in Palestine; the only difference lay in the language. This literature was, according to Brandstaetter, a natural consequence of *Galut* (exile), which, once it had fulfilled its mission to awaken the national consciousness and help create a homogeneous Hebrew national culture, would lose its purpose and disappear: 'We would prefer . . . to write in Hebrew', wrote Brandstaetter in 1933, 'and to be read by a Hebrew audience, but we are the emanation of our whole political and cultural condition and this is why we can neither be blamed nor accused.'

The programme proposed by Maurycy Szymel opposed that of Brandstaetter and his followers. Szymel emphasized the role of the Diaspora and Yiddish. Poetry, in his opinion, has to be uninvolved, and Szymel criticized all signs of Zionist exaltation: 'To be a good Polish Jewish poet one has to know the language and the culture of the Jewry. Someone who writes a few little poems about psalms and *halutsim* is not a Polish Jewish poet.' For Szymel, the manifestation of Jewishness in literature did not mean the presence of ideology, but involved the expression of cultural and traditional values. Yet no matter how heated the controversy was between the supporters of Brandstaetter and Szymel, and which concept of Jewish literature or, in a broader sense, Jewish culture one agreed upon and was ready to promote, they all had one thing in common: as far as their national identity was concerned, they always stood apart from Polish society, even while becoming closer to Polish culture.

In the inter-war period, acculturation led to Polonization in a cultural, but, in Prokóp-Janiec's opinion, rarely national, sense. The creativity of Polish Jewish writers belongs to both cultures, Polish and Jewish, easily detectable by taking a closer look at its journalistic and literary achievements. The press especially constitutes a junction where elements of both cultures actively interact. Alongside details of Hebrew and Yiddish literature, Jewish theatre, film, and art, translations of Mendele Mocher Seforim, Sholem Aleichem, Perets, An-ski, Bialik, Tchernichovsky, Ash, Opatoshu, the Singer brothers, and many others, the Polish Jewish press addressed many issues of Polish cultural life.

What Prokóp-Janiec refers to as the 'invasion' of the literary world by Polish

raises the question of whether writing in languages other than Jewish ones should be considered part of Jewish culture. Two opposing opinions were championed by Polish Jewish writers: one promoted the concept of pure Jewish culture free from distortions of *Galut* and writing exclusively in Hebrew, while the other saw a multilingual, heterogeneous culture as a natural consequence of living in the Diaspora.

Some perceived in the neo-romantic tendencies of the inter-war period a means for interpreting Jewish art in the Diaspora and for defending multilingualism. According to Maurycy Szymel, 'We are the most authentic emanation of Jewish spirit, its nobly broad road and desire to encompass all. And the Jewish spirit speaks in all the languages of the world.' Similarly, Chaim Low argued, 'If Jewish literature is possible in Aramaic or German, why not in Polish? This is a good intention and above all deeply rooted in our national tradition.'

Looking at Polish Jewish literature from ideological and artistic angles, it is possible to distinguish two major tendencies. On the one hand, there is a literature that focuses on the traditional culture of the shtetl, deriving its inspiration from Jewish folklore and Yiddish literature. Its sentimental tone is revealed through pictures evoking childhood and feelings of security, serenity, and a special dimension of Jewish folk-beliefs and customs. On the other hand, there is a very different kind of literature reflecting various trends in Zionist ideology. This literature adopts various literary forms (educational novels, agitators' songs, etc.), is critical of traditional culture, and focuses on a future that would bring a partial restitution of biblical patterns. What is interesting, if hardly surprising, in both cases is that their connections with contemporary Yiddish and Polish literary traditions may be traced independently of their separating tendencies.

Prokóp-Janiec's book offers one of many possible ways of describing and reading inter-war Polish Jewish literature, or, more accurately, its particular aspects. Her work reveals a new area of Jewish creativity, and in this way contributes to a better, deeper understanding of Polish Jewish thought. According to David Rosenthal, 'The vibrant, variegated cultural life of Polish Jewry was expressed not only in the sphere of ideas, but also in the sphere of language. Polish Jews lived in three languages: Yiddish, Polish, and Hebrew.'

While there has been a reasonable amount of research on Hebrew and Yiddish, so far very little is known of the Polish part of trilingual Jewish culture in Poland, and much work in this field still remains to be done. Polish–Jewish relations have recently aroused considerable interest in Poland, as well as among western scholars of Jewish studies, because of the cultural and social importance of the problems they address. Despite this, Prokóp-Janiec's book is the only attempt to explore this particular part of Polish Jewish creativity. The language barrier makes most of it a *terra incognita* to western scholars; it is also surprisingly unfamiliar to the Polish reader as well.

The last part of the book contains biographical notes of Polish Jewish writers whose existence has never been mentioned in any Polish literary compendia. They do not appear in the curriculum of Polish students of literature, and this is one of the reasons why young Poles still learn next to nothing about Polish Jewry.

The cultural trends among Jewish intellectuals in Poland, so vivid especially between the two world wars, might have borne fruit in the form of much more sophisticated literary works if events had turned out differently. The list of those who perished in the Holocaust is endless, and, as Henryk Grynberg, one of the post-Holocaust Polish Jewish writers, said, 'in fact the number of murdered is higher than the number of those who are dead'. Those who survived and remained in Poland after the destruction are very few, and their writings are over-shadowed by the Holocaust. Grynberg has called it the 'life after death' of Polish Jewry. After the Holocaust, Polish Jewish literature still exists. This phenomenon both astonishes and raises serious and very bitter controversies, especially within the context of certain authors' decisions to remain in Poland after the destruction. Nevertheless, the importance of this literature as a source for historical and socio-logical analysis must not be ignored. We hope that the work of Prokóp-Janiec will not be the last of its kind and will open up a new area of scholarly research.

JOLANTA KISLER-GOLDSTEIN
*Brandeis University*

JOEL RABA

# *Bein zikaron lehakhehashah: Gezerot tah vetat bereshimot benei hazeman ubere'i haketivah hahistorit*

(Tel Aviv: Center for the History of Polish Jewry, Tel Aviv University, 1994)
pp. vii + 381. ISBN 9653380176

Until the events of this century, 1648 had been perceived by Jews as Polish Jewry's darkest hour. It was then that Jewish communities in the Ukraine were destroyed. Many thousands of civilians were murdered, and untold numbers of others were terrorized and forced to flee. Some no doubt succeeded; others, stripped of their assets and, too often, their loved ones, languished.

Yet not everyone shared this perception of the fate of the Jews in south-eastern Poland in the mid-seventeenth century. Joel Raba's book is not an attempt to reconstruct the events of 1648 and the Swedish invasions that followed in their wake. Rather, it traces the changing perceptions of the fate of the Jews who lived

---

This book has now appeared in an English translation: *Between Remembrance and Denial: The Fate of the Jews in the Wars of the Polish Commonwealth during the Mid-Seventeenth Century as Shown in Contemporary Writings and Historical Research* (Boulder, Colo.: East European Monographs, 1995); pp. 519; ISBN 0880333251.

in Poland during those years in the consciousness of subsequent generations, primarily of Poles, Ukrainians, Russians, and Jews.

After an introductory chapter on the development of historical consciousness, Raba meticulously gathers material concerning the fate of the Jews during the mid-seventeenth century in the Polish–Lithuanian Commonwealth. He searches the works of observers and historians of peoples that were directly involved in the events (except for Swedish sources), as well as foreign reports such as contemporary diplomatic and personal accounts from the seventeenth century up to and including the post-Holocaust period. He also wisely includes historical views expressed in popular Ukrainian poetic works from the first half of the nineteenth century, before professional historians had emerged in this region.

Raba's survey shows that each people and each age viewed 1648 and its aftermath from its own perspective. The generation of Jews that actually endured the destruction was most concerned with recording the horrors and the scope of the disaster. For those who suffered, the catastrophe was not part of a long legacy of Jewish tribulations, but a unique and dreadful experience that was expressed with great emotion by people such as Natan Hannover. Soon after, Jews connected the events with a legacy of suffering that went back much earlier to the Middle Ages. Yet the plight of the Jews was only of marginal interest to authors of the other nationalities involved. Polish writers, according to Raba, sought to use the events of 1648 to incite the Polish population against the Cossacks and had little interest in recounting the victimization of their religious and economic competitors, the Jews. Raba argues that while Jews and Poles died together, Jews soon dropped to the periphery of Polish historical consciousness and eventually became nonparticipants, despite the fact that they were ultimately blamed by Poles for the tragic events. By the nineteenth century Jewish responsibility for the events of 1648 had become even more pronounced in Ukrainian historiography, where the Jew came to be viewed as the immoral oppressor of the Ukrainian people, an oppressor who had brought the troubles on himself. The denial of Jewish victimization in 1648 and its aftermath reached an extreme in the twentieth century when Ukrainian and later Soviet historiography were almost unwilling to admit to the atrocities of 1648; the claim was that Hanover's account of the events was simply fantasy.

Perhaps Raba's use of the survey format does not facilitate a concurrent evaluation of the sources; nor does it allow him to place them in their historical context. To be sure, Raba does take notice of the role of romanticism in shaping Polish and Ukrainian historiography, but what of the role of Zionist historiography—a school that certainly existed well before the establishment of Israel—in moulding the views of Ben-Zion Dinur and his student Shmuel Ettinger? Did their propensity to view Jewish life in the Diaspora as fraught with dangers for the Jew skew their view of 1648? Similarly, did not Ettinger's focus on antisemitism also shape his perception of the events? Raba does not say. Only where there seems to be a deliberate attempt at disinformation, such as by the influential Theodore Mackiw, is Raba moved to examine the historian's sources carefully and discredit them. It is a pity that a thorough analysis of other sources that have been equally important in shaping public opinion through the ages was not included. Although Raba showed the traditions and sources that constitute the historiography of 1648 and its aftermath, he did not describe the selection process (even if he claims to have done so in his conclusion on page 332). Such an evaluation would have defined the transmission of historical messages and the evolution of various historical consciousness more clearly and left fewer blanks for the reader to fill in.

Raba's work, with its extensive bibliography, is an indispensable reference tool for students of the events of the mid-seventeenth century in the Polish–Lithuanian Commonwealth. Although a subject index would have made the book of even greater practical use, there are few scholars who could have accomplished the yeoman tasks of gathering and presenting such a broad range of information gleaned from eight languages. Yet in many ways the work essentially remains a source book, written by a historian saddened by what he believes to be an injustice perpetrated by historians of all cultures (including some Jewish ones) to the memory of Jewish victims. It would have strengthened Raba's moral stance if he showed similar feelings about the other innocent victims of the Cossack uprisings, who have been ignored by Jewish and non-Jewish historians.

EDWARD FRAM
*Ben-Gurion University of the Negev*

MAREK ROSTWOROWSKI (ED.)
## Żydzi w Polsce: Obraz i słowo

(*Jews in Poland: Image and Word*)

(Warsaw: Wydawnictwo Interpress, 1993)
pp. 347; 460 illustrations. ISBN 8322326300

This sumptuous volume, the first in a two-part series, is devoted to depictions of Jews by Polish artists, both Christian and Jewish, as well as by several non-Polish artists who worked in Poland. Its splendid reproductions range from the Middle Ages to the present, although most of the works are from the nineteenth and twentieth centuries. The book has four principal sections. The two larger sections portray the religious dimension of Polish Jewry (Jews at prayer, images of synagogues) and the role of Jews in Polish life (including images of Jews in various economic roles, Jews participating in the struggle for Polish independence, and portraits of Jewish artists and intellectuals). The other two sections contain antisemitic images (including a horrifying eighteenth-century depiction on page 106 of Jews torturing a Christian child for ritual purposes) and depictions of the Holocaust.

Some of the material presented by Rostworowski can be found in the pioneering work of Halina Nelken, *Images of a Lost World: Jewish Motifs in Polish Painting* (London, 1991)—both Nelken's book and the one under review derive from exhibitions first held in Poland. But *Żydzi w Polsce* is a more ambitious and more inclusive study. It clearly belongs to a popular contemporary genre, the representation of the 'other', much as images of Arabs were popular in nineteenth-century France (for example, numerous works by Delacroix), and American blacks are now equally popular among art historians, as evidenced in the remarkable book by Peter H. Wood and Karen C. C. Dalton, *Winslow Homer's Images of Blacks* (Austin, Tex., 1988). There is another, more specific context for this book: it is the investigation of Polish–Jewish relations via the medium of the arts. Works in this category include Magdalena Opalski and Israel Bartal's book *Poles and Jews: A Failed Brotherhood* (see review), on the image of the Jew in Polish literature and of the Pole in Jewish literature; and Alina Cała's *Wizerunek Żyda w polskiej kulturze ludowej* (Warsaw, 1992; English version: *The Image of the Jew in Polish Folk Culture* (Jerusalem, 1995)), on the image of the Jew in Polish popular culture.

The book under review here can also be seen in the context of efforts by a new generation of Polish scholars and publicists to come to terms with the Jewish dimension of their own history. Marek Rostworowski, son of the inter-war Polish writer Karol Rostworowski, has taken upon himself the task of explicating for his Polish readers who 'know not Joseph' the remarkable history of Polish Jewry, its rich cultural (largely religious) heritage, and its efforts to maintain an autonomous existence as well as to integrate to some degree in Polish life. Rostworowski's introductory text and elucidation of the images is in part an exercise in *Wiedergutmachung*; the author is engaged in a rehabilitation of Polish Jewry, which becomes a glorification of Jewish spirituality. The book is not entirely free of Polish apologia, however: he admits the existence of antisemitism but points out that in the 1930s the Poles had no monopoly on antisemitism. He also emphasizes the affinity between Judaism and Christianity. In general Rostworowski writes from the perspective of the new Catholic attitude towards Jews (the spirit of the Polish Pope is palpable) and in the philosemitic tradition of Mickiewicz and other Polish writers. He looks back nostalgically to the brief periods of Polish–Jewish *rapprochement* (as in 1861–3), and deplores the misunderstandings and hatreds that have tragically characterized much of Polish–Jewish relations. The image in the book that best represents his standpoint is Maurycy Gottlieb's painting of Jesus preaching at Capernaum on page 222, in which Jesus is shown wearing a *talit* (prayer shawl).

What can we learn from the images that are so beautifully presented in this book? On one level the visual dimension we confront on these pages serves to

complement what is already well known about modern Polish Jewish life: the
essential roles of Jews as merchants, traders, innkeepers, artisans, and even
musicians, and the intensity of religious life. Those interested in the material culture of Polish Jewry will find a wealth of information on traditional Jewish dress,
while those who study synagogue architecture will welcome the various images of
Jewish houses of worship assembled here. Scholars dealing with the modernization of Polish Jewry will be able to follow the emergence in modern times of the
Europeanized Polish Jew who has discarded traditional garb for the dress of the
Polish bourgeoisie. In one remarkable painting on pages 288 and 289 by the writer
and artist Bruno Schultz, we are shown an encounter between the proverbial 'two
worlds' that emerged within Polish Jewry. It shows a hasid with his head down,
furtively glancing at two modern women in high heels, while they do not see him
at all. Historians of Polish Jewry searching for illustrations to accompany their
texts will find them here in abundance, most notably in the depictions of Jewish
participation in the revolutions of 1830 and 1863 (for example, the portrayal of the
Jewish guards organized in 1831 on page 159) and the well-known painting on
page 181 by Aleksander Lesser of the burial of the five martyrs killed by the
Russians in 1861, which includes a portrait of the rabbi and Polish patriot Ber
Meisels.[1]

*Żydzi w Polsce* also traces the emergence of Jewish artists in Poland, devoting
ample space to the most important ones: Maurycy Gottlieb, the Galician-born
pupil of Matejko, Samuel Hirszenberg, and Jankiel Adler.

The images collected in this volume testify to the ubiquitous presence of
Jews, to their penetration of the public, if not the private, space of the country. A
beautiful painting by the Italian-born artist Bernardo Bellotto (the Polish
Canaletto), who worked in Warsaw in the second half of the eighteenth century,
shows this clearly. The painting, reproduced on pages 124 and 125, is called *Ulica
Miodowa w Warszawie* (Miodowa Street in Warsaw) and dates from 1777. It portrays an elegant Warsaw street, with a horse-drawn carriage conveying a member
of high society. In the foreground are Jewish men in traditional black garb, talking. Like the traveller in the carriage and the other figures on the street, they are
an integral part of the Polish scene. This motif is repeated in many other paintings
reproduced in the book. In the little towns and villages of Poland, the Jews are
present. They can be seen witnessing Polish funerals and religious processions (as
in the painting by Wacław Koniuszko on page 209), entertaining the public in a
Warsaw park (on page 206), selling their wares at the city gates, watching Polish
workers from a distance, and standing near the Roman Catholic Cathedral in
Wilno. They are everywhere.

But who are they? The overwhelming impression conveyed from representa-

[1] This painting serves to illustrate Opalski and Bartal's book. A second image from this book was
also used: Artur Szyk's portrait of Bronisław Mansperl, who died in 1915 fighting for Polish independence; see my recent study *On Modern Jewish Politics* (New York, 1993).

tions of Jews by non-Jewish artists in the nineteenth century is that, while Jews live in Poland, they are not really of Poland. They are often seen observing a scene from afar, bearing witness to a society to which they as outsiders do not belong. In the paintings it is their dress that most clearly marks them off. Consider the reproduction on pages 56 and 57 by Wincenty Smokowski from 1852 called *Wesele żydowskie* (Jewish Wedding): there is a bizarre crowd of men and women (in exotic headgear) led by three musicians, all marching through town on the way to a wedding ceremony. What would a Pole happening upon this scene make of it? He might well compare it to an invasion of gypsies or other foreigners, and yet these people were not newcomers to Poland; they had been living there for centuries. The grotesque nature of the Jewish image created by Polish artists, embodied in this painting of the three *klezmorim*, is much in evidence in this book. Thus, for example, the Jewish figures in Piotr Michalowski's *Jarmark w Mościskach* (The Fair in Mościska) on page 165 are shown running and gesturing, while several Poles stand calmly by, one smoking a long pipe. Is this perhaps an attempt to show national types, nervous Jews contrasted against placid Poles? Then there is Stanisław Lentz's painting from 1897 on page 211 showing a Warsaw merchant. Interestingly, a Jewish artist, Jankiel Adler, also portrays an image of the nervous Jew in his portrait of a Jewish cellist on page 254.

If nineteenth-century Jews are often portrayed as exotic, bizarre foreigners in their own land, that is not the whole story. In his study of the black image in American art, Guy C. McElroy writes that African Americans appear as 'grotesque buffoons, servile menials, comic entertainers, and threatening subhumans'.[2] For the Jews, however, the situation was much more complex: this book has many portraits showing modern Polish Jews, or Poles of Jewish origin, including some by important artists such as Henryk Wieniawski and Julian Tuwim, that are not intended to be grotesque or comic; nor are many of the portrayals of traditional nineteenth-century Jews demeaning or derisory. On the contrary. Consider the painting by Piotr Michalowski called *Jews*, which is used on the jacket of the book and reproduced in the introductory section. It shows the faces of five Jewish men of different ages radiating pride and inner strength. These are faces from the mid-nineteenth century, but there is nothing subservient or laughable about them. No less dignified is the brilliant painting by Aleksander Gierymski on pages 22 and 23 depicting the Jewish New Year *tashliḥ* ceremony (a somewhat different, but better version of this work is reproduced in Nelken's book; here it is too dark to make out the figures distinctly). There is a general aura of dignity, of the profundity of religious feeling, which is also echoed in the portrait of *A Jew at Study* on page 40 by the French-born artist Jan Piotr Norblin de la Gourdaine. This work from the 1780s is suffused with an inner tranquillity and piety. Many of the traditional Jews depicted in the art included in this book seem

[2] Cited by Henry Louis Gates, Jr., in his essay in Guy C. McElroy's *Facing History: The Black Image in American Art, 1710–1940* (San Francisco, 1990), p. xxix.

sure of themselves and of their integral culture and civilization. They are members of a proud nation, not in the modern Zionist sense, but in the old, pre-modern Jewish sense.

Of course it is impossible to generalize. One of the great strengths of the Rostworowski book is that the material it contains is so rich, so variegated, so multifaceted, that no generalization is adequate. The Jews portrayed here are dignified and grotesque, distant from Polish society and part of it, exotic and impossible to distinguish from their Polish neighbours, rich and poor. That this is so is a tribute to the visual feast Marek Rostworowski has made available, for his book provides us with the visual dimension of a highly complex, variegated story, the story of the Jewish nation's history in the Polish lands and of Polish–Jewish relations.

EZRA MENDELSOHN
*Hebrew University, Jerusalem*

JEAN W. SEDLAR
## *East Central Europe in the Middle Ages, 1000–1500*
### (*A History of East Central Europe*, iii)

(Seattle: University of Washington Press, 1994)
pp. xvi + 556. ISBN 0-295-97290-4

The concept of east central Europe as a separate entity is relatively recent. Though it has roots in medieval times as the area east of German- and Italian-speaking territory and west of Russia, it is only since the collapse of the Soviet Empire and the subsequent reorientation of most of the countries in the area west of Russia (i.e. central Europe) that east central Europe emerged as a politically self-conscious part of Europe. Nevertheless, its frontiers are not easily drawn.

The book under review, *East Central Europe in the Middle Ages*, is the third in the ten-volume series, *A History of East Central Europe*, under the general editorship of Peter F. Sugar and the late Donald W. Treadgold. It is comparable to W. Conze's posthumous *Ostmitteleuropa: Von der Spätantike bis zum 18. Jahrhundert* (Munich, 1993), although the German historian's chronological range was wider and his focus narrower. Most of the ten volumes in the *East Central Europe* series have already appeared: only volume ii, on the beginnings of history in east central Europe, volume iv, on the Polish–Lithuanian Commonwealth, 1386–1795, and volume x, on east central Europe since 1939, have yet to be published.

The volume by Sedlar, although somewhat arbitrarily limited to the period 1000–1500, covers its complex theme less chronologically than by topics. To be sure, chapter 1 deals largely with the first millennium AD, and at least two major events occurred in the year 1000: Emperor Otto III visited Poland and the archdiocese of Gniezno was established, and Hungary converted to Christianity. The cut-off year of 1500, however, boasts no such momentous events.

The book is divided into fifteen chapters: 'Early Migrations'; 'State Formation'; 'Monarchies'; 'Nobles and Landholders'; 'Peasants, Herders, Serfs, and Slaves'; 'Towns and Townspeople'; 'Religion and the Churches'; 'The Art and Practice of War'; 'Governments'; 'Laws and Justice'; 'Commerce and Money'; 'Foreign Affairs'; 'Ethnicity and Nationalism'; 'Languages and Literatures'; and 'Education and Literacy'. Three useful appendices provide a chronology of important events (from 681 to 1699), a list of monarchs mentioned in the text, and place name equivalents in various languages. A bibliographic essay covers the literature consulted, as well as some suggested readings. Finally, the volume concludes with an extensive name and subject index using bold-face type and asterisks to facilitate identification.

While the appendices add to the value of the book, as does the initial note on pronunciation (despite its imprecision in describing the Polish nasal vowels and some palatalized sounds in Polish and Czech), the three maps are more confusing than helpful. The second map, which shows east central Europe *c.*1250, and the third map, *c.*1480, were adapted from volume i, P. R. Magocsi's historical atlas. Some puzzling aspects of the maps include the omission of the Baltics, Belarus, and western Ukraine from east central Europe in 1994. It is also unclear why the Lithuanian boundaries for 1250 do not include Lithuanians living in the area to the west of Lithuania proper, or why the mass of Rus' is designated as 'Kievan', even though Kiev had fallen to the Mongels in 1240. Equally puzzling is why Dubrovnik is located in Serbia on this map, contrary to fact and Magocsi's original, or why all European portions of the Ottoman Empire, including Greece, are considered part of east central Europe in 1480, while in 1994 Greece and all of Turkey are excluded. No less confusing is the inclusion of Albania, Macedonia, and Bulgaria. The drawing of these borders is arguable, notwithstanding the close ties of some of the peripheral regions with the core of east central Europe (e.g. Poland, later, Poland–Lithuania; Hungary, including Slavonia, Croatia, and Dalmatia, as well as Slovakia; and Bohemia and Moravia, the Czech lands which, as part of the Holy Roman Empire, can claim membership in central Europe as well).

This brief review cannot assess all the details of such a rich presentation, but what can be said is that the organization of the complex subject over fifteen chapters makes good sense and that checks of some select items confirm the overall favourable impression of the author's vast knowledge and general reliability. Thus, her treatment of the Jews in medieval east central Europe, notably in Poland and Bulgaria, is unbiased and well informed. It is interesting to learn how Władysław Jagiełło turned against the Jews after Casimir III showed them tolerance and protection and encouraged them to settle in his realm. Yet the Polish–Lithuanian ruler, born a pagan but with a Greek Orthodox mother, continued the tolerant policy of Casimir toward the many adherents of Orthodoxy in his dual monarchy, even though he converted to Catholicism to ascend the Polish throne. The attitude of Jagiełło's son Casimir IV was not as uniformly hostile towards the Jews: after first protecting them, Casimir revoked their privileges in response to the clergy's reproaches for having lost a battle against the Teutonic Knights. It was also in Casimir IV's reign that the Renaissance entered Poland. During this period, the Germans who came to Poland and other east central European countries also encountered difficulties. Although they brought many improvements in crafts and mining, as well as in legal regulations (including the Magdeburg town law), they were identified with the hostile Teutonic Knights, which led to Polish–German tensions in some border areas, especially Silesia. A minor detail: although it is acceptable to refer to the two Bohemian kings as Ottokar I and Ottokar II, the author should have mentioned that these rulers are also known as Přemysl-Otakar I and II, respectively.

Sedlar's chapter on education and literacy is excellent, even though the terms 'Old Slavic' and 'Church Slavonic' (p. 459) could have been defined more precisely (Old Slavic is not the common term used in English but is rather a literal translation from the French or Russian). Sedlar does use the more common term on page 146, however. Regarding the relationship of *Der Ackermann in Böhmen* and the much longer *Tkadleček*: while the German piece is usually considered the model for the Czech allegorical novel, which came first has not yet been definitively settled. Sedlar's remarks on languages and literatures are otherwise on the mark, even though her use of secondary literature—especially for Hungarian (and, to some extent, Croatian) sources—does not attest to her familiarity with what is first-class scholarship. Nevertheless, the paucity of typographical errors in the bibliographical essay is quite impressive.

In the chapter on state formation, the distinction between a 'White' and a 'Red' Croatia on the Adriatic coast by the end of the eighth century is not well founded (White Croatia echoes a presumed former Croat homeland north of the Carpathians). In the chapter on religion and churches, a few critical remarks are in order. It is unfortunate that in listing the names of important Slavic pagan deities the author in two instances uses the Polish spellings, *Swarożyc* and *Światowit* (the latter, moreover, incorrectly for *Świętowit*), instead of *Svętovit* (or *Sventovit*) and *Svarožic*, which would have been preferable here. The date of 866 for Khan Boris's conversion to Christianity on page 145 is surprising, as scholars usually place this event in 864 or 865. Not sufficiently stressed is the Bulgarian ruler's flirtation with Rome (after converting to the Orthodox faith) in frustration over not having been granted an independent (autocephalous) Bulgarian patriarchate. In discussing early saints of east Central Europe, the author lists St Vitus as if he had been Czech (the historical Vitus was Italian, venerated, it is true, in Saxony and Bohemia), and, while St Virgil is properly identified as Irish, his function as founding missionary bishop of Salzburg should have been pointed out. Furthermore, although it is perhaps understandable in view of the limitation to east central Europe that the earliest saints of Kievan Rus', the slain brothers Boris and Gleb, are not mentioned among the indigenous saints of the Eastern Church (they were venerated in Bohemia as well), the activities of St John of Rila in Bulgaria were about as far removed from central Europe as the martyrdom of the Kievan saints was. Despite these small lapses, Sedlar's treatment of both the Bogomils and the Bosnian Church is excellent.

All in all, this is a reliable and well-informed survey of medieval east central Europe. The time and space limitations may well have been imposed on the author by the editors of the series, and, compared to Conze's work, Sedlar's is more comprehensive—even if it is somewhat less original and thought-provoking.

HENRIK BIRNBAUM
*University of California, Los Angeles*

JERZY TOPOLSKI

## *Polska w czasach nowożytnych: Od środkowoeuropejskiej potęgi do utraty niepodległości, 1501–1795*

(*Early Modern Poland: From Middle European Power to the Loss of Independence, 1501–1795*)

(Poznań: Uniwersytet Adama Mickiewicza w Poznaniu, 1994) pp. 943. ISBN 8323205361

This brilliant work by Jerzy Topolski, an internationally renowned Polish historian and historical methodologist, is the second volume in the great series entitled The History of the Polish Nation, State and Culture currently being produced by a team of historians at the Adam Mickiewicz University in Poznań. This book analyses the causal processes at work in the history of the Polish–Lithuanian Commonwealth. Topolski treats Polish history in an integral manner, taking account of the complex issues affecting all the national groups living in what was formerly Commonwealth territory. As an outstanding scholar, he is well aware that a synthetic approach to the history of Poland in the fifteenth to eighteenth centuries, incorporating the guide-lines for research methodology that he himself has advocated as well as the very wide range of conclusions arrived at in this book, requires inclusion of all national groups. The author treats the history of Polish Jews as an integral part of Polish history, presenting their circumstances as a part of the social, economic, and political changes occurring in the Polish–Lithuanian Commonwealth. He deals with all of the basic aspects of the history of Polish Jews during the period, including demography, professional structure, and the attitudes towards the Jewish community of Polish society and the various ethnic groups living in the Commonwealth, as well as such issues as local Polish Jewish self-government (*kehila*) and central self-government (the Council of Four Lands), culture, language, and hasidism. Indeed Topolski devotes much more space to the Jews than to the remaining national groups and in no other published synthetic account of Polish history have issues connected with the Jewish community been given so much attention.[1]

Topolski underlines the significance of the fact that the largest Jewish community in the world at that time was to be found in Poland. He bases his population statistics on available estimates and concludes that as a proportion of the population the Jewish community rose from 0.6 per cent in 1576 to 4.5 or even 5 per cent in 1648. Topolski also writes about the decline in the Jewish population in the middle of the seventeenth century and the losses it suffered as a result of the Cossack uprising and the Swedish wars, pointing out that these were among the factors responsible for the process of radical general decline of the demographic potential in Poland, others being natural calamities and economic regression. He emphasizes, that, however, in the case of the Jews the losses were more than made up. Between the middle of the seventeenth century and the second half of the eighteenth century, Jewish numbers increased two- or threefold the middle of the second half of the century. The author also points out the differences between the percentage of Jews and the remaining non-Polish ethnic groups, noting that in the second half of the eighteenth century the Ukrainian and Lithuanian populations together comprised approximately 25 per cent, whilst Germans, Armenians, Tartars, and other national groups taken together were less than 5 per cent of the total. Jews at that time, according to Topolski, made up 8–10 per cent of the population of the Polish–Lithuanian Commonwealth. He is not content, however, merely to supply demographic data, but lists certain factors which contributed to such a significant increase in the Jewish population. He goes back to well-established claims from the annals of Polish history that the main contributing factor was the tolerance and protection extended to the Jews by Polish kings and magnates as early as the Middle Ages. About the magnates he adds that it was 'their aristocratic mentality, which had a sizeable cosmopolitan component', that influenced their attitude to the Jews, and not simply economic considerations. In his view the appellation 'Polonia paradisus Iudaeorum' (Poland the paradise of the Jews) had a basis in reality. One might add, however, that the belief that life in Poland offered them more safety and freedom than they were likely to find elsewhere was not particularly widely held among the Jews.

Topolski emphasizes that Jews contributed to the 'intensification of the economic life of the country' since they 'actively contributed to the development of trade and manufacturing crafts'. They leased mills as well as inns and breweries from the gentry and magnate estates, and were able to make a living from various

---

[1] The subject of the inseparability of Jewish and Polish history has also been discussed by A. Wyczański, *Polska Rzecząpospolitą szlachecką*, 2nd edn. (Warsaw, 1992).

other sectors of the economy; they also acted as landowners' agents, and assisted in their trading activities. But the author does not just offer a cursory glance at this aspect of Jewish life; he also analyses the differences in the professional distribution of Jews in the eastern and western territories of the Polish–Lithuanian Commonwealth. In relation to the role played by Jews in the colonization of Ukraine and Belarus, he provides new information about some 4,000 Jews employed in various branches of the economy of the Ostrogski estates in the seventeenth century. Based on his own research, he maintains that two factors brought about the formation of the distinctive professional structure of the Jewish population in the Wielkopolska region: first, there were many fewer Jews here than near Poland's eastern borders; and secondly, the urban centres in this region were more developed than in the east. This situation made it easier for them to find sources of income in the cities so that, in contrast to the numbers of Jews leasing country inns in other regions of Poland, only very few did so here.

The author also attempts to answer the question why some Polish towns were granted the prerogative of *de non tolerandis Iudaeis*, which has hitherto not been explained in any historical writing. Topolski concludes that these privileges were regarded as an additional source of income, since records testify to cases in which, on payment of a sum of money, Jews were allowed to live in a town where restrictions based on such documents were in force. Topolski's hypothesis, however, does not take account of the fact that the majority of these prerogatives were granted in the sixteenth century, at a time when the still-powerful Polish townsmen were was using this as a means to eliminate competition from Jewish merchants. On the other hand, these towns were not keen to face the increasingly negative consequences of implementing such restrictions, as the complete elimination of Jews would have threatened a total collapse of trading activities. For this reason the prerogatives granted permission to Jewish merchants to attend fairs and to remain in town for three days after the fairs were over.

In addition to the *de non tolerandis Iudaeis* prerogatives, Topolski mentions the practice in several towns of designating a number of separate Jewish residential streets and districts, a measure that he points out increased the well-documented feeling of social and cultural isolation which could be observed in Poland to a much greater extent than in other European countries. The assertion that the 'interdependence of both nationalities living in the same territory was so great that there could be no question of any isolation' seems to relate mainly to various unsuccessful attempts to introduce a general ban against Jews employing Christian servants.

Topolski also confronts the widespread problem of the Jewish stereotype, both among the various national groups and among the Polish population in some regions of Poland. His comparison of this stereotype with others accepted in Poland at the time reveals that the Jewish stereotype was more conspicuous and had deeper roots in Polish society. Topolski also points out the similarity of some defects ascribed to both Jews and inhabitants of the Mazovia region, citing the widespread contemporary belief that both of these groups were born blind.

In addition to descriptions of the attitudes of various classes of Polish society to Jews, Topolski's book also usefully deals with Jewish attitudes to Poles, though it is arguable whether, as the author maintains, Jewish elders in Warsaw during the period of the Four Year Diet, in striving to achieve a higher degree of autonomy, really did obstruct co-operation with the city magistrates and the co-ordination of activities being pursued by both sides: for it must be acknowledged that representatives of Warsaw's citizens took an uncompromisingly negative stand towards Jews.

The few criticisms offered here should be understood in light of the fact that Topolski often found it necessary to try to clarify issues which have not been investigated thoroughly in the scholarly literature. Nevertheless this work by an outstanding historian might serve as a model for historical syntheses of other nations, if only because it underlines the need to give a fair and balanced account of the place of Jews in the history of Europe.

JACOB GOLDBERG
*Hebrew University, Jerusalem*
*Translated by Theresa Prout*

LAWRENCE WEINBAUM
## *A Marriage of Convenience: The New Zionist Organization and the Polish Government*

(New York: East European Monographs, 1993)
pp. xiii + 295. ISBN 0880332662

Until now, the important and interesting problem tackled by Lawrence Weinbaum has not been discussed in a thorough study. The history of co-operation between Polish governments and the New Zionist Organization, whose course might seem appropriate to the plot of an action-adventure film, was sometimes mentioned in the biographies of such Jewish politicians as Vladimir Jabotinsky, Menachem Begin, and Abraham Stern. Among Polish writers, Władysław Pobog-Malinowski devoted the most attention to this issue. He maintained close contacts with the 1930s establishment. In his *Najnowsza historia polityczna Polski*, ii (London, 1956), Malinowski used information obtained from leading Sanacja (movement to 'clean up' Parliament after 1926) politicians. As long as the archives remained inaccessible, it was difficult to verify this data, which consequently had to be treated very carefully.

Lawrence Weinbaum engaged in a wide-ranging archival investigation, with the most important sources being the seldom examined collection of the Polish Ministry of Foreign Affairs in the Archiwum Akt Nowych (Archive of Modern Documents) in Warsaw and documents in the Jabotinsky Institute in Tel Aviv. His work also makes use of copies of documents from the Foreign Office (the private archives of Mr Shmuel Katz in Tel Aviv) and material from the Central Zionist Archives in Jerusalem.

The collected documents disclose certain important gaps, especially the author's lack of familiarity with material in Polish military institutions. For the New Zionist Organization, the General Staff and Military Intelligence were the part-ners next in importance to the Ministry of Foreign Affairs. It was the army that organized training courses for Jewish fighters and was involved in arms sales. The archives of Polish Military Intelligence, closed to historians for several decades, were made available in 1990 (contrary to the author's belief, the material in the Centralne Archiwum Wojskowe (Central Military Archive) in Warsaw is hardly 'extremely scanty').

Since the events described in the book had a broad international context, similarly interesting results can be expected from research carried out in archives of other countries. British and German intelligence and American authorities were certainly interested in the activities of the New Zionist Organization. Equally important material must be contained in Soviet and Romanian archives (the New Zionist Organization maintained lively contacts with the authorities of the latter two countries), as well as the information gathered by the Arabian side.

The first two chapters serve as an introduction. The author discusses the situa-tion of the Jewish population in Poland, the premises for emigration plans pre-pared by the Polish Ministry of Foreign Affairs, and the motives that led revisionists and Polish authorities to co-operate. This section of the work is largely a recapitulation of facts and information from other studies rather than new findings.

Weinbaum correctly notes that the new approach of the Polish authorities towards the Jewish issue after the death of Józef Piłsudski in 1935 came from a group of officials working in the Consular Department of the Ministry of Foreign Affairs (older works on this subject attributed the new approach to the Camp of National Unity). Up to that time the Sanacja sought (albeit not always con-sistently and energetically) a certain *modus vivendi* in relations with the Jewish population, but after 1935 the Polish government claimed that a 'basic contradic-tion of interests' existed between the Poles and the Jews in Poland. Emigration of the Jewish population on a massive scale was the only solution to the Jewish ques-tion. The author accurately presents the position of the Ministry of Foreign Affairs, but he omits the reasons for the Piłsudski camp's views (although the existing literature on the topic makes it possible to speculate about this particular issue).

The author's arguments about the Sanacja cabinets' constant sympathy for the

Zionist movement should be formulated more precisely. In the course of everyday political work, for instance during parliamentary elections, the Sanacja considered the Zionist movement to be a part of the opposition to its rule. On the other hand, the authorities responded favourably to the Zionist-launched slogans calling for the emigration of the Jews. One should emphasize, however, that these slogans were also well received by the overwhelming majority of other Polish political groups, including the nationalist National Democrats.

The author presents an interesting history of the origin of the New Zionist Organization and its ideology, a subject that clearly fascinates him. None the less, he also depicts the basic reservations of the opponents of revisionism on the reality of the 'ten-year plan', as well as their doubts that Poland was capable of influencing British policy towards Palestine, with a justified scepticism. In light of subsequent events, how should the controversy be seen today? It is certainly difficult to judge the policy pursued by various Jewish groups exclusively according to the categories of traditional realism. In large part it was the emotional product of a tragedy experienced by the entire Jewish community, the drama of a people unwanted in Europe, yet for whom the gates to their promised national homeland remained locked. Seen from this perspective, the policy of Jabotinsky and his co-workers was just as much a symptom of revolutionary dynamics, the viewpoint stressed by the author, as a desperate reaction to a feeling of helplessness.

Chapters dealing with diplomatic activities connected to the Palestinian question, the emigration of the Jewish population from Poland, and military aid from the Polish government to the New Zionist Organization are the heart of the book, as well as the best-prepared sections. Weinbaum uses interviews with living Jewish fighters throughout his discussion of the military aspects of the co-operation between Polish authorities and the revisionists. In his use of this material he discloses his skill as a historian. Even if undiscovered archival material comes to light in the future, this book already contains such valuable information presented in a clear, concrete way that it unquestionably adds much to the field. The most interesting finding is the way the author undermines prevailing myths, especially those still flourishing in Poland. Polish assistance was somewhat less important than Pobog-Malinowski described in his highly suggestive but rather general portrayal. For example, some of the arms purchased in Poland never reached Palestine because of organizational obstacles.

All in all, this is an important book, even though certain problems still call for further research. It is written in a lively and lucid way, enhanced by excellent photographs, though the overall favourable impression is somewhat marred by the careless spelling of surnames, names of organizations, and titles of Polish-language publications.

ANDRZEJ CHOJNOWSKI<br>*Institute of History, Warsaw University*

E. THOMAS WOOD AND STANISŁAW M. JANKOWSKI
# Karski: How One Man Tried to Stop the Holocaust

(New York: Wiley, 1994)
pp. 316. ISBN 0-471-01856-2

The story of Jan Karski is well known. A Polish courier to the French-based and later London-based Polish government-in-exile, Karski undertook dangerous missions from Poland to the west. On his final mission he became a messenger from the Jewish community of Warsaw, and was sent to a concentration camp he once described as Bełżec. He was, in short, an eyewitness to the inferno who requested immediate and urgent action on behalf of Poland's beleaguered Jews.

In London in 1942 he had meetings with British government officials from Anthony Eden on down—though not with Winston Churchill. He was then sent to the United States, where he met all the relevant American leaders from President Franklin Delano Roosevelt and members of his cabinet to the Jewish leadership, the press, and public leaders. He told them what he had seen, and forwarded specific requests from the Jewish community. He published articles and a best-selling book telling the story of the Holocaust. He informed those who wished to be informed. He was a faithful messenger, and his message was not heeded while there was still time. Mission accomplished—the story was told. Mission failed—nothing changed.

E. Thomas Wood and Stanisław M. Jankowski have written a gripping biography of Karski. Were it not true, the book could read as a work of fiction, a tale of conspiracy and machinations. Part spy story, the sections on Karski's suicide attempt and escape from a Polish hospital are riveting. Part tale of intrigue, one sees how different factions of the Polish community played one another off against each other and how differences over the past, even more than over the future, made co-operation difficult at best—and often impossible. This was true even while a common enemy should have united the community—exiles as well as natives. I was struck by the parallels with the struggles within the Jewish community and the absence of unity. As Jews absorbed much of Polish culture and Polish ways in their seven-century sojourn in Poland, the converse is also true.

This is a work of scholarship. The authors, one American and one Polish, are both journalists. They write without jargon and with a breeziness that permits quick reading, but they have done their homework. They have examined documents and records of the Polish government-in-exile and the Office of Strategic Services among many others. Thus, the recollections of oral history are enhanced by documentary material, and each memory is weighed. Confirmation is sought. Speculation is described as such.

The authors clear up one misidentification in Karski's testimony. Prior to his departure from Poland, he was sent to a concentration camp previously identified at Bełżec; but the story of his visit was not credible. Small details did not add up, and they called into question his entire testimony, which was clearly so valuable. The authors identify the town as Izbica, midway between Lublin and Bełżec, some forty miles from each locality, and a sorting-point.

Adventure, political intrigue, and scholarship aside, what *Karski*—the man and the work—document with clarity is that, in addition to antisemitism, other factors were at work that prevented the Allies from acting on the information they received. The events Karski described were just incredible—in the most literal sense of the word—to people such as Justice Felix Frankfurter. They were indeed difficult, nay impossible, to comprehend. So, upon hearing the young messenger, the influential judge confessed that he *could not* believe what he was hearing. Decades later Zbigniew Brzezinski, who as a young boy heard Karski relate to his parents what he had seen and heard, described it as staggering and numbing. The only analogy offered by the former National Security Adviser to President Carter, who had sat for years within proximity to the 'black box' containing the codes for launching a nuclear strike, was to nuclear armageddon.

Credibility occurs only within a context. The real struggle, *Karski* demonstrates, was for the future of Poland. Most officials were interested in this, and the spoils of war and the shape of the post-war world. When the Jewish question was raised it was a side issue, worthy of a passing reference, but not of major attention. Poor Karski, who had seen what he had seen, and who had been a faithful messenger. He carried the truth to people who could not comprehend what he was saying; nor could he hold their attention. Historians cannot answer the question 'What if . . .?', but it burns through each page of this book.

Many years ago I honoured my colleague and friend Jan Karski by saying that he had 'redeemed the image of humanity precisely at the moment when by his very being, by his heroic deeds he indicts that image of humanity'. So too this book, so worthy of the life it depicts.

MICHAEL BERENBAUM
*United States Holocaust Memorial Museum*

STEVEN J. ZIPPERSTEIN
*Elusive Prophet: Ahad Ha'am and the Origins of Zionism*

(Berkeley and Los Angeles: University of California Press, 1993)
pp. xxv + 386. ISBN 0-520-08111-0

A bitter, gloomy, carping, defensive, unoriginal, vain, self-absorbed, arrogant, jealous, depressive, demanding, priggish, self-righteous man, who was generally unwilling to lead those who wished to follow him, who was cruel and exploitative towards his father, cold and distant towards his children, and often dismissive and patronizing towards his disciples, Asher Ginzberg, or Ahad Ha'am (One of the People), the pen-name by which he was generally known, never even began the masterpiece he planned to write. He did not seem destined for greatness.

He failed to recognize any value in Theodor Herzl's contributions to Zionism, was blind to the potential of the kibbutz, and sensed none of the power of Yiddish or Jewish folklore for the east European Jewish masses. He tended to disdain those masses and to fear democracy; his own followers frequently ignored his teachings. He vastly underestimated the import of the Balfour Declaration. Indeed, who would have guessed he was destined for Zionist canonization?

All of these character flaws and misperceptions notwithstanding, Ahad Ha'am was enshrined in the Zionist pantheon early in his career, and he has remained secure there since his death in 1926. This unlikely apotheosis is the subject of Professor Zipperstein's masterly work.

Unlike most earlier books about Ahad Ha'am, this is not a hagiography. It is also not an intellectual biography; the sources of Ahad Ha'am's ideas, the author asserts, are too readily recognized by anyone conversant with nineteenth-century European thought to make such an exercise worth while. Nor, for that matter, is Zipperstein concerned with his subject's personal life, although some of the book's most convincing passages describe the Ginzberg family and the relationships of 'the elusive prophet' to his acolytes. In large measure *explication de texte*, the book examines Ahad Ha'am's writings in the context of his public life.

The personification of truth in the Jewish world (p. 242), Ahad Ha'am was a mythologizer of himself. He was a writer who saw (or at least depicted) his life's work as neatly constructed and all of a piece, with a beginning, a climax, and a conclusion, as if written beforehand by a skilful novelist. (In fact, Zipperstein shows, there were many loose ends.) According to this vision, his career and public life began in 1889 with the essay 'This is not the Way', which outlined his plan 'to replace Judaism's theological foundations with national–cultural ones' (p. 35), and peaked with the essay 'Truth from Palestine' (1891), which disavowed the 'emigrationist policies' of the practical Zionists, many of whom thought they were living out his ideas in building the Jewish homeland institution by institution. It culminated with the essay 'Summation' (1912), in which he celebrated some of the achievements of the Jewish colonists in Palestine while casting doubt on the probability of their ever becoming truly rooted in its soil, one of Zionism's most fundamental goals.

In between and afterwards came other essays, including two, 'Moses' and 'The Supremacy of Reason', in which he discussed the nature of Jewish leadership and implicitly justified his own behaviour, as well as journalistic pieces; the founding and editing of a Hebrew journal, *Hashiloah*; an attempt to shape Zionism (the word had not yet been coined) through a secret society, the Bnei Moshe; and close work during the First World War with Chaim Weizmann on the negotiations that led to the Balfour Declaration. Ahad Ha'am acquired his Zionist fame on the strength of these after-hours activities. (He earned his living managing his father's enterprises until they failed, probably because of him; later he worked for the Wissotzky Tea Company in Russia and London.) But his essays aroused fierce controversy with their harsh, cranky criticism of any and all Zionist achievements; he had to be removed as editor of *Hashiloah* because his uncompromising standards were pushing the journal to bankruptcy; the Bnei Moshe disintegrated, partly because of his own equivocating leadership; and his role as Weizmann's adviser was not much publicized. What then accounted for his stature in the Zionist movement?

According to Zipperstein, some of Ahad Ha'am's weaknesses and failures were also his strengths. The dyspeptic, thoroughly cerebral, ambivalent approach that ensured he would not succumb to the euphoria or the single-mindedness that gripped Zionist enthusiasts like Herzl allowed him to serve as the conscience of the movement. Although much resented, that function often brought about the re-evaluation and improvement of policies. As 'the preeminent intellectual of Jewish nationalism' (p. 253), he was not always able to comprehend the problems of the masses; but he could weigh judiciously the proffered solutions to those problems.

He had other strengths, too, as Zipperstein points out. Despite the appearance of rigidity, he often displayed flexibility and realism, qualities that helped to keep Weizmann from committing an irredeemable *faux pas* during the First World War. Ahad Ha'am proposed a secular Judaism to Jews whose faith was waning, but he had no ambivalence regarding his Jewishness. His lack of self-hatred resonated even with opponents. As much as anything else, time proved him right with regard to Palestine. In the end, the building-blocks of Jewish settlement there proved to be the colonies and the cultural institutions that he had insisted on; and they had been built in the careful, gradual way he proposed. When the charter first sought by Herzl was achieved in the Balfour Declaration, it was the institutions built by his followers that provided the infrastructure for its realization. Although he was too sour, and by then too ill, to gain much pleasure from it, he did acknowledge his ultimate triumph.

One cannot help but doubt any explanation of the success of such a negative personality. But if Zipperstein has not quite squared the circle here, he has come as close as possible. There are some technical problems with the volume: the occasional ponderous sentence; references to pages in the collected works, not to individual essays, making for confusion; errors in Hebrew translation and transliteration; the misreading of a poem ostensibly in memory of Ahad Ha'am's father (it is even more disrespectful than Zipperstein claims). But these are quibbles. *Elusive Prophet* is a very significant book that provides a definitive reading, for now at least, of some of Zionism's seminal texts, and a fresh look at their creator and his world.

MICHAEL BROWN
*York University*

# Bibliography of
# Polish–Jewish Studies 1994

The bibliography is arranged according to the framework listed overleaf.
Readers should note related headings.
All titles are given in their original languages.
The list includes supplementary items that appeared in 1993 but were omitted
from the list for that year.

## REFERENCE WORKS

CASTELLO, ELENA ROMERO, and KAPON, URIEL MACIAS (eds.) *The Jews and Europe: 2000 Years of History* (New York: Holt, 1994); pp. 239. ISBN 0805035265.

CURTIS, GLENN E. (ed.), *Poland: A Country Study*, 3rd edn. (Washington: Library of Congress, 1994); pp. xlix + 356. ISBN 0844408271.

ELYASHEVICH, DMITRI A., *Dokumental'nye materialy po istorii evreev v arkhivakh SNG i stran Baltii: Predvaritl'nyi spisok arkhivnykh fondov* (St Petersburg: Acropolis, 1994); pp. 134. ISBN 5865850237.

*Kto był kim w drugiej Rzeczypospolitej*, ed. J. Majchrowski, G. Mazur, and S. Kamil (Warsaw: Polska Oficyna Wydawnicza BGW, 1994); pp. 579. ISBN 8370665691.

LENIUS, BRIAN JOHN, *Genealogical Gazzeteer of Galicia* (Anola, Man.: Lenius, 1994); pp. 375. ISBN 0969878303.

PAUL, BARBARA DOTTS, *The Polish–German Borderlands: An Annotated Bibliography* (Westport, Conn.: Greenwood, 1994); pp. xii + 201. ISBN 0313291624.

SANFORD, GEORGE, and GOZLECKA-SANFORD, ADRIANA, *Historical Dictionary of Poland* (Metuchen, NJ: Scarecrow, 1994); pp. xii + 339. ISBN 0810828189.

SCHEDRIN, VASSILY, and BANCHIK, NADEZHDA, *Dokumental'nye istochniki po istorii evreev v arkhivakh SNG: Putevoditel'* (Moscow: Izd-vo Evreiskoi Nasledie, 1994).

## FESTSCHRIFTEN AND COLLECTED STUDIES

CIESIELSKI, STANISŁAW, KULAK, TERESA, and MATWIJOWSKI, KRYSTYNA (eds.), *Polska–Kresy–Polacy: Studia historyczne* (Wrocław: Wydawnictwo Uniwerstytetu Wrocławskiego, 1994); pp. 358. ISBN 8322911297.

ETTINGER, SHMUEL, *Bein Polin leRusiyah* (Jerusalem: Merkaz Zalman Shazar and Mossad Bialik, 1994); pp. 467. ISBN 9652270938.

## LITERATURE, LINGUISTICS, AND THE ARTS

### Belles-lettres

BRANDSTAETTER, ROMAN, *Ja jestem Żyd z 'Wesela'*, new ed. (Cracow: Baran i Suszczyński, 1993); pp. 67. ISBN 8385845011.

FORMAN, FRIEDA, WOLFE, MARGIE and SWARTZ, SARAH (eds.), *Found Treasures: Stories by Yiddish Women Writers* (Toronto: Second Story, 1994); pp. 391. ISBN 0929005538.

GOLD, AVNER, *Le'or hadimdumim: Meye'ush letikvah* (Jerusalem: Yaḥdav, 1994); pp. 174.

HIRSH, AZRIEL, *Miyom kipurim zeh* (Jerusalem: Reuven Mas, 1994); pp. 357.

SACHER-MASOCH, LEOPOLD, RITTER VON, *A Light for Others and Other Jewish Tales from Galicia*, trans. Michael T. O'Pecko (Riverside, Calif.: Ariadne, 1994); pp. vii + 338. ISBN 0929497937.

SINGER, ISAAC BASHEVIS, *Meshugah*, trans. I. B. Singer and Nili Wachtel (New York: Farrar, Straus, Giroux, 1994); pp. 232. ISBN 0374208476.

WIATER, STANISŁAW JÓZEF, and WIATER, PRZEMYSŁAW (eds.), *Przemyśl w oczach pisarzy: Antologia XX wieku* (London: Poets and Painters, 1994); unpaginated. ISBN 898923051.

## Literary Studies and Criticism

ADAMCZYK-GARBOWSKA, MONIKA, *Polska Singera: Rozstanie i powrót* (Lublin: Wydawnictwo Unywersytetu Marii Curie-Skłodowskiej, 1994); pp. 197. ISBN 8322706243.

ALTER, ROBERT, *Hebrew and Modernity* (Bloomington: Indiana University Press, 1994); pp. xi + 192. ISBN 0253208564.

KITOWSKA-ŁYSIAK, M. (ed.), *Bruno Schultz: In Memoriam, 1892–1942*, 2nd ed. (Lublin: FIS, 1994); pp. 242. ISBN 8385671102.

KLANSKA, MARIA, *Aus dem Schtetl in die Welt, 1772 bis 1938: Ostjüdische Autobiographien in deutscher Sprache* (Vienna: Bohlau, 1994); pp. 470. ISBN 3205980247.

LÖW, RYSZARD, *Hebrajska obecność Juliana Tuwima: Szkice bibliograficzne* (Tel Aviv: Hasefer, 1993); pp. 48.

MARKIEWICZ, HENRYK, *Literatura i historia* (Cracow: Universitas Kraków, 1994); pp. 376. ISBN 8370522173.

WEINTRAUB, WIKTOR, *O współczesnych i o sobie: Wspomnienia, sylwetki, szkice literackie*, ed. Stanisław Barańczak (Cracow: Znak, 1994); pp. 556. ISBN 8370061273.

WERSES, SHMUEL, *Relations between Poles and Jews in S. Y. Agnon's Work* (Studies of the Center for Research on the History and Culture of Polish Jews, Hebrew University, Jerusalem; Jerusalem: Magnes, 1994); pp. 128. ISBN 9652238732.

## Linguistics

GELLER, EWA, *Jidysz: Język Żydów polskich* (Warsaw: Wydawnictwo Naukowe Państwowe Wydawnictwo Naukowe, 1994); pp. 261. ISBN 8301112670.

## Visual Arts

AN-SKI, SEMYON, *The Jewish Artistic Heritage: An Album*, intro. Abram Efros, comm. Alexander Kantsedikas (Moscow: RA, 1994); pp. 128. ISBN 5851640243.

KÖPPEN, MANUEL (ed.), *Kunst und Literatur noch Auschwitz* (Berlin: Erich Schmidt, 1993); pp. 411. ISBN 3503030700.

*Painting and Sculpture*

BUDZIAREK, MAREK, *Judaica łodzkie z zbiorach muzealnych i zasobach archiwalnych* (Łódź: Museum Historii Miasta Łodzi, 1994); pp. 204. ISBN 8390185105.

HOSHEN, SARAH HAREL (ed.), *Otsarot genuzim: Osefei omanut yehudit miGalitsiyah mehamuzeion le'etnografiyah ule'omanut beLevov* (Tel Aviv: Beit Hatefutsot, 1994); pp. 57. ISBN 9654250039.

*Film and Photography*

KLANSKA, MARIA, *Jüdisches Städtebild, Krakau*, photographs by Stanisław Markowski (Frankfurt-on-Main. Jüdischer Verlag, 1994); pp. 276.

## HISTORY

### Documents and Sources

BORZYMINSKA, ZOFIA (ed.), *Dzieje Żydów w Polsce: Wybór tekstów źródłowych XIX wieku* (Warsaw: Żydowski Instytut Historyczny, 1994); pp. 130. ISBN 8385888039.

*Pamiętniki Reba Dowa z Bolechowa, 1723–1805*, ed. and trans. Roman Marcinkowski (Warsaw: Formica, 1994); pp. 120. ISBN 8390014603.

ZARIZ, RUTH (ed.), *Mikhtevei ḥalutsim miPolin hakevushah, 1940–1944* (Ramat Efal: Yad Tabenkin and Beit Lohamei Ha geta'ot, 1994); pp. v + 319. ISBN 965282044X.

ZBIKOWSKI, ANDRZEJ, *Ideologia antysemicka, 1848–1914: Wybór tekstów źródłowych* (Warsaw: Żydowski Instytut Historyczny, 1994); pp. 142. ISBN 838588808X.

### Biographies

ALFASSI, YITSHAK, *Sarei hatorah: Me'orot me'olam harabanut* (Jerusalem: Karmel, 1993); pp. 370. ISBN 9654070553.

BAUMOL, YEHOSHUA, *A Blaze in the Darkening Gloom: The Life of Rav Meir Shapiro*, trans. and ed. Charles Wengrov (Jerusalem: Feldheim, 1994); pp. xxiii + 408. ISBN 0873066758.

DANSKY, MIRAM, *Rebbetzin Grunfeld: The Life of Judith Grunfeld, Courageous Pioneer of the Bais Yaakov Movement and Jewish Rebirth* (Brooklyn: Mesorah, 1994); pp. 336. ISBN 0899061192.

GAVISH, GALIA, *Makom tov legadel devorim*, ed. Aviv Meltser (Tel Aviv: Yaron Golan, 1994); pp. 134.

GLÜCKEL OF HAMELN, *Die Memoiren der Glückel von Hameln*, trans. Bertha Pappenheim (Weinheim: Belz Atheneum, 1904); pp. xvii + 320. ISBN 3895470406.

KORNBLUTH, WILLIAM, *Sentenced to Remember: My Legacy of Life in pre-1939 Poland and Sixty-Eight Months of Nazi Occupation*, ed. Carl Calendar (Bethlehem, P. A.: Lehigh University Press, 1994); pp. 228. ISBN 0934223300.

STIFTEL, SHOSHANAH, 'Darko shel Nahum Sokolow min hapositivism hayehudi-polani el hatenu'a hatsiyonit', Ph.D. dissertation (Tel Aviv: Tel Aviv University, 1994); pp. 240.

SVIDERCOSCHI, GIAN FRANCO, *Letter to a Jewish Friend: The Simple and Extraordinary Story of Karol Wojtyla's Jewish Friend* (London: Hodder & Stoughton, 1994); pp. 93. ISBN 034061014X.

TUSZYŃSKA, AGATA, *Singer: Pejzaże pamięci* (Gdańsk: Marabut, 1994); pp. 344. ISBN 8385893040.

WEINTRAUB, JACOB, *Jacob's Ladder: From the Bottom of the Warsaw Ghetto to the Top of New York's Art World* (Lanham, Md.: Madison, 1994); pp. x + 285. ISBN 1568330359.

WINAWER, H. M. (ed.), *The Winawer Saga* (London: Winawer, 1994); pp. 444. ISBN 095241290X.

WOOD, E. THOMAS, and JANKOWSKI, STANISŁAW M., *Karski: How One Man Tried to Stop the Holocaust* (New York: Wiley, 1994); pp. 320. ISBN 0471018562.

YARON, HAYYIM YEHUDAH, *Toledot mishpaḥat Grosman miLodz, Polin, umikhtavim le'erets Yisra'el: MiNovember 1935 ad sof August 1939* (Jerusalem: Yaron, 1994); pp. 240.

ZAMIR, ISRAEL, *Avi: Yitshak Bashevis Singer* (Tel Aviv: Sifriyat Poalim, 1994); pp. 192. ISBN 9654480379.

ŻEBROWSKI, RAFAL, *Mojżesz Schorr i jego listy do Ludwika Gumplowicza* (Warsaw: Żydowski Instytut Historyczny, 1994); pp. 205. ISBN 8385888047.

## Historiography

FRANKEL, JONATHAN, *Reshaping the Past: Jewish History and the Historians*, Studies in Contemporary Jewry, (New York: Oxford University Press, 1994); pp. 384. ISBN 0195093550.

RABA, JOEL, *Bein zikaron lehakhehashah: Gezerot tah vetat bereshimot benei hazeman uvere'i haketivah hahistorit* (Tel Aviv: Center for the History of Polish Jewry, Tel Aviv University, 1994); pp. vii + 381. ISBN 9653380176.

## General Works

CANTOR, NORMAN F., *The Sacred Chain: The History of the Jews* (New York: HarperCollins, 1994); pp. xxii + 472. ISBN 006016747.

CRAMPTON, R. J., *Eastern Europe in the Twentieth Century* (London: Routledge, 1994): pp. xx + 475. ISBN 0415053463.

ETTINGER, SHMUEL, *Bein Polin leRusiyah* (Jerusalem: Merkaz Zalman Shazar and Mossad Bialik, 1994); pp. 467. ISBN 9652270938.

MATWIJOWSKI, KRYSTYN (ed.), *Z historii ludności żydowskiej w Polsce i na Śląsku* (Wrocław: Wydawnictwo Uniwersytetu Wrocławskiego, 1994); pp. 250. ISBN 8322910568.

ROSMAN, MOSHE, *Hayehudim bekalkalat Polin: Defusei irgun vehanhagah, Polin: Berakin betoledot yehudei mizrah-Eiropah vetarbutam*, Units 3 and 4 (Jerusalem: Open University of Israel, 1994); pp. 154. ISBN 9653026380.

STEPHAN, INGE, SCHILLING, SABINE, and WEIGEL, SIGRID (eds.), *Jüdische Kultur und Weiblichkeit in der Moderne* (Vienna: Bohlau, 1994); pp. 351. ISBN 3412004928.

TRAVERSO, ENZO, *The Marxists and the Jewish Question: A History of a Debate, 1843–1943* (Atlantic Highlands, NJ: Humanities Press, 1994); pp. ix + 276. ISBN 0391038060.

TURNAU, IRENA, *European Occupational Dress from the Fourteenth to the Eighteenth Century* (Warsaw: PAN, 1994); pp. 202. ISBN 8385463267.

TURNIANSKY, CHAVA, *Lashon, hinukh, vehaskalah bemizrah Eiropah, Polin: Perakim betoledot yehudei mizrah Eiropah vetarbutam*, Unit 7 (Jerusalem: Open University of Israel, 1994); pp. 96. ISBN 9653026402.

WOLFE, ROBERT, *Remember to Dream: A History of Jewish Radicalism* (New York: Jewish Radical Education Project, 1994); pp. 368.

WOLFF, LARRY, *Inventing Eastern Europe* (Stanford, Calif.: Stanford University Press, 1994); pp. xii + 419. ISBN 0804723141.

## To 1648

BOGUCKA, MARIA, *Staropolskie obyczaje XVI–XVII wieku* (Warsaw: Państwowy Instytut Wydawniczy, 1994); pp. 229. ISBN 8306023471.

GORECKI, PIOTR, *Economy, Society, and Lordship in Medieval Poland, 1100–1250* (New York: Holmes & Meier, 1994); pp. 336. ISBN 0841913188.

ROWELL, S. C., *Lithuania Ascending: A Pagan Empire within East Central Europe* (Cambridge: Cambridge University Press, 1994); pp. xx + 375. ISBN 052145011X.

SEDLAR, JEAN W., *East Central Europe in the Middle Ages, 1000–1500* (Seattle: University of Washington Press, 1994); pp. 552. ISBN 0295972904.

## 1648–1795

CLARK, CHRISTOPHER, *The Politics of Conversion: Missionary Protestantism and the Jews in Prussia, 1728–1941* (New York: Oxford University Press, 1994); pp. 390. ISBN 0198204566.

GOLD, AVNER, *Shenat haherev: Eruei hadamim vehagezerot shel 5408–5409* (Jerusalem: Yahdav, 1994); pp. 181.

LESZCZYNSKI, ANATOL, *Sejm Żydów Korony, 1623–1764* (Warsaw: Żydowski Instytut Historyczny, 1994); pp. 184. ISBN 8385888063.

LIBERA, ZDZISŁAW, *Rozważania o wieku tolerancji rozumu i gustu* (Warsaw: Państwowy Instytut Wydawniczy, 1994); pp. 400. ISBN 8306021118.

MĄCZAK, ANTONI, *Klientela: Nieformalne systemy władzy w Polsce i Europie, XVI–XVII wieku* (Warsaw: Państwowy Instytut Wydawniczy, 1994); pp. 229. ISBN 9306023471.

MICHALSKI, JERZY (ed.), *Lud Żydowski w Narodzie polskim: Materiały sesji naukowej w Warszawie, 15–16 Wrzesień 1992* (Warsaw: Instytut Historii Polskiej Akademii Nauk and Center for Research on the History and Culture of Polish Jews, Hebrew University, Jerusalem, 1994); pp. 120. ISBN 8390084686.

## 1795–1918

BORZYMINSKA, ZOFIA (ed.), *Dzieje Żydów w Polsce: Wybór tekstów źródłowych XIX wieku* (Warsaw: Żydowski Instytut Historyczny, 1994); pp. 130. ISBN 8385888039.

GONEN, RIVKA (ed.), *Back to the Shtetl: An-Sky and the Jewish Ethnographic Expedition, 1912–1914* (Jerusalem: Israel Museum, 1994); pp. 156 Hebrew + pp. 20 English. ISBN 9652781525.

HOEDL, KLAUS, *Als Bettler in die Leopoldstadt: Galizische Juden auf dem Weg nach Wien* (Vienna: Bohlau, 1994); pp. 331. ISBN 3205981510.

## 1918–1939

BARZILAI, ZVI, *Tenu'at haBund bePolin bein shetei milhamot ha'olam* (Jerusalem: Karmel, 1994); pp. xvi + 251.

CRAMPTON, R. J., *Eastern Europe in the Twentieth Century* (London: Routledge, 1994); pp. xx + 475. ISBN 0415053463.

HELLER, CELIA S., *On the Edge of Destruction: Jews of Poland between the Two World Wars*, 2nd ed. (Detroit: Wayne State University Press, 1994); pp. xvi + 383. ISBN 0814324940.

KAHAN, ME'IR, *Homat hashetikah nifretsah: Koho shel iton*, ed. Yitshak Alfassi and Yosef Kister (Tel Aviv: Makhon Jabotinsky, 1993); pp. 174. ISBN 9654160013.

KAMIŃSKA-SZMAJ, IRENA, *Judzi, zohydza, ze czci odziera: Język propagandy politycznej w prasie 1919–1923* (Wrocław: Towarzystwo Przyjaciół Polonistyki Wrocławskiej, 1994); pp. 231. ISBN 8370910084.

KORNBLUM, JOSEF, *Ziemia przeobiecana* (Cracow: Oficyna Literacka, 1993); pp. 444. ISBN 8385158855.

MICH, WŁODZIMIERZ, *Obcy w polskim domu: Nacjonalistyczne koncepcje rozwiązania problemu mniejszości narodowych, 1918–1939* (Lublin: Wydawnictwo Uniwersytetu Marii Curie-Skłodowskiej, 1994); pp. 144. ISBN 8322706367.

MODRAS, RONALD, *The Catholic Church and Antisemitism: Poland, 1933–1939* (Reading: Harwood, 1994); pp. 250. ISBN 3718655683.

ZYNDUL, JOLANTA, *Zajścia antyżydowskie w Polsce w latach, 1935–1937* (Warsaw: Fundacja im. K. Kelles-Krauza, 1994); pp. 96. ISBN 838583821X.

## 1939–1945: The Second World War and the Holocaust

### General Works

CESARANI, DAVID (ed.), *The Final Solution: Origins and Implementation* (London: Routledge, 1994); pp. x + 318. ISBN 0415099544.

GRYNBERG, DANIEL, and SZAPIRO, PAWEŁ (eds.), *Holocaust z perspektywy półwieczá. Pięćdziesiąta rocznica powstania w getcie Warszawskim: Materiały z konferencji zorganizowanej przez ŻIH* (Warsaw: Żydowski Instytut Historyczny, 1994); pp. 368. ISBN 8385888055.

HARTMAN, GEOFFREY (ed.), *Holocaust Remembrance: The Shapes of Memory* (Oxford: Blackwell, 1994); pp. xi + 306. ISBN 1557861250.

KATZ, STEVEN T., *The Holocaust in Historical Context*, i: *The Holocaust and Mass Death before the Modern Age* (New York: Oxford University Press, 1994); pp. xv + 702. ISBN 0195072200.

PACY, JAMES S., and WERTHEIMER, ALAN P., (eds.), *Perspectives on the Holocaust: Essays in Honor of Raul Hilberg* (Boulder, Colo.: Westview, 1994); pp. vii + 195. ISBN 0813320348.

### Reference Works

*A Catalogue of the Dr David Azrieli Holocaust Collection at Concordia University* (Montreal, 1994); pp. iii + 304. ISBN 0889472068.

DREW, MARGARET A., *Annotated Bibliography* [Holocaust] (Washington: US Holocaust Memorial Museum, 1994); pp. 32.

EDELHEIT, ABRAHAM J., and EDELHEIT, HERSHEL, *History of the Holocaust: A Handbook and Dictionary* (Boulder, Colo.: Westview, 1993); pp. xix + 524. ISBN 0813314119.

FRIEDMAN, SAUL S. (ed.), *Holocaust Literature: A Handbook of Critical, Historical, and Literary Writings* (Westport, Conn.: Greenwood, 1993); pp. xxx + 677. ISBN 0313262217.

SILVERSTEIN, LEAH, *The Holocaust: A Selected Monographic Bibliography* (Washington: Silverstein, 1994); pp. 259.

### Special Studies

BARTROP, PAUL ROBERT, *Australia and the Holocaust, 1933–1945* (Melbourne: Australian Scholarly Publishing, 1994); pp. xvii + 304. ISBN 1875606122.

BENDER, SARAH, 'Yehudei Bialystok bemilḥemet ha'olam hasheniyah, 1939–1943', Ph.D. dissertation (Hebrew University, Jerusalem, 1994); pp. 401.

BRECHER, ELINOR, *Schindler's Legacy: The Stories of the List Survivors* (New York: Dutton, 1994); pp. xxxvii + 442. ISBN 0525939415.

DOBROSZYCKI, LUCJAN, *Reptile Journalism: The Official Polish-Language Press under the Nazis, 1939–1945* (New Haven: Yale University Press, 1994); pp. 192. ISBN 0300052774.

ENGELKING, BARBARA, *Zagłada i pamięć: Doświadczenie Holocaustu i jego konsekwencje opisane na podstawie relacji autobiograficznych* (Warsaw: IFiS PAN, 1994); pp. 318. ISBN 8301110708.

FOGELMAN, EVA, *Conscience and Courage: Rescuers of Jews during the Holocaust* (New York: Doubleday, 1994); pp. xx + 393. ISBN 0385420277.

FRIEDMANN, T. (ed.), *SS- und Polizeiführer Globocnik in Lublin und ein Bericht über de Judenvernichtung im General-Gouvernement in Polen, 1941–1944: Dokument-Smmlung* (Haifa: Institute of Documentation in Israel for the investigation of Nazi War Crimes, 1994). Various paginations.

GRILAK, MENAHEM, *El hagardom uveḥazarah: Sipuro hanorah shel maḥaneh hahashmadah Treblinka* (Tel Aviv: Kesharim, 1994); pp. 360.

GRYNBERG, HENRYK, *Dzieci Syjonu* (Warsaw: Karta, 1994); pp. 166. ISBN 8390067625.

GUSHEE, DAVID P., *The Righteous Gentiles of the Holocaust: A Christian Interpretation* (Minneapolis: Fortress, 1994); pp. xiv + 258. ISBN 0800629027.

GUTMAN, ISRAEL, *Resistance: The Warsaw Ghetto Uprising* (Boston: Houghton Mifflin, 1994), pp. xx + 277. ISBN 0395601991.

JADACKI, JACEK JULIUSZ, and MARKIEWICZ, BARBARA (eds.), '... A Mądrości zło nie premoże: Wybór tekstów* (Warsaw: Polskie Towarzystwo Filozofie, 1993); pp. 180. ISBN 8390130408.

LACAPRA, DOMINICK, *Representing the Holocaust: History, Theory, Trauma* (Ithaca, NY: Cornell University Press, 1994); pp. xiii + 230. ISBN 0801429978.

LANGBEIN, HERMANN, *Against all Hope: Resistance in the Nazi Concentration Camps, 1938–1945*, trans. Harry Zohn (New York: Paragon House, 1994); pp. 502. ISBN 1557783632.

LUKAS, RICHARD C., *Did the Children Cry? Hitler's War against Jewish and Polish Children, 1939–1945* (New York: Hippocrene, 1994); pp. 263. ISBN 0781802423.

MEIRTCHAK, BENJAMIN, *Jewish Military Casualties in the Polish Armies in World War II*, i: *Jewish Soldiers and Officers of the Polish People's Army Killed and Missing in Action* (Tel Aviv: World Federation of Jewish Fighters, Partisans, and Camp Inmates and Association of Jewish War Veterans of Polish Armies in Israel, 1994); pp. 108.

PELED, YA'EL, *Krakov hayehudit, 1939–1943: Amidah, maḥteret, ma'avak* (Kibbutz Loḥamei Hageta'ot: Beit Loḥamei Hageta'ot, 1993); pp. 360.

POLEN, NEHEMIA, *The Holy Fire: The Teachings of Rabbi Kalonymus Kalman Shapira, the Rebbe of the Warsaw Ghetto* (Northvale, NJ, Aronson, 1994); pp. xix + 208. ISBN 0876688423.

RINGELBLUM, EMMANUEL, *Ketavim aḥaronim: Yaḥasei polanim-yehudim, Yanu'ar 1943–April 1944*, ed. I. Gutman, Y. Kermish, and Y. Shaham (Jerusalem: Yad Vashem and Beit Loḥamei Hageta'ot, 1994); pp. ix + 391. ISBN 9653080229.

ROKEAH, MORDEKHAI, *Kuntres haderekh* (Jerusalem: Makhon meḥkar ve'arkhiyon keter malkhut, 1994); pp. 45.

SAKOWSKA, RUTA, *Die zweite Etappe ist der Tod: NS-Ausrottungspolitik gegen die polnischen Juden, gesehn mit den Augen der Opfer: Ein Historischer Essay und ausgewälte Dokumente aus dem Ringelblum-archiv* (Berlin: Hentrich, 1993); pp. 278. ISBN 3894680776.

SCHWEID, ELIEZER, *Bein ḥurban leyeshu'ah: Teguvot shel hagut ḥaredit lasho'ah bizemanah* (Tel Aviv: Hakibbutz Hame'uḥad, 1994); pp. 264.

SCHWEID, ELIEZER, *Wrestling until Day-Break: Searching for Meaning in the Thinking on the Holocaust* (Lanham, Md.: University Press of America; Jerusalem: Jerusalem Center for Public Affairs, 1994); pp. xxvi + 367. ISBN 0819193585.

SEEBER, EVA, and FELDMAN, MARIAN, *Beiträge zur Geschichte des Warschauer Ghettos* (Leipzig: Rosa Luxemburg Verein, 1994); pp. 66. ISBN 3929994135.

SHAMIR, YOSEF, *Shemu'el Breslav: Hama'avak vehatikvah, geto Varshah, 1940–1943*, ed. Levi Deror (Tel Aviv: Moreshet, 1994); pp. 102.

SWORD, KEITH, *Deportation and Exile: Poles in the Soviet Union, 1938–1948* (New York: St Martin's, in association with the School of Slavonic and East European Studies, University of London, 1994); pp. xiii + 269. ISBN 0312123973.

TILL, BASTIAN, *Auschwitz und die 'Auschwitz Lüge': Massenmord und Geschichtsfalschung* (Munich: Beck, 1994); pp. 102. ISBN 3406374484.

TOMASZEWSKI, IRENE, and WERBOWSKA, TECIA, *Zegota: The Wartime Rescue of Jews* (Montreal: Price-Patterson, 1994); pp. 171. ISBN 0969577168.

TUCHEL, JOHANNES, *Die Inspektion der Konzentrationslager, 1938–1945: Das System des Terrors* (Berlin: Hentrich, 1994); pp. 232. ISBN 3894681586.

URBANSKI, KRZYSZTOF, *Zagłada ludności żydowskiej Kielc, 1939–1945* (Kielce: Kieleckie Towarzystwo Naukowe, 1994); pp. xviii + 196.

WOOD, E. THOMAS, and JANKOWSKI, STANISŁAW M., *Karski: How One Man Tried to Stop the Holocaust* (New York: 1994); pp. 320. ISBN 0471018562.

YOUNG, JAMES E. (ed.), *Holocaust Memorials: The Art of Memory in History* (Munich: Prestel, 1994); pp. 194. ISBN 3791313223.

ZARIZ, RUTH (ed.), *Mikhtevei ḥalutsim miPolin hakevushah, 1940–1944* (Ramat Efal: Yad Tabenkin and Beit Loḥamei Hageta'ot, 1994); pp. 319. ISBN 965282044X.

*Photographic Records*

PLANK, KARL ANDREWS, *Mother of the Wire Fence: Inside and Outside the Holocaust* (Louisville, K. Y.: Westminster and John Knox, 1994); pp. xii + 169. ISBN 0664252192.

*Memoirs*

BLADY-SZWAJGER, ADINA, *A więcej nic nie pamiętam* (Warsaw: Volumen, 1994); pp. 135. ISBN 8385233482.

BOCIAN, TOSIA, *Raḥashei haberosh* (Tel Aviv: Hakibbutz Hame'uḥad, 1994); pp. 184.

BRANDWEIN-ZEMIN, JANINA, *Ne'urim vetushiyah bamilḥamah: Zikhronot miyemei hasho'ah* (Tel Aviv: Golan, 1994); pp. iv + 147.

BREWSTER, EVA, *Progeny of Light, Vanished in Darkness* (Edmonton: NeWest, 1994); pp. viii + 268. ISBN 0920897754.

CHECINSKI, MICHAEL, *My Father's Watch* (Jerusalem: Gefen, 1994); pp. 246. ISBN 9652291129.

CHIRURG, RIVA, *Bridge of Sorrow, Bridge of Hope*, trans. Arlene and Jerry Aviram (Berkeley: Judah L. Magnes Museum, 1994); pp. xi + 192. ISBN 0943376610.

DEUTSCH, MINA, *Mina's Story: A Doctor's Memoir of the Holocaust* (Toronto: ECW, 1994); pp. 184. ISBN 1550222120.

DRIX, SAMUEL, *Witness to Annihilation: Surviving the Holocaust, a Memoir* (Washington: Brassey's, 1994); pp. xvi + 249. ISBN 028810872.

DRORI, YA'AKOV, *Hashevu'ah* (Tel Aviv: Hakibbutz Hame'uḥad and Beit Loḥamei Hageta'ot, 1994); pp. 141.

FAITELSON, ALEX, *In shturem un gerangl* (Vilnius: Lituanus, 1993); pp. 420. ISBN 5899570164. Hebrew version: *Basufah uvama'avak*, trans. A. Brauner (Tel Aviv: Perets, 1994); pp. 384.

FINEGOLD, YEHUDA ARYEH, *Ikh bin geblibn lebn: Shviderlikhe shilderungn fun a Yid vas hat durkhgelebt di shreklikhe yahrn fun 5699–5705 in Lodz, Varshaver geto, Treblinka, Auschwitz, Bergen Belsen* (Jerusalem, 1993); pp. 228.

FINKELSTEIN, GENYA, *Genyah* (Tel Aviv: Yediot Aharonot, 1994); pp. xvi + 145. ISBN 9654480646.

FRIEDMAN, PESKA, with Fayge Silverman, *Going Forward: A True Story of Courage, Hope and Perseverance* (New York: Mesorah, 1994); pp. 269. ISBN 0899066151.

FRIEDRICH, OTTO, *The Kingdom of Auschwitz* (New York: Harper Perennials, 1994); pp. xiv + 112. ISBN 0060976403.

GABEL, DINA, *Arayot basheleg* (Jerusalem: Feldheim, 1994); pp. 507. ISBN 1560621273.

GINSBURG, BERNARD L., *A Wayfarer in a World in Upheaval*, ed. with intro. by Nathan Kravetz (San Bernardino, Calif.: Borgo, 1993); pp. 128. ISBN 0809504006.

GOLDBERG, CHAIM, *I Remember Like Now: The Odyssey of a Polish Jew*, as told to Jo Atkinson (Windsor, Ont.: Black Moss, 1994); pp. vii + 74. ISBN 088753239X.

JACOBS, BENJAMIN, *The Dentist of Auschwitz* (Lexington, Ky.: University Press of Kentucky, 1994); 240 pp. ISBN 0813118735.

KARAY, FELICJA, *Hamavet hatsahov: Maḥaneh ha'avodah Skarzysko-Kamienna*, ed. Y. Rav (Tel Aviv: Tel Aviv University and Yar Vashem, 1994); pp. ii + 436. ISBN 9653080288.

KEGEL, ME'IR, *Kenafayim herukhot* (Kibbutz Loḥamei Hageta'ot: Beit Loḥamei Hageta'ot, 1994); pp. 222.

KOMBLUTH, WILLIAM, *Sentenced to Remember: My Legacy of Life in pre-1939 Poland and Sixty-Eight Months of Nazi Occupation*, ed. Carl Calendar (Bethlehem, P.A.: Lehigh University Press, 1994); pp. 228. ISBN 0934223300.

KRAKOWSKI, AVRAHAM, *Counterfeit Lives*, with Avraham Yaakov Finkel (New York: CIS, 1994); pp. 317. ISBN 1560622687.

LASMAN, NOAH, *Hakevish*, trans. Aryeh Ben-Menahem and Yosef Rav (Tel Aviv: Misrad Habitaḥon, 1994); pp. 190. ISBN 9650507205.

LEITNER, ISABELLA, and LEITNER, IRVING A., *Isabella: From Auschwitz to Freedom* (New York: Anchor, 1994); pp. 223. ISBN 0385473184.

LEWIN, KURT, *A Journey through Illusions* (Santa Barbara, Calif.: Fithian, 1994); pp. 461. ISBN 1564740579.

LILIENBLUM, HENRY, *The Aftermath: A Survivor's Odyssey through War-Torn Europe* (Montreal: DC, 1994); pp. xi + 181. ISBN 0919688454.

MANDEL, EDMUND, *The Right Path: The Autobiography of a Survivor*, as told to Lynn K. Egerman (Hoboken, NJ: Ktav, 1994); pp. x + 389. ISBN 0881254983.

MARGOLIS-EDELMAN, ALINA, *Alla z Elementarza* (London: Aneks, 1994); pp. 137. ISBN 1897962045.

MATZNER, DAVID, with David Margolis, *The Muselman: The Diary of a Jewish Slave Laborer* (Hoboken, NJ: Ktav, 1994); pp. ix + 166. ISBN 0881254576.

MEIR, SIMHAH, *Ani Io Stashek: Ben yeshivah besherut ḥeil ha'avir haNatsi* (Jerusalem: Hamaḥlakah leḥinukh uletarbut toraniyim bagolah shel haHistadrut hatsiyonit ha'olamit, 1994); pp. 192.

MORGENS, FRANK, *Lata na skraju przepaści*, trans. J. Holzman (Warsaw: Alfa, 1994); pp. 216. ISBN 8370017452.

RAZIEL, ELIYAHU, *Boded bemistor* (Tel Aviv: Moreshet, 1993); pp. 119.

RONEN, AVIHU, and KOKHAVI, YEHOYAKIM, *Guf shelishi yaḥid: Biyografiyot shel ḥavrei tenu'ot no'ar bitekufat hasho'ah* (Moreshet, Beit Loḥamei Hageta'ot, and Yad Ya'ari, 1994); 2 vols. ISBN 965222510X.

RONEN, SHELOMOH, *Telyavnovkeh [Terebovlia] giv'at hamavet: Sefer te'udi* (Tel Aviv: Ronen, 1994); pp. 160.

ROSENFELD, OSKAR, *Wozu noch Welt: Aufzeichnungen aus dem Getto Lodz*, ed. Hanno Loewy (Frankfurt-on-Main: Neue Kritik, 1994); pp. 323. ISBN 3801502724.

ROTEM, SIMHA (Kazik), *Memoirs of a Warsaw Ghetto Fighter*, trans. Barbara Harshav (New Haven: Yale University Press, 1994); pp. 192. ISBN 0300057970.

RYMKIEWICZ, JAROSŁAW, *The Final Station*, trans. N. Taylor (New York: Farar, Straus, Giroux, 1994); pp. 327. ISBN 0374154953. Polish version: *Umschlagplatz* (Paris: Instytut Literacki, 1988); pp. 223. ISBN 2716801029.

SANIK, LEIBEL, *Someday We'll Be Free* (New York: CIS, 1994); pp. 303. ISBN 1560622679.

SEVERIN, GABRIEL, *Beḥurevot Varshah* (Tel Aviv: Yaron Golan, 1994); pp. 95.

SHAMIR, YOSEF, *Shemu'el Braslav: Hama'avak vehatikvah—Ghetto Varshah, 1940–1943*, ed. Levi Deror (Tel Aviv: Moreshet, 1994); pp. 190.

SHOHAM, BELLA, *Arukah hayetah haderekh* (Tel Aviv: Yaron Golan, 1994); pp. 297.

SLOWES, MIRA, *Moje trzy życia* (Tel Aviv: Kontury, 1994); pp. 235.

SZAJN-LEWIN, EUGENIA, *Aufzeichnungen aus dem Warschauer Ghetto: Juli 1942 bis April 1943*, trans. Roswitha Matwin-Buschmann (Leipzig: Reclam Verlag, 1994); pp. 133. ISBN 3379014974.

TENENBAUM, SAMUEL LIPA, *Lekh lekha: Get thee out of thy country* (New York: Shengold, 1993); pp. 266.

TESTYLER, JO, *Yaldei Slavkov*, intro. by Elie Wiesel, trans. Dinah Vintrob and Mikhael Bar-Tsevi (Tel Aviv: Yaron Golan, 1994); pp. 155. French version: *Les Enfants de Slawkow: Récit autobiographique* Paris, 1992.

WAWER, POLA, *Poza gettem i obozem* (Warsaw: Volumen, 1993); pp. 164. ISBN 8385233253.

WEISS, MOSHE, *From Oswiecim to Auschwitz: Poland Revisited* (Oakville, Ont.: Mosaic, 1994); pp. 182. ISBN 0889625581.

WIDAWSKI, CELINA *The Sun will Shine Tomorrow* (Hawthorn, Vic.: Essien, 1993); pp. viii + 120.

WIESEL, ELIE, *Tous les fleuves vont à la mer: Mémoires* (Paris: Éditions du Seuil, 1994); pp. 564. ISBN 2020215985.

WILDFEUER, EDGAR, *Auschwitz 174.189: Testimonio de un sobreviviente* (Cordoba, Argentina: Lerner, 1994); pp. 365.

YELIN, ME'IR, *Bay di gliyendike koyln* (Tel Aviv: Leivik, 1994); pp. 302.

ZELKOVITS, YOSEF, *Bayamim hanora'im hahem: Reshimot migeto Lodz*, ed. Mikhal Unger, trans. Aryeh Ben-Menahem and Yosef Rav (Jerusalem: Yad Vashem, 1994); pp. 370. ISBN 9653080385.

ZILBERBERG, TOVAH, *Imah: Bakashati nitkablah*, ed. Menuḥah Toker (Benei Brak: Zilberberg, 1994); pp. 282.

*Belles-lettres, Visual Arts, and Literary Studies*

BACHI, RUTH, *Tik Yozefinah* (Tel Aviv: Misrad Habitaḥon, 1994); pp. 207. ISBN 9650507124.

GREENBERG, BLU, *Black Bread: Poems, After the Holocaust* (Hoboken, NJ: Ktav, 1994); pp. xiii + 120. ISBN 0881254908.

GROSS, NATAN, *Poeci i szoa: Obraz Zagłady Żydów w poezji polskiej* (Sosnowiec: Offmax, 1993); pp. 191. ISBN 839001439.

GRYNBERG, HENRYK, *Prawda nieartystyczna* (Warsaw: Państwowy Instytut Wydawniczy, 1994); pp. 258. ISBN 8306024133.

HARTNETT, D. W., *Black Milk* (London: Cape, 1994); pp. 261.

MAGEN, MIRA, *Kaftorim rekhusim heitev* (Jerusalem: Keter, 1994); pp. 227.

PEROOMIAN, RUBINA, *Literary Responses to Catastrophe: A Comparison of the Armenian and Jewish Experience* (Atlanta, Ga.: Scholars Press, 1993); pp. x + 238. ISBN 155540894X.

RAHAV, NEHAMAH, *Haseret ha'adom: Asarah sipurim al yaldah begeto Vilna* (Tel Aviv: Moreshet, 1994); pp. 52. ISBN 9652225071.

RENGLICH, SZLOMA, *In the Heart of Warsaw: An Autobiographical Novel*, trans. Zigmund Jampel (Montreal: Véhicule Press, 1993); pp. 326. ISBN 1550650378.

ROSENBERG, JACOB BEN GERSHON, *My Father's Silence* (Melbourne: Focus, 1994); pp. ix + 48.

RYMKIEWICZ, JAROSŁAW, *The Final Station*, trans. N. Taylor (New York: Farar, Straus, Giroux, 1994); pp. 327. ISBN 0374154953. Polish version: *Umschlagplatz* (Paris, 1988).

SHEDEUR, AVRAHAM, *Korot A-11667:5741–5745* (Jerusalem: Karmel, 1994); pp. 224. ISBN 9654070901.

SIEDLECKA, JOANNA, *Czarny ptasior* (Gdańsk: Wydawnictwo Marabut; Warsaw: Wydawnictwo CIS, 1994); pp. 156. ISBN 83855458042.

TAIKHTEL, YISAKHAR SHELOMOH, *Emunah tserufah bekhur hasho'ah: Pirkei zikhronot* (Jerusalem: Hayyim Menahem Taikhtel, 1994); various paginations.

TEICHMAN, MILTON, and LEDER, SHARON, *Truth and Lamentation: Stories and Poems on the Holocaust* (Urbana: University of Illinois Press, 1994; pp. 526. ISBN 0252020286.

ZYCH, A. A. (ed.), *Na mojej ziemi był Oświęcim: Oświęcim w poezji współczesnej*, ii (Oświęcim: Państwowy Muzeum w Oświęcimiu, 1993); pp. 446. ISBN 8385047026.

### 1945–present

BRAHAM, RANDOLF (ed.), *Anti-semitism and the Treatment of the Holocaust in Post-communist Europe* (Social Science Monographs; Boulder, Colo.: Columbia University Press, 1994); pp. vii + 253. ISBN 0880333022.

DOBROSZYCKI, LUCJAN, *Survivors of the Holocaust in Poland* (New York: Sharpe, 1994); pp. x + 164. ISBN 1563244632.

GRUBER, RUTH ELLEN, *Upon the Doorposts of thy House: Jewish Life in East-Central Europe, Yesterday and Today* (New York: Wiley, 1994); pp. ix + 310. ISBN 0471595683.

KLESS, SHLOMOH, *Baderekh Io selulah: Toledot haberiḥah, 1944–1948* (Givat Havivah: Moreshet; Beit edut al shem Mordekhai Anilevits; Hamakhon leyahadut zemaneinu, Hebrew University, 1994); pp. 378. ISBN 9652224979.

KURLANSKY, MARK, *A Chosen Few: The Resurrection of European Jewry* (New York: Addison-Wesley, 1994); pp. xiv + 410. ISBN 0201608987.

LILIENHEIM, HENRY, *The Aftermath: A Survivor's Odyssey through War-Torn Europe* (Montreal: DC, 1994); pp. xix + 181. ISBN 0919688454.

MICGIEL, JOHN, *'Frenzy and Ferocity': The Stalinist Judicial System in Poland, 1944–1947, and the Search for Redress*, Carl Beck Papers, no. 1101 (Pittsburgh: University of Pittsburgh, 1994); pp. 48. ISSN 08899-275X.

PACZKOWSKI, ANDRZEJ, *Aparat bezpieczeństwa w latach, 1944–1956: Taktyka, strategia, metody* (Warsaw: Instytut Studiów Politycznych, PAN, 1994). ISBN 8385479589.

ROZPĘDOWSKI, HENRYK, *Był chamsin* (London: Aneks, 1994); pp. 288. ISBN 1897962029.

URBAN, KAZIMIERZ, *Mniejszości religijne w Polsce, 1945–1991* (Cracow: Zakład Wydawniczy NOMOS, 1994); pp. xi + 299. ISBN 8385527133.

WEBBER, JONATHAN (ed.), *Jewish Identities in the New Europe* (London: Littman Library of Jewish Civilization for the Oxford Centre for Postgraduate Hebrew Studies, 1994); pp. xix + 307. ISBN 1874774153.

WISTRICH, ROBERT S. (ed.), *Terms of Survival: The Jewish World since 1945* (London: Routledge, 1995); pp. 461. ISBN 0415100569.

### Special Topics

*Regional and Community Monographs; Memorial Books*

ADLER, HILLEL, *Mémoires d'une ville juive éteinte: Ozarow* (Published in France by the author, 1994); pp. 247.

BONUSIAK, WŁODZIMIERZ, and BUSZKO, JÓZEF (eds.), *Galicja i jej dziedzictwo*, i: *Historia i polityka* (Rzeszów: Wyższa Szkoła Pedagogiczna, 1994); pp. 262. ISBN 8386246006.

BUDZIAREK, MAREK, *Judaica łódzkie z zbiorach muzealnych i zasobach archiwalnych* (Łódź: Muzeum Historii Miasta Łodzi, 1994); pp. 204. ISBN 8390185105.

CARTER, FRANCIS W., *Trade and Urban Development in Poland: An Economic Geography of Krakow, from its Origins to 1795* (Cambridge: Cambridge University Press, 1994); pp. xxii + 509. ISBN 0521412390.

DOMAŃSKA, HANNA, *Kadisz gdańskich kamieni* (Warsaw: Agencja Wydawnicza Tu, 1994); pp. 128. ISBN 8390297108.

MELAMED, VLADIMIR, *Evrei vo L'vove: XII-pervaia polovina XX veka. Sobytiia, obshchestvo, liudi* (L'viv: Sovmestnoe ukrain'ko-amerikanskoe predpriiatie Tekop, 1994); pp. 263. ISBN 5770723149.

*Our Roots: In Memory of the Hrubieszów Martyrs and the Jewish Victims of the Holocaust, 1939–1945* (Tel Aviv: Organization of Former Residents of Hrubieszów in Israel, 1994); pp. 62.

PRZEMSZA-ZIELINSKI, JAN (ed.), *Żydzi w Zagłębiu* (Sosnowiec: Sowa-Press, 1993); pp. 92. ISBN 8385876006.

RADZIK, TADEUSZ, *Yeshivah ḥakhmei Lublin*, trans. Artur Blaim (Lublin: Maria Curie-Skłodowska Press, 1994); pp. 27. ISBN 8322706405.

SIMHAH BEN ARYEH NAFTALI, *Imrei Maharshah al masekhet Bava Metsia im korot ha'ir Książ [Wielki] verabaneiha* (Brooklyn: Yaakov Matityahu Zeligfeld, 1994); pp. 505.

ZGRZEBNICKI, JACEK, *Cracow's Kazimierz Jewish Town—Żydowski Kazimierz* (Cracow: Agencja Promocyjna Patchwork and Agencja Turystyczna Wiktor, 1994); pp. 144. ISBN 83902398.

## Emigration

BERROL, SELMA, *East Side–East End: Eastern European Jews in London and New York, 1870–1920* (Westport, Conn.: Praeger, 1994); pp. xiv + 159. ISBN 0275947726.

HOERDER, DIRK, and RÖSSLER, HORST (eds.), *Distant Magnets: Expectations and Realities in the Immigrant Experience* (New York: Holmes & Meier, 1994); pp. 320. ISBN 0841913021.

JACOBSON, MATTHEW, *Special Sorrows: The Diasporic Imagination of Irish, Polish and Jewish Immigrants in the United States* (Cambridge, Mass.: Harvard University Press, 1994); pp. viii + 321. ISBN 0674831853.

## Cultural History

LEDERHENDLER, ELI, *Jewish Responses to Modernity: New Voices in America and Eastern Europe* (New York: New York University Press, 1994); pp. ix + 232. ISBN 0814750842.

NOBLE, SHLOMO, *A Storyteller's Worlds: The Education of Shlomo Noble in Europe and America*, interviews and comment by Jonathan Boyarin (New York: Holmes & Meier, 1994); pp. xv + 231. ISBN 0841913439.

PRUSSAK, MARIA, *Świat pod kontrolą: Wybór materiałów z archiwum cenzury rosyjskiej w Warszawie* (Warsaw: Wydawnictwo Krąg, 1994); pp. 187. ISBN 8385199292.

SZCZUCKA, A., and BUJAK, A., *Świątynia: Rzecz o budowlach sakralnych różnych wyznań w Polsce* (Warsaw: Spotkania, 1993); pp. 239. ISBN 8385195661.

TURNIANSKY, CHAVA, *Lashon, ḥinukh, vehaskalah bemizraḥ Eiropah, Polin: Perakim betoledot yehudei mizraḥ Eiropah vetarbutam*, Unit 7 (Jerusalem: Open University of Israel, 1994); pp. 96. ISBN 9653026402.

### Polish–Jewish Relations

BŁOŃSKI, JAN, *Biedni Polacy Patrzą na Getto* (Cracow: Wydawnictwo Literackie, 1994); pp. 157. ISBN 8308025765.

FOGELMAN, EVA, *Conscience and Courage: Rescuers of Jews during the Holocaust* (New York: Doubleday, 1994); pp. xx + 393. ISBN 0385320277.

KORWIN, LUDWIK (pseud.), *Szlachta Mojżeszowa*, i: *Szlachta Wyznania Mojżeszowego w Europie* (Warsaw, 1993); pp. 200. ISBN 83850690977.

RINGELBLUM, EMMANUEL, *Ketavim aḥaronim; Yaḥasei polanim-yehudim, yanu'ar 1943–april 1944*, ed. I. Gutman, Y. Kermish, and Y. Shaham (Jerusalem: Yad Vashem and Beit Loḥamei Hageta'ot, 1994); pp. ix + 391. ISBN 9653080229.

TOMASZEWSKI, IRENE, and WERBOWSKA, TECIA, *Żegota: The Wartime Rescue of Jews* (Montreal: Price-Patterson, 1994); pp. 171. ISBN 0969577168.

VOGLER, HENRYK, *Wyznanie mojżeszowe: Wspomnienia z utraconego czasu* (Warsaw: Państwowy Instytut Wydawniczy, 1994); pp. 124. ISBN 8306023552.

WERSES, SHMUEL, *Relations between Poles and Jews in S. Y. Agnon's Work* (Studies of the Center for Research on the History and Culture of Polish Jews, Hebrew University, Jerusalem; Jerusalem: Magnes, 1994); pp. 128. ISBN 9652238732.

### Other Countries

BRYM, ROBERT J., with Rozalina Ryvkina, *The Jews of Moscow, Kiev and Minsk: Identity, Antisemitism, Emigration*, ed. Howard Spier (New York: New York University Press, in association with the Institute of Jewish Affairs, 1994); pp. xvi + 142. ISBN 0333617525.

CLARK, CHRISTOPHER, *The Politics of Conversion: Missionary Protestantism and the Jews in Prussia, 1728–1941* (New York: Oxford University Press, 1994); pp. 390. ISBN 0198204566.

GREENBAUM, ALFRED ABRAHAM, *Rabbanei Berit Hamo'atsot bein milḥamot ha'olam: homer leleksikon biyo-bibliyografi* (Jerusalem: Centre for Research and Documentation of East European Jewry, Avraham Harman Institute of Contemporary Jewry, Hebrew University, 1994); pp. iii + 73.

*Juden in Sachsen: Ihr Leben und Leiden* (Leipzig: Evangelische Verlaganstalt, 1994); pp. 120. ISBN 3374015239.

LEVIN, DOV, *Baltic Jews under the Soviets, 1940–1946* (Jerusalem: Centre for Research and Documentation of East European Jewry, Avraham Harman Institute of Contemporary Jewry, Hebrew University, 1994); pp. 393.

LUKIN, VIKTOR MIKHAILOVICH, KHAIMOVICH, B. N., and DYMSHITS, V. A., *Istoriia evreev na Ukraine i v Belorussii. Ekspeditsii, pamiatniki, nakhodki: Sbornik nauchnykh trudov* (St Petersburg: Peterburgskii Evreiskii Universitet, 1994); pp. 220.

SILBERFARB, MOSES, *The Jewish Ministry and Jewish National Autonomy in Ukraine*, trans. David H. Lincoln (New York: Aleph Press, 1994); pp. xi + 115.

VAKSBERG, ARKADY, *Stalin against the Jews* (New York: Knopf, 1994); pp. 408. ISBN 0679422072.

## SOCIAL SCIENCES

### Sociology

BAR-ON, DAN, *Bein paḥad letikvah: Sipurei ḥayim shel ḥamesh mishpaḥot nitsolei sho'ah, sheloshah dorot bamishpaḥah* (Kibbutz Loḥamei Hayeta'ot: Beit Loḥamei Hageta'ot, 1994); pp. 301.

IRWIN-ZARECKA, IWONA, *Frames of Remembrance: The Dynamics of Collective Memory* (New Brunswick, NJ: Transaction, 1994); pp. xiv + 214. ISBN 1560001380.

WŁADYKA, W. (ed.), *Inni wśród swoich* (Warsaw: IBL and PAN, 1994); pp. 158. ISBN 8385605193.

### *Antisemitism*

MODRAS, RONALD E., *The Catholic Church and Antisemitism: Poland, 1933–1939* (Singapore: Harwood Academic Publishers for the Vidal Sassoon International Centre for the Study of Antisemitism, Hebrew University, Jerusalem, 1994); pp. xvi + 429. ISBN 3718655683.

### Political Studies: Parties and Movements

BARZILAI, ZVI, *Tenu'at haBund bePolin bein shetei milḥamot ha'olam* (Jerusalem: Karmel, 1994); pp. xvi + 251.

### Education and Pedagogy

BORZYMIŃSKA, ZOFIA, *Szkolnictwo żydowskie w Warszawie, 1831–1870* (Warsaw: Żydowski Instytut Historyczny, 1994); pp. 335. ISBN 8385888748.

COHEN, ADIR, *The Gate of Light: Janusz Korczak, the Educator who Overcame the Holocaust* (Rutherford, NJ: Fairleigh Dickinson University Press, 1994): pp. 360. ISBN 0838635237.

WALASEK, STEFAN (ed.), *Studia o szkolnictwie i oświacie mnieszości narodowych w XIX i XX wieku* (Wrocław: Wydawnictwo Uniwersytetu Wrocławskiego, 1994); pp. 164. ISBN 8322910487.

### Women's Studies

DANSKY, MIRAM, *Rebbetzin Grunfeld: The Life of Judith Grunfeld, Courageous Pioneer of the Bais Yaakov Movement and Jewish Rebirth* (Brooklyn: Mesorah, 1994); pp. 336. ISBN 0899061192.

### Folklore

*Book of Fables: The Yiddish Fable Collection of Reb Moshe Wallich*, ed. and trans. Eli Katz (Detroit: Wayne State University Press, 1994); pp. 305. ISBN 0814324495.

HILLEL, MOSHE (ed.), *Mifalot Elohim: Pe'ulot usegulot . . . mikitvei Eliyahu Ba'al Shem, Yo'el Ba'al Shem, Yitshak Ḥazak, Naftali Kats* (Jerusalem: Makhon Benei Yisasskhar, 1994); pp. 206.

HILLEL, MOSHE (ed.), *Toledot adam: Pe'ulot usegulot . . . mikitvei Eliyahu Ba'al Shem, Yo'el Ba'al Shem, Yitshak Hazak, Naftali Kats* (Jerusalem: Makhon Benei Yisasskhar, 1994); pp. 197.

NIGAL, GEDALIAH, *Sipurei dibuk besifrut Yisra'el*, 2nd ed., rev. (Jerusalem: Mass, 1994); pp. 300. ISBN 9650900209.

SHADUR, JOSEPH, and SHADUR, YEHUDIT, *Jewish Papercuts: A History and Guide* (Berkeley: Judah L. Magnes Museum; Jerusalem: Gefen, 1994); pp. 111. ISBN 0943376548.

### JUDAISM AND OTHER RELIGIONS

**Religious Thought**

JACOBS, STEVEN L., *A Child of a Survivor Responds* (Albany: State University of New York Press, 1994); pp. 151. ISBN 0791419576.

PAIMER, YOSEF, *Derashot rabeinu Yoself miSlutski: Hidushim uve'urim al hatorah* (Jerusalem: Mif' al torat hakhmei Lita, 1994); pp. 24 + 202.

RIVLIN, HILLEL BEN BENJAMIN OF SZKŁÓW, *Kol hator, vehu shitat haga'on rabeinu Eliyahu miVilnah . . . 'al tekufat ha'athalta dege'ulah*, new edn., rev. enlarged (Jerusalem: Mefitsei kol hator, 1994); pp. 151.

*Kabbalah*

POSY, ARNOLD, *Mystic Trends in Judaism* (Middle Village, NY: David, 1994); pp. 238. ISBN 0824603680.

*Hasidism*

ALFASSI, YITSHAK, *Mamlekhet hahokhmah: Toledot beit Ropshits-Dzikov* (Jerusalem: Karmel, 1994); pp. 376. ISBN 9654070693.

——*Me'orot me'olam hakabalah vehahasidut* (Tel Aviv: Da'at Yosef, 1994); pp. 574.

ANKORI, MIKHA, *Meromei reki'im vetahtiyot she'ol: Masa'ei hanefesh shel Rabbi Nahman miBratslav* (Tel Aviv: Ramat, 1994); pp. 120.

BARTAL, ISRAEL, ELIOR, RACHEL, and SHMERUK, CHONE (eds.), *Tsadikim ve'anshei ma'aseh: Mehkarim behasidut Polin* (Jerusalem: Mossad Bialik, 1994); pp. 397. ISBN 965342184.

BAUER, JULIEN, *Les Juifs hassidiques* (Paris: Presses Universitaires de France, 1994); pp. 127. ISBN 2130462286.

BUXBAUM, YITSHAK, *Storytelling and Spirituality in Judaism* (Northvale, NJ: Aronson, 1994); pp. xvii + 255.

COHEN, LAURENT, *Le Maitre des frontières incertaines: Rabbi Nahman de Bratslav* (Paris: Éditions du Seuil, 1994); pp. 152. ISBN 202020133X.

DRIKERMAN, YA'AKOV, *Temimei derekh*, ed. Gedalyah Nigal (Jerusalem: Karmel, 1993); pp. 140. ISBN 9654070642.

EDELBAUM, ME'IR, *Hamaggid miMezerich [Międzyrzecz]: hayav, pa'alo, utenu'at hahasidut bitekufato* (Tel Aviv: Edelbaum, 1994); pp. 336.

ELIEZER BEN YISRAEL MIVIZNITSA, *Damesek Eli'ezer: Amarot . . . asher hishir aharav*

*Eliezer miViznitsa* (Benei Brak: Hamakhon lehotsa'at vehafatsat sifre rabboteinu hakedoshim, 1994); pp. 311.

EPSTEIN, KALONYMOS KALMAN BEN AHARON, *Sefer ma'or vashemesh hashalem*, ed. Menaḥem Avraham Braun (Jerusalem: Makhon or hasefer, 1994); pp. 444.

FINKEL, AVRAHM YAAKOV (ed.), *Contemporary Sages: The Great Chasidic Masters of the Twentieth Century* (Northvale, NJ: Aronson, 1994); pp. xxiii + 219. ISBN 1568211554.

FRENKEL, HAYYIM (ed.), *Zikaron kodesh leba'al 'Esh Kodesh'* (Jerusalem: Va'ad hasidei Piastczena-Grodzisk, 1994); pp. xxiv + 132.

GELLMAN, JEROME I., *The Fear, the Trembling and the Fire: Kierkegaard and Hasidic Masters on the Binding of Isaac* (Lanham,: Md. University Press of America, 1994); pp. xxi + 123. ISBN 081919364X.

HALBERSTAT, HAYYIM OF SACZ, *Sefer besefer ḥayim* (Benei Brak: Makhon Beit Sanz, 1994); pp. 332.

HESCHEL, ABRAHAM YEHOSHUA, *Sefer torat emet* (Emanuel: Makhon lezikhron kedoshei Polin, 1994); pp. 241.

HIRSH, HAYYIM (ed.), *Hai go'ali: Torat hage'ulah shel rabbi Zadok hakohen miLublin* (Jerusalem, 1994); i: pp. lxv + 456; ii: pp. 493.

HOROWITZ, ELI'EZER BEN YA'AKOV, *No'am magidim ukhevod hatorah*, ed. Shim'on ben Kalonymos Weiss, 2 vols. (Brooklyn: Ateret, 1994); pp. 1087.

HOROWITZ, YA'AKOV YITSHAK OF LUBLIN, *Sefer pitgamim kadishin al hatorah mitorato shel Ya'akov Yitshak Halevi miLancut hanikra haḥozeh miLublin, melukat misefarav umisifrei talmidav* (Monsey, NY: Rosenfeld, 1994); pp. xvi + 218.

IDEL, MOSHE, *Hasidism: Between Ecstasy and Magic* (Albany: State University of New York Press, 1994); pp. 480. ISBN 0791417336.

LEVI ISAAC BEN ME'IR OF BERDICHEV, *Kedushat Levi hashalem . . . menukad umefusak im tsiyunim umarei mekomot*, 2 vols. (Jerusalem, 1994).

MOSKOVITS, YISRAEL MOSHE, *Sefer Akh Tov le Yisra'el al hatorah umo'adim* (Benei Brak: Hamakhon lehotsa'at sefarim vekitvei yad shel ḥasidei Alexander, 1994); pp. 241.

MYKOFF, MOSHE, *The Empty Chair: Finding Hope and Joy. Timeless Wisdom from a Hasidic Master, Rebbe Nachman of Breslov* (Woodstock, Vt.: Jewish Lights, 1994); pp. 114. ISBN 1879045168.

NIGAL, GEDALYAH, *Magic, Mysticism and Hasidism: The Supernatural in Jewish Thought* (Northvale NJ: Aronson, 1994); pp. xiii + 289. ISBN 1568210337.

——*Sipurei hasidut Czernobyl* (Jerusalem: Karmel, 1994); pp. 202. ISBN 9654070723.

PIEKARZ, MENDEL, *Bein ideologiyah lemetsiyut: Anavah, ayin, bitul mimetsiyut udevekut bamaḥshavatam shel rashei haḥasidut* (Jerusalem: Mossad Bialik, 1994); pp. 316.

POLEN, NEHEMIA, *The Holy Fire: The Teachings of Rabbi Kalonymus Kalman Shapira, the Rebbe of the Warsaw Ghetto* (Northvale, NJ: Aronson, 1994); pp. xix + 208. ISBN 0876688423.

ROKEAH, MORDEKHAI, *Kuntras haderekh* (Jerusalem: Makhon mehkar vearkhiyon keter malkhut, 1994); pp. 45.

ROTNER, MORDEKHAI (ed.), *MiLizhensk le Yerushalayim: Harebbe Elimelekh, toledotav, torato, ufa'alo ledor uledorot* (Jerusalem: Igud Hatse'etsa'im shel R. Elimelekh, 1994); various paginations.

ROTSTEIN, SHMUEL YITSHAK, *Dos malkhusdike khsidus: A bashraybung fun dem Rizhiner rebbe Yisrael mit zayne kinder* (Brooklyn: Sharf, 1994); pp. 346.

SAFRIN, YITSHAK YEHUDA YEḤI'EL, *Sefer ma'aseh haShem hashalem: Uvedot vesipurim mige'onei erets: HaBesht vetalmidav* (Muncey, NY: Makhon or haganuz, 1994); pp. vi + 253.

SCHOCHET, ELIJAH JUDAH, *The Hasidic Movement and the Gaon of Vilna* (Northvale, NJ: Aronson, 1994); pp. xv + 257. ISBN 1568211252.

SOFER, YA'AKOV BEN ME'IR ZE'EV, *Sipurei Ya'akov*, ed. Gedalyah Nigal (Jerusalem: Karmel, 1994); pp. 218. ISBN 9654070812.

STAIMAN, MORDECHAI, *Niggun: Stories behind the Chasidic Songs that Inspire Jews* (Northvale, NJ: Aronson, 1994); pp. xv + 294. ISBN 1568210477.

VAINBERG, SHELOMOH ZALMAN, *Netsaḥ shebanetsaḥ: Toledot hayav ufo'olo shel . . . David miTolna* (Jerusalem: Vainberg, 1994); pp. 285.

VALAKH, SHALOM ME'IR BEN MORDEKHAI, *Ha'esh dat me'ozerov: Korot ḥayav shel . . . Rabbi Moshe Yeḥi'el Halevi Epstein . . . Admor meOzerov-Checiny* (Tel Aviv: Keren lehotsa'at sifrei Esh Dat, 1994); pp. 448.

WEINTRAUB, NOAH GAD BEN YA'AKOV DAVID, *Sofer biyeshishim ḥokhmah; Mekhil ke'elef imrei kodesh ve'uvedot pele, hanhagot vehadrakhot me'et kem'atayim talmidei haBesht asher ne'esfu venirshemu mipi ziknei veyeshishei Polin, Galitsiyah, veRomanya* (Jerusalem: Makhon Har Naḥli'el, 1994); pp. ii + 424.

WISKIND-ELPER, ORA, 'Hamemad hafantasti beyetsirat rav Naḥman miBraslav', Ph.D. dissertation (Hebrew University, Jerusalem, 1994); pp. 352.

# Notes on the Contributors

PAUL COATES is Reader in Film Studies in the English Department of the University of Aberdeen. His publications include *The Realist Fantasy* (1983), *The Story of the Lost Reflection* (1985), and *The Gorgon's Gaze: German Cinema, Expressionism and the Image of Horror* (1991), as well as articles on aspects of Polish literature and cinema. He is currently editing a volume of essays on Krzysztof Kieślowski.

ARTUR EISENBACH (1906–1992) was a distinguished historian of the Jewish experience in Poland. His numerous publications centred mainly on the Holocaust and on the social and legal changes during the nineteenth century.

TOMASZ GĄSOWSKI is a Lecturer at the Institute of History of the Jagiellonian University in Cracow. He has written extensively on the history of Galicia.

JACOB GOLDBERG is Professor Emeritus of the Hebrew University in Jerusalem and *doctor honoris causa* (1993) of the University of Warsaw. He taught previously at the University of Łódź and has been Visiting Professor at a number of European universities. He specializes in the history of Polish Jews and the history of Poland in the sixteenth to eighteenth centuries. Among his publications is *Jewish Privileges in the Polish Commonwealth* (1985).

ZENON GULDON is Professor Emeritus of the University of Warsaw at Kielce. He is engaged mainly in research on the social and economic history of Poland and Polish Jews in the sixteenth to eighteenth centuries.

THOMAS C. HUBKA is Professor of Architecture at the University of Wisconsin, Milwaukee.

GERTRUD PICKHAN is a member of the research staff at the German Historical Institute in Warsaw, where she is working on the history of the Bund in the interwar period. She gained a doctorate at the University of Hamburg on medieval Russian history.

MOSHE ROSMAN is Professor of Jewish History at Bar Ilan University. His most recent book is *Founder of Hasidism* (Berkeley and Los Angeles, 1995).

CHONE SHMERUK is Professor Emeritus of Yiddish Literature at the Hebrew University in Jerusalem. In recent years he has been Visiting Professor at both Warsaw University and the Jagiellonian University in Cracow. Among his publications are *Prokim fun der yidisher literatur-geshikhte* (1988) and the edition, together with Irving Howe and Ruth R. Wisse, of *The Penguin Book of Modern Yiddish Verse* (1987).

DANIEL STONE is Professor of History at the University of Winnipeg. He is a specialist in Polish history.

ISRAEL M. TA-SHMA is Professor of Talmud at the Hebrew University in Jerusalem and Director of the Institute for Microfilmed Hebrew Manuscripts of the Jewish National and Hebrew University Library. Among his publications is *Minhag Ashkenaz hakadmon* (1992).

NECHAMA TEC is Professor of Sociology at the University of Connecticut. She has published numerous studies of Holocaust-related subjects including *Defiance: The Bielski Partisans* (1993).

CHAVA WEISSLER holds the Philip and Muriel Berman Chair of Jewish Civilization at Lehigh University. Her monograph on prayers in Yiddish for women, *Voices of the Matriarchs* will be published shortly by Beacon Press.

ELIMELECH WESTREICH is Lecturer in Jewish Law and Family Law at Bar-Ilan University.

JACEK WIJACKA is Lecturer in History at the School of Higher Education in Kielce. His research has concentrated mainly on the history of Polish–German relations in the sixteenth century and the history of Polish Jews in the sixteenth to the eighteenth centuries.

# Glossary

**Ashkenaz(i)** Although in its narrowest sense 'Ashkenaz' denotes German lands, the term 'Ashkenazi' is generally used to denote Jews who share in the cultural legacy that derives initially from northern France and Germany and spread eastward to include Poland–Lithuania and the other lands of east central Europe.

**Ban** (Hebrew: *herem*) Denotes various degrees of religious and social ostracism imposed by rabbinical courts. Frequently used as a deterrent; transgressors would be threatened with the ban when an edict was promulgated.

**Bund** General Jewish Workers' Alliance. A Jewish socialist party founded in 1897. It joined the Russian Social Democratic Labour Party, but seceded when its programme of national autonomy was not accepted. In independent Poland it adopted a leftist anti-Communist posture and from the 1930s co-operated increasingly closely with the Polish Socialist Party (PPS).

**Commonwealth** (Polish: Rzeczpospolita) The Polish term is derived from the Latin *respublica*. It is sometimes translated as 'commonwealth' and sometimes as 'republic', often in the form of 'Nobleman's Republic' (Rzeczpospolita szlachecka). After the Union of Lublin in 1569 it was used officially in the form Rzeczpospolita Obojga Narodów (Commonwealth of the Two Nations) to designate the new form of the state that had arisen. In historical literature this term is often rendered as 'The Polish–Lithuanian Commonwealth'.

**Council of Four Lands** (Hebrew: Va'ad Arba Aratsot) Founded in the second half of the sixteenth century and disestablished in 1764, the Council of Four Lands was the institutional representative body of Polish Jews. Made up of lay and rabbinical delegates from an increasing number of communities and regions, its chief tasks were to negotiate the level of Jewish taxation with the Royal Treasury and to apportion the tax burden among the regions and communities. In addition, it passed laws and statutes on internal education and economic matters and other general Jewish concerns. There was a similar council in the Grand Duchy of Lithuania.

**Four Year Sejm** The extended session of the Polish parliament in Warsaw in 1788–92 that most notably adopted the Constitution of 3 May 1791 which reformed the government of the Polish state. Also known as the Four Year Diet.

*gematriyot* (sing.: *gematriyah*) Every Hebrew letter has a numerical value. *Gematriyah* denotes the explanation of the significance of the numerical value of words and phrases in sacred texts.

**geonic period** (from the Hebrew *ga'on*, pl. *ge'onim*) The period of influence of the heads of the great religious academies in Babylonia (Iraq), Sura, and Pumbeditha, between the eighth and eleventh centuries.

**Habad** An acronym based on the Hebrew mystical terms *hokhmah*, *binah*, *da'at* (lit. 'wisdom', 'understanding', 'knowledge'). It was applied to a hasidic group founded in the Grand Duchy of Lithuania by Shneur Zalman of Lyady. He and his descendants espoused a more intellectualized mystical doctrine than was characteristic of many other hasidic groups. Also known as the Lubavitch hasidim, the group was led until recently by the close family of its founder.

**halakhah** (Hebrew, literally 'the way') A word used to describe the entire prescriptive part of the Jewish tradition. It defines the norms of behaviour and religious observance.

*ḥalitsah* The ceremony of taking off a brother-in-law's shoe by the widow of a brother who has died childless, through which he is released from the obligation to marry her, and she becomes free to marry whomever she wishes (Deut. 25: 5–10).

**Ḥasidei Ashkenaz** (Hebrew: pietists of **Ashkenaz**) Groups of hasidim (pietists) who appeared chiefly in the Rhineland in the twelfth and thirteenth centuries. They followed a highly ascetic regimen and their doctrines stressed humility and the pursuit of esoteric knowledge. Except in terms of their general and profound influence on **Ashkenazi** culture, these hasidim are not connected to the hasidism that arose in Poland–Lithuania in the second half of the eighteenth century.

**hasidism** A mystically inclined movement of religious revival consisting of distinct groups with charismatic leadership. It arose in the borderlands of the Polish–Lithuanian **Commonwealth** in the second half of the eighteenth century and quickly spread through eastern Europe. The hasidim emphasized joy in the service of God, whose presence they sought everywhere. Though their opponents pronounced a series of **bans** against them beginning in 1772 (*misnagdim*, literally opponents, i.e. of hasidism), the movement soon became identified with religious orthodoxy.

**Haskalah** (Hebrew, literally 'learning' or 'wisdom' but used in the sense of Enlightenment) A movement that arose in the wake of the general European Enlightenment in the second half of the eighteenth century and continued to the second half of the nineteenth century. Its adherents were known as **maskilim**. Its most prominent representative was Moses Mendelssohn (1729–86). The Haskalah was particularly important and influential in German and Slavic lands. It advocated secular education, the acquisition of European languages, the adoption of productive occupations, and loyalty to the state. In eastern Europe there was considerable emphasis on Hebrew as opposed to Yiddish, which was rejected by most maskilim.

*ḥerem* See **Ban**.

*kahal, kehilah* Although both terms mean 'community', *kahal* is used to denote the institution of Jewish autonomy in a particular locality while *kehilah* denotes the community of Jews who live in the town.

**Maimonides** Moses ben Maimon (1135–1204), the outstanding figure of medieval Jewish theology and **halakhah**. Also known by the acronym Rambam, he was the author of numerous works including the theological work *Moreh nevukhim* (Guide of the Perplexed) and the compendious halakhic code *Mishneh Torah*.

**Małopolska** (Polish, literally 'Lesser Poland') Southern Poland, the area around Cracow. Also referred to under the Habsburgs as (western) Galicia.

**maskil, maskilim** See **Haskalah**.

**Naḥmanides** Moses ben Naḥman (1195–1270), also known by the acronym Ramban. A Spanish rabbi and scholar who wrote influential works in the areas of **halakhah**, biblical commentary, and kabbalah.

**notarikon** A Greek word used in Hebrew deriving from the same root as the English 'notary'. It is a method of interpretation, chiefly of scripture, in which each of the letters of a word is taken to stand for a whole word, or words are divided into constituent parts, each of which is read as a word. Sometimes the order of the letters is reversed or otherwise manipulated. Thus, the last letters of the first three words in the Bible can be made to spell *emet*—truth.

**piyyut** Jewish liturgical poetry.

**Rabbenu Tam** Jacob ben Meir Tam (*c.*1100–71). The grandson of **Rashi**, he was the leading French talmudic and **halakhic** scholar of the twelfth century.

**Rashi** Acronym for Rabbi Shlomoh (Solomon) ben Isaac (1040–1105). An outstanding **halakhic** scholar, he was the author of the standard commentaries on the Bible and the Talmud.

**Sejm** The bicameral parliament of the Polish–Lithuanian **Commonwealth**.

*Shulḥan arukh* (Hebrew: literally 'The Set Table') The last comprehensive code of **halakhah**, it was written by Joseph Caro (1488–1575) in Palestine. The custom arose of publishing it together with the *Mapah* ('Tablecloth'), the commentary of Moses Isserles (1525–72) of Cracow, who supplemented the work of the Sefardi author by adding reference to **Ashkenazi** practice.

**Shum** An acronym denoting the Jewish communities of Speyer, Worms, and Mainz, the leaders of which met together from time to time.

*starosta* (Polish: 'elder', 'sheriff') Territorial administrator appointed by the king.

*takanah, takanot* An edict or directive enacted by **halakhic** authorities or the leaders of a *kahal* acting together with rabbinical judges that has the force of law. Its authority is derived from that of the body or individual who issues it and does not depend on the interpretation of a scriptural verse or talmudic passage.

**tosafot, tosafist** Collections of talmudic commentary deriving mainly from French and German lands in the twelfth to fourteenth centuries. The tosafists in their comments generally took as their point of departure not a talmudic passage but the comments on it of **Rashi** and other earlier commentators.

*tsadik* (Hebrew, lit. 'righteous man') The leader of a **hasidic** group was called *tsadik* or *rebbe*. Often his hasidim credited him with miraculous powers, seeing him as a mediator between God and man.

**Wielkopolska** (Polish, literally 'Greater Poland') Western Poland; the area around Poznań.

*wojewoda* From the thirteenth century this term designated a royally appointed provincial authority. From the sixteenth century, he conducted the dietine, led the *levée-en-masse* of the *szlachta* in times of danger to the state, and had particular authority in cities. The assistant *podwojewoda* often acted as Judge of the Jews. The position of *wojewoda* entitled its holder to sit in the senate.

*wójt*   Town headman, a hereditary official presiding over town administration.

**Zohar** (Hebrew, literally [Book of] Splendour)   The fundamental work of kabbalistic literature comprising various related compositions in Aramaic and dating mainly from the last decades of the thirteenth century in Spain. The main author was Moses ben Shem Tov de Leon (d. 1305).

# Index